*This book is dedicated to my mother,
brother, grandparents, my wife Jill,
Rocky and the Bushranger boys, who were
all there when it mattered.*

Nick Bleszynski was born in Scotland and grew up in central and eastern Africa. After returning to the UK and graduating from Anglia University, he went into television where he has worked for the past eighteen years as a writer, producer and director. This is his first book. He is married and now lives in Sydney, Australia.

SHOOT STRAIGHT,
YOU BASTARDS!

The truth behind the killing of 'Breaker' Morant

Nick Bleszynski

RANDOM HOUSE AUSTRALIA

Random House Australia Pty Ltd
20 Alfred Street, Milsons Point, NSW 2061
http://www.randomhouse.com.au

Sydney   New York   Toronto
London   Auckland   Johannesburg

First published by Random House Australia 2002

National Library of Australia
Cataloguing-in-Publication Entry

  Bleszynski, Nick.
  Shoot straight, you bastards! : the truth behind the killing of
  'Breaker' Morant.

  Bibliography.

  ISBN 1 74 051217 0.

  1. Morant, Breaker, ca. 1865–1902. 2. Trials (Military offenses) –
  South Africa. 3. South African War, 1899–1902. I. Title.

  968.048

Front cover photograph: Harry 'The Breaker' Morant courtesy of
  The Bulletin.
Back cover photograph: still from the movie *Breaker Morant* courtesy
  of the South Australian Film Corporation.
Internal design by Midland Typesetters
Typeset by Midland Typesetters, Maryborough, Victoria
Printed and bound by Griffin Press, Netley, South Australia

10 9 8 7 6 5 4 3 2 1

Contents

Acknowledgements

Although I am credited with being the author, no book is written by a single person. Firstly I'd like to thank Brian Meldon, the current Tenterfield Saddler, for introducing me to 'The Breaker', his staunch and unwavering support throughout and the beers. Likewise, Rob McAuley, my producer on what started out as a documentary film, deserves a special mention in dispatches for always giving me sound advice on story development and enduring the long struggle with a fortitude deserving of a medal. We'll get there yet, mate. *The Bulletin*'s Anthony Hoy has also been there from the beginning. His championing of the cause and unstinting support were also vital factors in getting this story told.

This book simply could not have been written without the tenacious and thorough research skills of both Ted Robel and Joe West. Their pursuit of the historical minutiae and forthright opinions forced me to constantly reappraise various sections. No-one could have done it better. I would like to thank my mother, Iris Bleszynski, Steve Playford, Bill Woolmore, Max Chamberlain and Julian Putkowski for their insightful critiques into the various drafts, which kept this bastard honest.

I am also indebted to many others who generously gave of their time and kindly shared material with me (in alphabetical order): the Anglo–Boer War study group in Melbourne, Max Chamberlain, Rodney Constantine, Julian Fellowes-Kitchener, Friends of the Boers Internet group, Beryl and Cathie Morant,

Dr John Mordike, Dora Murrant, Dr Tony Phol, Neil Speed, Ian Spence and the Thomas family. I would also like to thank Susan Lloyd and Jennifer Broomhead at the Mitchell Library, Sydney, for help with documents and illustrations, the Duke and Lady Hamilton for graciously allowing me to quote from the diaries of RM Poore, and the Admiral Blake Museum in Bridgwater for the photograph of the Union Workhouse.

Random House Australia has been a fantastic Publishing House to work with. Always supportive and enthusiastic, special thanks must go to Jeanne Ryckmans for seeing the potential, giving me the chance to write the book and backing the project to the absolute max. Also, thanks to Lydia Papandrea who with Jeanne gave sound advice at the editing stage and steered me through my first excursion into publishing. Sincere thanks also to my agent, Margaret Gee, for taking on an unknown and for all the support, advice and lateral thinking.

Last but not least I'd like to thank Tim Fischer for his generous comments about my book and providing a heartfelt and insightful Foreword.

Foreword

There was some significant opposition to Australia's participation in the Boer War or to be more precise, the participation of various detachments from the State colonies as Federation had not been formed when the first troops went to South Africa.

However the opposition, whilst publicly stated, was not sufficient to deter Breaker Morant and Peter Handcock from entering forth into fierce battle in the area north of Pretoria, culminating in the capture of several Boer prisoners and the killing of the German missionary Heese.

This story is one of detail with regard to these aspects of the Boer War, which in turn led to a trumped up court martial, a conviction of guilty and subsequently the execution of two brave Australians on a clear blue morning, thousands of kilometres from their homes, in February 1902.

There is no doubt this book is about a hundred years too late, but it is certainly a case of better late than never. A magnificent writing involving comprehensive research relating to one of Australia's greatest military controversies, the author has left no stone unturned in getting to the bottom of what exactly happened, especially with the conduct of the court martial.

The Boer War was not just some form of African Dutch rebellion against the British Commonwealth Forces and governmental administration. It was something much deeper than that and it is doubtful, all things considered, whether Australia had a particular role to play militarily even before the nation of Australia had been officially formed.

There were some extraordinary leaders on both sides of the Boer War, such as Horatio H Kitchener, known as Lord Kitchener, a man not courageous enough to stay at post in Pretoria on the day of the executions of Breaker Morant and Peter Handcock. On the other side there were leaders like General JC Smuts who went on to become a great builder of the modern South African nation and in an extraordinary twist of events was, as a Senior Minister of the National War Cabinet during World War II, for a brief period Acting Prime Minister of Great Britain.

There are two particular reasons why Australians and people beyond Australia should follow with interest this exciting story. On the one hand, this was the first war in which the media played an important and huge role. Helped by the activities of crisp and colourful writers such as Winston Churchill, along with the advent of the telegram, battles were covered in some considerable detail back at home. Indeed, upon the news of the release of Mafeking after a 217-day long siege by the Boers, there were celebrations right around the Commonwealth in a matter of hours thanks to the telegram and journalists being on hand.

The point should be made that this media coverage was a double-edged sword. The British Government and Kitchener were under pressure, generated by the media, to see that there was adequate punishment dished out to those Commonwealth troops who went beyond the bounds in the conduct of this bitter war. It could be said from a careful reading of this excellent book, that it was the advent of detailed media coverage that led to Kitchener needing scapegoats and two Australians being designated as those scapegoats. The evidence is there that Kitchener wanted a hanging court martial and nothing too much should be allowed to interfere with that result.

The second overall element is one for Australia alone, and that is how two of our citizens could have been slaughtered or shot dead on the altar of political expediency of a military flavour. One hundred years on, this must represent unfinished business, and as much for ensuring proper precedent as anything else, Australia and the Australian Government should take steps to render a Measure of Honour for these two iconic soldiers.

Guerrilla war and the war against terrorism, in an extraordinary parallel, are once again unfolding upon the world a century after the Boer War. It is essential that honour be restored to Morant and Handcock, because they did not deserve to die as a consequence of a curious court martial. Also, it should be a reminder that Australians under the command of British, United States, Thai and other international force leaders, are still deserving of vigorous support by the Australian Government, and overarching scrutiny of any disciplinary action taken against them.

This book represents a mighty step forward in the right direction. But whilst various people may reach different views as to who actually killed whom and why, even if Breaker Morant killed Boer War prisoners in cold blood, even if Peter Handcock dealt with and killed Heese, undeniably there were mitigating circumstances whereby at no stage should they have been sentenced to death by firing squad.

Lastly, the book uncovers in detail a third Australian victim, namely Tenterfield solicitor and lawyer JF Thomas. This Australian Army Officer, called on to defend Morant and Handcock at short notice, did a sterling job in all the circumstances but was absolutely destroyed by the verdict and the carrying out of the verdict. In a crucial letter written on the day of the exe-cutions, it was already apparent that JF Thomas was going to assume a cross of burden over this matter and carry it to his grave.

It is now well known that he returned to Tenterfield crushed by the outcome of the court martial with a sense that he had personally failed and let down Morant and Handcock. This of course was not the case as he had valiantly defended the two Australians, however his legal practice in Tenterfield gradually declined, he with-drew from the local community and became a hermit suffering from huge bouts of depression. He now rests on a gentle slope in a magnificent setting of the Tenter-field cemetery in far north New South Wales.

At least when I last saw his grave I did not trip over, but when I visited the graves of Morant and Handcock, I stepped back to get a better photo and tripped on the edge of the masonry work and fell heavily to the ground. As I lay in the dust of this strange corner of the Preto-ria cemetery, I smiled to myself and thought the Breaker and his mate would be happy enough to know that they still had the ability to bring a measure of authority crashing to the ground.

I salute the author Nick Bleszynski on this magnifi-cent account of a truly momentous saga in Australian military history. I hope that the likes of this arbitrary justice involving unfair and unjust execution never occurs again, and whilst Morant, Handcock and even Thomas were no saints, as this book makes out in chapter and verse, they simply did not deserve the fate that befell them.

2Lt, the Hon Tim Fischer (RL)
February 2002

'A brave race can forget the victims of the field of battle, but never those of the scaffold. The making of political martyrs is the last sanity of statesmanship.'

Sir Arthur Conan Doyle

Author's Note

The story of 'Breaker' Morant is both an intriguing historical subject and a rattling good yarn. A novelist or screenwriter would be hard pressed to invent a story with as much pathos and drama, and I wanted this book to reflect that. The human and political intrigue that surrounded the execution of Harry Morant and Peter Handcock reads like the wildest fiction and the controversy and the conflict of emotions this story generated still has the power to move a century later. The hardest thing about writing this book was not the three solid years of full-time research and writing, but *how* to capture all the elements that emerged during the research. To either convict or acquit Morant, it was necessary to go beyond the historical facts surrounding his controversial trial one hundred years ago and examine his spirit and character. After all, if someone is convicted of murder today, the first questions asked are: Who was he? Why did he do it? What in his character or background caused him to act the way he did?

Writing this book presented me with two major challenges. The first was to discover the truth about the events surrounding the trial and execution of Morant and Handcock. Was it justice or murder? The second was to find out who Breaker Morant really was. Surprisingly, the second challenge turned out to be more difficult than the first. As soon as the first reports of Morant's death reached Australia in 1902, the romantic gown of the martyr was draped across his shoulders.

When a heroic figure dies young and in tragic circumstances there is a tendency to read his life backwards as if everything in his life led inevitably and irrevocably to his premature demise. This is how most authors have chosen to approach the life and death of Harry Morant. It was his inevitable fate, his date with destiny. His story could not have ended any other way.

His first biographer, Frank Renar (Fox), discovered how seductive the romance of the Morant story really is. One moment he was decrying him in *The Bulletin* as a murderer who got his just desserts and worse still a lacklustre poet whose infamy would elevate his verse above its proper station. Perish the thought! Yet, barely two months later, he released a racy best-seller on Morant entitled *Bushman and Buccaneer: Harry Morant – his 'ventures and verses* chock full of chivalric imagery. Since then, Morant, the man, has by and large been explored through the same series of anecdotes and coloured black or white depending on the political leanings of the author. He was either a hero or a villain with nothing in between.

However, the plain truth is that we do not know everything (yet) about the life and death of Breaker Morant. Certain intimate details about his origins and the events leading up to his death were either destroyed, suppressed due to guilt, embarrassment or decorum, or still await discovery in some dusty archive. Although I found answers to many crucial questions, some still remain. That presented me with a problem – how to tell the *whole* story when in some parts we only had fragments of historical fact. I came up with a hybrid style that allowed me a little latitude to put those fragments – which would otherwise have been left out – into a series of reconstructions. *These scenes are clearly identified by the use of italics.* I felt they were vital in enabling the reader to get a clearer understanding of the underlying motivations of key characters. One of the problems with the historical analysis of Morant is that he has been divorced from ordinary human feelings and we don't see how his own personal tragedy fitted into the bigger picture of his life. Hopefully, this book will put some flesh on his bones. Perhaps it didn't happen *exactly* the way I have imagined, but the evidence that follows makes that supposition a reasonable one. To my mind, these passages are vital to a clear understanding of how this great drama unfolded. They do not materially affect the facts of Morant's life and death as presented – they only provide an understanding of how and why they came about. The substance of the book is still factual.

For example, the influence of Daisy Bates (nee O'Dwyer) on Edwin Murrant was, I believe, far more considerable than has been previously thought. During their short liaison in Queensland she persuaded him (for her own selfish ends) to claim the name of Morant, which set him on a collision course with the destiny that awaited him in South Africa. But Daisy was as enigmatic as Edwin Murrant and has bamboozled the many seasoned historians who have tried to fathom the secrets of her soul. However, her background, the sexual power she exerted over men and her chameleon-like talent for changing her identity to suit her surroundings were all real traits and, I believe, are the key to understanding where, when and why Edwin Murrant metamorphosed into Harry Morant. I could have started each sentence with 'possibly', 'maybe' or 'perhaps', but the *italics* make all those qualifications instead and allow us a glimpse at the characters behind the story.

This will, doubtless, offend the puritans and *purists*, but this book was not written for them but for those

Frank Renar called 'the great, unreasoning, unthinking people' who have never let this story die. This is my personal reading of an extraordinary life – warts and all.

Nick Bleszynski
Sydney, Australia
2002

Cast of Principal Characters

Daisy May Bates – an Irish émigré who met, married and left Morant in quick succession in Charters Towers during 1883–1884. Bigamously married Jack Bates and Ernest Baglehole before abandoning Bates and her son Arnold, and going off to the Nullarbor Plain, Western Australia, to live with the Aborigines. Spent over forty years chronicling their culture, language, customs and history. Was appointed West Australia's first Commissioner for Native Affairs and was awarded a Commander of the British Empire for her work in 1934.

Lieutenant Alexander Best – a friend of both Morant and Hunt. Was killed during an attack on a train at Naboomspruit in which seventeen Gordon Highlanders were killed. It was the last straw for Kitchener who issued Hunt, through Hamilton, with orders to take no prisoners shortly afterwards.

Major Charles Bolton – Assistant Provost Marshal in Pietersburg who helped frame the case against the BVC officers. Forced to take over as chief prosecutor after the Visser case when the original prosecutor, Major Burns-Begg, was recalled to London. Ended up feeling great sympathy for Morant and they became good friends. Was entrusted to see that his personal effects were returned to his family in England. Bolton's daughter was present when Morant's effects were returned and her story is one of the key pieces of evidence that

Morant was who he said he was – the son of Admiral Digby Morant.

St John Brodrick – Secretary of State for War during the South African conflict. Said to be the author of orders to shoot Boers found guilty of atrocities, following the killing of British soldiers at Vlakfontein and Graspan during May and June 1901. But as part of the executive which confirmed the death sentences on Morant and Handcock, he showed no mercy. Favoured shooting Lieutenant George Witton as well as Morant and Handcock and refused to release the courts martial transcripts after the executions became public knowledge.

Bennet Burleigh – war correspondent for the London *Daily Telegraph*. Morant was poached by Burleigh from General French as a dispatch rider. They became firm friends as they followed Field Marshal Lord Roberts' advance through South Africa all the way to Komaitipoort where Roberts famously declared the war was 'practically over' when it still had eighteen months to run. Burleigh was recalled in late 1900 after filing some pro-Boer dispatches.

Joseph Chamberlain – Secretary of State for the Colonies before and during the Boer War. Colluded with Cecil Rhodes and the 'gold-bugs' in the abortive 'Jameson Raid' – a stage-managed uprising which aimed to unseat the Transvaal Government – but escaped censure. His Edinburgh speech in October 1901, accusing Germany of war crimes, inflamed German public opinion and increased British Government sensitivity to any allegations of British war crimes. Part of the executive that confirmed the death sentences on Morant and Handcock with the enigmatic lines 'two ought to be sufficient'.

Lieutenant James Edwards – Australian Adjutant who obtained an independent witness statement from

German farmers who saw Boers kill and kick a wounded Captain Hunt after the attack on Duwielskloof. According to Major Lenehan he was intimidated into dropping the evidence and would not speak to British officers unless in the presence of another Australian.

Sergeant Frank Eland – a local Irish recruit who served first with Morant in the BVC B Squadron and then moved to Fort Edward with him. Became firm friends with Morant and was killed alongside Captain Hunt during the attack on Duwielskloof. The deaths of Lieutenant Best, Sergeant Eland and Captain Hunt in quick succession and in brutal circumstances convinced Morant to start following orders to 'take no prisoners'.

Colonel Francis Hall – a veteran of India and Afghanistan, he was made Commanding Officer of the BVC – a desk job based in Pietersburg. Although he was the senior officer, he had no control over the appointment or activities of Captain 'Bulala' Taylor who was controlled directly by Kitchener. Received reports about the killings in the Spelonken and forced Captain Hunt's predecessor, Captain Robertson, to resign, but took no further action, despite receiving reports that more Boers had been shot. When the BVC scandal broke he was transferred to India to prevent him being called as a witness at the courts martial and implicating Kitchener.

Lieutenant-Colonel Hubert Hamilton – Kitchener's Military Secretary. Captain Hunt told Morant that it was Hamilton who issued him with orders to take no prisoners on Kitchener's behalf. Hamilton also denied this at the courts martial, on Kitchener's behalf.

Sergeant-Major Ernest Hammett – present when Visser was shot and part of the shooting parties who executed first eight and then three Boers. Arrested along with other BVC officers, but like Lieutenant Hannam, acquitted after the court of inquiry.

Lieutenant Charles Hannam – in charge of a BVC unit who fired on Boer wagons, despite their attempts to surrender, and killed two children. Arrested with other BVC officers, but acquitted after the court of inquiry. Given the new evidence it would appear that Hannam escaped because he, unlike Morant, followed the 'take no prisoners' order correctly and shot before the Boers surrendered.

Major Jack Hindon – a drummer boy who deserted from the British Army and joined the Boers. After distinguishing himself as a scout by holding the Boer line at Tugela – thereby allowing the siege of Ladysmith to continue – he became a notorious train-wrecker who disrupted British traffic along the Delagoa Bay and Pretoria lines. There was a price on his head and Kitchener ordered that he should not be taken alive. Only the placing of Boer civilians on trains stopped his wrecking activities.

Captain Percy Hunt – Morant met this ex-Hussar from a wealthy English family during his sojourn in Devon in 1901. They became firm friends and were engaged to two sisters. It was Hunt who suggested Morant join the BVC. Hunt was appointed senior officer following the dismissal of Captain Robertson in May 1901 and had Morant transferred to Fort Edward. Morant claimed that Hunt told him that Army HQ had given him orders to take no prisoners. Morant avenged Hunt's death after he was killed and mutilated following a raid on a farmhouse on July 6, 1901.

Major-General Sir Edward Hutton – first served in Australia during 1893 to 1896 overseeing the re-organisation of the New South Wales volunteer defence forces. Hutton was a firm believer that Australian forces should be deployed in defence of the Empire under Imperial command – a policy he pursued covertly after being appointed General Officer Commanding of the Australian Army in 1902. Hutton took the side of Britain during the Morant and Handcock affair and refused to allow Major Lenehan back into the Australian Army, despite the orders of the Australian Minister for Defence to do so. He was removed for his wilful disobedience of ministers and the discovery that he was sending messages to London via secret cipher. He was regarded as a 'failure' on his return to England and put 'out to grass'.

Major-General William Kelly – Adjutant General and Kitchener's second-in-command at Army HQ. Oversaw discipline in the British forces. Kelly told Major Thomas on the night of the executions that there was no hope of a reprieve because the case had stirred up 'grave political difficulties', which started the widely believed rumour that Germany pressured Britain into ordering the executions.

Herbert Horatio Kitchener 1st Earl of Khartoum – after gaining a certain notoriety for his handling of the Sudan campaign, he succeeded Field Marshal Lord Roberts as Commander-in-Chief and commanded British and colonial forces until the conclusion of the war in May 1902. Noted more for his organisational skills than his tactical ability in the field, where he tended to sacrifice men needlessly, he was dubbed 'K of chaos'. Pursued a much harsher campaign against the Boers in which he stepped up farm and crop burnings, herded women and children into detention camps, built a vast network of blockhouses to limit Boer mobility and founded irregular units – such as the BVC – to counter Boer guerrilla units in remote areas. Kitchener made the executive decision to prosecute and execute Morant and Handcock. At the trial he had his Military Secretary, Lieutenant-Colonel Hamilton, deny Morant's claim that orders were issued by Army HQ to shoot Boer prisoners – although this has now been contradicted by new evidence. He was appointed Commander-in-Chief in India before serving as Minister of War during World War I and was lost at sea when the *HMS Hampshire* was torpedoed off the Orkney Islands in 1916.

Major Robert Lenehan – a lawyer in the New South Wales Supreme Court before the Boer War. Made Officer Commanding in the field of the BVC and recruited Morant whom he knew socially from the Sydney hunt clubs. Was Kitchener's original choice as 'scapegoat' when news of BVC killings became public. Morant and Handcock refused to implicate him to save themselves. At the courts martial, Lenehan was found guilty of not reporting a murder, for which no-one was ever found guilty, given a reprimand and sent back to Australia. He informed the Australian Government of the executions. After due investigation, the Australian Government decided to reinstate him into the Australian Army. General Officer Commanding of the Australian Army, Major-General Hutton did not approve of this and spent two years trying to get him dismissed. Lenehan was eventually allowed to take up his position in 1904.

Alfred Milner – a hardline imperialist who served as High Commissioner to The Cape Colony during the Boer War. Shared Cecil Rhodes' view that the only way to resolve the issue of who ruled South Africa was to crush the Boers. Represented Britain at the various conferences leading up to the war and did his utmost to engineer a conflict with the Boers. Wielding immense political influence, he agitated against any peace deals during the war. Milner derailed the plan Kitchener hammered out at Middleburg in early 1901 and prolonged the war by another eighteen months.

Francis Enraght-Moony – appointed as the first civilian Commissioner for Native Affairs in northern Transvaal. Very quickly exposed the murky deeds of his military predecessor Captain Taylor and his imminent presence at Fort Edward was one of the key factors in Kitchener's decision to prosecute the BVC officers for murder.

Admiral Sir Digby Morant – the man Harry Morant claimed was his father. A Lieutenant at the time of Harry's birth in 1864, he rose through the naval ranks to become an Admiral and received a Knight Commander (of the order) of the Bath in 1901. Although he denied Morant was his son on a number of occasions and no conclusive link can be proved (as yet), there are a number of pieces of strong circumstantial evidence linking them.

Sergeant-Major Kenneth Morrison – stationed at Fort Edward and in charge of the patrol dispatched to shoot the first six Boers on the orders of Captain Taylor. Morrison questioned the 'take no prisoners' policy and fearing for his life fled to Pietersburg where he informed Colonel Hall about the killings in the Spelonken. He was dismissed along with Captain Robertson, but was called as a defence witness at the courts martial and implicated Taylor in the first seven killings in the Spelonken.

Edwin and Catherine Murrant – the parents of Edwin Murrant. Catherine was his biological mother, though there is doubt that Edwin, who died from rheumatic fever two weeks before his son's birth, was the father. They were Master and Matron of the Bridgwater Workhouse. After Edwin's death, Catherine continued to work there until she was dismissed for drunkenness in 1882. She died in 1899 whilst her son was in South Australia.

Sir Henry Parkes – an ex-Premier of New South Wales and member of Parliament who became the 'father' of the Federation movement. In a historic speech at the Tenterfield School of Arts on October 24, 1889, he urged Australia to federate into one nation and take responsibility for its own affairs.

Major Robert Montague Poore – as Provost Marshal he was responsible for discipline in the field, investigating alleged crimes and prisoner movements. Having been asked by Kitchener to form the Bushveldt Carbineers in February 1901, Kitchener then asked Poore to invest-igate them when news of the killings came in from the Spelonken. He collected evidence against them and was responsible for their security whilst they were in custody, for transporting them to Pretoria and for drilling the firing party. His diaries reveal that despite the denials of Kitchener and the British Government, orders did exist to shoot Boers wearing khaki and those taken prisoner.

Reverend Fritz Reuter – German predikant who lived at the Medingen Mission near Duwielskloof. He warned Captain Hunt not to attack Viljoen's Farm, however Hunt ignored his warning and died. Reuter washed and cleaned Hunt's body before he buried him on his prop-erty and testified at the courts martial that the body had been mutilated.

Cecil Rhodes – a British-born imperialist of boundless ambition whose dream was to see Britain claim the whole continent of Africa. He trekked north and founded the central African state of Rhodesia, which was named after him. His Chartered Company had a finger in every pie – from Kimberley diamonds to the Rand goldmines – and he was not afraid to use his polit-ical office, Prime Minister of The Cape Colony, to gain commercial leverage. Architect of the abortive 'Jameson Raid' of 1895, a thinly veiled coup d'état to oust the Transvaal Government and deliver the gold-rich Rand into British control. He was removed from political office as a result, but remained immensely influential. Rhodes died in 1902 and was hailed as a hero.

Field Marshal Lord Roberts – controversially replaced the first Commander-in-Chief of British forces, Sir Redvers Buller, in December 1899 and served in that capacity until November 1900. Roberts turned the war around and in less than a year took all the major cities, but was regarded as being too gentlemanly in his dealings with the Boers. He failed to crush them at Johannesburg and then Pretoria, which allowed the Boers to retreat to the veldt and begin fighting a guerrilla war. He left for England declaring that the war was 'practically over'. The so-called 'guerrilla war' ran for another eighteen months.

Captain James Huntley Robertson – first senior officer of BVC A Squadron at Fort Edward. Described as weak and effeminate, he deferred to Captain Taylor who ordered the killing of the first six Boers and the BVC trooper Van Buuren. He was removed by Colonel Hall and allowed to resign without being charged. He was then retained as a star witness by the prosecution during the courts martial where he admitted that orders to 'take no prisoners' existed and he also implicated Taylor in the killings. Despite being dismissed from the Army, he was later re-employed as a Lieutenant.

Captain Alfred Taylor – an Irishman who emigrated to Rhodesia and helped put down the Matabele uprising. Known for his hatred of natives, who dubbed him 'Bulala' (killer). Worked for Cecil Rhodes and was appointed native commissioner cum intelligence agent to the BVC at Fort Edward by Kitchener. According to various accounts, Taylor was the real man in charge. He instigated the first Boer killings in the Spelonken, tried and executed many natives and terrorised and murdered the local Boer population. However, despite there being sufficient evidence, Taylor escaped punishment and went on to occupy senior positions of responsibility.

Major James Francis Thomas – a lawyer, newspaper proprietor and Captain of the local volunteer force in Tenterfield before the war, Thomas was a pillar of the community and a great supporter of Federation. He served with distinction at the siege of Elands River before being asked by Major Lenehan, whom he knew from Sydney, to defend him at the BVC officers courts martial. On arriving in Pietersburg he discovered that the other accused had no representation and offered to defend them – which he did with a day's preparation. Despite his best efforts, the accused were found guilty and Morant and Handcock executed. He campaigned for George Witton's release, but the trial had a serious psychological toll on Thomas and on returning home, he spiralled downwards into bankruptcy, prison and disbarment. The final blow was Witton's 1929 'confession' in which he revealed that Handcock had admitted to killing Reverend Heese. Thomas died alone and impoverished in 1941.

George Whyte-Melville – how the young Edwin Murrant came into his care is not known, but this monied Scottish author, soldier, hunt master and golfer who was regarded as England's greatest equestrian expert was the man who brought up, educated and made the young Henry Murrant into the great horseman he became. A seminal influence on Morant's early life.

Lieutenant George Ramsdale Witton – sailed with the 4th Contingent early in 1900. Joined the BVC in mid-1901 and arrived in the Spelonken just as Hunt was killed. He got caught up in Morant's campaign to avenge Hunt and was part of the 'drum-head' court martial that sentenced Visser to death. He shot one of the eight Boers who went for his rifle and for this he was court martialled along with the other BVC officers and sentenced to death. Kitchener commuted his sentence to life in prison. He served two years and was released in 1904. Following his return to Australia, he wrote the controversial inside account of the BVC entitled *Scapegoats of The Empire*. He later changed his mind and told Thomas in a letter that Handcock had admitted to him that he killed Reverend Heese.

Prologue

HE'D RUN AND RUN UNTIL HIS LUNGS *were on fire, but still he was pursued down the long dark tunnel that he knew could only lead to hell itself. In front of him, blocking his path, the face appeared again, but though he struggled hard to focus through swollen eyes blinded by sweat, he could put no name to it.*

The man's mouth ballooned in size until it seemed to take up his entire field of vision. The thin lips hidden beneath the drooping, almost burlesque moustache formed a single word.

'Fire!'

The answer came in a thunderous volley from an eighteen-barrell rifle looking oddly like a menorah, every one of its cold, steely, empty eyes pointed right at him. Looking down the barrels, he watched in morbid fascination as, in slow motion, the trigger released the spring that propelled the firing pin into the base of the cartridge case and began the complex chain of chemical reactions that would ignite the cordite. Simultaneously, eighteen cherry-red spurts of fire bloomed like fleurs du mal in the darkest recesses of the gun chambers and were followed by a dull rumble of thunder that got progressively louder as the terrific gas pressure the explosions produced forced the bullets up the barrel towards him. Instinctively, he threw up his hands in a futile effort to ward off the hail of flesh-tearing bullets that he knew would follow.

But before the bullets could reach their target, Harry Morant snapped awake. Gasping for breath, his heart hammering and straining below his rib cage, he realised that he had cheated death . . . for another hour at least. His relief was short-lived. Before the chill early morning air had even begun to cool the slick of hot, clammy sweat bathing his entire body, the reveille bell sounded in the distance. A cold hand clutched at his heart as he realised what day it was. The nightmare was not over; it was only just beginning. The bell tolled for him. This was the day he was to die. No phantom dream this time, just cold hard reality.

His rude awakening to the day of his death was in direct contrast to the peaceful figure of Peter Handcock, whose large frame lay huddled under the thin blanket on the cot opposite, barely visible in the gloom of the sullen dawn. Nothing would wake Peter, no distorted dreams haunted his sleep. A solid, reliable mate – God bless him. Only wish he'd shave that moustache off – it reminded him of Lord bloody Kitchener!

Outside, Morant could hear the detail methodically checking and loading the firing party's rifles, with standard issue .303 rounds. How ironic! In court, he had claimed he shot the Boers under 'Rule .303' and now Provost Marshal Poore, who oversaw all matters of discipline and punishment, had drilled a firing party to impose that same rule on them.

The click of the breeches was followed by the dull sound of two heavy objects thudding onto the rough ground and being scraped along. He closed his eyes briefly. Those would be the two wooden coffins they'd built in the workshop for the occasion. Yesterday evening, as darkness fell like a shroud on their final day, he'd seen them through the bars of the cell window standing on their ends in the courtyard – silent shibboleths to the great hereafter.

Morant rose from the table, measured the twelve paces across the cell to the washstand and dashed some cold water from the tin bowl onto his face. Curiosity caused him to look one last time at his reflection in the cracked mirror that Jailer Morrow had given him. Good bloke. They'd come out from Adelaide to South Africa together to fight the Boers. He'd done what he could . . . what more could a man ask? He saw that his ruggedly handsome face had lost some of the athletic leanness and his skin had paled in the five months since his arrest, but he still had most of his hair and hadn't changed much over the years. Later, biographer Frank Renar would write of Harry Morant:

> Only a little more battered, more worn with ten years of roving and rioting; with only a very little of shiftiness in his frank eyes to mark the desperate straits navigated by this accomplished good-for-naught, the sorrow of his family, the solace and menace of his friends.

Now, in that timeless pre-dawn moment of February 27, 1902, similar sentiments drifted through his mind as he thought briefly of the girl he'd left behind in Devon. Dear sweet thing, she'd be heartbroken . . . After a lifetime of roving he might have gone back to her, but he'd needed this last hurrah to come home in a blaze of glory and make things right with his family. Too late now . . .

He turned to the table and picked up the papers lying there. Whilst Peter had written a simple one-page note to his family, he, Harry Morant, otherwise known as 'the Breaker', had occupied himself during his last night on earth by writing one final bilious ode to the British Empire.

It was a biting satirical poem on the double standards of an army that sent a man all the way from Australia, an outpost of the Empire, across the world to South Africa to kill Boers, the perceived enemies of

*that Empire, then tried and sentenced him to death
for carrying out those very same orders . . . As he'd
remarked in a farewell letter to Major Lenehan, his
commanding officer:*

> Had I known as much two months ago as I know
> today, there would be a lot of Dutchmen at large
> that are now in Hell, or lazing in the Bermudas.

*At the further end of the courtyard, approaching foot-
steps started out towards their cell, ominous doom in
their ponderous tread.*

*Morant stared hard at the page clenched in his hand
and the words leapt out at him, their jaunty defiance at
odds with the sinking feeling flooding him. His final
riposte was entitled,* Butchered to Make a Dutchman's
Holiday – The Last Rhyme and Testimony of Tony
Lumpkin – The Breaker:

> In a prison cell I sadly sit,
> A damned crest-fallen chappie!
> And own to you I feel a bit –
> A little bit un-happy!
>
> It really ain't the place nor time
> To reel off rhyming diction –
> But yet we'll write a final rhyme
> Whilst waiting cru-ci-fiction!
>
> No matter what 'end' they decide –
> Quick-lime or biling ile, sir?
> We'll do our best when crucified
> To finish off in style, sir!
>
> But we bequeath a parting tip
> For sound advice of such men,
> Who come across in transport ships
> To polish off the Dutchmen!

If you encounter any Boers
You really must not loot 'em!
And if you wish to leave these shores
For pity's sake, Don't shoot 'em!

And if you'd earn a D.S.O.,
Why, every British sinner
Should know the proper way to go
Is 'Ask the Boer to dinner!'

Let's toss a bumper down our throat,
Before we pass to Heaven,
And toast: 'The trim-set petticoat
We leave behind in Devon!'

Its bitter satire was quite a departure from the roistering exploits of the Brigalow Boys *or his odes to loves lost which had made him such a fixture in the pages of* The Bulletin *back in Australia, but Morant justifiably felt proud of his final effort. It would make a fine epitaph and raise a few cheers back in old Sydney town.*

When Peter had asked him to read through his letter, its simple heartfelt honesty brought a tear to even the Breaker's jaundiced eye. It ended:

I will go to meet my Maker certain that I did my duty. If I overstepped the mark, I can only ask my country and my family to forgive me . . . God save Australia.

In spite of himself, a smile cracked Morant's face. We wouldn't be needing God if they'd only thought to take charge of their own blokes instead of leaving it to the bloody Poms . . . I sound like a bloody Aussie . . . *The thought came to him in a wave of ironic humour quickly swamped by the hard reality of his life. But when it comes to it, who will there be to claim the body of old Harry Morant and see he gets a decent burial, sparing* him the ignominy of a pint o' quicklime and an unmarked grave – the usual fate of those who fall short of the British military's high ideals?

What wouldn't he have given to wake once more in that wide brown land on the other side of the world to the mocking call of the kookaburra and the medicinal scent of eucalyptus that drifted in on the cool morning breeze? Oh, he had cursed that damned Brigalow many a time when he felt the Dante-like monotony of its straw-coloured spinifex, stunted gums and cathedral-like red ironstone outcrops bounded by seamless blue skies stifling his freedom-loving spirit. But even the shit, dust and flies kicked up by a mob of cattle in the searing heat of summer would be preferable to this.

'This is what comes of Empire building!' The wry words he had uttered with a sigh and a curse to Peter as they'd been shackled in irons for the journey to Pretoria to receive their sentences of death came back to haunt him now.

His reverie was interrupted by the rude clash of keys opening their cell door. Doom had arrived and spoke with a thick Scottish accent. The two Cameron Highlanders detailed to escort them had muted their native belligerence today in respect for the occasion. The sergeant met Morant's gaze squarely and nodded.

'Let's be haein' ye, gentlemen!' came the polite request, sounding for all the world like the maitre d' at the Mount Nelson in Cape Town summoning them to dinner, rather than an executioner to their deaths. Well, they'd had their 'Last Supper' at any rate, as he had reminded George and Peter last night when they raised their glasses one last time and drained the dregs of Jailer Morrow's native whisky.

Peter came awake in an instant and swung his legs onto the floor, his giant frame dwarfing Morant as he rose unsteadily from the cot, still lost on the edges of sleep. For one crazy moment Morant thought about rushing the two men at the cell door and making a bolt for it. No! he thought, savagely . . . that's what they'd like, prove 'em right what they said about Harry Morant. Well, if they want a fucking show, that's what they'll get, he resolved as he crossed the cell to stand by Handcock.

He was surprised at the slight tremble in his knees as if the weight of his powerful, stocky frame was suddenly too much for them. Instead he said coolly, eye to eye with the senior member of the escort: 'You'll give the man time to come to himself, have a wash and brush up. Go out like a soldier should. His bloody Majesty's Army can wait.'

It was not a request, more like an order. The bushy eyebrows of the Cameron Sergeant raised and lowered only a fraction before he nodded in agreement.

Morant turned to Handcock, who was already bent over the washstand splashing water onto his face.

'Take your time, mate. Dawn's slow in coming today, for a change.'

At last it was time. To cover up his emotion, he made one of the famous off the cuff quips which had always sprung easily to his lips.

'Come along then Peter, me old mate, will sir be havin' the bacon or the grilled kidneys this mornin'?'

'Both, me good man, I thinks!' threw back Handcock, entering into the spirit with a grin as he finished buttoning up his tunic. 'Seein' how the day looks to be turnin' out so fine!'

The two jailers threw each other quizzical glances as they closed ranks behind them.

Halfway down the corridor, the white, frightened face of George Witton appeared at the serving hatch of one of the cell doors. Tears streaked the young, fresh *features that once burned with patriotic pride as his transport ship cast off from the quay at Melbourne. His eyes were puffed and red. Why's he crying? He's off to England . . . unlike some! Morant thought uncharitably, then softened as Witton reached his hand through the hatch and stammered:*

'Good . . . goodbye, Harry.'

Morant squeezed the lad's warm, sweaty hand and replied: 'Goodbye, George. Take care of yourself. Remember what I said in court.'

He had no need – every detail was indelibly imprinted on Witton's memory. After the court of inquiry, at which bitter accusations flew around, The President, Colonel Carter, told them that they were to be court martialled. Morant jumped to his feet with his fists bunched and a wild look in his eye. Focusing on Carter he snarled, 'Look here Colonel, you have got us here now; take us all out and crucify us at once, for as sure as God made pippins, if you let one man off he'll yap.'

And Witton did yap. Following his release from Lewes prison in 1904, he wrote an account of his experiences entitled Scapegoats of The Empire.

Before they were hustled away by the guards, Peter Handcock stepped forward and clasped George's hand in mute farewell. Poor George, he'd been spared from the firing squad but had taken the verdict harder than them.

Down the long flagstone corridor now, towards the open door, the sound of their army boots echoing, marking each step away from the sterility of the cell where they had spent the last five days of their lives. Somewhere beyond the doorway, out there in the bush, a jackal howled in the rustling dawn wind that had risen with the first streaks of light.

MORANT SLOWED AT THE DOORWAY *and appreciatively drew in a long breath of the clean cold air of the veldt morning.* Should've taken up that offer of a horse and a clear passage to Laurenco Marques, when I had the chance.

Even as the thought came to him, he dismissed it. Wouldn't that just have been delaying the inevitable? He'd known deep down all his life that this day would come. It wasn't so much a matter of how it would end, more a case of where and when.

Better this way. They'd never be able to forget old Harry Morant now. Born a nobody . . . died a hero . . . in some quarters at least. *He straightened his shoulders and matched his step to that of Peter Handcock.*

As they marched across the courtyard, a British officer approached them. The two Camerons saluted him, but Morant and Handcock kept their hands by their sides. Ignoring the slight, he asked with stiff formality, tapping his swagger stick against the fine khaki twill of his breeched thigh, 'Would you like a priest?'

'No, *thank you, I'm a pagan,*' Morant *replied jauntily, the corner of his mouth curling into his trademark grin. The officer's barely suppressed annoyance at the sight of the condemned colonials amused him no end.* Pompous bastards. Pompous Poms. *His smile widened but his eyes were hard and fierce. The officer's gaze flickered and retreated in the face of his contempt.*

'What the blazes is a pagan?' *asked Peter, innocently, his open face registering incomprehension. Taking his cue from Morant's wicked wink, he closed ranks quickly and added softly,* 'Me too, mate.'

Dear loyal Peter. Who else would you have at your side on your final walk? *As they left the officer in their wake, Morant's quick eyes noted the fresh furrows made by the coffins in the earth as they were dragged towards the veldt, tracing the same path as they now did*. Though I walk in the shadow of the valley of death, I fear no evil. Not long now, *he thought, pursing his lips in a soundless whistle.*

The Kaffirs are noticeably absent this fine morning, *he thought. Their usual curiosity about the strange doings of the mulungus did not extend to the method in which they executed their own warriors, it seemed. Bad juju in anyone's language. Normally they would be in the background of every occasion, as much part of the landscape as the kopjes and the flat-topped acacia trees, watching and listening, trying to piece together the unfolding events of the white man's history in their land. Not today.*

As if on cue, a screech owl hooted a mournful requiem from the thorn thickets away to the east where the new day was struggling to break through in streaks of dull gold and angry scarlet. Harry Morant felt the shiver run down his back under the stiff serge of his tunic. To the natives the pale blur of the owls often glimpsed at dusk or daybreak was the harbinger of bad news or an omen of death. No surprise there, mate. *No doubt they'd seen or heard them in the trees and, fearfully superstitious of tribal lore, stayed away. His glance flickered towards the low cluster of beehive huts on the periphery of the military camp. They stood silent and aloof in the chill of misty dawn, huddled low down against the earth as if the inhabitants inside were willing them, with all the patience at their disposal, to pass on by into history.*

Unseen eyes from both thorn trees and kraal tracked Morant and Handcock as they appeared together on the veldt in the grey half-light of dawn and walked, flanked by the two armed sentries, towards the small knot of dun uniforms that had gathered a few hundred yards into the veldt. This was it, then. The small corner of God's earth reserved for executions.

Ahead of them, the eerie silhouettes of the waiting

Cameron Highlanders were black against the lightening sky, as if pasted onto a theatre backdrop, their funereal black tartan kilts flapping against their bare knees in the stiff breeze like the wings of the assvogels that hovered hopefully overhead.

The shooting party made up of eighteen riflemen and a major stood apart from the rest of the party and awaited the deliverance of their victims. Major Thomas Souter, whose men had the dubious honour of carrying out the sentence, resisted wiping away the beads of perspiration that had formed on his brow despite the coolness of the early hour.

One of the rifles had a blank in its breech, but he knew that some of the men would still fire to the side rather than live with the possibility that theirs had been the fatal shot that had ended the life of a soldier who was, at the end of it all, one of their brothers in arms. Who could blame them?

Souter watched the prisoners approach. The shorter, stocky Morant was known by reputation, if not by name. The Australians called him 'the Breaker' – a great horseman by all accounts. He was a cool customer, no doubt about it.

Standing in the forefront was Victor Newland, who served with the South Australian Mounted Rifles. He had caroused long and hard with Morant during their wild outback days and they had joined up on the same day in Adelaide. Later he would pay testimony in his diary to the courage with which his cobber Harry Morant faced death:

> I can see it so plainly yet . . . his debonair swagger out into the damp coolness of morning; his bright greeting to all.

But for now, Newland had no words – only a hard, stiff knot in the pit of his belly as he wondered what his final words to his friend would be.

As the prisoners and their escort came level with the Cameron Major, Morant stopped and reached into the breast pocket of his tunic. Opening a beautiful ornate silver cigarette case, he carefully selected a cigarette for himself. Lighting it, he handed the case to Souter and said, 'A souvenir of this auspicious day, Jock. I won't be needing it where I'm going.' The defiant smile had just a hint of sadness in it. The Highland Major just nodded.

Morant said loudly enough for all to hear, his voice steady, 'I was given orders to shoot Boers, but only did so after the Boers murdered my CO Captain Hunt, the best mate I had in the world.'

That sent a frisson through the Cameron ranks like a message down a telegraph wire. Some of them twitched uneasily and Souter cursed inwardly as he heard McPhail's muttered obscenity in the ranks. Trust that wee shite stirring Heilan' teuchter tae get a haud o' it.

'Whar's Lord Kitchener the day, then?' hissed the small, feisty, red-headed McPhail, his sun-reddened face showing his open contempt for all authority, and especially the titled variety.

'Awa' fechtin' Boers, nae doot,' came the sarcastic reply from somewhere in the ranks of the shooting party. There was the raucous clearing of phlegm and a soft splat as the glob of saliva and mucus hit the ground.

The Major decided to ignore it and raised his chin to ease his neck away from the cutting edge of the military jacket that had suddenly become too tight. Rumour had it Kitchener had gone up country once London had confirmed the men's sentences – just to be sure there'd be no last minute appeal or reprieve. Major Thomas, the Australians' lawyer, had been told that General Kitchener could not be reached . . .

'Aye, an' leavin' us tae dae his dirty work,' complained Private McPhail sourly.

'Haud ye're wheest min, afore we're kilt 'an a',' came the urgent reminder that they were within earshot of the top British military brass who would not tolerate dissent in the ranks. Dirty work, aye there was something in that right enough, *thought Souter reflectively* . . . though it was best never said out loud.

Major Souter had attended the courts martial himself, out of curiosity and, if the truth be known, not a little sympathy for the accused. He did not consider himself especially well educated and had little more than a rudimentary knowledge of military law, but even he could see what was going on. Oh, it all looked and sounded fine enough, but it was what was not said that concerned him. They'd all been told what to do with Boer prisoners. As many serving men had testified at the trial, they'd shot many a Boer themselves on patrol under what Morant had termed 'Rule .303' – the bullet calibre of their Lee-Metford rifles. It was common knowledge that the Gordons, the other Highland Regiment serving in the Transvaal, had taken revenge on the train-wreckers who claimed some twenty of their men in a single raid.

Glancing sideways at his own men, he counted half a dozen who, but for the grace of God, could be standing at the wrong end of their own rifles right now. There's mair tae this than meets the eye, but it's o'er late fir these twa noo. They'll hae tae settle wi Kitchener at that higher tribunal in their ain time.

He was jolted back to the present by Provost Marshal Robert Poore stepping forward and nodding curtly for him to proceed. Such military occasions lacked the ceremony and theatre of their civil counterpart. There was no reading of the charges and sentences, no priest to deliver their last rites and no last testimony from the accused, but Morant wasn't going to let that stop him. He launched a broadside of fiery invective at

*the Provost Marshal, who returned a little too quickly
to the bosom of his fellow officers with the harsh words
nipping at his tail.*

*Then, in stark contrast to the bombast he'd shown
all the way through this terrible ordeal, Morant reached
out and took Handcock's hand and together they
walked their last few steps across the veldt to where two
chairs had been placed side by side.*

*Before they blindfolded him, Morant stared down
his executioners across the twenty-five paces of rough
ground that separated them. As though he had tele-
pathically intercepted their earlier thoughts, he rolled
the fag, whose life expectancy was now about as short
as his own, to the corner of his mouth, and called out
nonchalantly to them, 'Better fire all those bullets lads,
or I'll come down those fucking barrels looking for
'em!'*

*Feet shuffled nervously as the directness of the words
found their mark among the uneasy men. It was as if
he'd been privy to their innermost thoughts. Souter
looked across at Morant in sudden respect and saw no
hint of fear in those bright blue eyes. He's nae mocking
us either. The mad bastard is gaunae go oot wi a' guns
blazin' . . .*

*He also noted that Handcock said nothing, just sat
with his head down. Mibee thinkin' aboot his wife and
bairns oot in Australia.*

*The lightening sky over the faraway hills signalled
that it was time for the final scene. The best thing was
to end it quickly. The Major straightened his shoulders
and moved forward to take charge of his men.*

God! How dreadful it was when they bound his
eyes and sat him in the chair, square and fearless, a
dead man yet alive.

More of Victor Newland's words that were destined for

another day. All that tumbled to his lips in the last moment of farewell was a quick 'God bless, Harry,' as he had passed within earshot, that and a hand on his shoulder, pressing hard.

'Ready!' shouted Souter, looking along the row of men, rifles at the ready, youthful faces pale, the usually belligerent McPhail looking as if he was ready to spew. He prayed that a return to military drill would banish the spectres of doubt that had been mingling about this sorry gathering for too long.

There was one last exchange between the two blind-folded men out on the veldt.

'Goodbye, Peter,' said Morant, a half smile creasing up the corners of his mouth.

'So long, Harry, mate,' replied Handcock, raising his head and turning his blindfolded eyes towards him.

'Pre-sent arms!'

As the Camerons raised their rifles in a ragged reluc-tant row, Major Souter glanced instinctively towards the prison, as if half expecting to see someone sprinting across the veldt waving a last-minute reprieve. But only the red, white and blue of the 'Butcher's Apron' – the mocking term used for the Union flag – fluttered impa-tiently above the ramparts as if to remind him that any order given under its Imperial authority would be expected to be carried out, as was his bounden duty as a servant to the Crown.

Morant used that momentary pause to great dramatic effect. The line of silent, waiting muzzles had given him a strong sense of deja vu, but this time he saw the face that had appeared in front of him in his dream.

He saw no compassion in those cold cobalt eyes. As those thin lips below the lustrous moustache again formed that single word, he knew that this time he would not wake up and cheat the bullets, and decided to go out in style. Victor Newland described what happened next, a moment of pure theatre, the kind of performance the Breaker had been famous for:

> Then from the chair rises the Breaker – down flutters the blinding kerchief: I catch a glimpse of tawny fearless eyes alight with understanding and pity for the man who must call death upon him. Lightly swings his hand to his breast . . . Smartly drop his arms to his sides, square set his shoulders: a steady, motionless figure he stands.

With his heartbeat roaring in his ears like a herd of runaway brumbies, Harry 'the Breaker' Morant knew his moment of destiny had arrived. He opened his mouth, sucked in one last sweet, clean breath and let his final eulogy rip through the still morning air. Last words – no plea for redemption, only a command mixed with a prayer, not only for himself, but for Peter who had walked every inch of the way with him.

'Shoot straight, you bastards! Don't make a mess of it.'

'Fir fucks sake, min!' hissed McPhail savagely, squeezing his eyes shut as Souter granted Morant's final request. Victor Newland stood by helplessly as his mate drew his last breath:

> Then comes the word of his doom, 'Fire!'

The wooden stocks of eighteen rifles slapped back hard into their shoulders as they discharged the deadly volley that threw the two men backwards into the dust and sent flocks of screeching, cawing birds wheeling into the air in alarm.

The Cameron Highlanders slowly brought down their rifles and listened to the rumble as the celestial chariots, bearing away the souls of the dead warriors, rolled down the veldt towards Valhalla.

A mile away, George Witton and Henry Picton, who had only been cashiered for his part in the killings, also heard them pass overhead as he stood on the railway platform where he had been taken to await the train to Cape Town, and closed his eyes in silent prayer. He later wrote:

> [T]he death knell of my late comrades . . . out went two brave and fearless soldiers, men that the Empire could ill afford to lose.

The sun chose that moment to rise in salute above the far horizon and bathed the scene in a watery golden light. Souter stepped forward and drew his revolver in case a final coup de grâce was needed. Thankfully, it was not.

Morant lay on his back with eyes wide open and a surprised expression on his face. Souter could have sworn he was about to speak, but where his eyes had been defiant before, they were now vacant. The Breaker was dead and his soul departed. He'd taken most of it down the left side, his right arm crossed over his chest above his heart in an oddly Christian gesture for a 'pagan'.

Souter bent down and closed his eyes on this world, so that in the next he could face his maker with his eyes wide open – an old Pictish superstition that well befitted a man who insisted he was a pagan. Except for the gaping wounds in his chest, Peter Handcock looked as if he had just turned over and gone back to the sleep he had been so abruptly disturbed from at dawn.

The Major straightened, and with a terse nod to the Provost Marshal confirmed that the sentence had been carried out. Satisfied, Poore led the officers back to their mess for a cup of tea to wash away the caustic taste of cordite and guilt.

Despite their outward disdain, their diaries admitted a grudging respect for the men they'd just consigned to history. 'Died game' was the overall verdict. Poore noted:

> Major Souter (Cameron Highlanders) who was in charge of the firing party conducted operations very badly.

Only Major Thomas, who had been the men's defence counsel, remained still, white-faced and shocked. With a heavy heart he watched a group of slouch-hatted Australians lug two wooden coffins out from behind the clump of trees. Paraded on the square during the execution amid rumours of a mutiny, they were given leave to claim the bodies before the blowflies and rigor mortis began their grim work. On his return to Australia, he never again used the title of Major.

Souter turned and dismissed the firing party who had gone quiet since they discharged their volley, no doubt taking the time to absorb what they'd just done and silently praying for God's forgiveness. The Almighty was not far away from his own thoughts as Souter looked at the face of Harry Morant for the last time.

'Nane'll judge ye noo, but the Lord himsel',' he whispered by way of a final benediction.

He was wrong about that.

JUST OUTSIDE OF HARRISMITH, SOME *two hundred miles south of Pretoria, Lord Kitchener was sitting on his favourite chestnut mount watching the long line of captured Boer wagons and cattle filing slowly across the horizon under the watchful eye of his mounted corps. A staff officer galloped up, saluted and placed a cable in his hand. It was a concise one-line message befitting both military custom and the rudimentary nature of telegraph technology at the end of Victoria's reign.*

EXECUTIONS CARRIED OUT AT DAWN STOP

Kitchener inwardly breathed a sigh of relief, tapping the paper reflectively against the pommel of his saddle.

'Majuba Day' had been a great success. On this very day, twenty-one years before, the Boers had defeated the British forces at Majuba Hill and wrested back control of the Transvaal. Today would go down in history as the day he, Lord Kitchener, restored the Empire's honour . . . twice! Once in Sudan and now in South Africa.

A sudden breeze blew across the dry vastness of the veldt and spun dust devils of whirling grit into the faces of the Boers, just to add further insult to injury. The rogue wind also ripped the cablegram from the General's distracted hand and carried it away across the coarse grass. As Lord Kitchener watched it tumble off into the distance, he thought it wholly appropriate. It was the last the world would ever hear of Harry Morant.

Lord Kitchener – like Major Souter – would also be proved to be very wrong. A century after Kitchener ordered those executions, Harry 'the Breaker' Morant is an Australian legend, and the issue of their innocence and guilt is still being fiercely debated. History, not Lord Kitchener, will have the last word on that.

'What is it about the politics of this country that turns us all into blackguards?'

Lord Kitchener

1

'Breaker' Morant –
Man of Mystery

Born of a thoroughbred English race,
Well proportioned and closely knit,
Neat, slim figure and handsome face,
Always ready and always fit,
Hardy and wiry of limb and thew,
That was the ne'er-do-well Jim Carew . . .

'Jim Carew' by 'Banjo' Paterson

MOST BIOGRAPHIES END WITH THE death of the subject, but given the turbulent nature of Morant's personal life and military career, there were always going to be loose ends, unresolved issues and many questions. Indeed, the mystery and secrecy that still shrouds the circumstances of his death has sustained public interest for a century. Amid rumours of lies, cover-ups and conspiracies, the dubious threads of this tale lead back to the highest echelons of the British military and top government figures of the day. Morant keeps appearing like Banquo's blood-spattered ghost – refusing to die until justice is done.

Morant and Handcock's defence counsel, Major JF Thomas, said, 'The story of Morant and the Bushveldt Carbineers is a romance and a tragedy.'

It was all that and a lot more.

23

The true story of 'the Breaker' began to unravel on March 28, 1902, the day the *SS Aberdeen* docked in Melbourne. Standing anxiously at the rail was Major Robert Lenehan, the Commanding Officer of the Bushveldt Carbineers. Held incommunicado in South Africa by Lord Kitchener, following his discharge Lenehan was bundled aboard the troopship in Cape Town, but not before he ran into lieutenants Witton and Picton and learned of the terrible fate that had befallen Morant and Handcock.

On the long voyage back to Australia he'd paced the deck for a restless, sleepless month with the sensational news he carried burning a hole in his conscience. By the time he arrived in Melbourne, Lenehan's pent-up emotions were like a coiled spring ready to be released.

To the vigilant newspapermen waiting on the dock, this was just another troopship arriving home from the war. There'd be a good yarn here and there – stories of heroism, sacrifice and loss but in the two and a half years since the First Australian Contingent sailed, they'd heard plenty of those.

If they'd looked more closely, they would have seen a stout, moustachioed, middle-aged man dressed in a borrowed, ill-fitting civilian suit hurrying down the gangplank. The flags, the gaily coloured bunting, the energetic military band playing the popular anthem *Soldiers of the Queen* were just a blur of noise and colour as Lenehan shoved through the cheering throng of families, friends and well-wishers in their Sunday best, packed like sardines on the quay. Little did those reporters know that the most sensational Australian story of the whole war had just jumped on a train and was headed for the city of Melbourne.

Shortly after his arrival, Lenehan had a meeting at Army headquarters with Major-General Sir Edward Hutton. The diminutive grey-haired general blew a long sigh through his neatly trimmed moustache once Lenehan had finished telling him about his ordeal in South Africa. Hutton had only been General Officer Commanding of Australian forces for a month, though before the Boer War he had commanded New South Wales' volunteer forces between 1893 and 1896. He led some of them in battle with great distinction in South Africa.

The Major-General tried to dissuade Lenehan from telling the Prime Minister the sordid details of the courts martial and the executions. It was a curious reaction from the commander of the Australian armed forces who had just been told that two of his men had been wrongly executed, but Hutton was not all he seemed. He had a reputation as a 'fiery little soldier' and an Englishman right down to his cotton underpants. He also had a flair for the dramatic. He once went to a meeting with an Australian Cabinet Minister with a loaded pistol concealed in his jacket because he was convinced the minister would try to attack him.

After Lenehan stood firm, Hutton relented. But, as Major Lenehan later discovered to his cost, Sir Edward Hutton fully deserved his reputation.

On hearing the news, the grim-faced Australian Prime Minister, Edmund Barton, was forced to admit in the House of Representatives that he had not been informed about the executions and knew little more than the newspapers did.

By now, excited journalists had also got wind of the executions from returning soldiers and from stories that had begun to appear in the London press. The wires ran hot, the presses rolled, and the headlines screamed:

A SENSATIONAL STORY – EXECUTION OF AUSTRALIAN
OFFICERS

SHOOTING OF SURRENDERED BOERS – IRREGULARS
EXECUTED

Whilst the Australian press and the Government tried to ascertain the hows, whys and wherefores of what had happened in South Africa, a small insert appeared in the London *Times*. It reported that Admiral Sir Digby Morant had denied that the officer of the same name recently executed in South Africa was his son.

Anxiously scanning the English papers for information about the executions, this denial was picked up by people from *The Bulletin* – the Sydney journal Morant had spent the past decade writing poetry for. Morant had told them he was the son of an admiral and of good English stock, but their research now revealed that no-one had ever entered Australia under the name 'Harry Harbord Morant'.

Local Queensland newspaper *The Northern Miner* took up the cry and revealed that Morant's signature matched that of the Edwin Henry Murrant who married a Daisy O'Dwyer in Charters Towers in 1884. *The Bulletin* concluded that the same hand had written both the Morant and Murrant signatures. A modern handwriting expert has confirmed this suspicion. In other words, Harry Harbord Morant appears to have started life as Edwin Henry Murrant.

Perhaps this revelation is not that surprising to those who know something of this story already. Like most legendary figures, the Breaker was a deeply flawed man with two very different sides to his character. On the one hand he was a violent, reckless, risk-taking, debt-making, drunken larrikin, while on the other he was the brave, fearless horseman of popular myth, a generous, cultured gentleman at ease in high society and blessed with the ability to write fluent verse with scarcely a need for correction.

But who was Edwin Henry Murrant? What terrible event or dark family secret caused him to change his given name? Why had the man he claimed was his father forsaken him? As Australian historian Manning Clark, put it, 'The facts of his life, like the secrets of his heart, were always shrouded in mystery.'

Discovering his true identity is as important as the events that led to his execution. In order to fathom his true character, we need to know what forces shaped him and if he suffered a double injustice – first at the hands of his family and then in the service of his country. Was he a cold-hearted killer, or just a little boy lost?

BREAKER MORANT BEGAN LIFE AS PLAIN Edwin Henry Murrant in the town of Bridgwater, England on December 9, 1864, according to the British records of births, deaths and marriages. Newspaper reports said that was the coldest winter since records began.

ICICLES HUNG LIKE GLITTERING DAGGERS from eaves and guttering all over the town and the frost hung in the air in tangible clouds of ice particles, painful to breathe in. Fresh water was a scarce commodity, as all the taps and pumps were encased in ice, and people were reduced to shovelling up snow from the ground and melting it in pots.

Within the foreboding red brick walls of the Union Workhouse, Catherine Murrant had just given birth to a son barely two years after the birth of her daughter Annie. Cradling the newborn babe in her arms, she decided to call him Edwin Henry after his recently departed father who had died just two weeks and two days before the birth. It was the least she could do. Aged just thirty-one, he had been taken abruptly by rheumatic fever.

Its origins were unknown in 1864. It began as a common sore throat, which was easily caught from the cold and damp that clung to the mean buildings of the workhouse. Suddenly and dramatically his condition worsened and the fever wracked his body. A skin rash and aching, swollen joints were the external symptoms, but it was an inflammation of the heart that finally killed him. It was a silent killer and showed neither fear nor favour to inmates or their keepers and would continue to claim victims for another century.

She played over the helpless agony of his final hours in her mind again. Is this God's punishment for my infidelity? she wondered, glancing guiltily over at the Bible that sat next to her on the bedside table. The only mercy was that her late husband would never have to look at his son and see the face of someone else's bastard staring back at him. Casting a worried eye to where Annie was toddling about in a corner of the shabby room, Catherine Murrant clutched her baby closer, as if to ward off the desperation that threatened to engulf her.

Looking out of her solitary bedroom window, the young mother felt no joy at the coming Yuletide. In the distance she could see that a new fall of snow had softened the hard outlines of the smoke-blackened factories to which this godforsaken town owed its recent prosperity. She knew it wouldn't last. Evil black smog still spewed from those blackened cancerous chimney stacks and by morning would have remade Bridgwater in its own image.

All over the country, dour hardworking people in little towns like Bridgwater toiled to produce the raw materials for Great Britain, then rapidly rising to the height of its Imperial and commercial powers. Bridgwater could legitimately claim that it was playing its part in the building of this great land as it supplied the nation with bricks, tiles and mortar from its many factories. Not that there was any accolade or reward attached to such an economic feat, for this was the England inhabited by Oscar Wilde's Dorian Gray –

gilded palaces for the rich, and gin palaces, opium dens and workhouses for the poor.

If Australia was the land of blue sky and red earth, then Britain was the land of brick. The wide picture windows of any train travelling through the industrial heartland of England were filled by endless vistas of brick. The bright eye of the architects who envisioned brick mosaics of browns, oranges, reds, whites and blues had seen them muddied by the dull eye of the factory owners and their sentinel-like chimneys, which had reduced them all to an amorphous soot-covered industrial mass. Brick was a perfect metaphor for the working class of Bridgwater who spent their lives shuffling back and forth between streets of identical back-to-back brick dwellings and brick factories where they produced yet more bricks.

Catherine Murrant felt an overwhelming sense of that gripping bleakness as she wondered how she could have invested everything in something that now seemed so ephemeral in the harsh light of the reality she now faced.

Instinctively, she reached back into her past for comfort and meaning. 'What if . . .' had been a game she had played many a time with her friends when she had still been a girl dreaming of the future. Once again she lost herself in the childhood game, now a sad one.

She had been an elementary schoolteacher in Fleet, Lincolnshire, before she met and married Edwin. Was it only four years ago?

Through the good offices of Edwin's father, also a workhouse master in nearby Boston, they had first found work in Devon before securing positions as Master and Matron here in Bridgwater three years ago. Edwin and she had so many plans and dreams . . .

Losing her husband was a cruel blow, financially as well as personally. Now she would have to find food, clothing and shelter for herself and two children. From *now on life would be a continual struggle which, if lost, would land her back within these unforgiving walls, not as a Matron, but as an inmate. The religious homilies 'God is Good', 'God is Truth', 'God is Holy' and 'God is Just' had been carved into the roofing beams above the heads of the oakum-picking paupers, but even a god-fearing woman like herself knew there was nothing very good, holy or just in this place.*

EVEN AS THE PRESENT MATRON OF Bridgwater Workhouse, she was not immune to the fetor of whitewash, urine and overboiled cabbage that permeated her every waking moment. That was the smell of poverty and should she now find herself unable to provide, she knew only too well what lay in store – not only for herself, but for her little children.

The *Poor Law Amendment Act* of 1834 and the Protestant work ethic were the main weapons of the recently elected Whig Government which intended to end three centuries of ruinous Poor Law legislation. Land enclosure and rapid industrialisation had drawn huge numbers of rural dwellers to the cities and quadrupled the cost of benefits to the poor between 1780 and 1820. It had drained the economy and demoralised the honest working man by rewarding the poor for being what the British authorities described as 'vicious, idle, dissolute, prone to laziness, drunkenness, debauchery and to mutinous and indecent discourses . . . a brutish sort of people'.

These new reforms intended to instil a new morality and thrift into the common man and to turn workhouses into 'Bastilles' – a deterrent to able-bodied paupers. Instead of allowing the poor to receive benefits at home, they now had to enter a workhouse where their standard of living was to be lower than the lowest paid worker.

However, social theories driven by political policies rarely work in practice, and the aims of the *Poor Law Amendment Act* were never realised. Only a third of those receiving poor aid ever entered a workhouse and, as the century progressed, instead of 'Bastilles', the workhouses became refuges where the flotsam and jetsam – the old, wretched, sick, abandoned and insane – could seek shelter from the harsh realities of Victorian life. So concerned were the authorities with their policy of deterrence that they did not take the care of the afflicted into account.

Instead, workhouses provided plenty of material for the novels of Mr Dickens. During his 1836 visit to a 'foul ward' in the Wapping Workhouse, he observed women, riddled with venereal disease, lying listlessly on filthy bedsteads and on the floor. This visit inspired many of his literary characters and made him a champion of the poor and oppressed. Public perception of workhouses was forever coloured by Oliver Twist holding out his bowl and asking for 'more'. One newspaper reported how hunger forced inmates at Andover to gnaw rancid gristle from the bones they were supposed to be pounding into fertiliser.

Fortunately for Catherine Murrant, she was well thought of – a hard worker who conducted herself well. The Workhouse Board, which comprised of fifty guardians, passed a vote of sympathy to Catherine, describing her late husband Edwin as '. . . a most efficient officer and an excellent master', and retained her as Matron, despite the fact that her position required her to be married to the Master. They advertised for a new Master, and widower Thomas Baker was appointed shortly afterwards. However, as she rightly predicted in the sad aftermath of Edwin's birth, life was going to be tough from now on. Despite the sympathetic treatment she received from the Board of Guardians, Catherine Murrant was forced to make ends meet on her single salary of £40 per annum, compared to £100 when her husband was alive.

Although Edwin was *from* the workhouse, but not *of* it, he spent his first eight years in this Dickensian atmosphere. It undoubtedly rubbed off on him. He grew up both greatly fascinated and equally afraid of what lurked in the shadows of that dank, rat-infested place.

The punitive nature of the 1834 legislation had also made workhouses places of 'unresolvable tension' where violence, drunkenness and rioting were commonplace. Children grew up quickly in such an environment and the workhouse urchins were a rough and uncultured rabble. During that era, children on remand for criminal offences were held in workhouses.

In the Bridgwater Workhouse, the pauper children led by criminals applied a crude social Darwinism to their relations with the Matron's boy with no father. The choices facing Edwin Murrant were stark: 'Tell your mother . . . or fight!' Not only did he throw his first punch there, but he kissed his first girl, took his first puff of tobacco, and stole his first apple. He quickly learnt the 'black arts' of the Artful Dodger – a character trait that would later surface in the Breaker's complex make-up.

Although the education of pauper children became compulsory from 1862, Edwin and Annie were not educated in-house. The teachers were of a poor standard, judging by the discipline problems that came to light during the Murrants' tenure. In January 1862 they reported the schoolmaster for 'exciting the boys to acts of insubordination'. The man was forced to resign. In June of the same year, his successor was reported for 'having destroyed and misappropriated property for his own use and otherwise misbehaved himself'. He was merely reprimanded. In any event, the rules of the workhouse dictated that the Master and Matron's children were not allowed to live on the premises once they had reached the age of eight, which was the official school age. The details of their early education still remain shrouded in the mists of time. However, young Edwin Murrant received an education far above his station as a lad born and brought up in a workhouse.

The issue of his education is vital, because in later life it was apparent to all who met the Breaker that he was the beneficiary of a first-class British public school education. He was also an exceptional horseman with literary talents and the social 'polish' to enable him to move effortlessly between hard-drinking bush larrikins and the rarefied atmosphere of British colonial high society.

Workhouse records show that at the age of twelve, Edwin was either a boarder or living away from home. In December 1876, the workhouse guardians resolved that '. . . Matron be not called upon to pay anything for her son whilst residing with her during his Christmas holidays'.

In 1881, when Edwin and Annie, then aged seventeen and nineteen, appeared in the national census for the first time, both were recipients of a first-class education. Annie gave her profession as a 'Professor of Music' and Edwin as 'Tutor' at the exclusive Silesia College in High Barnet, North London. This was remarkable, as there was a major discrepancy between their standard of education and their mother's limited financial means.

In 1881, sixteen years after the death of her husband, Mrs Murrant's salary still remained at the same level of £40 per annum, ample proof that the guardians considered retaining the services of the widow an act of charity on their part and refused to countenance any further wage rises. Therefore, she was becoming progressively poorer each year as the cost of living rose and her children grew up.

In February 1881, Mrs Murrant received a serious reprimand from the workhouse guardians for having both Edwin and Annie living with her, albeit for a very short period. Workhouse regulations forbade anyone who was not a resident or employee from living there. Annie had been there since September of the previous year and Edwin was back for the holidays. She responded with a very apologetic letter dated February 22, 1881, stating that both children had now left. The following day, Catherine was officially reprimanded and told that the children were not to reside at the workhouse, even for one night, without the express permission of the guardians.

The Bridgwater Union Workhouse and Silesia College in Barnet provided two very disparate points of reference at opposite ends of the social spectrum for Edwin Murrant. As Silesia College was only founded in 1876, the earliest Edwin could have started there would have been at the age of twelve. That leaves three critical years of his young life to account for, during which time he received an education which enabled him to gain entry to a first-rate public school. Given his mother's circumstances, how was the boy from the workhouse able to defy the social conventions of the time that decreed that only the privileged received a good education?

THE MURRANT FAMILY TREE, WHICH can be traced back to the early 18th century, shows they were a Hampshire family of good yeoman stock, but with no apparent connections to either land or money. Edwin's branch of the family had been concentrated in and around Portsmouth since at least 1688.

His grandfather, George Murrant, brought up young Edwin, or so the present-day Murrant family believes. Although an earlier census in 1871 doesn't place him within George's household at that time, it must be considered a possibility. Grandfather George had been a schoolmaster prior to becoming a workhouse master, however sometime between 1871 and 1881 he had retired to Somerset to become a shopkeeper. Whilst he would have been able to offer young Edwin shelter and intellectual stimulus, he does not appear to have had the financial means to give young Edwin a private education.

George Murrant had at least eleven siblings, three other sons (Henry, William and George) and a daughter called Louisa. Census information for 1861, 1871 and 1881 shows Edwin's relatives to have been schoolmasters, coopers, workhouse masters, soldiers and sailors. Well down the social pecking order, they would have been described as skilled working class/lower middle class – unlikely to be able to afford such a scholastic luxury for any of their own family.

Edwin's mother was born Catherine Reilly in Killarney, County Kerry in 1837 and moved to England during her youth. Her father was a farmer and she became an elementary schoolteacher before her marriage, again, a lower middle-class occupation. Given Catherine's worsening financial straits, particularly after the death of her husband, it is very unlikely that the Reilly family was able to finance a private education.

If neither the Murrants nor the Reillys had the financial means, then young Edwin Murrant's education must have been secretly funded by an anonymous benefactor – perhaps by the man he claimed as his true, biological, father, the dashing young naval officer Digby Morant.

The Morants were one of England's oldest families, with branches stretching from Ireland through to Devon, Hampshire and Scotland, and with outposts as far apart as India, Jamaica and Australia. They were at the other end of the social spectrum to the Murrants and the Reillys. Descended from a long line of landed gentry, the Morants could boast amongst their descendants a number of titles – Members of Parliament, high-ranking military and naval officers, High Sheriffs and an aide-de-camp to the reigning monarch, Queen Victoria. If Edwin Murrant really was a Morant, how could a member of such a noble house have fathered the son of a workhouse matron?

The Breaker had openly stated on a number of occasions that Admiral Sir Digby Morant was his 'guv'nor', but we know for a fact that Catherine Murrant was his mother and she was married to Edwin Murrant. The logical explanation is that Edwin was born 'on the wrong side of the blanket' – a predicament not unknown in an era as famed for its hypocrisy as for its supposed virtue. This theory is supported by the fact that two of the three key ingredients of any successful seduction were present – geography and timing.

Around the time of Edwin's conception, Catherine's father-in-law, George, had returned from Boston, Lincolnshire to Lee-on-Solent, Portsmouth. Lee-on-Solent lies on the foreshore of the British Navy's main base and is only some thirty miles from Roydon Manor, the then Morant family home in Brockenhurst. Doubtless, Catherine would have taken her new daughter on the train to visit her grandfather whilst her husband Edwin carried out his duties at the workhouse.

According to Royal Navy records, after six months of active service in the Crimea, Lieutenant Digby Morant spent the period during which Edwin was conceived in England. He joined his ship at Pembroke Dock on March 12, 1864, exactly nine months before the birth of Edwin Murrant.

The third ingredient of any successful seduction is

opportunity. How and where would a young upper-crust naval officer meet a young married mother and matron of a workhouse – especially as they would have travelled in very different social circles. There are a number of possibilities. George Murrant was Master of the Union Workhouse in Portsmouth at the time and had managed workhouses in other parts of England. Digby was later president of the Royal Humane Society. There may well have been a social event where a common interest would have transcended the normal social barriers and an introduction between Catherine and Digby could have been affected.

On the other hand, a purely chance encounter between Digby and Catherine, both known to have been in the same area at the same time, is not that far-fetched. Romance often starts in the strangest of places – a face in the crowd, a stolen glance, a chivalrous gesture. The voracious media of today reminds us on a daily basis that human resourcefulness in the pursuit of sexual gratification knows no bounds. Contrary to popular belief, things were no different in Victorian times; the thrill was perhaps even more heightened because of the high risks and secrecy involved in carrying out clandestine affairs. As it later emerged, Catherine did have a wild side to her character.

A 'window of opportunity' did exist geographically and biologically and, given the size of that 'window', Digby would have left England unaware that Catherine was pregnant. Perhaps Catherine never intended to tell Digby, even if she were sure that the child was his and only did so after her husband died and she found herself in dire financial straits. By then, Digby had every reason to deny it. He was a Lieutenant in the British Navy and had married Sophia Georgina Eyres in 1866. She produced two of her seven children in quick succession. Sophia's father and Digby's father were good friends and both were senior officers in the Grenadier Guards.

The revelation that he had sired a 'bastard son' by a married woman of lower social standing would not only have damaged Digby Morant's career, but also his marriage and his father's social standing. Social conduct was of paramount importance to a man's professional and social aspirations during the Victorian era. A scandal could be extremely costly. Similarly, an admission in 1902 that he had not only sired a bastard, but a murdering one who had been court martialled, found guilty and shot by his own side, would have been totally ruinous! Little wonder that it has remained a dark family secret. However, as the story unfolds across the next four decades, a succession of incidents, coincidences and documentary evidence will confirm that a secret liaison did take place between Digby and Catherine and that the deep emotional scars it left created Edwin Murrant's dual identity. *The Bulletin* and *The Northern Miner* were right, he was both a Murrant and a Morant.

By the time Edwin was born, the day was long passed when bastards were publicly recognised and advanced. Whilst this might have been the case a hundred years before, by the 1860s the most a bastard son could have expected was a reasonable education and an introduction to a respectable trade. He would not normally meet his father's family and this would appear to have been what happened in Edwin's case. Digby kept his distance, but helped Edwin through an intermediary. Morant revealed that he had been brought up by an 'uncle'. One of his old Hawkesbury mates named him as George Whyte-Melville and described how he taught Morant to ride:

> It may not be known that the late Lieut. H.H. Morant, 'The Breaker', took his first riding lessons on the knee of the Devonshire sport and author,

G.J. Whyte-Melville. Poor Morant. [His tutor was] [h]ot-headed, violent at times [and] a great horseman. He jolted the hard faced youngster up and down, and on his head he put a hunting-cap, and in his chubby hand a riding crop, then man and boy rode a great burst over imaginary fences, with a 'Tally-Ho!' for a finish. Morant was very reserved, but at times he talked to this sorrowing mate of Devonshire and childhood, when at eight years of age he rode to hounds.

Roger Evans' book, *The Forgotten Heroes of Bridgwater,* also places young Edwin Murrant with Whyte-Melville during his formative years.

George Whyte-Melville hunted with the Stevenstone Hounds, previously known as the Mark Rolle Hounds, who rode out of Bideford, North Devon. Digby must have explained his predicament to his close circle of friends and prevailed upon one of them to take the son he could never openly acknowledge under their wings. This type of 'guardianship' was widely practised amongst monied families during the Victorian era.

Under their watchful eyes and through their patronage, the penniless Edwin Murrant received a good education, a love of literature and the equestrian skills that later established him as an Australian bush legend. Whyte-Melville was the 'uncle' the Breaker referred to during his time in Australia. His childhood reminiscences also included references to Devon, Fife and Leicestershire. Whyte-Melville was associated with hunts at Bideford, Tiphook, Pytchley Hounds, Malmesbury and St Andrews. He was renowned for turning young horses into finished hunters – a skill the Breaker was also noted for in Australia. In those days, horsemanship, like a good education, was for those to the 'manor born', not for those to the 'workhouse born'. In the Australian bush during the latter part of the

19th century, to be accepted as a horseman you'd have to be 'good', to be known for your horsemanship you'd have to be 'very good', but to become a legend you'd have to be 'bloody good' – and that from the lips of men not known for faint praise.

In the company of his 'uncle', Edwin Murrant would also have had the opportunity to mix with high society and learn the ways of a gentleman – a skill which he exhibited with much aplomb in both Australia and England. When he returned to England in 1901, his association with Whyte-Melville *et al* led him back to Devon where he was accepted back into the north Devon social scene and hunted with the Stevenstone Hounds again.

WHYTE-MELVILLE CAST AN APPROVING eye over young Edwin, who sat in a leather armchair by the crackling fire immersed in a book. His initial resolve to treat him like the other grooms in his charge, despite his parentage, soon crumbled when he discovered that Edwin had a bright and inquiring mind and gave Edwin Murrant, his personal attention. Now and again he'd catch a glimpse of Edwin's father in the lad's profile. 'A chip off the old block', he told Digby in one of his yearly reports. Pity they'd never met. Maybe when he got older, but for now he seems content.

During the day, Edwin worked in the stableyards with the other grooms, but at night he retired to the big house to eat dinner with George and continue his education. Edwin soaked up information like a sponge and George had plenty to impart. He was the prolific author of some thirty books on horses, hunting and literature as well as novels, reviews and countless poems for the noted London publisher, John William Parker. Whyte-Melville always seemed to underestimate his literary talent, but it was an era when it was unseemly for a gentleman to be too concerned about working, far less actually making money from his endeavours – not that royalties ever concerned George Whyte-Melville. He was a man of substance and imbued with the Victorian spirit of self-improvement and philanthropy. He used all the royalties from his books to provide reading rooms and educational facilities for grooms and stable boys. It was under the tutelage of Whyte-Melville that his love of literature and poetry that would later become such an integral part of Breaker Morant was awakened. It might even be argued that the Breaker could have stepped right out of the pages of one of Whyte-Melville's novels.

He was an extremely popular author in his day and his novels sold well to his readership of predominately well-to-do sporting military gentleman. His stories were set in the social, sporting and military circles he moved in and almost invariably featured a classical-style odyssey or adventure undertaken by strong, chivalrous, horse-riding heroes who behaved with reverence and respect towards the fair sex.

As in the workhouse, Edwin's privileged position elevated him above the others and caused quite a bit of resentment, but his quick fists and ability to survive against all odds – skills from an early life in the workhouse – inevitably won the day. After pulling him off one unfortunate wisecracker who'd collected a bloody nose and a shiner for his trouble, George realised the workhouse had left a wild streak in the boy he was grooming to be a gentleman.

The master himself introduced Edwin to the three H's – horses, hunting and hounds. George was a tall, slender man who always dressed immaculately and sported a fashionable pair of mutton chop whiskers down to cheeks ruddied by over half a century of exposure to the elements and the finest whisky his native land had to offer. Whyte-Melville looked every inch the Hunt Master and was widely acknowledged as England's foremost expert on horses and hunting. His sanguine advice to Edwin on horses was: 'Treat them like a mistress, lad – rein them in hard, give them a bloody good ride and don't forget to give them a pat and a good feed at the finish.' Edwin learned well and his rapport with both horses and the ladies were often remarked upon.

The discipline and skills George's coaching instilled in him, allied to his natural combativeness, made Murrant appear fearless, even reckless in the saddle. George often spied him through his study window betting his weekly allowance against his ability to clear some seemingly impossible hurdle, then heard the groans of the grooms and servants as Edwin sailed over with plenty to spare before cheekily offering them 'double or quits'.

Edwin became the son Whyte-Melville never had. He'd married Charlotte Hanbury-Bateman, the daughter of the first Lord Bateman of Northants, but it was not a happy marriage, which accounted for the sad, almost melancholic air that hung about him and permeated the very words of his novels. Nonetheless, they produced a daughter. But he kept his wife and daughter at home like dolls in Tetbury, in the style to which they were accustomed – though his daughter had now grown up and married. Truth was, he'd always preferred the company of men – the legacy of a military and sporting life.

After leaving Eton, George had bought a commission in the 93rd Highlanders and later served in the Coldstream Guards where he rose to the rank of Major. After resigning his commission, Major Whyte-Melville later volunteered for service with the Turkish Irregular Cavalry during the Crimean War and was awarded the Turkish Order of Mejidie (fourth class) before returning to England and sporting life. However, in one of his books, The Old Gray Mare, George said of his own life, 'I freely admit that the best of my fun I owe it to horse and hound'.

To young Edwin, George was an entree into a glittering new world of possibilities far away from the oppressive atmosphere of the Bridgwater Workhouse which was now just a bad memory and the location for a Christmas visit. He loved roaming around Devon's wide open spaces and accompanied Hunt Master Whyte-Melville all around England to hunts in Oxfordshire, Leicestershire and Nottinghamshire.

Edwin's favourite trip came every summer when they went to London, boarded the Flying Scotsman at Kings Cross and steamed through the night to Edinburgh. Whyte-Melville was the Fife Hunt Master and club captain of the Royal and Ancient St Andrews golf club. To pass the long night, George taught him the old Scottish standard Maggie Lauder.

Many years later, Brigalow Mick, one of the Breaker's Australian bush mates, wrote to The Bulletin saying that Morant was unusually 'well tubbed' for a Pom, and when washing in a billabong he would sing Maggie Lauder – the only song he knew all the words to. When asked, Morant said that he had learned the song during his childhood holidays in Fife. His knowledge of the Scottish vernacular in his later poem Reprobate's Reply also suggests more than a passing acquaintance with the dialects spoken in the east of Caledonia.

From Edinburgh, the Aberdeen train traced the winding Fife coastline past villages of squat slate and sandstone houses with tiny windows, bunched together for protection against the cruel gales that whipped unchecked across the North Sea from the frozen waste of Siberia. They disembarked at St Andrews where a hansom cab took them the rest of the way to the Melville ancestral home at nearby Monimail where George had been born half a century before.

'Eight–teen twenty–one!' exclaimed Edwin when George told him the year of his birth. 'Fifty-three . . .

I don't think I'll ever be that old,' he said, shaking his head, little knowing the truth of his own words.

Built to a design by noted architect James Smith at the end of the 17th century for George's grand-father, the first Earl of Melville, Melville House was the 'Kingdom' of Fife's first and greatest monument to classical architecture. Its neo-Palladian facade was a radical departure from the conservative Jacobean and Dutch influences preferred by the more dour, self-effacing Scots. A huge H-shaped structure, its windows, gables and cavernous front entrance were described in characteristically ornate detail and was topped off by 120 tall chimney pots – one for each room. An imposing 16th century medieval tower of stone, Monimail tower, which had been incorporated into the surrounding walls, dominated the local skyline.

Set in a hundred acres of lush, verdant fields and forests that were teeming with game and fowl, Melville House was the rallying point for local hunters. Resplendent in scarlet jackets and white breeches, they mingled at the front entrance which stood high above the swirling maelstrom of barking hounds that eddied round their horses' legs. After fortifying themselves with a 'wee dram', the bugles sounded and they galloped off in pursuit of their unfortunate quarry.

It was also the perfect setting for the legendary dinner parties and balls which invariably followed those hunts. Done up to the nines, Edwin loved those big social occasions the best.

George had shown him which knives and forks to use for each course and Edwin had also learned about old-fashioned chivalry – how to bow and kiss the hands of the ladies, and some of their daughters too. After the men had retired to the smoking lounge, he amused them all with little ditties and rhymes he had made up during the day's hunt. George had noted with some alarm that they became more ribald with each passing year. Oscar

Wilde was a distant Irish cousin of the Morants and whilst to him the hunt fraternity were 'the unbearable in pursuit of the uneatable', these were salad days for Edwin, times he would often recall with fondness out in the harshness of the Australian bush. He would strive to recapture the magic of those extraordinary days for the rest of his short but eventful life.

The years drifted by and the day for him to leave his 'uncle's' sanctuary came all too quickly. Now almost twelve he was growing into a fine-looking young man and it was time for him to go off to college.

Silesia College had opened in Barnet, north of London, and was run by a former Bridgwater Master, James Russell. Catherine Murrant had heard about it when one of the workhouse guardian's sons was accepted there.

The guardian, who had been impressed with Edwin's manners, self-assurance and obvious intelligence when he visited his mother in the holidays, agreed to write a letter of recommendation. Catherine asked George to do the same. As much as he would miss the lad, George knew it was time for him to make his own way in the world. Eton had been the making of him and Silesia would be the making of the boy. He wrote the letter with a heavy heart.

When the day came, George Whyte-Melville was barely able to fight back a tear as he pumped Edwin's hand. 'Bye, lad. Do yourself proud.'

The boy just nodded as he stepped into the cab, and though George waved until the carriage disappeared, Edwin never looked back and kept his eye firmly fixed on the future.

SILESIA COLLEGE WAS WHERE EDWIN developed his literary talents, which became such a central part of the Breaker legend, and refined the social graces George Whyte-Melville had instilled in him.

Silesia College was originally Oakmead, a private house, then variously used as an orphanage and a school. In the 1861 census, a Reverend Henry S Wood, formerly master of Barnet Workhouse, was operating it as the Silesia House Orphan Asylum Royal Patriotic Fund. It housed 120 boys and was funded by public money donated to children left fatherless by the Crimean War. In 1873 it became the Silesia House School when it was taken over by a Charles Presdee, former principal of the Queen Elizabeth Grammar School. In 1876 it became Silesia College as the new proprietor, James Russell, took it upmarket.

The school was situated at Bells Hill, on the edge of Barnet, in four acres of rolling green fields. The classrooms and dormitories were housed in the large, white, three-storied house. 'The most salubrious air in London' was its proud boast. Silesia was no fly-by-night institution and Russell determined that it would be a seat of excellence right from the outset. It was one of a new breed of private schools that had sprung up around the country and would soon become as well known as venerable public schools like Winchester, Rugby and Eton.

Unlike the old schools that were supported by endowments and shares, local businessmen and landowners funded these new colleges. However, the extensive newspaper advertisements, which appeared in the local *Barnet Gazette* made clear Silesia College's intention to emulate those elite establishments. Its curriculum offered a mix of the classical and the modern; the Classics, the Arts and foreign languages as well as the 'Foundation' subjects of reading, spelling, writing and arithmetic, book-keeping and land surveying. Its pupils were intended to be educated for a profession, careers in commercial trading or farming and some would go on to sit the 'local' exams for entry into Oxford or Cambridge.

However, private education doesn't come cheaply and fees have to be paid promptly. In 1876, the fees were twenty-four to thirty-four guineas per annum for boarders – almost as much as Edwin's poor mother's entire annual income. So, how did Edwin Murrant, son of a poorhouse matron, gain entry into Silesia College? Clearly, it required the *largesse* of a well-heeled uncle or father.

Where Edwin acquired his early education is still not known. Banjo Paterson's *Jim Carew* says he '. . . Gained at his college a triple blue' – the kind won at public schools, and a short story Morant wrote for *The Richmond and Windsor Gazette* entitled *Billy Murdoch's Farewell* alluded to the fact that he might have been educated at England's oldest school, Winchester. Whilst there is no Murrant, Morant or Murdoch in the Winchester school records, what is certain is that it was a first-class education.

In the 1881 census, the fifteen-year-old Edwin described himself as a 'Tutor' at Silesia College. He was, in effect, a pupil teacher who earned his board, lodgings and school fees by helping the masters tutor the pupils. This would have involved him giving tutorials as well as supervising and checking homework. A position of such responsibility would require a high standard of education in the first place and would have been earned by merit. However, as fifteen was the earliest he could have been given such a responsibility, his fees during his first three years at Silesia can only have been met by either his father or Whyte-Melville.

EDWIN WAS ALWAYS A NOCTURNAL creature. At night, when everyone else was in bed, he liked to walk the corridors of the former manor house. He knew every inch of it, but never tired of gazing up at the twinkling reflections of the crystal chandeliers that graced the ornate, high stucco ceilings and perusing the dusty, leather-bound tomes in the great library. Poetry and literature were his favourites.

Edwin would pull a different book down each night and spend the remaining hours till dawn cracked the eastern sky immersing himself in the great literary works of the past. The Greek epics, whose Gods ventured out on great odysseys and endured torturous ordeals just to discover their true selves, greatly intrigued him. Such truths were never far from his own thoughts, to the very end of his days in the prison cell on the Transvaal. Sometimes, as he returned to his room, he stopped in front of one of the long mirrors that had been strategically placed to remind pupils that those who aspired to the higher orders must always look their best.

His vision blurred as he searched the deepest recesses of his memory for the one faded, dog-eared snapshot he kept of his past life – him posing, in front of his mother's mirror in his hob-nailed boots and long shorts, his sparrow chest sticking out defiantly and a soggy roach hanging from his bottom lip. The image of the scrappy workhouse urchin receded into the past as the present came back into focus. He had come a long way since then.

Edwin was fast developing into a strong young man. In his well-cut formal tail coat, sharply creased trousers and with his well-groomed hair worn fashionably long, he cut quite a dash and didn't look a bit out of place amongst the sons and daughters of the well-to-do who attended Silesia College. If only they knew! Amazing what a bit of spit and polish can do.

When the moon was full, Edwin often sat in the window seat and gazed out at the silvered fields and gardens lying peacefully in the moonlight. The contrast between his surroundings and those of his early childhood often worked their way to the front of his mind. Lest he forget, the Barnet Workhouse was right next to *the school. Though he would never have to endure the stench of whitewash, urine and overboiled cabbage again, it seemed to Edwin that he'd never escape its long shadow. Some would argue that he never did.*

DESPITE THE SCHOOL'S GROWING academic reputation and strong sporting ethos, there is no mention in its advertisement or the local paper of any equestrian activities. So, where did Murrant continue to develop his riding skills? Where did he learn the horsebreaking, bare-knuckle fighting and general hell-raising which so clearly distinguished his 'Hyde' from the more refined and intellectual 'Jekyll'?

The answer lay outside the narrow bounds of school and curriculum in a place beyond the school gates where Edwin would sneak to indulge his love of horses, supplement his meagre allowance and enjoy the illicit pleasure of a 'walk on the wild side' – a temptation that would eventually be his downfall.

Letters and papers belonging to one of Edwin's former pupils, Charles H Mabey, confirms that Edwin did lead a 'double life' at Silesia College. Murrant was his English tutor and Mabey recalled that although his name was Edward (sic) he liked to be called 'Harry', a common derivative of his middle name Henry, and the name he would later make famous in the Australian bush. Harry gave boxing lessons 'down the field' after school at sixpence a time and Mabey suspected he gambled away that money at the horse track. He also recounted how they were occasionally visited by two of Edwin's family – George and Annie Murrant. George was remembered because he always brought them sweets and would address them, 'Hello my fine scholars. How are you today?' The boys would respond, 'We are well sir. You are well received sir.' His sister Annie also visited, in a professional capacity.

According to Mabey she played the piano, harp, flute and violin, sang, spoke French and Italian and like her brother had a very fiery temper.

The town of Barnet has a long and distinguished equine tradition going back many centuries and, as the last country town before the suburbs, it became the principal horsetrading centre for London. Horses were broken in, trained, stabled and traded at its main showcase, the annual Barnet Horse Fair, which was one of the largest horse shows in the country. The local stables were where Edwin honed the skills he learned from Whyte-Melville and also learned the practical, no-nonsense business of handling, training and breaking in horses.

Barnet had a famous racing track that drew huge crowds from London and all over the surrounding area. It attracted not only a rough and ready crowd willing to have a flutter, but also sharp local characters only too ready to part a fool from his money. Unlicensed betting was illegal but widely practised in those days. A pint of porter, a few bob on the horses and the faint hope he'd backed a winner at long odds was the only solace of the working man eager to escape the drudgery of his life for a few hours. These equestrian pursuits drew Edwin back to the shadowy world of the workhouse and the more mundane pursuits he learned there.

There were also other local tracks, such as Finchley, that would have given a game amateur jockey a ride. The Breaker won many a race in Australia and was much in demand as a jockey. Barnet is where Edwin earned his 'spurs'.

As a result, he was a first-class horseman by the time he reached Australia. The bush was no place to begin to learn the basics of horseriding and the handling of temperamental horses. Tales of Morant's daredevil stunts, his skill at polo, his daring on the racetrack and courage as a 'breaker' of brumbies – the fiery Australian wild horses – were legion. They may even have inspired the greatest legend of them all – 'Banjo' Paterson's *The Man From Snowy River*.

Barnet was also famous for its pugilism and boasted a number of English champions. There is a photograph of Morant in Australia boxing with a mate out the back o' Bourke and many anecdotes were told of how he trained with a punching bag and practised on un-suspecting Aboriginal stockhands. Doubtless a hard shoulder and a quick pair of fists were also de rigueur in the shady, dog-eat-dog world of Barnet turf management.

A later fusion of these experiences in Bridgwater, Bideford and Barnet created the colourful alter-ego known as Breaker Morant.

THERE IS ONE MORE VITAL INGREDIENT, without which the colourful legend of Breaker Morant would never have been created – scandal! Every historian who has written about the legend of the Breaker has referred to the 'scandal' that pitched Edwin Henry Murrant head-long towards Australia and the annals of history. This story, like many that have become attached to Morant, has been repeated so often that it has become an accepted truth. Details of that scandal have proved elusive. Local newspapers in Barnet, North Devon and Bridgwater yielded no clues and his Aussie cobbers gave little away. After news of his execution reached Aus-tralia one commented, 'To the end of his wild and stirring life Harry Harbord Morant clung to the secret which made him an outcast for so long.'

In the years leading up to his exile from England there were many destabilising factors that may have led to a sudden indiscretion. First, he lost the only steady-ing male influence in his life, George Whyte-Melville. He was killed instantly on December 5, 1878, two years after Edwin started at Silesia, after being thrown from his old horse Shah whilst out hunting.

The sudden downturn in his mother's fortunes may also have been the catalyst for his sudden fall from grace. In January 1882, after twenty-one years of faithful service, she walked through the red brick portals of the Bridgwater Union Workhouse for the last time. Both she and the Master, James Winterson, had been dismissed after being brought before a Local Government Inquiry Board earlier that same month.

Ever since Winterson's appointment in 1878, there was bad blood between the two of them. Reading between the lines, Winterson wanted his wife to be Matron and set about trying to get Catherine dismissed. It all came to a head in November 1881 at a stormy meeting of the guardians, during which Catherine accused the Master of lying about his marital status when he applied for the job and being abusive to her. She was described in the minutes of the meeting as being disrespectful, violent and defiant to the guardians. It also emerged that Winterson was responsible for reports about Catherine for having her children at the workhouse. The complaints began in 1879 and earned her a reprimand in January 1881.

A history of drunkenness was also revealed. Winterson reported that Catherine had been drunk after the Bridgwater Carnival in November 1880 and an independent witness testified that he had recently seen Matron Murrant staggering around drunk on the workhouse premises blowing a tin whistle and throwing towels around.

'Hitting the bottle' appeared to be something of an occupational hazard at the Bridgwater Workhouse. On May 11, 1881 Catherine noted:

> I have to report that Nurse Mary Walsh left the house on Saturday night without my permission and was brought back drunk by PC Goodrich at 10.50 pm.

Nurse Walsh was dismissed, and now it was the Matron's turn. The years of toil and struggle within the oppressive atmosphere of the workhouse had finally taken their toll.

At the time of her dismissal, Catherine Murrant was forty-eight years old, had few prospects and nothing in reserve for the rainy day that had now arrived with a vengeance.

The 1891 census shows Catherine and Annie Murrant had moved from Somerset to Devon and were living at a salubrious address at Wellswood Park, in Torquay. Catherine worked for retired military people of means as a live-in housekeeper or servant. The census also revealed she was the retired Matron of the Country Asylum, which is where she went after being dismissed from Bridgewater Workhouse. Annie is described as a private organist, twenty-eight years old and single.

Some of Morant's previous biographers have speculated that the reason for Morant's Australian exile was 'a card debt'. In fact, Morant's great 'crime' was to fall in love with the wrong girl. As the shock of Morant's execution reverberated around Australia in early April 1902, many who knew him felt compelled to write to the newspapers or talk to journalists. Early press reports were full of wild rumour and speculation, but an article which appeared in Sydney's *Town and Country Journal* contained personal information that came from someone who served in South Africa and knew Morant intimately. Although the paper did not disclose its source, the newly returned Major Lenehan must be the prime candidate. Perhaps Lenehan finally learned the secrets of Morant's heart during those dark hours they spent together awaiting trial. The article revealed,

> The son of vice-Admiral Digby Morant who served with distinction in the Crimea – young Morant was himself destined for the navy, and serving his

probation as a mid-shipman, he was appointed A.D.C. to a prominent personage shortly after receiving his commission. While still a minor himself, Lieut. Morant fell in love with a young lady who was a Ward in Chancery, and eloped with her. Being liable for a heavy term of imprisonment for contempt of court, Morant abandoned his career in the navy and left England for Australia.

Whilst this would explain his departure for Australia in April 1883, nothing about the life of Henry Murrant alias Harry Morant is ever that straightforward. Although Morant himself claimed to be a 'navy man', there is no trace of a Harry Morant or a Henry Murrant in the British naval records. However, two Morants *did* enter the officer's training course on *HMS Britannia* during the 1880s. Anthony Morant enrolled in January 1883 and in 1886, Edgar Robert Morant, Digby's first son to Georgina Eyres, enrolled on the same course and passed out in 1888. Edgar followed in his father's illustrious footsteps and also became an Admiral. However, any thoughts that Anthony Morant might have been 'Tony' alias Harry Morant (Morant was known as 'Tony' during his second tour of duty in South Africa) were dashed as Anthony Morant's naval career after he graduated is easily traced.

Naval training, which usually began at twelve years of age as a midshipman, does not tie in with what we know of Edwin Murrant's formative and later years – which were undoubtedly spent on *terra firma*. The alternative, an officer's course for the beneficiaries of a good education, took two years to complete and even a commissioned officer would require some naval experience before being made an aide-de-camp. The most likely explanation is that the navy rumour was either a

'Chinese whisper' or it was started in Australia by Morant himself as part of his search for legitimacy as Digby's son. Morant always portrayed himself as a man of good breeding and education. A naval commission would point to the social and personal influence of his real father, Captain Digby Morant, and mask the truth that he was only his illegitimate son.

However, the second part of the statement from the *Town and Country Journal* about Morant's involvement in a romantic tryst has a ring of truth about it. The girl in question was a Ward in Chancery. She was most probably an heiress, not yet old enough for marriage, without living parents. Such a scandal would ruin her social reputation and make marriage within the higher echelons difficult. If she did not marry she would forfeit her inheritance. The alternative was to allow her to marry her seducer, who would then gain access to her fortune, or, as was more common, marry a foreigner who was not bound by British social mores. Whether Edwin did it for love or money, her guardians obviously felt that he was not a suitable match and as she was still a Ward in Chancery, the threat of legal action would have ensured Edwin's speedy departure.

A number of items published after Morant's death point to a woman as being the source of the scandal. One old bush mate reported that he always carried an engagement ring which was given to him by a girl in England before his exile. Another who knew 'warm-hearted Morant' wrote to *The Bathurst National Advertiser* after his death and signed the letter 'B.A'. It said:

> Morant did not leave England under peculiar circumstances and has suffered until his tragic death mental pain that only the strong can face. But he was guilty of no crime, he left the land of his birth accused of a social transgression and – rather than

destroy the good name of one who had a chivalrous claim upon him – he destroyed himself.

The same theme was touched on by his close friend, JCL Fitzpatrick, owner/editor of *The Richmond and Windsor Gazette* and Member for Rylstone. He wrote a poem for Morant after he left Windsor in 1898 entitled *Bon Voyage* that ended with the lines,

> Your big heart, with a bare wound showing –
> Mate o' mine! by the cool creek flowing,
> None but I got a chance of knowing,
> Your hidden misery.

His 'crime' certainly weighed heavily on his shoulders and he spent the rest of his life trying to repair the rift it caused between him and his father. As the story of Breaker Morant develops, it will become clear that his desire to make reparations for this youthful indiscretion was at the heart of his desire to seek glory in South Africa and led directly to his fateful decision to join the ill-starred Bushveldt Carbineers (BVC).

His indiscretion was treated as a betrayal by his father and left him with few immediate prospects. He had a good education, but no money to attend university or buy into a profession, the chance of a commission in the navy was lost forever and he was facing imprisonment over his affair. In the late 19th century there was only one thing to do with a 'black sheep' – buy him a one-way ticket to Australia, the last refuge of many a ne'er do well.

The papers of his former pupil at Silesia College, Charles H Mabey, also shed some light on Murrant's departure. It would appear he was a tutor right up until the time he left for Australia. According to Mabey, 'something happened' and he was gone. The next thing they heard he was in Australia. He does speculate that the controversy may have involved owing money to the bookies, which is most likely where the rumour of a debt originally started.

THIS FIRST CHAPTER OF HIS LIFE ENDED on April Fool's Day, 1883 when Edwin Henry Murrant kissed his mother and sister goodbye on Plymouth quay and boarded the *SS Waroonga,* bound for Townsville. At the last moment, his mother had pushed her Bible into his hands, hoping it might offer some comfort in the wild and godless land that lay at the end of her son's long journey.

Whether he was a Morant or Murrant, the supreme irony is that both families originated from the same French root, *demorant,* which means 'a stranger or sojourner'. This description certainly fitted nineteen-year-old Edwin Murrant as he stood on the deck of the *Waroonga,* watching through tear-clouded eyes as his homeland receded below the horizon between the grey scudding clouds and the rolling waves of the Atlantic Ocean. As it finally disappeared, did he close his eyes and surrender himself to the forces of destiny, just like the Greek odysseyers he had read about in the Silesia College library?

Edwin could never have guessed it would be seventeen long years till he set foot in dear old England again, or imagined the adventures, tragedies and glories that lay ahead of him. Such is the stuff of legends.

He would become famous as 'Breaker' Morant and his deeds of derring do would inspire poets. A decade later, when Australia's most celebrated bard, Banjo Paterson, came to write *Jim Carew,* he saw that the seeds of Morant's despair and eventual destruction had been sown during this first stanza of his life:

Born of a thoroughbred English race,
Well proportioned and closely knit,
Neat, slim figure and handsome face,
Always ready and always fit,
Hardy and wiry of limb and thew,
That was the ne'er-do-well Jim Carew.

One of the sons of the good old land –
Many a year since his like was known;
Never a game but he took command,
Never a sport but he held his own;
Gained at his college a triple blue –
Good as they make them was Jim Carew.

Came to grief—was it card or horse?
Nobody asked and nobody cared;
Ship him away to the bush of course,
Ne'er-do-well fellows are easily spared;
Only of women a sorrowing few
Wept at parting from Jim Carew . . .

2

The Vanishing Point

He will leave when his ticket is tendered
A bundle of debts, I'm afraid –
Accounts that were many times rendered
And bills that never will be paid.
Whilst the tailor and the riding boot maker
Will stand with their thumbs in their mouth,
With a three cornered curse at 'The Breaker'
When 'The Breaker' is booked for the South.

'When "The Breaker" is Booked for the South'
by Will Ogilvie

EDWIN MURRANT'S FIRST GLIMPSE of Australia came after two long months at sea – long enough for the small community of 536 aboard the *SS Waroonga* to mourn a death and celebrate two births. The voyage on the British India Line's newest ship, recently commissioned from the world-famous Glasgow shipyards, had taken them down through the Suez Canal which, along with the rest of Egypt, had recently become a British 'Protectorate'. It offered the navy a safe and speedier route to her Middle and Far Eastern colonies should the predatory Russians or Germans show any territorial ambitions. This direct route cut three thousand miles and about a month off the old sailing schedule for the passenger and trading ships that used the old explorers' route around the Cape of Good Hope.

As they periodically put into ports like Aden, Colombo and Singapore, Edwin became increasingly aware of the distance he had put between himself and England. Standing at the rail gazing across the wide blue azure, he wondered what he would find at his journey's end. He was travelling light and only had what his mother was able to scrape together in his pockets.

The other passengers must have shared his apprehension, as they all rushed to the rail as they approached Cooktown, a busy port in northern Queensland. They probably viewed the mysterious palm-fringed coastline with the same trepidation as the man who had given the town his name a century before. In 1883, Australia was still something of an unknown quantity, *terra incognita*, to most Britons.

Before the age of photojournalism and newsreels, impressions of this furthest outpost of the British Empire were coloured by men like journalist and traveller Frank Fowler. Fowler had visited Australia to do a book on the new prosperity being enjoyed there since the discovery of gold. The former convict colony now boasted one of the highest standards of living in the world.

Edwin read his account at college and was held in thrall as the intrepid Fowler traversed the continent and revealed that, 'Australia is not the level and unvaried waste that some have represented'. He described how he 'walked through rich and ever-changing scenes – verdant valleys, zoned with blue-capped hills – and but for the somewhat dusty foliage, the ring of the cicada, the guffaw of the laughing jackass, or the rattle of the snake, might have imagined myself in the fairest and fairyest spots of the Mother land'. The 'foul-mouthed bush men' and 'frivolous, talkative and over-dressed . . . colonial damsels' irked him, but not half as much as the, 'Flies – black, blue, bumble and blow – musquitoes

[sic], cockroaches, spiders, tarantulas, and even cen-
tipedes' which were sent to, 'annoy and terrify the new
arrival'. Worst of all were the 'musquitoes' who gave
him no respite, even when he slept fully clothed, and
'whose corpses now stencil the walls of my bedroom'.

However in the cities, Fowler found a blessed relief
from the vicissitudes of the bush. 'What first took my
attention in Sydney, after I had sufficiently recovered
from the bites of the mosquitoes to show myself in
public was the air of well-to-do-ness which character-
ized every thing about me. The carriages passing
through the streets were quiet and elegant; the people
were well and soberly dressed . . . noble public buildings and palatial dwellings that Belgravia or Tyburnia
might proudly own . . . It was London in good spirits –
as if every man had turned up a nugget or two in his
back garden', but whose less salubrious areas still held
out the promise of 'sin in its bizarre and most lurid
aspects' to any unworldly young man still seeking to
embark on that particular rite of passage.

In slightly less florid terms, Edwin knew that many
thousands, guilty of everything from petty pilfering to
murder, had been transported to Australia during the
first half of the 19th century. Transportation ended
when gold was discovered in the 1850s and the British
authorities realised that convicts now saw being sent to
Australia as a boon rather than a punishment. The last
convicts were sent to Western Australia in 1861.

The recently commissioned *Waroonga* was one of
an expanding fleet of ships servicing the burgeoning
immigrant run to and from Australia. Judging by the
average age of Edwin's fellow passengers, the ships were
more crowded on the outward rather than the return
legs. Like Edwin, many were in their late teens and early
twenties and spoke of escaping the drab, uneventful
years of toil that awaited them in one of Blake's 'dark

satanic mills' to take their chance as free settlers in the
'lucky country'. Word had it that, for all its 'hardships',
Australia was a wide brown land of opportunity where
an honest man, or even a dishonest man, could make
good and where birthright counted for nothing.
However, despite all their gritty optimism, when they
docked at Townsville, Edwin was relieved to see a
Union Jack fluttering above the Customs House and
a reassuring predominance of white faces on the
crowded quay below.

The name on the ship's log was 'Edwin Murrant',
the date of his arrival June 5, 1883 and he was described
as a 'free' (settler). There was one final act in the in-
glorious life of Edwin Henry Murrant before his
metamorphosis into 'Breaker' Morant began.

His exceptional horse riding skills quickly secured
him a 'pick up' job with one of the travelling circuses or
rodeos that had begun to ply their trade up and down
the eastern seaboard. Acrobats, jugglers and buckjumpers were all part of travelling caravans such as
Ashton's and Wraith's, but, as with so many things in
Edwin's life, it was a short-lived fancy, and he parted
company with the circus in the gold-rush town of Charters Towers – only seventy-five miles down the road.

THE AUSTRALIAN GOLD BOOM WAS as sudden and dramatic as the seismic activity that produced the precious
metal deep beneath the earth's surface. The lone shout
of 'Eureka!' in New South Wales in 1851 was echoed
down in Victoria and during the next forty years reverberated round the continent like a shockwave – up
through Queensland, across the Top End and back
down the other side to Western Australia. Following in
its wake was a reluctant population who had predominantly hugged the east coast during the first

century of white settlement. Gold, more than any other single factor, changed the course of Australia's destiny and it went from convict colony to 'lucky country' almost overnight.

These 'strikes' mostly occurred in or around remote bush towns with small populations, but as soon as news of a strike got out, 'diggers' or prospectors descended in their thousands to burrow into the ground like worker ants. Edward Hargraves, whose discovery started the gold boom, named the first diggings 'Ophir' after the biblical city of riches, but it was cold, naked greed that drew men away from kith and kin and kept them on the gold trail for years. Once the alluvial or surface deposits had been ripped out of the earth by sweat, toil and manual tools, news of fresh discoveries further north would arrive and they moved on to keep alive their dream of striking it rich in the lucky country. The diggers were a unique breed; they lived in hope, but most died in despair. Almost as soon as they had disappeared over the far horizon, towns with sleepy names like Hill End, Gympie, Palmer River and Turon slowly sank back into the obscurity they'd come from.

However, Charters Towers was an exception to the rule. An Aboriginal discovered gold there in 1871 and by the time Edwin hit town with his travelling show, Charters Towers was the country's most prolific goldfield and the population had swelled from 8,000 to 33,000 at its peak. With its gold and wealth, its one hundred working mines and one hundred pubs and a stock exchange that was open round the clock, Charters Towers became known as 'the World'. The vivid paintings of Peter Lawson and early black and white photographic images captured the boom years for posterity. They show elegant Federation-style stores, banks and hotels all jockeying for position along the bustling High Street like its many 'working girls' who hoped to catch the eye of the nouveau riche, but seldom turned anyone away. By the grace of God, that sweat-soaked digger lying on top of them tonight could be a sweet-smelling millionaire tomorrow. The throng of bullock carts, horses and traps and well-heeled pedestrians also gave the town an unmistakable air of prosperity whilst the beer-swilling diggers hanging out of hotel doorways had an unmistakable air of optimism which lasted until well after the Great War.

Hard yakka on the goldfields was not for Edwin Murrant. Instead he found work as a stockman at Fanning Downs, a cattle station twenty-five miles from town where the torment and heartbreak of being forced to leave his girl behind in England was swiftly repaired. Within weeks he met a young slip of an Irish girl called Daisy May O'Dwyer, who was the governess at Fanning Downs, and was only six months out from England herself. Daisy told him that she had been compelled to come for health reasons. She was by any standards a striking girl and they had much in common. To Edwin's delight he found she also enjoyed riding and hunting.

Edwin, or Eddie as he had now been renamed with typical Aussie economy, was entranced as the golden light made the emerald in her eye sparkle and accentuated the fineness of her porcelain-white complexion. As always, despite the heat of the Australian outback, she was immaculately dressed in the latest British fashion. She was by her own confession a passionate woman and 'Nature had endowed her face and body with the beauty deemed appropriate for those who claimed to belong to the higher links in the chain of being'.

No more than a gentle gallop from Charters Towers, there is a look-out called Cornishman. Although not that imposing by Australian standards, it still affords intrepid walkers a magnificent panorama of the surrounding bush that stretches uninterrupted out to the Burdekin River.

It was here that Eddie proposed to Daisy and told her all about his convoluted family background, about the Murrants and the Morants and the cruel twist of fate that had cast him upon this fatal shore. However, Eddie had much more in common with Daisy than he ever could have suspected. Daisy probably already knew all about the Morants from her home county of Tipperary where she had been dragged screaming into the world on October 16, 1860.

Lydia and Malvina Hempill were the daughters of local landowner Baron John Hempill of Cashel, Tipperary. Digby Morant's father, George, a senior officer in the Grenadier Guards, married Lydia, and his brother Charles subsequently married her sister Lavina.

Through those marriage ties, the Morant name would be well known in the rural communities on the Celtic fringes where people lived in both awe and contempt of the big local landowners on whose continued benevolence most of them depended for employment, shelter or land. They literally held the power of life and death over the largely peasant population of Ireland. Little wonder that their comings and goings were the stuff of local gossip.

SHE LOST COUNT OF THE TIMES THAT she, little Daisy May, raised her envious eyes to the imposing facade of Emill Castle, ancestral home of the Andersons and Lady Outram, whom she would later claim raised her. She imagined the fine furnishings and gilded rooms, the expensive clothes and jewels, good food and wines that lay within. It was everything that a girl born into an overcrowded 'midden' of a turf-roofed cottage to an ailing mother and a feckless drunk of a father could possibly dream of.

Every Sunday, she stood in the throng and watched the Anderson's fine horsedrawn carriage pull up outside the church. As they all craned their necks to get a glimpse, the liveried driver would alight, throw back his cape and pull open the door like a magician revealing a secret portal to a mythical kingdom of grace and favour.

Daisy was not yet five years old on the day they lowered her mother's roughly hewn coffin into the frozen earth. Through the tears that scalded her eyes she thanked God that her father, James Edward O'Dwyer, had abandoned his children, taken a new wife and joined the legion of habitual Irish drunks who had gone 'across the water' to comb the streets of Boston on their hands and knees looking for the promised land they'd been told about. In any event, James O'Dwyer arrived in the 'New World' feet first. He died during the crossing. Like Ed, Daisy was left with a deep-rooted insecurity and it was noted that 'The slight tremble of her lower lip betrayed some hurt in her life, some wound about which she could speak to no-one'.

THE ELDEST O'DWYER DAUGHTER, Maria, was old enough to fend for herself, but it was left to Grandma Hunt to bring up Daisy May, Jim, Kathleen and the newborn babe whose arrival in this world had coincided with the departure of their mother. Daisy kept her fears and insecurities at bay by retreating into a rich fantasy world that she created from Grandma Hunt's great fund of stories of goblins, ghosties and leprechauns.

Daisy May also learned how to reinvent herself on the knee of her grandmother. Grandma Hunt had always regarded the O'Dwyers as drunkards and wastrels, so she renamed the children the O'Dwyer-Hunts. It was that simple – change your name, leave your past behind, and create a new identity. Little Daisy May obviously took that salutary lesson to heart as, later in life, she gave wildly contrasting accounts of her early years, in which names, dates and places of birth were all interchangeable.

Following the death of Grandma Hunt, the children were split up and sent to live with various relatives. Daisy claimed in one account of her early life to have been brought up with the children of the wealthy Outrams, who were friends of her family, and in another to have lived with her father who was a lawyer of note in Dublin. She also claimed to have travelled Europe in the company of the Outrams and attended a European finishing school where she learned languages, poetry and science.

The truth, as is so often the case, was a lot less glamorous. Daisy was sent to Dublin but not, as she claimed, to live with her rich lawyer father and attend an exclusive girl's school, but to an orphanage where she attended a charity school and was trained to become a governess. With the help of the society 'bible', Debrett's, Daisy had simply transposed a glamorous life with the Outrams over the Hunts, the O'Dwyers and the orphanage. The Outrams later denied any connection with her, but she maintained the same pretence on her arrival in Australia, and would do so till the end of her days.

HAD EDDIE TROUBLED HIMSELF TO LOOK closer, he would have seen the furrowed brow, the firm set of her jaw and that steely look in her eye. Even though Daisy passed herself off as a girl of good breeding by always dressing as though she were in Dublin or London rather than the Australian outback and by sheer force of personality, she knew what being on the bottom of the pile was all about. Life's few opportunities must be grabbed with both hands because life would always come back later, knock you down, shit all over you, stand you up and do it again. Daisy, like Edwin, had felt the pain of rejection and loss, but she believed that by aspiring upwards to a higher station in life she could shape her own destiny. Mere birthright would be no obstacle to her grand plan, particularly in a land where origins were never challenged. Daisy had no claim to title, but Edwin did and here he was dithering over who he really was.

She distilled all her worldly experience into a few words. Letting her carefully arranged façade slip for a moment or two, she berated him in her rough Irish brogue which owed more to the bogs than Emill Castle, 'Ah, fuck the lot of 'em, Edwin! It's your birthright. Claim it! Sure I would, God help me!'

As well as his rugged good looks, quick wit and devilish charm, it was the lure of belonging to a titled family that attracted Daisy to Eddie in the first place. Daisy's whole raison d'etre was to:

[A]ppear to the world as one of God's elect . . . one of the few who 'rightly do inherit Heaven's graces'.

It was Daisy who persuaded Eddie that Murrant and Morant were similar semantically but worlds apart socially, and that such an elevation would help him escape his inauspicious start in Australia. After all, he was entitled to take the name of his real father . . . and it might serve them both very well. She also warned him she would not take a husband without at least the prospect of title or means. Faced with the prospect of losing her, Edwin Murrant finally found the courage, after nineteen years, to take his real father's name and go out into the world as his legitimate son. His transformation from Eddie Murrant to Harry Morant had begun.

BUT EDDIE WASN'T THE ONLY MAN to be caught in the intricate web of this femme fatale. In truth, it was an ill wind not ill health that had blown Daisy out to Australia.

She said that when a tuberculosis spot was found on her lung it was thought best that she went to live in warmer climes. She also claimed that Bishop Stanton, who had been her chaperone in Ireland and was now the Bishop of Townsville, had invited her to Australia.

Again, the truth had been sacrificed on the altar of convenience. After finishing her education and aged eighteen, Daisy took a job as a governess with a well-to-do family, which is probably where she learned her airs and graces. Her rare beauty and free spirit bewitched the young master of the house, but when he realised he could never have her he commited suicide in a fit of depression. Between 1880 and 1920, there was a great demand for single women under Australia's Assisted Female Immigration policy and also for good Christians to help settle Australia. Daisy was most probably sent to Australia under the auspices of the Catholic Church who ran the orphanage where she was brought up in Dublin. The Bishop Stanton of Townsville may have been responsible for the welfare of Daisy and the many like her who came to Australia, but were she really a lady of substance, it is unlikely Eddie would have found her working as a governess at Fanning Downs cattle station. Governess was a position that a working-class girl, not a member of the upper-classes, would aspire to.

But Daisy was no more lucky in love in Australia. Once again, she became the object of a young man's affections. Arnold Knight Colquhoun was the son of a wealthy American family who was reputed to have jumped ship in Australia and worked for the Charters Towers paper *The Northern Miner*. Once again, Daisy became embroiled in a tragic death. Colquhoun poisoned himself with opium on October 31, 1883 – a few months before Eddie and Daisy were married. He wrote his last letter to Daisy and although the contents were never revealed it was strongly suspected at the time that he took his life because his love for Daisy was unrequited. However, Eddie was not the only one vying for Daisy's hand at that time. She had promised to marry Philip Gipps, a relative of the former Governor of New

South Wales, but in yet another tragic twist of fate he was killed in a riding accident at Inverell, New South Wales, on February 22, 1884.

So, Daisy and Edwin, both on the rebound from tragic, broken romances, found themselves thrown together in the dusty corner of Australia by the fickle hand of fate. Daisy was a practical girl. Australia, even more than Ireland, was a man's world and she needed a man of substance to make a home for her and to help her ascend the social ladder. So, she shrugged her shoulders and accepted Edwin's proposal.

UNDER THE WATCHFUL AND NO DOUBT disapproving eye of her guardian, Bishop Stanton, Daisy and Edwin married on March 13, 1884. He was Church of England and she was a Catholic and it was as much an Irish comedy as a tragedy that such an 'unholy union' could not be blessed in either house of the Lord, so the ceremony was performed by an Anglican minister at the house of Mr and Mrs John Veal. Edwin married Daisy as Murrant and despite later claims about his parentage, also gave his father's name as Edwin Henry Murrant.

Alas, the course of true love did not run smoothly and the writing must have been on the wall from the moment Edwin 'duded' the Reverend Barlow out of his £5 wedding fee. The good reverend was due to move to a new parish the following week and Murrant obviously didn't think he would wait around for it. It was a bad omen and within a couple of weeks the newly weds' domestic situation began to disintegrate.

On April 16, 1884, a warrant was issued for Edwin's arrest in Charters Towers Police Court after he was accused of stealing a saddle from a Mr Brooks on April 3 and stealing thirty-two pigs from a Mr Riordan on April 7. It seems that you could take the boy out of the workhouse, but not the workhouse out of the boy. A Constable Quinn tried to serve a summons on Murrant and his co-accused, Palmer, but Murrant, still living at Fanning Downs, could not be contacted. Palmer was served, but failed to appear.

The two accused were finally brought before the court on April 21. Murrant had been arrested on the 19th, on the Dalrymple road sixteen miles from Charters Towers. He said he was not running away because of the saddle or the pigs, but because he had written cheques that had not been honoured and was told he could be prosecuted for it. Although bail was set at £40 with two sureties of £20 each, he remained in custody until the 23rd when he was acquitted of stealing the pigs. Magistrate PF Sellheim concluded that no act of larceny was proved and the accused were acquitted, 'till the pigs fly'. However, Murrant was remanded until the 25th on the charge of stealing the saddle.

This time, sub-inspector Meldrum said that a prima facie case had been made out. Murrant had asked Mrs Brooks if he could borrow a saddle, but then had helped himself to a better one. Murrant had later sold the saddle on to Mr Palmer for £4, although he never received the money for it. Murrant was discharged because the Magistrate did not think the Attorney-General would prosecute and ordered the return of the saddle to Mr Brooks.

Details that emerged during the court case suggest that Ed and Daisy's marriage was 'on the rocks' even before he was arrested. When Constable Quinn apprehended Edwin, he apparently told the policeman that he planned to flee west to Cloncurry and admitted that 'if he had got the horse they would not have seen him for some time'. The fact that his wife was not with him, she hadn't posted bail for him, and Mrs Brooks had said that Murrant was living at her house on April 13 when he stole the saddle, seems to confirm that Edwin and Daisy had already parted company.

Those suspicions were well founded, because on the day Edwin was acquitted, Daisy made the decision to leave him, barely five weeks into their marriage. She told him that she wanted a husband who would make her a home and suggested a trial separation of two-and-a-half years. Daisy returned some jewellery he got her on the 'never-never' and told him to come and find her again once he'd mended his ways. Daisy thought she was marrying a gentleman, but once she discovered that his often-mentioned remittance was never coming, and his only real prospect seemed to be prison, her passion cooled.

Although Daisy's feminine influence failed to curb his larrikin ways, Murrant's metamorphosis into Morant clearly took place during his brief sojourn with her. When Edwin bought two horses and signed the cheque 'Morant', it was the first time he used the name he would make famous. However, where finances were concerned, Morant picked up where Murrant left off, because both the cheque and the horses had to be returned.

The Charters Towers police and court records chart his gradual transformation from Murrant into Morant. During the time of his arrest, they have him down as both EH Morant and Ed H Morant. However, the newspapers consistently refer to him as Murrant. Murrant may have started calling himself Morant, but as far as *The Northern Miner* was concerned, the leopard had not changed its spots. He had not yet changed his Christian name to the soon to be familiar Harry. There are only two Harrys in the Morant family tree – George, Edward and John being the most common Christian names – but it was his choice of the very distinctive middle name Harbord that offers further proof of his Morant origins.

The Morant family tree shows quite a few Horatios and Huberts, but only four Harbords; five including Harry Harbord Morant alias the Breaker. To chose that rare family name would require an intimate knowledge of the Morant family tree.

The reason he chose or had been given this name was revealed in a letter from Julian Fellowes-Kitchener, whose grandmother, Madelene Morant, was Digby's sister. His letter confirms:

> Digby's grandmother was a Mary Shelly who married George Morant in 1813. She had a sister, Emily, who married Edward Harbord, 3rd Lord Suffield. There are no other connections between the families of Harbord and Morant and so it does suggest that this is the correct branch of the Morant family to look for Harry Harbord Morant's roots.

Indeed, that same branch of the Morant family used the name Harbord for the first time in the next generation. George and Mary's second son, Digby's younger brother, Horatio, was given the middle name Harbord. He went on to distinguish himself in the army, becoming a Lieutenant-Colonel and aide-de-camp to Queen Victoria. Harbord does not appear in the next generation, other than in Harry Harbord Morant. Since his execution, the Morant family has never used the name again. However, this is not the last word on his origins. Far from it. As the story of the Breaker unfolds over the next two decades, there are many more clues to his true birthright and meetings with members of the Morant family, all of whom confirmed his lineage.

DAISY AND EDWIN HAD COME TO A FORK in the road of life and went their separate ways to carve out their niches in the history of Australia. He became a bush legend and executed martyr, whilst she, better known as Daisy Bates, became *Kabbarli* – 'the white-skinned grandmother' of the Aboriginal peoples, gaining honours for her role.

Edwin left her with a kiss and the promise that he would come back when he'd recovered his fortunes ringing in her ears. He never did.

Once, whilst fording a dangerously swollen river in an effort to reach a nearby pub before 'swill time', the Breaker summarised his life philosophy with the words 'I never turn back'. He stayed true to that motto, even at the end when he might have saved himself from the firing squad. But the same could also be said of Daisy.

Despite having left the door open for a possible future reconciliation, less than nine months after leaving Edwin, Daisy risked a seven-year prison sentence to bigamously marry Jack Bates, celebrated horseman and former head stockman of the world's biggest woolshed, Tinneburra Station. There was no time to get a divorce and being a Catholic presented certain moral as well as legal problems. Daisy solved the problem by marrying Jack using her maiden name – O'Dwyer – in Bathurst on February 17, 1885. However, no sooner had they married than Jack went off droving for six months.

In his absence she turned her attentions to Ernest Clarke Baglehole, a merchant seaman. She committed bigamy for a second time when she married him in the Sydney suburb of Newtown on June 10, 1885. She again got round the fact she was inconveniently married to both Edwin Murrant and Jack Bates by presenting herself at the altar, for the third time, as the virginal, spinster Daisy O'Dwyer. Ernest was her third husband in little over a year, but like Edwin and Jack he proved unsuitable and was quickly discarded so she could be at home when Jack returned from the bush.

Daisy ended a tumultuous two years by giving birth to her only child, a son called Arnold, on August 26, 1886. However, given the tangled nature of her love-life either Jack or Ernest could have been the father with the possibility that the boy was named after another lover – the tragic Arnold Knight Colquhoun.

Daisy left Jack and Arnold in 1894 and spent five years in England working as a journalist before returning to Australia where she and Bates tried to repair their relationship. By 1903, the year after Morant's execution, their differences had become irreconcilable and they separated for good. Whilst acknowledging that Bates had been a 'fine man . . . superb rider' she admitted, 'I could never run in double harness'.

She saw men as a means to achieve her ends – wealth and social position – but eventually she reached her 'goal' without the help of a husband. She found fame through her long and lonely vigil with the Aboriginal people, whom the white colonists believed were a dying race. Was it a supreme act of kindness or a self-imposed exile from her own race 'which could not provide her with the satisfactions she craved, [and] continued her role of queen . . . [in] a land where her will would be sovereign'?

A tent in Cannington, Western Australia, would never be Emill Castle, but her work with the Aborigines did get her the recognition from high office she craved. In May 1904, the West Australian Government asked her to record the customs, languages and dialects of the Aborigines at the Maaba reserve in Cannington. It took nearly six years to compile and arrange the data. Many of her papers were read at Geographical and Royal Society meetings and she started writing articles for newspapers and journals. The Commander of the British Empire medal she received in 1934 for her services to the Aboriginals completed her re-invention of herself, which, it must be said, was eminently more successful than

Morant's. Daisy's maxim was that the truth is only what you can get others to believe. She never left that fantasy world of her childhood and changed the details of her date and place of birth, her upbringing, social status, marriages and her life at will. Rarely do any two accounts of her life agree. At the end of a poem she wrote later in life she said: 'I have never grown out of my longing for you and my playmates of long ago.'

However, it has also been said that her fantasy world 'was her open sesame into the Aboriginal mind'.

Although Daisy never mentioned that she was married to the Breaker to any of her biographers, she did try to find out what became of her estranged husband. Though, technically, she was his next of kin, Daisy was apparently unaware he was one of the executed officers who had excited such controversy across three continents.

Even more bizarre was the *ménage à trois* Daisy later became entangled in whilst corresponding on the subject of the Aboriginals. She not only exchanged letters with one of her husband's prime accusers, Ramon De Bertodano, but also his embittered defence counsel Major JF Thomas, without realising their common connection.

After he left Daisy, Morant sowed his 'wild oats' far and wide, but at the time of his death was engaged to the 'trim-set petticoat' in North Devon who was mentioned in the final poem he wrote in his cell 'Whilst waiting cru-ci-fiction!'.

Neither of them was lucky in love and what fun the gods must have had toying with the destinies of those star-crossed lovers, the Romeo and Juliet of Australian history.

NO PHOTOGRAPH OF EDWIN MURRANT has ever come to light and we shall never know whether there was any actual physical metamorphosis when he reached the 'vanishing point' at the edge of Charters Towers where Edwin Henry Murrant became Harry Harbord Morant. Did Edwin Murrant shave off his beard, cut his hair or change his clothes? He may have changed his name and even his appearance, but not his personality. According to the local newspapers Edwin Murrant had not been a popular character. He was a thief and a trouble-maker. It is noticeable that at the time of his leaving and after his death, when it was known that Morant was once Murrant, there were no tears shed in Charters Towers, no humorous anecdotes or fond memories of Edwin Murrant. It was now time for Harry Morant to come to the fore, but Edwin would always be there, waiting in the shadows, and would re-emerge later in South Africa during his darkest hours. But, for now, Harry Morant sat taller in the saddle as he put some distance between himself and the wife whose social aspirations he could never hope to fulfil, and all the inadequacies of his old life in England.

Perhaps another good reason for changing his name before he 'went bush' was that Edwin is no name for a horse-breaker or drover in the outback of Australia. Too Pommy, by far! Harry had a more familiar, universal ring to it and suited the rough and ready mateship he found in the bush.

Edwin left the Bible his mother had given him on the quayside at Plymouth in Charters Towers with Mrs Hapgood-Veal, the woman in whose house he had been married. '*I won't need it where I'm going,*' he told her. Armed with little more than a swag, a billy can and a stockwhip, Harry Harbord Morant rode off confidently into the endless, godless dusty stretches of the Australian bush without looking back, to begin the Breaker legend in earnest.

The bush had forged many legends and the Breaker arrived just as the era of the bushranger ended. Ned Kelly had been hung just four years before and more

recently Captain Thunderbolt had died in a hail of
police bullets like Ben Hall, Johnny Gilbert and Mad
Dan Morgan before him. Captain Melville, John Dunn,
Captain Moonlite and the Clarke brothers had all
dangled at the end of the hangman's noose and Frank
Darkie Gardiner had rotted in prison. But despite the
brutal nature of some of their crimes, these so-called
'barbarians of the bush' enjoyed great public sympathy
and there were vacancies for a new generation of
Australian heroes in the anti-authoritarian mould.

They would be created by the so-called 'bush poets'
who articulated the first distinctively Australian literary
voice. The best known were the 'Holy Trinity' of Banjo
Paterson, Henry Lawson and Will Ogilvie and, to a
lesser extent, the Breaker, who wrote and inspired many
a legendary verse. But all this, and a lot more, lay ahead
of him.

3

The Wild Colonial Boy

Well-known on the border, strong, handsome and straight,
A reckless, wild liver, but true-hearted mate –
What his name is I'm not in a position to swear,
But we called him – it suited him – Devil-may-care!

Drink! He drank Bullocky Jim out of breath!
Dance! He could dance the red stars to their death!
Ride! There was nothing in hide or in hair
Too rough to be ridden by Devil-may-care! . . .

'Devil-May-Care' by Will Ogilvie

THE NEWLY CHRISTENED HARRY HARBORD Morant began his sixteen-year odyssey in the Australian bush by heading southwards to the country town of Hughenden – the next sizeable town down the line from Charters Towers. With a fine education, a ready wit and a way with words, Morant felt that journalism might be a good outlet for his prodigious talents. He tried to buy a share in the local newspaper, assuring the owners that he could get the funds from a 'titled gentleman in England'. He spent quite a lot of money sending a cable to England with all the details of his proposal. But the wound that caused his Australian exile was still too fresh and the money never materialised. Some sixty years later, Digby's nephew John Morant revealed that

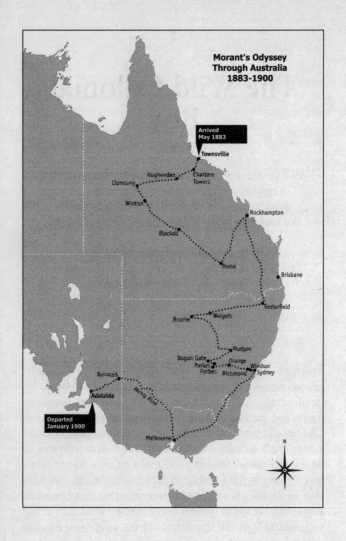

Morant's Odyssey
Through Australia
1883-1900

Arrived
May 1883

Townsville

Hughenden
Cloncurry
Charters
Towers

Winton

Rockhampton

Blackall

Roma

Brisbane

Tenterfield

Bourke
Walgett

Mudgee

Bogan Gate
Parkes
Forbes

Orange
Richmond

Windsor
Sydney

Renmark

Murray River

Adelaide

Departed
January 1900

Melbourne

N

Digby had been given a copy of that letter, which confirms that the 'titled person' was someone within his social circle; Digby Morant did not get his Knight Commander (of the order) of the Bath until 1901.

Morant was forced to withdraw from the venture due to the lack of funds, and after some trouble with a hotel bill left town, not for the last time, with the curses of creditors nipping at his heels. He has often been described as a 'remittance man', but he never received a penny from England. Had he done so, perhaps his life might have taken a different turn. Indeed, his good friend 'Banjo' Paterson asked in his valedictory, 'What is it that such men lack – just a touch of determination, or of caution maybe – to turn their lives from failures to successes?' In Morant's case, about £100.

He fared no better in Winton and Cloncurry – the other one-horse towns he passed through. Realising that it was pointless to keep hoping for money from England and that he'd have to make it on his own, he surrendered to the inevitable and turned his horse towards the bush.

The late 19th century was a great era of expansion for Australia in every sense. She was discovering her own identity and shaping, in the words of the father of Federation, Henry Parkes, 'the Australian continent we can call home'. The wild Australian interior was being opened up by squatters and gold, silver and mineral prospectors who were literally following in the footsteps of the great explorers Wills and Burke, Stuart and McKinlay. Men of vision like Sid Kidman, the 'cattle king', were seizing the day and building their empires, whilst the fledgling BHP Company was sinking its first mineshaft at Broken Hill and building a city in the outback. By the last decade of the century, the railways were probing further inland to service the flourishing sheep, timber, cattle and mining industries and had connected four of the five major cities.

The map of Australia looked very different one hundred years ago. Country towns like Bourke, Parkes, Orange, Windsor and Richmond were the thriving cattle capitals of Australia. Harry Morant drifted southwards down the 'bush route' taking a succession of jobs, mostly horse-breaking and droving, and spending up big in the nearest town when he got his cheque.

The large cattle stations and the small squatters alike relied on a large army of itinerant bush labour to fence their land, cut timber, deliver supplies, shear sheep, muster their cattle and drive the cattle to market. The shearers, 'breakers' and overlanders migrated like birds with the changing seasons from the Northern Territory down through Queensland and New South Wales, into Victoria and across to South Australia as their fancy took them.

Despite the huge distances involved, news travelled fast in this tightly knit community. Employment opportunities came through word of mouth and when one job was over, the news would come of another one via the 'bush telegraph'. References were verbal and a good horseman was always worth his weight in gold. This nomadic lifestyle fulfilled the need for freedom and adventure for men like Morant who were too restless or frivolous to squat their own land or work a claim. Henry Lawson summed up that wanderlust in his poem *Ballad of a Rouseabout*:

> Some take the track for gain in life,
>   some take the track for loss,
> And some of us take up the swag
>   as Christ took up the cross.

Further inland at Esmerelda station, Morant found gainful employment as a storeman, but the novelty of weighing out tea and sugar for stationhands and passing 'swaggies' soon wore off. He continued to drift and turned his hand, instead, to droving and overlanding. His job was to muster the cattle that roved free in the huge outback properties and drive them to market. These cattle had been born in the wild and often had never been mustered before. Being feral, they were much more aggressive than normal, domesticated cattle.

Amongst the horsemen who herded the mob across the country were the 'nuts' – young jackeroos who would perform dangerous manoeuvres to keep the cattle moving or get them across a river, which made this a risky profession. The 'nuts' were commonly described as, 'long, lank, lantern-jawed, whiskerless colonial youth with an insolent and aggressive manner. His most common appearance was in a "terrific uproar" at the local shanty where he would drink, swear, brawl with his peers.'

It was whilst he was 'on the wallaby' that Morant struck up a lifelong friendship with a tough drover and blade shearer called Sam Nicker. He described them as 'mischievous twins' always trying to outdo each other, whether it was riding, composing verse or reciting passages from classical texts round the campfire. Nicker remembered Morant as a great drover but something of a show-off. 'Doing a Harry', was Sam's affectionate term for Morant's habit of carefully setting his hat at a jaunty angle over one eye like some gunslinger from the Wild West. In one of his short stories, *The Honourable Harry*, which, like much of his poetry, appears to be autobiographical, Morant described his own unique droving technique and demonstrated this tendency for 'flashness':

> We uster call him 'the Honourable Harry' – part because he was the son of a Dook or a Major General, or something of the sort, at home in England; and part because he was very honourable

in the matter of his liquor, for he'd never take a nip without asking everyone there 'what his poison was?' No we never passed a shanty but what the Honourable Harry acted honourable! But the two most notorious things about 'the Honourable' was the wonderful, white, baggy riding-pants he wore, and his everlasting habit of smoking cigarettes . . . But the Honourable Harry's wonderful pants and his cigarettes came in handy before the trip was finished and the bullocks delivered.

One of the big problems the overlanders faced was the sudden stampeding of cattle.

Bad Cattle – you can just bet your last pipeful that they was bad. A falling star, or a black duck flying over, would start 'em any minute of the night. They knocked down more gidgee in one night's rush than would make new posts for the Border Fence; whilst this side the Barwon they 'carried away' enough wire to fence all Tyson's cattle-country into small sheep-paddocks.

During the night, the thousand head of bullock they were delivering to market stampeded:

Well, the Honourable and me were riding slow around the cattle, when all of a sudden they was off, sailing helter-skelter in the direction of a thick bit of timber, and coming my way. There was no moon, nor no stars that night, and you could hear a lot better than you could see; but I recognised an old white-backed brindle bullock – a notorious rogue – in the lead, and a couple of 'ballys' close up behind him. I kept the greenhide going pretty free, and 'WHAAY WHOOPED' till I was getting hoarse, when all of a sudden, like a condensed bit of lightning, up slides the 'Honourable' on old Yanalong, and whips by me like a swallow. Then I sees him lean over his horses off-side, and – galloping all the time – he strikes a match on that old white-backed brindle bullock's near horn, and lights the cigarette which he had in his [the Honourable Harry's] mouth! Strike me Imperial Crimson purple! – if the cattle, catching sight of them white baggy pants as the Honourable Harry struck the match, didn't steady down straightaway. We flogged 'em back on to camp, and they never rushed after; and we put them into Muswellbrook yards like as if they was a mob of milkers' calves, instead of being the dirtiest lot as ever crossed the Queensland Border. Ah, the Honourable Harry was a fine horseman!

But it was as a horse-breaker that Morant made his name in Australia. Banjo Paterson, no slouch in the saddle himself, said of him: 'he was an excellent rough-rider and when he was young, with a nerve unshaken, he was a first-class horse-breaker and a good man to teach young horses how to jump fences.'

He was also described as 'reckless' and 'having no regard for his personal safety', but great horsemen always walk that fine line – that daring is what separates the great from just the good.

Morant was popular for his dash and courage, and he would travel miles to gain the kudos of riding a really dangerous horse.

He described many such feats in his colourful letters to Banjo Paterson:

Filled up some leisure by breaking in a four-year-old colt by the Levite (a Yattenden horse) out of an old mare by The Drummer. The colt was a man-eater when I first tackled him, but has turned out a beautiful horse to ride, and I may get a race out of

him, as his old mother has won both over hurdles
and on the flat.

But it was for the feat of riding the most dangerous
brumby ever corralled in Australia that earned him the
nickname by which he became popularly known – 'the
Breaker'.

*DARGIN'S TRAVELLING SHOW WAS camped somewhere
out the back o' Bourke just a few clicks south of
nowhere. It was around noon when owner and chief
spruiker Arthur Dargin spotted a lone figure riding in
slowly. He knew it was noon because the cattle dogs
had crept off in search of shade and lay there panting,
their pink tongues hanging out as dry as sandpaper. The
blast-furnace heat evaporated the moisture on your eye-
balls in the time it took to blink and rivulets of sweat
slalomed down your back, and that from just sitting
still. Nothing moved at midday during summer, unless
it had to.*

*Arthur squinted into the blinding light. Maybe it was
the way the hot air rose in waves and created a strange
mirage effect around the approaching stranger, but he
had an uncanny feeling that something dramatic was
about to shake them out of their torpor.*

*'Mad bastard,' croaked the ragged throat next to
him, the words carefully chosen both for their economy
and effectiveness. Big and bulky with a mass of black
hair and an overlander's bushy beard, Mick Lynch was
not built for a tropical climate. From the high-backed
wooden chair which groaned under his great weight, he
had also been following the progress of the stranger. He
shielded his eyes with one shovel-like hand and used the
other to fend off the big black bush flies whose sole
mission between dawn and dusk was to explore the
deepest recesses of his nasal passages.*

'Mad bastard,' repeated Mick. A thunderous snort

and a stream of precious spittle returned an intrusive fly to its natural habitat and acted as a punctuation mark. He continued, 'Five bob says he keels over before he gets in.' The chair groaned in protest as he slumped back, spent by the sheer effort of the past few moments. It was two months since Mick had been to the track and he'd have bet on a cockroach race to break the monotony of those endless hot days.

'Yer on,' said Arthur, who had been shrewdly watching the silhouette approach with growing interest.

Twenty minutes later, Arthur pocketed Mick's five bob as the stranger brought his fine-looking black horse alongside them. He reckoned the man to be in his mid-twenties, around five foot seven inches, powerfully built, with the broad shoulders and the muscular forearms of a horseman, or a sportsman. His nut brown bushman's tan and expertly packed 'drum' also told him he was no 'new chum'. Arthur digested this information as the stranger tipped his hat in greeting, revealing a pair of twinkling blue eyes with a hint o' Irish devilry in them. But this stranger wasn't so easy to pick.

'G'day.' Though it was only two words, the local greeting only accentuated his pronounced English accent.

'Stone me, he's a Pom!' exclaimed Mick, regaining some energy and humour after briefly mourning the loss of his hard-earned coin. Ignoring the jibe, the stranger continued: 'Word at the shanty is that you might have some work.'

'What kind of work would that be, mate?' asked Arthur steadily.

'Well, I've been breaking and training horses over by Cloncurry and Winton.'

'Is that right? What'd they call you, mate?' he asked cautiously, careful not to break the first rule of the bushman's code, which respected the anonymity of a stranger who didn't want to be found for whatever

reason. Some went under an assumed name and some preferred just to use a nickname. It was never challenged.

'Harry, Harry Morant,' said the stranger, fearlessly giving his whole name without a moment's hesitation.

'Is it Harry "the Breaker" Morant, then?' said Mick with a wink. 'I reckon we could do with a breaker round here,' he added, tilting his head sideways towards the stockade. Arthur could see where Mick was headed, so he nodded and added, 'Got a brumby fresh out of the bush yesterday arvo. Doesn't seem too flighty. Game to give it a go?' Arthur sensed that his instinct about the approaching stranger was right.

'Certainly,' replied Harry, coolly sensing their game.

'Certainly,' mimicked Mick, rolling his eyes and sensing an opportunity for some good sport and a chance to get his five bob back, maybe with a bit of interest.

They led Morant to the small square stockade where they challenged the public to ride buckjumpers. Brumbies were wild and it was the job of the breaker, a freelance equine troubleshooter, to get up on its back and make it buckjump – kick its legs in the air until it couldn't arch its back anymore. That was the theory, at least. Penned in by eight-foot timber rails, horse and rider fought it out on fifty square feet of hard-packed, sun-dried red earth that felt like solid rock to those unfortunate enough to land on it.

'Strewth, they're putting the bloody Pom on Dargin's Grey,' called Charlie, the diminutive horse wrangler, as he scuttled out of the barn with a burst of speed that belied his seventy years.

'Fair dinkum?' asked a stockhand and ran off to spread the news.

Dargin's Grey is said to be the maddest, baddest brumby ever to be brought in from the Australian

bush – and that was a big claim. Harry Morant is said
to have been 'one of the most reckless riders who ever
threw a leg over a wild horse in Australia' – which was
also a big claim. Two immovable forces of nature were
about to collide, but Mick, Arthur and Charlie, who had
perched themselves on the top rail like crows on a fence,
didn't know that . . . yet.

'Mad bastard,' came Mick's motif.

'Who, the Pom or the 'orse?' cracked Charlie, keen
to get in on the act.

'Both,' said Mick and cackled like an old witch.

Arthur watched Harry slowly approach the horse.
He'd noticed something in his gait as he rode in, and
now he saw it in his walk. He picked him as a man who
knew horses.

'What d'ya reckon Mick?' he mused.

'Quid on the 'orse,' came the tense reply. All around
them, similar wagers were being laid with nods, winks
and grunts.

Harry knew at once by the sudden appearance of
every performer and handler in the show that this was
a rogue horse. Judging by the wild look in the horse's
eye and the fresh spur marks on his sides, a few brave
souls had come to grief trying to tame this wild spirit.

Dargin's Grey was in fact the star turn at Dargin's
travelling show which specialised in feats of daredevil
horsemanship. 'Out bush', horses were all they knew,
all they talked about and all they'd part with their hard-
earned coin to see. As chief spruiker, Arthur's job was
to cajole, entice and bully the breakers, rough riders and
local blowhards with a shot of grog in them to saddle
up, using the lure of £5 prize money and the kudos of
being the only man to ride Dargin's Grey. Over the
years, he'd seen a few good ones, some average ones
and more bad ones than he cared to remember.
Dargin's Grey had recently acquired the added distinc-

tion of being a 'killer horse' – a local horse-breaker had broken his neck after being tossed. Tragic, but 'he knew the go', would be the epitaph on the fresh grave he occupied under the shade of a big gum tree a few towns back. Such was a breaker's lot – hazardous at best, fatal at worst.

Nonetheless, he was a magnificent beast – a huge, solid lump of muscle with a dark grey coat the colour of rough granite. His unkempt sandy brown mane and straggly tail had never seen a stable boy's clippers or brush. Morant's shrewd eye told him he stood at least eighteen hands high. Its powerful looking front and hindquarters were a legacy of a life on the hoof. He was born in the wild, where only the strongest survive. New foals had only a few hours to get up and run before the dingoes sniff them out.

Harry moved warily towards him, slowly whispering softly, wary that he might buck suddenly or lash out with his hooves. He recalled Old George Whyte-Melville's well-worn adage: steady as she goes, lad, nice and gentle. They like to be courted before they're ridden, just like a proper lady.

'What's he up to?' asked Mick anxiously.

'Sweet-talking him,' smiled Arthur. This Morant was no greenhorn.

'It ain't a bloody sheila, mate,' Mick thundered, earning a reproachful glance from Harry who now stood behind the horse. Dargin's Grey feigned indifference, but he rolled his eye backwards periodically, keeping him in close check. Both were still pretending that nothing was going to happen. Harry was still talking soothingly to him as he ran a hand down his powerful flank. He snorted at the impertinence of the sudden touch and the horse's muscles rippled with tension under his hand, but he did not lash out. Closer and closer, Harry moved up his flank towards his head, *still talking. As they drew level they looked each other in the eye for the briefest of moments, but they knew they were going to duel. Man and horse – adversaries and best mates since the dawn of time. Then, in what appeared to be a primal show of machismo, Dargin's Grey suddenly unsheathed its huge black penis, which dropped down and dangled heavily between his hind legs. That raised a riotous cheer from the onlookers and Mick's basso profundo came sailing over the top of them all, 'I think he likes ya, mate!'*

Harry ignored the sideshow and nodded to a young jackeroo, who threw a lasso round the horse's neck with a practised flick of his wrist and took up the slack as Dargin's Grey reared up. Two other men quickly joined him whilst the others dodged the flailing hooves to quickly blindfold, saddle and bridle the beast before retreating for cover.

The three rope men were already covered in a film of red dust as they hung on grimly.

'Quick, mate! We can't 'old him all arvo,' shouted one anxiously as the greenhide rope strained to breaking point.

Without warning, Harry mounted Dargin's Grey in one fluid movement, catching not only the 'crows' but the horse completely by surprise. Harry grinned as he caught a glimpse of Mick's open mouth. There was a brief pause, as if time had stood still, but it was only the eye of the storm. Harry dug his spurs into the horse's meaty flanks, giving the jackeroos time to get the rope and blindfold off. With a loud whinny, Dargin's Grey arched his back and sent a shower of earth heavenwards as he lifted his hindquarters high. A roar went up from the makeshift grandstand, hats went into the air and the onlookers whooped like Buffalo Bill's cowboys.

The power of the horse's first thrust nearly unseated Harry, who had never felt such raw power under his 'pigskin'. The beast arched his back, leapt straight up in the air, lifting all four legs off the ground and propelling Harry skywards. Clinging to the reins, gravity brought him slapping back into the saddle, just as Dargin's Grey reared up on his hind legs. The horse-breaker's greatest danger was that if he pulled on the bit too hard, his mount might come right over backwards and crush him. Three times he felt the stirrups smack off the ground as the horse lurched sideways – very nearly overbalancing on each occasion – but by deft use of his knees, shifting his weight, anticipation and a light rein, Harry managed to maintain his balance. But Dargin's Grey had only just got started. His front hooves raked the ground as he pirouetted and leapt coiling and uncoiling like a tightened spring in a series of almost perfect circles, then throwing his weight forwards and kicking his hooves high in an effort to throw Harry clean over his head. Shaking its head and frothing at the mouth, Dargin's Grey used all its wiles – twisting and turning, galloping and coming to a skidding halt, which Harry countered by leaning back, pulling hard on the reins and ramming his knees hard into the horse's sides.

Having failed to dislodge the unfamiliar weight on his back by fair means, Dargin's Grey then resorted to foul tactics. He raced along the fencing, perilously close to the rails, scattering the 'crows' from their perch. In desperation, he crashed sideways into the stock rails, which knocked the wind out of Harry. That was a new one, he thought, and grimaced as the numbness spread through his shoulder, but still he hung on. He heard George's steadying voice in his head, 'Ride the storm, lad, she'll blow herself out.'

As always, old George was right. After sixty tense minutes, Dargin's Grey began to tire and the balance of power shifted gradually, but instead of allowing the tiring horse any respite, Harry forced the pace by squeezing the grey's huge barrel chest with his knees. But its manic energy was spent and fifteen minutes later, Dargin's Grey came to a standstill, gave a huge snort and conceded defeat. The tempest had subsided – he had ridden the storm. Harry saw Mick's shoulders slump and his hand go to his pocket in a reflex action as though he had just received some mortal wound.

As the dust cleared, the red, iron-hard earth beneath them had been ploughed and churned by the stampeding hooves – fitting testament to the titanic struggle that is still talked about 'out bush' to this very day. Harry the showman milked the admiration of his peers by trotting the grey round the paddock and putting him through his paces like a show pony. He patted the thick neck. He was a lovely horse and would make a great hunter. He brought him to a stop in front of Arthur, dismounted with the same smooth action and handed him the reins. Nodding at Mick, he said unsmilingly, 'Take the bastard for a fiver next time!'

Arthur grinned widely for the first time since he realised his star attraction had been tamed and tipped the front of his wide-brimmed hat in salute, 'Breaker Morant, ya'll do me.'

'Ya knew him, didn't ya?' asked Mick, his faced crumpling in despair and his eyes darting back and forth accusingly from one to the other.

'Nah, mate, but I'd heard tell of him,' confessed Arthur. 'Not too many Pommy buckjumpers in these parts – least none that can keep their arses in the "pig-skin" for more than a minute,' he added with a chuckle.

That night, Arthur shouted the grog at the local pub with his winnings and Harry Morant showed he could drink as well as he could ride, while Mick sat in the corner watching them with an expression that would sour milk. He'd had quite enough of Harry Morant for one day.

By the time they were finally evicted by the landlord,

somewhere between midnight and 3 am, the legend of Dargin's Grey had passed into Australian bush folklore. From that day on, Harry Harbord Morant was known as the Breaker and Will Ogilvie, the young Scots poet with whom he later rode, immortalised it in a poem he wrote about his mate simply entitled Harry Morant:

> 'Breaker Morant' was the name he earned,
> For no bucking horse could throw
> This Englishman who had lived and learned
> As much as the bushmen know.

THE ONLY OTHER MAN WHO EVER tamed Dargin's Grey was Harry Rydell, better known as the notorious bushman Captain Starlight. He said that Morant was a man of great courage and strength who never betrayed a mate or broke a confidence and was 'capable of spitting in the eye of the devil'. Starlight's assessment of Morant would turn out to be uncannily accurate.

The Breaker cemented his reputation with a series of daredevil stunts and outrageous bets. The backblocks from Queensland to South Australia are littered with such legends – some of them verifiable. Tales are still told of the time he jumped a complete bullock train over the bar at Jericho, and the time he drove a mob of cattle hell for leather down the main street of Orange at 5 am, and how he cleared a six-foot fence illuminated only by a lantern on a blindfolded horse at Parkes.

It was said, 'Harry Morant's deeds of daring were the outcome of someone's saying he "wasn't game".' Another factor was his perpetual lack of funds. In the convivial atmosphere of a pub he would boast loudly that he could perform some seemingly impossible equestrian feat. He would invariably find a taker keen to cut a tall poppy down to size and the whole pub would adjourn outside to watch Morant lift his horse over the obstacle, then repeat it just to prove the point. The bloke who laid the wager would then learn that a 'round of drinks' meant one for everyone in the pub, which further endeared the Breaker to one and all.

His jump over a series of six-wire fences outside the Barwon Inn in Walgett on Christmas morning 1896 is perhaps his best known feat. According to the local *Upper Murray and Mitta Herald*, around sixty wandering bushmen had gathered at the pub to wet the head of the infant Jesus when, 'Suddenly from up out of the river bend rode Harry Morant, who was greeted by all and sundry with a, "Merry Christmas Harry!".'

He had no money, as usual, but had his mind set on a good Christmas drink, so he threw out a bold challenge. He claimed that he could jump his blindfolded horse over the two stout six-wire fences that skirted the road.

> The wager was made, whereupon his mount was securely blindfolded and, when Morant put his heels to the mount, the colt made some spectacular bounds, and just as it seemed as though he must crash into the wires, the rider lifted his hands and yelled 'Over'. The noble animal leapt as if propelled from a giant catapult, and landed feet beyond the danger zone. He was then sent pell mell across the road to the opposite fence and repeated the same tactics. 'The colt made a wonderful leap and cleared the fence', according to an old bushie, 'by a full twenty feet!'.

It is now a proud part of Walgett's local history and a plaque marks the spot where the jump took place.

On another occasion he was arrested by police in Windsor, who put him and his favourite horse, Cavalier, in a compound surrounded by high walls and a gate illuminated by a single light. When they returned from their rounds, they couldn't understand how horse and rider could have escaped.

Other yarns have a similar theme, with pubs, grog and a bet being the common denominators. In Clarendon he bet his horse, Cavalier, 'the one thing he really loved' that he could jump 'an old picket fence with a ragged, heart-scarring top . . . reported on sober word to be seven feet high', and in Parkes he bet he could clear a solid four-railed fence that stood five feet high. 'Needless to say, the Breaker didn't have to shout.'

But the greatest of all the Breaker yarns must be the time he tried to jump Govetts Leap in the Blue Mountains. During the mid- to late-1890s, Morant spent a few years around the Hawkesbury, Richmond and Windsor area just outside of Sydney. On one occasion he visited the Blue Mountains with a mate and went to inspect the yawning chasm, which is many hundreds of feet wide and deep. His mate was leaning over the wooden safety rail commenting that you'd have to be mad to want to leap that when he heard thundering hooves approaching from behind him. He whipped round in time to see Morant and his horse hurtling towards him. Open mouthed, he watched as the Breaker nudged his horse with his knees. The horse sailed over the safety rail, executed a perfect 180 degree turn in mid-air (an old hunting trick) and brought them up just short of the precipice.

As he revealed in his letters to Banjo Paterson, Morant was also an amateur jockey and a polo player of note, and also enjoyed 'pigsticking' and hunting.

> I have a dingo-skin here, the biggest I have ever seen, and all the local liars say the same of it, which same I will send down to you at the first opportunity. Do for a mat – heads, pads and all attached. Considering the 'strychnine and stiffening' character of the

country my dingo died a sporting death. The local talent had tried with poison since Christmas last to kill him, but I pulled him down with a couple of cattle-dogs in the moonlight about a week ago, after a couple or three miles gallop, finishing him with that good old weapon, the stirrup-iron. Killed him within a few hundred yards of a tank-sinker's camp, the pick and shovel men turning out of their bunks . . . I brought a Lancer's spear back with me from Sydney, and find it a first-class weapon for pigs, which are fairly numerous in the lignum of the Culgoa. With a handy horse pigsticking is not bad fun.

MOST PEOPLE HAVE TO WAIT FOR THEIR legend to be created by the hand of others, but under the pseudonyms of the Breaker, Harry Morant, HM, The B, B, and Apollo Beledere, he simply wrote his own. Starting with *A Night Thought* in September 1891, he wrote over sixty verses for *The Bulletin*, before his departure for South Africa in 1900, and became a popular bush poet. He also published verse, short stories and worked as a journalist in Hughenden, Walgett, Orange, Coonamble, Windsor, Richmond and Penrith, and had odd pieces published in assorted country newspapers such as *The Pastoralists Review*.

Although there were a number of Australian journals publishing the same mix of radical politics and verse, such as *The Truth*, *The Worker* and *Boomerang*, the Breaker stayed loyal to *The Bulletin* – a weekly paper with a national circulation.

A redoubtable Scot called JF Archibald founded it in 1880, the same year Ned Kelly was hanged. Archibald took on the rebel mantle, but where the bushrangers had raged against police corruption and the inequity of the land distribution system by turning to murder and

robbery, Archibald saw knowledge and organisation –
the ideals of Socialism – as the keys to effecting lasting
social change. *The Bulletin* became known as the
Bushman's Bible. Both radical and nationalistic, it was
the favourite publication in the bush. It was described
as being 'within the one set of covers an entertainer,
popular educator in the progress of radical thought, and
medium of exchanging bush folklore'.

Sam Nicker remembered Morant as being very well
read in the classics, military history and politics. During
the course of a long run, the few books they could carry
and journals like *The Bulletin* were read from cover to
cover many times before being swapped. Station sheds
were said to be better stocked than most Mechanics
Institutes and Schools of Arts, with the result that
people in the bush were not as ignorant as the 'squat-
tocracy' claimed. One English observer of the time said,
'the new bush worker was a reader and to some extent
a thinker'.

This much was evident from the rising political
consciousness in the bush. Morant and Nicker were
amongst the early members of the Shearers' Union.
Nicker family legend has it that the pugilism Morant
learnt at Barnet came in useful as their union member-
ship landed Harry and Sam in quite a few fist fights
around Blackall in south-eastern Queensland. Blackall
was in the heart of sheep country and a unionist strong-
hold during the Shearers' strike, which was to be a
defining moment for the Australian Labor movement.

Unions with their code of mateship and egalitarian
ideals were seen as the work of the devil by pastoralists
who needed to keep wages low to turn a good profit. A
fall in wool prices in 1885 saw a cut in the rate paid to
shearers, who then followed other industries and
formed a union to protect their interests, as the old
Masters and Servants Act was weighted heavily in

favour of the employer. The introduction of machine clippers allowed station owners to use less skilled labour and issue the *Pastoralists Agreement*, which set down new terms and conditions for employees. The unionists countered with the *Bushmen's Official Proclamation*, which urged unionists not to sign as they claimed it proposed to reduce wages for casual labour, made the pastoralists the sole arbiters of who got hired and fired, removed any right of appeal against sacking or wages deduction and proposed to make shearers pay for any damage to combs and cutters. It also predicted that 'The Queensland bush is to be a battle ground whereon it is to be decided whether Capitalism can crush Australian Unionism altogether into the dust'.

The Shearers' strike, which rumbled on from 1890 to 1894, brought violent clashes between union and imported non-union labour, or 'blacklegs', the burning of woolsheds, strikes and go-slows and acts of sedition. The deployment of troops, police and volunteers by the Queensland Government pushed Australia to the brink of serious civil unrest for only the second time in its history – both times over workers' rights. The shearers also flew the rebel flag of the Southern Cross, but unlike the 'diggers' at the Eureka Stockade,[†] there was no bloody showdown. History records that one of the many confrontations, which would determine that very issue, did take place at Terrick Terrick Station near Blackall on September 9, 1891.

TERRICK TERRICK STATION IS THIRTY-FIVE miles south-west of Blackall in Queensland as the crow flies. Right

---

† *Fourteen striking gold miners were killed when Victorian troops bombarded then stormed the Eureka stockade on December 3, 1854. The 'diggers' were protesting over the introduction of prospector's licences and police corruption.*

in the heart of sheep country, Terrick Terrick was one of the big stations rivalling Tinnenburra and Meteor Downs, owned by sheep baron James Tyson. Morant and his mate, Sam Nicker, had that morning driven in a flock of jumbucks for shearing by their good mate and champion bladesman, Jackie Howe, whose record of 321 merinos sheared in a single shift stood for sixty years after the introduction of electric clippers.

They were damping down the dust that had caught throats during the last thirsty leg of their long haul with some sweet black tea when they heard silver shillings rattling in Fred Bilby's battered felt hat as he wordlessly shook it under the noses of the drovers and shearers who had also gathered in the yard for their morning smoke-oh. Most dutifully thrust their hands deep into their pockets for small change, though Bilby's frosty glare ensured that it wasn't too small. It was for a good cause.

In a couple of weeks two fellow shearers, Harry Riley and William McKenzie, were up before the Judge. During the rioting in Clermont in May of that year they had tried to blow up a bridge to stop the police and troops getting in. 'Sedition' screamed the newspapers, pastoralists and Queensland Government in harmony. Judge Harding had been dispatched from Brisbane to nip the Shearers' strike in the bud and ensure that justice was done – in that order.

Though it was part of the bushman's code that you always helped a mate, this strike had split them and pitted mate against mate. It had been easier when it was the workers and the squatters – them against us – but the union had changed all that. Some held that the forming of a union would make sure they got a fair dinkum wage for their hard yakka. Others didn't like being told when, where and who they could work for by a union any more than a squatter. They liked things just as they were.

Mick McCarthy and Bill Martin were two such men.
They remained motionless when Bilby passed the hat
under their noses. Bilby was not a handsome man and
his short cropped black hair and thin moustache emphasised a prominent bone structure, which could only be
described as Neanderthal. Lifeless grey eyes were sunk
deep in their sockets and his dead, undertaker's stare
settled most arguments long before he raised his great,
shovel-like hands. His history as a bar room brawler
was written in scar tissue across his face like a map of
outback Australia; head cut by a shovel in Porooga, eye
busted open by a police truncheon in Muttaburra, cheek
slashed by a broken bottle in Kyuna and, appropriately,
his scarred, disjointed red nose broken by a Scotch head-
butt in McKinlay. He fixed McCarthy and Martin with
one of his trademark stares and jangled the coins again.
No movement. Bilby condescended to a rare exchange
of the Queen's English.

'Youse blokes blind as well as deaf?'

'Nah, we're just fussy who we give our coin to,' came
Martin's even reply.

Bilby rose to their bait. 'No decent bloke would
think twice about putting his hand in his pocket for a
mate,' he observed upping the ante.

Turning to McCarthy for support, Martin retorted,
'But no decent bloke would ask a mate to put his hand
in his pocket for a union man neither.'

'Too right,' chimed in McCarthy with the soft
brogue of southern Ireland. The blow was so quick and
so devastating that when McCarthy came to he thought
he was still in Tipperary and was astonished to find that
a single punch had landed him in Australia.

That first blow shattered the thin veneer of calm that
appeared to exist in the yard just moments before. The
cramped living conditions at Terrick Terrick kept men
who should have been kept apart in close proximity and

soon the fists and boots were swinging as rhythmically as the swarthy arm of the station's blacksmith. There was no need for words or accusations. The arguments had been rehearsed over and over again these past few years and the pent-up hatreds soon stained the dust red. The station-owner rushed across the yard shouting in alarm. Whilst the men were wasting their energies fighting, no sheep were being clipped and no profit being turned. As he arrived at the edge of a fracas he was sent sprawling in the dust by a vicious hook. Jumping to his feet, his face flushed with anger he yelled, 'Ah, fuck it!' and started swinging away with the rest of them.

The violence spread like a raging tropical fever and soon every man had been forced to take sides. Sam and Jackie, union men through and through, stepped up to the mark, but Sam put a restraining hand on Harry's arm as he went to follow.

'Leave it, mate. There's no need for you to get involved.'

Though kindly put the implication was clear. He was a Pom and the son of a gentleman. This wasn't his fight. Little did they know. He had learned everything he needed to know about the struggle of the working man from those grey shrouded ghosts of the workhouse that still visited him in his dreams. What of his mother – sapped of all joy and spirit and driven to drink by twenty years of soulless toil for the same wage she got when her husband was Master, whilst the workhouse trustees stood in the boardroom with their backs to the fire sipping sherry and congratulating themselves for discouraging the poor from seeking help. To kill the tedium of the long journey to Australia he had read the Bible his mother had given him from cover to cover and one of the psalms had stuck in his head: 'I was made in secret and curiously wrought in the lowest parts of the earth.'

Snapping back to the present, Morant gave one of

his wide smiles, his face betraying no hint of the dark secrets of his past that had just bubbled up to the surface.

'What, and miss out on a good scrap?' he exclaimed. Any further argument was cut short when an enraged Martin, bleeding from a head wound, rushed them like a wounded bull. Instinctively Harry raised his fists, transferred his weight from the soles to the balls of his feet and adopted the wide-legged stance of a boxer. With almost no backlift he caught the onrushing Martin a sharp left jab full in the mouth that rocked the giant back on his heels.

'Queensberry rules is it sir,' sneered the bloodied phizog in what Morant now recognised as a sonorous Somerset burr. Morant jinked sideways to avoid a wild windmill-like swing, as Martin continued with the verbal assault, 'Why you siding with these here union blokes? A gent like you should be on our side. Gone native 'ave we?' he taunted as he tried to cut off Harry's deft circular movements.

High on a mixture of pain and adrenalin Martin bellowed, 'Stand still and fight!' and threw his arm in another wide arc. Morant bent his knees sharply allowing the haymaker to sail over his head, then sprung back up and swung a stout riding boot into the groin of his off-balance adversary, which connected with a meaty thud. The blow expelled the air from his lungs with a whoosh and the roaring bull dropped first to his knees and then rolled onto his back in the dust like a supplicant puppy, clutching his ruptured manhood. Martin's face whitened and frothy spittle appeared on his lips as he silently entered that realm of pain even the bravest warrior feared. Winking broadly at Sam and Jackie's open-mouthed expressions, Morant rolled up his sleeves and furrowed his brow.

'I'm sure the Marquis would have approved in this

case . . . Now, what was it we're fighting for again?' As they waded in Sam shook his head in wonderment. A rhyming, horse breaking English gentleman running wild in the Australian bush who could charm the knickers off the hardest-hearted whore, drink the bloody Irish under the table and punch like a prize fighter. Was there no end to this man?

It took a troop of burly Blackall policemen to finally separate the warring parties. The station-owner blamed the unionists and the unionists blamed the station-owner, but the police carted off the unionists. Ironically, the jailed unionists who sparked the Terrick Terrick riot, McKenzie and Riley, were acquitted, whilst Fred Bilby was found guilty of riotous behaviour and fined £20 with £26 costs.

THE SHEARERS' STRIKE WAS EVENTUALLY crushed and fourteen strikers given three years' hard labour, but the political genie was out of the bottle. The Australian Labor Party emerged from the ashes of the Shearers' strike and it was Lane and Lawson's bushmen, not Marx's proletariat, who led Australian workers towards proper political representation. Just a decade later, in April 1904, Australia elected the world's first Labor Government.

It is not known whether Harry Morant was amongst the sixteen charged, but Sam Nicker is said to have 'bailed him out' on a number of occasions. Although Nicker did not specify whether he got him out of debt or out of prison, Morant did appear in Rockhampton Central court on July 3, 1889 on charges of obtaining money under false pretences and larceny. Morant was in Muttaburra in January that year when John Henry Grimshaw had agreed to purchase four horses from Morant for £20 on the proviso he would buy them back for the same sum. However, Morant reneged on the deal when he took back the four horses and sold one of them to another party. Found guilty on both counts he was sentenced to three months hard labour in Rockhampton gaol.

This episode again reveals the two contradictory sides of Harry Morant. He was known throughout the bush as the son of a British Admiral and a gentleman of good breeding, yet he joined the union movement, which stood against the very privilege and patronage he had enjoyed in England.

As WELL AS EDUCATING AND RAISING political consciousness, *The Bulletin* also launched the careers of the 'Holy Trinity' – Banjo Paterson, Henry Lawson and Will Ogilvie. It published Paterson's *El Mahdi to the Australian Troops* and Lawson's *Sons of the South*. Both were protests against the sending of a New South Wales expeditionary force to Sudan in 1885 to avenge the killing of General Gordon during the siege of Khartoum.

Politics apart, Henry Lawson said the importance of *The Bulletin* in creating a distinctive Australian literary style cannot be overestimated and would never have been invented without it. In the late 19th century, an Australian author's best prospect of being published was to go to London. Author and poet Norman Lindsay went even further and saw *The Bulletin* as an important catalyst in creating the national identity.

> Up to its appearance the Australian born were wandering in a limbo begotten by a nostalgia in the early settlers who called England 'home'. The 'Bulletin' initiated an amazing discovery that Australia was 'home' and that was the anvil on which Archibald hammered out the rough substance of the national ego.

Bush poetry was the first distinctively Australian literary genre and Morant became a small but celebrated part of it. By all accounts, he composed his verses in his head as he drove along a mob of cattle, shouting out rhymes and jingles to a droving mate as they came to him, wrote them down later and sent them in for publication with no revisions. However, through his Morant lineage he could claim quite a literary pedigree – Lord Alfred Tennyson was a distant relative and Oscar Wilde a cousin.

His verses were popular and well recited throughout the bush community, which was his intended audience. Round the campfire and during smoke-ohs, rhymes, jingles and yarns were the common currency.

Often self-effacing, sharply observed and populist, Morant's work tells us much about both his character and his life in the bush, which shaped him more than has been previously admitted. In the main, his verses were loosely autobiographical accounts of long days in the saddle droving cattle in the outback, his hellraising adventures with the 'Brigalow Brigade' and the loves he won and lost along the way. His 1893 composition *While Yet We May* set down in words his devil-may-care attitude to life:

> Years may bring a dole of sorrow,
> Give enough to fast and pray,
> From the present pleasures borrow,
> Let the distant future pay;
> Leave the penance for the morrow,
> Sweetheart, love and laugh today!

Morant's day-to-day life in the bush provided plenty of material for his fertile imagination. For long months beneath peerless blue skies he endured searing heat, persistent flies, lumpy swags and bad tucker as he drove cattle or sheep through the unforgiving harshness of the outback, through mulga to Mitchell and saltbush to Brigalow, zig-zagging from one water hole to the next, trying to second-guess the weather gods and avoid the droughts. Though it was never going to satisfy a man who had such pressing business back in England, this roving life at least spoke to his restless spirit, and out in the wild he occasionally found some solace.

> Camped out beneath the starlit skies –
>   the treetops overhead,
> A saddle for a pillow and a blanket for
>   a bed,
> 'Twas pleasant, mate, to listen to the
>   soughing of the breeze
> And learn the lilting lullabies that stirred
>   the mulga trees.

But any feeling of peace was shortlived and in his ballads there is a constant longing for the trip to be over and the agents to settle up so he could get into town and into trouble.

> Of afternoons at Randwick! of night haunts
>   painted red!
> Of garish deeds of drover men some six
>   months 'mulga fed'!
> O pale-faced sons of Sydney town, who
>   don't find Sydney gay,
> You should have been where we have been
>   these many months away!

A sizeable portion of Morant's work tapped into the rich vein of roistering that was always a close companion of his pay cheque. Amongst his most popular works were *Slewed!*, *Westward Ho!* and *The Brigalow Brigade* which tell of the hellraising antics of Morant and his fellow drovers – gnarly bush characters like Paddy Magee, Brumby Bill and Brigalow Mick who hit town with their cheques already burning a hole in their pockets. One early rejection note from *The Bulletin* complained that his recent submissions 'seem to be a dreary list of your old friends who broke their necks while drunk'.

Morant did write requiems for Paddy Magee and Brumby Bill later on, but whatever their initial reservations, *The Bulletin* published *The Brigalow Brigade,* which became a best-loved Morant piece. It was a backhanded tribute to those free-spirited souls who preferred the swag to a feather bed and the solace of the Birdsville track to the bustle of Sydney's George Street. Morant and the many others who wrote about the bush in the late 19th century placed it at the heart of the emergent national consciousness. The rapidly growing cities would have to wait for the 20th century.

There's a band of decent fellows
On a cattle-run outback –
You'll hear the timber smashing
If you follow in their track;
Their ways are rough and hearty,
And they call a spade a spade;
And a pretty rapid party
Are the Brigalow Brigade.

They are mostly short of 'sugar',
And their pockets, if turned out,
Would scarcely yield the needful
For a decent four-man 'shout'.
But they'll scramble through a tight place
Or a big fence unafraid,
And their hearts are in the right place
In the Brigalow Brigade.

They've painted Parkes vermilion
And they've coloured Orange blue,
And they've broken lots of top-rails
'Twixt the sea and Dandaloo;
They like their grog and palings

Just as stiff as they are made –
These are two little failings
Of the Brigalow Brigade.

The Brigalow Brigade are
Fastidious in their taste
In the matter of a maiden
And the inches of her waist;
She must be sweet and tender
And her eyes a decent shade –
Then her ma may safely send her
To the Brigalow Brigade.

But women, men and horses,
With polo inbetween,
Are mighty potent forces
In keeping purses lean;
But spurs are never rusty,
Though they seldom need their aid –
For the 'cuddies ain't to dusty'
In the Brigalow Brigade.

And as he recalled in *Stirrup Song*, all too soon his
money was spent, his mates all tapped out and the town
snowed under with his IOUs.

We've drunk our wine, we've kissed our
    girls, and funds are getting low,
The horses must be thinking it's a fair thing
    now to go.
Sling up the swags on 'Condamine', and
    strap the billies fast,
And stuff a bottle in the bag, and let's be
    off at last.

After roving and roistering, women and horses were the
other major themes running through his work.

Rumour had it that his behaviour to other human
beings resembled the methods he employed so successfully with horses: that he was a tormentor of
horse flesh – and a tormentor of the human heart,
especially the hearts of women.

Contrary to such 'rumour', Morant loved both horses
and women. His horses – Cavalier, Condamine, Harlequin and Bideford Boy – are all mentioned fondly in his
poems and letters. On one famous occasion he broke
his shoulder after falling off a horse he was trying to
jump over a five-foot fence outside Windsor courthouse.
On regaining consciousness, his first thought was said
to be for the welfare of the horse. In a poem called *A
Departing Dirge* he imagined his feelings if he was able
to leave Australia and return to England by boat. He
ends the poem with the lines:

> Here's the burden of my song:
> 'Good-bye, old girl! Old chap, so-long!'
> Hardest loss of all I find
> To leave the good old horse behind.
> So-long, 'Cavalier!'

Morant's marital track record indicates that he was very
much a ladies man. He had been engaged in England
before being forced to leave for Australia, married and
separated from Daisy O'Dwyer in Australia and finally
engaged to the Devon girl we only know as 'trim-set
petticoat' on his return to England in 1900.

As no doubt Nell, Margaret, Kitty and the other
women he featured in his poems would testify, women
found such a charismatic character with all his shades of
light and dark irresistible. As a footloose young man
passing through country towns, he left a number of

broken hearts in his wake, but anecdotal evidence suggests that where affairs of the heart were concerned, he was chivalrous and kind – more Morant than Murrant. In fact, his romantic verse marked him out from the other bush balladeers, who never wrote about women. Horses, cattle, countryside, mates or adventures involving all or some of the above were popular themes, but there weren't many women in the bush. Of the bush balladeers only Morant and Ogilvie, both immigrants, wrote about women. Some of his verse veered towards the sweetly sentimental or melancholic – like his 1894 ode to a love lost entitled *Much A Little While* that became one of his best-loved works. Although it runs contrary to his macho roistering image, some of his verse and his sustained efforts to reconcile with his family reveal Morant to be a man with some emotional depth.

> 'Love me little, love me long'
> Laggard lover penned such song
> Rather Nell! – in other style –
> Love me much, A little while.
>
> If that minstrel ever knew
> Maid so kissable as you –
> (Like you? – There was never such)
> He'd have written, 'Love me much.'
>
> Other loves have pass'd away
> Springtimes never last always!
> Twill be better – will it not
> To think that once we lov'd 'A lot.'

So delighted was editor AG Stephens with Morant's tender musings, that he commissioned a revised version for *The Bulletin*'s 1894 Christmas special. It was illustrated, as were many of his early works, by noted cartoonist Benjamain Edwin Minns, who also contributed to *The Sydney Mail* and the English satirical journal *Punch*. The Breaker had more illustrated Christmas verses than any other bush bard – a tradition that continued until 1906 – four years *after* his death. However, Morant's work never enjoyed the longevity or acclaim of his illustrious friends, and *The Bulletin* never published a volume of his collected works as they did for Paterson, Lawson and Ogilvie.

The critics have largely disparaged Morant's work. Biographer Frank Renar didn't think, in light of his war crimes, that he had the nature to be a poet and that his infamy had elevated his work to a level that it did not merit. But could the same not be said of many of the greats? Such people have been around for centuries and have always been disparaged as 'folk' or 'popular' by the pompous purveyors of high culture. Morant himself had no pretensions about his literary talent and said of his own work in *Station Songs and Droving Ditties*:

> Jingles! – neither good or clever –
> Just a rover's random rhymes,
> But they'll serve their turn if ever
> They recall the old bush times.

Morant's literary exploits further embellished the chivalric image his horsemanship and tales of derring-do had created for him. To Banjo Paterson, he was 'the perfect idea of a beau cavalier' and his legend was further emblazoned on the public consciousness by his friendship with Paterson and Ogilvie who, along with Lawson, were the poetic clan of the day.

To them, Morant was the real thing – a Renaissance man in the bush with bottle of grog in his saddlebag next to his volumes of Byron and Browning. His eclectic choice of reading matter was also testament to the two distinct sides of the Morant character. Browning appealed to the lyrical and sophisticated Morant, whilst Byron spoke to the darker Murrant side that craved action like the notorious bard and was also 'mad, bad and dangerous to know'. His later metamorphosis back into Murrant, during the South African war, would see him damned like the quixotic heroes in Byron's colourful classical tales.

The bush ballad reached its zenith during the last decade of the 19th century when the legends of *Clancy of the Overflow*, *Waltzing Matilda*, *The Man from Snowy River* – and Breaker Morant – were all created. Bush poetry was the first uniquely Australian literary movement and was in marked contrast to the metropolitan culture of the day which was little more than a pale colonial imitation of the motherland – part of that neverending search for legitimacy and acceptance. The monumentalist architecture of the Victorians and the latest Knightsbridge fashions all met in Australia by way of Oxford Street, Paddington and Kings Cross . . . Sydney.

The earlier claim that Morant might have been the model for *The Man From Snowy River* will be anathema to many. The story has become synonymous with good, clean, chivalrous values and Paterson has become Australia's poet Laureate. However, Paterson, like any artist, took inspiration from what he saw around him and there are many examples of the Breaker providing both him and Ogilvie with inspiration for some of their most famous verses.

NELUNGALOO STATION NEAR PARKES, New South Wales, is famous for being the place where police shot bushranger Ben Hall, and is where Will Ogilvie met Morant in 1896. Morant then left Nelungaloo and rented a paddock near Birthday Mine where he broke horses for the townsfolk. Morant, Ogilvie and a group of locals cleared some land near the Bogan Gate Hotel, which they re-named The Selector's Arms, and turned it into a polo field. Morant taught Ogilvie and other locals the finer points of the game, but the wielders of the sticks were as inexperienced as their mounts and it was, at best, what Morant described as 'polo in the crude'.

It was in this paddock that they staged the first un-official Australia v Great Britain polo international in December 1896, drawing a huge crowd from far and wide. Morant captained the British team and Mark Foy (of the Sydney department store family) was captain of the Aussies and put up a handsome purse for the winner. Ogilvie also played for the Great Britain team, repre-senting Caledonia. After a hard-fought contest, Britain triumphed 4–2.

Using his nom de plume, 'Glenrowan', Ogilvie penned an epic one and a half page verse entitled *The Glory of The Game* which was published in *The Richmond and Windsor Gazette* on February 6, 1897. One of the stanzas lionises Morant's extraordinary courage

> Then somehow in a scrimmage, a face and
>   stick got linked,
> And the timber broke in pieces, though the
>   Breaker never winked,
> The mallet went to hospital, whilst the
>   Breaker bathed in gore,
> Went sailing through the scrimmages more
>   fiercely than before.

The occasion also moved Paterson to verse. He wrote *The Geebung Polo Club* with its play on the name of the club, and also wrote *Jim Carew* about Morant. So, the Breaker could have been the model for Australia's greatest horseman.

It has been argued that Morant was nowhere near Victoria during 1894, when Paterson wrote the story, but neither was Paterson! Since when did a writer only draw inspiration from what he had to hand at the moment of creation? The creative writing process is a fusion of experiences past, present and imagined – geography is irrelevant. If Richard Magofin is right, then *Waltzing Matilda* is a powerful political allegory which was inspired by Samuel 'Frenchy' Hoffmeister, an Austrian anarchist who committed suicide during the 1894 Queensland Shearers' strike. Paterson was in Queensland during the strike, heard the story but never met 'Frenchy'.

But the Breaker knew Paterson well; they shared a few adventures together and corresponded until the Boer War sent them their separate ways. Morant certainly had the equestrian credentials and his verses *The Nights at Rocky Bar*, *On the Warrego* and *After Horses – A Reminiscence of the Queensland Warrego* all describe how he trapped mobs of brumbies. Morant himself makes reference to *The Man From Snowy River* in a letter to Paterson written between August and December 1895, shortly after *The Man from Snowy River and Other Verses* was pulished:

> Apropos of 'The Man from Snowy River', there is a small sultry border township, _____ to wit, where, just a year ago, a horse owned by an alleged steward ran a bad second to a shearer's moke, and was declared the winner by the biased judge.
>
> I have done a bit of brumby running in mountain country although most of my cleanskin experience has been in mulga or Brigalow, and I have noticed that a good man on a plucky horse can always beat brumbies, when going down a declivity. A horse with a rider on his back goes with confidence, whilst brumbies are never all out then. When going uphill the naked horse gets away. Weight tells then, I suppose, though, of course, there

is the chance of a smash going down. I must now saddle up for my ride home.

With best wishes, –
Yours truly

H.H. MORANT.

Morant clearly identified with Paterson's book and relates his own experiences to the climatic downhill scramble. Did Paterson, as he did with *The Geebung Polo Club* and *Jim Carew*, draw inspiration from Morant's yarns about his brumby running which clearly happened before Paterson wrote his book?

At the other end of the literary scale, Morant may also have been the inspiration for 'Foreskin Fred', the hero of Lawson's infamous *The Bastard of The Bush*.[†] When the Captain asks him if he'd uphold the shabby values of the Push:

> Would you have a moll to keep you; would
>   you swear off work for good?
> Said the Bastard: 'My colonial silver-
>   mouthed oath I would.'

If the manner of Morant's death gave his verse an eminence it did not deserve, it also coloured his eventful life and made the minor indiscretions he committed in the Australian bush seem mere preludes to murder. The bracketing of Morant with bushrangers only began once the circumstances of his death became known. Australian historian Manning Clark likened him to his hero Ned Kelly because both were believers in 'the fearless, the free and the bold', but bemoaned the fact that the legend of the Breaker has taken hold during the past century because it:

---

† *The poem has been credited to Lawson although there is no substantial proof that he was the author.*

> [P]ortrayed Morant as a hero in the Australian bush, where hard drinking was no sin, roving recklessness was held in high esteem and the love of the horse more commendable than the love of Christ . . . Once again Australia and its savage past caused its victims to celebrate as a folk hero a liar, a thief and a drunken lout, a scoundrel, a believer in the rule of fist and a murderer of innocent people.

However, whilst Morant fits into the same anti-authoritarian mould as Kelly et al. and some of his infamy was richly deserved, it is a lazy comparison. A roisterous larrikin he may have been, a leaver of debts, a breaker of hearts and a few teeth even, but he was not a bushranger. Had he not died in such controversial circumstances, he would have remained just that. His crimes were decidedly petty and he robbed no banks and shot no troopers. The killings he ordered were in the theatre of war and in controversial circumstances far removed from the hum-drum of the Australian bush. To link his larrikinism to the killings that took place in South Africa is to ignore the effect of the traumatic events that caused Morant to behave quite out of character. Nonetheless, the bushranger tag has stuck and has resulted in him being connected, erroneously, to various unsolved crimes.

For example, his change of identity from Murrant to Morant has raised the suspicion that Harry Morant was also Thomas Day – a man suspected of four brutal murders in southern Queensland committed during November and December 1898. John Meredith makes this claim in his 1996 book *The Breaker's Mate – Will Ogilvie in Australia*.

Between 1895 and 1898 Morant had been working as a journalist for *The Richmond and Windsor Gazette* and *The Nepean Times* in Penrith. In November 1898, the Breaker disappeared suddenly from Windsor. Money worries, women trouble or itchy feet? Whichever it was, he made his exit in classic Morant style according to the locals who watched him go. He was making his way up the main street when the Salvation Army band playing in the middle of the road spooked the young polo pony he was leading. When Morant's polite requests to let him by were ignored, he rode at them full tilt. *Abide With Me* ended in an unholy row as startled Salvos abandoned their instruments and dived for cover and watched Morant gallop away across the fields towards the mountains.

At about the same time, a swagman called Thomas Day appeared in Gatton, South Queensland. He told locals that he had come from Sydney to Brisbane by boat, arriving on December 6 and had taken ten days to reach Gatton with his swag.

Four days after that swaggie left Brisbane, a fifteen-year-old youth called Alfred Hill was murdered just outside Oxley, which is half-way between Brisbane and Gatton. Both he and his pony were shot through the head with a .38 bullet. It was suspected by police that the boy was killed to conceal 'an unnatural act'. The police arrested a local suspect.

Day found a job as a slaughterhand in Gatton and three more murders took place on Boxing Day evening. Michael Murphy and his sisters Norah and Ellen rode six miles into town to attend a dance. The function was cancelled but they never returned home. A search party found their blood-spattered bodies in a paddock the next morning. Michael and his horse had both been shot in the head with a .38 bullet and his two sisters had been raped and then clubbed to death. The modus operandi was the same as the Oxley murder – a sexual assault, a bullet in the head and a spent cartridge left at the scene. The perpetrator was both a sexual deviant and a cold-

blooded serial killer. The police again arrested a local
suspect, recently released from prison for attempted rape.
A later inquiry concluded that Thomas Day was responsible, but the police investigation failed to follow up leads
on a number of suspects at the time.

Day collected his wages and left shortly after the
murders but, unusually for a suspected serial killer, he
remembered to pay a quarter's subscription to the
library. Despite his disagreeable character, Thomas Day
had an incongruous love of literature! He borrowed
Rienzi – a racy 14th century romance by Lord Bulwer
Lytton – from the local library. This tenuous literary
connection seems to be one of the prime pieces of evidence that Day was, in fact, the Breaker.

The details of Day's physical appearance were also
somewhat hazy. Fellow worker Bob King said he was
'about 30 and weighing 13–14 stones and skilled in handling carcasses', but local policeman Sergeant Arrel had
him at 'about 5 ft 9 in' and thought he was 'in his early
20s'. Either of these descriptions could have fitted any one
of a thousand swaggies or itinerant workers passing
through the Australian bush at that time.

But whether Day was guilty and fled, or just felt that
a stranger in a small town was the most likely to be made
a scapegoat for unsolved murders, we will probably never
know because the trail ran dry shortly afterwards.

Thomas Day disappeared and Morant reappeared
again on Paringa Station in South Australia and began
working for the Cutlack family who were tenants on the
land. Where had he been? Merely making his way from
Sydney to South Australia, or murdering innocents in a
shadowy guise?

Regardless of the painfully thin evidence, Meredith
supports his claim by saying Morant had both a revolver
and a 'sadistic streak'. He cites a letter to Banjo Paterson describing the slaughter of a heifer:

Last week my mate and I went beef-hunting. We were riding colts and had but four revolver cartridges. Four bullets failed to drop the cleanskin heifer we selected, and I got alongside the heifer to knife her. She turned and charged in her tracks, and the colt not being up to the game, his bowels came out instead of the heifer's, whilst I was hurled headlong. The colt went off (died that night, poor brute!), and I just managed to put a tree between me and the heifer as she charged. After one or two narrow squeaks – though no beast can catch a man if there is a tree handy – I managed to hamstring her, and the cuddy's misfortune was avenged.

Morant's reference to the 'poor brute' seems to have gone unnoticed, and 'beef-hunting', 'pigsticking' and hunting were all established blood sports during the Victorian era. The .38 revolver used in the murders was the most common pistol in circulation at the time and widely used by bushmen. However, the implication is clear. Morant was capable of changing identities, had a revolver, a 'sadistic streak' and a literary bent, and was later executed for murder, therefore he fits the profile of Thomas Day. However, with the cutting, pasting and juxtaposition of circumstantial evidence, you could produce Morant, Thomas Day or any number of other unsavoury characters.

Incidentally, after Morant left the Richmond and Windsor area he went to Melbourne to enjoy the company of his old mate Victor Foy. The local papers reported how he caused a sensation at The Prince's Theatre by settling a fight between two strangers in the dress circle. Having heard both arguments he stood up and knocked down the man he disagreed with.

Paterson used this 'give a dog a bad name' theme in his 1939 article *An Execution and a Royal Pardon – Dramas of Yesterday*. In it, he drew a parallel between the Breaker, Alfred Dreyfus and Edmund Galley, whom he knew as a boy. The French convicted Dreyfus of treason because he was a Jew, Galley was suspected of murder because his mate died in unknown circumstances and he had a previous conviction for murder. After proper examination in each case, it was found that Dreyfus was not a traitor and Galley was not a murderer. Having been sent all Major Thomas' legal papers, Paterson said, 'I happen to know all that was to be known about Morant's trial and execution', and believed that if the Morant case were properly re-examined, it would be found that it was deeply flawed.

The bard of the bush, Banjo Paterson, was the one who knew the best and worst of Morant. He paints quite a different picture of the errant Morant, though his two public statements about the Breaker are nearly always taken out of context. As a close friend, he knew all of Morant's faults, but as a bush balladeer and war correspondent, he also knew that Morant was not the only larrikin in the Brigalow and not the only soldier to kill in anger.

Morant and Paterson first met in 1893 or early 1894. Paterson's uncle, Arthur Harton, a tough Queensland grazier and Morant's employer at the time, introduced them. Assuring Morant that his nephew would be able to show him around on what must have been his maiden voyage to Sydney, he wrote to Banjo about his visitor:

There is a man going from here to Sydney and he says he's going to call on you. His name is Morant. He says he is the son of an English Admiral and he has good manners and education. He can do anything better than most people; can break in horses, trap dingoes, yard scrub cattle, dance, run, fight, drink and borrow money, anything except work. I don't know what is the matter with the chap. He seems to be brimming over with flashness. He will do any dare devil thing as long as there is a crowd to watch him. He jumped a horse over a stiff three-rail fence one dark night by the light of two matches which he placed on the posts.

By the time it came for him to write the Breaker's valedictory piece, Paterson more or less echoed his uncle's sentiments.

Both being lovers of horses and hunting, they hit it off immediately in Sydney, even after Banjo declined to cash one of Morant's infamous 'rubber' cheques. Paterson's first impression of Morant proved to be a lasting one:

He talked like a man without a care in the world. I found myself comparing him with the picturesque heroes of the past who fought for their own hand. Nowadays we would call him a case for a psychologist. Yet he was no Micawber – he didn't wait for something to turn up, he tried to turn it up for himself.

Banjo, a successful flat and steeplechase rider and part of the New South Wales Hunt Club championship-winning team, took Morant hunting with his club. Morant's superb horsemanship and English social connections soon made him the darling of the Sydney hunting set. He was as much at home with gentlemen in the Hunt Club bar as he was with the rough diamonds he met in the outback. Further proof of the social polish he gained during his formative years in England was his courtship of the noted horsewoman Dorothy Brand, daughter of Henry Robert, 2nd Viscount Hampden, 24th Baron Dacre and former Governor of New South Wales. Morant dedicated two verses to her (*An Enthusiastic Sportsman Enthuses* and *To Dorothy – The Dolorous*), but she returned to England with her family in 1899 and married someone else the year he was executed.

However, Paterson did not detect in Morant the air of a man trying to preserve a facade:

> [H]e never affected the 'swell' in his manner, and he never tried to dress himself up to act the part of the well-connected 'adventurer'. Such as he was, he was the same to all men.

That observation is best illustrated by Paterson's yarn about the time Morant was invited to stay with Sydney's 'best people'. He turned up on a pony with his luggage balanced on the saddle in front of him. 'This was a great act and went over big', recalled Paterson. He then borrowed some clothes from the son of the house, who was about his size.

Some time later, the same family were having a charity gymkhana and wanted someone who could 'provide buckjumping as well as Mr Morant'. The Breaker extracted £10 from the organising committee to cover transport expenses for a celebrated grey horse that he intended to bring from Dubbo. Unfortunately, the owner refused to part with it and with time passing he was forced to secure another grey horse. The replacement knew 'no more about buckjumping than it did about Einstein's theory' and the show was a disaster. The committee decided to hold onto the horse until the £10 was repaid, which suited Morant fine. In due course, the owner turned up from Dubbo and threatened to bash the chairman unless he got his horse back. Paterson continues:

> After this our hero's reception at this temporary home was anything but enthusiastic, but with his queer flair for theatricalism, he managed to make an exit with a certain amount of glory.

Announcing that he had to return to Queensland on urgent business, he made a gift of a horse to the son of the house who had kindly lent him his clothes:

> He did the handover with a sort of Arab's farewell to his steed – a touching scene which lingered in the memories until the owner turned up and reclaimed it – saying he'd only given Morant a couple of quid to quieten it for a little girl.

Despite such distractions, the disenchantment he felt with his lot spilled over from his verse into his letters to Paterson:

> Had an English letter the other day from an old schoolfellow who is presently yachting in The Hebrides to put in time ere stag-hunting commences in Devon. Stag-hunting starts this week there. How I hate this _____ Brigalow desert sometimes! Thirty years next Christmas, but feel fifty! Would like one whole open season, well carried in Leicestershire, and wouldn't growl at a broken neck at the finish. A better lot than dreary years in the bush with periodical drunks!

When Morant fell asleep under the Southern Cross, he dreamed not of the bush but of the green fields of England, and of returning home to reclaim his place in his family's affection and to hunt and ride with the hounds again. During his sixteen years of wandering in the outback, getting older and shabbier with each passing year, it was a dream he never let go of. And when it was finally dashed from his hands in South Africa, his resultant rage brought about his final downfall.

Christmas and his thirtieth birthday both came and went, and a letter to Paterson saw him more restless than ever. Morant, unlike most of his mates in the bush, had experienced the big wide world. He had a good education, a sense of history, an appreciation of the arts and high culture, and knew he was wasting his potential:

> In the course of a month or six weeks, I intend departing from these regions to try Coolgardie. If I don't find it prosperous over there, next Christmas will find a prodigal turning up in England with a request for prime veal.

Morant didn't try his luck in Western Australia, but did try and work his passage back from Sydney to England on the *SS Ornsay*. He was unable to get a berth and the minimum fare of £25 was beyond his slender means. Perhaps he was also finding the risks on which he had built his reputation harder to face:

> They have an outlawed mare, the Witch, over at Bundaleer station. The boss there gave a fellow a note to ride her twelve months ago. She slung him, and had been spelling since. She was in the yards the other day and I had a go at her. I have not, as a rule, much respect for sheep-station outlaws, but this one was pretty bad. Up on her hind legs, then backward bucks, and occasionally one or other stirrup banged on the ground.
>
> The worst part of her was that one couldn't pull an ounce on her mouth. If you did, the brute would come back with you. I rode her for about an hour, and she was just as bad at the finish as when I got on her, though she would stop when she got the double of a whip round her. I'm not keen on riding her again, anyhow.

His reputation now depended not just on a strong heart, but a strong liver as 'he was close to perilous forty; and felt it. He was losing his nerve, and needed a peg or two to screw him up for a stiff mount.'

Paterson's cautionary tale *Jim Carew* was written during the period Morant was sending him those letters of woe from the bush. Paterson saw how the tragedy of his past and his toil in the bush was dragging him down, but he also warns his friend where Jim Carew will end up if he keeps going down the same path:

> Gentlemen Jim on the cattle-camp,
> Sitting his horse with an easy grace;
> But the reckless living has left its stamp
> In the deep drawn lines of that handsome
>   face,
> And the harder look in those eyes of blue:
> Prompt at a quarrel is Jim Carew.
>
> Billy the Lasher was out for gore –
> Twelve-stone navvy with a chest of hair –
> When he opened out with a hungry roar
> On a ten-stone man, it was hardly fair;
> But his wife was wise if his face she knew
> By the time you were done with him,
>   Jim Carew.
>
> Gentlemen Jim in the stockmen's hut
> Works with them, toils with them, side
>   by side;
> As to his past – well, his lips are shut.
> 'Gentleman once,' say his mates with pride,
> And the wildest Cornstalk can ne'er outdo
> In feats of recklessness Jim Carew.
>
> What should he live for? A dull despair!
> Drink is his master and drags him down,
> Water of Lethe that drowns all care,
> Gentleman Jim has a lot to drown,

And he reigns as king with a drunken crew,
Sinking to misery, Jim Carew.

Such is the end of the ne'er-do-well –
Jimmy the Boozer, all down at heel;
But he straightens up when he's asked to tell
His name and race, and a flash of steel
Still lightens up in those eyes of blue –
'I am, or – no, I was – Jim Carew'.

But with characteristic disregard for his own wellbeing, Morant gleefully adopted the name Carew and used it, as one of his many pseudonyms, in the short story *Billy Murdoch's Good-bye*. Despite all his failings, Paterson saw Morant not as a bushman but a fully-fledged member of the fourth estate and, as such, did not condemn him for his scapegrace ways. He described him as living the 'curious nomadic life of the Ishmaelite . . . money he never valued at its true worth; he was a spendthrift and an idler, quick to borrow and slow to pay – as many literary and other Bohemians have been from time immemorial.'

But Paterson fretted about his trips into town to 'see life' that, 'involved borrowings and difficulties that would have driven differently constituted men out of their minds . . . But Morant managed to keep his place amongst friends – and they were many – but how he managed it was always a problem.' Paterson could equally have been describing Morant's hero, Byron, or his own great rival, the 'people's poet', Henry Lawson, a habitual drunk and a shameless borrower who charged his admirers a toll for a yarn or a poem.

Despite the initial press reaction, in which it was felt he got his just desserts, the general consensus amongst his friends was that it was hard to reconcile the Breaker they knew with the executed war criminal they had read about. To them, he was a menace to nobody

but himself and his worst fault was his proclivity for not
paying debts and his tendency to borrow right left and
centre from his friends and never repay them. As Paterson said, 'drink is his master', and it released his
doppelgänger – the reckless, foul-mouthed Edwin
Murrant, who was a bit too ready with his fists. Mind
you, that description would have fitted half the transients
in the bush during the last decade of the 19th century.
But his wild ways and inability to hold his drink did not
make him the devil incarnate – the slow and insidious
poison of rumour and innuendo did that.

LOCAL LEGEND HAS IT THAT A WASTREL known as Harry
'the Breaker' Morant worked briefly at a cattle station
called Barney Downs, a few miles from Tenterfield,
where the infamous bushranger Captain Thunderbolt
was once a stockman.

This small country town is known as the birthplace
of modern Australia because on October 24, 1889,
Henry Parkes made a famous speech in the local School
of Arts which called for the federation of the Australian
states into a nation.

The issue that prompted this call was national
defence. Australia's armed forces had recently been
thoroughly reviewed by Major-General Sir James Bevan
Edwards, whose report called for the federation of all
Australian forces into one army of thirty to forty thousand men. Although he did not say it directly, it was also
implied that these forces could be deployed overseas in
the defence of the Empire under Imperial command. The
nationalistic *Bulletin* produced a cartoon likening
the British Army to a vulture and Australia to a lamb,
but even the normally conservative Australian press
could read between the lines and recognised that such
a notion involved certain 'policy difficulties'.

Parkes bitterly opposed the New South Wales contingent being sent to Sudan in 1885 on the orders of the acting Governor, William Bede Dalley, without gaining either the consent of the state parliament or the troops who had only volunteered to defend their state. His comment, 'This is not patriotism, this is not loyalty . . . this is the cry of wolf when there is no wolf', warned of the danger of setting such a precedent. He used his Tenterfield speech to argue that it was time Australia federated and took responsibility for matters of such import.

This issue arose because, although surrounded by sea, Australia could now no more remain in 'splendid isolation' than could Britain. The opening of the Suez Canal, and the coming of steam and telegraph communications had made armies and navies more mobile and the world smaller. Britain was faced with the perennial problem of how to defend its huge Empire in the face of growing Russian, German and French Imperial ambitions.

Britain's foreign policy had also been undergoing progressive change, mirroring the more liberal, laissez-faire thinking that characterised the latter half of the 19th century. The aggressive conquer and colonise or 'forward' policy of old had been replaced by a more sophisticated kind of imperialism. It advocated a more liberal attitude towards the self-government of its white colonies, whilst simultaneously developing its black colonies. These modern imperialists were men like Chamberlain and Milner who saw the colonies as part of a 'Greater Britain' – a supreme world state with its defence and trade controlled by a single grand Imperial parliament, which would consolidate the power of the Empire and the English race. The alternative was to try to hold on to her empire and watch her colonies drift away like America.

The Colonial Defence Council, set up in 1878,

thought that the rapidly growing colonies should contribute to their own defence and, by extension, the Empire that protected them. 'The defence of Australia begins in India' was how one Imperial officer put it. However, the Council recognised that Australia traditionally regarded her military units as for internal defence only and there was a strong nationalistic streak that would resist any Imperial interference. And so Britain began a covert campaign to persuade Australia to adopt its strategy.

Country solicitor John Francis Thomas, who helped organise Parkes' visit, was in the audience the night Parkes gave his Tenterfield speech. Even in his wildest dreams, Thomas could never have imagined that he would defend the case that would bring the issues that Parkes raised that night to the forefront of the national consciousness.

In 1890, Thomas moved to Tenterfield from the tough tin-mining town of Emmaville where he had unsuccessfully tried to establish a Solicitor's practice. During the next decade, Thomas became a cornerstone of this small rural community as he established a thriving solicitor's practice and rose quickly through the ranks to become Captain of the local defence unit, the Tenterfield Rifles. Thomas was a first-class shot and was regarded by his superiors as non-excitable, principled and a good leader. An extract from his record in 1894 says:

A very high standard of efficiency has been reached by the Tenterfield Half Company and the excellent Military spirit which exists and with extra work predicts that they will, '. . . achieve a standard of efficiency which should be second to none in the colony'.

If proof was needed, Thomas led the Tenterfield Rifles to two Hutton Shield victories.† The annual competition was named after Major-General Hutton, who conceived the idea after taking charge of the New South Wales forces in 1893 following a critical defence review. During his three-year tenure, Hutton not only reorganised the New South Wales forces but tried to advance Britain's secret agenda by recommending the federation of the six colonial forces into one united Australian Army. However, the Byzantine rivalries between the colonies made this an impossible task, at least until political union was achieved.

In 1898, Thomas became proprietor of the local newspaper, *The Tenterfield Star*, which he used to support Parkes's Federation campaign and highlight rural issues such as the population drift from the country to urban centres.

Given the close proximity of Barney Downs to Tenterfield and the Breaker's celebrated fondness for grog and 'trim-set petticoat', the chances are that he visited the town. Morant and Thomas may have passed in the street and even said 'G'day'. Neither could have known that their destinies would collide again halfway round the world but, given the dramatic circumstances of their next meeting, there would have been little time for deja vu.

South Africa was still a long way off for Morant – he still had half a decade of hellraising in the bush ahead of him – but perhaps some hidden hand of fate was at work. Such freakish historical coincidences or portentous events can only be seen with the benefit of hindsight and prove nothing in themselves, but they give an epic quality to the most humble of lives.

† *There is some debate as to whether the Tenterfield Rifles won the Hutton Shield outright in 1895. There is documentary evidence to suggest that they attended the presentation, indicating that they at least shared it. They did win it outright in 1893.*

4

The Call to Arms

He went to fight in a foreign land
and I know that he only went
To fight with the cares that were creeping
close and stealing his heart's content . . .

'To The Memory of One Dead' by Will Ogilvie

THE FINAL LEG OF HARRY MORANT'S Australian odyssey
began in late 1898 when he slipped down into Victoria
and spent some time in Melbourne with his friend Victor
Foy. As always, once his funds were exhausted and his
mates tapped out, he returned to the cattle runs looking
for work. Following the mighty Murray River, which
forms a natural, meandering border between New South
Wales and Victoria, 'the Breaker' crossed into South Australia in early 1898. He turned up looking for work at
the Paringa Station just outside Renmark, where the
Cutlack family were tenant farmers. They bought young
cattle at market, fattened them up and then sold them
on for beef.

Morant was employed as a stockman and charged
with mustering the cattle during that year's unusually
dry season and driving them out of the rough outback

down to the river frontage or out to the waterholes. The Cutlacks' young son, Frederick, who accompanied the men and drove the spring-cart with the supplies, recalled how Morant passed the long journeys reciting rhymes and jingles.

Morant soon became firm friends with his employer and told him about his origins and efforts to reconcile with his family. Frederick Cutlack remembered:

> My father wrote letters for Morant and did a lot to persuade a Colonel Morant, a Renmark settler, to recognise the Breaker and his golden opportunity to restore himself in the eyes of his family in England. The Breaker was deeply appreciative and confided in my father about those English connections and showed him letters from his sisters. There was no doubt in my father's mind about the identity of Morant's people; but proof of the evidence he had was never kept, for the matter was never under challenge.

Charles May Allen Morant was the son of a reverend in the British Army and was born in 1874 in Bangalore, India. He followed his father's footsteps into the army and rose to the rank of Lieutenant-Colonel in the Madras Cavalry. On retiring in 1891, he emigrated to Australia and bought a fruit farm in Renmark, which he named after his birthplace.

Beryl Morant, now ninety years old, still lives on 'Bangalore' – one of the few remaining examples of a pioneer station in the Riverland area of South Australia. She recalls being told that Harry was a frequent visitor and became good friends with both the Lieutenant-Colonel and his two sons, Arthur and Charlie. Beryl's father, Arthur, used to refer to Morant as 'that charming devil'.

According to Beryl, the Lieutenant-Colonel was also

convinced he was a Morant. On hearing the Breaker's family saga, he wrote to Digby's sons in England. They wrote back and gave exactly the same reply: 'No comment'. It was by no means an admission but, perhaps more significantly, it was not a denial either. If Morant was a charlatan, why would he press his claim with the very people who might expose him? If the Brockenhurst Morants knew he was a liar, why did they not warn the Lieutenant-Colonel? After Harry's execution, Arthur's older brother, Charlie, also wrote to England asking the Morants to recognise Harry as family. His request was also refused. Charlie's companion in later life, Hilda Truman, recalled:

> Charlie seemed to have an inexpressible fellow feeling for the Breaker who evidently was not looked on favourably by the family and relatives, but Charles always referred to him as a very brave man – but then he came from very brave stock.

Following the Breaker's death, an old mate from his Hawkesbury days wrote to *The Richmond and Windsor Gazette*. Identified only as 'The Breaker's Mate', he was responding to the newspaper reports of Admiral Morant denying that the Breaker was his son. Recalling conversations he had with Morant, he said:

> [F]amily matters were touched upon, and left no doubt in my mind as to his identity . . . I was with Morant when he interviewed a lawyer, and prevailed upon him to write to the irreconcilable Admiral and intercede for him. Will Ogilvie, at present in England, and others, could bear out the writer's statement if he cared to.

He also claimed to have seen letters from Morant's mother, Catherine, and sister, Annie, written from

Marseilles and Naples. Whilst it solves the mystery of Catherine's whereabouts after she left Bridgwater, how could a jobless widow afford the luxury of foreign travel? The most likely explanation is that her daughter Annie found employment as a musical tutor or a governess on the continent. In the 1881 census, Annie had given her profession as 'Professor of Music'. According to the Royal College of Music, there is no record of her studying there or at any other institution. However, the title of 'Professor' did not necessarily mean that she had attained a formal qualification in music. Many people set themselves up as self-styled professors of music to cater for the burgeoning interest in the arts. The late Victorian era was the high water mark of the performing arts before the technological age of cinema, radio and television slowly killed live entertainment.

But Morant would soon push aside the thorny issue of family as events on the other side of the world took a turn for the worse.

THE CAUSES OF WARS ARE COMPLEX and multifarious, but the greed for land, resources and the power that comes with them are prime factors in most. These were the root causes of the fractious relationship that existed between the British and the Boers ever since they both set foot on the Cape. The Dutch East India Company arrived first in 1652 and established a supply station for its trading ships. A few Dutch farmers settled there before the British decided the Cape was of vital strategic importance to its Far Eastern Empire and annexed it in 1806.

The Great Trek of 1835–1837 saw five thousand Boers leave the Cape to escape the rigidity of British laws and institutions that had governed them since annexation.

The Boers particularly objected to Britain's abolition of slavery, which they relied on for cheap labour. One half trekked east to Natal, the other half north to the Orange Free State and Transvaal.

The Boers trekked north into the Orange Free State and Transvaal before a splinter group broke off and headed down to Natal. When the British then annexed Natal in 1843, the Boers were forced to return north to join their brethren. Though Britain had formally recognised the two Boer republics, The Orange Free State in 1852 and the South African Republic (Transvaal), she then annexed both over the next decade – in an effort to create a federation – though on this occasion bankruptcy forced the Boers to ask for Britain's help. In 1881, Paul Kruger led a rebellion against British rule known as the First Anglo–Boer War, in which the Empire suffered a rare bloodied nose at Majuba Hill. Britain restored the Boer republics, though they retained suzerainty over foreign policy. But that defeat stung the military. They would avenge it, as they had avenged Gordon in Sudan, when the time was right.

Almost predictably, peace was shortlived. When President Kruger and General Joubert were told in 1886 that gold had been discovered in the Transvaal, Joubert smiled, but Kruger admonished him, saying that it was the worst news he had ever heard. He warned, 'every ounce of gold taken from the bowels of our soil will yet have to be weighed up with rivers of tears, with the life-blood of thousands of our best people in the defence of that same soil from the lust of others yearning for it solely because it has the yellow metal in abundance'.

Kruger also said that he only feared four men – God, the Devil, General De La Rey and 'that damned Englishman Rhodes'. Rhodes' comment 'I would annex the planets if I could' sums up the restless and relentless energy and philosophy of the man who intended to claim the entire continent of Africa for the Empire. However transparent his underlying intention, public opinion and the niceties of international relations demanded a reasonable pretext at least.

The pretext for Britain's intervention in the Orange Free State and Transvaal was voting rights for the foreign gold workers, or *Uitlanders* as the Boers called them, who had arrived by the shipload to seek their fortune in the Transvaal goldfields. Within a short space of time they formed the majority of the previously sparsely populated Transvaal and the British Government demanded that they be given voting rights. Kruger refused, seeing it as a thinly veiled attempt at annexation through the back door and imposed tough criteria. There was a genuine need for political reform but, as so often happens, the slow process of mediation is held ransom by expediency.

The 1895 'Jameson Raid', was a coup d'état cooked up by Rhodes and Milner and covertly supported by Chamberlain and the so-called 'gold-bugs' – the two largest gold companies, Wernher-Beit and Rhodes' Chartered Company. Sir Leander Starr Jameson read out a manufactured letter from the *Uitlanders*, begging for help, but the raid failed because there was no real popular support for it. The *Uitlanders* made peace with Kruger and not one rode out to meet Jameson's raiding party as planned. Also, as 'Banjo' Paterson discovered during his brief time in South Africa as a war correspondent, few British settlers were prepared to give up their British citizenship to vote in Transvaal. Nonetheless, voting rights was the issue the British used to try and draw its colonies into the conflict as Britain and the Afrikaaners began trading military threats and ultimatums.

Even though the Jameson Raid failed, it irreparably damaged the political process and patience was wearing thin on both sides by the time they met at Bloemfontein in June 1899. The British representative, Lord Milner, demanded self-government for Transvaal at a time when the British were not prepared to even consider home rule for Ireland. President Kruger of the Transvaal told Milner bluntly: 'It's our country you want.'

After Bloemfontein, Kruger did not trust the British or believe that the issue could be resolved by negotiation, so he put his trust in 'God and the Mauser', as Ben Viljoen put it. Knowing he would not be able to resist the British Army at full strength, he issued a four point ultimatum of his own. It gave Britain forty-eight hours to agree to arbitration on all points of difference with the Transvaal, remove its troops from the border of the republic, send back all reinforcements that had arrived since June 1, and turn back those already at sea. It wasn't that the British misjudged the mood of the Boers, they simply never considered it worth judging. They expected them to back down – 'they always do' said a confident Milner. Britain saw its military power as an extension of its foreign policy and was used to having its own way. The deadline passed unheeded, and the Boers launched a pre-emptive strike on British forces in Natal and the Cape on October 11, 1899.

Ironically, both sides went to war believing God was on their side. The Boers believed they had a 'Covenant' with him, whilst the British had long invoked the name of God in its quest to rule the world claiming, on one hand, it was spreading enlightenment and civilisation, whilst shoving the heads of their own impoverished children up chimneys with the other. Despite the name of the Almighty being bandied about, this unholy struggle would last two and a half years with neither side showing much in the way of Christian charity.

The British press cheerfully declared that the war would be over by Christmas, but Queen Victoria was not so sure. She wrote to Kitchener:

It must however be borne in mind that this is a very different type of warfare of the Indian and Egyptian. The Boers are a horrid brutal people, but are skilled in European fighting and well armed.

The doughty monarch showed a caution seemingly lacking in her generals. She would not have been amused at the way the Boer attack caught the British totally unawares and, as she had predicted, it became quickly apparent that it was going to be no push-over. By the end of October, the British had been driven out of Dundee and found themselves under heavy siege in the key centres of Mafeking, Kimberley and Ladysmith. The war would not be over by Christmas, as some optimists had suggested, and there was worse to follow during what would become known as 'black week' in January 1900. But whatever Britain's agenda was in South Africa, the Empire was under attack and the call went out to defend her honour.

AUSTRALIA WAS NOT ALWAYS AS passionately committed to the South African cause as ANZAC legend would have us believe. In the year preceding the Boer War, the Colonial Office and British military worked hard to engineer support from her larger colonies in the event of a war they knew to be inevitable in South Africa.

Expressions of Australian public support for the *Uitlander* cause were lukewarm at best, as were 'spontaneous offers of support' sought by the British Government from both military volunteers and the parliamentary executives of the two largest states, New South Wales and Victoria. The lack of enthusiasm was due to both the cost and the Australian perception that war in a faraway land over an issue they knew little about was not yet inevitable. The home press was also divided. Whilst it was a defence of democratic rights to the monarchists and jingos, it was empire-building to the Republicans, Labor and *The Bulletin*. Only the Sydney *Daily Telegraph* correctly saw 'British prestige' as the real issue. It saw that now the argument had begun, Britain had to have its way in order to maintain its 'paramountcy' in Africa. Anything less would send out the wrong signals to its Imperial rivals. As the situation worsened in the Transvaal, intensive lobbying by British officials and representatives led to protracted discussions amongst the states. In the end, just three weeks before war was declared, the first commitment to supply volunteers by any colonial government in the Empire came from Victoria. Ten days before war, a meeting of the state commandants was still debating whether to send a single federal force or allow each state to make its own arrangements.

In the end, Chamberlain settled the issue with his infamous October 3 cable accepting Australian troops for service in South Africa, even though they had not yet been formally offered. He stated a preference not for a federal force, but two units of 125 men from Victoria and New South Wales and one from South Australia to be commanded by no-one higher than the rank of Major. This dashed any notion of a federal force. As it was, the Australian contingent was shortlived in South Africa. It was split up into units and deployed within Imperial forces.

The motions to send contingents to South Africa were still being debated in some state parliaments when the first shots of the war were fired. Reasoned debate on the rights and wrongs of Australia's involvement in this Imperial adventure and who had executive control over Australian troops was abandoned as Britain suffered a series of dramatic early reversals. It was, ultimately, to Britain's benefit that the Boers attacked first, because

Chamberlain knew that unless the Boers were seen as the aggressors, the war would be very unpopular in Britain.

The *Uitlander* issue had also failed to spark colonial enthusiasm for a fight. Whether it was because the Boers attacked first, or because the motherland found itself unexpectedly against the ropes, the tide of public opinion in Australia turned suddenly and decisively in Britain's favour. Suddenly, latent warlike passions were aroused and issues that had been clouded by doubt and suspicion of Britain's motives became clear. Soon there were only a few discordant voices left wailing in the political wilderness. The Member for Grenfell, WA Holman, who said during the New South Wales debate that he thought 'this to be the most iniquitous, most immoral war ever waged with a race' and finished by saying he 'hoped the English may be defeated', was later dragged from the podium during a speech in Hobart and assaulted. In one particularly ugly incident, a member of the public was set upon and killed for not believing the British cause. Later in the conflict, the pro-war lobby tried to get Professor George Arnold Wood of the University of Sydney dismissed for his public statements criticising Australia's participation in the war. Had the colonies passed formal resolutions on their participation *before* the war began, the course of history may have been very different. But the people had spoken and war it was.

In a near carnival atmosphere, recruitment bands marched round the country signing up men as they went. Country boys, craving adventure and finding work hard to come by in recession-torn Australia, rushed to the cities to sign on, eager to do their bit for what still was Queen and country. Australians they may have been geographically, but British they were constitutionally and emotionally. An eighteen-year-old battery gunner called George Ramsdale Witton was one of those who answered the call to arms and joined the 4th Victorian Imperial Bushmen in early 1900. His heartfelt eulogy spoke for the vast majority of young men in Australia:

> When war was declared between the British and the Boers, I, like many of my fellow countrymen, became imbued with a warlike spirit, and when reverses had occurred among the British troops, and volunteers for the front were called for in Australia, I could not rest content until I had offered the assistance one man could give to our beloved Queen and the great nation to which I belong.

His involvement in the Morant affair would later cause him to regret such zeal, but like Australia itself, he responded to his first instinct, to serve the motherland. The opportunity to fight in a real war also had an important national dimension. In 1853, political maverick William Wentworth had lamented:

> It has been the misfortune of all my countrymen, that we have not lived in troublous times, when it became necessary to subdue unrest at home or pour out our chivalry to seek glory and distinction in foreign climes. This has been a privilege that has been denied to us. It is a privilege which can only belong to our posterity.

He didn't have long to wait before Victorian Government troops spilt blood on home soil at the Eureka Stockade, but it was almost another half century, not counting the brief skirmish in the Sudan, before Australia got to prove itself in that tribal rite of passage called war.

This was the chance that Australia and Wentworth had been waiting for, a chance to prove their loyalty and to rid themselves of the stain of their origins. Like some pagan rite, they sent forth their young to be sacrificed on the altar of war believing that once anointed with the sacrament of blood all past sins would be atoned for and nationhood would be rightly theirs.

Not only were these young men going to war with the nation's blessing, but, apparently, with God's too. The prince of the Catholic Church in Australia, Archbishop Cardinal Patrick Francis Moran of Sydney, said during a service shortly after the outbreak of war that if a volunteer died on the battlefield, Heaven's portals would be open to receive him. He would gain salvation in the eyes of his fellow man and God. As Australian national biographer Manning Clark put it, 'Religion sanctified, elevated and ennobled the profession of arms'.

Tenterfield was typical of the country towns that answered the call to arms and military headquarters requested that Captain Thomas raise a contingent for South Africa. On October 28, 1899, just three weeks after the declaration of war, the 1st New South Wales Mounted Rifles, composed of men from nearby Toowoomba, Warwick, Stanthorpe, Glen Innes and ten from Thomas' Tenterfield Rifles, set sail from Sydney aboard the *Kent*. The First Contingent also comprised volunteers from Victoria, Tasmania, Western Australia and South Australia who sailed that same day from Melbourne.

War fever seized Tenterfield. For the first time, telegraph technology enabled even a provincial paper like *The Tenterfield Star* to follow the progress of the local boys, give blow by blow accounts from the front and produce pull-out maps of South Africa to help the eager public follow field reports from places with all manner of strange names. A satirical cartoon appeared in *The Bulletin*, the only Australian newspaper to take an anti-war stance, showing public interest in the war outstripping cricket – and this in a country which had a Test team before it had a government.

As an act of patriotism, a Victorian gentleman of means called John McLeod Cameron raised a twenty-five man unit of scouts at his own expense. Cameron colourfully summarised the virtues of the Australian horseman in an interview with *The Tenterfield Star*:

> As horsemen, Mr Cameron rightly claims that they have no equals in the world, and their shooting abilities are of a high order. And he also insists on their natural instinct for learning the lay of the land and their ability to endure any hardships. They possess, indeed, the same qualities which, badly employed, enabled the KELLY gang to defy the Victorian Government for years, and to traverse vast tracts of country with speed and a certainty which confounded all pursuit. It is hardly too much to say that men of this type should be a match or more than a match for the Boer, and as scouts and raiders, they deserve to rank with those cowboys of the States who, under the leadership of Buffalo Bill and his companion, have again and again, under somewhat similar circumstances, rendered incalculable service to The United States war authorities.

Those comparisons to Ned Kelly and the Wild West would be commented on many times by the end of the war.

Captain JF Thomas had become a pillar of the Tenterfield community and the local mayor, William Reid, said as much at the smoke concert they held for Thomas the night before he departed for the war:

> This . . . is the eve of your departure for South Africa . . . At first when we heard you were going to the war we felt we could not let you go without some act of courtesy and that were justified, and indeed in duty bound to offer you the attention we are showing you this evening. In addition to this

concert it will be my duty to present you a purse of sovereigns in place of a gift. You will understand when we heard of your departure we felt anxious to tender you a gift of some sort so that whenever your eyes fell on it you might think of the many friends you are about to leave in this district. You have been here many years, and though not given to flattery I can conscientiously say no man in our midst would be more missed than you will be. We know duty calls you, and Tenterfield must think itself highly honoured in providing for the Empire a gentleman who has risen to the position of Captain in one of the finest armies going to South Africa. You will be accompanied by a number of the best young fellows we have, and it will be a grand advertisement for our district to supply such a gentleman as you to fight for The British Empire.

With those fine words, the sound of the brass band and hearty cheers of the good folk of the town ringing in his ears, Thomas left Tenterfield's picturesque little station on a train to Sydney to join his men. This scene was being repeated in country towns all over Australia.

Amongst the first cinematic images ever recorded in Australia was grainy, black and white footage of soldiers parading at barracks, marching through the streets and leaving on boats for war. Even without sound, an invention still some twenty years away, the crowded wharves and waving hats and flags still manage to convey the sense of excitement and history in the making as the Australians left en masse for the first time to fight in foreign lands.

Captain James Francis Thomas and the A Squadron of the New South Wales Citizens' Bushmen embarked on the transports *Atlantian* and *Maplemore* at Sydney on February 28, 1900. The Second Contingent, like the First, had been raised by public subscription and on leaving Sydney its strength was thirty officers and 495 other ranks, 570 horses and ten carts.

AS HE LOOKED ACROSS THE SEETHING MASS *of cheering, upturned faces that had shoe-horned themselves onto Circular Quay, Thomas felt his heart beating in time to the throbbing steam engines and suddenly increase in tempo as the ropes which still umbilically connected them to their homeland were cast off and the ship he was on pushed away from the crowded quay towards South Africa. He felt a lump of pride swell in his throat as the great cacophony of cheering that rose from the quay was met with an impromptu chorus of* Waltzing Matilda *from the deck and those who had climbed up into the rigging. Paterson's ditty was already a firm favourite with home-sick diggers in South Africa.*

The two ships ploughed a furrow along the long Sydney Harbour foreshore and out through the Heads – the same route the founding fathers had arrived by a little over a century before. Now their sons had grown up and were off into the world to become men.

Thomas turned around and caught a last sight of Sydney before they slipped into the open sea. For one sombre moment he wondered if he would see home again, but he had committed himself to a worthy cause and he knew there was no turning back.

TEN THOUSAND MILES AWAY SIMILAR thoughts were running through the mind of Harry Morant as Table Mountain hove into view. After seeing the recruitment poster in the pub window, he decided to go to Adelaide to join up with four other Renmark blokes – but not before he left his mark on the quiet fruit-growing town of Renmark.

The Renmark Hotel has been rebuilt since its Federation days when it boasted one unusual architectural feature – the pub was upstairs instead of on the ground floor. However, there has been a 'Breaker Bar' in the hotel ever since the night in 1899 that Morant rode his horse into the upstairs bar for a bet. That was to be his last riotous act on Australian soil, and young Frederick Cutlack who wrote a biography on the Breaker sixty years later, remembered the day he left after working for nearly ten months on Paringa Station:

> After the Boer War broke out in October 1899 there was a morning when for the last time he boiled his quart pot on the river bank while he and the others waited to catch the down-river steamer for railhead to Adelaide, and he gave me that quart-pot as a parting gesture.

He also gave the Cutlack family the famous photograph of himself taken in uniform and distinctive slouch hat, which by strange coincidence was designed by Morant's aunt, Caroline Emily Clarke, during a trip to Australia in 1885 to review Australian forces with her husband, Sir George Sydenham Clarke. Morant might have been born an Englishman, but he was going to war as an Australian. *Bulletin* writer Frank Renar (Fox), who would later write the first biography on Morant, said of his enlistment: 'To Harry Morant the opening of the gates of The Temple of War was as the opening of prison gates to a captive'.

The war in South Africa offered him just the opportunity he had been waiting for all these long years – a chance for the prodigal son to recast his reputation in the heat of war and return home to England a hero to start afresh. Will Ogilvie, who had an intimate understanding of Morant's need for redemption in the eyes of his family, knew that it was not lust for war or glory that caused Morant to sign up. The real reason was revealed in a poem entitled *To the Memory of One Dead*, which he wrote after Morant's death:

He went to fight in a foreign land,
And I know that he only went,
To fight with the cares that were creeping
    close,
And stealing his heart's content . . .

On January 13, 1900, *The Adelaide Advertiser* recorded
the enlistment of Harry Harbord Morant in the 2nd
South Australian Contingent. It listed the men who
signed the contract below. Harry Harbord Morant was
thirty-seventh out of ninety-three. Of those who also
signed that day were, number fifty-eight, Victor Marra
Newland, and number seventy-three, John Henry
Morrow, both of whom would bear witness to
Morant's final performance. The report also detailed
their conditions of service. The contract was the same
as the one signed by the First Contingent.

South Australian Volunteer for South Africa –
Army Act 44 and 45 Victoria, Cap. 58. The
Defences Act, 1895.
    – We the undersigned, do hereby solemnly,
sincerely and truly severally declare that we will be
faithful and bear true allegiance to Queen Victoria,
her heirs and successors according to law, and that
we will faithfully severally serve as members of the
South Australian Volunteer Contingent enrolled for
service in South Africa, and we hereby severally
bind ourselves from the 17th day of October, 1899,
and until discharged to be subject to the provisions
of the Army Act in force for the time being in Her
Majesty's Army, in like manner as if we had been
severally duly enlisted and attested for Her Majesty's
Army for general service, and as if the said South
Australian Volunteer Contingent formed part of Her
Majesty's Army, and that we in like manner during
such time severally be subject to the Queen's rules

and regulations, the rules and articles of war, and to
all such other rules, regulations, and discipline of
whatever nature or kind to which Her Majesty's
Army is for the time being subject, and to all laws,
rules and regulations in force within the Province of
South Australia under the Defence Act 1895; and
also to all rules and regulations re: general orders
and of any general officer commanding Her
Majesty's forces in South Africa in which we may
severally for the time being be serving.

The contract signed by the Australians was not subjected
to any great scrutiny at the time, though following the
executions of Morant and Handcock, many questions
were asked about their rights and the constitutional
position of Australians serving in the British Army. By
signing the above document, Morant and the other Australians effectively agreed to serve in Her Majesty's Army
and be subject to their rules, regulation and military law
'in like manner as if we had been severally duly enlisted
and attested for Her Majesty's Army for general service'.

Britain had not secured the undertakings it had been
seeking prior to the declaration of war. The Colonial
Secretary, Joseph Chamberlain, had insisted at the 1897
Diamond Jubilee talks that Australian troops come
under the *Army Act*, where matters of discipline were
concerned, when serving with Imperial units. His request
had been declined, but as George Reid, Premier of New
South Wales, told Major-General Hutton, in the event
of war the states would back the Empire to the last man
and forget all their narrow prejudices. He was right, and
the exigencies of war ensured Chamberlain got his wish.

Australia had not yet achieved political or military
union and had no Defence Act of its own. Also, Chamberlain's unwillingness to accept any Australian above
the rank of major ensured that it would be Imperial
officers who would dispense justice. Although their

long-term goal of creating a colonial expeditionary unit for Imperial service still remained elusive, the British had secured executive command and control of Australian units in South Africa. They effectively brought the sixteen thousand Australians who volunteered during the course of the war under British military law, despite Parkes's reservations and the lively discussions about this very matter that had surfaced during the Federation talks. But it mattered little to those volunteers who were burning with patriotism and ready to serve the Empire to which they believed they belonged. They could never have imagined that they would ever have cause to question the integrity of the British military.

MORANT'S HORSEMANSHIP AND CHEERFUL disposition soon made him a favourite in the barracks and he was quickly promoted to Corporal. He was nicknamed 'Buller' because he bore a striking resemblance to the then Commander-in-Chief of the British forces in South Africa, Sir Redvers Buller. And like Buller, Morant would also make an ignominious exit from the British Army.

The Adelaide Observer produced a special weekend supplement on the Contingent that featured a group photograph of the non-commissioned officers and a short profile of Morant. In keeping with the confusion that surrounds his origins, it describes him as a 'journalist', says he was 'born at Devon, England, December 9, 1870' and was the 'son of Vice-Admiral Morant', and, in direct contravention of the rumour that he had been in the Royal Navy, says he 'served in the West Somerset Yeomanry and Cavalry'.

Whilst billeted in Adelaide, Morant also made the acquaintance of Lord and Lady Tennyson. Lord Tennyson, son of the famous poet, Alfred Lord Tennyson, had been appointed Governor of South Australia in 1899 before he became the second Governor General of Australia from 1902 to 1904.

Lady Audrey Tennyson was a Lushington, who regarded the Morants as cousins. Harry was invited to Marble Hill, their summer residence in the picturesque Adelaide Hills, for dinner. Being in his element amongst the good and the great of Adelaide society, he made quite an impression on them all. Never one to miss a chance of a bit of sport, he used an Army open day at Montefiore Park, where they were camped, to stage a three-a-side polo match, in the finest Geebung tradition. The team of AA Murray of the Adelaide Polo Club, Corporal Morant and Trooper Lee won the match.

The day before the Contingent's departure, Morant visited Marble Hill for the last time. The whole Contingent rode through Adelaide and as they wound their way up into the steep escarpment into the hills, they enjoyed the breathtaking panoramas that had inspired Colonel William Light, the architect of Adelaide.

In his report, the local *Adelaide Observer* reporter waxed lyrical about the 'loyal response' of the volunteers and quoted one of the freshly minted patriotic verses that captured the feeling of pride and patriotism which had swept the country and would have been music to the ears of the Colonial Defence Committee.

> Britain's myriad voices call –
> 'Sons be wedded, each and all,
> Into one Imperial whole,
> One with Britain, heart and soul!
> One life, one flag, one fleet, one Throne!
> Britons hold your own!

After refreshments, the Governor gave an impromptu but colourful speech to the shortly departing troops which reiterated their patriotic duty and stuck to the official British line on the reason for the conflict:

I am sure you are feeling proud of going to serve
your Queen and country and to fight alongside our
British troops in South Africa among the best in the
world and – and captained by highly trained scientific
officers . . . You are leaving your homes and all that
is dear to you in order to join in a great work –
that of freeing your kinsfolk from the tyranny of The
Boers, of winning for them their civil, political and
religious liberties and of overthrowing those who have
remorselessly broken their solemn pledges and treaties,
and who have ruthlessly invaded our territories.

He finished by reminding them to write home 'as cheerfully as possible', despite the dangers, discomfort and
difficulties, to keep up morale at home, and read out
a letter of gratitude from Queen Victoria. Lord and
Lady Tennyson then moved down the long khaki file,
shook each soldier by the hand and wished them the
best of luck.

But as Morant and the Contingent rode back to
barracks from Marble Hill in the gathering gloom,
rhyming and singing as they went, Morant felt very
up-beat. A new century had arrived and with it the
prospect that he might redeem his reputation at last.
The Morants in Renmark and Lady Tennyson in Adelaide had accepted him as kin, he had made a good start
in the armed forces and Britain would be grateful to
him in its hour of need.

Before he left he just had time to dash off a letter and
a bit of verse for his old bush mate, Sam Nicker, who
had resisted the call to arms. The middle verse has been
lost, but the first and last verses read,

> The minstrel boy to the war has gone,
> In a Sydney bar you'll find him.
> The stumpy mare his pack has on
> And the Warrego lies behind him . . .

> . . . and he'll drink one straight
> For Sam his mate
> And damn old Bobby Warner†

The Contingent left for South Africa on January 25, 1900 from Port Adelaide amid now-familiar scenes of jubilation. On the day of Morant's departure, Ogilvie wrote to *The Bulletin*'s editor AG Stephens from Parkes and enclosed the following poem. He did not regard it as 'good literature' and thought that it 'jumps' and was 'very jingo – very jingle', but as it turned out, Morant was just 'another reckless devil for the front'.

> (News Item – H. Morant 'Breaker' leaves
>   with S.A. Contingent)

> Whatever they may say
> You're a fighter all the way
>   (Goodbye, Breaker!)
> Let us put your faults behind
> Let us put your better qualities before,
> For we're glad to hear you've signed –
> And we'll drink the red night blind
> To another bulldog fighter for the War!

> Whoever may deny,
> You're a plucky sort, say I,
>   (Good luck, Breaker!)
> We have seen you go ahead
> In the rattling polo-rally and the hunt,
> So we'll hope you dodge the lead
> And we'll fill the wine cup red
> To another reckless devil for the front.

Morant was a popular figure on board, where his cheery disposition helped break the monotony of the

---

† *Bobby Warner was a local shopkeeper that Morant owed money to.*

long trip. The soldiers filled their endless days at sea by
stealing whatever small home comforts they could from
the ships stores, drilling, exercising and having target
practice at boxes thrown over the side of the ship.
Artillery gunner George Witton who sailed with the
Fourth Contingent also recalled that in keeping with
the rapid and makeshift nature of their military education, a Lieutenant-Colonel read out extracts from
the Queen's Regulations and Military Law, 'specially
impressing on us . . . the first duty of a soldier, obedience to orders'.

*After skirting the African coast for days, which had
been little more than a smudge of land on the distant
horizon, Morant spotted spray rising off the top of the
rolling breakers which crashed onto the teeth of the
unforgiving reefs. He recalled his father, Captain Digby
Morant, telling him about the 'wild coast' just west of
Durban, the graveyard of many an incautious mariner.
Morant's calculations proved accurate, as the next day,
against the fading orange light of a magnificent African
sunset, they finally sighted the imposing silhouette of
the flat-topped atoll known as Table Mountain. The
slouch-hatted Australians pressed onto the deck, keen
to get a glimpse of this famous landmark.*

*The benevolent beauty of the Cape of Good Hope,
its sweet water and fresh supplies, had long been a
welcome haven for jaded seafarers on their long journeys from Europe or Asia. However, it was also the
confluence of the Atlantic and Indian oceans, currents
and prevailing winds that could also make rounding the
Cape a treacherous journey. During the next two years,
Morant would come to know Africa and all its moods.*

At the end of the month-long voyage, a cartoon of
the Breaker was sent back to *The Bulletin* along with

the news that he had been promoted to Sergeant during the voyage. On a postcard to Australia, Morant wrote rather prophetically: 'Gawd knows when I'll see any old Hawkesbury fellows again. Probably when we wear a halo.'

5

The First Shots

Oh, chant me a lay of the days of old;
Of the days when men were brave –
When they loved the strife that brought no gold,
No fief, but a hero's grave;
When a woman's love was a noble prize –
But not for a woman's sake;
When a kiss, and a glance of a leman's eyes,
Were on show for a Man to take.

'The Song of the Bushveldt Carbineers'
by FJ Broomfield

DURING THE PRELUDE TO THE WAR, the War Office felt
they had enough British regulars to deal with the Boers
and that the colonial forces were not really needed. They
were only taken after pressure from Chamberlain's
Colonial Office, who requested Australian infantry
rather than cavalry. Whatever the truth of this, the
British were grateful the colonials had arrived, and the
reasons for their spectacular failures during the first
phase of the war soon became apparent to Morant and
the other Australians.

Britain's battlefield tactics, honed by centuries of
set-piece European wars, had proved adequate in sub-
duing poorly armed native forces in India, Burma,
Sudan and South Africa. However, the British strategy
proved hopelessly outmoded when it came to fighting

well-armed foe of European origin who knew the terrain intimately and had a native cunning about them. President Kruger had spent some of his huge gold revenues on the latest German armaments, such as Mauser rifles and the fearsome 'Long Tom' – a siege gun with a huge range. However, his greatest weapon was the element of surprise.

The Boers knew they did not have the organisation, discipline or numbers to take the British head-on. In colonising the wild interior, they had fought many bloody battles against hostile African tribes and developed a hit and run tactic that was difficult for a conventional army to counter. They would watch the ponderous advance of large British columns from miles away and have an ambush laid by the time they arrived. The traditional British response was to fix bayonets and send in foot soldiers under an artillery barrage, but by the time they got to the Boer positions, they had vanished. Despite British accusations of it being a 'cowardly practice', it proved a very effective tactic. What the British needed were their own mounted infantry units who could also shoot and ride and live off the land. It was in this area, in particular, that the Canadians, Australians and New Zealanders proved invaluable.

It has been said that Morant was part of the First Australian Regiment attached to General French's column that turned the tables on the Boers. Taking the lead in Roberts' advance, they outflanked Cronje at Magesfontein, relieved Kimberley, destroyed the Boers at Paardenberg and then captured Bloemfontein. However, the *Surrey,* with Morant on board, didn't arrive in Cape Town until February 27, 1900, eight days after the relief of Paardenberg and, in another of those strange historical coincidences, exactly two years to the day before he was executed.

The *Surrey* transportees were first sent to Prieska in the Cape Colony to join a force under Kitchener, then back to De Aar where they were moved up to Bloemfontein to join the First Australian Contingent and the main advance north under Roberts. This was not what Morant imagined war to be. There were few straight battles to fight and few chances for him to shine, until his knowledge of horses came to the notice of General French.

The British had not anticipated the Boer tactics and as a result there was a shortage of horses with which to carry the war to the enemy. Those they did have were heavily laden with the kind of cumbersome equipment a soldier might need in a European theatre of war. Many of the inferior mounts the British had acquired from Hungary and Argentina buckled quickly under the strain. Hardly surprising given what 'Banjo' Paterson, in South Africa as a correspondent for *The Sydney Morning Herald*, Melbourne's *Argus* and *The Adelaide Advertiser*, was told about the appointment of the British director of remounts:

> [H]e had to have some job so they made him director of remounts. He's a soldier all right but what does he know about remounts? As much as I know about dancing the Spanish cachucha to a pair of castanets.

This is where Morant came into his own. He was able to break in the wild horses that were being shipped in from overseas and had a knack of acquiring the better staff mounts under the cover of darkness. Such practices were common and General French felt that he better have the best on his staff, and seconded Morant as a 'galloper' or dispatch rider.

WHILST MORANT LANGUISHED IN THE remount section and put his dubious talents to good use, other Australians were distinguishing themselves in the field. Lieutenant NR Howse won the first of the six Australian Victoria Crosses in July 1900 at Vredefort. The following month, Captain JF Thomas and the Tenterfield troopers were part of the heroic defence of Elands River, which confirmed the fighting qualities of the Australians and was arguably their finest hour in the whole campaign.

Serving under General Plumer, they were part of the relief of Mafeking, which was greeted with great euphoria and relief in Britain. Coupled with the breaking of sieges at Kimberley and Ladysmith, the British had wrestled away the Boers' early advantage. The war now entered its second phase – almost a year of British advances through the Orange Free State and Transvaal fighting a more familiar series of European-style battles.

After the relief of Mafeking, Captain Thomas and the A Squadron started a drive eastwards to Rustenburg with General Baden-Powell's column, under the command of Lieutenant-Colonel Hore. This unit was a mixture of Australian Bushmen, Queensland Mounted Rifles, Plumer's Rhodesians and Protectorate troops, who were part of a bigger column of two thousand men. They got to Rustenburg with little incident on June 20 and took the town. Hore's unit, including Thomas, were left to guard the town, but were advised to evacuate on July 3 by Baden-Powell, who had information that a Boer force of two thousand with field guns planned to attack. They decamped to Elands River, forty miles away. A diary, written by an unnamed officer with access to official communiqués, kept a detailed description of the siege. Captain Thomas' pluck and cool efficiency on patrol is mentioned three times before the siege even began.

On July 29, the anonymous keeper of an Elands River diary remarked that when the order to entrench themselves was issued, 'They were not very keen on it and did not realise the absolute necessity of cover, but this was down to a large number of them (mostly of the Australian Contingent) never having experienced shell-fire. However, in a few days their skill & capacity for work in entrenching improved in a most miraculous manner.'

That improvement began on August 4, the day the siege began. The three hundred men of A Squadron, assisted by fifty other men, defended Elands River post against De La Rey's eighteen hundred men and field guns. For the first few days they were shelled from sunrise to sunset, and the Tenterfield contingent suffered their first fatality. Sergeant-Major Mitchell was hit by flying shrapnel and died a few days later after sustaining further injuries in the field hospital, which was also hit by a Boer shell. During the course of the war, Mitchell was joined by four other Tenterfield boys who would never go home. Thomas also had a narrow escape when his horse was shot from under him. God, plainly, had other designs for him.

On August 9, General De La Rey, commanding the Boer forces, sent the following letter, addressed to Lieutenant-Colonel Hore, offering them the chance to surrender:

> I wish to submit to your very serious consideration that the time has come to avoid further bloodshed and to end your defence which you have carried on with so much courage. In the event of your handing over to me the camp with all that it contains without concealing or destroying anything in it then I am prepared and pledge myself to allow you and the troops under you to proceed to the nearest force of British troops wherever you may choose to go. The commanding officers will in that case keep their arm as a recognition of the brave defence of your camp. Kindly answer me as soon as possible. If

necessary I am prepared to have an interview with you in order to further discuss the matter and settle details.

J.H. De La Rey
Commanding General

Despite the terrific odds they faced, the answer was short and sweet.

To Ass. General De La Rey

Sir,

I beg to acknowledge the receipt of your letter 9/8/00 concerning your demand for the surrender of the British troops under my command at Elands River camp + in reply must inform you that as this post is held by Her Majesty's Forces I decline to surrender.
C.O. Hore
Lieut. Col.
Elands River 9/8/00

Bill Woolmore's book *The Bushveldt Carbineers and The Pietersburg Light Horse* reveals that although it was signed by Hore, the veteran of Egypt, Sudan and the recently lifted siege of Mafeking was stricken with malaria and the job of making the decisions fell to Major Turnbridge of the Queensland Mounted Rifles. Both agreed that it would be better to face De La Rey's guns and die, than live to face Roberts' wrath, if they surrendered and the supplies they were defending fell to Boer hands. Turnbridge was also under pressure from his fellow Australians who told him in no uncertain terms that they would not be party to any surrender.

Turnbridge suspected that the Boers were short of ammunition after the fusillade of shells they had dispatched during the first few days. The last week of the siege was largely restricted to rifle fire, surprise attacks and cruder methods such as setting the veldt on fire. Shell-fire coming from other directions also suggested that British troops were trying to relieve them.

The siege was lifted on August 16 by Lord Kitchener's force, supported by Lord Methuens' column. Again, in one of those strange historical coincidences, Thomas cheered Kitchener's arrival, little knowing that his champion would soon become his nemesis. Both Kitchener and Roberts inspected them after the siege and they were congratulated on their plucky defence. The ever-modest Thomas said, 'we thought the praises were unduly great', but it was a great moment for Thomas and the Australians. As Gavin Souter put it in *Lion and Kangaroo – The Initiation of Australia*:

> 300 mixed Aussies, together with 200 Rhodesians covered themselves in glory at Elands River. They were pinned down by 1800 Boers with Pom Poms and heavy artillery. Although more shells were fired into their camp than Mafeking – they held out for 12 days until relief arrived. 75 Aussies died and that great chronicler of the Boer War – Sir Arthur Connan Doyle wrote,
>
>> 'When the ballad-makers of Australia seek for a subject let them turn to Elands River, for there was no finer fighting in the war'.

But as Souter observed, Elands River was more than just a military victory, 'It was exactly what Australia wanted – a chance to blood itself with honour next to seasoned Imperials with the mother country grateful for prompt assistance loyally given.'

However, their moment of glory was spoiled by an inexplicable decision by the War Office not to award the colonials a clasp or bar for their heroic defence –

despite Roberts' assurance they would be rewarded. *The Times* commented that a failure to recognise a defence widely acknowledged as one of the most heroic acts in the war would be a slight to the colonies, but the War Office was unmoved, despite a formal request from the Australian Government. As Captain Ham of the Victorian Bushmen pointed out, 'bars and recognition had been plentifully given to English troops for occasions in which not half the gallantry, endurance, etc, had been shown, and we can only arrive at the conclusion that it was because we were colonials'.

However, another piece of the fatalistic jigsaw was put in place in the aftermath of the Elands River siege when Thomas chanced upon Major Robert Lenehan, who was a member of the relieving force. Before the war, Lenehan had been a lawyer in the New South Wales Supreme Court when Thomas was doing his articles in Sydney. They wished each other 'godspeed' and hoped they'd meet again after the war. Little did Thomas know that the next time they spoke, it would be through the bars of a prison cell.

MORANT'S 'LOT' IMPROVED IMMEASURABLY with the arrival of Bennet Burleigh, war correspondent for London's *Daily Telegraph,* in June 1900. Burleigh was one of the most respected war correspondents of his era. He got out of Ladysmith just before the Boers laid siege to it, attracting criticism from some quarters, but while those who stayed spent months on one story, Burleigh was riding on Roberts' coat-tails, reporting on the British fight-back.

The good-humoured, avuncular Burleigh was introduced to Morant and discovering their mutual love of horses, literature and a good time, they hit it off at once. Recognising that he was articulate and intelligent, as

well as a first class galloper, Burleigh soon poached
Morant from French as his assistant/dispatch rider.
Burleigh must have pulled strings to get Morant out of
the Army, as the newspapers employed dispatch riders
and Morant's last Army pay was drawn on July 31,
1900. He was also able to leave for England before he
had served the regulation twelve months.

Roberts' most serious tactical error was not to finish
off the Boer forces when he had them encircled at Johannesburg. This has remained one of the great mysteries
of the Boer War. Major Robert Montague Poore, who
would later become intimately involved in Morant's
destiny, was part of Roberts' column. His diary captured the frustration felt throughout the army:

> Wed 30th May 1900,
>
> This morning Lord Roberts sent an officer into
> Jo'burg to demand the surrender of the place and
> sometime after he returned with Dr Krause, who is
> commandant, the arrangement having been made
> that 24 hours law would be given the Boers to allow
> them time to evacuate, Dr Krause refusing to
> answer for the safety of anyone under that . . . This
> made everyone awfully sick, as it was giving the
> Boers time to do what they wanted, a Jo'burg paper
> also came out and in it was described a fight in
> which our Cavalry was severely mauled. This added
> to the fact that we have heard nothing of our
> Cavalry made us feel uneasy and the 24 hours law
> seems to us to be sheer madness. Of course the
> supply question may have something to do with it
> and perhaps there is something Lord Roberts knows
> we do not.

What Roberts knew was that Dr Krause was, like
himself, a Freemason. Roberts himself was a Past Grand
Warden and despite the fact they were at war, both he

and Kitchener attended Lodge meetings during the course of the war with their Boer brethren.

Royal Warden Brother Kitchener was at the time District Grand Master of the Egypt and Sudan Lodge and attended one meeting. The meeting was on April 23, 1900 at Rising Star Lodge No. 1022, Bloemfontein and became renowned throughout the Masonic world. The meeting was to celebrate the escape of MW Grand Master of England – Prince Edward of Wales – from an assassination attempt.

The thirty-nine members and sixty-one visitors were an incongruous mix of Boer generals on parole, Boer brethren, all the chief Masonic Generals in the British Army, and also present was a brother of ex-President Steyn of the Orange Free State. The host, Brother Haarburger, was German by birth and not one man from that Lodge fought on the British side, but three actually took up arms against them. The minutes also show Lord Roberts sent his apologies, as he was indisposed, and in his stead Lord Kitchener proposed a thanksgiving. At the meeting Haarburger said:

> It seems evident judging from the spectacle which presents itself to us at the present moment, that freemasonry offers a common ground for those who, in other respects, are in opposite camps, and that the grand principle of extending the right hand of fellowship, is no ideal dream. Freemasonry, like St. George, is symbolic of the strife against the power of evil, yet we must not forget that the power of our order is merely conciliatory, striving as it does towards peace and harmony. Therefore, you, my visiting brethren, will gladly join us this evening in reviewing our pledge of fidelity to the cause of freemasonry, which will ever remain dear to us all.

The fraternal spirit of Masonic brotherhood was recognised by Roberts and Special Commandant Dr Frederick

Krause, who was a founder of the Kaiser Friedrich Lodge No. 86, Netherlands (No. 20 in the Grand Lodge of South Africa) when they met at Germiston to discuss the surrender of Johannesburg.

Krause had gone against the Boer generals who wanted to blow up the goldmines. He personally overpowered and arrested the extremist Judge Kock, who drew his gun and threatened him. Krause negotiated twenty-four hours for Boer forces to leave Johannesburg to avoid street fighting which would have taken a high toll of civilians and soldiers. It was Krause who led Roberts into Johannesburg on May 31, 1900, where the surrender took place.

Did Krause bluff the gentlemanly Roberts by using the Masonic code of chivalry to buy the Boers time? That twenty-four hours' grace allowed Kruger to escape with his best men, his heavy guns and gold reserves totalling some £500,000, which he used to fund the continuing struggle. This episode has since been described as Roberts' 'supreme blunder', as it was later revealed that the Boers never intended to destroy the mines. But Roberts saw the taking of Johannesburg as a key objective, and his June 2 letter to Krause displayed all the hallmark Masonic formalities:

Dear Dr Krause,

I desire to express to you how fully I appreciate the valuable assistance you have afforded me in connection with the entry into this town of the force under my command. I recognise that you have had difficulties of no ordinary nature to contend with of late, and any weakness in the administration of the town and suburbs at such a juncture would doubtless have been taken full advantage of by the disorderly element which necessarily exists in a mining community. Thanks to your energy and vigilance, order and tranquillity have been preserved, and I congratulate you heartily on the result of your labours. Permit me to tender you my personal thanks for the great courtesy you have shown me since I have had the pleasure of meeting you.

Believe me to be,
Yours very truly,

Roberts

The Boers used the same delaying tactics at the surrender of Pretoria. Whilst Roberts enjoyed his triumphal parade through the Transvaal capital on June 5, the British war correspondents felt cheated. There had been no Armageddon, no final crushing defeat of the enemy, but they had no inkling of why their leader had held back.

Again, Roberts showed that the British found it hard to think outside of conventional war strategy by waiting a week in Pretoria for a Boer surrender that never came. He had repelled the attackers, advanced and taken their capital and, according to the gentleman's rules of war, he had won. But the Boer nation was struggling for its very survival and cared nothing for convention. It had defied all the odds from the outset and was about to do so again.

The Boers decided that it was the veldt and not the cities that were the real symbol of the *volk* and adopted the guerrilla tactics De Wet had always favoured. Realising his error, Roberts sent his men back into the field to finish the job. The war took a bitter twist as the Boers enjoyed some early successes and Roberts was forced to show the less chivalrous side of his character.

The arrival in South Africa of Mrs Roberts coincided with the beginning of a program of farm burnings designed to deny food and shelter to the guerrillas. She, like many of her husband's officers, believed that the womenfolk were more bitter than their menfolk and had kept them in the field long after many would have surrendered. At least three Boer 'Amazons' are known to have taken up arms and fought alongside their menfolk. This grim determination was perfectly illustrated by a letter from a Nurse Robinson to *The Birmingham Post*:

> I was a nurse through the war in South Africa, and heard the following story from the lips of two soldiers who were concerned in the incident. On a Boer farm, far over veldt, dwelt a Boer farmer, his Scotch wife and their baby. When the late war broke out the farmer went to assist the Boers in defending his country; so bidding his wife be faithful to him and his cause, he left her in the lonely homestead, with only a weak-minded Boer girl to assist her. Some month afterwards the man broke from a detachment of Boers that had been defeated, and fled to his home. After a few hours rest and refreshment he took another fond farewell of his loved ones, and started off again up the country. He had departed but a few hours when a regiment of English soldiers came up, and some of their number dismounted and entered the farmhouse. By the aid of an interpreter he had with him, the officer in command inquired which way the woman's husband and his companion had gone.
>
> 'I cannot tell you,' the brave woman replied, her Scotch accent taking the soldiers by surprise.
>
> 'And you a Scotch woman, siding with the enemies of your country?' inquired the officer, 'Why don't you tell me where the traitor that lives here has gone to?'
>
> 'He is my husband,' the woman simply said.
>
> 'Husband or no husband,' shouted the irate officer, 'I demand to know his whereabouts, or you and your baby will suffer for their silence.'

Irritated beyond measure the soldier advanced towards the women, when the Boer girl, who had been sitting in the Boer corner, yelled out to the interpreter, 'Stop, I'll tell' and was proceeding to describe the way the Boers had fled, when the mother suddenly produced a revolver from her pocket and shot her dead. Thereupon a soldier, at the instigation of the officer, in hopes of effecting his purpose by intimidation, snatched the baby out of its mother's arms, and the officer, pointing his revolver at it, said that he would shoot it if she didn't tell.

For a minute she wavered, then casting a hungry look of love into her darling's eyes, the brave woman shouted, 'No' and discharged one barrel of her still smoking revolver into the child and another into herself before the soldiers could arrest her tragic purpose.

With tears streaming down their faces the soldiers took the bodies out and buried the woman and child in a grave, with all the honour that be paid to such an example of heroism and devotion.

'Her husband deserves to live,' said the officer in choking tones; and the pursuit was not persisted in.

The determination of the so-called 'bitter-enders' to continue the war was only matched by British incompetency in the field. There was a third crucial failure to trap De Wet during August 1900 as he tried to flee north from The Rand into the relative safety of northern Transvaal. This elusive figure became a constant thorn in the side of Roberts' successor, Kitchener's penance for his part in allowing him to escape.

Kitchener, who had secured himself the ignominious title of 'K of chaos', used four columns to box in De Wet, but allowed him to slip by at Schoeman's Drift when he crossed the Vaal River. General Ian Hamilton compounded Kitchener's error when he instructed to use his 7600 men to block the pass at Olifants Nek to prevent Steyn and De Wet escaping into northern Transvaal. But Hamilton went instead to The Rand to try and cut him off before the Nek. However, Hamilton only covered thirty miles per day, to De Wet's forty-five, with the result that the Boers were able to side-step Kitchener, outrun Hamilton and escape. Like Johannesburg, it was a golden opportunity missed, and *The Times* correspondent who followed the action described the desolation that followed:

> No-one can describe the feelings of both officers and men. Here we had been enduring forced marches, heavy days of fighting, privations of all sorts . . . but of these we had thought nothing when we believed that we at last had our man. And then to find the bird had flown! Never during the whole war have we encountered a man of such vital importance as De Wet is today and never has there been such a flagrant piece of mismanagement as the evacuation of this all-important position. Why is it that even today these mistakes are made?

As a result of that failure, the new generation of Boer leaders – De Wet, Botha, De La Rey, Viljoen, Smuts and others – was able to divide the remaining 'bitter-enders' into commandos and establish their guerrilla operations in the remote, inhospitable regions of Transvaal north of the Delagoa railway, which the British had not yet subdued. Kitchener was bitter, and would have cause to be, but Roberts refused to criticise Hamilton. Colonel Henry Rawlinson, who had been at Roberts' elbow during the whole De Wet debacle, had a dark foreboding about the continuing struggle. But even he could not have anticipated how long it would take to finally subdue the Boers:

> We ordered Johnny [Hamilton] to go to Olifants
> Nek but he did not go there and in consequence
> De Wet has eluded us. This will prolong the war
> considerably I fear, and we are all down on our
> luck . . . the war could last for a good many months
> more. The enemy will, as I have always said, break
> up into small parties and take to guerrilla war,
> which will entail much time and blood to conquer.

Rawlinson's gloomy prediction did not prevent Roberts
proceeding to Komaitipoort on the Portuguese East
African border and securing the Delagoa Bay railway,
which cut the Boers' only link to the sea and the outside
world. Bennet Burleigh, with Morant in tow, had shad-
owed Roberts' advance and was present in Durban to
hear Roberts declare the war was *practically* over.
Lieutenant Lachlan Gordon-Duff of the Gordon Highlanders was also there, but like Rawlinson saw the war
very differently:

> At midnight 28/29th November 1900 Lord Roberts
> laid down his command in favour of Kitchener,
> saying at once that the war was over. At this
> moment the Boers were at the peak of their opera-
> tional strength and were poised to invade the Cape
> from two directions. They had a government which
> functioned, though with no fixed seat, and were
> acting upon a common plan in defence of their
> beloved country. They were united. To quote Rayne
> Kruger again: 'What Roberts had won was a
> shadow. He left Kitchener to grapple with reality.'

On the strength of Roberts' bold statement, Conan
Doyle rushed his history of the war into print. He could
never have dreamed that it would be another two years
before he produced *The Final Edition*, nor that the
10,000 men Britain had lost to date were only half
the blood price they would have to pay to defeat the
Boers and claim South Africa.

In October 1900, the Second South Australian Contingent returned to Australia, having completed nine months' active service, but Morant stayed on. The Commanding Officer of the Second South Australian Contingent, Colonel CJ Reade, wrote him a farewell letter of recommendation:

My Dear Morant,

There seems to be an immediate probability of the S.A. regiment returning either to Australia or going to England, so I hasten to send you a line wishing you 'Au Revoir.' I desire to wish you most heartily every success in your future career, and to express my entire satisfaction with your conduct while with the South Australians.

Your soldierly behaviour and your continual alertness as an irregular carried high commendation – and deservedly – from the whole of the officers of the regiment. I trust that in future we may have an opportunity of renewing our pleasant acquaintanceship.

Morant's first tour of duty in South Africa ended when Bennet Burleigh, like Banjo Paterson, was sent home after expressing some pro-Boer views in his dispatches.

The Boer War might have been the 'last gentleman's war', but it was the first media war. For the first time there was a well-organised anti-war movement, a sign of the more liberal-minded, educated times. No Imperial adventure had ever been subjected to such public scrutiny and the skirmishing was almost as bitter in the pages of the British and international press as it was on the veldt.

Morant decided that this would be an opportune moment to take some leave and make his long-awaited return to England. But before he sailed, Morant checked into the palatial Mount Nelson Hotel, one of Cape

Town's finest, and held court there for a week or so, running up a bill of £16.13.0. As was his wanton way, he left for England with Burleigh without settling his account. However, he did leave a forwarding address: c/o GD Morant Esq., New Forest, Hampshire. Oddly, Digby Morant lived in London.

It may have been a clever ruse to avoid paying the bill or a cheeky reminder that he was still alive, but the unpaid bill did find its way to the correct branch of the Morant family, along with a demand for payment from the Mount Nelson. According to Digby's grandson, Edward Morant, Digby's sister, Lydia, called a family conference, which indicates that it was regarded as more than a hoax. The meeting included Digby Morant who, in Harry's absence, had now risen to the rank of Vice-Admiral. He denied all knowledge of Harry Morant, but had little choice, as the chances are that Digby's wife, Georgina, knew nothing of her husband's bastard offspring. Given the social standing of the Irish Morants, who were part of the 'ascendency',[†] the existence of a low-class bastard would be a severe embarrassment and ruinous to his promising career in the navy. The Mount Nelson had asked, 'we shall esteem it a favour if you will let us know what course we had better adopt'.

The reply said that no-one by that name lived there and suggested that they present the bill to his employers – The British Army! However, as they huddled around the hearth in conference, those Morants who knew the truth must have been alarmed at the prospect

---

† *The Irish Morants, from whom Digby was descended, were part of the Protestant 'ascendency', that is, they were a family who concerned themselves with improving their social status generation after generation. They came after Ireland was amalgamated into Great Britain and saw themselves above the native Irish who were predominately Catholics. They became the new elite.*

of the return of the prodigal son who had now taken his father's name. Morant was now fulfilling the prediction he made to Banjo Paterson five years before: 'Christmas will find one prodigal turning up in England with a request for prime veal.'

6

The Return of the Prodigal

Now I'm leaving Sydney's shore
Harder up than e'er before;
A keen appetite I feel
To taste a bit o' British veal;
And let's truss, across the foam
They have a fatted calf at home.

'A Departing Dirge' by Harry Morant

SEVENTEEN YEARS AFTER EDWIN Murrant *had set sail from Plymouth, Harry Morant returned there again in October 1900. As he disembarked, handsome and tanned, wearing his khaki uniform and slouch hat, he paused for a moment and looked around, drinking in the familiar sights and sounds of England. Even the low squat cottages with their furiously smoking chimneys, the numbing pre-Christmas cold and the wheeling, screeching gulls that provided the only splash of colour in a grey and lifeless sky all seemed beautiful to him.*

At Plymouth quay he boarded a furiously puffing steam train that carried him to Bideford via all points north and west. Having no need for an umbrella these past seventeen years he took the ritual soakings, as he waited

*for connecting trains on rural platforms, in good part.
During the final leg across the English Channel he had
braved the rain and spray to stand out on deck. After the
heat and dust of Australia and then Africa, the cold piss
and damp of an English winter was a welcome change.
Nothing, not the dark rolling clouds overhead, nor the last
few russet leaves that autumn hadn't yet claimed could
dampen his mood today. He had got home before Christmas and had the whole hunt season ahead of him.*

*By the end of the day he stood and stared at the neat
stone façade of the station which bore the name he had
longed to see – Bideford, Devon – the place of his childhood, which had assumed almost mythical proportions
during those long, lonely years of exile. Home, home at
last. A familiar English accent brought him out of his
reverie. 'Would you be needing a cab sir?'*

*Morant smiled at the memory of the distinctive
Devonian twang. He had enjoyed a few good nights
with some lusty Devon lads in South Africa, but there
was nothing like hearing it spoken on home soil.*

*'Yes my good man I would,' Morant replied striding
off towards the waiting hansom cab, leaving the cabbie
in his wake to struggle with his luggage.*

*'Where to Sir?' he said puffing slightly from his exer-
tions and the biting wind which whipped at them
mercilessly.*

*'The Kings Head, and don't spare the horses!' said
Morant with a flourish, settling back in the comfortable,
well-worn leather upholstery.*

*'Right you are, sir!' replied the eager cabbie, seeing
a big fare. Money was not uppermost in Morant's mind,
but it never was, whether he had it or not. After six
months' service in South Africa, with nowhere to spend
his pay, he was flush and he intended to enjoy himself.
What little he had seen of war had only reiterated his
own personal philosophy that life was short and should*

*be lived to the full. As if to reinforce the point, he leaned
out of the window, 'A guinea extra if we get there before
opening time!' he yelled up at the cabbie, who wielded
the lash with renewed vigour.*

*His heart filled with an inexpressible joy as they
raced through the ancient streets of Bideford past familiar, reassuring landmarks. The blackened, weather-
beaten battlements of Chundleigh Fort still perched
imperiously on the hill overlooking the town, and he
saw St Mary's spire looming up ahead as they rattled
over the medieval cobbles and twenty-four arches of the
Long Bridge that spanned the river Torridge and neatly
bisected the town. The cab turned sharply at the end of
the bridge and charged along the quayside past the creak-
ing, ghostly hulls of the trading ships that waited patiently
like faithful old dogs outside the quaint old hostelries for
their masters to tumble out. They skidded to a halt in
front of the pub with minutes to spare. Morant gave the
sporting cabbie his fare and his well-earned tip and patted
the noses of his two sweating horses.*

*'You've had a good pay, take them home easy now,'
he advised the cabbie, who tipped his hat in acknowledgement. Morant scooped up his luggage and headed
towards the welcoming warm light of the King's Arms,
where he had supped his first ale so many years ago.*

*Perhaps it is indicative of Morant's character that
he enjoyed a night of revelry in the quayside pubs he
had known so well as a young man before going down
to pay his respects to his late mother. He had worked
up a fiercesome thirst during his long exile, and every
hoary old seadog in Bideford that night stood his hand
for that soldier of the Queen who could out-drink,
out-talk and out-dance the devil. Better yet!*

*Annie Murrant was living in Torquay when Cather-
ina, as she was called on her death certificate, passed
away in July 1899, aged sixty-six, when Harry was still*

in South Australia. The next-door neighbour was the only one with her at the end and registered the death. She died of Bright's disease, a kidney disorder. The news had hit him hard.

As he stood before her modest tablet, he felt a great sobering wave of sorrow wash over him. He had vowed to both her and Annie on that windswept Plymouth quay that he would return one day with his fortunes restored. That he'd done, but a year too late. For the first time in many, many pitiless years, he felt tears prick his eyelids as he recalled all the struggle and hardships she had endured in the workhouse and remembered how she stood waving on the pier at Plymouth until he had disappeared from sight. Eyes closed and head bowed, he struggled through a wordless prayer, feeling guilty for leaving her Bible in Charters Towers. He stood a moment staring at the simple stone that bore her name, but not her sorrows, struggles or disappointments, before putting his hat back on and crunching his way back down the gravel path to the waiting cab.

'Death for the dead, and life for the living,' his mother had always said, and Morant did his best to live up to that philosophy during the next few months. He went hunting again with the Stevenstone Hounds who gathered, as was tradition, at Roborough.

As always, his horsemanship marked him out, but a returning war hero with childhood connections to the famed George Whyte-Melville needed no social introductions. After a few bracers, courtesy of the Master of the Hunt, the fox was sighted, the horns sounded and with a cry of 'Tally Ho!' the red-coated army set off in pursuit of their single quarry. 'If the Hawkesbury boys could only see me now!' he thought with a smile as he joined the throng. Morant was pleased to find that his long absence had not dulled the thrill of the chase.

George had passed away many years before, but Harry
felt his spirit still there, racing alongside him on the
wings of the blustery yuletide breeze that whistled
through the leafless, skeletal trees.

AT ONE OF THOSE HUNTS, HE MET Lieutenant Percy Hunt,
with whom he'd served in French's Scouts. Like Morant,
Hunt had recently returned from the fray and would
become both Morant's best friend and the prime instrument of his destruction.

Although he was some seven years his junior, Morant
found Hunt to be a kindred spirit with his love of horses,
hunting, fine wine, fine clothes and ladies. Where
Morant used his devilish wit and racy humour to win
them over, Hunt wooed them with his sheer good looks.
Next to the nuggetty Morant, he was tall, elegant and
well-dressed, but like all good double acts, they played
off each other and soon won the hearts of two sisters of
good social standing – their father being a local squire.
Both announced their engagement on the same day.

There is a photograph of Morant taken during his
brief sojourn in Devon by a local Bideford photographer
called WH Puddacombe. Perched on a stone balustrade,
he is resplendent in smart jacket, waistcoat, cravat, fashionable riding boots and breeches and looked every inch
the gentleman he always claimed to be. The soft focus
backdrop of green trees and rippling stream completes
the bucolic air of the English countryside. For that one
brief moment, frozen in time by the photographer's
magnesium flash, he had finally fulfilled all the hopes
and dreams that had sustained him during those long
years in the outback. Harry Harbord Morant had come
home, at last.

❖

NEW YEAR'S DAY, 1901 PROBABLY saw Morant so full of
festive good cheer, that it's likely he didn't realise

Australia had become a Federation. Lord Hopetoun read out the proclamation that created the Commonwealth of Australia at Sydney's Centennial Park in front of thousands of cheering people.

But the sombre ceremonies, august declarations and colourful parades belied the scramble that had gone on behind the scenes. Five of the six querulous states had finally agreed to become one nation, but the fate of the rich, gold-producing state of Western Australia hung in the balance until the eleventh hour before a referendum delivered a resounding vote in favour of joining the Federation.

Negotiations with the British had been no less fraught. On the vexed issue of defence, they had demanded that the Queen remain Commander-in-Chief of Australian forces, effectively ceding executive control to the British military. However, the Australian view that power should be invested in the Governor General prevailed in the end.

When the Federation Bill was passed by the House of Commons on May 21, 1900, the Australian delegation, including the man who would be Australia's first Prime Minister, Edmund Barton, are said to have joined hands and danced round the office of the Attorney General like children. But did they understand the huge weight of responsibility such an undertaking entailed?

Australia was a nation at last, but in name only. It had no flag, no written history, no stamps, no anthem – in short, none of the trappings of nationhood that might distinguish Australia from Great Britain. With *The Bulletin,* asking 'why not a twang?' in its campaign for a distinctive Australian accent, it appeared that Australians had not yet even learned to love their own cadences and colloquialisms. More importantly, for a nation at war, it had no Defence Act governing its troops – a shortcoming that would soon prove significant.

By spring, the hunting season in England was over and the novelty of holidaying was wearing thin – as was Morant's bank balance. Around this time, a ditty appeared in the poetry column of *The Bideford Weekly Gazette*. It bears his trademark self-deprecating, tongue-in-cheek style, which perfectly reflected Morant's attitude to money and which featured in many of Morant's Australian verses.

> Broke, Broke, Broke!
> I have squandered the utmost sou,
> And have failed in my efforts to utter
> One last IOU.
>
> Oh, well for the infant in arms,
> That for ducats he need not fret,
> Oh, well for the placid corpse,
> That he's settled his final debt.
>
> And dun after dun comes in
> Each brings his little account
> And oh for the touch of a five dollar bill
> Or a cheque for a larger amount!
>
> Broke, Broke, Broke!
> My course as student is run,
> I'll back to my childhood days, and act
> The role of The Prodigal son.

However, any thoughts Morant had of returning to the family fold were quickly dashed. The prodigal son in the Bible may have been welcomed back by his father with rings, robes and sandals like a man returned from the dead, but despite sixteen long years of exile, and one of military service in which he rendered the country of his birth good service and had earned a commission, the soon-to-be Admiral Digby Morant would not forgive his youthful indiscretion. This treatment was harsh in light of the fact that Digby was guilty of a similar 'crime' – at a more mature age. Father like son one might say. However, during a visit to England some years later one of the Australian Morants visited their Hampshire kin. She remarked that she was shocked by their coldness towards each other and declared that the boys were 'brought up as if they were on deck' and concluded that once you had been cut – you remained cut.

His failure to repair relations with his family was expressed by his cryptic use of the name 'Tony Lumpkin' from this time on. Tony Lumpkin was a fictional character that featured in two well-known literary works that Morant would have been familiar with – Oliver Goldsmith's play *She Stoops To Conquer* and a recently published novel by E Sommerville and M Ross called *Some Experiences of an Irish R.M.*

Tony was said to 'look like a gentleman amongst stable boys and a stable boy amongst gentleman' and spent his life being doted on by his mother and at loggerheads with his stepfather. Despite his best efforts, Tony was never able to heal that rift.

Morant, no stranger to alienation by family, began using the name at the end of letters and would become to be known as 'Tony' Morant. But then again, Edwin Murrant had gone under many pseudonyms in his short but eventful life.

Morant's thoughts turned to South Africa. The talk everywhere was about the recent death of the beloved Queen Victoria and the war, which still rumbled on in South Africa months after General Roberts had declared it over. He was still holding an offer of a commission in Baden-Powell's Transvaal police, and was considering taking it up. Percy Hunt had already returned to South Africa; he'd joined the South African Mounted Irregulars – one of the 'special forces' that were now operating in the remote districts of the Transvaal. He wrote home to Morant and told him about a new unit called the Bushveldt Carbineers, which he intended to join. Morant knew it was time to rejoin the fray.

'Tony' Morant felt that if only he could do one more term of service and distinguish himself in the heat of battle, as his father had done in the Crimea, perhaps a Distinguished Service Order would melt the old boy's heart. But while the police commission offered relative safety, security and the prospect of promotion through the ranks, it did not offer the freedom and swashbuckling adventure his soul and reputation craved.

So as he had done eighteen years before, he kissed a woman goodbye on Plymouth quay and promised her he would return soon with his fortunes restored. He waved until she disappeared from sight, little knowing that the prodigal son would never return home.

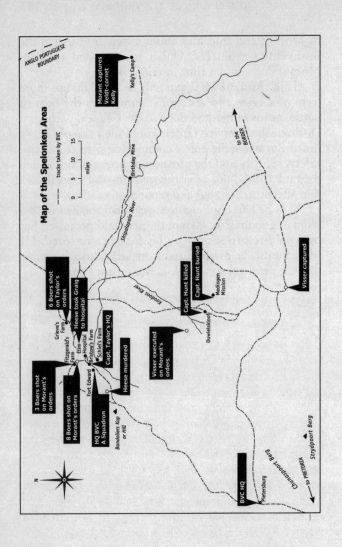

Map of the Spelonken Area

- - - - tracks taken by BVC

0 5 10 15
miles

Morant captures Veldt-cornet Kelly

Kelly's Camp

ANGLO PORTUGUESE BOUNDARY

Shipalapola River

Birthday Mine

to the BORDER

6 Boers shot on Taylor's orders

Grieve's Farm

Heese took Graig to hospital

Elim
Hospital
Fitzgerald's Farm
Bristow's Farm
Schiel's Farm

Capt. Taylor's HQ

Koodoos River

Capt. Hunt killed

Capt. Hunt buried

Medingen Mission

Duiwelskloof

Visser captured

3 Boers shot on Morant's orders

Fort Edward

Visser executed on Morant's orders

Heese murdered

8 Boers shot on Morant's orders

HQ BVC A Squadron

Bandoliers Kop or Hill

N

to PRETORIA

Chinaspoort Berg

Strydpoort Berg

BVC HQ

Pietersburg

7

The Dogs of War

Harry Morant was a friend I had
In the years long passed away,
A chivalrous, wild and reckless lad,
A knight born out of his day.

Full of romance and void of fears,
With a love of the world's applause,
He should have been one of the cavaliers
Who fought in King Charles's cause . . .

'Harry Morant' by Will Ogilvie

ONCE AGAIN THE GREAT PROMONTORY of Table Mountain announced to Harry Morant that he had arrived in South Africa. He never took up his commission in Baden-Powell's South African constabulary. Armed with his letter of recommendation from Colonel Reade, Morant approached Colonel McKay, the staff officer for the colonial troops, seeking work connected to the Australian units. McKay told him the war had taken a new turn since Morant had left South Africa.

Lord Roberts had left for England in November 1900, declaring that the war was 'practically over', but his claim was being rapidly reassessed in light of a renewed Boer resistance. Roberts had taken all the major population centres and the British laughingly described the government of the former Boer Republics as the 'Cape Cart' government, holding session on whichever kopje they camped and still tendering a worthless currency. However, they had not broken the Boers' fierce pride, and under Botha, Steyn, De Wet, De La Rey and a large number of able Boer field commanders, they still had the veldt.

The war had now entered a third distinct phase as the Boers reorganised and continued their fight using guerrilla tactics. Even as Roberts ploughed his way homewards across the Atlantic, the Boers were enjoying their first real success of the new campaign, De La Rey and Beyers routing General Clements at Nootgedacht.

As Roberts' successor as Commander-in-Chief, it had fallen to Lord Kitchener to finish the war, and it had taken on an increasingly bitter nature. It was felt amongst the troops, younger officers and the press that Roberts had been too gentlemanly towards the Boers. Kitchener was expected to be tougher. The *Black and White Budget* urged a repeat of England's most infamous and bloody military victory over the Scots:

> Now that Roberts has left, it is to be hoped that these people will be dealt with in the proper and only way. For months they have treated the British nation as people of 'Jugginses'. Now it is time to show the mercy exhibited at Culloden.

Captain David Miller wrote home with his opinion from the front: 'The Government should declare the war over and shoot anyone found with arms – this is the way to treat them.'

When his peace terms were rejected by the Boers at Middleburg in February 1901, Kitchener retaliated by unleashing a devastating total war against them. Like Roberts, he was also a Freemason, but never let it interfere with his declared intention of ending the war – one way or the other. Although he attained one of the highest ranks in the Masonic fraternity, it would appear

Kitchener viewed Freemasonry as a necessary social connection that could aid his rise through the ranks, rather than an expression of his own personal beliefs.

The advent of photography catalogued the human cost of war for the first time. Grainy black and white images of blazing farmhouses and the distraught faces of women and children being herded into detention camps where they died in their thousands betrayed the politicians' smooth speeches. No longer was the truth the preserve of the victor.

Kitchener also built an elaborate system of eight thousand blockhouses interconnected by ten thousand miles of barbed wire, which transformed the Transvaal into a series of grids to be systematically cleared one by one. These draconian measures were designed to deny the Boer guerrillas the food, shelter, space and mobility they had used to such great effect during the campaign.

Also, for the first time in its history, the British Army employed irregular units such as the 1st and 2nd Kitchener's Fighting Scouts and Steinaker's Horse to pacify the remote regions of Transvaal and quash any activity along the Portuguese border. It would be against this backdrop of an increasingly bitter war that the final act of Morant's military career would be played out.

Colonel McKay suggested that Morant pay a visit to a Major Robert Lenehan. He was recruiting an irregular unit to counter the Boer guerrillas in northern Transvaal. Morant's spirits lifted immediately. Lenehan was a name he knew well. They had known each other through the hunt clubs back in Australia, where Morant on Harlequin had raced Lenehan on Satan across half of New South Wales. Morant had even written a verse entitled *The Hunt Club at Windsor* to commemorate the visit of the Sydney Hunt Club, which included Paterson and Lenehan, to Windsor, where Morant was working as a journalist in 1898.

As MORANT ROUNDED HIS DOOR, *he saw the stocky, pugilistic figure of Major Lenehan hunched over a thick sheaf of papers. He was still sporting his walrus moustache but the rigors of active service had seen him shed a few pounds since they had last met in Sydney.*

'Robbo!' called Morant, and Lenehan, who had been absorbed in the papers in front of him, looked up, surprised to hear his nickname reverberating around the austere colonnades of Army HQ. But when he saw Harry's beaming phizog peeping round his door, he broke into a smile, rose from his seat and offered his hand.

'Harry! How are you, mate?'

'Good, mate . . . good,' replied Morant, who always enjoyed the informal way the Australians greeted everyone from the new Prime Minister to a tram conductor.

'What brings you to Pretoria?'

'This prodigal son has a burning desire to serve the Empire and restore the honour and glory of the motherland,' quipped Morant, clutching his slouch hat to his heart and rolling his eyes heavenwards.

'You've come to the right place then,' Lenehan said, motioning to a chair opposite him.

As Morant regaled him with tales of his recent trip to England, Lenehan recalled the last time they'd met.

A few years before, Morant had ridden Bay Lady for the Master of the Sydney Hunt Club, Colonel Airey, in an amateur steeplechase at Sydney's Randwick racecourse. During the race, Morant fell at a fence. But never one to waste a valuable social opportunity, he turned up bandaged and bruised to dinner and a theatre party, in a dress suit belonging to a man a size smaller than him.

Morant had obviously come up in the world since then. In his fashionably wide breeches, knee-length riding boots and smart uniform, he looked to be well set up and every inch the English gentleman he had always claimed to be.

LENEHAN TOLD MORANT ABOUT A LOCAL Jewish shop-keeper called Levy from Pienaars River who had proposed a local defence unit. Levy claimed that he had loyal British subjects ready to serve in a corps to subdue the Boers in that area and contributed £500 to the venture. At that point, the British had only penetrated as far as Nylstrom. Between there and the Rhodesian border, the Boer commandos ran wild.

Provost Marshal Robert Poore was charged with the task of forming an irregular unit, which became known as the Bushveldt Carbineers. In his diary, Poore notes that the only way to defeat the Boers was to ruthlessly fight them on their own terms, and recalls:

> A man called Levy came to see me, he had been sent by Lord Kitchener to raise a corps called the Bushveldt Mounted Rifles . . . and I am supposed to organise the corps . . . After dinner I went to the Transvaal Hotel to discuss the raising of the Bushveldt Mounted Rifles . . . I set forth the object of the corps and the proposed composition . . . At Lord Kitchener's instigation I am forming a Boer Commando of those who have surrendered voluntarily, their object is to loot from the enemy.

Although the new unit came into being on February 21, 1901 as the Bushveldt Mounted Rifles, the name was changed to the more familiar Bushveldt Carbineers two days later. Lieutenant Peter Handcock, with whom Morant would later become acquainted, was one of the first to join on February 28. Poore noted what proved to be a rare show of unity in this unhappy corps: 'I arranged to have the Bushveldt Carbineers sent North . . . they were entrained at 6 pm, I went to see them and found them all singing.'

However, Surgeon James Kay, who like Provost Marshal Poore was destined to play an important cameo in the denouement of the Carbineers, tells of the real, less-than-patriotic reasons for Levy's generosity. In his journal dated October–December he noted:

> The original mover in the raising of this corps was a canteen keeper who subscribed 500 pounds towards equipment, and as a reward he was transformed from a publican to a Captain and paymaster. Within a week of donning his uniform he applied for liquor licenses at all (the ten) stations between Pretoria and Pietersberg and was both surprised and indignant when his 'mild' request was refused.

The British had attributed the general good behaviour of their troops to the lack of alcohol, so Levy didn't get his grog licence and only thirty of his 'loyal British subjects' came forward to serve King and country. The original idea of filling the ranks with loyal subjects and disaffected Boers failed to produce enough bodies, and Major Lenehan, who had distinguished himself with General Anderson's mounted infantry units, was made field commander and ordered to start a recruitment drive. Newspaper advertisements were placed seeking 'Recruits who can ride and shoot . . . For Special Service in Northern Districts of Transvaal'.

However, even the lure of 'special inducements' (pay of 7/- per day, 2/- above the regular colonial rate) failed to boost numbers to full strength. Lenehan suggested to Kitchener that he recruit time-expired Australians. Kitchener agreed, as he believed that the colonials were better suited to this type of work than the British militia or yeomanry whose mishaps only 'gave heart' to the Boers. Harry Morant had happened along at an opportune moment.

Knowing Morant to be an excellent horseman and a seasoned bushman, Lenehan agreed to make him a Lieutenant in the new unit. He sent him north to Pietersburg on the next train. Ironically, Morant signed on for service with the Bushveldt Carbineers on April 1, 1901 – eighteen years to the day since he set sail for Australia. April Fool's Day would again mark a major turning-point in his life.

Roughly forty-five per cent[†] of the Bushveldt Carbineers (BVC) were Australians and they contributed all but two of the officers. The rest of the unit was made up of various Boers, Americans, New Zealanders, Canadians, Germans, Rhodesians and British. However, whilst the character of the unit was Australian, its origins were Imperial.

Because of the problems of raising men for such service, and the resultant high turnover, the BVC never reached its proposed full strength of 500. During the eight months the unit was in existence, it only used some 630 men in total, with no more than 350 on the roll at any one time. One of the reasons for its unruly reputation and bitter demise was that they took whomever they could get. Adjutant James HV Edwards, an Australian from Orange, New South Wales, joined the BVC at the outset and said of some of the other recruits:

> The Carbineers are composed of a mixed lot, the pickings of the men of every corps who were left behind . . . In fact, I might add that many of the men

† *Percentage calculated by adding together the number of men who enrolled in the BVC and who were either born in Australia, resident in Australia, or gave their next of kin as living in Australia. Morant was counted as an Australian. Of the 630 men that signed up for the BVC, there were 141 Australians out of a typical unit strength of around 350.*

forming the BVC had been charged – when in other contingents – with shooting surrendered Boers, had been court-martialled and still got off.

The BVC was based at the Pietersburg garrison along with the 2nd Wiltshires, 2nd Gordon Highlanders, the Highland Mounted Infantry and a section of the Royal Garrison Artillery. Lieutenant-Colonel Francis Henry Hall of the Royal Artillery was made Commander Lines of Communication for the BVC. His was a desk job, with the fieldwork being left to Major Lenehan. Hall's service record shows he was a seasoned soldier with plenty of field experience. He had spent thirty years as an artillery officer and saw action in India, Afghanistan and South Africa. He was mentioned three times in dispatches during the South African campaign.

Kitchener had decided that it was time to carry the fight into the remote parts of Transvaal, where the Boer guerrillas operated freely. The BVC had acted as scouts ahead of Plumer's mixed force of 2nd Wiltshires and 2nd Gordons.

The brutal pattern of this phase of the war was established during the first major action the BVC was involved in. On April 8, 1901, the BVC was involved in the taking of Pietersburg which until recently had been the Boer seat of government and the last remaining large town under Boer control. During the occupation, a Boer sniper picked off two Tasmanian Bushmen, Captain AA Sale and Lieutenant CH Walker, then, as their mates stormed the sniper's nest, he calmly stood up, threw aside his gun, put his hands up and called out 'I surrender!'. The on-rushing troops took no notice and ran him right through with their bayonets. The victim, GC Kooijker, was a local schoolteacher who had taken up arms and, in the view of the Tasmanians, deserved no quarter, even though the *Army Act* specified that he should be treated as a prisoner of war as soon as he surrendered. The Australian Bushmen and the New Zealanders then sacked Pietersburg like some barbarian horde.

This was followed two months later on June 6 by the razing of Louis Trichardt some ninety miles north of Pietersburg. Captain Alfred Taylor, who would play no small part in the controversy that was about to unfold in northern Transvaal, did this on Kitchener's orders. It proved to be a bad omen for the BVC campaign in those remote territories.

Morant began his tour of duty in charge of No. 2 troop of B Squadron, defending the south-eastern passes at Strydpoort and Chunesport. Based at an out-post commanded by Major MacDonald of the 2nd Wiltshires, he raided farms used by the local Boer commandos under the leadership of Veldt-cornet Beyers. Morant proved to be an excellent choice as leader and the experience he accumulated during sixteen hard years in the Australian outback served him well. Living off the land and Boer beef, they travelled light and often rode through the night so they could attack the Boers at first light whilst they were still in *laager*. He soon had a string of prisoners and herds of cattle to his name. The Boers came to fear Morant and kept well away from his 'beat'. Major Lenehan later said of Morant during this period, 'I was glad to have him serving under me . . . he was just the man for the job.' In an early letter to Lenehan, Morant seemed to be happy enough with his lot.

Strydespoort
9/5/1901

Just an unofficial note to let you know my where-abouts, Midgley is 16 miles E. of me with a troop. I am 30m. S.S.W of Pietersburg with another troop.

Patrolling the country on damned awful bits of
horseflesh. But with judicious nursing I've got the
horses a lot fitter and better than when they were
supplied to us. On my way over from Pietersburg I
heard of 5 Boers, armed and in a very nasty position to attack, in a terraced kloof. As our horses
then could hardly raise a walk, I should hardly have
been able to snap them – certainly not without the
loss of some men, so I came on to camp and
reported them to Major MacDonald of the Wilts
here; and, leaving camp at 3a.m. next morning we
got the five. Surprised them at daybreak. Got 'em
without any loss. Five Mausers and whips o' ammunition. There are other Boers reported about. With
luck we'll secure their scalps. As I said, our horses
are greatly improved, but if you can get us better
ones for the Lord's sake do so. I'm using natives
(Kaffir boys) as much as possible to save horseflesh . . . The men I've got here are very satisfactory.
Eland is an excellent sergeant and the Afrikander
troopers are invaluable owing to their thorough
knowledge of Dutch and Kaffir.

Morant became good friends with Sergeant Frank
Eland, a rare Irishman who had sided with the Imperial cause. He and Morant enjoyed hunting and went on
a number of anti-guerrilla missions together. Morant's
swashbuckling, no-nonsense style made him popular
with his men and Eland recalled how the men of
B Squadron turned out to cheer Morant as he went
past with a patrol. Again, there was no hint of trouble
or the drama that lay ahead. He had picked up where
he left off on his first tour of duty. The atmosphere in
B Squadron was described as 'cheerful'.

On July 5, Eland noted they were paraded and new
orders from Kitchener read out. They were told that 'as
the enemy persisted in holding out it behoved every

officer, NCO and man to use any endeavour to put an end to armed resistance'.

Although 'any endeavour' was not clearly defined, in the context of Kitchener's increasingly severe prosecution of the war, it became clear that the BVC had been recruited for these remote regions at a higher rate of pay to undertake a different class of work than that of the regular troops. This new *diktat* came in the wake of one of the most infamous Boer actions of the war at Naboomspruit, which would bring Hunt and Morant together at last.

THE TOWN OF NABOOMSPRUIT IS *roughly halfway between Pretoria and Pietersburg. It was an unremarkable small town where the close-knit local farming community came to sell their livestock and produce and exchange news. However, as the town clock chimed at 2 pm on July 4, 1901 and a supply train with an armed escort of 2nd Battalion Gordon Highlanders pulled out of its neat, white-washed, colonial-style station bound for Pietersburg, Naboomspruit was about to claim its place in history. As the train disappeared into the distance beneath a blanket of acrid black coal smoke, the telegraph wire above trembled as the news of its departure was broadcast up the line to Pietersburg.*

Julius Brand sat back in his saddle, as he often did, watching the white whispers of cloud drift aimlessly across the endless horizon. The wide, dry, brown veldt was dappled with soft winter sunshine. A sudden breeze rippled the long, dry strands of khaki-coloured spinifex grass, disturbing a lone 'bok which suddenly popped its head up out of the grass. Although its fawn coat was excellent camouflage, certain predators enjoyed a similar advantage. It immediately swivelled its black and white-patterned head, crowned by a set of magnificent horns, looking and listening for a tell-tale rustle of grass or a sudden blur of movement. Very wise my friend. You never know who's waiting for you. *Brand smiled at the obvious analogy and nodded his head as he continued his survey.* This is God's country right enough. Even the rooinecks knew it.

Brand released a brown stream of tobacco juice onto the hard pan of the veldt as he dragged his mind back to the more practical matter of ensuring that it would still belong to the volk at the end of this war. The pale sun was suspended in a clear sky just at his shoulder and he knew the train would be along soon. It was time to position his men. That thought was confirmed by the raised thumb of one who had shinned up the nearest telegraph pole and intercepted the telegraph message from Naboomspruit. Stupid rooinecks. Still hadn't realised we were tapping their wires and leading them a merry dance.

Brand raised his arm and motioned for his force, which numbered some one hundred and fifty, to move forwards. He might be the son of the former President of the Orange Free State, but that didn't guarantee their respect. His rag-tag army pointedly finished their conversations and moved in their own time, which was typical of the stubborn Boer attitude to authority. Like him, they were bearded and dressed in a threadbare collection of ancient greatcoats and jackets, patched trousers and an assortment of footwear, all of which had seen better days. There was even a smattering of flour-sack jackets, which De Wet had made popular. It would never have caught on during peacetime, but in times of war, needs must. Their dishevelled sartorial state belied the fact that they were amongst the best commandos in the Transvaal, and all cradled Mausers to prove it. These were Conan Doyle's 'tough frontiersmen living in a land where dinner was shot, not bought'.

'Jack man, have you set the charges?' *asked Brand, his English heavily accented by Afrikaans.*

'Aye, man, ready to go,' replied the slight, sandy-haired Scotsman who crouched down before him coiling the trigger wire that led down to the charge he had laid on the railway line.

Thirteen years after drummer boy Jack Hindon deserted from the British Army, he still had a distinctive Scots burr and he still preferred the fashionably British handlebar moustache to the full set of whiskers favoured by the Boers. But no-one doubted his loyalty. In one famous incident, he and two other scouts had held the Boer line and prevented the early relief of Ladysmith. He was now veldt-cornet of a Boer commando and had become the infamous British turncoat who wreaked havoc along the Delagoa Bay and Pretoria lines. He had once wrecked three trains in the one morning.

The railways were vital to the British and the Boer war effort. They were the principal means of reinforcing and supplying their huge army. The British had stuck close to the tracks as they advanced through South Africa and Viljoen once joked that the British would never leave the railways because they would be deprived of condensed milk for their tea. Looted supplies from wrecked trains also helped sustain the Boer campaign, especially since the British cut their access to Delagoa Bay and the outside world.

The Provost Marshal vowed that he would see the treasonous Hindon dance at the end of a hangman's noose. The railway men of the military had vowed to 'fling him into the firebox of the nearest engine' should they catch up with him. In a captured camp newspaper, Hindon had seen with his own eyes Kitchener's printed orders: if he or any of his wreckers were caught, they were not to be taken prisoner.

White plumes appeared on the horizon like Red Indian smoke signals to announce the arrival of the train, and Hindon knew the price on his head was about to go up.

They heard the asthmatic wheeze of the furiously puffing engine before they saw it round the bend dragging four carriages into the deep cutting where they had set the trap. Brand's intelligence told him that the soldiers would be in the rear compartment. Hindon saw that their car was not armoured, coiled his hand around the wire to take up the last of the slack and studied the approaching train with the focused intensity of a big-game hunter. Hindon had picked out a spot on the rails. He would pull the wire and detonate the charge as soon as the front wheels passed over it.

The usual so-called 'Cremer method', invented by and named after a German wrecker in Hindon's unit, was to wedge a bag of dynamite and a Martini-Henry rifle, with its barrel and trigger guard sawn off, just under the tracks. The rifle fired as the weight of the locomotive passing overhead depressed the trigger, and the bullet detonated the dynamite.

It was not one hundred per cent reliable, and this newer manual detonation method and the ambush that followed were both Hindon's inventions – designed to improve the accuracy and effectiveness of the blast and to rupture the armour-plated steel that usually protected the troop carriage.

Inside, the twenty men of the King's Gordon Highlanders and the three soldier passengers were totally unaware of the maelstrom that was about to engulf them. They were engrossed in a penny card game when Jack Hindon expertly blew their engine's wheel piston with a sharp tug of his wrist. The crippled train came screeching to a halt as it left the tracks and ploughed into gravel and hard-baked earth, pitching the Gordons on top of each other.

They were still scrambling for their helmets and guns when one hundred and fifty Boers stood up on the high banks on either side of them and fired down into the train below. It was like shooting at a watermelon. Their explosive dum-dums, designed to expand on impact to do maximum damage, pierced the thin metal skin, and judging by the screams and cries from within, they were finding their mark with deadly accuracy.

Within minutes, the Gordons' carriage resembled a butcher's slab, slicked red with the blood that flowed freely from great gaping wounds out of which bone, muscle and sinew rudely protruded. Amid the stench of burning flesh and cordite mingled with sweat and an almost palpable sense of fear, the living stumbled over the wounded and the dying who screamed and thrashed around on the floor. It seemed that every whine of a Mauser swelled the ranks of the cabaret macabre below them. Their shouted gibberish was lost in the cacophony of screams, ricochets and volleys of gunfire they poured blindly into the sun, which the Boers used to maximum effect.

After five minutes of sustained fire, Brand held up his hand and it stopped after a fashion – a few cursing him for not letting them finish the rooinecks off there and then. Fingers were eased off triggers and Mausers red-hot from continuous firing lowered from shoulders as an uneasy silence descended over the carnage below.

Brand cupped his hands together and called, 'You are surrounded, surrender now!'

Inside the car, Lieutenant Alexander Archibald Dunlop Best, commander of the Gordons' unit, had sustained a wound to his leg, but his only thought was to get the engine moving and to pull them clear of this murderous fire.

Given the insurmountable odds, the most sensible thing to do would be to surrender, but he couldn't, even if he had wanted to. 'Surrender' was not a word that featured in the long and illustrious military tradition of the Gordon Highlanders. The Gordons refused to abandon their guns at Leekoehoek, despite the retreat being ordered by Kitchener. Their commander, Colonel MacBean, sent them in to get the guns after dark. Many, including Captain Younger, died, but they retrieved the guns.

When General Smith-Dorien visited the gallant wounded Gordons, he met Private Docherty who got a Distinguished Conduct Medal for his bravery during this action. When told he had done very well, he replied, 'Aye, we may have done weel eneuch, but ay dinnane haud wi yon rinnin' awa'.'

'Running away?' exclaimed Smith-Dorien 'We retired by order of the Commander-in-Chief.'

'Aye sir, you'll mibee ca' it retirin', but I ca' it rinnin' awa'!'

Infused with the spirit of Docherty, Best raised himself up and shouted, 'No surrender' defiantly through a broken window. Rushing for the door, he called for covering fire. Brand was in no mood for heroes and a thunderous volley of gunfire from both sides of the cutting answered Lieutenant Best's bold move. Despite his gallantry, Best never made the engine. He was cut down by two Boer bullets and died instantly on the trackside.

Seeing their lieutenant go down, the Gordons tried to fight their way out of the car after him but sustained heavy losses in the process. There were only four left by the time they got down onto the tracks, and despite having no cover and being completely surrounded, they kept firing. Finally, twenty minutes after the ambush began, the last Gordon fell forwards and the Boers ceased firing.

An eerie silence descended on the carnage below as Mars, the god of war, rumbled away across the veldt, the only sound now the soft moans and sobs of the wounded.

'Crazy Scotchmen,' muttered Brand, then paused to look over at Hindon. His work was over once the piston was blown and he'd watched the carnage below impassively. These were his countrymen they had slaughtered. Brand had ordered the execution of brother Boers who were caught working for the British, but always with a heavy heart. He detected no flicker of emotion in Hindon's face. Handlebar moustache and slight Scots burr apart, he had burned all his bridges.

As he waited for the pall of gunsmoke that had gathered in the hollow below to clear, he wondered what turns a man into a traitor – money, hatred, revenge, or the simple realisation that you agreed more with the philosophy of your adversaries than your own side? This cursed war had taxed the loyalty of many men. There were English, Irish, Boers and Americans fighting on both sides, so why not Scots? The English had also taken their land and they owed no loyalty to the British crown.

He led his men down into the cutting where Private Nicholl, one of the four who had made it onto the tracks, lay on his back with a pool of blood, as crimson as an African sunset, radiating out around him. He'd been shot through the lungs and was breathing heavily, but was still alive. But his final day was fast drawing to a close. Poking him with the toe of his boot, Brand said, 'Hey, man, why didn't you surrender? You were surrounded.'

Using the last of his precious energy, the young private raised himself up on one elbow so he could look Brand in the eye, and said defiantly in a thick and impenetrable Highland accent, which, he noted, had none of Hindon's soft lowland lilt, ''Cause we're the Gordon Highlanders min.'

Brand just nodded. These were the Transvaalers of Scotland and he knew them to be fearsome warriors *who would never give up easily. But whatever momentary respect he felt for that young private was soon forgotten as the Boers counted five of their own dead and rounded up the survivors. With emotions still running high and talk of vengeance still hot on their lips, things got a little out of hand and the badly wounded Private Aitken was shot in cold blood for not putting up his hands quickly enough. As night drew a discrete veil over the terrible carnage, Brand paraded the fireman, the driver, the guard and two natives who had been on the train and read them their last rites.*

'You people have helped our enemy take our land and kill our people as if you yourselves had carried guns. For this you will die as a warning to the others who come after you.'

Before they could protest, they were mowed down where they stood by a volley of gunfire.

The Boers then stripped the dead and looted the living before ransacking and setting fire to the train. They then melted into the darkness without offering the remaining four wounded Gordons so much as a drink of water. Help finally arrived at 10 pm, but Private Nicholl died of his wounds a few days later.

NEWS OF THE NABOOMSPRUIT massacre was received with dismay and anger at Army HQ. Kitchener flew into one of his famous rages and locked himself away in a darkened room for three days. This is what his staff called 'churching it'. He would stay in there and refuse to eat or to see anyone. The only person who could coax him out was 'the Brat', aka aide-de-camp Frank Maxwell, and things would return to normal, until the next disaster. However, disaster was turned into glory when news came in of the Gordons' heroic resistance.

On August 10, 1901, Lord Kitchener cabled King Edward VII, who was the Colonel-in-Chief of the Gordon Highlanders:

> As C-in-C of the Gordon Highlanders Your Majesty may be pleased to know that Commandant de Villiers who was present and who has just surrendered informs me that at the attack on the train on 4th July at Namboomspruit the guard of Gordon Highlanders under Best, who was killed, behaved with upmost gallantry. After the train had been captured by 150 Boers the last 4 men though completely surrounded and with no cover continued to fire until they were killed and the forth wounded. On Boers asking the survivor the reason they had not surrendered, he replied, 'Why man we are the Gordon Highlanders.'

The King replied on August 12:

> Delighted to hear of the gallant conduct of the Gordon Highlanders. Proud to be their C-in-C.

Naboomspruit was written into the annals of Gordon history, alongside their fixed bayonet charge at Doornkop that owed more to the 14th than the 20th century. The sight of those kilted Valkyries bearing down on them with fixed bayonets and skirling pipes put the Boers to flight and moved *The Morning Leader* to proclaim, 'There was no doubt that they are the finest regiment in the world'.

Much to the chagrin of those who performed so heroically at the defence of Elands River, but received nothing for their courage, a rare medal was struck with King Edward's head on one side and a Highlander on the other, inscribed with the immortal words of the wounded man: 'Because I'm a Gordon Highlander.'

ON JULY 7, SERGEANT ELAND MENTIONS in a letter to his wife that Morant was very cut up when the news of the Gordons' disaster reached them. Lieutenant Best had been a good mate of both Hunt and Morant. The mood of the patrol that Morant led in search of Brand and his brigands that night was clear to Eland: 'the Boers who outnumbered our fellows nearly twenty to one seem to have shot men down in cold blood. If we had come up with that party of Boers that night we would not have taken any prisoners.'

However, as will be illustrated later, the Gordons proved more than capable of getting their own revenge. But as Morant later testified in court, the Naboomspruit incident was an important factor in his decision to start shooting prisoners. It also illustrated the brutal nature of the guerrilla warfare that was taking place in the Transvaal and that vengeance was something taken by units other than the BVC.

Naboomspruit was also the last straw for Kitchener. Although he had managed to give the slaughter of the Gordons a positive spin, it was a serious blow to his pride to have to inform the King of a major Boer success in a war that was supposed to be over. The press and the government were turning up the pressure on him to finish the war, whilst tying one hand behind his back. Almost monthly he inundated London with requests to take ever more drastic measures against those who continued the struggle, and every month they refused. The new rising stars of the army had been selected from Kitchener's inner circle – men like Colonel Henry Rawlinson, who had no doubt about what should be done:

> This war is fast degenerating into some kind of dacoit hunt we used to have in Burma. The Boer is becoming just as cold-blooded a ruffian as the dacoit was and his wholesale slaughter of

Kaffirs . . . has I think forfeited his right to be considered a belligerent. I found four Kaffir boys none
of them over 12 years of age with their heads
broken in by the Boers and left in the kraal of their
fathers. Strong measures will be required to stop this
slaughter.

But neither the slaughter nor the train-wrecking
stopped. In fact, their success at Naboomspruit only
encouraged the Boers. There was a second attack on the
same line on August 10, 1901 using the same ambush
tactic. This time, however, the Gordons' escort was in
an armoured car and drove off the Boers. A third serious
incident on the Pretoria to Pietersburg line came
on August 31 at Waterval – only eight weeks after
Naboomspruit and three weeks after the failed attack
on the Gordons.

A large provision train from Pretoria was delivering
supplies to all stations along the line to Pietersburg.
Between Waterval and Haman's Kraal the train slowed
suddenly as they saw a native running alongside the
track waving at them. The warning came too late. A
large explosion sent trucks flying into the air. As they
had done at Naboomspruit, the Boers fired into the train
until all resistance had been crushed. One officer, twelve
soldiers and two natives died. The twenty wounded
were then dragged from the wreckage and stripped of
all their weapons and clothing. A trooper then described
what happened to the two ladies with babies and a nurse
who had also been on the train:

The Boers took all their money and valuables and
their clothes and even the little babies clothing
and left them nearly naked. Then, as I lay wounded,
I saw a young Boer go up to the nurse and tell her
to hand over her money which she hesitated to
do . . . The Boer then deliberately shot her through

the body. I shall never forget the woman's screams. It has been ringing in my ears ever since. How I longed to get up and knock the brute but my wounds would not allow me.

After they had finished their task of murdering they set fire to the train and burnt everything they could not carry away with them.

Despite Kitchener's protestations, train-wrecking was not a new ploy. The Boers had employed it to great effect during Roberts' command and made a hero of a young, red-headed correspondent called Winston Churchill who was captured helping to save a train from wreckers at Chievely. Kitchener also received a legal opinion from Judge Advocate General, Colonel James St Clair that said train-wrecking was not illegal. Veteran Boer Commandant Ben Viljoen retorted that the British had no room for complaint, as General Woolsley himself had recommended its use in his handbook on the methods of warfare. Nonetheless, train-wrecking, more than any other single activity, increased the bitterness between Boer and Briton.

It was the BVC who found an ingenious, if brutal, solution to the problem during their advance towards Pietersburg under General Plumer when they adopted a tactic first used thirty years previously by the Germans in the Franco–Prussian War. The BVC put small groups of burghers in a wagon in front of the engine to discourage wreckers. Roberts had tried the same tactic following the fall of Pretoria twelve months before, but the resultant uproar in Britain had forced him to abandon it. However, Kitchener confided to one of his fellow officers, 'We may have to start doing this.' A British officer again objected to the renewed use of civilians as 'human shields', as it clearly contravened the *Army Act* and every human rights convention that came before and after it. However, attitudes had hardened considerably in the year since it was last tried and it soon became official policy as the Gordon Highlanders, who had borne the brunt of many wreckings, noted: 'From today (September 10th) two prominent burghers are to travel on every train (to prevent wrecking). The first train under these orders arrived today.'

Although it was an illegal order and against the conventions of war, Provost-Marshal Robert Poore's only complaint was not about its legality, but its effectiveness:

> Everybody is very keen about putting people (Boers) on trains but I think out here it is all nonsense. The Germans put influential Frenchmen on trains, these men were mayors and men with some influence, but out here the only Boers in our hands are what their fellow Boers call 'Hands Uppers' and consequently are men with no weight at all, and more than that the Boers in the field would enjoy putting a bullet into them, I therefore consider it more of an encouragement than otherwise.

Poore was proved wrong and the Boers were forced to stop train-wrecking after they blew up a few of their own civilians. To Boer War historian Arthur Conan Doyle, this tough policy was long overdue:

> Considering that these tactics were continued for over a year and that they resulted in the death or mutilation of many hundreds of British officers and men, it really is inexplicable that the British authorities did not employ the means used by all armies under such circumstances – which is to place hostages upon the trains. A truckload of Boers behind every engine would have stopped the practice forever. Again and again in this war the British have fought with the gloves when their opponents used their knuckles.

Colonel Rawlinson, one of Kitchener's up-and-coming officers, agreed with Doyle and also recommended executing 'cold-blooded ruffians' like the Boers out of hand. 'It will be no congenial task to fight white men under those conditions, but I do not see there is any alternative . . . it is certainly best for the future peace of the country.'

But Kitchener had hardened his policy not just to please the military and the chroniclers, but because his own position was under threat. As we have seen, he had bombarded London with radical ideas for ending the war on a monthly basis, but as Provost Marshal Poore noted on June 30, 1901:

> I'm afraid Lord K. isn't getting much encouragement from home, they say they have changed their policy so often that they don't feel disposed to change it any more, so we are to proceed in the old, old way, so now it's quite certain the war will not end as soon as we expected and further it's pretty certain Lord K. will not go home when Lord Milner comes out. So we must simply face the future.

For Kitchener to be removed from the field like that old war-horse Buller was unthinkable and would dash any dream he had of becoming Viceroy of India. He knew drastic steps were necessary and although London was not aware of it, he had instructed other irregular units to 'take no prisoners'.

From both recorded and anecdotal evidence, which will be presented later in this book, it is clear that Kitchener had taken the decision at a meeting of his 'inner-circle' early on in his command. There were frequent meetings to discuss tactics, intelligence and discipline. Discipline in the field was constantly reassessed as the situation deteriorated. For example, there were Boer abuses of the white flag and the use of British khaki to lure British troops into ambushes.

It was the job of the Provost Marshal to report back on such issues so that new local edicts, reflecting the current realities, could be issued. The prevailing feeling amongst both the officers and the ranks was that Roberts had been too soft on the Boers, especially after they had issued their own orders to take no prisoners. De Wet made a proclamation on October 6, 1900 stating that British soldiers caught burning farms or deporting women and children to camps are to be shot. De Wet's own farm was destroyed by British troops.

KITCHENER LOOKED ROUND THE TABLE *at the dozen or so men whose responsibility it was to deliver a quick victory. Amongst them were Major-General Kelly, the big, bluff Irishman who was his deputy, Major Robert Poore, Provost Marshal, Lieutenant-Colonel Birdwood and Colonel David Henderson, Director of Intelligence – all good men who knew the realities of war.*

They discussed how Boer tactics such as trainwrecking, wearing khaki and the white flag had been used to lure British soldiers to their deaths and resulted in certain units, like the Canadian Scouts, seeking vengeance. The Canadians' popular leader, 'Gat' (Gattling Gun) Howard, had just been shot in cold blood when he went to accept a white flag from the Boers. They had joined together and vowed to take no more prisoners, regardless of orders from HQ.

Then there was the issue of prisoners. The war was now being fought on lots of isolated fronts by small mobile units, often with no base. Getting supplies to them was difficult enough without having to cater for Boers and then tie up men to bring them in. One of the greatest criticisms levelled at Roberts was that this system allowed the Boers to surrender, rest up and then go back out to join their commando again.

The nature of the war had clearly changed and new rules were needed to deal with its ongoing realities. The Army Act didn't cover some of the situations that they were now having to face. They had been forced to constantly change their field tactics in South Africa and now they would again have to adapt to the new rules. Doing nothing could be dangerous. Given the nature of war, men seeking vengeance would take matters into their own hands and should it come to light, the Provost Marshal would have to arrest and courts martial them. It was difficult enough getting men for the BVC and such a scenario would make the irregulars less willing to end this wretched war. Better to harness that malign energy in the great cause.

Kitchener fixed them with his steely blue eyes. 'So, gentlemen, we are agreed. Irregular units are to be instructed to take no prisoners. No quarter is to be given to Boers surrendering, waving white flags or wearing khaki and we make it known that any man who does so will be protected.'

IN LIGHT OF THE EVENTS AT Naboomspruit, Kitchener decided that it was time to convey this information to the BVC. He knew Hunt had suffered a deep personal loss at Naboomspruit, and just a week afterwards, in this highly charged atmosphere, was about to take charge of A Squadron of the BVC. He would be another willing conduit for his unofficial policy to end the war.

THE OPPORTUNITY TO TACKLE Hunt presented itself the night before he headed north. Hunt had arrived at HQ to deliver two polo ponies that Kitchener had bought from him. Like Morant, Hunt was a celebrated horseman who bought and trained polo ponies. It was during this visit that he was issued with the controversial orders by Kitchener's ever-faithful chief of staff, Lieutenant-Colonel Hubert Hamilton, who had served him in Egypt.

Seeing Hunt out at the stables, he slipped out into the darkness on the pretext that he was going out for his evening constitutional. It was a cold, still night illuminated only by a half moon and a soft twinkling from the bejewelled heavens. There was no sound bar the nocturnal chorus of crickets, punctuated by the odd laugh or shout from the silhouettes huddled round the native campfire. Satisfied no-one would overhear them, Hamilton approached Hunt, who was stroking the long nose of one of the ponies he'd delivered to Kitchener.

'Evening, Percy,' said Hamilton lightheartedly.

'Evening, Colonel,' replied Hunt, continuing to pat the muzzle of the bay who had become his favourite.

'Grown quite attached to them, I see,' observed Hamilton, standing next to Hunt.

'Very. Lovely ride. Ideal for a bit of rough and tumble on the polo field,' Hunt expanded.

Drawing in a sharp, nervous breath, Hamilton drew closer to avoid having to raise his voice, 'The chief asked me to pass on his best wishes for your new posting and to inform you that . . . there has been a change of tactics you should be aware of.'

There was nothing in what Hamilton had said to alarm Hunt, and he continued to pet the horse. Hamilton pressed on.

'That dreadful incident with the Gordons sent the chief wild . . .'

As he suspected it would, the mention of Naboomspruit hit a raw nerve. Hunt turned to Hamilton, his face already clouded with rage.

'I'll bloody say. Archie . . . Lieutenant Best, was a damned decent sort and the bloody Boers responsible will be brought to book yet, mark my words.'

Hunt's eyes blazed with anger but he bit his lip, realising he was cursing a senior officer, and Hamilton moved on smoothly.

'Yes, the chief mentioned Best's dash when he cabled the King. Sorry old chap. The Johnnies have been getting a bit full of themselves lately. Train-wrecking is the work of brigands, not soldiers and . . .'

'They deserve to be strung up, the lot of them,' said Hunt, *finishing Hamilton's sentence while staring morosely out into the darkness.*

'Exactly what the chief said,' added Hamilton *reassuringly. Having steered the conversation to where he wanted it, he got straight to the point.* 'The lot you will encounter up north are of the same ilk so when you take charge of the Carbineers you are instructed to treat all Boers as hostiles. By that I mean do not allow them to surrender. White flags and the wearing of khaki have been used to lure our chaps into an ambush on many occasions and should be ignored. Spies should also be dealt with summarily.'

Hamilton let his statement hang heavy in the air whilst Hunt stared at him for a moment then simply said, 'I leave in the morning.'

Hamilton nodded and held out his hand, 'Godspeed Percy and good hunting. Captain Taylor's a good man. He'll keep you right.'

Hamilton, well used to making these clandestine missions on Kitchener's behalf, scurried back through the darkness to warm himself wordlessly at the log fire that burned in the hearth of the officers' mess.

Up at the crack of dawn, as usual, to deal with cables and correspondence, Hamilton and Kitchener watched Hunt ride out from the breakfast table together. Hamilton nervously tapped at his hard-boiled egg as he considered the possible ramifications of the new orders he had given Hunt. It was a bold tactical move, a radical *departure from London's softly, softly approach which had frustrated their efforts to finish the war.*

'*That man could be either the making or the ruin of us,*' *mused Kitchener intercepting Hamilton's anxious semaphore with a remarkable perception that only served to further unnerve him.*

CAPTAIN HUNT WAS NOT THE ONLY one in the BVC who had received special orders. On July 2, two days before Naboomspruit, there was a meeting of officers of the BVC A Squadron at Sweetwaters Farm. Sweetwaters was over a hundred miles north of Strydpoort, where Morant was serving at the time. Orders were given for a unit to meet and shoot an incoming group of six Boers surrenderers. Under no circumstances were they to be brought in alive.

The character of A Squadron was very different to that of Morant's. Following the capture of Pietersburg, his had been ordered northwards to counter the Boer commandos in an area of Zoutpansberg known as the Spelonken. Rugged, mountainous, semi-tropical and malarial, the environment was as about as welcoming as its inhabitants – tough farmers living right on the very edge of white civilisation, nothing between them and Rhodesia to the north but inhospitable terrain and war-like native tribes. The men the BVC were up against were a very different type of fighting man, strange even to the Boers. The Boer Commandant Dennys Reitz described a meeting between Ben Viljoen and his officers:

> The astonishing assemblage looked very much like a cannibal fancy dress meeting. One officer wore a jacket of monkey skin, hair to the outside, another officer a jacket of leopard skin. One looked like a cross between Attila the Hun and Sancho Panza. Others wore garments of sheep, goat and deerskin,

and of green baize and gaudily clad Kaffir blankets.
Quite evidently the apparel does not here proclaim
the man.

Conan Doyle described the Zoutpansbergers as:

> Shaggy, hairy half savage men, handling a rifle as a
> medieval Englishman handled a bow and skilled in
> every wile of veldt craft, they were formidable
> opponents as the world could show. They were
> known as takhaaren who were strange and wild to
> other Boers. Even Boer leader Schikerling said,
> 'These people are wretched indeed — some I am told
> hardly till the soil, subsisting mainly on stam
> vruchten and other wild fruits and even eating
> monkeys.'

The controversial order to shoot the incoming Boers
was issued by Captain Alfred Taylor.

An Irishman by birth, he'd settled in Rhodesia as a
young man and prospected for gold in remote areas.
Although he hated natives, his greatest attribute was his
knowledge of their many dialects and customs. After he
helped guide Rhodes into Rhodesia, he then helped
crush the Matabele uprisings. In 1893 he was a scout,
but by 1896 he was commanding a unit of Plumer's
Scouts, which also became known as Taylor's Scouts.
Before the outbreak of the South African war, Rhodes
also used Taylor's unique talents in the Spelonken in yet
another effort to destabilise the Transvaal. His orders
were to offer local tribes support if they would rise
against the Boers.

The war in South Africa again saw Taylor active in
the Spelonken. He and a few hand-picked men from
Plumer's Scouts came down and took the lightly
guarded Fort Botha and wrecked the Boer communications systems for northern Transvaal. Forced to hide
in the hills by the presence of Boers, they emerged

when the irregular Rhodesian unit, Kitchener's Fighting Scouts, arrived in Louis Trichardt, which, it is said, Taylor then burned to the ground. Taylor tagged along with Kitchener's Fighting Scouts and showed his value by negotiating the surrender of a Boer force under siege at Rensburg. His good work and previous experience in the Spelonken area led to Kitchener personally appointing him Area Commandant of the Spelonken – a 'native commissioner' cum intelligence officer. A detachment of BVC was deployed to assist him. Under the aegis of the intelligence division he set up his HQ at Sweetwaters or Bristow's Farm, which was a mile from the BVC base, and appointed his own team of intelligence officers. He may have been Captain Taylor to the British Army, but the natives knew him as *Bulala* – the killer – and *Bamba* – he who takes. During his tenure in the Spelonken, Taylor proved himself a worthy recipient of both monikers.

Captain James Huntley Robertson commanded A Squadron, in name at least. Somewhat effeminate in character, he had a penchant for wearing shirts with frilly cuffs and stood on a plank to avoid getting his boots dirty. He was patently unfit to lead such a motley crew in such harsh environs. His inability to impose order was soon evident as the troopers began bringing in native spirit from local stills, treating captured Boer cattle and horses as their own and even selling British khaki uniforms to the Boers. Insubordination, drunkenness and anarchy 'bordering on mutiny' were rife in A Squadron. In his diary, Trooper McInnis says: 'We have a lazy time; plenty of Kaffir boys to cook our scoff, fetch wood and water, groom, feed and water our horses, and fetch coffee to us in bed – all this on active service.'

Sergeant-Major Kenneth Morrison, surprised both by the order to shoot the incoming party of Boers and the source it came from, asked Taylor to repeat the order, which he did, and added that they should ignore any white flags. Morrison then asked Robertson if he should take orders from Captain Taylor. Robertson replied, 'Certainly, he is commanding officer at Spelonken.'

Despite a deep sense of unease, Morrison repeated the orders to Sergeant Oldham, who was to lead the patrol. Instead of the usual custom of taking the required number of men from the right flank, Morrison hand-picked six men and a corporal who he knew would obey such orders.

The BVC patrol lay in wait at the side of the road as two Boer wagons with a hundred head of oxen came lumbering into view. Once they were well within range, they unleashed a withering volley on Oldham's command. Almost immediately, white flags of surrender were shown and Sergeant Oldham led his men in to see whether there were women or children in the wagons. Closer inspection revealed only six men, including an old man who was lying on a stretcher, seriously ill with fever. The Boers had bandoliers of bullets and rifles, but did not resist when disarmed. Oldham, in line with Taylor and Morrison's orders, ordered a firing party to shoot them all by the side of the road, except the sick man who was killed where he lay. Though they were not present at the shootings, Taylor and Robertson both arrived later and saw the bodies lying on the road. Sergeant Oldham reported, 'All correct; they are all shot.'

Van Buuren, a Boer member of the BVC, had been present and was shocked by the brutal killings. He was later seen pointing out the men responsible to the grief-stricken relatives who came to Fort Edward to claim the bodies. Little did he know, he had just signed his own death warrant.

But Taylor was not finished. The six Boers had been shot near a native kraal and as three native witnesses had buried the bodies, he rode in and told them what to say if questioned. The witnesses proved unwilling to keep quiet and fled, so Taylor dispatched a patrol into the *bhundu* with instructions to run them down and shoot them in the back.

Taylor's malign influence was soon felt again. It was common knowledge that Taylor distrusted the Boer members of the BVC and it was widely felt that Van Buuren could not be trusted. Some of the men refused to go out on patrol with him, fearing that he would give them away, and he had been seen pointing out the men who had shot the six Boers the previous day. There were also his long unexplained absences from Fort Edward. Rather than gather evidence of his complicity with the enemy and then arrest him, Taylor decided that suspicion was evidence enough. He acted as judge and jury and appointed Lieutenant Peter Handcock as executioner. Following a meeting between himself, Captain Robertson and Lieutenant Handcock, Robertson ordered Handcock to take Van Buuren on patrol and shoot him on July 15.

Taylor led and Robertson was also present as the patrol containing Handcock and Van Buuren rode out to harass a Boer commando that had supposedly been seen in the area. On arriving in the target area, they split into two groups and Handcock went up the left flank with Van Buuren. Trooper Muir Churton,[†] who was also on the left flank, witnessed what happened next:

> Once into the bush Handcock ordered the left flank
> to fan out ... Van Buuren turned to observe him
> [Handcock] as he rode up alongside. Before he
> could utter a word the Lieutenant drew out his

---

† *Trooper Muir Churton did not volunteer this information until almost seventy years later when interviewed by author/film-maker Frank Shields. Perhaps fearing for his own safety, he made no mention of this incident in the sworn deposition he made in 1902.*

revolver and put three shots in quick succession into the Dutchman, then without slackening his pace, he rode on.

Handcock returned with Van Buuren's horse saying that a Boer had shot him, but Trooper Edward Powell, who had climbed a tree to get a better view of the area supported Churton's allegation of foul play. He said that he saw no Boers in the vicinity that day.

Reports were compiled for Colonel Francis Hall. The first claimed that the six Boers had resisted and were killed in a fair fight. Captain Robertson even felt confident enough to write to Colonel Hall saying he felt he deserved a Distinguished Service Order after this action – an honour he was rightly refused. Hall returned the first account they submitted with a note to the effect: 'This report will not do. How could disarmed men assume the offensive? Send something more probable – Hall.'

Handcock was asked to write a report on the Van Buuren incident. Handcock, born on a farm at Peel near Bathurst, had been a blacksmith and railway worker and was now a farrier. He was, by his own admission, a simple man with no military aspirations. Not realising the need for deceit, he wrote down exactly what happened, and on reading it Robertson was heard to remark, 'That's no good to us,' and compiled his own. Robertson's version claimed that Van Buuren was killed during a skirmish with a Boer commando. Despite Hall's rejection of the first report on the six Boers, there was no reaction from Pietersburg on either count. These two incidents, later attested to by a number of witnesses, clearly establishes that before Morant and Hunt ever arrived in the Spelonken, a culture of murder already existed and appeared to be sanctioned and approved by HQ. Whilst the killing of seven people in

such circumstances was shocking enough, it was a mere
prelude to what was about to follow.

ON JULY 13, ELAND'S LETTERS MENTION that he and
Morant, and sixty other men from B Squadron, were to
be moved up to Fort Edward to replace most of A
Squadron who had been recalled to Pietersburg. Eland,
Morant and an English lieutenant, Picton, were all
hand-picked by Hunt to help him restore order. In the
poisonous atmosphere of the Spelonken, it did not take
Eland long to acquaint himself with what had been
going on.

> 'A' squad were not pleased to see us; discipline was
> very lax with them and there were several nasty
> rumours with regard to the conduct of several of
> them. I believe a courts martial will be held and if
> they do their duty, a verdict of murder ought to be
> returned. Don't mention this to anyone out there.
> There are several fellows in this crowd who would
> stop at nothing; they'd shoot and rob their own
> mother!

Eland's first impression turned out to be correct and was
backed up by Trooper Silke, who had also been moved
up from Strydpoort with Eland and Morant:

> Captain Hunt came out in command and with him
> came Lieutenant Morant . . . We relieved Captain
> Robinson [sic] and party (BVC) who had to go to
> Pietersburg to attend an inquiry on four charges:
> murder, cowardice, rape and robbery. The first
> charge was founded on fact, for with his knowledge
> and maybe his consent and approval, six surren-
> dered Boers were shot after their arms were taken
> from them . . . The other three charges were not
> raised at the inquiry.

According to Silke, Robertson was being investigated for murder, not the lesser charge of rape as is often stated. That Hall knew about the murders in the Spelonken cannot be doubted – as both Eland and Silke knew within days of their arrival.

For reasons never disclosed, Hall decided not to prosecute Robertson for the seven murders that had occurred under his command. By failing to prosecute Robertson, Hall was tacitly condoning the covert policy of the BVC.

The lawlessness that Robertson had allowed to take root in the Spelonken gave Hunt and Morant early discipline problems. Shortly after Morant arrived, Lieutenant Picton reported that some of the men had got at the rum he had brought up from Pietersburg with other stores. They evidently hid it nearby, as during the next few days some of the men were seen leaving the fort and returning drunk some hours later. Hunt placed the offenders, including Sergeant-Major Morrison, under arrest, but they escaped and returned to Pietersburg. Hunt sent eight men after them. The patrol soon caught up with the deserters, but instead of arresting them they all got drunk and carried on into Pietersburg.

Hunt reported what happened to Lenehan, who tracked them down and arrested them in Pietersburg. At the subsequent inquiry, sergeants Morrison and Grey made allegations against Captain Robertson and other officers with regard to the shooting of six Boers and Van Buuren.

Again, Hall failed to act and decided 'in the interest of all concerned, to discharge them from the regiment and let them go'. Despite further allegations and ongoing inquiries into the seven murders, Captain Robertson was never investigated. He was finally allowed to resign his commission on September 10 and refused further military employment. The only conclusion that can be drawn is that Hall tacitly approved of the BVC's special mission of destruction, or was following a covert policy that had been decreed by Army HQ. Even after such flagrant breaches of the *Army Act*, there is no evidence that Hall issued orders to discontinue the practice of shooting prisoners or issued any warnings to A Squadron. Indeed, Hunt was heard issuing the order to shoot prisoners on many occasions. It was later testified in court that Hunt reprimanded Morant when he brought in prisoners and told him that in future he would have to feed the prisoners out of his own rations.

In an effort to make a new start they re-named their base Fort Edward. The core of their defences was a captured mobile Boer steel fort called Fort Hendrina, which arrived from Louis Trichardt shortly after Hunt, Morant and the rest of B Squadron. It was a nine yard wide hexagonal steel box with firing slots and big double doors into which the BVC could retreat if attacked. On June 19, it was re-christened Fort Edward with a bucket of whisky, but after the party Hunt and Morant smashed the illegal stills and confiscated the stolen Boer cattle in an effort to restore some semblance of order. However, it was going to take more than a change of name to quell the remaining unruly elements of A Squadron who resented the new order and wanted a return to the lax regime they had enjoyed under Captain Robertson.

The BVC resumed their work of clearing the area of Boers and Morant exemplified the new spirit by going out on patrol with twenty-two men and coming back with nineteen prisoners. However, it proved to be a false dawn. If July had been a bad month for the BVC, it was going to be nothing compared to August.

8

The Heart of Darkness

The Bushveldt Seddoneers
Thrice a thousand cannibals
Silent men and stark,
We can smell our quary well,
And track him in the dark –
We, the Lion's next of kin,
We, the tiger's peers,
Point the foe, and let us go,
The Bushveldt Seddoneers!

We need no commissariate,
We make no useless fuss:
Blood-hot, fresh-human flesh –
meat and drink to us!
We are ruth and pity,
What are children's tears,
Age, or sex to Richard Rex
And his seddoneers . . .

The Bushveldt Seddoneers by 'WM'

2 AM – AUGUST 5, 1901 – VILJOEN'S FARM, APPROXI-
MATELY 40 MILES SOUTHEAST OF FORT EDWARD.
*It was a typically cold, clear winter's night in the Trans-
vaal, but Captain Percy Hunt didn't feel the cold as
he crept towards the quiet, dark silhouette of Viljoen's
Farm. The adrenalin was coursing through his system
and he felt a slight sweat break out on his brow.*

Although he was only twenty-eight years old, he had been a Hussar, a member of French's Scouts with Morant and now commanded a squadron of the Bushveldt Carbineers, but still regarded a bit of fear as a healthy thing.

As Captain Hunt and his force of sixteen soldiers and natives crept through the tough bush grass and thick scrub that covered this area of northern Transvaal, the partial moon peeped out periodically between thin wisps of cloud overhead, as though it was too afraid to watch their advance. Their progress was slowed when they blundered into a low-lying area of boggy ground and as the heavy mud sucked at their boots Hunt was reminded why the area was known as Duwielskloof. The local Boers declared that the boggy ground gripped at their wagon wheels like the claws of the devil to stop them leaving this accursed, malaria-ridden country. The Gothic theme was echoed by the prominent landmark that he used to keep his bearings, the eerie, claw-like rock whose silhouette loomed above them like a bad omen. He shuddered slightly as they passed into its dark shadow.

Breathing hard, Hunt crouched down a few hundred yards from the farmhouse where he had been told the Viljoen commando stayed every night. Viljoen was one of the two Boer commandants in the area. Beyers was the other. The BVC had been after them both for a while. A few weeks ago, Reverend Fritz Reuter, a German missionary, had come to Fort Edward and said that the Boers had been worrying farms loyal to the British cause. Hunt sent out a scouting patrol which reported back that Viljoen's commando spent every night at their farm. When Hunt announced his plan to raid the farmhouse, Captain Taylor had warned him against interfering with Viljoen.

All seemed quiet. Lifting his left hand, he waved his men closer, and with the other pulled out his Webley

Mk III service pistol. He had almost reached the wooden stoop at the front of the house. Once we've got 'em surrounded we'll soon flush 'em out. *That was the last thought that flashed through Percy Hunt's mind before a silhouette suddenly loomed up in the window in front of him.*

He leapt up onto the veranda and shouted, 'Surrender! We've got you surrounded!'

He saw the long shape of a rifle being raised up to a shoulder and he instinctively pointed and squeezed the trigger of the pistol he was holding, twice. Almost simultaneously, a flash leapt out of the darkness directly in front of him, closely followed by a sharp crack and then he felt a hammer blow to his chest which knocked him backwards. As he lay on the damp ground, a fusillade of flashes illuminated the night sky above him; it was like Guy Fawkes night. Thinking he was just winded, he tried to get to his feet, but a sharp pain forced him back down. He gingerly explored the wound inside his tunic, and the sticky residue he felt on his hand told him his fight was over. Looking around him, he saw Sergeant Eland lying nearby. He had been right behind him when the firing began. Hardly surprising, as one of the farms the Viljoen commando had been menacing was his mother's.

Judging by the barrage coming from the house, there were a lot more than the fifteen Boers reported by intelligence. Hunt saw Trooper Mercer crawling towards him and motioned him back.

'Get out of here Charlie, I'm alright.'

Mercer[†] was one of Morant's recruits, and like all

---

† *Although no Mercer appears on the BVC roll, he is quoted extensively in Australian newspaper accounts. His detailed knowledge of events suggests he was present. It is thought that Mercer may have been confused with Mertens, another Australian in the BVC.*

Australians, never short of an opinion. But for once he did as his superior officer told him without question.

Hunt had felt a terrible foreboding about this mission and told the men that if anything happened to him to get out of the Kloof before first light.

Soon the firing stopped and he could hear the order for the BVC patrol to pull back. Hunt lay back and looked up at the stars twinkling above. He could hear raised voices shouting in Afrikaans, and the brittle stems of grass crunching underfoot as the voices came closer, and he smelt the rough tobacco the Boers smoked. Suddenly he felt very tired and surrendered to the darkness that wrapped itself around him like a warm blanket.

As soon as the shout 'Rider incoming!' went up, Morant sprang to his feet with his heart thumping. He knew instinctively it was bad news. He'd also had a bad feeling about the mission and had begged Eland not to go. His worst fears were confirmed as he marched towards the exhausted rider who was being helped from his saddle. The pitying look on the man's face as he approached said it all. Under Morant's intense stare, the trooper struggled to find the words.

'Trooper Haslett reporting, sir. There was . . . a fight, early this morning, at Viljoen's . . . Captain Hunt and Sergeant Eland are dead,' he added flatly, military protocol forgotten. The men waited intently for Morant's reaction. Through the numbing wave of shock that had broken over him, he calmly said, 'Thank you, Trooper. Dismissed. Get yourself a tea from the billy.'

Morant didn't wait for a salute, but turned on his heel. Operating on remote control, he shouted to the nearest man, 'Tell the men to saddle up. All the men.'

'But sir . . .'

But before the man could explain that he was only a private, Morant swung round, fists bunched and *mouth twisted in an angry snarl. It was the first sign of emotion he had shown. Barely able to restrain the volcanic anger welling up inside him, his eyes burned into the face of the hapless trooper and he repeated his order in a voice quivering with emotion, 'Fucking well do it now, soldier!' He lifted up a muscular right arm as if to strike him, but instead held it in front of his face. 'You've got five fucking minutes!'*

There was a strange light in Morant's eye which told the unlucky soldier that he wasn't going to take no for an answer.

'Company, saddle up!' the trooper shouted vainly and Morant continued to his tent.

He stared into the glass containing the stiff tot of whisky he had just poured. Random disconnected images flashed through his mind – him and Percy hunting together, his girl waiting patiently for him, a smile spreading across her face as she turned her face towards the warm spring sunshine, and then Percy lying cold and lifeless and alone on the veldt. Tears pricked his eyelids and he looked again at the glass. He knew who was waiting patiently for him at the bottom of it – the same person who was always there. Edwin.

Morant drained the glass with one swallow, then another . . .

Five minutes later, he burst through the flaps of the tent, the rough native whisky still burning his guts, but it had dulled the pain. Naturally, the men had ignored the hapless trooper who, fearing the wrath of Morant, had tried to get them to saddle up.

His face flushed with whisky and anger, Morant whirled round the square like a dervish, yelling, pushing men towards their horses, cursing and threatening them with terrible violence. He led them the short mile to Sweetwaters Farm in sullen silence. It had not yet sunk in that Hunt's death meant he was now in charge.

On arriving at the farm Captain Taylor used as his headquarters, Morant stepped up on the smooth-topped, sun-baked ant hill which served as a rostrum, and stood for a moment, head bowed, composing himself. Then he straightened up and looked out over the sea of expectant faces.

'This morning, at round 3 am, Captain Hunt led a patrol to flush out a Boer commando bailed up at Viljoen's Farm. During the course of the fight, Captain Hunt and Sergeant Eland were killed . . .' But he couldn't go on. He bowed his head, and with shoulders shaking, wept uncontrollably. Tears fell unashamedly from his face as the assembled men stood in shocked silence. Morant came with a reputation as a hard nut, and he was the last bloke they expected to see crying.

Seeing the thought that Morant had 'lost it' running through their minds, Captain Taylor took his place on the mound. At thirty-eight he was short, stocky and dark, and his short, stiff handlebar moustache, which seemed to bristle with static, gave him the sinister air of a pantomime villain. His hooded black eyes were dark bottomless pools of sin and gave him the lazy, malevolent look of a predator. As soon as he spoke the murmur died down. His rough Irish brogue was tinged with guttural Dutch – testimony to his many years in Rhodesia.

'Captain Hunt and Sergeant Eland were murdered by Boers yesterday morning, but we're not going to let those bastards get away with it. You are going to saddle up, get out there after them and avenge your brother officers.'

A man of few words, he paused and looked around while his words sank in. There was no murmur of agreement or shouts of encouragement, the kind of esprit du corps you'd expect amongst a group of men living in the shadow of death. But the Bushveldt Carbineers was no ordinary unit. There was a fierce antagonism between the *officers and men, and this mission of destruction would be the source of yet more bad blood. Such was the atmosphere that nearly everyone in A Squadron left as soon as their initial six months was up and few returned.*

But Taylor commanded the respect, or the fear, at least, of every man jack in Fort Edward. He was Kitchener's man; the real boss, and everyone knew it. He shot natives like rabbits and his distrust of the Boers in the BVC was no secret. He had no hesitation in getting rid of Van Buuren and they all suspected the same fate awaited anyone foolish enough to cross him. He was 'Bulala' and up here his word was law. An hour later, Morant led a strong patrol out of Sweetwaters.

The patrol included Lieutenant George Witton, who had enjoyed an eventful first few days in the Spelonken. Such were the Carbineers' ongoing recruiting difficulties, that Major Lenehan had offered Witton a commission if he could personally raise the thirty men needed for a BVC gun detachment. Having pulled together the requisite number and been discharged from the Victorian Imperial Bushmen, he travelled up to Pietersburg. In another strange twist of fate, Witton was posted to Fort Edward after Captain GW Baudinet hurt his leg playing polo and was unable to accompany the other nineteen reinforcements.

Witton's first inkling of what was to follow came during the train journey to Pietersburg when they passed through Naboomspruit and saw the nineteen freshly dug graves of the Gordons at the side of the tracks. Now came the dramatic news of the death of their commanding officer, and though he had never met Captain Hunt, Witton was now on the way to avenge his death.

Gone was the jocular, devil-may-care Morant he'd met only recently. He was now a hollow-eyed avenger. He kept them moving at quite a lick, only stopping to menace the German guide with his carbine when he periodically lost his way. The guide looked beseech-ingly at the others to save him from this madman, but no-one was keen to cross Morant in this mood. Witton dismissed the involuntary shiver that suddenly ran down his back and urged his mount onwards as they rode away from the setting sun and into the darkness like the horsemen of the apocalypse.

After riding all night and most of the next day through some of the most rugged country in Africa, they finally arrived at Medingen, also known as Reuter's Mission. They saw the men who had been on patrol with Hunt returning from his grave. They had missed Hunt's funeral by an hour. Eland had been buried at his mother's nearby farm, Ravenshill.

Reverend Reuter broke the news to Morant that Hunt had been kicked to death and his body mutilated. Morant's shock turned to anger as he demanded details.

'What do you mean, mutilated?' he asked angrily, and shrugged off the comforting hand the small, portly missionary tried to lay on his arm. Taking a deep breath, Reuter told him about the marks he'd seen on Hunt's body.

'I myself prepared the bodies for burial when they were brought in. We noted that in addition to the first wound in his chest, there were also slash marks on his legs . . .'

Morant avoided Reuter's sorrowful gaze and scanned the faces of those who had been at Duwiels-kloof the previous night. He was sure people answering the religious calling practised that look in seminary for such sombre occasions. His gaze came to rest on the face of Charlie Mercer, who had been there that night. Mercer didn't wait to be asked and blurted out what he'd seen.

'He was alive when I last saw 'im Harry. Told me to fall back and get the blokes out of the kloof before

dawn. Next time I saw 'im he was lying naked in a gutter, his neck all twisted and his eye had popped out of its socket. The ground around 'im had been torn up by heavy boots . . . He had a bootmark right 'ere,' he added, slapping his forehead with his palm.

Knowing how close Morant had been to Hunt, Reuter had hoped to spare him the uglier details and had withheld the fact that both Hunt and Eland's genitals had also been mutilated. He suspected native witchdoctors, but decided to say nothing. Morant looked round the group of other soldiers present and nodded to himself bitterly. Must have been some bloody wastrels out there with him that night. *Struggling to control his emotions, Morant looked down as a great wave of sadness welled up inside him.* Bad enough he was killed in a fair fight, but murdered and mutilated and left in the gutter like a dog? *Suddenly feeling it too hot in the crowded room, he barged his way to the door.*

The cold night air cleared his head like a wet sponge at the end of a tough round in the boxing ring. He had barely lit a fag with trembling hands and drawn down that first calming puff deep into his lungs when Adjutant James Edwards, who was stationed at Pietersburg, appeared out of the gloom leading a native boy who Morant recognised as Aaron, Hunt's 'boy'.

'I'm sorry Harry. Bloody terrible business . . .'

Seeing Morant staring hard at Aaron, Edwards continued.

'Aaron here saw the whole thing . . . Tell Bwana Harry what you saw.'

Stuttering tearfully, the young boy told Morant what he'd seen in his pidgin English.

'I . . . I see Bwana Percy shot, but he still livin'. I go over to help him, but the Boers come out the house and I hide in the bushes. They no see me. They very angry. They beat him good and jump on his head.'

With that, Aaron covered his face with his hand and turned away.

'I thought you ought to know the facts, mate,' said Edwards apologetically.

Morant nodded. 'Thank you Edwards,' and vanished into the darkness.

It was a sombre Morant who walked alone up to the mound of fresh earth, scarcely able to believe that Percy lay beneath it. Whilst he grieved for him, he also grieved for himself. A few days ago, the future had seemed rosy. He and Hunt would see out the war, return the conquering heroes, marry their sweethearts and he'd reclaim his place in the bosom of his family. For Morant, Hunt was an embodiment of the paradise lost which he never regained – an entree back to the England he had known.

Morant looked up at the silhouettes of the distant Drakensberg Mountains bathed in the brilliance of the pale moon. They stood shoulder to shoulder like sentinels, as stolid and unmoved as the Boers that inhabited them. A flash of anger penetrated his numbed senses, but Harry Morant, man of letters, could only mumble, 'Rest easy, Percy. We'll settle your score.'

He knew if the positions were reversed he would expect and get no less.

Best, Eland and Hunt – three mates killed in a month. Like most Australians, he'd always thought the Boers a decent lot, no different to their own bushmen, and had paid little heed to the wild yarns about Boer brutality. He recalled walking through Cape Town in the wee small hours listening to Paterson littering the silent streets with treasonous talk of press conspiracies and British imperialism. No wonder they sent him home.

But things had changed and the old biblical dictum came suddenly to mind: 'He who lives by the sword will perish by the sword.' A cold detachment settled over him as he resolved wordlessly to make those responsible pay. As he later recalled, *'I felt most horribly angry, in fact, I felt savage.'*

He spent the rest of the night sitting sleeplessly by the dying embers of the campfire, fuelling his growing anger with strong ersatz coffee laced with whisky, going over and over the ifs and buts.

As soon as first light cracked the eastern sky, he was up in his saddle and riding in and out of the groups of blanketed figures shouting, *'Let's be having you, you lazy bastards!'*

Bleary-eyed from the few hours of sleep they had managed to snatch, they saw their new commanding officer towering above them, impatient for the off.

He challenged, *'Get up you bastards! Or do I have to go out and get 'em all myself?'*

Muttering beneath their breath, they scrambled to their horses. Another morning without breakfast. But they did so with some trepidation. Like Witton, they had seen a change come over Morant. Bad things happen in war, but as Morant led the forty-five-man patrol into the sunrise at a fair lick, they all had a bad feeling in their guts about what was going to happen next.

Morant pushed them on the whole day, only stopping to give the horses a rest and to examine the campsite where the Boers had camped the previous night and the two freshly dug mounds they left behind. Percy must have winged a couple on the way down, thought Morant with a grim satisfaction that brought him little comfort.

The trail got even warmer when they put a group of Boer horsemen to flight. They not only abandoned their camp and precious food supplies, but also a cart. A mournful groan attracted their attention and to their *horror they discovered Trooper Yates tied naked to one of its wheels. He was the one man not accounted for after the attack on Viljoen's Farm and had been presumed dead or deserted. His body was covered with angry blue and purple bruises and as they untied him he told how he'd hidden after the attack on Viljoen's Farm had broken up, but had run into a couple of Boers as he was making his way out of the kloof. They'd taken him along and he had endured some pretty rough treatment in the days since the raid, but left him behind as they fled the BVC attack.*

Morant listened grimly as Yates told him, 'I had a fearful time of it. They kicked and knocked me about something terrible. I was expecting every moment to be my last.' However, Yates was luckier than Hunt and ended up in a hospital bed rather than a shallow grave.

The pieces began to come together in Morant's mind. Yates' treatment confirmed what Reverend Reuter, Charlie Mercer and Hunt's boy, Aaron, had told him back at Medingen about the manner of his death and the state in which they found Hunt's body. The morning after the attack on Viljoen's farmhouse, Hunt's patrol had returned to Duwielskloof and discovered the battered, mutilated bodies of Hunt and Eland lying outside in the gutter, and the white, stiff bodies of Veldt-cornet Barend Viljoen and one of Viljoen's two sons, Jappe, inside the house. Hunt had shot both clean through the head before he was hit. The rest of the commando had obviously taken their revenge for the death of their leaders, first on the wounded Hunt and later on Yates.

Sensing that the main party must be near, Morant decided to push on and just as dusk was closing in around them they spotted a distant flicker of fire from a Boer camp that was situated behind a low range of hills. Sending Lieutenant Picton down the right flank they split into two groups and climbed the hill – a good position from which to attack. As soon as he caught sight of the wagons and heard the strangulated vowels of Afrikaans drifting up from the campfire, vengeance started gnawing away at his reason. Instead of allowing Picton to close in and catch them by surprise, Morant gave the order to fire when they were still twelve hundred yards out.

The phantom volley caught the Boer completely by surprise and seeing the ghostly figures of Picton's patrol bearing down on them, urgent shouts of, 'Oopsaal' (saddle up) went up. Their half-eaten dinners and cups of coffee were still hot when the BVC reached the laager, but the Boers, well used to speedy exits, had long gone. They had left everything behind in their panic to escape, including a twenty-year-old man named Visser, who was found under a wagon. He had been hit on the heel by a stray bullet and couldn't stand up.

Revenge was very much on Morant's mind after a search of the camp uncovered Hunt's water bottle, binoculars and other personal effects and Eland's carbine, collapsible knife and fork, belt, pouch, spurs, bandolier and field glasses. The evidence connected Visser directly to Hunt's death and Morant's first instinct was to shoot him on the spot. He was persuaded not to do this for fear of attracting other Boers in the area. They bivouacked in a safer place for the night and resolved to run down the rest of Viljoen's commando the next day.

A shout of 'Who goes there?' woke the whole camp at first light on August 11. They turned out, still fully dressed with guns at the ready only to find that the intruder was a runner from Fort Edward. They were to return at once, as a Boer commando was menacing the few men who had remained at the fort.

Before they turned and headed for home, Morant

*questioned Visser about Hunt's death. He prefaced the
question by saying that if he told the truth, he'd be
spared, otherwise he'd be shot. Morant studied Visser
closely as Trooper Botha translated Morant's statement
and the reply in a heavily accented Afrikaans. Under-
neath the heavy dark beard and unkempt hair there was
the fresh complexion of a young man and judging by
his nervous hand movements he knew his fate was being
decided. Botha translated his first reply.*

*'He said Captain Hunt died in a fair fight and was
shot through the chest.'*

*Morant replied testily, 'Then how is it that when we
found him his neck was broken?'*

*Visser's animated hand movements negated the need
for Botha's reply. 'He says it's not true.'*

What a surprise!, thought Morant.

*'What about the rest of his mates. Where are they
headed?' pressed Morant.*

*'He says they won't stay here now, but go to Wood-
bush to join with Beyers' commando.'*

*When they stopped for a makeshift lunch of tough
trek ox steak at a place called Mamehelia the officers –
Morant, Handcock, Witton and Picton – held a meeting
at which Morant announced his intention to shoot Visser.*

*Witton and Handcock were silent, but Lieutenant
Picton said, 'Harry you can't shoot this man. We've had
him prisoner too long. The red book says that you can't
shoot him once he's surrendered and you've taken him
prisoner.' Picton was the most seasoned soldier amongst
them. He'd won a Distinguished Conduct Medal whilst
serving with Loch's Horse and claimed he'd been in the
Congo with the French Foreign Legion.*

*But Morant was having none of it. He spat into the
fire and it hissed back angrily as he told them, 'Bugger
the book! He was there when they murdered Hunt and
we found him wearing a khaki shirt and using Hunt's*

*trousers as a pillow. In any case, I've got orders direct
from headquarters not to take prisoners, and Kitchener's
not long sent out a proclamation saying that all Boers
captured wearing khaki were to be summarily shot.'*

He stood up, indicating the discussion was over. He
repeated what he'd just said to the men and ordered
Sergeant-Major Clarke to assemble a firing party of ten
men. Intelligence Officer Ledeboer was dispatched to
tell the prisoner his fate.

Visser protested that he'd told the truth and was
promised he'd be spared, but Morant waved away the
objection. Some of the men also objected, but fearful of
Morant's reaction, Clarke asked Witton to speak
to Morant.

Morant was unmoved by Witton's pleas. Staring
deep into the fire, as though he was drawing strength
from it, he said, 'You didn't know Percy, George. He
was my best friend . . .'

Morant looked him straight in the face for emphasis, and Witton could see that the spirit of forgiveness
did not live in those cold, blue eyes.

Morant turned and pointed at Visser, who was
slumped in the cart, his eyes closed and lips twitching
in silent prayer.

'If the men make any fuss, I'll shoot the bastard
myself,' said Morant.

After much grumbling, enough men were found to
make up a firing party and Lieutenant Picton was
put in charge. George Witton could stand no more.
Knowing nothing would stop Morant killing this Boer,
he walked away. But Visser wasn't the only one afraid
for his life. As the firing party huddled together in a
small group, Botha confided to Trooper Jas Christie,
who had also been chosen to deliver Morant's retribution, or what he would later describe in the courts
martial as 'Rule 303', 'I know this man good. We go to

the school together. I don't like to do it, but he shoot me if I don't.'

Visser had pleaded for help during the interrogation, but Botha had kept quiet. Being too sympathetic to the Boers had got Van Buuren killed.

'Poor bastard,' said Christie, shaking his head, but was overheard by one of the English troopers, who had no such qualms.

'What's wrong with you lot? Quicker we finish 'em off, quicker we get out of 'ere. Oo's side you lot on anyway? Thought you lot would be glad to do you bit for Queen and country,' he said with a distinctive Cockney twang.

Christie replied by going up to the cart where Visser sat writing a final note. He was trying to appear unconcerned, but every so often the corner of his mouth twitched involuntarily, which betrayed the fear that must have been coursing through him.

Lieutenant Picton ordered the firing party to fall in, and as they lined up, Christie had made his mind up that he was going to shoot wide.

Some of the natives lifted Visser out of the cart in a blanket and set him down some twenty yards away with his back to the firing party. Most of the men were secretly glad they didn't have to look at him as they took aim. Visser, who had struggled to a kneeling position, said nothing, but clasped his hands in front of him in silent prayer as Lieutenant Picton announced the moment of his doom. As the volley rang out, he fell backwards from his sitting position. Then, even before the smoke had cleared, Picton stood over Visser, put his revolver to the side of his head and blew out his brains for good measure.

There was a sullen silence amongst the men afterwards, none of the usual banter.

Morant came over to where Jas Christie was sitting

with a cup of tea and said, 'I know it's hard lines for him, but it had to be done. They knocked Hunt about something terrible.'

Christie glanced up at Morant, who towered over him, but felt no fear. They had been good mates, up to now.

'That's bullshit Harry. Hunt died a soldier's death. He was killed in a fair go.'

Morant kneeled down suddenly so his face was only a few inches from Christie's.

'So, you call killing a wounded man, then mutilating him "a fair go"?' snarled Morant.

'I didn't see any marks on 'im,' retorted Christie.

'Not what Reuter told me, and I reckon the word of a man of God is worth ten of yours any day,' Morant spat and jerked his thumb over his shoulder to where Visser lay on the ground, stiffening and forgotten by everyone but the flies that were swarming busily over his corpse.

'And what was that bloke doing with Hunt's trousers and Eland's gear – minding them?'

Christie felt light spittle on his face, the surfeit of Morant's vehemence, but he persisted.

'But he wasn't wearing 'em . . .'

Morant cut him short and pointed his finger right into his face, 'But he had 'em . . . and that proves he was in that house when Hunt and Eland died, no matter what you chicken-hearted bastards say.'

He glared round at the rest of the men he now commanded.

'What kind of bloody mongrels are you? Your bloody mates get murdered and you feel sorry for the Boers . . .'

Christie also stood up suddenly, his face flushed with defiance, 'He was no mate of ours! He was an officer and you lot just look after yourselves and don't give a stuff about us blokes. If this is soldiering, I don't want any part of it.'

With that, Christie turned on his heel.

In a British unit, such behaviour would have seen Christie put on a charge immediately, but blowing off a bit of steam, even at officers, was a part of the more relaxed colonial culture.

Morant pointed at the rest of them, then swept his arm round in an arc and laid down the law with an edge of menace creeping into his voice.

'I thought I'd weeded out all the lazy, boozing, blowhard bastards in this unit, but I was wrong. I'm in charge now and we'll do things my way . . . or else.'

The undefined threat hung heavily in the air as Morant watched Christie saddle up with the anger still burning inside him like a furnace. They won't stop me. Percy is going to be avenged or my name isn't Harry Morant, *he resolved.*

They began the long trek home in silence. The only sound was the scraping of shovels on hard earth as the natives dug a narrow trench for Visser out on the lonely veldt.

JAS CHRISTIE WAS THE FIRST TO DISPUTE Morant's story. He later made a statement that denied Hunt was mutilated and Visser was wearing khaki or had Hunt's trousers. Their conflicting accounts would become a key issue at the courts martial and would be bitterly disputed long after the court delivered its verdict.

By the time Morant's patrol reached Fort Edward, they found a detachment under Lieutenant Neel had arrived from Pietersburg in time to help Taylor drive the Boers off. During this action they had entered a native kraal and Taylor summarily executed a native for refusing to tell him which way the Boers were headed. His defence in court was that he had intended to shoot over his head to scare him, but had aimed too low. The court accepted this as a defence and he was acquitted of murder.

Things would never be the same again at Fort Edward. Visser's execution signalled an important turning-point in the story of the Bushveldt Carbineers. The simmering tensions that existed between the officers and the men, even before Morant's arrival, now spilled over with Morant's adoption of the take no prisoners policy advocated by Hunt. There were now two factions in Fort Edward – the officers and a section of troopers either willingly or reluctantly following orders to shoot prisoners, and those, like Christie, who distrusted the officers and were prepared to defy their orders. It would be they, rather than the intelligence department or HQ, that would bring about Morant's downfall.

And the Visser issue was no guilty secret. Witton says that Morant reported it to Taylor, as did Picton to both Lenehan and Hall in person.

Morant's letter to Lenehan shortly after Hunt's death confirms his policy of open disclosure, but its tone and mood was markedly different to the one he wrote whilst in charge of B Squadron.

17/08/01

My Dear Major,

A runner goes to Pietersburg this morning, so just a hasty note, as I happen to be in camp. You know how cut up we must have been over poor old Hunt's death. I'll never get such a good pal as he proved himself to be. I wish to the Lord that I'd been out that night, he might have got wiped out all the same, but the d___d Dutchman who did it would never have left the house. We've killed 13 of them to date now – and that crowd haven't a blanket left to wrap themselves in. It was a d_____d hard job to write to Hunt's girl, which same I did after we returned. Poor old Hunt! God rest his soul! but he 'died decent.' I've lost my best mate, and you've lost your best officer.

We're getting along very well up here. Whips o' work. News comes in every day of small parties of Boers; and out we go out to harry them like b____dy cattle dogs. We've given this quarter a pretty hot name for The Boers and they are all drifting to the WATERBERG: gathering up there to some considerable number by this time. We're whipping them in: 'getting them together' and IT WANTS A STRONG FORCE – column – to smash them once they get consolidated there. One great requirement here is HORSE SHOES. For the Lord's sake send up half-a-dozen boxes at least. We've got the shoes literally worn off the horses' hoofs – with work. I make the men out on patrol walk and lead at every opportunity; and considering the work done the horses last out and look well. The Sgt.-Major [Hammett] you sent up is an excellent man: has a big grip of the men; knows his work and makes them do theirs! With the men getting 7/- per day they ought to be pretty freely 'culled' and get a better quality of soldier without damaging the numbers to any extent! By G_____, there must have been some wastrels out there the night poor old Hunt went under. I suppose Mortimer has told you that his body was stripped, neck broken, etc., etc., by the Boers. I've straightened some of them up. They stand cursing! But you cannot make a crooked stick straight, or make a d_____d coward a good plucked one. I fancy you've heard some fairy tales to the detriment of Taylor! You must remember the source they came from. Hunt got on famously right from the first, and I, Handcock, and the rest of us couldn't

wish for better fellow to work with. We work ourselves, men and horses d___d hard, but Taylor
lends us every assistance, and his 'intelligence' is
the most reliable I've struck in South Africa. Handcock you know, and I find him worth the other two
in himself. You must excuse my apparent carelessness in the matter of letter writing, but I have not
had any chance of scribbling. If I ever sat down to
write then some d___d Boers bobbed up and we
had to go out and 'worry' them. By the way if there
are any scattered things of Hunt's about Pietersburg camp, will you look after them personally?
Poor old chap – he left his ponies and all his gear
to me, and I've got something to fix up for him,
which as it's a very private matter, I will not write:
but will inform you privately as our C.O. when I
see you.

Good-bye Major!
Yours obediently,

HARRY H. MORANT. 'Tony.'

Mystery surrounds Morant's claim to have shot thirteen
Boers, as according to the statements given by BVC
troopers and non-commissioned officers that were used
to charge the BVC officers with murder, only Visser had
been shot by the date on the letter. However, Witton
told his brother in a letter that on the day they returned
from Duwielskloof: 'The detachment returned to Fort
Edward, and on August 11 made another attack on the
Boers, and captured six, who were wearing khaki. These
were all court martialled and shot.' Was the court
martial of those six Boers any different to Visser's? Why
these six Boers were never mentioned in later depositions or cited at the courts martial as proof that orders
to shoot Boers wearing khaki did exist is a mystery.
On August 13, two more Boers were killed in another

skirmish. If the eight killed after their return are added to the two who died at Duwielskloof, the two graves found during the chase that led them to Visser – the total is thirteen. However, Morant clearly thought nothing of admitting the killings and if the number had alarmed Major Lenehan or Colonel Hall, the BVC would have been reeled in long before things got out of hand. On the other hand, if they wished to destroy the stubborn Boer commandos, then letting an embittered Morant loose on them was the best policy.

In any event, Morant received a letter from Hall saying he was now the officer commanding at Fort Edward and congratulating him on the good work he had done. To Morant, who later quoted this letter to troopers who questioned his new tactics, this was official approval of the special mission of destruction he had embarked on. Despite the sacking of Robertson and the murder of Hunt, Hall felt no need to caution Morant about conduct at Fort Edward. By his own admission, Morant had already accounted for thirteen, and had been given no reason to believe he should not continue.

MORANT'S TRAIL OF VENGEANCE continued on August 23 after news reached Fort Edward that eight Boer prisoners were being brought in. Trooper Petrie and an intelligence officer had been returning from a special mission to the Portuguese border when they came across and captured eight Boers. Halfway back to the fort they were met by Trooper Wrench and twelve other men, who brought them back to the Swiss Mission Hospital at Elim six miles from Fort Edward.

Morant asked Witton to accompany him on patrol along with Lieutenant Handcock and Sergeant-Major Hammett. En route to meet the prisoners, Morant stopped for a private meeting at Taylor's HQ at Sweetwaters

Farm. None of the others were privy to what was said between Morant and Taylor, and shortly after leaving Sweetwaters, Morant announced that it was his intention to shoot the prisoners. Hammett, who like Witton was a relative newcomer to A Squadron, asked if he was sure he was right, to which Morant replied that he had his orders and dismissed Witton's concern that they were shooting prisoners too close to Fort Edward.

They met Sergeant Wrench's patrol with the prisoners about six miles from the fort at the Swiss Mission Hospital, Elim. Morant instructed the escort to go ahead while the officers and troopers Botha, Duckett and Thompson brought up the rear with the prisoners.

While the party was stopped, a thirty-four-year-old missionary called Daniel Heese, who had been at Elim Hospital, spotted the eight Boers sitting in the wagon. According to an investigation conducted later by the Berlin Mission Society, Heese then made the fatal mistake of approaching the wagon because:

> Among them he immediately recognised a fine Dutchman, named Vahrmeyer, the teacher of village children at Potgietersrust, about whose whereabouts he had already quite often been worried. Recognising and greeting him was naturally one action. The latter complained to him that they were in great disquiet regarding their life and every moment were running the risk of being shot, as they believed they could conclude from their expressions they had heard. But Heese comforted him (by saying) that according to Martial law nothing more could happen to them than to be taken away, seeing that they had laid down arms. Then suddenly two officers stood up, who had been lying in grass alongside the wagon and snapped at Heese how he could make so bold as to speak to prisoners, he should immediately climb into the wagon, for he

was herewith arrested. Heese naturally refused and referred to the pass from the commandant. So then they let him go but they also obtained from him his word of honour to present himself personally at 10 o'clock before the Captain of Fort Edward.

The two soldiers who challenged Heese were Morant and Handcock. About three miles out from Fort Edward, Morant stopped the Boer's wagon, lined the men up at the side of the road and questioned them. It was later alleged that some of the eight were wearing items of clothing belonging to Hunt. When asked if they knew anything about Captain Hunt, one replied that he was dead. Morant then ordered them shot. One big, powerful Dutchman, seeing what was about to happen, grabbed the barrel of Witton's rifle. As Witton put it:

> I simplified matters by pulling the trigger and shooting him. I never had any qualms of conscience for having done so, as he was recognised by Ledeboer, the intelligence agent, as a most notorious scoundrel who had previously threatened to shoot him, and was the head of a band of marauders.

The remaining seven were then shot on Morant's orders. As they stood over the bodies Morant was heard to say, 'That's for Captain Hunt'. He fingered a letter in his breast pocket that had recently arrived for Hunt from his girl in Devon. It was full of gay chatter and Devonshire gossip, the author totally unaware that he would never read her tender musings. By now she would have received his letter bearing the news of his tragic death and though he had spared her feelings, Morant knew that she would take it hard. He swore to her that he would hunt them down and make them pay for Percy's death.

The Boer's wagon, mules and between twenty and thirty head of cattle was handed over to Taylor so they could begin the long, slow drive up to Mangwe, Rhodesia where he owned a farm entirely stocked with stolen Boer livestock. Morant and Handcock stayed behind to arrange the burial of the bodies before returning to Fort Edward. However, fate would again play a hand when the Reverend Heese happened by shortly after Morant and Handcock left.

> Heese [on his way to Fort Edward] naturally still saw the poor victims, for after several days their hats and other articles were still lying scattered about by the thoroughfare.

Trooper Phillip, who was on guard duty at the fort, spoke to Heese as he arrived for his interview with Captain Taylor. He was greatly agitated and said words to the effect that there had been a fight that morning and several people had been killed. However, during his meeting with Taylor, Heese is said to have sworn at him and threatened to report what he'd seen when he got back to Pietersburg.

> Captain Taylor let him leave and warned him against driving alone, since the Boers were suspected of being on the way, but of those Heese had not need have any fear; they at the most might have taken from him his draught animals. Nevertheless, on the advice of the English officials he at least still fixed a white flag to his wagon, in order to be made safe against surprise attacks by robbers by this signal.

It was at this point that Morant saw the hooded buggy drawn by two mules passing the fort on its way to Pietersburg. As passes had to be obtained by civilians wishing to travel about the countryside, Morant saddled up and went to investigate. He warned the missionary that Boers had been seen in the area and advised him to attach a white flag to the side of his cart. He returned, telling Witton that it was a missionary from Potgietersrust returning home. That was the last connection Witton had with the incident which, he believed, was the reason he was sentenced to death. Eyewitnesses who saw Lieutenant Handcock ride out about an hour after the missionary say he headed out, but in the opposite direction, whilst others say he headed in the same direction, but took a different track.

Morant's movements were also the subject of speculation. He maintained that he went to Sweetwaters to see Taylor and then onto Mrs Bristow's. However, it was claimed that he went out the afternoon that Heese was killed with a patrol of twenty to Bandolierskop, near where the missionary was killed, left them for a while and rejoined them in a highly agitated state. None of the twenty troopers he was supposedly on patrol with recalled any of this.

By Sunday evening, Heese had not arrived in Pietersburg and Superintendent Krause, head of the Berlin Missionary Society, was informed of his absence by a missionary called Endlmann, who also informed Taylor. Their first thought, that Heese had been kidnapped by Boers, was replaced by trepidation as the days passed.

Endlmann was allowed to send out a patrol of his own and on Wednesday, August 28, five days after Heese had left Fort Edward, they found his wagon with his personal effects covered in blood. But of Heese, however, there was no trace. The natives had not seen him either.

Colonel Hall was informed in Pietersburg, and on Thursday a patrol left Fort Edward to search for the missing man. They had searched the place where the wagon was found again, and seventy yards away in dense scrub and high grass, they found the body. Peter Handcock made the following report:

Report by Lieut. P J Handcock

To Capt. Taylor for OC L of CN
OC Spelonken, Sweetwater

29-8-01

Sir,

I beg to report as follows Re Rev Heese. On morning of 29/8/01 under orders I proceeded to investigate the presence of a Cape Cart reported at Bandolier Kopje and its surroundings. It being reported or rumoured a man was shot in the vicinity I proceeded with my patrol in open order and when at Bandolier Kopje one of the troopers reported a spider being crushed into the trees with the pole broken. On examining same I found as follows (2) two pipes, one table napkin marked H with red thread, one white cuff and stud, one collar size 15½, one spider wrench, and half bottle of salad oil, a few biscuits in a small sack. In the back compartment of spider between seats was a considerable amount of clotted blood. I found traces of horses being tied to trees about the spider. My suspicions being roused to the fact some foul play had taken place I spent some time with my men searching the surroundings.

After following the wheel tracks to and from the road bearing evidence of a rambling attitude we found the body of a man lying in a cramped position and in a state of decomposition rendering it difficult to judge his height or complexion. He had a wound in left breast and a wound on left hand. His whiskers of about medium length, brownish colour slightly turning grey and as near as I could judge a man of medium build. Articles found on the body were as follows: ordinary cotton shirt, drab coloured waistcoat, black trousers, white shirt front, small white tie, braces, khaki socks, brown shoes, and a truss. There were three rugs thrown on the body, 2 striped bright coloured, one a sort of tweed with ravelled edges.

Two passes were found by the body one signed by Capt. Taylor OC Spelonken, permitting the Rev Heese to return to Pietersburg and one signed by Capt. Bolton of 2nd Wilts passing Rev Heese to town and back. Captain Bolton's signature was written in blue pencil.

The pockets of the clothes were turned out, the only article of jewellery found was the stud in cuff above-mentioned which I herewith enclose.

The body was about three hundred yards from the spider and about ¾ of a mile from the main Bandolier Kopje on the Spelonken side. The mules and part of the pole and harness I found later about 3 miles from the spider. I examined the natives of nearest Kraals they would not admit having any knowledge of the occurrence. It is quite possible to have happened unknown to the natives, they are over two miles from the scene.

The mules were tangled up in the harness in a cruel manner, four or five horse tracks were traced about the scene.

Sir – If this is not sufficient Major Lenehan of BVC has a sworn statement from me and some of the men on patrol with me.

I buried the body where it laid by the telegraph line before returning to camp.

I have etc

P J Handcock Lieut. BVC

Hall forwarded on a copy of Handcock's report to Reverend Krause along with the stud that was found on the body.

Heese's wife only found out about the death of her husband on Monday, September 2. On Thursday, Missionary Sontag, with the blessing of Mrs Heese, travelled to Bandolierskop to search for the grave with Missionary Endlmann. They found the grave, erected a simple cross and read a service for him.

Heese's body was moved some months later to a more appropriate resting place by the detachment that replaced the BVC, the Pietersburg Light Horse. He was re-interned in the graveyard at the Swiss Mission at Elim next to his friend Mr Craig, who died following his operation.

Heese remained there until August 1904, when he was at last brought home to Makapanspoort, in keeping with his oft-expressed wishes, so that he might rest there among his beloved Matabeles.

There have been various theories about what happened to Heese between the time he left Fort Edward and met his death at Bandolierkop, some 15 miles west of Fort Edward. The most popular theory is that either Handcock, or Handcock and Morant, knowing that Heese had seen the bodies of the eight Boers and was on his way to Pietersburg to report it, ambushed and killed him. However, despite all the suspicion and rumours that circulated round the increasingly nervous population of Fort Edward, there was not a shred of evidence to connect either Morant or Handcock to the crime. This theory seems to hinge on the fact that Morant was seen speaking to Heese on the road just after he left for Pietersburg, and after a conversation with Morant, Handcock was seen leaving the fort about an hour after the missionary. But Trooper Van Der Westhiuzen said Morant ordered Handcock to saddle up right away and overheard part of their conversation in which Morant said, 'Mr Handcock do your best', to which he replied, 'All right, I know what to do'.

Morant's summary execution of the eight Boers and the fact that no Boers had been reported in the area that day also aroused suspicion.

Despite the misgivings of both the BVC troopers and the missionary community, Colonel Hall again turned a blind eye. On August 25, the British authorities had telegrammed to tell him that there was some concern about Heese's whereabouts. A week later he wrote the following letter to Reverend Krause, Superintendent of the Berlin Missionary Society, at whose house Heese had made a will before journeying into the Spelonken. Hall's letter was based on Handcock's report, which indicated that Hall was prepared to accept his version of events without further investigation.

2/9/01

Dear Sir,

I have had some particulars from the Spelonken about the death of the Reverend Mr Heese.

Captain Taylor warned him that the road was unsafe and strongly advised him to wait, but Mr Heese was anxious to get home and thought as he had come along the road a few days before that it was free from danger. Lieut. Morant BVC states that shortly before noon on the 23rd (August) he saw [a] buggy near the Fort at Sweetwater, as it had been stopped by a sentry he went up and found the occupant Mr Heese who had his pass all in order. Lieut. Morant warned him that Bandolierskopjes was unsafe and advised him to wait until a patrol was going down, but Mr Heese said that he wanted to get back as quickly as possible and at Lieut. Morant's suggestion he tied a white flag on his wagon and went on.

On the 27th (August) news reached Capt. Taylor's office that a missionary had been shot. Enquires were made and a patrol was sent out. The party went to Bandolierskopjes and about ¾ of a mile on the north side of it they found a trap and nearer the kopje a body. On it were passes issued to the Rev. Heese. There were bullet holes in the left breast and hand. There was no coat, but a waistcoat, harness and cotton shirt and a tie, khaki socks and brown shoes. There was a truss. The body was covered up with two rugs. There were traces of five horses which had evidently been tied to the trap for some time. The horse's tracks led to the Zoutpansberg Mountains. All the native kraals were visited without getting any information. The nearest was 2½ miles east of the trap. Two mules were found in a donga, about 3 miles from the trap. The officer gave instructions for the body to be buried and took the patrol back to the camp. There was a small stony kopje about 40 yards on the east side of the road and as Mr Heese was shot in the left side it is probable that it was from [that] spot that the bullet came. If I get any further information I will let you know it.

Yours truly

I.K. Hall
Chief Commandant

Reverend Krause did not share Hall's opinion that marauding Boers murdered Heese. He replied on September 9, enclosing a copy of a statement made to him by a native boy, Silas, which Hall had asked him for.

During the course of the afternoon at approximately 3 o'clock, he (Heese) drove off with his small black driver. On the way he met a Christian from Keuzburg named Silas, who wanted to go the same way. They exchanged greetings, and Heese drove on. Then it occurred to Silas how comfortably he could have gone along with him if he had asked the missionary for this. So, as quickly as his feet would carry him, he ran after the vehicle, if possible to overtake it. Meanwhile, an English officer rode past him. His horse was fatigued, the rider seemed to be in a hurry. Because otherwise he would not unnecessarily strain his little horse on this road, which continually went uphill and downhill. Still the black greeted the Englishman respectfully and also received from him a greeting in reply.

When Silas had again got on to the top of a rise and looked for Heese's wagon, he saw it stopped in the distance, the mules were unharnessed and were being watered. He also noticed an ox-wagon, which drove past him and whose occupants – as was later ascertained – made enquires regarding the safety of the road. The farmer, named van Rooyen, then also addressed Silas and thereby delayed him a little.

When the latter hurried on, he noticed from the tracks that the rider had dismounted and turned off with the horse into the trees, which at that spot stood fairly densely to the right and left of the road. Heese's wagon had in the meantime again disappeared from his view. Then suddenly he hears shots fired in quick succession. He stops short, and then slowly goes on. At the bend in the road he looks around in amazement for the wagon; he sees it in front of him, but to the side of the road between the trees. Surprised, he slowly draws closer. He got an uncanny feeling. For now he does [not] see any mules any more in front of the wagon, but on the other hand the saddled horse of the rider whom he had noticed earlier is standing behind it. Otherwise, no trace of a human being is to be found. Frightened to the core by this sight, he takes no notice of the road. Then, with his foot, he strikes against the corpse of the little driver. Horrified he cries out, 'What is that, here a murder has taken place!' – and as quickly as his feet can carry him he hurries away full of dread. To his good fortune and by God's dispensation – for if the murderer had got wind of him, he would have dispatched him out of this life as quickly as possible, and we would have had no trace of the perpetrator. At least we can infer that from the fact that the body was removed soon afterwards. For when other travellers came on the same road soon afterwards they could not detect anything of the murder.

Although he established the presence of someone in military uniform, Silas failed to identify either the mysterious rider or the murderer. As far as Hall was concerned, that was the end of the matter, but the killing didn't end there. Another fatal incident involving the BVC took place two weeks after the death of Heese on September 5. A patrol, under the command of Lieutenant Hannan, had been sent back to Reuter's Farm to keep an eye out for the return of Viljoen's commando or reprisals against Reuter's Mission or Eland's Farm. Trooper Christie, who was with the patrol, recalled:

We heard Boer wagons to the south and east of us, and presumed, as usual, that they were trekking in to surrender. We had been some four or five days out of camp, when the Corporal told eight of us that we were to go out and bring in three wagons with four men with them, and some women and children. We said: 'Leave them alone, they are trekking up this way out of the fever country, and will come in'.

'No,' he says, 'we are to go out. None are to be brought in'. 'What do you mean?' 'Oh', said he, 'we've got to blot a lot out'.

'What! Shoot kids?' 'Yes, of course'. 'Whose orders are those?' 'Never mind, that's orders.' Next day the patrol went out, and the sequel was that two children were shot dead – one three and another nine years and a girl of nine was shot through the neck, and the lobe of her ear taken off. Some cows were also shot. This was done about 5 o'clock at night, and, Although the men and women called out that they surrendered, the firing still went on, and when it finally ceased the above were the casualties. With the exception of three men, all the others told me before they went out they would not fire on the women and children. They were about 200 yards or 250 yards off the wagons when they opened fire. Next day I was ordered out, with a Transvaaler called Cootzee, to go to Koodoo River and take over the wagons from Corporal Ashton, and take them to the fort.

The Boers were made to inspan in the darkness and trek away, in case the firing might have been noticed by some other Boers, and a dead infant and a dying one were put on board and trekked away to where I was to meet them. The second boy only lived two hours, and the grief of the parents was loud and pronounced. The three wagons now contained four men, four women, and twenty-two children (all of tender years), and two dead bodies. Father Piet Grobler asked leave to bury them, and a coffin was made out of some boards lying about the store. The Kaffirs were put on to dig the grave, and the men themselves made the coffin. I felt we were round one of the saddest sights of the war – sad because quite unnecessary.

Christie's account conflicts with Witton's, which said that Hannam's patrol came across the wagons in the laager and called on the Boers to surrender. They then saw figures running away and when they opened fire were not aware there were women and children in the wagons. On hearing their screams, they stopped firing. Witton continued:

> I afterwards escorted these prisoners to Pietersburg, and in conversation with the parents of the children they told me that they in no way reproached Lieut. Hannam or his men for what had happened; they were themselves to blame for running away from their wagons when called upon to surrender. This is the only foundation for the wicked reports as to the wholesale shooting of women and children by the Carbineers.

Which of the two versions is correct is open to speculation, but Hannam was not prosecuted for this incident. And, again, there was nothing from Colonel Hall in Pietersburg.

The final three killings took place two days later on September 7 at Fitzgerald's Farm, close to where the eight Boers were killed. They followed a by-now familiar pattern. Intelligence was received that a party of Boers was coming in to surrender and a patrol was dispatched from Fort Edward to shoot them. On this occasion, lieutenants Morant and Handcock, Sergeant-Major Hammett, Corporal McMahon and troopers Botha and Hodds all went out together. They arrived at Elim and asked if they'd seen three Boers passing by. Around 3.30 pm they found them sitting by their wagon eating. There was an elderly man, a man in his thirties and a boy around fourteen to fifteen years old who was lying in the wagon racked by fever. All three were unarmed. The two older men were made to walk in front of the patrol for a little way and were then shot. Trooper Botha asked if he could shoot the boy, which he did as he lay in the wagon. As in the cases of Van Buuren, the eight Boers and Reverend Heese, Boers were blamed for the shootings the BVC had just carried out.

When Morant returned to the camp, he found Major Lenehan had arrived from Pietersburg. He asked Morant, 'Been shooting buck?'

'Something better than buck,' replied Morant. It was later alleged that Morant summoned Botha that same night to the officer's mess to settle an argument about the loyalty of the Boer Troopers in the BVC. Morant is said to have asked him, 'Well, Botha, did you shoot the damned Dutchman today?'

'Yes, sir, I shot him,' he confirmed, before Lenehan intervened.

'I do not want such things talked of at mess. Botha, you can go.'

Morant denied at the courts martial that any such exchange took place, but no questions were asked and still no reprimand was given, even after Lenehan returned to Pietersburg. However, unbeknown to Lenehan and the officers at Fort Edward, a dissident faction amongst the non-commissioned officers and troopers were plotting their downfall.

They did not believe that HQ had given orders to shoot prisoners and did not want to be part of the execution squad the BVC had become. It later emerged that a group of them had planned to mutiny and take the officers hostage if there were any more killings. It didn't come to that, because the shootings on September 7 were to be the final bloody entry in the short but infamous history of the Bushveldt Carbineers. Army HQ had been preparing to move against the officers at Fort Edward, even before the final killings took place.

9

Rough Justice

They say his debts he oft forgot,
    But one he settled up,
They say he used to drink a lot,
    – His last was a bitter cup.
And right or wrong, or weak or strong,
    I can't keep back the tear
For the Devil-heart, the rebel-heart
    That ceased its beating here . . .

'A Gaol-Wall Inscription' by 'Mousquetaire'

AUSTRALIAN BORN CAPTAIN RAMON De Bertodano, a thirty-year-old intelligence officer had been keeping a keen eye on events in the Spelonken, despite Colonel Hall's apparent disinterest. According to his much quoted memoir, written a half-century after the events, the heir to the Spanish title Marquis del Moral, grew up in Australia, attended the University of Sydney and worked in a solicitor's office in England before moving to Rhodesia and becoming involved in the Matabele rebellion. During this conflict, he met Captain Taylor and formed some strong opinions about his character:

> [Taylor] was known as a sadist. He frequently stirred up trouble in native kraals and then shot some natives 'in self defence', as he always stated. He was notorious and was distrusted by most white

men he came into contact with . . . I had met him
in Bulawayo during the Matabele Rebellion in
1896. Neither his face nor his eyes prepossessed me
and his reputation stank to Heaven.

It therefore came as a shock to De Bertodano when he
discovered Taylor acting as 'second in command' of the
BVC in Lenehan's absence during March 1901.

Immediately on my return to Pretoria I reported to
the D.M.I. [Director of Military Intelligence], Col.
Henderson, and told him of 'Bulala' Taylor's reputation. I urged him to see if it was possible to cancel
Taylor's appointment, as trouble was bound to
ensue! The D.M.I. reported to Lord Kitchener and
the matter was discussed, but it was found to be
very difficult. Major George Milne and I discussed
the matter at length as I was perturbed; however,
told to 'keep an eye' on Bulala Taylor.

However, despite the rumours of foul play circulating
in Pietersburg, following the dismissal of Captain
Robertson and Sergeant-Major Morrison from the
BVC, his much vaunted native intelligence network and
his spy in Fort Edward, De Bertodano failed to gather
anything concrete on Taylor's 'reign of terror'.

For some time rumours had been seeping into
Pietersburg of the behaviour of the Carbineers, but
nothing definite beyond the death of Capt. Hunt.

De Bertodano only took decisive action after the Reverend Heese was killed, and only then because he had
been party to arranging for Heese to bring Intelligence
Agent Craig to Elim Hospital and felt 'primarily responsible for having sent the poor man into the Spelonken'.

His suspicions were first aroused when he received
a telegram from his mission at Potgietersrust saying
Heese was urgently required at home. He cabled Fort

Edward to ask why Heese was being detained, received no reply, but then:

> About the 29th August a further wire came to say that the Rev. Heese had been shot by Boers at Bandolier Kopjes, 15 miles from Fort Edward on the Pietersburg road. This was a yarn I could not swallow.

Feeling sure that Taylor was somehow involved, he revisited Major George Milne and informed him, 'The Ball has commenced'. After failing to get a reply from Fort Edward about the circumstances of Heese's death, he sent two native scouts to find out what had happened. One returned after nine days saying that according to Morant's 'boy', Morant and Handcock killed Heese. De Bertodano claims that this and other intelligence caused him to switch his attention from Taylor to Morant and Handcock.

It was at this point that De Bertodano confronted Colonel Hall with his evidence and his conclusion that Lenehan, Taylor, Morant and Handcock were a 'coterie which apparently has no respect for life'. Despite his brief to keep an eye on Taylor, De Bertodano obviously knew nothing of what had been *really* going on in the Spelonken and his assumption that Hall also knew nothing appears to be based on no more than deference to a senior officer. But Hall knew that all the BVC's dirty deeds were about to become public knowledge because an investigation into the conduct of Taylor had been ongoing since the beginning of September. All Hall could do was feign innocence and sit tight.

But what really brought the 'house of cards' crashing down in the Spelonken was not the intervention of De Bertodano, as many contemporary historians have insisted. De Bertodano has been elevated to hero status in recent times, but he was not called at the courts martial, none of the main evidence used to 'nail' Morant and Handcock could be attributed to his efforts and his own reputation for truthfulness was somewhat dubious.

His previous tenure as Commissioner of Kroonstad ended early in 1901 with a court of inquiry in which he was accused of abusing his position. Among the twenty charges laid against him were fraud and embezzlement of government monies, trafficking Boer livestock, bribery and rough handling of the local population. In the end, although nine serious charges could not be explained away and the inquiry concluded that he was 'untrustworthy', he escaped punishment. He told the inquiry who had the power to order his court martial:

> No, you will not court martial me. Instead you will move me from this pestiferous little town and make me head intelligence officer in a much bigger place . . . otherwise I'll spill the beans about what's really happening in the Transvaal.

Although he did not elaborate, the threat was enough to get him moved to the Intelligence Department in Pretoria. In his forthcoming book, *The Bushveldt Carbineers and The Pietersburg Light Horse*, Bill Woolmore gives a detailed critique of De Bertodano's claims and concludes history must continue to treat both Captain De Bertodano and his error strewn version of events with great scepticism – at least until the present Marquis del Moral publishes or places his father's diaries in the public domain.

The BVC's downfall started with an innocuous sounding re-organisation of the Department of Native Affairs at the beginning of September 1901. Since the occupation and then annexation of the Transvaal by Roberts in late 1900, there was no single, cohesive body overseeing Native Affairs. The responsibility fell to a mixture of military, intelligence and civilian bodies and a Military Governor. Key administrative positions, such as magistrates, were filled by military personnel, and in the bush, intelligence agents, such as Taylor, had doubled as native commissioners under the Director of Military Intelligence, Colonel David Henderson.

Sir Godfrey Lagden was appointed Secretary for Native Affairs, with Francis Enraght-Moony in charge of Native Affairs in northern Transvaal. Enraght-Moony was now effectively Taylor's boss, at least where native affairs were concerned. The appointment was made by Kitchener's bête noire, Alfred Milner, whose consistent hard line in peace negotiations with the Boers had prevented Kitchener ending the war at Middleburg in February. There was no love lost between the two men. The involvement of do-gooding civilians in native affairs was tricky enough for the military, especially as Kitchener had secretly armed some 10,000 natives, contrary to the spirit of the conflict which the British and Boers had agreed was to be a white man's war. Even worse was the thought that Taylor's special mission of destruction might come to light.

In a letter to Colonel Henderson, Lagden confirms that Taylor was Kitchener's man in the Spelonken, by offering to order Taylor to communicate with Enraght-Moony on native affairs because 'He will not do so unless under instructions from those who appointed him'.

Kitchener later offered to let the Department of Native Affairs take over Taylor, but Lagden thought it unwise 'so as long as he is in command of men performing military service whose usefulness might be impaired at this juncture by conflicting instructions'.

Henderson wrote on September 2 to Taylor to inform him of these changes and asks him to keep Enraght-Moony informed of his actions. By way of reassurance he told Taylor, 'It is not the intention of the Minister of

Native Affairs to interfere with the administration now carried on by military officers in outlying districts.'

Henderson closed by passing on Kitchener's appreciation of his good work to date and his anticipation of 'further successes'. Taylor obviously interpreted this as 'business as usual' rather than a warning to tone things down, because on September 5, Lieutenant Hannam shot up a Boer laager, killing two children, and two days later, on Morant's instructions, three Boers were shot by the side of the road. But the days of official indifference to Taylor's murderous ways were numbered once Enraght-Moony reached Pietersburg.

Any undertaking Lagden had given Henderson about non-interference was brushed aside by Enraght-Moony, who quickly established what Taylor was up to before he had even set foot in the Spelonken – which further calls into question De Bertodano's later claim that it was he who uncovered the slaughter in the Spelonken. Within a week of Henderson's letter to Taylor, Enraght-Moony felt moved to write twice in one day, on September 11, to Lagden on the subject of Taylor, despite having no knowledge of his 'brief' or the scope of his operations.

> These instructions are noted, but appear to imply a desire from a Military point of view, to retain the services of Taylor in the Spelonken. This is to be regretted. From all the reports I have heard regarding the actions of this man, in his dealings with the Natives, the more I am convinced that he should be removed without delay. Some of the charges are so serious as to practically amount to murder. It is also reported that under the pretext of looking for Boer cattle hidden by the Natives he has seized numbers of their cattle which have been since, misappropriated. I believe this matter is in the hands of the Military.

Taylor is very rough and arbitrary in his treatment of the Natives and flogs freely. From all I can hear the Natives of the Spelonken and Zoutpansberg were very friendly disposed towards the British upon our occupation and the reports of their lawlessness were exaggerated; but, I fear, Taylor's administration is fast dispelling this friendly feeling and will in its place sow sullen antipathy. The people will associate his actions with a promised [sic] continuance of Boer methods. Another disturbing influence is the fact that Taylor uses the services of two aliens who fought against us – Schiel son of Col. Schiel formerly Native Commissioner and one Schwartz.

If you can send me a man for the Spelonken there is no reason why this should not be done at once as it is of the greatest importance to our future success in Native Administration. There is a small Military force in the Spelonken whose duty is to keep the district clear and our Native Commissioner could co-operate with this force in the matter of collecting intelligence etc. This is practically all Taylor does, for he is not in Military Command, I believe.

He followed it up with:

Your minute of 3rd only reached me yesterday as trains run at irregular intervals. I have written re Taylor again. This is a most important matter hence my insistence. I think that if we sent up a man who could co-operate with the officer in charge of the troops up there he could render as much assistance. He should have tact to be able to get on with the irregular forces – Bushfelt [sic] Carbineers – which is stationed there, in trying to put a stop to the irregularities practised by those men.

Col. Hall is in accord with me regarding the desirability – nay urgency – of removing Taylor.

He would send the best officer he could to take command and work with our man. This is of course confidential and not to be used in discussing the matter with C-in-C [Kitchener]. Taylor was sent up without reference to Col. Hall.

Two weeks after Enraght-Moony's double-barrelled blast at Taylor, Henderson wrote to Lagden on September 24:

The Chief wants to remove Captain Taylor, who is making trouble in the North. Lord K. thinks it is now time for your Department to take over the Native control of the Zoutpansberg, which is very nearly clear of Boers, and suggests that you should send up the man whom you intend to have the district finally, and let him take over now. The intention is that he should have control of Taylor's present force, about 100 men, as police and for protection . . . Please keep this quiet as possible as I do [not] wish Captain Taylor to have much warning.

On September 27, 1901 Henderson informs Lagden that Taylor has been recalled to Pretoria and Enraght-Moony is free to go up to the Spelonken. After a meeting with Kitchener, he set off and finally arrived at Sweetwaters on October 21. Having gained possession of all Taylor's files, it did not take him long to piece together the grim details of Taylor's 'administration' of the native population. On October 26 he provided Lagden with a list of Taylor's misdeeds – the third and fourth points being the most pertinent:

3.) Taylor during his administration here has adjudicated upon a number of Native cases and dealt out a rough and ready sort of justice; mostly the former. One case of Homicide was brought before him, and three Natives were sentenced to death and shot. He had no assessors on the bench with him. The notes on the case are very meagre. In another case the Natives were charged with being spies and one of them if not both were shot by Taylor's orders; while in a third instance another Native was shot, it is believed by his own hand [Taylor's] for, as it is, refusing to give information regarding Boers three.

4.) The case of Taylor is in the hands of the Intelligence department, and the notes taken in the murder case have been handed over to it, together with the Books.

The conversations that took place between these letters can only be imagined. This brief, open exchange before the court of inquiry began, gives a rare insight into the true machinations of power in the Spelonken and clearly establishes a number of key points.

Firstly, that Taylor *was* officer commanding of the BVC force at Fort Edward, which will become a crucial point as the story of the courts martial unfolds. According to Witton, Taylor admitted to this fact during the courts martial.

Secondly, Enraght-Moony revealed why Hall did nothing as the reports of BVC atrocities piled up on his desk.

But Colonel Hall did nothing about the killings, because Taylor had been installed by, and was responsible directly to, Kitchener. It would be a brave career soldier of advancing years who would challenge his commander-in-chief's orders. However, after his interview with Enraght-Moony, he knew that the killings in the Spelonken were going to come to light. It was no coincidence that he chose September 10, the day before Enraght-Moony informed Lagden of his suspicions about Taylor and the BVC, to allow Robertson to resign quietly from the BVC. He feared that if Robertson was tried, his complicity in covering up the first

seven killings would come to light. As soon as Enraght-
Moony arrived, however, he was keen to cooperate with
the civilian authorities to remove Taylor who, to his
mind, was the main protagonist at Fort Edward.

THE BVC WERE UNAWARE THAT THE net was tightening
around them and there was just enough time for one
last hurrah from Morant. In mid-September, Major
Lenehan arrived at Fort Edward to find out if there was
any substance to the rumours that were leaking out of
the Spelonken about the death of missionary Heese. He
noticed, as had others, that Morant's character had
changed since the death of Hunt. Where he had once
been cheery and gregarious, he was now irritable,
moody and morose. Lenehan even considered removing
Morant from his command.

Before he could do anything, news came in that the
notorious Veldt-cornet John Kelly and Commandant-
General Beyers had teamed up and were planning raids
in the Spelonken. Kelly was known as a great horseman, sharpshooter and – after capturing a quantity of
explosives and fuses – a dedicated train-wrecker. Intelligence said he was camped out on the Portuguese border
with two pom-pom guns and had boasted that no-one
would take him alive. For the British, it was a matter of
urgency that he be caught. Morant requested permission
to go after him. Lenehan replied, 'But we particularly
want this man brought in alive.'

'Alive!' exclaimed Morant. 'Don't you know what a
b____ scoundrel he is?'

Lenehan reiterated the importance of bringing Kelly
in alive, and on September 16, Morant led a patrol out
of Fort Edward to begin the long trek to the Portuguese
border through what the locals called 'death country',
due to the malarial mosquitoes, wild animals and hostile

tribes that inhabited it. After a wait at Birthday Mine for the scouts to join them with details of Kelly's where-abouts, they were in position and ready to strike by nightfall on September 22. Resisting the temptation of a night attack, they divided into three parties and lay in the bush grass to wait for first light. During the long night, a camp dog caught their scent and started to bark. They lay flat against the dew-drenched grass as a Boer got up and sent the dog yelping for cover with a well-aimed kick.

Morant was heard to mutter, 'A man never knows his luck in South Africa.'

In a letter to Colonel Hall dated September 25, Morant described what happened next:

There we lay till 4.30 am Monday 23rd inst. when we charged into camp with rifles loaded. The camp was taken completely by surprise. I took Kelly's rifle while he was still in bed and the camp put their hands up sulkily as the BVC collected their rifles etc. This occurred on the Thsombo River a short 12 miles from the Portuguese border and 130 miles from Fort Edward. Kelly had but a few days prior to his capture refused to surrender to the Portuguese authorities and threatened to give any English 'a warm reception' if they came after him. His rifles, with the exception of one Mauser, and his saddle gear are all British which his people have captured early in the war. I will give further details upon my arrival at Fort Edward. I hope to be in camp on Tuesday next 1st October. Kelly and the nine Boers are the last remnants of a commando which has caused much trouble in the Spelonken district, and his capture renders this district free from the enemy . . . Kelly's crowd are intact and I trust to give a safe delivery. As the country is now clear I should like permission to escort these prisoners personally to Pietersburg, leaving Lieut. Handcock in charge of the Fort, and if possible I would very much like to go to Pretoria for a couple of days to settle up the affairs of my friend, the late Captain Hunt, as he wished me to. I will write you upon my arrival at Spelonken.

Morant's claim to have captured Kelly was disputed by Trooper Silke. He recorded in his diary that *he* was the one waiting for Kelly when he popped his head out of the tent. There were other disparaging comments that Kelly was no big catch as his camp was full of women, children and dogs. Nonetheless, the credit went to Morant and despite his misgivings he brought Kelly and his whole entourage into Fort Edward alive and well. Morant then went on the two weeks leave he had requested.

Most probably 'The private matter' Morant told Lenehan he was going to fix on Hunt's behalf concerned Hunt's finances, which were in the same parlous state as his own. In that same letter, Morant told Lenehan that Hunt had left him his ponies and personal effects – which was just as well, as his tailor got what little was left!

It seems Hunt was not only 'one of the handsomest men in the British Army', but the best dressed too! In sartorial matters, at least, his profligacy rivalled Morant's. The letter of administration of Hunt's estate reveals that he died intestate and that his army tailor, John Henry White, applied to the High Court to wind up his estate which had a gross value of £193 6s 7d and a net value of nil – which meant he owed at least that amount to White. There were no other assets or property. Hunt had left his estate in good hands, Morant being no stranger to such financial imbroglios.

Notwithstanding Hunt's untimely death, Morant had every reason to feel satisfied with his lot as he rode

Bideford Boy, whom he named after his favourite Devon town, towards Pietersburg. He had turned the BVC into a formidable fighting unit and cleared the most trenchant Boers in South Africa out of their heartland. Kelly's capture earned Morant the plaudits he had come to South Africa to earn, and he received a message of congratulations from Colonel Hall: 'Very glad to hear of your success, and should like to hear an account of what must have been good bit of work.'

Kitchener, desperate for any success against the Boers, also sent his congratulations to the man he would shortly turn his guns on, and Kelly's capture made the national newspapers in both Australia and Britain. As Morant supped his first cold beer for many months, the thought probably crossed his mind that he'd bagged a Distinguished Service Order or a promotion, which might curry some favour with his obdurate father. He could never have guessed that he'd led his last patrol across the veldt.

Things moved swiftly in Morant's absence. With both Taylor and Morant out of the way, fifteen disgruntled troopers and non-commissioned officers who had recently returned to Pietersburg after serving at Fort Edward seized their opportunity. They, like most of the men who joined the BVC, had no intention of signing up for another six months. Together they made the following sworn deposition to Trooper RM Cochrane, who had been a Justice of the Peace in Western Australia.

To
Colonel Hall

Line of Communications
Pietersburg

We the undersigned non-commissioned officers and men of the Bushveldt Carbineers recently returned from the Spelonken district feel it is our imperative duty to ask you to kindly hold an exhaustive and impartial Inquiry into the following disgraceful incidents which have occurred in the Spelonken district in order that the exact truth may be elicited and the blame attributed to those responsible. These disgraceful incidents are:

1.) On July 2nd the shooting of six surrendered Boer prisoners who were entirely disarmed and who offered no resistance whatsoever.
2.) On July 15th the shooting of Trooper Van Buuren BVC by Lieut. Handcock BVC for reasons which will be detailed later on.
3.) August 11th. The shooting of a surrendered and wounded Boer prisoner, Visser, after conveying him 15 miles.
4.) August 23rd. Shooting eight surrendered Boer prisoners and one German missionary.
5.) September 5th. Lieut. Hannam BVC and party fired on wagons containing women and children although no resistance whatever was offered, in spite of remonstrations of the men, killing 2 children of tender years and wounding one little girl.
6.) Sept 7th. Shooting 2 men and a boy who were coming in to surrender.

Details
Charge No.1 July 2nd. Intelligence was received that six Boers were coming in 2 wagons to surrender. One of the six was a very old man very sick with fever. Sergeant Major Morrison instructed Sergt Oldham to kill all the prisoners alleging that the orders came from Captain Robertson BVC. The Boers were totally disarmed and did not, as alleged, offer any resistance whatever. When dead, bandoliers were placed on the bodies and rifles by sides. It was noticed by the rest of the patrol when it came

up that in the excitement and confusion of the
moment some of the bodies had been placed on
bandoliers with Mauser ammunition and by their
sides were Martini Henry rifles. In the wagon there
was supposed to be a box containing about £2000.
As will be proved by eyewitnesses it is entirely false
that these Boers made any attempt to escape or
offered any resistance whatever. The firing party
consisted of Sergt Oldham, Troopers Eden, Arnold,
Brown, Leath and Dale. This is probably the only
case in which there may be some trouble to get the
witnesses together.

2.) July 14th. Trooper Van Buuren disapproved of
the events of the 2nd July and communicated the
true facts of the case to the relatives of the murdered
men. Next day he was taken out by Lieut. Handcock BVC in a district where the patrol claims there
was not a single Boer to be seen. Trooper Van
Buuren never came back, Lieut. Handcock saying
he had been shot by the Boers, but it is the consensus of opinion of the men that Van Buuren was shot
by Lieut. Handcock and not by the Boers. This is
believed the more readily as Lieut. Handcock has
repeatedly threatened to shoot any man who spoke
a word of dissent from the questionable proceedings. The troopers who were nearest to the deceased
were Troopers Eden, Arnold and Brown.

3.) Aug. 11th. The wounded Boer prisoner, Visser,
on this occasion was conveyed about 15 miles. He
was then given a short period of time in which to
write home. He was told that he had been tried at
courts martial and condemned to death though he
certainly was never present at any courts martial and
we do not believe one was ever held. At the time he
was wearing an old British warm and was not clad
in the tunic of the late Capt. Hunt as Major Lenehan

BVC tried to prompt the witnesses to swear when he held a so-called 'inquiry' in the fort at Spelonken recently.

4.) Aug. 23rd. Shooting of eight surrendered Boer prisoners and one German missionary. This party of eight Boers was being marched into camp by Sergt Wrench. The Boers had of course been disarmed. The rifles of the Boers were on the wagon but the bolts of all had been withdrawn and were in the possession of the escort. The escort was met close to the hospital by Lieut. Handcock and Lieut. Morant, both of the BVC, who told Sergt Wrench to ride on with his men. A little later some shots were fired from a kopie (but not by Boers) to simulate an attempt at rescue. The whole of the Boer prisoners were immediately shot. The firing party consisted of Lieuts Morant, Handcock and Witton, Sergt-Major Hammett, Troopers A. Thompson and Duckett.

The Rev. Mr Heese was walking alongside the wagon conversing with the prisoners. He was ordered to depart. The shooting then occurred. If not an eye-witness he must have returned almost immediately, attracted by shooting, and must have seen the unburied bodies. Shortly after he passed the pickets in a state of great excitement. Lieut. Handcock shortly after left the camp armed. Three Kaffir boys in the district affirm that they saw Lieut. Handcock shoot the missionary. Later on when men had searched in vain for the body to bury it Lieut. Handcock went straight to the place where the body was found, itself a suspicious circumstance. Mr Pritchard, storekeeper, can produce the Kaffir boys who state they saw the missionary shot. Mr Bristow, farmer and storekeeper, Sweetwaters, can also give valuable evidence as to the shooting of the eight surrendered prisoners.

5.) Sept. 5th. Lieut. Hannam and party fired on 3 wagons containing women children and 4 men. When the first shot was fired by the BVC disclosing their presence the Boers shouted 'We surrender' but Although Lieut. Hannam knew that the Boers wished to surrender and that from first to last they never fired a single shot in token of their desire to surrender, he ordered his men to continue firing with the result that two little boys were killed and one little girl wounded. The casualties would have been more numerous but the bulk of the firing party disdaining to fire on women and children and men who had offered to surrender, deliberately fired over the wagons. Altogether from 200 to 250 rounds were fired by Lieut. Hannam's positive orders to keep on firing long after the Boers appeals to be allowed to surrender had been heard and the shrieks of the women and children had revealed their presence in the wagons.

6.) Shooting two men and a boy who were coming in to surrender. Sept. 7th. The afternoon Major Lenehan BVC arrived at the Fort, Lieuts Handcock and Morant, Sergt-Major Hammett, Corporal McMahon, Troopers Botha and Hodds went out and shot two old men and a youth of 14 who were on their way in to surrender. The youth was sick with fever and was being supported by the two old men. The orders given were: 'When I tell you to dismount you dismount and put a cartridge in the breach of your rifle: directly I say "Hands up" shoot them down.' In the evening Tpr Botha was called into the mess room and the following conversation took place:

Lieut. Morant: 'Well, Botha, did you shoot the damned Dutchman today' [meaning the sick boy]? Tpr Botha: 'Yes, sir, I shot him.' Major Lenehan: 'I do not want such things talked of at mess. Botha, you can go.'

From this and other reasons we believe Major Lenehan to be privy to these misdemeanours. It is for this reason that we have taken the liberty of addressing this communication direct to you.

Sundry civilian witnesses can give evidence of importance provided they are guaranteed protection for a veritable reign of terror has prevailed in this district. Their names are: – Mr Bristow, farmer; the doctor at the Spelonken hospital, Mr Hayes, storekeeper, Mrs Cooksley, Mr Petringh, farmer; Mr Van Seker (?), farmer and storekeeper; Mr Pritchard, storekeeper and others. Among the Bushveldt Carbineers there are plenty of troopers in the Spelonken district who if brought in would gladly give evidence.

Sir, many of us are Australians who have fought throughout nearly the whole war while others are Africanders who have also fought from Colenso till now. We cannot return home with the stigma of these crimes attached to our names. Therefore we humbly pray that a full and exhaustive inquiry may be made by impartial Imperial officers in order that the truth may be elicited and justice done. Also we beg that all witnesses may be kept in camp at Pietersburg till the inquiry is finished. So deeply do we deplore the opprobrium which must be inseparably connected with these crimes that scarcely a man once his time is up can be prevailed to re-enlist in this corps. Trusting for the credit of thinking you will grant the inquiry we seek.

We are, sir,
your obedient servants.

[Sdg]
ERNEST G. BROWNE Cpl
A. SKELTON Trooper
A.W.M. THOMPSON Trooper

J. HATFIELD Trooper
C. SHERIDAN Trooper
J.W. H. PENN Trooper
A. DUCKETT Trooper
JAS CHRISTIE Trooper
E. STRATTON Trooper
GEO D. LUCAS Trooper
F.C. HAMPTON Trooper
H.Y. COX Trooper
A. VAN DER WESTHUIZEN Trooper
A.R. MC CORMICK Cpl.
JOHN SILKE Trooper

The signatures of many other men now absent on
patrol can also be obtained.
Witness to all the above signatures

[Sgd] R.M. COCHRANE Justice of the Peace,
W. Australia
4 October 1901

The summary was accompanied by the following document which presented their complaints and allegations
in more detail:

Memorandum

The following memorandum is submitted to
amplify the preceding one, that having then
confined to statements to which we had all the
necessary in camp. This memorandum will suppl-
[ement]some omissions in the previous one.

Complicity of Capt. Taylor
Before the six prisoners were shot there was a
meeting of officers at Sweetwaters Farm. There
were present Capt. Taylor, Capt. Robertson, Lieut.
Handcock. Nearly the whole patrol could see them.
Immediately the council was over Sergt-Major Morrison was called up and received instructions from

Capt. Robertson to wipe out the prisoners. He and Capt. Robertson can alone prove whether Capt. Taylor was actually present when these orders were given him. Capt. Taylor was undoubtedly present at the council. It can be abundantly proved that Capt. Taylor also saw the dead bodies lying in the road.

The witnesses required in this case are: Capt. Robertson, at present in Pietersburg, was present at council, issued instructions to S.S.M. Morrison, saw dead bodies.

S.S.M. Morrison, address unknown, received the instructions and conveyed them to Sergt. Oldham. Must, address unknown, was left at Sweetwaters Farm in charge of the residue of the patrol. Sergt. Oldham, received instructions from S.S.M. Morrison and executed them. He was in charge of the firing party. Address Pietersburg.

Trooper Eden. Address unknown, member of firing party.

Trooper E. Brown. Address unknown, member of firing party.

Trooper Heath. Address unknown, member of firing party.

Trooper Dale. Address unknown, member of firing party.

Corpl. Primrose. He was a member of the firing party, but was sent back with a report before the actual firing took place. Address Pietersburg. It lies between Troopers Eden and Dale as to which shot the aged sick Boer who was unable to leave his bed in the wagon. Trooper Arnold, address Pietersburg, was a member of the firing party.

Other witnesses are:

Corporal Browne saw the dead bodies. Saw the Kaffir Voorloper alive after the shooting but, who with two other Kaffir eye-witnesses, was chased by small patrol and shot in their back on Bristow's Farm. Corporal Browne can testify that the order to shoot the six Boers was issued at a council meeting (or rather shortly after it) at Sweetwaters Farm. Corporal Browne's address, BVC Orderly Room, Pretoria. Trooper Penn, Pietersburg can probably supply the names of the patrol who shot the three Kaffir eye-witnesses.

Q.M.S. Venables, Pietersburg, superintended the digging of the graves in which were buried the six Boers. He can also probably give the names of the patrol who shot the Kaffir eye-witnesses. The above witnesses are concerned with the shooting of the six surrendered Boer prisoners on July near a Kaffir kraal by an empty house. The patrol travelled easterly from Sweetwaters Farm. It passed Dr Leyme's [Liengme's] private hospital some 6, or 7 miles till the aforesaid empty house was reached. There the tragedy occurred.

It should be stated that after the shooting Capt. Taylor rode alone to the Kaffir kraal and it is presumed instructed the Kaffirs what evidence to give. Three Inconvenient ones were chased and shot.

Shooting of Trooper van Buuren
The witnesses are:
Trooper Eden, member of patrol left flanks
Trooper Arnold, member of patrol left flanks
Trooper Brown, member of patrol left flanks

Regimental books will give full names of patrol if required. Address of Troopers Eden and Brown unknown. Trooper Arnold is at Pietersburg. Corporal Browne states that he could approximately indicate the site of the murder and if provided with an interpreter could probably find or trace the rifle, bandolier and body of the murdered man.

Shooting of the wounded Boer, Visser
The following troopers volunteered to shoot the wounded man:
Trooper Petrie, hospital, Spelonken
Trooper Gill, Pietersburg
Lieut. Picton BVC after the shooting stepped up to the Boer who was not dead and blew his brains out with a revolver.

Other witnesses are:
S.S.M. Hammett, Spelonken
S.S.M. Clarke, Pietersburg
Sergt. Wrench
Corpl. McCormick
Trooper Christie
Corpl. Sharpe, Spelonken
Corpl. Torquis, Durban (?)

The officers present were:
Lieut. Morant
Lieut. Picton
Lieut. Handcock
    It is believed that Lieut. Witton was also present though I am not absolutely certain of this. The fact can be easily ascertained.

Shooting eight surrendered Boer prisoners and one German missionary Aug. 23.
    This tragedy took place about half way between the private hospital and officers present were:
Lieut. Morant, who fired himself
Lieut. Handcock, who fired himself
Lieut. Witton, who fired himself
S.S.M. Hammett, who fired himself
Sergt Wrench who was in charge of the prisoners and who was asked to leave before the firing began.
Trooper A. Thompson was coerced into firing.
Trooper Duckett was coerced into firing.
Thompson and Duckett are in Pietersburg.

Shooting of the Missionary
Corpl. Sharpe, Spelonken, saw Lieut. Handcock, armed, leaving camp and could give the names of the others. Lieut. Handcock usually rode a chestnut pony about 13 hands, a stoutly built pot-bellied animal, no white marks, except under saddle.

On the day the missionary was shot a picket comprising Trooper Phillips, Wrangham and Benadie were at Cooksley's Farm, saw Van Rooyen [a farmer] who told them he had passed one of the BVC in the vicinity of Bandolier Kopjes.

Almost immediately after the tragedy Lieut. Handcock heard that Troopers Wrangham and Phillips knew of the murder of the missionary. He sent for them, cross-questioned them very minutely as to the extent of their knowledge and the source where they got it. All the time he seemed labouring under very great excitement.

Slaughter by Lieut. Hannam of two little Boer boys and the wounding of one little girl Sept. 5. The two principal witnesses in this case are:
Trooper Hatfield, Pietersburg
Trooper Hampton, Pietersburg
    They will call what others may be required and should be called upon to name them.
Shooting at Mr Bristow [ie. on his farm]
The witnesses are:
Trooper Lucas who was on guard. Address Pietersburg
Trooper Bonnie [Bonney] Address Pietersburg. Cook to officer's mess, has never had the opportunity yet to give evidence, but probably can give material evidence.

Shooting of two men and a boy Sept. 7th
    The officers and others present at this tragedy were:

Lieut. Morant
Lieut. Handcock
Sergt. Major Hammett
Corporal McMahon
Trooper Hodds

All of whom fired except Trooper Hodds who was sent back with two mules just before they met the Boers.

Of these S.S.M. Hammett and Corporal McMahon are in the Spelonken. Trooper Hodds is in Pietersburg and Trooper Botha in Pretoria.

The three shot are stated to have been grandson, father and grandfather. The boy was so sick with fever that he could not walk alone, but had to be supported by the other two.

Fabrication of evidence by Major Lenehan
When Major Lenehan was sent out to hold an inquiry he endeavoured to bounce the troopers into giving evidence which would exonerate the officers. Particularly he tried to make them swear that the wounded Boer prisoner Visser shot on Aug. 11th was wearing the tunic of the late Capt. Hunt where as the witnesses pointed out that the clothes of the late Capt. Hunt's had been continuously worn by Lieut. Morant who was wearing them himself at that moment. Lieut. Morant wore the late Capt. Hunt's British Warm, riding breeches, tunic and leggings. When the witnesses refused to swear what Major Lenehan required but swore that the prisoner was wearing an old British Warm Major Lenehan ordered the men out of the tent as if they had been dogs saying 'That kind of evidence is no good to us.'
The witnesses are:
Corporal Gibbons, Spelonken
Sergt. Robinson, Spelonken
S.S.M. Clarke, Pietersburg

Complicity of Major Lenehan

When the two Boers and a boy were shot Sept 7th, Major Lenehan heard the firing. As Lieut. Morant came in the following conversation occurred:

Major Lenehan: 'Have you been shooting buck?'

Lieut. Morant: 'Something better than buck.'

At the mess table, in Major Lenehan's presence, Lieut. Morant elicited from Trooper Botha the statement that he had that day shot the Dutch boy. The witnesses are:

Trooper Lucas, Pietersburg

Trooper Botha, Pretoria

and others whose names I have not booked but who will readily come forward if asked. The last outrages, of which only the barest information is yet to hand, occurred while Major Lenehan was in charge. For full information apply to Corpl Sharpe, Spelonken.

Attempts on the lives of Troopers whose deaths were desired to extinguish evidence.

The lives of the following were deliberately attempted:

Sergt. Wrench, address Pietersburg

Sergt. Rogers, address Spelonken

Trooper Lucas, address Pietersburg

Trooper Dale, address unknown

It is tolerably certain that Capt. Taylor was privy to the attempt to murder Sergt. Wrench.

Plot to murder forty-five prisoners at Fort Edward by shooting

A very plain hint was conveyed by Lieut. Hannam to Corporal Browne to the same effect, that the blotting out of prisoners was desired. Corporal Browne's address, Pretoria (BVC orderly room, Church Street).

Plot to murder the forty-five prisoners at Ford Edward by poison

When the men were 'too squeamish' the officers said, to shoot the Boer Prisoners, Ambulance Sergeant Baker was requested to poison them with strychnine (note: they may have been arsenic tabloids). These tabloids, whether arsenic or strychnine, were requisitioned from the doctor who was then living at the fort. His name can be ascertained. It is not believed that he was aware of the criminal purpose for which these tabloids were intended to be used. He had left the fort before any suggestion was made to Sergt. Baker to use the tabloids.

Baker consulted with Corporal Browne what he was to do to prevent himself being shot when the time came to refuse to poison the prisoners. He was advised by Corpl. Browne to procure some other tabloids of a mild and harmless nature and to substitute them for the poisonous ones.

The witnesses therefore are:

Ambulance Sergeant Baker, Spelonken
Corporal Browne, BVC orderly room, Pretoria

Thefts of Cattle

Considerable thefts of cattle have occurred from friendly Kaffirs and others, but principally from murdered prisoners. These cattle have been driven into Matabeleland to Capt. Taylor's farms there and Portuguese territory. Many of the BVC – I believe, can give some evidence on this point, but Capt. Taylor is known mostly to have employed his own Kaffir boys in the work. S.S.M. Morrison is believed to have been an interested party in this business.

The Gold Nuggets

The gold dust and nuggets taken from the wagon when the Boers were slaughtered on July 2nd is believed to be in Capt. Taylor's possession for subdivision after the war.

Object of these crimes

It may be asked what was the object of their crimes? The general belief is that it was actuated by lust for loot in Land, Cattle and Gold. The programme appears to have been to wipe out the holders of certain farms which they had hoped to get for themselves after the war in return for their distinguished services, to round up loot cattle for stocking the same and to provide a surplus for sale to get ready money and lastly to lay their hands on all ready money and portable valuables possible. Then after the war they could settle down as wealthy landed proprietors while all inconvenient evidence as to how the wealth was acquired would have been snuffed out with Lee Metford bullets. This last paragraph is of course a surmise but it is believed generally among the men to have been the main motive. A minor motive was also probably to avenge Capt. Hunt's death. The last was the motive assigned to the men by Lieut. Morant.

Antecedents of Major Lenehan

R.Q.M.S. Ross can prove that Major Lenehan was drummed out of the permanent Artillery in New South Wales. His cowardice in the field in this country has been commented on in the Bulletin, Sydney which nicknamed the 'Hero of Abram's Kraal' R.Q.M.S. Ross was an eye-witness of his cowardice at Abram's Kraal and subsequent engagements. Further testimony can be got From Lieut. Col. Knight, New South Wales Mounted Rifles.

Forgery of Col. Hall's Name

To make the men believe that these crimes had the sanction of Col. Hall sundry contemptible devices were practised. One time, when the men were showing their disgust very freely, Lieut. Morant and Handcock ordered Sergt. Rogers to tell the men

that, 'These proceedings are sanctioned at headquarters and the orders must be carried out.' But
for the fact that many men believed that they would
have no support at headquarters in refusing, and
they would have been sent to the Breakwater [Cape
Town prison] for two or three years penal servitude
for mutiny they would never have carried out these
orders. Another time to strengthen this conviction
a report of the illicit shooting of the six Boers on
July 2nd – an account of alleged resistance – was
left lying where it must have been seen by several.
It bore the following endorsement: 'This report will
not do. How could disarmed men assume the offensive. Send something more probable . . . Hall.' The
above words may not be verbatim as they are
written from memory and the initial is forgotten but
that was the purpose of the endorsement. It was also
insinuated that profits of the cattle thefts were par-
ticipated in at headquarters. Who the author of this
forgery is I cannot say. The presumption is that if
the idea did not originate with Lieut. Morant the
endorsement was written by him as Lieut. Handcock would not write or spell the simplest sentence
without disclosing his authorship; he was so grossly
illiterate. This statement has been compiled by me
from the statements given to me by those concerned.

[Sgd] R. M. Cochrane, Justice of the Peace,
W. Australia
7 October 1901

Dated October 7 and signed by all the men named, the
deposition was then sent to Colonel Hall in Pietersburg.
It must be said that most of the allegations made in the
preceding documents were dismissed without further
investigation and rightly so as it was, for the most part,
a witches' brew of rumour and half-truths with a generous pinch of malice aforethought.

Nonetheless, it is clear from their collective statement that the issue that caused the men to denounce their own officers was the 'take no prisoners' order. The reason they gave for making the statement was that as Australians, they did not want charges of murder to stain the good name of their fellow countrymen. Roughly translated this meant that they could not conceive that HQ would order the shooting of Boer prisoners or Boers in khaki and believed their officers had invented them to satisfy their own blood-lust. However, as these men were not without military experience and demonstrated an open dislike of their officers, a far more likely explanation is that the statement was intended to cover their own backs. In other words, they fully understood that shooting prisoners was one of the 'black' secrets of war and was condoned by the command if kept quiet. But the situation in the BVC had got completely out of hand due to Taylor's sadism and greed, Morant's thirst for vengeance and Handcock's blind loyalty. How long before the dark deeds of the BVC came to light and tainted them all?

With the Berlin Missionary Society, De Bertodano and Enraght-Moony all breathing down his neck, Hall had a reasonable expectation that what had been going on in the Spelonken was going to be discovered. The troopers' deposition had been sent to him without his prompting and it was his duty to pass it on to Army HQ in Pretoria. The onus was now on them. We will never know whether it was the BVC deposition, the death of Heese, the impending arrival of Enraght-Moony in the Spelonken or a combination of all three that forced HQ to act, but they wasted little time.

In a diary entry dated October 7, Provost Marshal Robert Poore records the arrival of the deposition:

At about 6 pm Bolton (Wilts Regt.) (APM [Assistant Provost Marshal] Pietersburg) arrived with some papers about rather bad things which have been taking place North of Pietersburg . . . I just gave the outline of the case to Lord K. but the case is a bad one as it's the officers who are implicated.

Shortly afterwards, the man who had founded the BVC only eight months before, was asked to convene a court of inquiry to investigate the allegations made against them. The men mentioned in the BVC deposition to Hall were brought down to Army HQ in Pretoria between October 9 and 14 and questioned by both Kitchener and Poore.

This was kept secret from Major Lenehan, who was dispatched in mid-October to Fort Edward to compile a report on what had been going on. They never found out what his report contained, because on October 21 all officers, non-commissioned officers and troopers were ordered to abandon Fort Edward and return to Pietersburg. On Poore's instructions, Lenehan was promptly arrested along with Sergeant-Major Hammett and Lieutenants Handcock, Hannam and Witton when they arrived in Pietersburg. Captain Taylor was already in custody and Morant was the last to be picked up on his return from leave.

All the accused officers were taken into custody on the day Enraght-Moony arrived in the Spelonken, on October 21, a week late owing to Moony and his fifty-two man escort having to turn back to Pietersburg due to 'a sudden movement of Boers' – not a month after the Director of Military Intelligence had assured him 'the area is nearly clear of Boers'. This delayed Enraght-Moony's arrival just long enough for the BVC to be recalled. A suspicious mind might suggest that it was more than mere coincidence. Enraght-Moony had been fearless and adroit at seeing through Taylor's thin veneer; how long before he discovered the rest? But by the time he arrived in the Spelonken, there was no-one left to tell tales.

According to a letter written by Lagden after the war was over, Enraght-Moony already knew or suspected the awful truth:

> You will remember that about a year ago there occurred in the Zoutpansberg District a series of horrible scandals for which Morant and Handcock were shot . . . Moony brought these stories to my notice long before they were heard of by the outside world. His presence up there no doubt tended to check entirely any recurrence of the atrocities.

Provost Marshal Poore took on the role of chief detective as the court of inquiry began sifting the evidence and taking the officers' statements on November 6. Throughout the court's deliberations, the accused were kept in close solitary confinement, with orders that they were not allowed to communicate with each other or see anyone. Even the prison chaplain, Reverend Joshua Bourgh, was told to keep away from them. The officers were offered no legal advice for their defence during this critical stage of the inquiry. Finally, after a fortnight, they were brought before the court and told what charges had been levelled against them. Witton, who survived to tell the tale in his book *Scapegoats of The Empire*, which remains the only detailed record of the trial, said of the court of inquiry:

> A great deal of pride is evinced in what is called British justice, but after that court of inquiry I doubted if such a thing ever existed. This piece of history could well be dated back to the days of the Star Chamber or the Spanish Inquisition . . . I always understood that a man was innocent until he was proved to be guilty; that position was here reverse, and we were adjudged guilty until we were proved innocent.

Poore recruited Corporal Sharpe of the BVC, who was a detective in the former South African Republic, to round up witnesses to give evidence. According to Witton, Sharpe had been arrested several times whilst in the BVC and reprimanded for selling khaki uniforms, and was later forced to admit in court that he had said he would be 'willing to walk 90 miles bare-footed from the Spelonken to Pietersburg to give evidence against Morant'.

For the prosecution, Sharpe was gathering men like Trooper Botha, who was known to have a strong animus against the officers. He had known Visser and resented being part of the firing party, and gave evidence against the BVC officers – even though he had asked to shoot the young, sick boy when the final three Boers were killed. In any event, Botha's treacherous nature caught up with him after the trial when he was shot dead in the street in Pretoria.

Jas Christie, who turned against Morant following the shooting of Visser and signed the letter to Colonel Hall, set himself against Reverend Reuter when he claimed that Hunt's body was not mutilated when he helped prepare it for burial. His comment after hearing news of the arrests, 'we've almost done the job, six of them are in clink', reveals more than just a passing interest in seeing justice done.

Witton also complained about the draconian methods of the court of inquiry who interviewed BVC men, wrote a statement for them and told them to sign it. Meanwhile, the witnesses requested by the accused could not be found, or it was deemed too expensive to bring them back from their new postings. And the disgraced former captain, Robertson, who but for Colonel Hall would have been facing similar charges to Morant, was retained as a witness by the prosecution at the princely sum of £1 per day.

Following his return to Australia, Major Lenehan tried for years, without success, to get the Australian government to hold an official inquiry into the executions of Morant and Handcock. During these efforts he made a great many depositions about the court of inquiry and revealed that Morant and Handcock were offered an immunity deal. According to Lenehan:

> Both Lieutenants Morant and Handcock informed me that the Court stated to them if they received orders from me to shoot prisoners, nothing could happen to them as I alone was responsible.

In other words, if Morant and Handcock were prepared to say that Major Lenehan gave them the order to shoot prisoners, they would be protected by military law which in 1902 decreed that receiving superior orders was a defence. If the blame could be attached to Lenehan, this would protect not only Morant and Handcock, but everyone above him, including Hall and Kitchener. Offering Morant and Handcock immunity was an *ipso facto* acceptance by the court of inquiry that orders to shoot prisoners did exist, but to Lenehan's obvious relief:

> They were, however, too honest to perjure themselves, and save their lives at my expense, and persisted in stating as they did to the hour of their death, where the orders did come from, viz:– Headquarters.

Morant, in particular, was in a volatile and emotional state after being arrested. He believed that he was being persecuted for following orders given to him by Captain Hunt, who had in turn received them from Lieutenant-Colonel Hubert Hamilton on Kitchener's behalf. Many witnesses stated Hunt had repeated the order many times and berated Morant and others for bringing in prisoners. That only changed when Hunt was murdered and mutilated. This was the simple and consistent basis of Morant and Handcock's defence from the day of their arrest to the morning Morant faced down the firing party.

Having failed to snare Lenehan, the court of inquiry turned on Handcock, who they saw as the more impressionable of the two. According to Witton, Handcock was staggered by the charges laid against him:

> He was so completely ignorant of military law and court proceedings that he asked the president what would be the best course for him to pursue; he was advised to make a clean breast of everything, as the responsibility would rest solely on Lieutenant Morant.

Again, there was an offer of immunity, but Handcock refused to make a statement and was returned to solitary.

According to Witton, Handcock did make a 'clean breast of it' later in a confession, to please Colonel Carter, who headed the court of inquiry. Although Morant got him to withdraw it later, a copy was supposedly sent to Kitchener, but it was never used in court and its exact content never made public. Instead, its existence was held over the accused like the sword of Damocles during the court of inquiry and courts martial that followed. Perhaps Handcock said too much, as he had in his report on the killing of Van Buuren. According to British military law, a statement made during a court of inquiry must be used in its *entirety* during the subsequent courts martial; extracts cannot be used to imply guilt on the part of the accused. The other possible scenario is that the judge advocate general ruled the evidence inadmissible given the manner of its acquisition. Its use may have tainted the courts martial.

Witton was of the opinion that the 'confession' was coerced out of Handcock:

> Is it possible to conceive such an iniquity perpetrated in these days of supposed civilisation? – a

man charged with numerous murders shut up alone, without a soul from whom he could seek advice; condemned before he was tried. There could only be one ending; Handcock's mind gave way, and when he was not responsible for his actions he was forced into making a statement which incriminated himself and Lieutenant Morant.

Lenehan also complained about the bullying tactics adopted during the court of inquiry:

Lieutenant Edwards, the Adjutant of the Regiment, was so pressed to give evidence against me; and such endeavours were made to intimidate him, that he refused to speak until an Australian representative was present.

The uncommon secrecy that surrounded the court of inquiry was obvious not just to the prisoners, but those who worked at HQ itself. In 1947, during one of the periodic revivals of the Breaker legend, a former Australian officer recalled the atmosphere around Army HQ and questions Kitchener's later claim that the BVC officers were prosecuted as soon as the details of their misdemeanours were known. It seems stories of their misdeeds were common currency around both Pietersburg and Pretoria long before charges were laid:

During the Morant affair I was a very junior officer in the British Army attached to the staff at HQ Pretoria. The Bush Veldt Carbineers were a tough mob, but no worse than the mob they were supposed to pacify, vengeful and bitter Dutch from all over South Africa . . . Those doughty antagonists recognised no rules. Stories of their supposed doings drifted in from the bush veldt and caused no little excitement in Pretoria and Army circles generally. The occasional BVC officer who drifted into the Officers' Club in Pretoria was viewed with alarm by the old guard, but we juniors were always ready to buy drinks in return for stories with plenty of local colour. Morant was a frequent enough visitor to be known by name and sight to quite a lot of us, so that when news of his arrest came through we were intensely interested . . . It would be hard to convey the secrecy that surrounded not so much the court martial as the preparation of the case and all the details – the guarding of witnesses and the threats of punishment if any talking was done.

However, given the tenor of Morant and Handcock's defence, it became obvious that Colonel Hall would be a liability to the prosecution case. How could they justify prosecuting Lenehan when he let Captain Robertson resign his commission with the blood of seven men on his hands? In defending himself, Hall would have to admit that Taylor's orders came not from him, but from Kitchener at Army HQ. Sometime between the start of the court of inquiry and the courts martial, Colonel Hall was posted to India. It has been claimed that it was a legitimate posting, but the fact remains that *the* key witness was allowed to leave the country without ever making a statement or being interviewed by the defence counsel. It should also be noted that the posting can only have been ordered and approved by the Commander-in-Chief himself!

Oblivious to the machinations of the legal department, which was sifting information and framing the case against them, Morant concerned himself with the whereabouts of his horse and personal property, and fretted about missing the fox-hunting season in England:

11/12/01

DEAR MAJOR,

I received from a Captain Bell a memo about my horse 'Bideford Boy' being on the Pietersburg Light

Horse lines. Do you remember a black that Hunt left in charge of Anderson. when we first navigated towards Spelonken? The black, which was a private horse of Hunt's, was a very fair polo nag, and that is why he did not take it on trek with us. I have an idea that the horse was returned to BVC lines and that Neel had care of it. I should like to find out what has become it. Everything of mine and Hunt's in Pretoria had been looted from our house.

I blame Johnson for d_____d carelessness; even fox marks and brushes were taken! Talking of marks and brushes! __ this is December ___ they're killing foxes down in Devon with Mark Rolle's hounds whilst I am 'helping to save the Empire', in d_____d D_____d solitary confinement. Of such is the Kingdom of Brass Hats! Can you tell me what became of the black? as I wish to get the nag before a Government brand is applied – if that has been done someone will have to compensate. I haven't written home or to Hunt's people since I've been knee-haltered.

Thine,

'TONY'

Please answer; or who would know what became of that horse?

On December 21, the news came down that Morant, Handcock, Witton, Picton and Taylor would be charged with murder and Major Lenehan with failing to report a murder to his superior officer.

Sergeant-Major Hammett and Lieutenant Hannam, however, had no case to answer – despite the latter being involved in the incident in which two children died.

Other interesting opinions to come out of the court of inquiry include a clear admission about Taylor's role:

> I think that taking all circumstances of Case No.1
> (the 6 Boers) into consideration the responsibility
> should rest with the officer 'Captain Taylor' who
> gave the order to this N.C.O. through Sgt. Major
> Morrison . . . The idea that no prisoners were to be
> taken in the Spelonken appears to have been started
> by the late Capt. Hunt and after his death contin-
> ued by orders given personally by Capt. Taylor.

In a later memo to Major-General Kelly, Colonel St Clair
confidently predicted they would get the desired result:
'The summary has been carefully taken and should
I think be sufficient to prove several charges.'

No mention is made of Handcock's 'confession' in
which he supposedly admitted to killing Reverend Heese
on Morant's orders. In a telegraph to Adjutant General
Major-General Kelly, Major Bolton, who had been
appointed prosecutor, asked, 'In case of missionary I can
obtain no further evidence stop Can I withdraw charge
against Morant absolutely no evidence in his case'.

The request was denied. On hearing the news that he
was to be tried, the mercurial Morant could not
contain the frustration that had been building up inside
him during three months of solitary confinement and he
offered Colonel Carter some sobering advice: 'Look
here Colonel, you have got us all here now; take us all
out and crucify us at once, for as sure as God made
pippins, if you let one man off he'll yap.'

The two other accused, Lieutenant Hannam and
Sergeant-Major Hammett, were released without charge
whilst Morant spent Christmas in his cell, brooding and
thinking back a year to Devon when life seemed so
perfect. But in a letter he wrote to Lieutenant Hannam,
the legendary Morant wit is undiminished:

> I'm getting fat – showing embonpoint – owing to
> confinement. Hell! All on account of unity of Empire!

Should the Lord allow that I see Ushant light
4 points on the starboard bow once more, and steam
safely into Southampton Water or Plymouth Sound,
the only Empire I'll acknowledge is where
   At quarter to eight they open the doors
And the promenade's flooded with London's
whores.

God save Oireland!
Thine,

Tony

But behind the bluster and bravado, Morant was a
worried man. Although he is credited with writing
Butchered to Make a Dutchman's Holiday and *Who
Are the Guilty* on his last night on earth, it also appears
that he made a few other attempts at a final piece. The
first three verses below are new, but he grafted them
onto two verses he wrote a couple of years previously,
before he left Adelaide. It was scribbled on a page from
a dairy dated January 3, 1902. The courts martial were
still a fortnight away, but did Morant already know that
it was not going to end well?

> The days of the Breaker are over
> The days of the Buccaneer.
> He lived the life of a Rover
> And now lies buried here.
>
> And Peter lies within the grave
> And Percy rests on the hill.
> And though their lives I could not save
> I love their memory still.
>
> The reckless one, 'The Breaker'
> Sleeps beneath this sod.
> The Bravest one, True Peter,
> Went with him to God.
> Envoi.

When the last rounding gallop is ended,
And the last post and rails been jumped
And a cracked neck that cannot be mended
Shall under the yew tree be dumped.

Just leave him alone in God's acre –
And drink-in wine, whisky or beer –
May the good angels above give the Breaker
A horse like good old Cavalier.

Witton remained upbeat and also did not seem to realise the seriousness of his situation. He wrote to his brother in Melbourne:

We can prove justification for dealing with them summarily. The 'Johnnies' (Johnnie Boer) were concerned with Hunt's death and were wearing khaki and has his uniform and property in his possession. The lives of these Boers were already forfeited if they were wearing a British uniform. In the Franco–German War the Germans made no scruple about shooting 'franc tireurs' who were masquerading as harmless persons and were yet carrying on the tactics of guerrilla warfare. The two cases are precisely parallel, in fact several Boers have been court-martialled and shot for this transgression of rules. I reckon it is hard for any man who offers his service and his life to assist to end this war to be tried for his life when he wipes out a few of these Dutch gentlemen. No more empire-building on these terms for me. I shall come out of this all right, they can't surely crucify me. I reckon it will be rough if I'm cashiered.

British justice was also uppermost in the minds of another group of Australians at that very same moment. Earlier in the year, on the night of June 12, 1901, a force of 350 men, part of Brigadier-General Beatson's column, had been operating south of the town of Middleburg. Together with the Argyll and Sutherland Highlanders and the Duke of Cornwall's Light Infantry, they formed a column commanded by General Sir Bindon-Blood who were clearing country around Carolina and Amsterdam in Eastern Transvaal. They were employed in the countryside burning farms and crops, commandeering livestock and driving Boer commandos into wire and blockhouse lines.

The force comprised 270 men of the 5th Victorians, the rest being Royal Field Artillerymen accompanying their two pom-pom field guns. The force was commanded by Major CJU Morris of the Royal Field Artillery. They received a heliograph message from Beatson to stop and make camp for the night. Captain Watson deployed pickets as procribed by Beatson to keep an eye on the roving party of Boers they had exchanged sporadic fire with throughout the day.

Suddenly, at about 7.45 pm, a whistle sounded and the camp was attacked and overrun by around 120 Boers with half as many again in reserve. The Boers, commanded by General Meuller, sneaked past the pickets and caught them unawares. Many were cut down as they scrambled for their weapons. Major McKnight, the senior 5th Victorian officer, described in his report how he managed to get his weapon, but was ambushed by Boers wearing khaki whom he took for British troops. The fire-fight lasted less than ten minutes, and when the smoke cleared the British force counted two officers and sixteen men killed with four officers and thirty-eight men wounded. The final toll increased by one when a Victorian later died of his wounds.

The Boers released their British captives after heading off with two pom-pom guns, 2,500 rounds of pom-pom ammunition, 250 horses, thirty mules, rifles, small arms ammunition, carts and wagons.

A dozen British had escaped during the melee and managed to find Brigadier-General Beatson, who did not arrive until the next morning. He conferred with Major Harris and Major Morris took command of the Victorians. The officers made some disparaging remarks, but nothing was said until they trekked to Middleburg two weeks later.

The war was at a critical stage with a vocal British press and anti-war movement scrutinising every action. The protocol after such field disasters was to hold a court of inquiry at which statements were taken from any witnesses and a report sent to Army HQ and London. This was done whilst the column was making its way to Middleburg.

The inquiry, which included no representatives from the 5th Victorians, called some sixteen witnesses. There were Victorians amongst them and they said that Beatson set the pickets too far apart, cavalry style, rather than close together to stop the Boers, expert at infiltration, surprising them. There had also been no means of communication between pickets in the pitch-dark night. The pickets didn't even see the Boers, which was confirmed by the diary of the Boer General Meuller, who was later killed in another raid by the British. In a report to Commandant Ben Viljoen, he said, 'We charged to within 30 yards without their knowledge. We all fired simultaneously and completely routed the enemy so that they hardly retaliated at all. I was fortunate enough to make them surrender.'

Meuller, however, underplayed the level of resistance. Despite the element of surprise he still lost ten who were killed and thirty who were wounded. That gave the Victorians a better kill ratio than Gough's Mounted Infantry at Blood River Poort, who, even with the advantage of being the attacking force, in broad daylight, mounted, rifles in hand, flanked by a supporting regiment and with field gun support, still only bagged one and wounded four.

However, the report from General Sir Bindon-Blood, who like Beatson was an old India hand, did not mention any of this. He maintained that arrangements for defence were not sufficient – pickets were too weak, fires were burning, the pom-pom guns were too close to the perimeter and some of the pickets had not done their duty for the want of vigilance or cowardice. In general terms, his report blamed the Victorians and praised the British. Nothing was said about Beatson's wide cavalry picket placings and Major Morris, as commander, received a censure. However, in mitigation of Morris's failure, Blood also blamed the disaster on 'the chicken-hearted behaviour of the officers and men generally of the Victorian Mounted Rifles on this occasion. We must remember that they were all a lot of recruits together, and that their behaviour was only what was to be expected in the circumstances.'

Morris was censured and Kitchener told Secretary of State for War St John Brodrick that the bitter lesson the pickets had learned from this experience was punishment enough. The Victorians were not censured, although they received some criticism in the Australian press for tarnishing the otherwise good reputation of the Australian forces. Suggestions that they were not of the same quality as earlier contingents ignored the fact that they all underwent training and testing and that, up until the Wilmansrust debacle, the 5th Victorians had received high praise for their soldiering. They were also one of only four Australian units to win a Victoria Cross in the Boer War. But what was to become known as the 'Wilmansrust affair' did not end there.

Blood's criticism of the Victorians would never have come to light but for Beatson. Perhaps emboldened by Blood's criticism, Beatson rode past a group of

5th Victorians who were out 'sticking' bush pigs and commented, 'Yes, that's just about what you men are good for. When the Dutchmen came along the other night you didn't fix bayonets and charge them, but you go for something that can't hit back.'

He then launched a tirade, calling them, as one 5th Victorian later reported to *The Adelaide Advertiser*:

> '[A] fat-arsed, pot-bellied, round-shouldered lot of wasters', and continued that, 'all Australians were alike'. Major Harris took a note of it and the Col. [Beatson] said, 'you can add dogs too'.

Major Harris told him he was sorry to hear that and intended to take down his words. Beatson replied, 'Do by all means and you can add if you like that in my opinion they are a lot of white-livered curs.'

Major Morris reported this to Major McKnight, the senior officer of the 5th Victorians. McKnight's reaction was to report the incident to the Victorian Government and ask for leave to go to Pretoria. He intended to ask for a full inquiry into what really happened that fateful night.

Beatson tried to apologise, but as his comments were now public knowledge, McKnight insisted it was too late. He was refused permission to go to Pretoria and posted to Balmoral, fifty miles away, instead. Beatson then appealed to Major Umphelly, the Australian officer nominally in charge of the 5th Victorians, and McKnight was forced to drop the matter.

McKnight paraded the Victorian officers and read out a memo from Major Umphelly containing an apology from Beatson, but his men were not placated. He knew feelings were running high over a number of issues. In his report to Major-General Downes, Commandant, Victorian Military Forces, McKnight said,

I tried my best to keep the matter straight, as I knew it was the intention of the men to lay down their arms unless they could get another command. I also spoke to a number of NCOs, advising them to be careful what they did. They said they could not serve with confidence under the present General . . . The men felt that there was no regard shown for their lives and in some cases the punishments awarded were of a most humiliating character . . . I was at all times loyal to General Beatson but when it became a question as to the reputation of the Victorians and consequently of the State that sent me out to Africa, I was compelled to protest strongly against General Beatson's universal condemnation of our men . . . I could see that the treatment of the officers and men from Victoria by the Chief of Staff, Major Waterfield, and afterwards by General Beatson, must eventually cause trouble.'

It was also alleged that when Beatson took command he ignored the Australian officers and complained about their drill and dress. He didn't like volunteers (the Boer War was the first major conflict in which volunteers fought alongside regulars in the British Army). He wanted them to be like crack cavalry corps. He was also something of a disciplinarian and during his first week a trooper was courts martialled and sentenced to twelve months' imprisonment for refusing to obey a sergeant's order to withdraw from a farmhouse. Two others got two years each for surrendering to Boers and another was pegged out all night as a punishment. The Australians resisted his attempts to impose British-style barrack-room discipline by putting Imperial officers over them insisting that it 'does not work with our grain'.

Letters to the national press from other units told of simmering tensions between the British and the Australians.

A trooper in the 2nd New South Wales Mounted Rifles was courts martialled for stealing a case of officers' whisky. At the trial, the officer said that he saw 'a man' carrying a case, though it was too dark to positively identify him, however he recognised his voice. On that evidence alone the private was sentenced to forty-two days' field imprisonment – or 'crucifixion', as it was known in the ranks. This meant the prisoner had his arms lashed to a wagon wheel and was left in the sun all day. His mates were unhappy with the punishment and cut him loose. They were lined up and told by a Major Lydiard that 'they were small in numbers and as much as said he'd turn the guns on us'.

The Australians ignored the threat, cut their mate loose a second time and were again lectured on the consequences. They replied, 'we are satisfied to put up with the consequences of our acts, at the same time telling him we would not stand by and see an Australian lashed to a cart-wheel like a dog by the orders of a "Tommy" officer'.

They also made it clear they intended to cut him loose if they tied him up again.

Australian units particularly detested farm-burning, and in another more serious incident a British officer pointed his artillery guns at the men of an Australian unit who stacked their guns after refusing to burn Boer farms. However, he withdrew when the Australians retrieved their arms and took up defensive positions.

Others criticised Beatson's abilities as well as his temperament. An unnamed officer claimed that, 'The senior officers have come from India and are learning to fight the Boers at the expense of the Victorian 5th.'

It was also claimed that under Beatson, the 5th Victorians had suffered a higher casualty rate. Beatson had spent the previous years in India where they fought a very different kind of war against poorly armed, native peoples who lacked the organisation and guile of the Boers. Another Victorian was of the opinion that, 'If we stop under this man, General Beatson, much longer there will not be many left of the 5th Victorian Contingent. He is absolutely murdering our men. He is not fit to be with white men, he ought to be with the Sikhs. Beatson does not know the Boers yet. He sends us to kopjes where no man ought to go. The other day we were surrounded by Boers for 7 hours and did not get out till dark.'

It all came to a head when loose talk landed three members of the 5th Victorians in trouble. On the night of July 7, 1901, despite McKnight's warning, six of the 5th Victorians were heard discussing the matter around the campfire and an Imperial officer overheard trooper James Steele say, 'We'll be a lot of fools if we go out with him again.'

It was also said that Steele urged his comrades to pile arms and not to go out with Beatson until he apologised in person. Three Victorians, J Steele, H Parry and A Richards, were charged with 'incitement to mutiny' and courts martialled.

On July 11, 1901, they were found guilty and sentenced to death, but Kitchener commuted the sentence to ten years' penal servitude for Steele and one year's hard labour each for Parry and Richards. They were transported to England to begin their sentences without either the Australian Government or their families being informed. Trooper Parry's father had a letter he had written to his son sent back with a note from his Sergeant-Major saying that he had left the contingent and his whereabouts were unknown. He cabled the British authorities, but only received the following cryptic reply, 'Shipped England. Message ends.'

The whole matter only came to light when an anonymous letter containing a copy of the charge sheet was

A previously unpublished photo of Harry Morant in Devon in 1900–1901.
(Photo: Courtesy The Public Records Office, London)

Union Workhouse, Northgate, Bridgwater c.1890 where Edwin Murrant was born in 1864. He spent the first eight years of his life here. (Photo: Courtesy Admiral Blake Museum, Bridgwater)

Daisy May O'Dwyer aka Bates around the time she married Edwin Murrant aka Harry Morant. (Photo: Courtesy West Australian Newspapers Ltd)

A rogues gallery. A group photo of the BVC officers just prior to the death of Captain Hunt. From left to right: Lieutenant Handcock, Lieutenant Morant, Surgeon Johnson, Captain Hunt, Captain Taylor and Lieutenant Picton. (Photo: Courtesy *The Bulletin*)

To the Revd. Canon Fisher
Pretoria

The night before we're shot

We shot the Boers who killed & mutilated our friend (the best mate I had on Earth)

Harry Harbord Morant

Peter Joseph Handcock

Harry Morant wrote this legend on the back of the above photograph of the BVC officers that was given to the Reverend Fisher of Pretoria in case their story never got out. (Image: Courtesy *The Bulletin*)

Horsemen of the apocalypse. Harry Morant (second from left) with some of the Renmark boys from the 2nd South Australian Contingent. (Photo: Courtesy *The Bulletin*)

Major James Francis Thomas who defended the BVC officers at the courts martial. Despite his best efforts, he could not save them. (Photo: Courtesy *The Bulletin*)

Captain 'Bulala' Taylor (back row, first on right) with Cecil Rhodes (second row, first on left) during the Matabele Uprising c.1896. Taylor was implicated in all twenty killings that took place in the Spelonken, yet was acquitted. (Photo: Author's collection)

Lieutenant George Witton, the other BVC officer implicated in the Spelonken killings. He was found guilty of murder, but Kitchener commuted his sentence to life. (Photo: Courtesy *The Bulletin*)

Francis Enraght-Moony. His appointment as native commissioner for Northern Transvaal and subsequent investigations led to the demise of Captain Taylor's operations and the BVC. (Photo: Courtesy Mrs H du Plessis and JD Enraght-Mooney)

LEFT: JF Thomas standing over the grave of the men he couldn't save. In a letter home shortly afterwards he confessed: 'I feel quite broken up. It is too painful to write about.' (Photo: Author's collection)

BELOW: The grave of Harry Morant and Peter Handcock in Pretoria complete with new centenary stone bearing the epitaph he originally requested. (Photo: Author's collection)

ABOVE LEFT: Provost Marshal Robert Montague Poore. He helped form the BVC, led the investigation into the Spelonken killings and was present when Morant and Handcock were executed. (Photo: Courtesy The Queen's Own Hussar Museum)

ABOVE: Major Robert Lenehan, Field Commander of the BVC. He broke the story of the executions when he arrived back in Australia. (Photo: Courtesy Mitchell Library, Sydney)

LEFT: Following the murder of their Commanding Officer, the Canadian Scouts vowed never to take prisoners again and those who honoured that pledge wore black feathers in their hats. (Photo: Courtesy Neil Speed)

Australian Prime Minister Edmund Barton (right) and Joseph Chamberlain (left) during a Colonial conference c.1903. Barton received a knighthood for his services during the Boer War, but Norman Lindsay's vicious satire for *The Bulletin* (below right) saw that his bauble was paid for with the blood spilt by Australian 'diggers' in South Africa. (Photo: Courtesy Mitchell Library, Sydney; Illustration: Courtesy *The Bulletin* and the Norman Lindsay Estate)

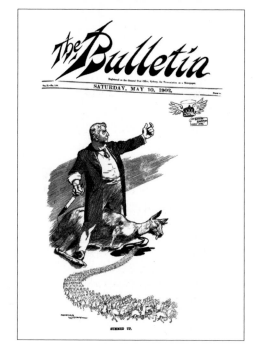

sent to *The Age*. It appeared on their front page on September 28, 1901 under the headline, *A Question of Treason?* Parry's father, who had tried for weeks to find out what was happening from the War Office and Department of Defence, said of his son, 'I am not altogether astonished that he is mixed up in the matter as I know him to be a true Briton and one who would stick to a chum or tent mate to his last drop of blood.'

JAM Fowler, a Western Australian Labor member in the Federal Parliament, asked about the press dispatches on Wilmansrust, whether what Beatson said was true, and if there would be an inquiry. Sir John Forrest, Minister for Defence, could only say that the Prime Minister had asked the Governor General to find out the facts from the Secretary of State for Colonies on 'the very regrettable matters'.

Meanwhile, Australians in London petitioned King Edward VII for a pardon and by the time the Member for Corio, Mr Crouch, had risen to request some information on behalf of Parry's father on October 9, a reply from Chamberlain had been received by the Governor General:

Referring to your telegram 3rd October. Privates J. Steele, A. Richards and H. Parry tried by courts martial for inciting mutiny sentenced to death. Sentences were commuted to 10 years penal servitude in the case of Steele, and one year's imprisonment, with hard labour, in other cases. Prisoners were sent to this country, but on receipt of proceedings of courts martial, Judge Advocate-General declared that there were legal flaws in the convictions, the men having been tried under a wrong section of the Army Act. Instructions have been issued for their immediate release, and joining provisional battalions shortly.

In effect, the charges had been quashed and Steele, Parry and Richards were returned home to Australia. General Sir Bindon-Blood went back to India and Brigadier-General Beatson was moved down to the Cape where, according to McKnight, he disgraced himself again. Other letters home suggested that Beatson's behaviour was not just an isolated incident:

> We were not sorry to lose him [Beatson] as he was 'led by the nose' – to use a vulgar expression – by his Brigade Major, Major Waterfield who had a strong dislike for the Victorian, and in consequence nothing we did was right.

On November 22, Prime Minister Barton asked if Lord Hopetoun would answer Mr Fowler's questions now that the Victorians had been released and the Australian people felt 'that their honour [had] been implicated in the charge which was brought against the men in question'.

By December 1901, when Steele, Parry and Richards arrived back in Australia aboard the *Oraya*, no reply had been forthcoming from either Beatson or the War Office. No answer is recorded in the archives and the Commonwealth Government dropped the matter. It would not be the last time the Australian Government would have to be satisfied by silence from London on such grave matters.

The 5th Victorians were put under the command of Colonel Coalville, and later in the same year, Lieutenant LC Magyer of the 5th Victorians became the first Victorian to be awarded a Victoria Cross and fully restored the unit's tarnished reputation. However, Major-General Hutton was determined to have the last word. At the celebration lunch – given in honour of the 1st Battalion who arrived home in April 1902 – Steele, Richards and Parry were singled out as troublemakers by Hutton who claimed he could not find a man who had heard Beatson make his controversial statement and that his removal to the Cape was, in fact, a promotion! However, the Victorians had the last word. A fine monument to the 5th Victorians, including the 'Wilmansrust 3' who served in South Africa, was built in the park opposite their Melbourne barracks which has since been described as 'a raspberry in sandstone' to the British Generals.

In a wider Australian context the so-called 'Wilmansrust affair' threw up a number of worrying questions. First, there was the treatment of Australian troops by British officers, which provoked the whole crisis. It was not an isolated problem. There were many recorded accounts of discord between the British and their colonial allies, mostly over matters of attitude and discipline.

But what gave most cause for concern was the way the system of military justice was so easily perverted. The court of inquiry quite clearly misrepresented the facts of the defeat at Wilmansrust, which impugned the honour of the 5th Victorians and directly led to the three Victorians speaking out of turn.

Considering the sentences later meted out to the Bushveldt Carbineers for crimes of much greater seriousness, the sentence of death imposed by the courts martial on Steele, Parry and Richards seemed unnecessarily harsh. Kitchener did commute their sentences, but the fact that they were tried and transported to England without any reference to the Australian Government should also have raised greater concern in Melbourne.

THE SPEED WITH WHICH THE MEN were released was remarkable once the whole business came to light in the Australian press – though the reason given for their release is suspect.

The case was framed by the Provost General's Department and the courts martial panel convened. The

Judge Advocate General then reviewed the sentences immediately after the verdict of the courts martial was handed down and a recommendation made to the Commander-in-Chief. In this case, the death sentence was commuted on his advice. Death sentences were used to keep discipline in the ranks and handed out for comparatively minor offences, but only around ten per cent were ever carried out.[†] However, the Wilmansrust case was only found to be unsound after a second review – three months after the Judge Advocate General's original report. This suggests either a monumental blunder, as the case would have passed through the hands of many trained legal staff both before and after the courts martial, or an expedient way out of what could be an embarrassing inquiry. Either way, it proves that British military justice was far from the infallible institution it was later claimed to be when the Bushveldt Carbineers were dealt their fatal hand.

On their return from South Africa, the Commonwealth Government declined to back the men's claim for back pay for the time they were wrongly detained. Parry took the matter up personally and got a reply from a Captain RM Collins, a Secretary in the Department of Defence:

> I am directed to state that the things to which you refer occurred during the men's service in The Imperial Army. The Commonwealth Government did not act as agents for the Imperial Government in raising or dispatching the Contingent, and neither the state nor the Commonwealth have any responsibility whatsoever for any military discipline or treatment to which the members of the Contingent had to submit in the service they undertook.

† *Average figure for World War I. No figures available for the Boer War.*

That rather tart reply clearly summarised the Imperial attitude towards its colonial troops where matters of discipline were concerned. Wilmansrust was merely a preview of what would ultimately be a much greater betrayal of the loyal service they offered.

Barton was concerned enough to ask Kitchener, through the Governor General, to keep him informed if he intended to try any other Australians. Kitchener's reply came on February 7, 1902, twelve days before the end of the courts martial of the Bushveldt Carbineers.

Army Headquarters,
Pretoria,
7th February 1902

My Lord,

I have the honour to acknowledge the receipt of your letter of the 5th December last with sentences passed by Courts-Martial on members of the Australian Contingents in South Africa.

In reply thereto I beg to forward a record of such trials to the 31st December 1901, and to inform you that a similar record will be furnished to you at the end of each quarter, so long as there is occasion to do so.

As regards the second request in your letter I would invite your attention to the column in the record forwarded herewith, which sets forth the sentences as confirmed with commutations and remissions. The number of Australian soldiers undergoing sentences on 31st December 1901, can be calculated from this column 'date of award'.

Given that it took Kitchener two months to reply to the Governor General and the evasive nature of his reply, it appears that Wilmansrust had also alerted Kitchener to the fact that the Australians were prepared to intervene, ask awkward questions in London and even petition the King. His method of accounting abrogated the need to tell the Australians about the ongoing prosecution of the Bushveldt Carbineers and ensured the sentences would be carried out before he was obliged to inform them.

DESPITE KITCHENER'S BEST EFFORTS to keep the prosecution of the Bushveldt Carbineers a secret, news of their misdeeds leaked out to London. Surgeon James Kay, recently returned from South Africa, had written to the Secretary of State for the Colonies, Joseph Chamberlain, asking him what became of the BVC officers charged with murder. In his journal for October to December, in the chapter entitled 'The Bushveldt Carbineers', Kay details the information he supplied Chamberlain with:

> The command of the corps was given to a major who had been dismissed from the Australian contingent and many of the officers were quite unfit to hold commissions and at the time of their appointments very unpleasant remarks were made on the subject and unfortunately the justice of these remarks is now apparent. The corps was raised for the express purpose of scouting and raiding cattle of the Boer commandos in the Bushveldt north and north east of Pretoria – much of it hilly and mountainous and most favourable territory for guerrilla warfare. As soon as the corps was raised they moved north to Pienaars River, about forty miles from Pretoria. After a short stay here they moved east (in the direction of Rhenosterkop).
>
> There was no discipline in the corps; the ration of rum was retained by the officers who had frequent orgies. At present it is impossible to

ascertain all details as the authorities are most anxious that nothing should leak out, but from various sources it is beyond doubt that twenty-three surrendered (Boer) prisoners were most brutally and treacherously murdered, including an old man very ill with fever. A German missionary named Hesse [sic] saw the bodies of some of the murdered men and was informed by Kaffirs of the full circumstances of their death. He was on his way to Pietersburg, and fearing that this German would give information to the authorities, members of the corps deliberately murdered him and his native servant.

Among the officers responsible for these murders (who are at present under arrest) are Lieutenants Handcock and Morant. A trooper in the corps, a Boer by the name of Van Buuren, on witnessing the first murders, remonstrated; whereupon Lieutenant Handcock fired three revolver shots at him; the first hit him in the mouth, the second in the body, and the third in the head; he then broke his skull with the butt of a rifle. It was the same man (Lieutenant Handcock) who shot the German missionary Hesse [sic] and his servant.

A Boer by the name of Smit who had surrendered and who had a valuable farm in the area was shot because one of the officers coveted his farm and openly stated that when the war was over he was going to apply for Smit's farm.

A Sergeant Rodgers was ordered to make an attack on some prisoners but refused. Next day he was ordered off to the left flank to scout. Someone had been told to watch him and shoot him. He was fired at but got away unwounded. A reign of terror existed among the men; it was understood that if a man was ordered to the left flank his doom was sealed. This was so well known that men refused to leave camp alone and invariably kept their rifles handy and loaded.

The object of some of the murders was to obtain cattle. According to proclamations which had been issued, Boers who surrendered were allowed to keep their cattle and belongings. But these officers decided that if the owners were shot their cattle could be sent to Rhodesia and sold there. It is said that thousands of cattle went there; the greater part stolen from the Government.

None of the officers concerned were Imperial men (they were recruited locally, mainly colonials). Their exposure was due to the troopers, who communicated with the authorities, who acted promptly and placed all the officers under arrest. It is lamentable that commissions should be given to men whose antecedents are not inquired into . . . and that we should have included in the corps a number of Boers to fight against their own people, which is wrong both morally and politically.

Kay revealed how he came by the information in a letter to a Mrs Shepstone, dated December 20, 1901: 'I discovered all this through the Portuguese Consul, who also told me that Lord Kitchener was trying to hush it up.'

Kitchener's predecessor, Field-Marshall Lord Roberts, who had returned to London to assume command of British forces, cabled Pretoria immediately:

Telegram   War Office, 8th January 1902
No. 594, Cipher

Mr James Kay in a letter to Mr Chamberlain, dated Box 162, Pretoria, makes allegations against Bushveldt Carbineers and states they are under arrest. Telegraph whether any foundation. Kay was suspected of being a deserter in September 1900; have those suspicions been dispelled?

Kitchener had not only neglected to inform the Australian authorities that he was about to try some of their servicemen for murder, but also his own government. In any event, he was forced to reply:

Telegram　　　　Johannesburg, 9th January 1902
No. S789, Cipher

Your no 594. Charges are framed and case is being tried. Would you give me grounds of suspicion against Kay as a deserter? I have no clue.

The allegations against Kay were baseless, but Kitchener was being less than honest with Roberts. The way he deliberately kept Roberts in the dark and his claim that the courts martial were in progress, a week before they even began, is more proof that a veil of secrecy surrounded this case and it was not the routine courts martial that has been claimed. His cover blown, Kitchener told his staff that 'The swift application of military justice' was required. His mood was not improved when Roberts again pressed him for further details:

Telegram　　　　War Office, 18th January 1902
No. 636 Cipher

My No. 594, and yours No. S789, Cipher. Further serious reports have reached me about the conduct of the Bush Veldt Carbineers. What has been done to them? What was the result of the trial?

Kitchener did not reply for another month until the trial was over. It would seem that it was his intention to secure a guilty verdict before releasing any details and only then as a fait accompli.

With the courts martial due to begin in mid-January,

the prisoners busied themselves trying to find someone to represent them. Morant asked a Captain Purland, Director of Prisons, who replied that he was astonished at such a request, as he hardly knew Morant, and his position would forbid it even were he inclined to defend him. Before the court of inquiry, Witton had asked about making arrangements for his defence, and was told not to bother; and a Captain Evans had advised 'You have nothing to fear or trouble about, you are bound to be exonerated'. That advice proved to be very wide of the mark and he considered asking John Rail to speak for him. Rail was from the National Mutual Life Association of Australia and was acting as the Victorian Government agent for military contingents. Neither Purland nor Rail had any legal training, but at a military court martial, during that era, proper legal representation was an uncommon luxury.

However, Major Lenehan, who was a lawyer himself, sent urgent cables to Major John Francis Thomas on January 6, 7 and 9 requesting that he defend him. They had known each other in Sydney as lawyers and had been reacquainted when Lenehan's force relieved Thomas at the Elands River siege. Now Lenehan needed Thomas to return the favour.

MAJOR LENEHAN WAS FORTUNATE that when his frantic cables reached Thomas, he was between military appointments. He was no stranger to the vagaries of British military justice and had even foreseen that Australians fighting in Imperial irregular units would run into legal difficulties.

Earlier the previous year, he had been involved in the Rhenosterkop debacle. On January 12, 1901, a group of around 300 Boers attacked a convoy of wagons his troop was escorting from Vlakfontein back to camp at

Rhenosterkop. Thomas was commanding a force of New South Wales Bushmen and West Riding Infantry who surrendered to the enemy.

At the court of inquiry the blame was attached to the Bushmen, and especially Captain Thomas. However, it emerged that Thomas only had twenty Bushmen and most of the fifty-three West Ridings that accompanied them had just been discharged from hospital, had been drinking and had few weapons and little ammunition. The defence of the convoy fell to the Bushmen and they held out for four hours. Although a rider went to Rhenosterkop camp for help and a signalling station watched the whole attack, no reinforcements were sent. The West Ridings surrendered of their own volition once they ran out of bullets, forcing the Bushmen to do the same once the Boers overran the West Riding positions.

Kitchener fully exonerated the Bushmen and Thomas, 'who was apparently not responsible for the raising of the white flag'. However, he did criticise the way Thomas deployed his small force and left the firing line to tend the wounded. General Wood was of the opinion that some allowance should be made for 'a man who has never been a soldier previously'. That minor reprimand did not prevent Thomas being promoted to major on May 2, 1901 after serving with Plumer's force which had taken Pietersburg on April 8. That concluded their twelve months' service and Thomas and the New South Wales Bushmen left Pietersburg for home on April 18, about the time Morant arrived in the Transvaal to begin his service with the BVC.

Thomas arrived in Sydney on June 11, 1901 and travelled to Tenterfield where he was given a hero's welcome in the town's gymnasium hall. Thomas M Walker, the new Mayor of Tenterfield, mindful of Tenterfield's historic role in creating the new

Commonwealth of Australia, declared, 'When those we are welcoming tonight left, Australia was a number of colonies; now it is a nation.'

This thought was uppermost in Thomas' mind during the next few months as he raised another detachment to return to South Africa. Although Thomas had signed on to serve in South Africa until April 1902, Brigadier-General Plumer had offered Thomas the opportunity to return to Australia with the Bushmen if he would undertake to return with another contingent of men. Recalling what Parkes had said in Tenterfield all those years ago, Thomas agreed, but with one important proviso:

> I had stipulated with the military authorities in South Africa that I should serve as an Australian officer and that the men should serve as Australians. In other words, I did not wish that we should sink our nationality by becoming South African irregulars.

His trip home and recruitment of another contingent has been mistaken for jingoism in some quarters, but there is nothing in his dispatches from the front to indicate that he saw his service as anything more than his patriotic duty to Australia. In fact, in the speech he gave on his return to Tenterfield he said, 'The Boers were farmers, something like ourselves, and so far as we have seen, they had been most kind to prisoners and the wounded.'

Thomas did recruit 200 returned servicemen for a second tour of duty, but only after his efforts to persuade the New South Wales government to find them employment or offer them land concessions in rural areas had failed. On August 20, 1901, just as the net was closing around the BVC, Thomas and his servicemen sailed for Cape Town on the *Britannia*.

However, any understanding Thomas thought he had with the Imperial authorities about serving in an Australian unit dissipated as soon as they landed in South Africa: 'when we arrived at Cape Town we were informed that the Marquis of Tullibardine had got authority to annex all the men and that the officers were not wanted. In the end, all the men who went over with me were scattered and lost their nationality as Australians.'

The issue of nationality clearly gave Thomas cause for concern, but the feeling that they had come out as Britons but would go home Australians was growing amongst Australian troops. Banjo Paterson captured this general feeling in *Our Own Flag*, which he wrote whilst in South Africa:

> T'was down with the saddle and spurs and
>   whip
> The swagman dropped his swag.
> And we hurried us off to an outbound ship.
> To fight for the English flag.
>
> And the English flag may flutter and wave
> Where the world-wide oceans toss
> But the flag the Australian dies to save
> Is the flag of the Southern Cross.
>
> If ever they want us to stand the brunt
> Of a hard-fought, grim campaign,
> We will carry our own flag up to the front
> When we go to the wars again.

Thomas became so disillusioned by the reaction of both Imperial and colonial units to his request that Australians be allowed to fight in a unit bearing their own name, that Lenehan nearly lost the man who was to provide his defence. He declined several offers to join irregular units, including the infamous Canadian Scouts unless they were renamed 'the Canadian and Australian Scouts' on account of the large numbers of Australians serving in their ranks. But Thomas was again disappointed:

> This was agreed to and I went to Pretoria, but the promise was not fulfilled and I resigned. I determined to have nothing more to do with the South African Irregulars. If I could not serve as an Australian and with Australians, I did not want to serve at all. I got a promise of a free passage back to Australia and arranged to leave for Cape Town early in January 1902.

Lenehan's telegram intercepted him in the nick of time and Thomas felt obliged to help: 'I did not like to refuse, so I got a permit to defend them and proceeded to Pietersburg, where I was engaged for about five weeks upon as difficult a task as I suppose ever fell to an advocate.'

Thomas arrived in Pietersburg on January 15, 1902, the day before the courts martial was due to convene. His original brief was to defend Lenehan, but on hearing that the other accused had no legal representation, he agreed to defend them too.

However, Thomas was a country lawyer who had never defended a serious criminal case, far less a capital case, in his life. His bread and butter were contracts, wills, trusts, and the buying and selling of businesses and property. He had occasion to defend the odd minor case in Tenterfield Police Court, but by the normal standards of British military justice, the BVC officers were better represented than most, who usually had to rely on their officers or a civilian of good standing to act as a so-called 'prisoner's friend' and say a few words on their behalf.

Thomas' record shows he was a seasoned officer who knew all about the bloody nature of war. Following the death of Mitchell, one of his Tenterfield boys at Elands River, he wrote in a letter home, 'This war is a sad, cruel business – but it is an unavoidable evil.' He was a pragmatist and didn't take on the BVC case out of some misguided sense of idealism, but rather out of the same compassion he showed in staying with Mitchell until he died.

THE FIRST COURTS MARTIAL BEGAN IN Pietersburg public court on January 16. It was not the austere looking building of popular imagination, but the rather grand, colonial-style residence of the British military authorities, which was set in its own gardens. The building still exists today and has retained its historic character. The cases were conducted in a rectangular room that measures nine metres by four metres. Given the number of defendants, legal representatives, witnesses, stenographers and so on, it is apparent that the accused and their accusers spent the five weeks toe to toe in the stifling summer heat. Given their sheer physical proximity to each other it is little wonder that the atmosphere was explosive.

After the preliminary proceedings and the swearing in of the members, an adjournment was called to allow a request for Thomas to defend the other accused to be sent to Pretoria. Only by virtue of this procedural point, and not to the largesse of the court or in the name of justice, was Thomas given one day's grace to prepare his defence. He spent that in conference with his new clients in a belated effort to prepare a plausible legal defence.

Permission had arrived by the next morning and the court sat to hear the first charge – the shooting of Visser. The accused officers – lieutenants Morant, Handcock, Witton and Picton – all pleaded 'not guilty' to the charge of murder.

The circumstances surrounding the death of Captain

Hunt on August 6 were examined. Ex-Sergeant Morrison, a witness for the prosecution, testified that Hunt had been killed during the attack on Viljoen's farmhouse and found the next morning lying in a gutter stripped of his clothing. Cross-examined by Thomas he admitted that his body bore marks of ill-treatment. This was corroborated by Reverend Reuter, who'd prepared the body for burial and said that Hunt's neck was broken, his body mutilated and the imprint of hob-nailed boots was on his forehead. Civil surgeon Johnson gave his professional opinion that Hunt's injuries were caused before his death. Captain Taylor said the Boers had threatened him with slow torture if they ever caught him.

The court was then told by Trooper Botha and Corporal Sharpe how Hunt's unit was reinforced by lieutenants Morant, Handcock, Witton and Picton and then set off in pursuit of the Boers. They caught up with them the following evening, attacked their laager and in the process captured the wounded Visser. Sergeant Robinson and Handcock said that he was wearing a soldier's khaki jacket and Morant added that Visser was using Hunt's trousers as a pillow and some of his personal effects were found at the scene.

Visser was carried along in a cart as they returned to Fort Edward the next day, but at around noon they stopped and the four officers held a court martial. It was decided to shoot Visser because he was involved in Hunt's murder and had been caught wearing khaki. Major Bolton of the 2nd Wiltshires said he knew of no order to shoot Boers wearing khaki. Witton said that he believed Visser knew he was being tried, but was not invited to offer a defence.

Picton said that he too had received orders from Hunt not to take prisoners and had been reprimanded by him for bringing some in. He had never shot any prisoners because he didn't like the idea. Hunt, he said, was bitter about the death of 'a friend' (Best). However, due to the shortness of his command, he had never had the chance to carry out those orders himself. Morant, he said, had never previously shot any prisoners, but after Hunt's death was much more severe on them. Picton also said he had opposed the execution of Visser on the grounds that, legally, he had been a prisoner too long and should have been shot the previous night.

Intelligence Officer Ledeboer said that he had translated the death sentence for the prisoner. Sergeant Robinson said he refused to have any part in it and asked Lieutenant Picton on whose authority Visser was being shot. Picton replied that they were Kitchener's orders and named a date from which all Boers found in khaki were to be shot. Robinson said he had never heard of such orders and that they had never been read regimentally. However, he did admit on cross-examination that Hunt had reprimanded him for bringing in prisoners.

Trooper Botha and Corporal Sharpe both confirmed the sequence of events and that they were both members of the firing squad. Botha said he had once lived on a farm with Visser and had objected to shooting him. Sharpe said that Picton had fired his revolver into Visser's head after he went down.

Picton confirmed that he had commanded the firing party on Morant's orders and had reported the facts to Major Lenehan and Colonel Hall in Pietersburg.

Called to the stand, Major Lenehan said that he was in command of the BVC but had no direct control over the corps, which acted on orders from Army HQ. From what he knew of Morant, he thought him incapable of murder or inciting others to do it. He confirmed that Picton had reported the shooting of Visser to him and said he had passed it on to Colonel Hall. However, he knew nothing about orders not to take prisoners.

During his testimony, Morant said that the BVC were ordered to clear the northern district of Boers by Captain Hunt, who was acting on orders given to him at Pretoria. On one occasion, Hunt had reprimanded him for bringing in thirty prisoners. Doctor Johnson, Lieutenants Picton, Handcock and Witton and Captain Taylor also confirmed this crucial point of evidence.

Morant had assumed command following Hunt's death and pursued the Boers responsible. Morant said that he had never carried out Hunt's orders because he regarded his prisoners as 'a good lot', but after discovering the nature of his friend's death, he told his men he had changed his mind. However, on cross-examination Morant admitted that the orders were always verbal, he had never seen them written down, but that Hunt had quoted precedents such as Kitchener's and Strathcona's Horse – who had both given Boer prisoners 'no quarter'. Morant was asked if he knew who gave the order to Hunt, but before he could give this vital evidence, the Judge Advocate objected and the court was adjourned until the next day.

The court reconvened the following day and decided to allow the question. Morant deposed that it was Lieutenant-Colonel Hamilton, Military Secretary to Lord Kitchener, who had given Hunt the order in Pretoria before he left for the Spelonken, so that he would be clear about their policy towards the Boer commandos operating in that area.

Morant then described how he captured Visser wearing khaki and in possession of an item of Hunt's clothing. He then held a 'drum-head' court martial and Visser was shot. Morant was then cross-examined by the President of the courts martial, Lieutenant-Colonel Denny, about the nature of this 'court': 'Was your court at the trial of Visser constituted like this?', asked the

President, 'and did you observe paragraph _____ of section _____ of the King's Regulations?'

Morant swept a scornful glance over the neatly pressed khaki uniforms and shiny buttons that had sent him out with orders to shoot prisoners and now stood in judgment against him.

> 'Was it like this?' he growled. 'No it wasn't quite so handsome. As to rules and sections, we had no Red Book, and knew nothing about them. We were fighting Boers, not sitting comfortably behind barb-wire entanglements; we got them and shot them under Rule .303.'

Witton described Morant's defence as 'plucky', but worried that he:

> [D]id not express any regret or have any fear as to what his fate might be. Driven almost to desperation, and smarting under the recent unjust acts of the court of inquiry, he, in his usual hot-headed manner, made disclosures which he believed would in all probability 'stagger humanity'. He vowed he would have Lord Kitchener put in the box and cross-examined as to the orders given to officers, and his methods of conducting the war. The folly of all this was apparent to everyone, as Lord Kitchener held Morant's life in his hands; but Morant would not be restrained and was prepared to suffer.

Anger vented, Morant then laid himself squarely on the line. He told the court:

> 'You can't blame the young un's. They only did as I told them. They just carried out orders, and that' – he raised his voice – 'they had to do. They were obeying my orders and thought they were obeying Lord Kitchener's . . . I did not carry out those orders until my best friend was brutally murdered. Then I

resolved to carry out his orders. But if anybody is to blame it is me.'

Morant's comment opened the way for Thomas's second line of defence. It didn't matter who gave the orders to shoot prisoners or where they came from, the fact that Captain Hunt gave them, as confirmed by many who testified, was sufficient to clear them as in any event, the order came from a superior officer.

When offering Morant and Handcock immunity, the court of inquiry stated that if they admitted they were given orders to shoot prisoners by Lenehan – a senior officer – nothing could happen to them. However, they refused and discovered what a double-edged sword British military law could be. The prosecution invoked a clause of military law that states that as an officer is responsible for the carrying out of even lawful commands that result in injury, he is *a fortiori* responsible for the carrying out of obviously illegal and improper commands from superiors. Orders to shoot prisoners, even if they were given, do not constitute a lawful command and need not be obeyed. Nonetheless, the fact that the orders did come from a superior order should have counted in mitigation against their sentences.

However, dramatic events were about to unfold outside of the courtroom that would give Thomas an even more potent argument for dismissing the charges against his clients.

A Boer commando attacked Pietersburg on January 23, 1902, mid-way through the Visser trial, and the court got a chance to witness first hand the courage and leadership that made Morant such an effective operative in the Spelonken.

Commandant Beyers re-entered the Spelonken and made his camp at Taylor's old HQ, Sweetwaters – just a mile from Fort Edward, which had been reinforced on December 1, 1901. Though the re-named Pietersburg

Light Horse contained many ex-BVC troopers, it showed none of the fighting qualities that made the BVC such an effective unit. They waited until a detachment of Field Artillery arrived from Pietersburg before driving Beyers away. A Boer captured in this chase said that Beyers had refused to go anywhere near the Spelonken as long as Morant was around, but when he learnt of Morant's arrest he felt it safe to return to the area.

NEWS OF THE IMMINENT ATTACK ON *Pietersburg reached the fort by galloper. As if to prove that in the absence of Morant he felt that he had little to fear, Beyers had made his way from Sweetwaters to Pietersburg where he liberated one hundred and fifty burghers from a detention camp by using women as a lure to distract the sentries. Major Copland, the Judge Advocate presiding at the courts martial was startled out of his sleep by the insistent shaking of the Fort Commander who awoke him with the news before dawn. Copland smashed his fist down on the stout wood table and exhaled deeply as he wiped what little sleep he had enjoyed from his eyes.*

'All I need in the middle of this bloody awful trial is a Boer attack. What if they overrun us? Pietersburg will be the first town to be taken back by the Boers. Christ, the Boss will have a fit! Court martial anyone the Boers don't shoot! Stupid buggers! Why can't they keep their minds on the job and their hands off those little Boer bitches?' he exclaimed.

Having already exorcised those same ghosts in a similar manner an hour earlier himself, the Fort Commander concentrated on the practical, 'I've deployed all our defences, but the truth is we're short of men. Beyers will attack with at least three hundred. We've not got near that.' He paused to allow Copland to join his train of thought.

'*You want to arm the prisoners? Absolutely not! If they bolt for it during the fight Kitchener will put us in the dock in their stead.*'

'*There's no choice,*' said the commander firmly. '*Six seasoned soldiers could make all the difference.*'

Seeing that he was damned whatever he did and knowing that military law allowed for such exigencies, Copland ran his hand over his ashen, sleep-deprived face and nodded.

'*Fair enough, but on your head be it,*' he warned.

The first silhouettes of horsemen were gathering on the far horizon as the heavy keys clashed in the lock of Morant's cell door. A tough looking, crop headed, Sergeant-Major called Knowles appeared in the doorway of Morant's cell holding a rifle. The smell of cheap tobacco and the pin-prick of light from the point of a cigarette drew his gaze to where Morant was already awake, lying on his bed in the gloom, his back propped up against the far wall. Exhaling a long, leisurely stream of smoke he preyed mercilessly upon the sergeant's obvious discomfort.

'*What's this sergeant? Can't wait 'till they do us up proper in court?*'

Clearing his throat the Sergeant-Major explained the reason for his presence in a Cornish drawl that was as thick as their famous clotted cream.

'*I have been instructed by the commander of the fort to give you this rifle and escort you and the other prisoners to the battlements. Pietersburg is about to be attacked by Boers,*' he said gravely.

But to Knowles' complete astonishment, Morant started laughing uncontrollably until tears ran down his face. Struggling to his feet, his voice still weak with mirth, Morant wiped his eyes with the back of his hand and enlightened the puzzled soldier.

'*Don't you see? You've got us in court for shooting*

them because they shot us and now they've come to shoot you, you want us to shoot them.'

'Very good Morant. Come along,' Knowles said testily motioning towards the door with his hand.

'That's Lieutenant Morant to you sergeant,' came the retort as Morant snatched the rifle from his hand and checked the breech.

'The bullets are safe with me,' said Knowles pointedly, opening his hand to reveal six long brass cartridges. Morant's chin jutted out defiantly at that slight of character and he continued to taunt his jailer. Having spent time in Devon himself, Morant pulled a rubbery face, rolled his eyes and said in a very passable Cornish accent, 'Cor, I once 'ad me bacon saved by that there Breaker Morant.'

Sick of his antics Knowles gave Morant a warning shove in the back as they left the cell, 'Just don't you be trying anything now.'

Morant rounded on him with the same incorrigibly stupid grin plastered across his face, 'Or what? Don't tell me . . . or you'll shoot me as well.' The prospect of getting out of the cell and back into action after the long months of inactivity had made Morant quite light headed and his laughter ricocheted off the stone walls as he climbed the steps to the battlements.

He was still chuckling when he emerged into the pre-dawn gloom where the mood was altogether more sombre and his light demeanour earned him a sour look from the irascible Major Copland. Rifles were being hurriedly loaded, ammunition stuffed into pockets and men ran back and forth carrying heavy boxes. Morant noted the irony that Britain's much-vaunted, superior firepower was nowhere to be seen. The Artillery had taken their guns when they had packed Colonel Hall off to India – before he could say anything about the killings in the Spelonken to the court of inquiry. Bugger should be here telling them the truth, *thought Morant bitterly as he spied Handcock, Witton and the others ahead.* Morant made his way across to them with a cheery call, 'Good morning gentlemen. Called on to defend King and country again. Let's hope they show a bit more appreciation this time,' he said loud enough to ensure that his words carried to the dun-coloured knot of British officers standing within earshot. None rose to his bait. They were more concerned with the forthcoming attack that was massing in the east.

Morant and Handcock expertly sized up the available vantage points. Pointing to the low roof of the guardhouse, which was situated down at the front of the fort, Morant asked Handcock, 'What d'ya reckon mate?'

Handcock sucked in a breath of cold, clear morning air, 'Bit exposed, but it'll give us a clear shot. Angle won't be too steep. We'll almost be able to look the buggers right in the eye.'

'That's settled then,' said Morant throwing one leg over the battlements. Hoisting his rifle onto his shoulder he prepared for the long climb down onto the rooftop below. Clearing his throat loudly he called out in a faux upper-class English accent, 'I say, could I have some bullets for my rifle now Sergeant-Major? They'd be awfully handy for killing Boers.'

A red-faced Knowles hurried over to Morant, ignoring the guffaws from the ranks and avoiding Major Copland's steely gaze who looked fit to burst at Morant's Pyrrhic victory. Once they loaded up with ammunition, Morant and Handcock disappeared over the side of the battlements.

'Where are they going?' asked Copland stepping forward in alarm, his hands flapping like flightless birds at the retreating figures.

'They're taking the suicide watch. No-one else will volunteer for that. But don't worry,' added the

Commander tilting his head up to the upper tier of the fort where the barrels of three anonymous rifles protruded through slots in the thick, stone walls. 'I've got my best shots up there. One false move and they'll take 'em down like game.' Copland nodded, mollified by the precautions that had been taken, but his nerves still jangled. If they escaped the consequences didn't bear thinking about.

No matter how many sunrises and sunsets you see, there is still something epic about nature's little cameos. Symbolising, as they do, the eternal cycle of night and day, life and death, they make a suitably dramatic backdrop for mankind to play out their own little tragedies. In those last moments of grey, chill pre-dawn there was silence – as though everything was waiting for a signal. Then, as the red eye of the sun peeked cautiously over the faraway hills, as, no doubt, were many others, the birds began their dawn chorus and the strange alien sound of crickets receded with the darkness. The changing of the guard was complete. The sound of approaching hooves started as a low rumble in the distance and built slowly like a drum roll as the sun rose. The first golden rays of sunlight filtered out over the veldt – briefly transforming this unyielding, barren stretch of land into a mythical, shimmering Arcadian golden harvest. As the drumming of hooves reached a crescendo the silhouettes of hundreds of Boer horsemen appeared on the horizon, framed against the new rising sun. The Boers regarded themselves as God's chosen people and there was certainly an air of the biblical about this early morning prelude to the battle between these two ancient warring tribes.

Usually the Boer relied on stealth, hit and run, but thinking they still had the element of surprise they came on unafraid. Sweat trickled down brows and fingers tightened round triggers, but a strong steady voice rang

out above the din, 'Steady . . . steady. Let 'em get to
fifty yards.'

Obediently they waited though their instinct was to
discharge every round they had into the rising sun
to relieve their pent-up tension. The drumming of hooves
got louder and louder as they came closer and closer, a
thick, black phalanx that almost blocked out the sun.
They could make out the heavy beards and the battered
felt hats by the time the order came at last – 'Fire!'

A few horses reared up as their riders were torn from
their saddles by the first fusillade of flying lead, but unde-
terred by their losses they kept on coming hell-for-leather.
Just as it seemed that they must crash into the battlements, they split in two and began riding round the fort
like redskins. Practised in the art of shooting from the
saddle, they picked off a few defenders, who returned
fire, but moving targets are always harder to hit.

Down on the most exposed position where Morant
and Handcock were keeping up a steady rate, they were
soon surrounded by spent brass cartridge cases and
bullets were singing off the stonework all around them.

'Strewth, these buggers are keen,' remarked Morant
as he rolled away from the Boers line of fire.

'Bloody oath,' murmured Handcock as he patiently
tracked another galloping rider across the veldt down
the sight of his rifle and then gently squeezed the trigger.
Morant watched a far away figure throw up his arms
and cartwheel away into the dust as he fell from his
horse. Handcock was later credited with 'bagging'
Beyers' fighting leader, Marthinus Pretorius.

AFTER AN HOUR OF FRUITLESS CIRCLING, the Boers realised
that there was little chance of taking the fort and Beyers
pulled his men back to lick their wounds and count
their losses. There was visible relief amongst the defenders, who offered not so much as a 'thank you' to the

prisoners before they were returned to their cells. If fate
had been kinder to Morant and Handcock, they would
have perished on that roof and their debt would have
been settled there and then. On another occasion, such
bravery might have yielded a medal or a mention in dispatches, but it was not even mentioned in court, offered
in mitigation of their sentences, or referred to in any
official report or any of the supposedly impartial newspaper reports of the trial.

To add insult to injury, they later learned that the
Pietersburg Light Horse had left Fort Edward and tracked
the retreating Beyers. Although some got within 150 yards
of him, their officer decided to wait until reinforcements
could be brought up before taking him. Needless to say,
Beyers escaped whilst they dithered and Morant mercilessly lampooned his unfortunate successor:

> A new foot-slogging Major has ventured
>   out of town,
> To spoil the mouth of 'Bideford', and break
>   the pony down,
> But when he sallies after Boers, it's different
>   now to then –
> He's got to let the Dutchmen rip, to muster
>   up his men.

The prisoners were back in court after little more than
a couple of hours respite, as if nothing had happened.
Witton noted that their early morning exertions had
little effect on the court, except to make them 'a little
more imperious'.

MAJOR THOMAS CAME STRAIGHT TO *his feet making out
a case for the prisoners' immediate release. As always
the thin, wiry Thomas crackled with nervous energy.*

'*I would like to draw the court's attention to what
Clode on military law says about this very issue: "The*

*performance of a duty of honour and trust after knowl-edge of a military offence ought to convey a pardon."
The precedent was, I believe, established by none other
than the Duke of Wellington . . .'*

Copland intercepted him smoothly, having already
been alerted to this custom by the very thorough counsel
for the prosecution, Captain Burns-Begg.

'*You would be correct in that assumption Major
Thomas, but not in thinking that this court would
regard it as sufficient grounds for dropping all charges
against the accused. Motion denied Major Thomas. This
court martial will proceed . . . come what may.'*

'*I must protest Major Copland . . .'* started Thomas,
but again was cut off by the raised hand of Copland.

'*Major Thomas, you will doubtless be aware that the
section of Clode you quoted is in fact a custom, not a
law. It is therefore up to the discretion of the court
whether we invoke the custom in question and on this
occasion I regret that I must decline to do so. That's the
last word on the matter. Let's move on.'*

'*It'll count in our favour, won't it though?'* Witton
asked in a low voice. Harry regarded Witton's wide-eyed innocence with weary indifference. Poor George!
He just doesn't get it. It's as Peter said, 'our graves were
dug before we left the Spelonken'. If we'd won the war
single-handed and delivered De Wet gift-wrapped it
wouldn't make any difference now.

THE FIRST ORDER OF BUSINESS WAS a return to Morant's
demand that Kitchener answer the charges he had laid
at his door, which had halted proceedings the previous
day. The wires to Pretoria had obviously been running
hot overnight as Copland announced that the whole
court was to be uprooted and transported down to Pretoria to hear the testimony of his military secretary,
Lieutenant-Colonel Hubert Hamilton.

As he watched the armoured train pull out of Pietersburg station, Major Bolton, the assistant provost
marshal, who would shortly take over as chief prosecutor from Captain Burns-Begg, confessed a terrible
foreboding:

> I have a terrible job on hand. I need a stiff whisky.
> Poor old Tony Morant and Peter Handcock are
> prisoners on the train.

MORANT WRUNG HIS HANDS TOGETHER, *which had been
oiled by a little of his own sweat. He had boldly made his
play when he accused Lord Kitchener of giving the orders
to shoot prisoners. A lot depended on this testimony.*

*A makeshift court had been assembled in a gloomy
room at the Pretoria Artillery barracks, which now
awaited the arrival of Lieutenant-Colonel Hubert
Hamilton who would answer questions on Lord Kitchener's behalf.*

*The Lieutenant Colonel was shown in. A tall, thin,
rangy man in his fifties, he had been Kitchener's Military Secretary for many years. As he stood before the
court he came face-to-face with those whose lives he
held in his hands. The strain was visible on his face and
his Adam's apple bobbed up and down nervously.
George Witton described him as:*

> [G]aunt and hollow-eyed, as though a whole world
> of care rested on his shoulders. He was apparently
> far more anxious than those whose fate depended
> on the evidence he was to give.

*Prosecutor Burns-Begg stepped forward and asked
in a loud clear voice, 'Lieutenant Morant has stated in
his evidence that the late Captain Hunt told him that he
had received orders from you that no prisoners were to
be taken alive. Is that true?'*

With a shake of the head and a purse of his lips, as though banishing the very thought from his mind, Hamilton answered, 'Absolutely untrue.'

That denial was all Burns-Begg needed. With a nod to Thomas, he deferred to the defence. Biting back the disappointment, the sandy-haired lawyer shuffled his papers whilst chewing the ends of his drooping moustache before heaving his tall, thin frame upward out of his chair and back into the fray. In a calm, clear voice that belied his frail, nervous appearance, he looked up and asked the gaunt figure of Hamilton who sat opposite him, 'If you do not recall those orders, then do you recall speaking with Captain Hunt when he brought two polo ponies to Army HQ last July?'

Willing this inquisition to be over with every fibre of his being, Hamilton gathered every ounce of conviction he could muster and replied, 'No. I do not recall speaking to Captain Hunt on that occasion, or ever discussing his duties in the Spelonken with him.' He sighed inwardly with relief as Thomas switched his attention to the court panel. His ordeal was over.

ROBBED OF THE CONFESSION WHICH would have seen his clients acquitted, Thomas was forced to change tack and argue that Hamilton's denial, in fact, made no difference. He tried to make out a technical defence arguing that the men who actually shot Visser must first be found guilty of murder, as his clients' guilt depends on the guilt of the firing party. As the firing party, like his clients, was only following the orders of a superior officer the correct charge should be conspiracy to murder, not murder.

Thomas also argued that Morant's vengeance was allowable under military law as there was evidence that Visser was part of the commando that killed Hunt, and because he was wearing khaki Visser was liable to be shot anyway, as it was against the customs of war.

With regard to the informal nature of Visser's court martial, Thomas said that there was no other way to conduct it in the field with the enemy nearby and that this practice was commonplace.

He also cited Captain Taylor's evidence that these men were marauders and outlaws and irregular forces deployed to deal with men of this nature must be given wide discretion and the benefit of the doubt if they made mistakes or erred in judgment.

The prosecutor, Captain Burns-Begg, rubbished Thomas' argument by saying that under both military law and English common law, the men can be tried as accessories before, after or with the principal felons regardless of their innocence or guilt, and where a common intent to commit a crime can be proved, the guilt of one can be applied to the others also.

As to the rest of Thomas' argument, Burns-Begg quoted the *Manual of Military Law*, which says that an officer is responsible for carrying out commands given by a superior officer, even if they are illegal. And even if they were being tried in a civilian court, they would still be liable to hang for illegally carrying out a death sentence.

With regard to Hunt's death, Burns-Begg said that their reaction was clear proof of their intent to kill. Retaliation under military law has a very specific application and does not shelter officers who use it to settle private grievances. If they do so they must accept the consequences. The Army prosecutor concluded his argument by saying that, in any case, there was no evidence to connect Visser with Hunt's death or to prove that Hunt was murdered at all.

The evidence was then summed up by Judge Advocate, Major Copland. He said that the accused felt their actions were justified by the orders given to them by

Captain Hunt and that they also acted under provocation and in ignorance of military law. It was Copland's argument that a person is responsible for any offence committed by another at his instigation. If several people are involved, they could all be charged with murder if the action resulted in a death. The charge could only be manslaughter if there was extreme provocation which at that moment deprived him of his own self-control. However, the manner of the crime, the time that elapsed between the act of provocation and retaliation and his state of mind at the time all needed to be considered. Copland indicated that the fact they had not acted on Hunt's order to shoot prisoners until after his death proved that the order had created the motivation for the killing.

He concluded by stating that military law dictates that an armed man could only be killed so long as he resists; once he surrenders, he must be treated as a prisoner of war. As to shooting Boers in khaki, it would have to be proved that the enemy intended to deceive by wearing the uniform.

The panel then retired to consider their verdict, and when they reconvened Witton noted that he saw tears in the eyes of one of the courts martial members, but did not attach any importance to it at the time.

It was customary to discharge the accused immediately if they had been acquitted of the charge.

But in this case, no verdict was given, indicating a guilty verdict.

The Visser case set the pattern for the other court martials. Many of the main points, such as the orders Captain Hunt allegedly received from Lieutenant-Colonel Hamilton and the customs of war, were revisited again.

During the journey back from Pretoria, some Boers had crossed the line ahead of the train and for the second time the prisoners were told to stand arms, but this time were not required to defend the lives of their accusers.

THE SECOND CASE, CONCERNING THE shooting of eight Boers, began on February 3, 1902. There was a change of prosecution counsel for this case. Major Burns-Begg was recalled to London and Major Bolton, who had been Assistant Provost Marshal in Pietersburg, took over. Morant, Handcock and Witton were accused of shooting or inciting others to shoot eight Boer prisoners on August 23. These facts were not disputed, but Thomas argued that they should be charged with conspiracy, not murder. The court rejected this.

Intelligence Officer Ledeboer told how he captured and handed over eight prisoners to a BVC patrol, but had no idea what happened to them after that.

Trooper Thompson said that he and troopers Duckett and Lucas had been sent for by Morant and asked if they were friends of Sergeant Eland, and had heard Lord Kitchener's proclamation that those who live by the sword must die by the sword. The Lord had delivered eight Boers into his hands and he was going to shoot them. Lucas objected, but Morant insisted that he would run the show and he had orders to obey. Thompson said that Morant gave the order and the prisoners were shot. Morant told him to stick to the story or there would be consequences. Thompson then changed the story he had given at the court of inquiry, and said that he had only heard of Hunt's orders second-hand.

Seargent-Major Hammett corroborated Thompson's story and told the court that Morant had told him he was going to shoot the prisoners the night before they were brought in. He'd asked Morant if he was exceeding his orders, to which Morant had replied that he had ignored them until then, but would do so no longer. The Boers were asked for information about Veldt-cornet Kelly, and one rushed Lieutenant Witton and seized his carbine. Witton fired and killed him. He said that Morant had always treated prisoners well until Hunt's death and had been a changed man since.

Sergeant Wrench told that on August 19, Intelligence Officer Ledeboer handed the eight prisoners in question to him and returned to Elim Hospital, where on August 23 Lieutenants Morant, Handcock and Witton, Sergeant-Major Hammett and troopers Duckett and Thompson arrived. Morant took charge of the prisoners and told him that Kelly's commando was about and to form an advance patrol. If Wrench heard any firing he was to gallop back to Morant. He did hear firing, but went instead to nearby Bristow's Farm, where he reported handing over the prisoners to Captain Taylor.

Later Morant sent for Wrench and told him that he'd made a fool of himself and that he'd be court martialled for it. He also said he knew there were those opposed to the shootings and had orders to weed them out. Morant told him he'd had letters of congratulations from HQ over the last fight (involving Visser) and intended to go on with it.

Wrench was asked by Thomas why Captain Hunt had reprimanded him for insubordination.

The prisoners did not testify, as the facts were not disputed, but they handed in written statements. Morant denied any such conversation took place with Wrench and again alluded to the orders given to him by the late Captain Hunt, the fact that he was reprimanded for bringing in prisoners and that up until Hunt's death he had not shot prisoners.

However, he admitted shooting prisoners after Hunt's death, as other irregular units had done. He believed that the men he shot were marauders and train-wreckers and were responsible for Hunt's death, and that he was justified in dealing with them summarily. As officer commanding at Fort Edward he took full responsibility. He admitted sending in an edited report of the Visser shooting, but did so 'for reasons which have actuated higher military authority' (that is, for the good of the corps). As to his state of mind at the time of the killings, he admitted,

> I have been told that I was never myself after the death of Captain Hunt, and I admit that his death preyed upon my mind when I thought of the brutal treatment he had received. This treatment of Captain Hunt's body, coupled with the train-wreckings which had occurred, made me resolve to act on orders and do as other officers have done under less trying circumstances than myself.

However, it would be another seventy years before post traumatic stress disorder was discovered and would be considered a mitigating factor in such cases. Lieutenants Handcock, Witton and Picton confirmed that they too had been told by Captain Hunt not to take prisoners, and all took it as read that his orders had proper authority. Captain Taylor recalled Morant being reprimanded for bringing in prisoners and being told they should have been shot. When cross-examined, he said the words Hunt had used were, 'What the hell do you mean by bringing these men in? We have neither room or rations here.'

Civil Surgeon Johnston and Sergeant Robinson confirmed Hunt's orders and members from other irregular units testified that those same orders had been carried out in their units.

Members of other irregular units then gave evidence that they had been reprimanded for bringing in prisoners and had dealt summarily with Boers caught wearing khaki, train-wrecking or murdering soldiers.

Sergeant Walter Ashton of Brabant's Horse testified that he had received orders not to take prisoners after acts of treachery by the Boers. Sergeant McArthur testified that he saw a Boer shot for wearing khaki.

Lieutenant Colin Philip said that the Queensland Mounted Infantry were in disgrace for bringing in Boers who were caught sniping. He said, 'Boers caught breaking the customs of war were shot summarily.' Instructions were published in the orders in Colonel Garratt's column that Boers caught in khaki were to be shot.

Captain King of the Canadian Scouts said that the Boers guilty of wearing khaki, train-wrecking and murdering (Empire) soldiers were dealt with summarily.

The Judge Advocate, Major Copland, protested that such evidence was irrelevant as it did not prove or disprove the charge of murder before the court.

Testimonies were also heard that Boers wearing khaki had been shot, and Australian newspapers were produced dated November 1901 with cablegrams saying that Kitchener had given orders that Boers found in khaki were to be shot. Even ordinary regulations stated that men wearing British uniform during a time of war could be executed. Despite this, Major Bolton went into the witness box and said he had no knowledge of an order issued by Lord Kitchener saying Boers wearing khaki were to be shot.

Major Thomas concluded by saying that the shooting of the eight Boers could not be regarded as a criminal act in a time of war and against men who should be regarded as lawless marauders and not a proper army. He said the BVC was formed with the special purpose of clearing the area of such brigands and it was necessary to recognise that different methods were appropriate for the different theatres of warfare in South Africa.

He contended that it was the Boers and their barbaric methods that had set in train the events that had brought them to this court. The killing of Best at Naboomspruit led to the death of Hunt, he said, and the taking of reprisals by Morant who up to that point had not followed Hunt's orders to shoot prisoners. Morant's attitude did change, said Thomas, and if this were a civil court he could be accused of being vengeful, but this was a time of war and 'war makes men's natures both callous and, on occasion, revengeful'. When the customs and rules of civilised warfare are departed from, he said, then reprisal follows reprisal. Thomas was of the opinion that if every crime committed in the war was dragged before the court, the courts martial would be in constant session.

The job of the irregular troops was to harry, hunt and shoot the enemy, and as such must be distinguished from regular soldiers, said Thomas. Irregular soldiers were fighting in irregular situations and some allowance must be made, he suggested. If they were to be restrained, then clear rules would need to be issued, instead of reprimanding them at one time for bringing in prisoners and at another time dragging them up as murderers for shooting them. He cited the Franco–Prussian War and the American War of Independence as recent examples where the rules were clearly laid down – guerrillas were executed summarily. Morant was not acting with criminal intent, said Thomas, but following orders of a superior, as were the other accused.

Thomas went to say that if the accused had overstepped the mark, they should be given the benefit of the doubt, not prosecuted. In this type of warfare, where the enemy hide amongst the general population, it was not possible to distinguish who was responsible for what – all those taking up arms must be regarded as the enemy. If the Boers wanted to engage in the type of warfare where they mingle with the general population, they had to accept the consequences. Thomas quoted a passage from the *Manual of Military Law* to support his argument. It stated that persons who did not wear the uniform of a regular army or fight under a recognised government run the risk of being treated as marauders and punished accordingly. He also reminded the court that, as they had heard, the members of the BVC were not the only ones to overstep the mark. Details of the Boers' train-wrecking activities in the area were also submitted.

The prosecution answered Thomas by declaring that the accused had admitted to killing the eight Boer prisoners on August 23, 1901, and that the defence's arguments were flawed because superior orders need not be obeyed if they are unlawful; the fact that other irregular corps shot Boers was irrelevant because two wrongs don't make a right; and regardless of the character of the Boers they had been fighting, they had to be protected and properly tried once they had surrendered.

The Judge Advocate agreed with the prosecution and, as in the Visser case, put forward the opinion that there was no place in war for personal revenge, that quarter must be given after a soldier surrenders, and even if their actions were deserving of death, they must be properly tried before the sentence is carried out. It is seldom permissible for a soldier to take the law into his own hands, he said. If they do and a death results, they must accept the consequences and be charged with either murder or manslaughter. Manslaughter would only be considered in cases of extreme provocation and only where it could be demonstrated the provocation had resulted in a loss of self-control. The manner of the crime and the length of time between the provocation and the killing would also be key criteria in considering the lesser charge, said Major Copland.

Again, the court retired and no indication of the verdict or the sentence was given.

MAJOR LENEHAN WAS NEXT ON THE stand on charges of neglecting to report what he knew about the Van Buuren killing and the shooting of the three Boers on August 25. Lenehan pleaded not guilty.

In the case of the three Boers the main evidence was given by Trooper Botha. He told how they were brought in by Taylor's police and shot by five BVC troopers on Morant's orders. Botha said he'd reported it to Morant in the presence of Lenehan, who had arrived that day from Pietersburg. Later, over dinner, the officers had been discussing the trustworthiness of Boers when Morant summoned Botha and asked him if he'd done his duty and shot the 'Dutchman'. Botha said 'Yes'.

Lenehan was also charged with not reporting the death of Trooper Van Buuren. He pleaded 'not guilty'. Ex-Captain Robertson, who had issued the order but was now a star witness for the prosecution said that he had been warned that Van Buuren could not be trusted and that men refused to go on duty with him. Robertson admitted that he had discussed it with Handcock and Taylor and it was decided to shoot him. He had submitted a false report, but did so in the interest of the corps. Taylor also knew the truth. He had told Lenehan that Van Buuren was shot because they had thirty prisoners and the Boers were near and they were afraid he'd give them away to the enemy.

Lieutenant Edwards said that he had received a copy of a confidential letter from Captain Hunt, the original having been sent to Pretoria. A postscript to the original had been torn off; it read 'Will write details of death of Van Buuren; Handcock shot him.' Major Bolton said he found the letter minus the footnote in Lenehan's kit. The footnote was not produced.

Lenehan said that Robertson had never told him the details of Van Buuren's death and didn't think that the postscript to Hunt's letter contained anything suspicious.

Taylor denied being party to the shooting of Van Buuren and said he didn't hear about it until later.

Handcock denied being part of the discussion, but carried out Robertson's orders and was told by the same officer to make out a report saying that Van Buuren died as a result of a skirmish with the Boers. The report didn't suit Robertson, who wrote one himself. However, he did tell Captain Hunt about his part in the death of Van Buuren and told him to pass it on to Lenehan.

Thomas objected to the fact that Lenehan, an officer, had been held for three months on a minor charge, and deposed that Robertson and Taylor were the guilty ones and should have been prosecuted, but Robertson had been allowed to resign.

THE CASE OF THE THREE BOERS WAS heard next and Lieutenants Morant and Handcock were charged with the killing of two men and a boy of seventeen on September 7. They again pleaded 'not guilty'.

Sergeant-Major Hammett confirmed that he was one of the patrol and that the signal to shoot the Boers was Morant's question, 'Do you know Captain Hunt?' Other witnesses confirmed that they too understood that no prisoners were to be taken.

In his defence, Morant said he had never asked the Boers to surrender. They were Dutchmen whom he was at war with and were part of the band that killed Hunt, so he had them shot.

According to Witton, Bolton then cross-examined Morant, who told him pointedly:

Look here, Major, you are just the 'Johnnie' I have been waiting to be cross-examined by; cross-examine me as much as you like, but let us have a straight gallop.

Handcock again reiterated Hunt's orders and Thomas said that it must have been common military knowledge that the Boers in the Spelonken made no pretence at carrying on recognised warfare.

FEBRUARY 7, 1902, SAW CAPTAIN TAYLOR tried, not by a court martial, but a military court. It had been successfully argued that Taylor was not a soldier, but a native commissioner, and because by the time the case came to court he had ceased to be employed by the army for more than three months.

The main prosecution evidence came from ex-Sergeant-Major Morrison, who told how Taylor had ordered him to shoot the first party of six Boers on June 2, 1901. He had asked Captain Robertson whether he should take orders from Captain Taylor. Robertson replied, 'Certainly, as he is commanding officer at Spelonken.' Morrison then asked Taylor to confirm the order, which he did, adding that if the Boers showed a white flag, they were to disregard it. He repeated those orders to Sergeant Oldham, who took a six-man patrol and shot the Boers.

Oldham said that Morrison had told him to make the Boers fight and on no account to bring them in alive. They ambushed the wagon, but stopped firing thinking there might be women and children inside. There were none and Trooper Botha said the six were shot at the side of the road.

Ex-Captain Robertson verified this version of events and told Morrison to take orders from Taylor, but did not hear what Taylor told him. It was usual for Taylor to give orders to patrols. He admitted that he was forced to resign from the Army and had been refused admission to any other corps.

Major Lenehan said that it had been Colonel Hall

who had held the inquiry into Robertson and Morrison's conduct, and it was his decision to dismiss them rather than prosecute them.

Taylor defended himself. He said that he had been a lieutenant in Plumer's Scouts and at the time of the shootings had been involved in native affairs and intelligence work in the Spelonken. He had no military command and had never been given orders not to take prisoners. He took his orders from Colonel Hall. He requested men for patrols, but never interfered with non-commissioned officers. He knew the six Boers were coming in, but never gave Morrison orders to shoot them. He said the first he knew of the death of those six Boers was the day before the hearing.

The court heard that the file containing letters telling Taylor about the six Boers coming in had disappeared, and the empty file was found at his successor's office (Enraght-Moony).

Taylor's Intelligence Officer, Otto Schwarz, said he told Taylor about the Boers coming in, but didn't know the number. Taylor had been angry about these shootings.

Evidence was taken to show that there was animosity towards Taylor on the part of Morrison.

The court then considered a second charge against Taylor – that of shooting a native. It was said that while in pursuit of a Boer commando, they stopped at a native kraal. Taylor asked a native for information and when he refused drew his gun and shot him in the head. When asked for an explanation, Taylor said that he had intended to shoot over his head, but had aimed too low. Despite documentary evidence discovered by Enraght-Moony, in Taylor's files, this was the only charge relating to his treatment of natives brought against him.

This time the court deliberated and, as was military custom, announced their 'not guilty' verdict and released the prisoner. Taylor was the only one to be acquitted.

THE HEESE CASE WAS THE LAST TO be heard on February 17, 1902, and was convened behind closed doors at Pietersburg Army HQ. Lieutenant Morant was charged with inciting Lieutenant Handcock to shoot the missionary Heese on August 23, 1901.

The prosecution said the motive for murdering Heese was that he had seen the bodies of the eight Boers Morant had ordered shot that same morning, and was on his way to Pietersburg to report the killings.

Trooper Thompson said he saw Heese speaking to the eight Boer prisoners before they were shot. Trooper Philips said he was on duty at Fort Edward on the day in question and saw Heese and his native driver heading towards Pietersburg. Heese showed Philips a pass signed by Captain Taylor and seemed very agitated. He had told Philips that there had been a fight that morning and several people had been killed.

Corporal Sharpe said that he saw Morant speaking to Heese before he left, around 10 or 11 am, and then observed Handcock go off in the same direction about an hour later. He was carrying a gun, a fact corroborated by two other witnesses, but they admitted that was not unusual for an officer. He was on a chestnut horse and did not take the same road as the missionary.

On cross-examination, Sharpe admitted going a long way to secure Van Rooyen, a Boer farmer who had been on the road to Pietersburg that day, as a witness, as he believed he may have witnessed the murder. Sharpe denied that he said he would walk to Pietersburg barefooted to be on the firing party that shot Morant. He admitted that he had sold khaki uniforms to the Boers and that it had resulted in Handcock issuing an order forbidding the practice. He claimed he had kept notes of what had been going on in the Spelonken.

Unusually, the testimony of a native called Silas was read out and admitted as evidence. Native evidence was generally regarded as unreliable, but this was overlooked as the statement contained a few salient details about the death of Heese.

Silas knew the Reverend Heese and had passed him on the road to Pietersburg. After the reverend had passed it occurred to Silas that he should have asked for a lift, and he ran after him. Further along the road a horseman on a brown horse passed and started following Heese, but he thought nothing of it. He stated:

> He wore khaki clothing such as the soldiers wear, a light coloured hat with a cloth of motley colours (red, blue, black and white), and had stripes like a corporal. He was a young, stocky man; his face was shaved except for the moustache that he wore. He wore two cartridge-belts crossways over his shoulders and his breast pockets were filled with cartridges. His horse was of a bay colour, had a long tail and was not particularly well-conditioned.

However, Silas's statement did little for the prosecution case and, if anything, suggested Handcock was not the culprit. Whilst the mysterious stranger Silas saw, but could not positively identify, had the same colour horse as Handcock, none of the photographs of the BVC or Handcock show him wearing the headgear Silas described and he certainly would not have been wearing a uniform with corporal's stripes because at the time of the killings he held the rank of Veterinary Lieutenant, which would entitle him to two pips on his epaulets. Also, it's unlikely that a farrier would own a horse in such poor condition. The proposition that he may well have been a Boer in one of the khaki uniforms being sold by troopers from Fort Edward has never been entertained. Sharpe, after all, was a Corporal.

Van Rooyen further confused the issue. He said he had passed Heese around 2 pm, spoken to Silas shortly afterwards and then pushed on. Around sundown he saw a man on horseback coming along the road from the direction of Pietersburg. The rider turned off the road into the bush and some time later a man approached him on foot and told him to move on as there were Boers about. When asked if the man he saw on horseback was the same man who approached him on foot, his answer was, 'I cannot say.'

But when asked if he could identify the man he saw on foot, he pointed to Handcock and said, 'It was that man.'

The case for the defence opened with Morant's account of the events that took place earlier that day. Morant stated that the eight Boers his intelligence said were guilty of train-wrecking and other crimes were shot on his orders. The Reverend Heese had disobeyed his orders and spoken to the prisoners. Afterwards, he saw Heese again, who produced a pass signed by Captain Taylor. Morant advised him not to travel as there were Boers on the road, but Heese insisted and Morant said he told him to tie a white flag to his cart. Morant then returned to the Fort, went to Captain Taylor's and later saw Handcock at Mrs Bristow's.

When asked if he ordered Handcock to shoot Heese, Morant replied, 'I never made any suggestion about killing the missionary, as I was on good terms with him.'

Handcock's statement was that he went to Mrs Schiels's, then to Mrs Bristow's till dusk, and then returned to the fort. Both Mrs Schiel and Mrs Bristow were called and confirmed Handcock's version of events.

With no other evidence, the courts martial immediately returned a 'not guilty' verdict in the final case on February 19. Morant and Handcock had been acquitted in the case reckoned to be the real reason they were tried at all. Two of the courts martial panel had half a dozen bottles of champagne delivered to the prisoners' cells. They popped every cork and toasted each other and everyone they knew ten times over. They would soon be free, or so they thought.

10

Shoot Straight, You Bastards!

For 'tis good to die as a strong man dies,
E'en though by the hangman's rope;
For nothing on earth so currishly cries
As the cry of a poltroon hope.
I will do as I will – as a strong man should:
I will reck when the reckoning comes;
Then march me to doom in the haltered wood,
Or brave the Rogue's March of the drums.

'The Song of the Bushveldt Carbineers'
by FJ Broomfield

ALTHOUGH THE PRISONERS HAD BEEN found innocent of killing the missionary, their fate still hung in the balance whilst the courts-martial panel deliberated the other charges. The general opinion was that the charge of killing Heese was the main one to answer and now that they had been acquitted of that, they would soon be free. It certainly never occurred to any of the accused that they might actually be shot.

On the evening of February 20, they were given even more reason for optimism. During a dinner party in Morant's cell at which all the accused were present, an orderly told them he'd overheard a staff officer saying that they had all been cleared.

351

That rumour proved to be false. The courts martial did, in fact, find them guilty on three separate counts of murdering Boers, but the panel of officers had cited six separate points of mitigation in their Recommendation to Mercy.

CASE 1 – VISSER CASE

The court sentence the prisoner	Sentence
Lieut. H. H. Morant Bushveldt Carbineers, to suffer death by being shot.	Death

Signed at Pretoria this 29th January, 1902.

H.G. Denny, Lieut.-Col, President
C.S. Copland

RECOMMENDATION TO MERCY

The court strongly recommends the prisoner to mercy on the following grounds;

1. Extreme provocation by the mutilation of the body of Capt. Hunt, who was his intimate personal friend.

2. His good service during the war, including his capture of Field-Coronet T. Kelly in the Spelonken.

3. The difficult position in which he was suddenly placed, with no previous military experience and no-one to consult.

Signed at Pretoria the 29th day of January, 1902.

Confirmed – H.G. DENNY, Lieut.-Col., President
KITCHENER, General
25th February, 1902

Promulgated at Pretoria, 26th of February, 1902, and extracts taken. Sentence carried out at Pretoria on the 27th, 1902.

HW HUTSON, Assnt. Prov. Marshall, Pret. Dist. Pretoria, 27th February, 1902.

EIGHT BOERS CASE
SENTENCE

The court sentence the prisoners –	Sentence

Lieut. H.H. Morant, Bushveldt   Death
Carbineers, to suffer death by being shot.

Lieut. P.J. Handcock, Bushveldt   Death
Carbineers, to suffer death by being shot.

Lieut. G.R. Witton, Bushveldt   Death
Carbineers, to suffer death by being shot.

Signed at Pietersburg, this 4th of February, 1902.

H.G. DENNY, Lieut.-Col, President.
C.S. COPLAND, Major, Judge Advocate.

RECOMENDATION TO MERCY.

The court recommends Lieut. H.H. Morant to mercy on the following grounds: –

1. Provocation received by the maltreatment of the body of his intimate friend, Capt. Hunt.

2. Want of previous military experience and complete ignorance of military law and military procedure.

3. His good service throughout the war.

The court recommends Lieut. P.J. Handcock and Lieut. G.R. Witton to mercy on the following grounds: –

1. The court consider both were influenced by Lieut. Morant's orders, and thought they were doing their duty in obeying him.

2. Their complete ignorance of military law and custom.

3. Their good services throughout the war.

Signed at Pietersburg this 4th day of February, 1902.
H.G. DENNY, Lieut.-Col, President.

DESPITE THE DIRECTION OF THE JUDGE Advocate during the courts martial, Thomas had won one of the key points in the case – that severe provocation had caused Morant to avenge his senior officer. Both the staff officer who was overheard speaking about the case and the courts-martial panel thought that those recommendations and an acquital in the Heese case would save them.

Whilst the prisoners celebrated, Kitchener burned the midnight oil. Once the courts martial had delivered a guilty verdict and any recommendations to mercy, it was the job of the commander-in-chief to weigh up the two and decide on the appropriate punishment. To help him, a senior legal authority, the judge advocate general, examined the trial and sentences to ensure they were technically sound and the sentence was justified.

In the Morant case, there were two Judge Advocate Generals to hand, Colonel James St Clair and Colonel AR Pemberton. They examined the papers immediately and concurred with the court's decision.

Legal Opinions
Pietersburg Cases

[To] A.G. (Major-General Kelly)

The procedure followed on these trials was by trying the prisoners jointly on each charge of murder and conducting each trial to its conclusion, including the sentence.

It resulted from this mode of procedure that

Lieut. Morant has been convicted three different times of murder and sentenced three times to death.

Lieuts. Picton, Handcock and Witton have been convicted once of manslaughter and sentenced to cashiering, Lieut. Handcock has been also twice convicted of murder and sentenced to death twice.

Lieut. Witton has been convicted of murder and sentenced to death. From the above it appears that the responsibility of these illegal acts were (sic) in the following order:

1. Morant 2. Handcock 3. Witton 4. Picton.

According to rules of procedure 48 and 62 the trial on the separate charge sheets should have proceeded up to and including the findings – but that one sentence should have been awarded each prisoner for all the offences of which he was convicted.

This irregularity has not in my opinion inflicted any injustice on Lieut. Morant but I am not prepared to say that it has not done so in the other 3 cases. A heap of irrelevant evidence was admitted by the Court on the part of the defence despite the rule of the Judge Advocate who I consider was justified in protesting.

[Col. St. Clair]
20.2.02

Col. Pemberton's Remarks

Lieuts Morant, Handcock, Picton and Witton BVC.

I consider that Lieut. Morant was properly convicted.

Murder of Visser

1. The so-called Court was not a Court at all; it may be more justly called a consultation between 4 officers which ended in a party of subordinates being ordered to commit murder.

2. The provocation theory will not hold water. Visser was captured on the evening of the 9th August – he was not shot until the next day; had he been shot at once there might have been a slight presumption that his execution was ordered on the spur of the moment – but the evidence discloses a totally different state of affairs – Visser was not shot until the next day. Lieut. Morant himself admits that the death of Capt. Hunt gave a bias to his mind. A stronger case of implied malice aforethought has rarely been represented before any tribunal – I fail to understand on what grounds the other 3 prisoners were found guilty of manslaughter only – I disagree with their finding; from the evidence adduced I consider the 4 officers are jointly and severally responsible for the death of Visser and guilty of murder. I do not think it proved that Visser was wearing British uniform.

(Sgd) A.R. Pemberton, Col.
I agree.
(Sgd) J. St Clair

8 Boers

I consider that the above officers were rightly found guilty of the charge preferred against them. The evidence shows they 'took the law into their own hands' an illegal proceeding for which they should take the consequences. The plea of justification falls to the ground.

(Sgd) A.R. Pemberton, Col.
I agree.
(sgd) J St Clair

3 Boers

Lieut.s. Morant and Handcock

I consider the prs [prisoners] were rightly convicted. Lieut. Morant evidently constituted himself the avenger of Capt. Hunt and should take the consequences.

(Sgd) A.R. Pemberton, Col.
I agree.
(sgd) J St Clair

Major Lenehan late Comm. of Bushveldt Carbineers

Convicted of neglecting to make a report of the illegal shooting of a comrade by one of his men which fact had been brought to his notice by his officers.

Sentenced to be reprimanded.

I am of the opinion that the evidence justified the finding. The prosecution was embarrassed by the absence of Lieut. Col. Hall, lately commdg. at Pietersburg to whom reports had been made from the Spelonken.

The action of Major Lenehan in this matter was probably caused by his anxiety to keep the scandals in his corps from becoming public and may possibly be looked on as a grave error of judgement.

Aside from St Clair's admission that finding the accused guilty more than once was a procedural error and may have inflicted an injustice on Handcock and Witton, the other noteworthy comment was Pemberton's reference to the absence of Colonel Hall. Many claims were made during the trial that reports of the killings were sent to Hall, and Pemberton implied that Hall was the key to discovering which reports were actually filed at Pietersburg. Indeed, as his conversations with Enraght-Moony indicated, Hall might have been able to shed light on a great many other things had he not been removed prior to the courts martial. Given his pivotal position between the BVC and Army HQ, his removal must be regarded as highly suspicious. After the trial, Major Lenehan did write to Colonel Hall asking him to confirm that orders to shoot prisoners did exist, but received no reply. But, unlike the officers he left behind in South Africa to face the music, Hall's career did not suffer. He was made a full colonel in 1903 and ended his career as a brigadier in 1909. He also received a Companion (of the Order) of the Bath and Commander of the Royal Victorian Order.

Kitchener had made no mention of the BVC since the courts martial began, but now it was time to inform Lord Roberts at the War Office in London of their outcome and his decision to execute Morant and Handcock and commute Witton's sentence to penal servitude for life.

Telegram   Pretoria, 21st February 1902
No. S877

Your No. 636. Lieutenant Morant, Lieutenant Hancock [sic], Lieutenant Whitton [sic],
    Lieutenant Picton and Major Lenehan, the Officer Commanding the Bushveldt Carabineers [sic], have been tried by General Court-Martial. Trial received today, resulted in convicting Morant of 3 separate murders, Handcock, 2 murders and 1 manslaughter; Whitton [sic], 1 murder and 1 manslaughter, Picton, 1 manslaughter; Lenehan neglecting to report knowledge acquired after the fact. The murders were of Boer prisoners, in a spirit of revenge, for alleged ill-treatment of 1 of their officers, Lieutenant Hunt, who was shot in action. No such ill-treatment was proved. Sentence, the first 3 death; Picton cashiered; Lenehan will be removed. As corps has been disbanded some time ago for

irregularities, dismissal of Lenehan not necessary and he will be ordered to Australia. I propose to confirm sentences on Morant, who originated crimes, on Handcock, who carried out several cold-blooded murders, and in the case of Whitton, who was present, but under influence, commutation to penal servitude for life. Do you concur? There are other cases against Morant and Handcock, including a charge of murder of German. Plea in evidence was not sufficient to convict.

Again, in this communication there was a sleight-of-hand by Kitchener. These 'other charges' against the accused were never laid and he also states that the 'alleged' ill-treatment of Hunt was not proved. This was not the finding of the courts martial, who cited the mutilation of Hunt in its plea for mitigation. One can only imagine the feelings of the panel when Kitchener ordered the death sentence and ignored their pleas for clemency, and in his later telegrams to Lord Roberts and Australian Prime Minister Edmund Barton, that there were he stated 'no grounds for mitigation'.

But what the prisoners and the panel didn't realise was that, in practical terms, a recommendation to mercy was meaningless. It carried little weight and effectively passed the responsibility further up the chain of command to Kitchener where the ultimate decision was made. For reasons that will become clear, only a 'not guilty' verdict on all counts would have saved them.

They were still celebrating at Pietersburg gaol when Kitchener was sending Provost Marshal Poore a telegram marked 'Pressing and Confidential'. Kitchener ordered Poore to: 'Send prisoners Major Lenehan, Lieutenants Morant, Picton, Handcock and Witton to Pretoria under an adequate escort commanded by a competent officer . . . Every precaution must be taken against possibility of escape.'

Morant's sweet dreams of freedom were rudely interrupted the next morning when he was roused at first light. Reality rushed in with the early morning light as they realised that the previous night's booze-fuelled optimism had been a false dawn. As the burly provosts of Wiltshire Regiment put heavy iron manacles around his wrists, Morant commented, 'This comes of Empire-building', and broke down.

Chained like convicts, the five prisoners were taken to the station under armed escort, split into groups of two and put into armoured carriages for the journey south. An officer and six soldiers guarded each carriage. Major Lenehan, who had only been reprimanded, the lightest of the three possible sentences for his 'crime', should have been free to go, but he was also put onto the train, though he was not chained. He later complained about the 'over-zealousness of the Provost Marshal'.

Whilst they were being loaded into the trucks, the 'competent officer' Kitchener had requested arrived on the scene. It was the chief prosecutor at the courts martial, Major Bolton. Lieutenant Picton raised his manacled hands and said, 'I have to thank you for these Major Bolton.'

Although Picton had good reason to feel bitter, Bolton, like the courts-martial panel, had come to feel great sympathy for the prisoners. Once the train was underway, Bolton countermanded Kitchener's draconian orders and had the guard release Morant's hands, on the promise he would not try to escape. Morant kept his word, but must have prayed that one of Jack Hindon's mines would cripple their train. Unfortunately for them, the train-wrecker's days were over.

Morant and Bolton spoke late into the night. Morant told him about his father, his disgrace and exile to Australia. He gave Bolton his watch and chain, notebook and a photograph of a girl which he asked him to return to his family if anything should happen to him.

They were not the only personal items that Morant gave away that night, however. When they broke their journey at Potgietersrust to ensure the line ahead was clear of Boers, he met an old acquaintance from Australia, a Yorkshireman called Arthur Keble Eastwood. They had met in the 1880s in Australia when Eastwood, a midshipman on the *Cutty Sark*, landed in Sydney and was given three weeks leave. Eastwood and his brother decided to go up country to hunt black swans. They met Morant at a cattle station en route and he joined them on the hunt. Eastwood was also a bit of a wild rover and by the time he went to South Africa in 1889 to try his luck as a 'digger' on the Witwatersrand, he and Morant had became firm friends.

It was in South Africa that they next met in early 1901. Morant had just returned from England, had joined the BVC and was stationed at Stydespoort, which is not too far from Potgietersrust. Morant tried to persuade Eastwood to join the BVC saying they'd have a great time together. Luckily, Eastwood declined the offer as he'd just joined the intelligence service. He was in charge of the blockhouses from Pietersburg to Potgietersrust, built to protect the railway from Boer train wreckers, and according to an elderly relative of Eastwood's, their third and final late night meeting took place quite by chance on that lonely platform at Potgietersrust.

After the only regular armoured train had passed through safely that day, Eastwood had gone down the line to Potgietersrust to have a drink with a friend called King. Suddenly it was announced that a train was coming in which had Major Bolton, Eastwood's commanding officer, on board. Afraid he'd be caught, he hid under a bed. Bolton came into King's tent and said,

'For God's sake give me a double whisky quickly; I'm on a frightful bloody job.'

'What is it?' Bolton replied.

'I'm taking poor old Tony Morant and Handcock to be court martialled and shot.'

Overhearing the conversation Eastwood emerged from under King's bed and said to Bolton, 'I know I shouldn't be here but you can court martial me too, I don't mind, but I must go and see old Morant, if you'll take me.'

Bolton agreed. 'Yes,' he said, 'it's a tragedy. They're in the truck behind and you can go and talk to them.'

Eastwood went out to the train and said, 'Tony what have you been doing?'

Morant, obviously in a bitter mood, told him about the murder and mutilation of Hunt and how it changed his attitude. 'I've shot those seven (sic) bloody Boers and I'll shoot every other one if they let me loose. But I know that I am going to be shot and I don't give a damn. I've done my job. I've shot those bloody Boers and buried them in their own graves.'

They had a cigarette together shook hands and said farewell for what they both knew would be the last time.

As they boarded the train again Morant gave Eastwood a leather cigarette case with the Morant family crest inlaid in tiny diamonds and emeralds. Morant said that it was a gift from his mother and to have it 'as a keepsake in my memory'.

If his claim that he was a Morant was a pretence, then he maintained it right until the end. Digby Morant was promoted to admiral in March 1901 and got a knighthood in November of the same year. In one of the many letters he wrote from prison shortly before his death, Morant referred to Digby's knighthood, saying 'the Governor got a KCB the other day in birthday honours'.

He made another reference to his 'Governor' on

arriving in Pretoria, where the security overkill continued. Major Lenehan was transferred to another train heading for Cape Town, where they put him on a ship back to Australia. He never saw them again. Morant had written him a last letter:

MY DEAR MAJOR,

– Hell to pay! Isn't it? – (you are all right and will live to go hunting again). If anything happens to me you write to my governor: and to my girl (_____, N. Devon). Also see Bulletin in Sydney town and tell 'em all the facts. How Hunt was shot by Boers, and how 'I carried on' – same as HE would have done – had I been shot that night at Viljoen's. Had I tumbled into Boer hands, I'd have gone on whilst I had a cartridge left, and then used the butt, and then have been wiped out. That's what I'd expect if I had fallen into Boer lines – wouldn't have 'groused' either – it would have been just part of the programme – War! But it is damned rough this treatment! from our own British (?) side! However I put my faith in the Lord and Headquarters, in Pretoria, and hope to see a fox killed and kiss a Devon girl, again.

Buck-up, old man. Had I known as much two months ago as I know to-day – there would be a lot of Dutchmen at large that are now in Hell, or the Bermudas. I've starved and trekked, and done my work tolerably successfully – from the Buck River to the Portuguese Border – and the result is:

D. S. O.
a i f
m l f
n l i
  y c
    e
    r

Hope we go home together, if not, Write to
My Guv'nor
Girl
and Bulletin
Thine,
TONY LUMPKIN.

If Digby was not his father, then who would Lenehan write to? His two other father figures, Edwin Murrant and George Whyte-Melville, were long dead.

FOR THE SHORT JOURNEY TO PRISON, they were transferred to a van flanked by mounted police armed with swords and revolvers. Witton commented that there were enough troops to form a bodyguard for Kitchener himself and that 'It wore an aspect that filled the prisoners with foreboding'.

Kitchener had not thought to inform Major Thomas of their transfer and he arrived on the next train to find they had been imprisoned in the old Pretoria Gaol where the Jameson raiders had been held following their failed coup. However, Morant and his co-accused would not get off so lightly. They waited five days to hear their fate whilst the telegraph wires between London and Pretoria hummed.

Kitchener's report, detailing the verdicts of the courts martial, passed across the desks of several Whitehall 'Mandarins' including Secretary of State for War, St John Brodrick, and Secretary of State for the Colonies, Joseph Chamberlain. On the day it arrived, Brodrick sought Chamberlain's advice on the matter. The Secretary of State for the Colonies returned it with the following handwritten observation: 'Two executions ought to be sufficient'. For what, he didn't say. Brodrick wrote back to Kitchener the following day, February 22, five days before the executions:

> My Dear Lord K,
>
> Your report on the courts martial on BVC came to hand last night. It is a most deplorable performance and, if it gets out, as I fear it will, even the strong measures we are taking will not undo the disgrace it reflects on our colonial forces. I should myself have been inclined to shoot all these officers – but you are in the best position to judge and I am agreeing with you.

Roberts, Commander-in-Chief of British forces, also replied on February 24 from London, but was much less gung-ho than Brodrick. He was prepared to allow Kitchener to use his own judgment, but wanted to see the transcripts and all the evidence. He also asked a number of searching questions about the murders and who was responsible for appointing the guilty parties to positions of responsibility. Like Brodrick, he foreshadowed the fact that the affair would become public and the colonials would be blamed.

> Telegram   War Office, 24th February 1902
> No. 642, Cipher
>
> Your No. S877. The circumstances of these deplorable occurrences and the evidence which has led to the conviction of these 5 officers, are not before us in sufficient detail to enable a judgement to be formed here of the relative guilt of those convicted. We are prepared to support the conclusion you have arrived at. If you have any doubt as to reprieving Whitton [sic], I could only express our opinion if all the facts and circumstances were

communicated, which would cause delay, and I fully rely on your judgement. As the incident will probably become public, I should like to be furnished with the fullest particulars and the evidence by mail. Meantime, please telegraph the number of murders committed in all, the authority responsible for the appointment of these Officers, and the name of the General responsible at the time. Were the murders all committed at one time and how long elapsed before the accused were placed under arrest? These disclosures will greatly affect the confidence felt in the administration of Martial Law by Colonial Officers. Can you restrict this by more stringent regulations?

Kitchener dispatched an immediate reply the next day, but once again his statement of the known facts was not entirely accurate.

Telegram   Pretoria, 25th February 1902
No. S886

Your No. 642, Cipher. Following are answers to your questions:– 20 murders were charged, of which 12 were proved. In Irregular Corps the Commanding Officer is appointed, and generally selects his own officers, but it is impossible to know that these officers, who had previously served either as Officers or non-commissioned officers, could have behaved in such a manner. Morant had been in the Navy and was a newspaper correspondent. Hancock [sic] had served as a non-commissioned officer in the New South Wales Contingent. Whitton [sic] was in Victorian Contingent. They were employed at the time under Officer Commanding at Pietersburg, Colonel Hall, Royal Artillery.

The murders were committed on four separate dates, 2nd July, 11th August, 23rd August and 7th

September. The accused were placed under arrest by my orders on 16th October, immediately the occurrence became sufficiently known to warrant their being charged. The crimes had nothing to do with Martial Law. They took place in the wildest part of the Transvaal, known as the Spelonken, about 80 miles north-east of Pietersburg. I do not think any regulations other than those existing can restrain from such acts, but punishment may deter. It is the only case of this sort that has occurred.

Again the information Kitchener gave London was riddled with inconsistencies and half-truths. Kitchener stated that there were twenty murders, but Morant and Handcock were only charged with thirteen. Morant was not even in the Spelonken during the first seven murders, and Handcock was not present when the first group of six Boers was shot. Kitchener does not mention that Taylor was directly implicated in seven of the murders, and consulted on nineteen, or that he appointed him directly. Neither does he mention that Colonel Hall had received reports of the killings in the Spelonken but still allowed Robertson to resign and escape justice; nor that he, Kitchener, was the general to whom the BVC were responsible, nor that he approved Morant's promotion to leader of A Squadron following the death of Hunt.

Nonetheless, Kitchener now had a mandate from London and acted swiftly. On Thursday afternoon, February 26, the prisoners were finally told their fate. One by one they were summoned to the governor's office. As Witton recalled, Morant was first:

He walked over and in a few minutes returned. His face was deathly pale; he looked as though his heart had already ceased to beat. I exclaimed, 'Good God, Morant, what is the matter?' 'Shot tomorrow morning was the reply.' Handcock was called next; when he returned he appeared quite unconcerned. 'Well, what is it,' I asked. 'Oh, same as Morant,' he wearily replied as though he was tired of it all, and felt relieved that the end had come at last.

I was next called, and walked across the yard quite prepared for, and fully expecting the same fate as the others. On being ushered into the Governor's office, I was taken before Captain Hutson, Provost Marshall of Pretoria. Glancing at me he said, 'George Ramsdale Witton, you have been found guilty of murder and sentenced to death.' He paused for a time, as if to give me the full grasp of that sentence. He then continued, 'Lord Kitchener has been pleased to commute your sentence to penal servitude for life.' I was then marched out, feeling quite resentful because my sentence had been commuted, as I felt that death a thousand times would be preferable to the degradation of a felon's life; I had already suffered a dozen times over pangs worse than death.

In his recently published book, *The Bushveldt Carbineers and The Pietersburg Light Horse*, Bill Woolmore added a footnote to this chilling scene. The former Captain Robertson used to dine out on the story that it was he, personally, who collected Morant and Handcock's death warrants from Kitchener. After signing them, he handed over the warrants, fixed Robertson with those piercing cold, blue eyes and remarked, 'Think yourself lucky you're not amongst them' – a tacit admission that the two men he had just condemned to die and would later pin the blame on for all twenty killings, including the seven Robertson should have paid for, were not guilty alone.

Morant immediately petitioned Lord Kitchener for a reprieve whilst Thomas rushed off to Army HQ at Montrose House to plead for their lives. Major-General William Kelly told Thomas that Kitchener was away and was not contactable. Thomas begged him to postpone the execution for a few days so he could appeal to the King. Kelly declined and told Thomas that the sentences had been confirmed by London and nothing could be done, as the case had stirred up 'grave political trouble'.

Morant also received a reply from Kelly through Thomas telling him that there was no hope of a reprieve – 'the sentence was irrevocable and he must prepare to bear it like a man'.

The speed of the executions and the lack of time for an appeal have troubled many, but it was army policy to carry out the death sentence within twenty-four hours of its confirmation to spare the prisoner undue mental anguish.

Thomas was convinced, based on previous evidence, that the King would spare them. King Edward VII had already shown himself to be a compassionate ruler, having exercised clemency for the 5th Victorians and he previously intervened on behalf of a young Englishman accused of deserting his post. Thomas's dilemma can best be summed up by Banjo Paterson's later comment that 'to try to upset a conviction in those days was like trying to take Gibraltar with a rowing boat'.

IN THE HISTORY OF THE BRITISH ARMY no-one successfully appealed a death sentence until 1951. But had word of the trials leaked out to Australia, the outcome might have been very different. Had Prime Minister Barton petitioned the King, the matter may have been investigated in more detail, as was the Wilmansrust affair. However, so tight was the security surrounding the prisoners, that both Witton and Lenehan were prevented from contacting family and Australian representatives. Telegrams marked as 'sent' were later found to have been suppressed.

Thomas's encounter with Kelly sowed the seeds of the great conspiracy theory that has prevailed for the past century. It has long been believed that Kitchener left Pretoria for four days so that he wouldn't have to face Thomas's last-minute appeals. It has also been suggested that he never left Pretoria and was there during the executions. Either way, his unexplained absence has been taken as an admission of guilt. This belief was fuelled by letters such as the one which appeared in *The Bulletin* in 1947:

> When he signed the death warrant Kitchener got on his train and disappeared from staff ken for four days. One day was spent by several high officers in feverish endeavour to find and persuade the C. in C. [Kitchener] to reprieve Morant and Handcock. But the German Emperor had to be appeased.

However, the truth lies in the papers of Kitchener's chief-of-staff, General Ian Hamilton, who took on the role in December 1901. Although Hamilton arrived too late to provide much insight into the BVC affair, his diary does provide an accurate record of Kitchener's movements around the time of the executions.

Hamilton records that Kitchener had been away quite often on field operations during early 1902 as he tried to bring the war to a conclusion. On February 27, Hamilton makes no mention of the execution or if, like many other officers, he attended it. However, he does note, 'Lord K. away at Harrismith' and that he received the following cable from him:

Harrismith Feb 27th 4.30 pm

Majuba Day so far produces 400 stop Hope for many more as I have received few reports stop

Country seen from Platberg is black with cattle being driven in.

On February 27, 1902, Kitchener was on the front-line supervising one of the biggest drives of the war. By the time Hamilton had received his cable, Morant and Handcock had been dead almost 11 hours and were about to be buried. Hamilton adds: 'I have heard nothing from Lord K. since, but I hear from Intelligence that there are over 600 prisoners there are also, Intelligence say, 18,000 cattle and 10,000 sheep. Altogether this is the biggest thing we have done for a long time.'

Kitchener also received and sent other communiqués during his sojourn in Harrismith. The day before the execution, Roberts had telegraphed him with his concerns about the irregular forces:

Telegram   War Office, 26th February 1902
No. 646, Cipher

Your No. S886. The point about Martial Law is that objection has been taken to Officers of Irregular Forces adjudicating in Cape Colony or elsewhere. This feeling will be strengthened by the grave misconduct of these Irregular Officers. If possible, Martial Law should in all cases be administered by Regular Forces.

Kitchener replied from his bolt-hole in Harrismith. Keen to insulate himself from any criticism after news of the executions became public, he drove home his belief (after the fact) that the colonials were not fit to command troops, ignoring the fact that he approved the appointment of Australian officers in the Spelonken where he feared British troops would not prevail.

Harrismith, 27th February 1902

Your telegram of 26th February. This is being done. I have for long objected to Colonial Officers administering Martial Law, as I think I have written you. I will send you numbers now doing so. I believe there are very few, as notwithstanding opposition in Cape Colony, I have carried my point.

This series of communiqués explodes the myth that Kitchener had gone into hiding, but it also contradicts Kelly's assertion that he was not contactable. The idea of the commander-in-chief, especially one as hands-on as Kitchener, being out of touch with HQ for days on end is unthinkable. It would appear that Kitchener had made up his mind and was deaf to any pleas for clemency. So, as Kitchener busied himself in Harrismith counting livestock, the executions went ahead as scheduled. A suspicious mind might also question the timing of the executions. On the same day as Kitchener's stunning success, which also avenged Britain's defeat at Majuba Hill twenty-one years before, which journalist would notice the execution of two colonials?

MORANT AND HANDCOCK WERE allowed to receive visitors on the eve of their execution. A strange cross-section of well-wishers shoehorned themselves into the tiny cell that the two condemned men would share on their last night on earth. There was Witton, Picton, their tireless defence lawyer, Major Thomas, Lieutenant Edwards and also the prosecutor Major Bolton. Morant's old mate and jailer, Henry Morrow, saw that they had a good supply of grog. The good company and the warming local spirit took their minds off the date with destiny that awaited them on the other side of darkness. They were only reminded when the disbelieving faces of the Cameron guards looked in through the open door as they did their rounds. To hear the singing, the laughter and the rhyming and the smell of whisky coming from the place, you would think that the King himself had just delivered a reprieve.

Inside the cell they had come to the conclusion that a royal reprieve was their only hope. Seeing the soldiers passing by the door an inebriated Morant called out to them, 'Hey Jock, come here a minute.' The two soldiers backed up suspiciously. Morant held up another half-empty bottle, 'Come away in. Have a dram . . . for the sake . . . for the sake of auld Lang Syne.'

The older one licked his lips at the prospect of a drink after months in the field without a drop, but shook his head, 'Sorry boys, we're on duty.'

Morant continued to wave them in, 'Come away with you. Would you deny a condemned man his last request?'

The older soldier looked at the younger one and then glanced about to make sure that there was no officer on the prowl and said, 'Weel, if ye pit it like 'at, we'll tak a wee nip fae ye.' Both men ducked inside the tiny cell and squeezed themselves onto the outer end of the bunk. Morant rapped the wall with his tin cup, momentarily deafening everyone. The kind face of Henry Morrow appeared in the doorway.

'Some water for these Scotch gentlemen if you please Mr Morrow,' said an ebullient Morant. Two tin cups of water dully arrived and Morant acted as toastmaster.

'Well gentlemen the whisky like our time on this earth has run out and its time for the last toast. Peter and I thank you for your good company and hope we meet again in the great hereafter.' There was a choked silence after his final valedictory, but Morant continued with a sweet, sickly smile on his face. 'There can only be one toast. The King. After all, he's the only one who could save our bacon now that Lord bloody Kitchener has turned tail.' Morant raised his glass and said loudly, 'The King!'

'The King!' came the chorus and they threw the last of the whisky down their throats then watched puzzled as the two Camerons passed their whisky over the tin cup in a circular motion before tipping it neat down their throats.

'Why the water?' asked Witton noting that they hadn't touched a drop.

Picking up his glass, the older Cameron repeated the toast and the circular movement over the tin cup. 'The King . . . o'er the water . . . The Stuarts . . . the rightful Kings of Scotland, exiled tae France,' he explained with a wink at Morant, who, having spent time there in his childhood, knew full well why the Scots always took water with their whisky.

Morant shook his head, 'Was there ever a race that brought more sorrow to this world than you perfidious Albion?' an edge of bitterness creeping into his voice.

The two soldiers stood and saluted Morant, 'Ye're a gentleman Mr Morant. Aw the best tae ye.' There was nothing more they could offer in the circumstances.

Morrow's native whisky had leavened the mood for a while, but could not dull the sorrow at the moment of their parting. There were firm handshakes, slaps on the back and words of encouragement. But there were also tears in the eyes of men who would later declare that they had seen bad things in war, but none worse than this. As Morant shook Witton's hand for the last time he said, 'Its hard lines and a sideways ending, thus being sacrificed to pro-Boer sentiments. Goodbye Witton; tell The Bulletin people the Breaker will write more verse for them; I'm going into laager in the morning.'

MORANT DID WRITE TWO POEMS THAT night as he sat in his cell wrapped in a shawl of darkness that got shorter by the hour and wished away the dawn. During those last few crowded hours, when all his instincts were at their keenest, he wrote *Butchered To Make a Dutchman's Holiday*. Its scathing, satirical, blatantly anti-war tone was radical for its time. The sense of waste and innocence lost in the works of war poets Rupert Brooke and Wilfred Owen still has the power to move almost a century later, but can't match the bitter sense of injustice that lay behind the jolly metre of Morant's last poetic testimony.

It has been claimed his Australian work lacked emotional depth, but the same could not be said of *Butchered*. It is a requiem for the forgotten men whose ghosts still march on Remembrance Day, whose names do not appear on the monuments where wreaths are laid and are never remembered 'at the going down of the sun'. This is the flip side of war. No glorious charge into history – official history at any rate.

Morant made only a modest literary mark, but in an age when sacrifice to King and country was not only taken for granted but expected, his dissident voice is at least there to remind us that war was *never* glorious or just. It exposes the double-standards and the rank hypocrisy that brought him to that condemned cell on the eve of his execution for crimes he believed had been commissioned and sanctioned by the very men who had the temerity to stand in judgment against him. To choose two men out of thousands of other worthy candidates could only be a political sacrifice. Byron, whose life and literary style he tried to imitate, was noted for his political satires, and although Morant had only written two[†] before *Butchered To Make a Dutchman's Holiday,* for this piece, if nothing else, Morant deserves the mantle of poet.

The second, though entitled *Bring on the Guns,* reveals the softer, more sentimental side of this two-headed Hydra:

† *Morant wrote two other political satires that were decidedly light hearted:* When Davey Rode the Mule *and* Untitled.

What tho' my life be many crimes!
Death hurts but once – Life a thousand
    times.
If thou should'st come to me with tales
    of Hell,
Pshaw! – I will go bravely, and say, 'Tis well!'
But if thou should'st come to me with tales
    of love,
With chant and song of kindness from above,
And kiss away my scalding tears of pain –
Then – oh, God, perhaps I'd wish to live
    again.

Bring on the Guns is often taken as a paean to some lost love, but he had won and lost the love of many women and was at the time engaged to the 'trim-set petticoat' from Devon. However, the one love he never won back was his father's.

It has also recently been revealed that during his last night on earth, Morant wrote a third verse to his old droving mate Sam Nicker entitled *Infinity*. Morant and Nicker had continued to correspond long after Sam did what Harry could never do – buy a station, start a family and settle down. Sam once remarked 'they should have put butter on his paws' in the hope that it would stop him wandering and getting into trouble. However, in his last poem, a philosophical piece in the style of *The Rubaiyat of Omar Khayyam*, Morant was no longer of the opinion that man was the master of his own destiny. He was thinking deeply about fate, destiny and the great secret he was about to discover in the hereafter:

Man is but <u>one</u> in this great Universe. That
    takes him back into her keeping so shalt
    thou rest.
But what if thou shalt pass into the Great
    Silence? from the living

And no friend mark
thy passing.
All that breathed shall share thy destiny.
For is man wholly incapable of forming his
    own future. There is within him a living
    principle that shapes his end;
So that when the summons comes for him
    to join that numberless caravan that
    mysterious realm, sustained by an
    unfaltering Faith Prince & beggarman
    alike, each in his appointed place will
    drape the covering of his couch about
    him & lie down in peace –
To Sleep.

The lines, 'For is man wholly incapable of forming his own future. There is within him a living principle that shapes his end', illustrates his conclusion that everything is pre-ordained and there is no point resisting the natural order of things. In those last desperate hours nothing could have seemed more certain. If Morant's theory is true, then putting 'butter on his paws' would not have made one iota of difference.

PROSE FLOWED EASILY FROM MORANT'S pen, but words came less easily to Peter Handcock as he crouched in the gloom trying to articulate his final thoughts. Like most country boys of that era, he only had a basic education, the prevailing view being that fine words would be of little use to a man destined for manual labour. But when they finally came, the words were simple and heartfelt, which belied the image of him, as expressed in the BVC letter to Colonel Hall, as Morant's simple, silent enforcer. However, his final letter was not addressed to his wife, but his sister.

The Handcocks' marital relations had been strained for some time before he left for South Africa. It later emerged that the reason for their estrangement was that Handcock's wife was having an affair with a distant cousin. Wounded by his wife's infidelity, Peter Handcock went down to Sydney and joined up without telling his wife or family. He later wrote from South Africa to tell his wife that he loved the soldier's life and would not return for some time. During his stint in South Africa there was precious little contact between them; so little, in fact, that Mrs Handcock wondered if he had been killed. On July 26, 1901, her local Member, Mr Young, asked the Premier of New South Wales, Mr See, if he would make enquiries as to the whereabouts of Lieutenant Peter Handcock. On October 3, Mr Young again pressed Mr See, as his constituent was sure he had disappeared and was now seeking support from either the Patriotic Fund or the State Board for the Relief of Destitute Children. Mr See informed Mr Young that he had information that Handcock had transferred to the Bushveldt Carbineers on February 20.[†]

Mrs Handcock finally received a letter from her husband a few months before he was executed. He did not tell her about his arrest and led her to believe he was in England visiting relatives.

Dear Sister,

I have but an hour or so longer to exist. And Although my brain has been harassed for four long weary months I cant refrain from writing you a last few lines, I am going to find out the great secret, I will face my God, with the firm belief that I am innocent of murder. I obeyed my orders and served my King as I thought best. If I over stepped my duty I can only ask my People and country for forgiveness.

† *Handcock actually joined the BVC on February 28.*

Tell poor Polly to take care of little Illem for me at all costs. They were my greatest comforts at Home & my greatest trouble now I hope my country will see my children cared for I will die bravely for the sake of all, God, forgive any enemies & give you peace for ever I have not heard if our Brother Eugene was killed in this retched war or not But if not tell him & Will I have gone to rest Tell Peter and Willie to be good for their sister, God be with you in your trouble.

from your fond brother
P.J. Handcock

Australia for ever

Amen

Having written their final testimonies, Morant and Handcock wrote one last message together. After they had been sentenced to death, they got a rise out of Assistant Provost Marshal Hutson when he asked if they wanted a priest. Morant had replied, 'No, I'm a pagan', and on finding out what it meant, Handcock declared, 'I'm one too'. However, on their last night they did feel the need of a priest. On the back of a photograph of the BVC, they wrote the following:

To The Reverend Canon Fisher, Pretoria,

The night before we're shot.
We shot the Boers who killed and mutilated our friend (the best mate I had on Earth)

Harry Harbord Morant
Peter Joseph Handcock

Following the release of the film *Breaker Morant* in 1980, author/historian Kit Denton, in trying to destroy the myth he felt he had been responsible for creating, tried to portray this last testament as some kind of death-bed confession. However, neither denied killing the Boers; what was in dispute was the reason and the circumstances in which they shot them. For them, the message to Canon Fisher was a simple statement of fact and, if anything, proves that their line of argument was clear and consistent until the end. The inscription was to ensure that their side of the story would become public – Morant and Handcock had been kept under close guard for six months and had no way of knowing what reasons would be given for their execution.

Having completed that final task, they blew out the candle and waited for dawn and death to come creeping in, hand in hand, under the door. They lay waiting in the darkness, drifting between sleep and stark reality, each footfall snapping them awake.

As they emerged from the gaol for the last time, in the grey light of dawn, the night air cooled the slick of perspiration that formed on their brows and their footsteps kept time with their thumping hearts as they marched to their deaths across the hard, sun-baked ground. Ahead they saw the eerie figures of the Cameron Highlanders waiting for them in the half-light, their kilts flapping in the breeze like the wings of the predators who watched from the surrounding trees with keen eyes.

How strange and melancholy it must have been to see the birth of a new day, feel the first rays of sun on your back and then die with the bitter taste of betrayal in your mouth, yet still have the presence of mind to breathe one final, unforgettable iconoclasm out into the ether, like a message in a bottle, in the hope that someone will hear it and try to find out why they really shot you. 'Shoot straight, you bastards! Don't make a mess of it.' The rest, as they say, is history.

THE FEATURE FILM *BREAKER MORANT*, which brought the legend of Morant to the forefront of public consciousness, vividly portrayed the events of that fatal last morning. Although some historians have expressed doubts about its veracity, a letter in the Melbourne *Argus* confirms that it did not take any historical liberties with Morant's final scene and, if anything, underplayed it.

Harry Morrow, who joined up in Adelaide on the same day as Morant and ended up as his jailer in Pretoria, wrote:

> Morant asked them to take off the blindfold, crossed his arms over his chest and looked them in the face. He said if they didn't fire he would look down the barrels of their rifles for the bullets! They fired and Morant got it all in the left side and died at once with his arms folded and his eyes open. You would have thought he was alive.

The film also did not portray the unease which the firing party, and in particular its commander, Major Souter, felt at having to perform that onerous task. There was no official firing party – one was selected from the regiment that happened to be guarding the garrison at the time. It was the Camerons' misfortune to be on garrison duty at that time.

That Morant died quickly and without the need for a final bullet in the head was largely due to Sergeant Robin Forbes, who was one of the firing squad that day. His great-niece, who was named after him, told me that although he had died in World War I, the story had been passed down through the generations of her family. Her great-uncle had described the officer (Morant) as a brave man who commanded great respect from the men. Forbes was chosen because he was a sharpshooter and when he picked up his gun he knew by its weight that it was loaded with real bullets, not blanks. He had served on, and would later serve on many more, firing squads and knew that men did not die immediately, even from fatal chest wounds. Forbes decided that Morant would not suffer and when the fateful order came shot him right through the heart.

Provost Marshal Poore, who was responsible for drilling the firing party and ensuring the execution order was carried out cleanly and efficiently, noted in his diary, 'I attended the execution of Morant and Handcock, they both took it very well . . . Major Souter (Cameron Highlanders) who was in charge of the firing party conducted operations very badly . . . Shot quail in the afternoon.'

However, despite his outward bravado, another observer noted that after the event Poore was 'visibly shaken'. Perhaps he felt the same sense of guilt as Director of Intelligence Lieutenant-Colonel David Henderson, who also had an intimate knowledge of the goings on in the Spelonken. Henderson revealingly remarked, 'I hope the Lord won't hold me responsible for the past sins of all the secret agents.'

The bodies of Morant and Handcock were reclaimed by the Australians, sparing them the usual fate of the disgraced soldier – a pint of quicklime and an unmarked grave within the walls of the gaol.

Feelings in Pretoria were running high at the time of the executions. Rumour had it that the Aussies were about to stage a demonstration, which would have amounted to mutiny, but were kept in the dark about what was going on and were too scattered to take any concerted action.

Morrow says that they were buried properly with a hearse and a mourning coach and thirty Australian officers were present at the funeral. One of those who attended the funeral wrote home:

His [Morant's] one desire was to be get buried decently outside. I heard a volley at 6 o'clock this morning, and was afterwards taken to see their coffins. I can tell you I don't feel too bright . . . Australians in Pretoria have felt pretty cut up over the affair, and are doing all in their power to give their comrades a decent and respectable burial . . . We were informed at the grave that both condemned officers kept up bravely until the end and died like men. Morant pulled up his handkerchief off his eyes a couple of minutes before they fired, and faced the firing party.

Another mourner described the funeral ceremony itself, which fell far short of the decency Morant had hoped for:

I followed the hearse to the cemetery and saw the funeral. The parson from the Cathedral here met the coffins at the gate and led the party to a detached portion of the ground, where a service took place after the bodies were lowered. The parson recited a preamble to the burial service which included the words, 'For as much as this is unconsecrated ground,' letting his hearers plainly know the difference between 'consecrated ground' and a 'dedicated grave'. Some of the service was omitted too. It was a woeful sight.

Major Thomas' last painful duty was to attend Morant and Handcock's funeral at the Church Street Cemetery in Pretoria where a haunting image of him standing over the freshly dug grave was taken. It can be called a 'grave', as Morant and Handcock were buried together. Though faded by the elements and the passing of time, it does not detract from the power of the image, which has a surreal, dream-like quality. It shows a tall, thin, dapper man standing over a freshly dug grave with an

Australian military flag draped over it. Though, due to the ravages of time, the expression on his face cannot be seen, his body language says it all. The weight of guilt and deep regret caused him to stoop sorrowfully over their grave, as though some terrible physical pain racked his body.

This event had ruined Thomas' life. That much I could see from the photograph. He might as well have been shot on the veldt with Morant and Handcock. At least their deaths were mercifully quick. It took him forty years to die from the mortal emotional and psychological wounds he received during those courts martial.

February 27, 1902 was also the day Arthur Morant from Renmark in South Australia arrived in South Africa. He was the son of the colonel who had treated Harry Morant as family, and to arrive on the very day Morant was executed was a cruel blow he never forgot.

THE BROWN, SCARRED EARTH HAS NOW been softened by lush, verdant grass. The sweeping avenues of trees that lead you past neat rows of gravestones have an air of tranquillity and the neatly clipped hedges ooze respectability. However, even the sanitary scent of pine cannot disguise the whiff of disgust you feel when you see that the grave of Morant and Handcock is well away from the hundreds of other servicemen who are also interned there. They were buried near the area known as *De Held Plats*, or The Heroes Acre which is reserved for heroes of the Boer nation. Soldiers executed by their own side were not thought to be fit company for those who had fallen in battle. In later wars, those who were executed were distinguished by the legend 'died', rather than 'killed in action' or 'died of wounds', but because Morant and Handcock were buried in a civilian cemetery they have the legend, 'To the memory of P. Handcock and H. Morant'. There is no reference to their military rank. It is a bittersweet irony that Morant, who always aspired to be amongst the great and the good, now lies in their midst, though it is Boers and not Englishmen who now keep him company. They were buried in the area reserved for heroes of the Boer nation and President Kruger himself, is a close neighbour.

However, given the riddle that is his epitaph, it would appear Morant would have preferred their company. The same line from Matthew 10 also appears on the headstone of Sergeant Frank Eland – who was killed with Captain Hunt at Duwielskloof: 'He that loseth his life, shall find it.' It is a perversion of the quotation from Matthew 10 – 'He that loseth his life [for my sake] shall find it.'

There has been much speculation about its cryptic meaning, but although this is the line that was inscribed on his headstone it is said that this was not the quotation that Morant originally chose for his epitaph. The one he is said to have chosen is also from Matthew 10, but three verses further back: 'And a man's foes shall be those of his own household.'

Whilst his mates were happy enough to ensure he was buried outside the prison, it was obviously felt that the quotation he had chosen was too pointed – especially given the nature of Morant's death. However, both quotations are interesting in what they reveal about Morant's feelings at the end of his life.

The modified epitaph, the one he originally chose, the fact he called himself 'Tony Lumpkin' and declared himself a pagan, all suggests a conscious rebellion by Morant against God and the sanctity of the family – both of which were a central part of the Victorian ethos. A comment in his last letter to Lenehan, 'But it is damned rough treatment from our own British(?) side' reiterated the feeling that Tony Lumpkin felt abandoned, not only by his family, but his very race.

There is further evidence that the issue of nationality was more than just a question mark in Morant's mind. Whilst his epitaph gives us a clue to his personal feelings, a new verse has come to light that suggests that whilst he was born in England, acted the part of an English gentleman in the bush and longed to return to England – he died an Australian!

To My Country appeared in *The Bulletin* on March 15, 1902 and although it was signed 'B. N.S.W.' like many of the poems he wrote, it has not, until now, been attributed to 'the Breaker'. The writer always put his location in the bottom left corner after the verse. For example, Morant's old mate Will Ogilvie was published regularly in *The Bulletin* during 1901–1902. At the end of 1901, he was still using 'N.S.W.', but following his return to Britain in early 1902 he began using 'U.K.' or 'ENG'. In the case of Morant the 'N.S.W.' would date it anywhere between the mid-1890s when he first arrived in New South Wales and late1898 when he left for South Australia. Why it appeared two weeks after Morant's death and two weeks before news of his death reached Australia, is a mystery. As no other balladeer signed himself 'B.' after the Breaker's departure in early 1900, the most likely explanation is that *The Bulletin* was working through a backlog of unpublished verses and this one just happened to surface, like some terrible prophecy.

A wind-blown, shimmering, shifting, awful
    waste,
Fringed by a broken edge of green and grey –
A ghastly field for devilish winds at play;
A painful tale of desperate men that faced
The loathly hell, of hard-won pathways traced

In dull white bones, of a race whose long decay
Gives warning to the pallid crowd to-day
To seek a land by greener beauty graced:

Australia! thou whose dust, made flesh, has
     given
Power to my soul to warn thy people now,
To me these horrors are a thing of naught.
O, nurse of serfdom, how shalt thy be shriven
Of threadbare knees and dust-enshrouded
     brow,
Mother of slaves who dare not speak their
     thought?

Depending which way you read it, the first stanza could be an allusion to England or Australia – both of which are islands of sorts and have an early history of grim, unremitting social struggle – and how the present generation would do better to seek their fortunes in a country with better prospects.

However, the second stanza undoubtedly refers to young Australia. Australia is called, by one who does not fear these hardships and is proud of it, to free itself of being shackled to Britain, and to listen to the voice of its people who are now calling for nationhood. These sentiments have a definite pre-Federation feel, which would place it in the 1890s.

It is always taken as read that Morant was an Englishman, but he fitted the profile of many Australians of the day – immigrants born in England to whom being Australian and British was the same thing. For Morant and many others who went, the Boer War was a watershed. The 'mateship' he showed the likes of Brigalow Mick, Sam Nickel and Major Lenehan was not learned in English public school, but in the dusty Brigalow he cursed so often. Perhaps more of Australia rubbed off on him than he knew.

Like his hero Byron, Morant always wanted to be part of the English establishment, though fate always conspired to keep him outside it, and in the end both turned reactionary. Byron left England and Morant ended one of his last letters with 'God save Oireland'. Feeling betrayed by the great cause he had fought for, it was his homage to both his origins[†] and the rebel Irish spirit that opposed the British Empire. England had been his talisman during his long Australian exile, but his failure to square things with his family and his prosecution by the army forced him to face up to the painful truth – however much he wanted England, it didn't want him.

Major Thomas concurred with Morant on the issue of whose side the British were really on. He wrote a letter to Witton just after the execution when his emotions were still raw:

> But though not guilty, Morant and Handcock would have not died over that case because our own (no not our own altogether) people would have them convicted before a trial.

Morant and Thomas articulated the feeling that had grown amongst many from the wide brown land during their service in South Africa – that they may have gone to war as Britons, but they would return home Australians.

Kitchener's curious game of cat-and-mouse with London continued the day after the executions, when he published news of the executions in the Army Orders which the press corps had access to.

---

† *The man he claimed was his father, Digby Morant, was born in Ireland as was his mother, Catherine Murrant nee O'Reilly.*

Army Order No. 506, 28 Feb. 1902 (extract)

1. – DISCIPLINE –

The following extracts from the proceedings of general courts martial held at Pietersburg, Transvaal, between 16th January, 1902, and 19th February, 1902, for the trial of the undermentioned prisoners are published for information:

1. H.H. Morant, P.J. Handcock, G.R. Witton and H. Picton, of the Bushveldt Carbineers, were charged with –
    Charge: When on active service, committing the offence of murder.
    Finding: The Court find the prisoner Morant guilty of murder, but find the prisoners Handcock, Witton and Picton guilty of manslaughter.
2. H.H. Morant, P.J. Handcock, and G.R. Witton, of the Bushveldt Carbineers, were charged with:
    Charge: When on active service, committing the offence of murder.
    Finding: The Court find the prisoners guilty of the charge.
3. H.H. Morant, P.J. Handcock, and G.R. Witton, of the Bushveldt Carbineers, were charged with:
    Charge: When on active service, committing the offence of murder.
    Finding: The Court find the prisoners guilty of the charge.
    Sentence: The Court sentence the prisoners Morant, Handcock, and Witton to suffer death by being shot, and the prisoner Picton to be cashiered.
    Confirmation: The General Commander-in-Chief has confirmed the sentence in the case of prisoners Morant, Handcock, and Picton, but has commuted the sentence awarded the prisoner Witton to one of penal servitude for life.

The sentences awarded the prisoners Morant and Handcock have been carried out.

4. Major R.W. Lenehan, Bushveldt Carbineers, was charged with:

Charge: When on active service by culpable neglect omitting to make a report which it was his duty to make.

Finding: The Court find the prisoner guilty of the charge.

Sentence: The Court sentence the prisoner to be Reprimanded. The finding and sentence have been confirmed by the General Commanding-in-Chief.

By Order,
W.F. Kelly, Major-General
Adjutant-General

On March 10, the military censor allowed the press to send a few lines to England, giving no more than the barest details.

Two members of the British irregular forces, who had been tried and convicted by a court martial of having shot Boers who had surrendered, have been shot at Pretoria.

The only way newspapermen could circumvent the censor was to send the story back to England by sea, which meant the first dispatches were not published for almost a month. Just after news of the executions finally broke in newspapers around the world, the Secretary of State for War, St John Brodrick, complained to Kitchener:

I have been a little embarrassed by not being told that the sentences on the Bushveldt Carbineers had been published in Army Orders of 28 February, as I had kept the whole matter quiet here. We have now published the main facts.

The 'facts' they published were the ones Kitchener had supplied in his earlier telegrams. As a result of Kitchener's early disclosure, there would not have been time for the courts martial transcripts and evidence to reach London and be evaluated. Perhaps this is why Brodrick wanted to keep 'the whole matter quiet here' until they knew all the facts. But it would appear from correspondence between the legal departments in South Africa that Brodrick would have had to wait a long time. Although a memo from Judge Advocate General James St Clair says that a full report was sent to Brodrick the day after the execution, that was different to 'the proceedings', the actual transcripts, which were being passed around the legal department in Pretoria.

Kitchener apologised to Brodrick the following day, claiming that it was standard practice to publish such items in Army Orders and that he had forgotten to request that it was not done in this case. This might have been the first media war, but all the way through this affair Kitchener showed that he understood the importance of controlling the flow of information and, by accident or design, had ensured that the British Government would now have to back his decision to execute Morant and Handcock. The story was now in the public domain and a century of controversy was about to begin.

11

Aftermath

S'long 'Breaker', you're gone for good,
Into the land 'outback',
Striking a line all bushmen should,
Taking the north-east track.
Send us word when the bush is sighing,
Wrapped in the heat of noonday dying,
Think when the swans are homeward flying,
Think of the Barracks 'Crack'!

'Bon Voyage' by JCL Fitzpatrick

NEWS OF THE EXECUTIONS ONLY REACHED Australia when
Major Lenehan's ship docked in Melbourne a month
later. Shortly after his arrival, he met with new General
Officer Commanding of the Australian Army, Major-
General Hutton, and Prime Minister Barton. Lenehan
was asked to say nothing whilst investigations were
being made. He had no wish to upset Hutton and told
the press that 'the whole matter was sub judice'.
However, when Lenehan asked for a court of inquiry
into the circumstances of his leaving South Africa, as an
alternative to speaking to the press, Hutton asked him
to resign within twenty-four hours or be dismissed.
Lenehan refused, but as damaging details began to
emerge, he commented to friends,

This absurd story should show Australians how easy
it is to libel the living and slander the dead . . . Wait
until you hear everything fairly and fully stated – the

charge and the defence. Then it will be time enough to say in their regard the harsh word or the kind and pitying one.

Sadly, human nature is such that a presumption of guilt comes before any presumption of innocence. Details reached Australia spasmodically through the British newspapers, as there had been no full-time Australian correspondents in South Africa since the end of 1900; they had either being killed, sent home sick, or like 'Banjo' Paterson, removed because of their increasingly pro-Boer reportage.

Some historical accounts have sought to downplay the impact of the executions, suggesting they caused little more than a ripple. However, even a cursory glance at the main international, national, regional and even country newspapers of the day suggests that was not the case.

In the likes of Sydney's *Daily Telegraph* and *The Sydney Morning Herald* the story ran prominently for over a month as the facts slowly emerged and claim followed counter-claim. It is hard to even imagine a story in the modern age that would merit such coverage, but this was the first war in which Australians got to shed blood in the Imperial cause. The expeditionary forces had arrived too late to see action in the Sudan and China, and after winning six Victoria Crosses and much praise from the British military top brass during the Boer War, such an event was viewed as nothing short of cataclysmic.

The first reports that two Australian officers had been executed were published on March 29, 1902, the day after Lenehan arrived back, and were met with disbelief in Australia.

The British press were scathing. *The Morning Leader* printed a damning account of wanton murder, greed and treachery. The main details found their way into the Australian press under the headline:

EXECUTED OFFICERS

STORY OF THEIR CRIMES

AS TOLD BY A TROOPER

SHOCKING DISCLOSURES

TEN BOERS MURDERED
FOR THE SAKE OF THEIR
WEALTH

'NIGGERS SHOT LIKE RABBITS'

The article went on to claim:

> [T]en unarmed Boers entered the camp and
> informed Lieut. Handcock who was the officer in
> charge that they were journeying in to Pietersburg
> to surrender. It became known that the surrender-
> ers possessed £20,000 and Lieut. Handcock and
> some of the other officers held a mock courts
> martial as a result of which they ordered the ten
> men to be shot . . . when the Boers were dead their
> wagons were ransacked and £20,000 (in Transvaal
> paper money) was found.

The Times also reminded its readers of the unimpeachable reputation of British justice:

> These men were fairly tried by a competent and
> impartial court and the decision in both cases must
> be accepted with implicit confidence until it is
> proved beyond demonstration that by some misad-
> venture a miscarriage of justice has taken place . . .
> The belief in the incorruptibility of the British court-
> martial is firmly grounded in the public mind of this
> country and it is gratifying to be able to believe that

as long as the public has confidence in the honest administration of justice – whether civil or military – these tribunals will fully deserve that confidence.

The overseas press praised Kitchener's firm hand and saw that in the wider context the executions would be beneficial to Britain's tattered international image. *The Commercial Advertiser* of New York said:

[T]he impartial punishment of colonials by Lord Kitchener ought to check the torrent of abuse on the Continent against Great Britain.

Perhaps more perceptively, *The New York Herald and Express* saw:

The course adopted by Lord Kitchener prevents the incident being charged against England.

These reports were supplemented by letters home and the testimonies of returning soldiers, such as the one that appeared in *The Sydney Morning Herald*:

A Liverpool man who formerly belonged to the Bushveldt Carbineers, declares that Lieutenant Morant shot and killed Trooper Van Buuren on the open veldt for speaking about the murders of Boers, and that the lieutenant then reported that Van Buuren had been killed in action while behaving with gallantry.

The men of the corps, the narrator continues, represented every nationality.

The missionary, the Rev. C. Heese, started for Pietersburg to report to the authorities the eight Spelonken murders, and he was shot.

The murders, the Liverpool man says, totalled between 30 and 40. In some instances the motive was robbery. In others the murders were committed in sheer recklessness through drink. Neither officers nor men were short of whisky.

The Times interviewed a British officer who had just arrived at Plymouth:

> [T]he BVC were not content with shooting Boers armed or unarmed, but wantonly murdered women and kids in cold blood with age and sex offering no protection from their merciless violence.

There were many other similar statements which all made for sensational copy, but the many basic factual inaccuracies betray the fact that their authors had never been anywhere near the Spelonken. After a few free beers they were only too willing to repeat second-hand gossip to news-hungry scribes and let a little of that reflected infamy rub off on them. Given the number of reports from 'ex-Carbineers', the public could be forgiven for thinking that they were a corps numbering thousands, not hundreds of men! Forced to break his silence, Lenehan remarked, 'You can easily answer a whole lie but it is difficult to answer half a lie.'

So virulent were some the comments against the Australians that the War Office were forced to step in and say the allegations made in *The Morning Leader* 'are for the most part untrue' and *The Times* tried to smooth ruffled colonial feathers with '. . . naturally, but quite wrongly, Australians feel the slur cast upon the good name of their soldiers in connection with the affair'.

But the damage had been done and some sections of the press set about separating the maverick BVC from the rest of the Australian contingents that had done Australia proud. Morant was even condemned by his old paper, *The Bulletin*, whose proud boast was that it 'howled for the undermost dog'. But this they did not do for Morant, initially. They renamed the Bushveldt Carbineers the Bushveldt Buccaneers, and before all the facts were known, said Morant was 'a man quite unfitted to act as referee even at a dog-fight . . . Just let anyone whoever knew "The Breaker" try to imagine him presiding over a court of life and death'.

That may well have been true of his roistering days in the bush, but nothing was printed about his meritorious service in the Bushveldt Carbineers and other units, or his capture of Commandant Kelly. *The Bulletin* lamented his passing thus:

> 'He died game'. That is the most charitable epitaph which a truthful acquaintance can put over the tomb of 'The Breaker' . . . 'Butchered to make a Dutchman's Holiday!' . . . Not a hint about the Dutchmen butchered to make a 'Breaker' (or was it a Bull) holiday. Mr Morant apparently had no conscience . . . Evidently he was absolutely incapable of comprehending that he had committed any crime; indeed his brain was puzzling sadly over the question why the laurel-leaves and the triumphal feast were not set out for him after his redoubtable slaughtering of many Boers, as for a David. A scientific mental analyst would have diagnosed the 'Breaker's' case as one of a complicated kind of madness, best turned to community use by employing him to hunt down noxious animals or to smash up disfiguring harbour hoardings.

It was signed FR – Frank Renar being the nom de plume of journalist Frank Fox, who then rushed out the first book on Morant, entitled *Bushman and Buccaneer: Harry Morant – his 'ventures and verses*.

However, the verdict from the literary fraternity was not so damning. Morant's great friend and Australia's unofficial poet laureate, Banjo Paterson, who last saw Morant in South Africa, weighed into the argument. Paterson's Boer War journalism had proved too partisan for the conservative Australian press and he had made it clear he had no love of the inscrutable,

'Sphinx-like' Kitchener. The farm-burning and block-houses filled him with revulsion and the plight of the Boers, who he saw as bush people defending their property, moved him to publish *Now Listen to Me and I'll Tell You My Views* in *The Bulletin* on March 29, 1902 – the day after Lenehan arrived back in Australia carrying news of Morant and Handcock's death. It reveals Paterson's feelings about Kitchener:

> And next let us join in the bloodthirsty shriek,
>   Hooray for Lord Kitchener's 'bag'.
> For the fireman's torch and the hangman's cord –
>   they are hung on the English Flag.
> In front of our brave old army! Whoop! the farm-house blazes bright.
> And the women weep and their children die – how
>   dare they presume to fight!
> For none dress in a uniform, the same as by rights
>   they ought.
> They're fighting in rags and in naked feet, like
>   Wallace's Scotchmen fought!
> (And they clothe themselves from our captured
>   troops – and they're catching them every week;
> And they don't hand them – and the shame is ours,
>   but we cover the shame with a shriek.)

However powerful Paterson's diatribe, the truth was that when put to the test, Australia preferred to believe the word of Kitchener over that of an itinerant rhyming buckjumper. Paterson also wrote a valedictory piece on Morant for *The Sydney Mail* entitled *The Late Lieutenant Morant – A Personal Sketch*.

In it he was candid about Morant's many faults, describing him as a ne'er-do-well and a 'scapegrace' who would tackle any sport and was afraid of nothing but 'hard work – or rather sustained steady work'. He never valued money, was a 'spendthrift and an idler,

quick to borrow and slow to pay . . . he never saved a
penny in his life, and the idea that he would take or
order the taking of the life of an unarmed man for the
sake of gain is utterly inconsistent with every trait of his
character'.

Paterson never condemned Morant because he saw
some of his darkness in himself, and although he had
never fired a shot in anger, he had the same sense of the
'but for the grace of God there go I' expressed by many
servicemen.

However, Paterson, always credited with being a
sharp observer of character, recognised the inherent
tragedy in Morant's life. Like Ogilvie, he saw that his
end was not inevitable – a bad 'un heading towards a
predictable end like the bushrangers – but a set of cruel
circumstances that might have been different, if his real
father had recognised him, if he hadn't transgressed in
England, if his remittance money had arrived in Charters Towers or Hughenden, if Hunt hadn't been killed.
A lot of ifs and buts, but history is testament to how a
man's life often turns on a single moment or a single
decision, for better or for worse. As we know, Morant's
decision to avenge Hunt, Best and Eland was a turn for
the worse and it cost him his life. Paterson saw that:

> He gambled with his chances all through life, and
> the cards ran out against him . . . What is it that
> such men lack – just a touch of determination, or
> of caution maybe – to turn their lives from failures
> to successes? His death was consistent with his life,
> for though he died as a criminal he died a brave man
> facing the rifles with his eyes unbandaged. For him
> Gordon's lines would make a fitting epitaph:

> > An aptitude to mar and break
> > What others diligently make
> > That was the best and worst of him

Wise, with the cunning of a snake;
  Brave, with the sea-wolf's courage grim;
Dying hard and dumb, torn limb from limb.

Will Ogilvie, 'the Breaker's' old bush mate and fellow poet who had marked his departure to South Africa with a jingle, now composed *To the Memory of One Dead* back in his native Scotland on hearing of Morant's execution. He prefaced it:

'This is the real epitaph of poor old Breaker Morant: and the sort he would have liked us to write above his grave. – W.H. Ogilvie.

When the horses broke for the stony ridge
  How his face would set in a grin,
As he shortened his hold of the brown colt's head
  And hammered the long-necks in!
And he drew his whip on the racing wing
  And was lost in the mulga trees,
His 'Get to the lead of the cattle, mate!'
  Came back cheerily on the breeze.

He went to fight in a foreign land,
  And I know he only went,
To fight the cares that were creeping close,
  And stealing his heart's content.
He went to fight with a foreign foe,
  And he fought them gallant and grey,
T'would be, 'Get to the lead of the cattle, boys!'
  As the scared Boers broke away.

They laid him low in a coward's grave,
  Somewhere out on the grey Karoo,
(Yet I know one mate would have called
    him brave
  And a woman who thought him true!)
And his hopes were spread like a scattered mob,
  But his pride was a crippled steed –

It was 'Get to the head of those cattle, there!'
<u>But he never got to the lead!</u>

Paterson and Ogilvie's sentiments were echoed by letters
that began to arrive from the bush outposts where
Morant had been a favourite son. Richmond, Windsor,
Walgett, Collarenebri, all sent their regrets and expressed surprise at the accusations which seemed at
odds with the character they had known.

After the early furore, other corrective accounts from
returning soldiers and ex-Carbineers also began to
appear in the press and it became clear that the case
was not as cut and dried as had been first thought.
They disputed the claims that Morant and Handcock
were ruthless profiteers, that Hunt had been killed outright, and said that the British had operated a 'take no
prisoners' policy. *The Bathurst National Advertiser*
printed a letter JF Thomas wrote to Witton's father
from Pretoria dated March 1902:

> Your son has been sent a prisoner to England and I
> think it will be wise to defer any active steps con-
> cerning him 'till the Australian government is in
> possession of the facts . . . The defence maintained
> was that under the customs of war the shooting of
> these Boers was allowable as they were merely
> running bandits or marauders. It was proved that in
> other cases exactly the same procedure was adopted
> and approved of by other officers. Consequently, you
> will see that from a soldier's point of view – at any
> rate – the crime was not so dreadful as might
> appear – though technically it was a crime. I only
> regret that poor Morant and Handcock did not
> receive a sentence of penal servitude, but poor fellows
> they were shot at 18 hours notice . . . As counsel for
> your son and other officers I should like to see that
> all the facts from the prisoners point of view are fairly

brought forward. When everything is known you will
not think the disgrace amounts to much, or anything.
War is war and rough things have to be done. Only
yesterday news came in of horrible barbarities on the
part of the Boers towards some of our colonials. I
say – they deserve what they get and with less nonsense and sentiment the war would be over.

The discrepancies between official statements and
the front-line information they were receiving from
servicemen began to trouble the press, as did the knowledge that as volunteers their ignorance of military law
with regard to 'drum-head' courts martials and the
customs of war, had contributed to their downfall.

The issue was also being debated at the highest
political level. On April 2, Member of Parliament Isaac
Isaacs, who would later become Witton's champion,
quizzed the Prime Minister in the House of Representatives about the 'matter which is agitating the minds of
the people of this country to an unprecedented degree'.
To his acute embarrassment, especially in light of the
assurances Kitchener gave him after Wilmansrust,
Barton had to admit for the second time in less than six
months that he knew nothing more than the newspapers about major incidents involving Australian
troops. His reply to Isaacs' question revealed how thin
the veneer of Australia's nationhood was. It had a grand
parliament, the institutions and all the trappings of
nationhood, but where its military affairs were
concerned, the power clearly lay in London:

> I am endeavouring to obtain information, but it
> rests entirely with the military authorities in
> South Africa as to the extent of the information
> which they will give, that being a matter for them
> exclusively to determine, having regard to the main-
> tenance of discipline in the Army.

Behind the scenes, Major-General Hutton and Governor General Lord Hopetoun were trying to find out what was going on. As Imperial representatives, they had been embarrassed that the Australian Government had not been kept up to date. Hutton, who could ill-afford a damaging Imperial backlash as he tried to persuade Barton to endorse his idea of a co-operative system of Imperial defence, involving the deployment of Australian troops overseas, wrote to Brodrick: 'It was a pity that the facts were not communicated here by the C. Chief [Kitchener], I think, as much adverse, and ill-advised comment would have been saved.'

After dispatching a strongly worded cable to Kitchener, the Governor General replied to Hutton rather more colourfully:

> If I fail to get proper satisfaction from him direct I shall turn the screw through Mr Chamberlain and St John Brodrick. These soldiers must not be allowed to have things their own way.

But Kitchener did have it his own way. His total silence on the matter and the mounting press speculation forced the War Office to pre-empt Kitchener's reply and made a statement backing him, which was published in *The Times* on April 5. It gave only a brief chronology and the barest facts, but was remarkable in a few of its comments:

> In July and August last, an irregular colonial force, the Bushveldt Carbineers, recruited in South Africa, but including other colonials, was employed in the wildest part of the Transvaal known as the Spelonken . . . No doubt exists as to the guilt of the accused, whose plea in extenuation that a member of their corps had suffered ill treatment at the hands of the Boers was not sustained by the evidence at the trial.

Notwithstanding the bold statement of guilt which in all likelihood was made before they had received any additional information from South Africa, and the fact that the courts martial panel had cited Hunt's ill treatment in their recommendation to mercy, the claim that the Bushveldt Carbineers was a 'colonial' unit was incorrect and little more than a cynical attempt to distance the Imperial authorities from any allegations of war atrocities. The War Office position also contradicted the reply Barton gave Isaacs a few days before in an equally cynical attempt to shift responsibility onto the British and cover his own embarrassment at not having been informed about the executions:

> They were not in any sense employed by Australia, nor were they a corps that was raised in Australia, or was distinctly Australian. They were liable to be treated according to the King's regulations.

As has been previously detailed, the BVC was raised as an Imperial unit by Provost Marshal Poore and contained British soldiers as well as various colonials. However, it could be described as Australian in character. Around forty-five per cent of the unit could be classified as Australians, as were all but two of the officers. As Australian biographer Manning Clark pointed out, 'No-one saw the lives of Morant and Handcock as part of the price Australians paid for the Imperial connection'.

KITCHENER'S REPLY TO HOPETOUN'S request for details arrived the day after the War Office statement. The telegram bore a striking resemblance to both the report Kitchener sent Roberts following the conclusion of the courts martials and the recent War Office statement.

Your telegram of 4th April, Hancock [sic] and
Witton were charged with twenty separate murders
including one of a German missionary who had
witnessed other murders. Twelve of these murders
were proved. From evidence appears Morant
was originator of crimes, which Handcock carried
out in cold-blooded manner. The murders were
committed in wildest part of Transvaal known
as 'Spelonken', about 80 miles to the north of
Pretoria, on four separate dates, namely 2nd July,
11th August, 23rd August, and 7th September. In
one case, when eight Boer prisoners were murdered,
it was alleged in defence to have been done in a
spirit of revenge for ill-treatment of one of their officers, Captain Hunt, who was killed in action.
No such ill-treatment was proved. The prisoners
were convicted after a most exhaustive trial, and
were defended by counsel. There were, in my
opinion, no extenuating circumstances. Lieutenant
Witton was also convicted, but I commuted sentence to penal servitude for life, in consideration of
his having been under the influence of Morant and
Handcock. Proceedings have been sent home.

Like Kitchener's previous statements on the issue, it was
also misleading. It sought to blame the accused for all
twenty murders committed in the Spelonken and failed
to mention that there were mitigating circumstances
as stated in the recommendations to mercy, and that
the court did accept that Hunt was the victim of ill-
treatment. A few days before, Barton confirmed in
parliament that the prisoners had helped to defend the
fort from a Boer attack during the trial. There was no
mention of this in Kitchener's statement to the Australian Government.

Recent research in Australia has suggested that
Kitchener's original telegram, which was sent in code,

was misinterpreted. According to the British wartime code book of 1898, the coded phrase 'sancile grovelling elucorum' should have been translated as 'there were extenuating circumstances'. That might have saved Witton, but Kitchener, who had the power of life and death, clearly saw no grounds for mitigation when he passed sentence on Morant and Handcock.

Up to now, everything in the press had been mere speculation, but Kitchener's telegram was regarded as the word of God. It was enough to satisfy some, but only inflamed rather dampened-down press and public opinion. The more detail that emerged, the more incon-sistencies emerged with it. Anyone seeking to discover the origins of the Morant legend need look no further than the ill-advised and badly co-ordinated attempts of British officialdom to conceal the facts from the Australian people.

The tragedy was given an unexpected human dimen-sion when it came to light that not only had the Australian Government not been informed, but neither had Bridget Handcock of Brilliant Street, Bathurst – the widow of Peter Handcock.

One of the lodgers she took in to help support her-self and her three children read about the executions in the paper. The early reports were sketchy and at first PJ Handcock was wrongly identified as coming from Western Australia. However the lodger, himself a returned soldier, knew Handcock and the corps he was serving in, and recognised his physical description. The lodger told his landlady's cousin, who was the man she had been having the affair with and would later marry. Rather poetically, Mrs Handcock learned of her husband's death from the lips of her lover. Her callous treatment and grief-stricken interview with *The Bathurst*

National Advocate further troubled the public conscience. In it she said she had not heard from her husband for a few months, but assumed he had been visiting relatives in England. As for the treatment she had received, she said:

> Would you think that the British authorities would treat a widow and three children as I have been treated? My husband has been dead a month, and not one of us has been acquainted of it. I've heard of the cruelty of the Boers spoken of, but could anything be more cruel than this treatment?

Thomas wrote to The Honourable John See, Premier of New South Wales, to demand an inquiry into the circumstances surrounding Handcock's execution and to grant his last request – that something be done for his children. It ended:

> But the matter of Vet. Lieut. Handcock wants special elucidation – especially in view of the lying and filthy statements made in some of the English papers which find ready sale here.
>
> I say, and will always say, that Handcock's life should have been spared – for he was a splendid stamp of a man with a young family. I also consider that Lieut. Morant should not have been put to death; but your Govt., of course, is specially concerned with Handcock. He was a man for whom I had the greatest regard.
>
> Meantime, I sincerely hope that the people of NSW will remember his children. I promised him that the latter would not be forgotten. I have done a little for them here and I hope that you will do what you can for this brave man's little ones. Whatever he did (and it was very little) was in conscientious obedience to orders received.

However, no inquiry was ever held into the executions
and Handcock's widow received nothing from the government of New South Wales, or the British government
to whom they appealed for his gratuities in 1905. It was
left to the faithful Thomas to help where he could.

IF MORANT'S EPITAPH BETRAYED HIS feeling about
the Morants, then he would not be disappointed by
their response to the news of his execution. On April 7,
sandwiched between more colourful accounts of
the Carbineers' blood-thirsty exploits, was a small
excerpt from *The Times*. It simply said:

> Admiral Sir Digby Morant K.C.B. denies that the
> late Harry Harbord Morant, of the Bushveldt Car-
> bineers, was his son, or that he was even related.

As outlined in Chapter One, Digby's rebuff was
picked up by Morant's old paper *The Bulletin* as they
began probing his background in conjunction with a
journalist called David Green from Charters Towers'
The Northern Miner. The *Miner* had been visited by a
Mrs Veal, in whose house Daisy and Edwin were
married. She showed them the family Bible he left in
her safe-keeping and some letters. A comparison of
signatures proved that Harry Harbord Morant had
indeed once been Edwin Henry Murrant – not that it
mattered. Many immigrants to Australia changed their
names to escape their pasts. Having raised the issue,
The Bulletin then concluded:

> As to Admiral Morant's cabled disapproval of
> Lieut. Morant's paternity, THE BULLETIN has
> received several letters attempting to refute the
> Admiral's statement. But after all what does it
> matter? What advantage to anybody if the body of

the son is hung around the neck of one particular old man? Morant has been executed. Is it necessary to also execute the family?

However, there were those amongst Digby's family who knew the truth. Following his execution, Lady Tennyson wrote in a letter to her mother in England confirming that she, like Lieutenant-Colonel Morant in Renmark, believed Harry to be a Morant:

> We have all been terribly shocked out here over a terrible case in South Africa. A young Mr Morant, a cousin of the Brockenhurst Park Morants, our friends, who has been out here in the Bush about 8 years – probably owing to being N'er do well – went out with the 2nd Australian Contingent & I remember very well talking to him up here, a very jolly and wild sort of fellow, immensely popular and very amusing – but a regular dare-devil sort of character.

Another piece of important information published at the same time further refuted Digby's claim, but was missed by *The Bulletin*. The Sydney *Daily Telegraph* also published Digby's denial and received an important counter-claim from an Adelaide source, which they published on April 6, 1902:

> It of course really matters very little indeed to the world at large whether the unhappy Lieut. Morant was or was not the son of the English Admiral who has repudiated him. But Admiral, then Capt. Morant certainly had a son Harry in the years 1875–1878 – a wild harum scarum lad of 14 to 16 years of age. Capt. Morant was at the time Chief Inspector of Irish lighthouses. In Australia, young Morant always passed as the Admiral's son. As such he, at the last, enlisted in the SA contingent with which he went to the front. One who knew

the present Admiral and his son in 1876 and who met the latter (or thinks he did) in Adelaide, asserts that, at all events, the so-called Harry Morant knew the Admiral well, and was thoroughly conversant with his life and habits when Inspector of Irish Lights.

Royal Navy records show that Captain Digby Morant was indeed Inspector of Irish Lights between 1875 and 1878. His eldest son, Edgar, was born in 1868 and would only have been eight or nine during the period in question. However, Edwin Murrant, who was born in 1864, would have been twelve years old, and the description 'harum scarum' certainly fitted Harry Morant. As revealed by Morant's former Silesia College pupil, Charles H Mabey, Edwin Murrant *was* using the name Harry prior to his departure for Australia. Did Digby choose the secluded coastline of his native Ireland to make the acquaintance of his illegitimate son? Morant, as we know, joined up in Adelaide, where the *Telegraph* correspondent claimed to have met him, and, if he was not the same Harry Morant he had met in Ireland all those years before, then it was a huge coincidence. If Morant was an impostor, how did he know about Digby and the Irish Lights?

If he was not a Morant, then why did Morant ask Major Bolton to deliver his personal effects to his family in Fordingbridge in Hampshire. Bolton's daughter was quoted in *The Bulletin* by a Reverend West as having said:

Father liked Morant and found him a sportsman in every sense of the word and felt intensely sorry for him. Morant gave my father his watch and chain, his notebook, and the photograph of a girl, which he asked him to send to his mother if anything should happen to him . . . Morant wrote a letter to

his mother which he asked my father to have sent
to her with the watch etc. Before he went out to be
shot he shook my father's hand and told him he had
done his duty and bore him no ill will. He refused
to be blindfolded and died with a smile on his face.

My father sent Morant's letter and belongings
home to my mother and asked her to go and see
Mrs. Morant and take her the things. One cold
March day we went down to Hampshire and drove
out to a lovely old country house where a pretty
woman with white hair received us. I was then a
child of about 10 and was told to occupy myself
elsewhere while my mother spoke to Mrs Morant.†

We were there a goodish time and I well remember saying goodbye and wondering why tears were
running down the lady's cheeks. It wasn't until
many years afterwards that the whole story was
explained to me. My mother said she sent the most
gracious and charming message to my father.

If Morant was an impostor, why did Mrs Morant, the
white-haired old lady, cry? Why did she accept his
personal effects and send a 'gracious and charming
message'? In correspondence with Australian author Kit
Denton, Hilda Truman, who was Charlie Morant's
companion during his later years, said that following
the execution the Morants held another family conference and argued for some kind of recognition. The

† *The white-haired old lady could not have been Catherine Murrant
as she died in 1899. The recently released 1902 census shows that
the only Morant at Fordinbridge during that time was Flora Morant
aged sixty-nine. Mrs Bagshaw must have assumed that she was
Morant's mother. Flora was widowed and later married John
Morant of Brockenhurst, who gave writer Frederick Cutlack information connecting Digby Morant and the Breaker which has been
reproduced in this book. This bears out the suspicion of a member
of the Morant family that Harry's effects were sent to Flora because
he knew she was probably sympathetic to his cause.*

Admiral, who did not want any scandal, vetoed this suggestion and disowned him.

The final twist came in 1907 when George Witton published *Scapegoats of the Empire* – his version of the Morant affair. After reading it, Digby Morant was said to be inconsolable. Did he realise too late that the son who he disowned may have been a scapegoat of the British Empire? Might an intervention by an Admiral of the Royal Navy who was also a Knight of the Realm and friend of the King have saved him? If any of those thoughts ran through his mind, he took them to his grave when he died in 1921.

Perhaps we will never know the whole truth about the tangled web of Harry Morant's origins, but maybe we don't need to. There is more than enough circumstantial and anecdotal evidence to suggest that Morant was more than the mere pretender modern historians have made him out to be. These critics saw the disputed claim that he was the son of Admiral Sir Digby Morant as part of a habitual pattern of petty pilfering, deception and recklessness that followed him from England to Australia and finally caught up with him in South Africa. Their logic was that if he could lie about his origins, he could lie about the events that led to his execution.

On April 17, a long account of the courts martial appeared both in *The Times* and the *Telegraph*. They outlined what they claimed were the charges and the main points of contention. Much was made of the fact that the court proceedings were open to the public and journalists. However, all press reports were subject to censorship by Kitchener, who had wielded his famous blue censor's pencil like King Arthur's 'Excalibur' ever since he took command.

Those members of the 'fourth estate' who imagined they were outside military control were quickly put

right. Banjo Paterson recounted the briefing he got from
Colonel Haig during his brief sojourn as a correspondent in South Africa. He was told that unauthorised
sending of reports, too many messages, getting in the
way or unauthorised trips would see him banished.
'Don't try and be too clever and you'll get on all right,'
was the great man's advice.

On February 7, 1901, Kitchener had Albert Cartwright, editor of *The Cape Town News* arrested on a
charge of criminal libel for daring to publish a letter
from a British officer which claimed he had received
orders from Army HQ to shoot prisoners in cold blood.
Cartwright got twelve months in prison and was not
allowed to return to Britain on his release. FS Mallan
and two other Cape editors also shared Cartwright's
fate for stepping out of line.

The single most important fact the public learned
from the summaries published in both *The Times* and
Telegraph was that the orders may have been given to the
BVC to shoot Boer prisoners. Witnesses disposed that
Captain Hunt had given such orders to the BVC, and
members of other corps testified that they had also
received and acted upon those same orders. Suddenly, the
question was being asked by *The Bulletin*:

> Why should stern justice be meted out to us whilst
> others go scot free? Why should the English officer
> who is a Bushveldt Buccaneer be a gentleman and
> a soldier whilst we Australians are scallywags only
> fit for a firing party? Our only fault is that we inter-
> preted your instructions literally. Others did the
> same and no word said . . . Already there are
> murmurs against the English court-martial on Aus-
> tralian officers.

The Bathurst National Advertiser published a letter from
a former *Bulletin* writer working as a correspondent for

a UK newspaper, which cast doubt on the accuracy of the published extracts:

> I have met a hundred of them – BVC who were mostly Aussies and with one accord they deny the blood-guiltiness of Morant and Handcock . . . What they had done was strictly in accordance with instructions and if they deserved death for the actions – at least a thousand others should have been shot in gloomy Pretoria gaol . . . I have seen the original evidence and compared it with the scant extracts and was amazed by the careful emasculation of the full report. In most essential points the facts were perverted and everything, which told in favour of the men, was carefully excluded . . . This story will stagger Australia and as a patriotic Australian I hope it will come out.

Other Australian servicemen in South Africa whose reaction was not recorded by the British press expressed similar sentiments in letters home:

> We wish that someone in Australia would take up the matter and do all they can to get the young fellow [Witton] off who is in prison at present. A great deal of bitter feeling is raging here against the execution. When all the facts of the case are known there will be a big how-do-you-do. You will think this is a rather melancholy letter, but it is enough to make a fellow depressed. It was two years yesterday since the second contingent arrived, and it seems strange that Morant should receive his death exactly two years from the date of his landing in South Africa.

Indeed, it emerged many years later that there were fears that the ill-feeling over the impending execution could boil over into mutiny. Trooper Hayes, formerly of the 1st Commonwealth Horse, said that the Australians in

Pretoria were made to form a square on the parade ground whilst the Breaker and Handcock were shot.

'Scapegoats' became a popular catchphrase in the press and calls were made in both Australia and in England for the publication of the full transcripts so that all the facts of the case would be known.

On April 8, Mr Swift McNeil, Irish National Party MP for South Donegal, requested the Secretary of State for War, St John Brodrick, publish the transcripts. Arthur Balfour, Leader of the House, denied this request on the grounds that he could not see that any public advantage would result from the publication of the proceedings.

McNeil pressed Brodrick again on April 28 and 29. This time Brodrick replied, saying that it was not usual practice to publish such papers and he did not intend to make an exception in this case.

McNeil, suspecting that the Government was not sure that the transcripts would bear out its version of events, then deftly exposed Brodrick's double standard by referring him to another infamous execution that had taken place only a few months before:

> I beg to ask the Secretary of State for War whether he will state what are the grounds on which he bases his refusal to publish the evidence submitted to the courts-martial by which Lieutenants Handcock and Morant were tried and convicted for the murder of Boers, having regard to his promise of the speedy publication of the evidence submitted to the courts martial by which Commandant Scheepers was tried and convicted of shooting blacks who were acting as spies for the British.

Now on the defensive, Brodrick replied that he had nothing to add to his previous statement and McNeil ended the exchange by saying if the honourable member

would not answer him then he would have to draw his
own conclusions.

In Australia, some sections of the media were doing
just that. The consistent refusal of the British Government, down the years, to publish the courts martial
transcripts and the suspicion that all the facts are not
yet known has done more than anything else to fuel the
ongoing 'scapegoats' theory.

The other important issue, which began to emerge
during this period of extraordinary revelations and
added yet more fuel to the theory of a conspiracy, was
the allegation that Morant and Handcock were shot
to appease the German Emperor over the death of
Reverand Heese.

The seeds of this particular myth, which still persist
to this very day, were sown when Kelly told Thomas he
could not delay the execution of Morant and Handcock
because the case had aroused 'grave political trouble'.
It all came out in a letter Thomas wrote just after attending the executions:

> Have you heard the news – the awful news? Poor
> Morant and Handcock were shot this morning at
> 6 am. It has broken me up completely. The order
> was signed yesterday sometime, and Lord Kitchener
> immediately left town and could not be approached.
> There was no time to do anything, but directly I
> heard the decision I went to General Kelly (AAG)
> and begged and entreated him to ask Lord Kitch-
> ener to defer the execution to enable me to cable the
> King on behalf of the Australian people for mercy;
> but he was obdurate, and said the order came from
> England and practically said grave political trouble
> had been aroused (apparently over the Hesse [sic]
> murder in particular). I begged especially for Hand-
> cock who was merely present as a Veterinary
> Lieutenant when Morant ordered the Boers to be

shot for outrages. I pleaded his want of education and of military knowledge and all that I could plead, but in vain.

Poor Handcock was right when he wrote two months or more ago: 'Our graves were dug before we left the Spelonken.' They were dug; I see it all clearly now, and why. I know what I cannot write in this accursed military-ridden country. My God! Poor Handcock, a brave, true, simple man; and Morant, brave but hot-headed. They took their sentence with marvellous braveness. Their pluck astounded all. Poor Handcock's only trouble was for his three children.

Edwards (adjutant BVC) and I were up with them up to 8 pm last night. They are to be buried together in the cemetery this afternoon and some trusty friends will attend. So will end another act of the tragedy. Witton gets penal servitude for life; Picton is reprieved and cashiered, and they both leave for England first transport; but I think Witton may be sooner or later released. Morant and Handcock were doomed – politically doomed – through the iniquities of the court of inquiry, proceedings of which got to Germany, I believe.

I am full of bitterness. I cannot here express my feelings . . . What I resented was dragging out a lot of details unless it was essential. I did not contemplate sudden and unappealable death sentences. I thought absolute acquittal in the Hesse [sic] case would mean at most a term of penal servitude, which could be remitted later on.

But, though not guilty, Morant and Handcock have died over that case because our own (no not our own altogether) people would have them convicted before a trial.

I will soon follow to Australia. I feel quite broken up. It is too painful to write about.

Poor brave fellows, nothing will worry them
again in this world, and if there be another world,
God will not think worse of them there than we do,
surely. May they rest in peace!

Yours sincerely,

J.F. Thomas

In this post-execution analysis, the signs of Thomas's
distress were already there, fuelled by his certainty that
they were victims of a cover-up. Did Thomas ever think
back to Henry Parkes's historic Tenterfield speech and
realise that this was exactly the type of scenario he
was alluding to? Australian soldiers under Imperial
command being tried under their system of justice with
no recourse to appeal to their own government who
were, as Barton had admitted during his speech in the
House of Representatives, powerless to act.

The belief emanated from Thomas's letter that
Morant and Handcock were shot at the behest of the
German Government to atone for the death of the Reverend Heese although they were found innocent of the
crime. To their eternal credit, the Heese family did not
subscribe to the biblical maxim of an eye for an eye and
signed a petition to Kitchener to ask that Morant and
Handcock not be executed. It was also known at a relatively early stage that Heese was, in fact, a British
subject at the time of his death, not a German.

Nonetheless, the rumour has persisted. On April 8,
the Under Secretary of State for Foreign Affairs, Lord
Cranbourne, denied that there had been any contact with
the German government over the Heese affair, which
was contradicted by the German Secretary of State for
Foreign Affairs, Baron von Richthofen, who said that
they had been in touch with the military authorities as
soon as the news of Heese's murder was heard.

The idea that the German Government had intervened made it seem like a political decision and the idea that a foreign government was involved behind the scenes was even more distasteful. *The Bulletin* sketched the outline of what it saw as a cover-up:

> Probably it was only after a conference with Germany that the fate of the men was absolutely sealed. If Germany would have been satisfied with a lesser punishment perhaps the crime of shooting Boer prisoners might not have been accounted so terrible . . . it seems reasonable to suppose that it was the first representations of Germany, and the publicity given on the Continent to the case, which induced Britain to take such action against Morant and Handcock as was not taken against murderers of other Boer prisoners.

However deep the public disquiet about many aspects of the case, it would be fair to say that opinion in Australia was divided on the issue and has been ever since. That dichotomy and the issues uppermost in the public mind were aired during the debate which developed when Morant's old friend and editor JCL Fitzpatrick, Honourable Member for Rylstone, brought up the issue of Major Lenehan's unfair treatment by the Imperial authorities in the Parliament of New South Wales on September 9, 1901.

Fitzpatrick declared that he had known Morant personally. Morant worked as a writer for his newspaper, *The Richmond and Windsor Gazette*, during the period of 1896 to 1898 and he had lived with him in a house on the Hawkesbury river. Fitzpatrick was one of the 'old Hawkesbury boys' Morant referred to in his postcard home shortly after he first arrived in South Africa.

> I had a very excellent opportunity for several years of knowing exactly the character of Morant, being

brought into close association with him for some two years, during the greater portion of which he lived in the same house as I lived in. I am convinced that, as far as the man is concerned, the charges which were levelled against him of unheard of brutality towards the Boer prisoners thrown in his way must assuredly have been highly-coloured.

The Member for Rylstone then questioned the British authorities' treatment of Lenehan and called for a royal commission to look into the executions of Morant and Handcock. He was supported by the Member for Ryde, Mr Farnell, who featured in the following exchange:

MR FARNELL: As a large number of people believe that those who were connected with the Bushveldt Carbineers were nothing but cold-blooded murderers, I think that in the interests of justice, and of those left widows and orphans, the whole of the truth should come out . . . The crimes for which Lieutenants Morant and Handcock were executed, and for which Whitton [sic] received a life sentence, and Picton was cashiered, were alleged to be due to their blood-thirstiness and desire to commit murders. It was also alleged that they had no authority or orders to shoot prisoners. From evidence that has come to light, and upon which I place the greatest reliance, I unhesitatingly say that orders were given by someone that no prisoners were to be taken . . . I had the pleasure of interviewing a captain lately returned from South Africa who alleges the orders went through the regiment with which he was connected, and he as well as others did not hesitate to carry out those orders which were received from headquarters.

AN HON. MEMBER: Does the Hon. Member mean to insinuate that orders went from the British Government that no prisoners were to be taken?

MR PARNELL: It is so alleged by officers and soldiers.

AN HON. MEMBER: I do not believe it!

MR ARTHUR GRIFFITH: It was sworn to by soldiers at British and colonial courts martials.

MR FARNELL: . . . It is a serious reflection on the British nation to think that any military commander should have given orders that no prisoners should be taken.

MR GORMLY: But would anyone believe it?

MR EDDEN: Does the Hon. Member for Ryde believe it himself?

MR FARNELL: Well, that is a question for inquiry. There are people ready to swear to it . . . it seems to me necessary that some commission of inquiry should be appointed; and in the interests of Australians and more particularly New South Welshmen, it is the duty of this Government to take the initiative, and urge the Federal Government to endeavour to induce the Imperial authorities to appoint a commission with a view to eliciting the facts.

AN HON. MEMBER: Does the Hon. Member consider that Morant was unjustly punished?

MR FARNELL: He was unjustly punished if he did carry out the orders of his superior officer. Others in South Africa say they did the same thing.

MR GORMLY (Wagga Wagga): The Hon. Member for Ryde in the course of his remarks, informed the House that a returned officer from the Transvaal had told him that a general order was given to take no prisoners. Any right-thinking person must see that a returned officer making such statements is not a fit man to be associated with. I do not believe, nor do I think that the Hon. Member himself believes, that such an order was ever given.

MR FARNELL: To shoot Boers in khaki and those using explosive bullets? I say yes!

MR GORMLY: To take no prisoners; that was what the Hon. gentleman said. Other people were to be taken prisoners beside these dressed in khaki and who used explosive bullets, and it is incredible that the authorities in the British army should have given the order attributed to them. Events have since demonstrated that the offences charged to the Boers were committed not by those people only. To carry out warfare under the conditions mentioned, and to shoot men in this cold-blooded way, is too much to accept, and I do not see that any returned officer from the Transvaal had any right to make the statement imputed by the Hon. Member for Ryde. I believe it to be untrue and uncalled for.

MR JESSEP (Waverly): (Referring to the summary of the courts martials published in *The Times* and *Telegraph*) The evidence goes to prove that all these alleged orders to shoot down Boers were from one man who was dead, namely Captain Hunt. It has been characteristic of the British army in all ages that they have displayed the highest qualities of humanity in dealing with a fallen foe . . . An inquiry was instituted by Lord Kitchener afterwards in order to satisfy the people of Great Britain and the House of Commons, who demanded that the fullest inquiry should be made into the charges of shooting these Australian officers. Consequent upon the report of Lord Kitchener, forwarded to the home authorities, a statement was made to the British Parliament by Mr. Brodrick, giving the whole of the details and showing that the fullest justice had been

done, and that these charges that men were ordered
to shoot in cold blood the prisoners who were taken
were unfounded.

Certain members of the New South Wales Parliament
may have been prepared to take Kitchener and the
British authorities at their word, but 'the great, unreasoning, unthinking people', as Renar described them,
were not. Though he was thinking of Boer rebels when
he wrote it, Conan Doyle's words could just as well
apply to Morant and Handcock: 'A brave race can
forget the victims of the field of battle, but never those
of the scaffold. The making of political martyrs is the
last sanity of statesmanship.'

Renar's biography, *Bushman and Buccaneer*, was in
bookshops just six weeks after news of the executions
reached Australia, even though he was not in a position
to write a definitive account, even with access to personal
letters, archive material and Major Lenehan's help.
Although Renar was sharply critical of the man his own
paper had made a bush legend, he could not resist the epic
quality of Morant's life. He drew heavily on the chivalric image of Morant as a knight out of time: 'But, unlucky
wight, this Devon man was born into the 19th century
with the spirit and temper of the 17th', and although he
tried fervently to avoid it, he helped write Morant's name
large on the Australian bush pantheon, as he predicted
would happen even before his book was published: 'He
will certainly be an Australian bush hero of the future,
his statue in the Valhalla where the venerated Ned Kelly
and Starlight wear their haloes unabashed.'

The year 1902 ended with *The Bulletin* once again
'howling for the undermost dog'. An article entitled
Those Bushveldt Scapegoats confidently stated:

Now that official censorship is relaxed we are
enabled to learn more of the real facts of the case

against the BVC . . . It bears out *The Bulletin*'s
assumption that Morant and Handcock were made
scapegoats of the British Army in South Africa.

Although *The Bulletin* had been rabidly anti-war from
the start, the majority of other Sydney and regional
papers shared the same general feeling.

GEORGE WITTON'S IMPRISONMENT FAR from home also
ensured that the issue of British (in)justice was never far
from the headlines during 1902. After hearing his comrades death knell whilst waiting on the platform at
Pretoria, he was taken, along with the cashiered Picton,
to Cape Town and put on board the *Canada* bound for
England. All the way home they refuted the allegations
made against them to reporters, returning servicemen
and anyone who would listen. Witton noted that there
seemed to be a good measure of genuine sympathy for
his plight, which gave him hope during the twenty-eight
long, dark months which lay ahead in Lewes and Port-
land prisons. In fact, from the time his sentence became
public, committees had been hard at work in both Australia and South Africa trying to secure his release.
Winston Churchill, then Conservative MP for Oldham,
was also a supporter and asked questions in the House
on his behalf.

In the background, Witton tirelessly petitioned the
British authorities to release him, or at least review his
case. He even requested a copy of the courts-martial
proceedings to help him plead his case. That correspondence is held under the hundred-year rule but, as
the transcripts have never been released, we need not
wait until 2003 to make an educated guess as to the
reply from the British authorities.

The Boer War ended on May 31, 1902 with the

signing of the Peace Treaty of Vereeniging. Kitchener ensured that this time Lord Milner, as he had done the year before at Middleburg, would not object to the terms and scupper the prospect of peace. The Boer peace delegation he met at Klerkensdorp had included two contentious statements in their draft treaty. The first was an acknowledgement that Britain started the war, the second a qualified recognition of the independence of the two Boer states. He simply put his blue censor's pencil through both, hit his bell and told his staffer to get the Boers' train ready as they would be leaving within the hour. The Boers crumpled in the face of his resolve.

Kitchener returned home to a hero's welcome and received a gratuity of £50,000 – which he promptly reinvested in the South African goldfields!

Peace gave Witton's supporters hope that a general amnesty might be declared. One by one the Cape rebels held in prison at the end of the war were released under an amnesty for prisoners of war, but Witton was to languish in prison longer than any of them. He also watched as Boers, accused of crimes similar to his, were acquitted.

In one infamous case, a Boer named Celliers was acquitted of murdering a British lieutenant. He did not deny the charge, but said he did so on the orders of Commandant-General Botha.

Lieutenant Boyle, in charge of Dewetsdorp during British occupation, was rude and obnoxious to the Boers in his charge and Botha had remarked in the presence of Celliers that if he returned to Dewetsdorp he would settle up with Boyle. However, Botha died before Dewetsdorp was recaptured by the Boers, but Celliers took it upon himself to settle Botha's score. He took Boyle out onto the veldt and told Boyle that he had five minutes to say a prayer, then shot him in the back whilst he was still on his knees praying. General De Wet, who did inquire into the case, decided to leave it as Botha, who he held responsible as superior officer, was dead. A civilian jury also found Celliers 'not guilty'.

Having told Witton's father that he would like to see all the facts in the public domain and the prisoner's point of view fairly represented, Thomas remained true to his word. Forfeiting the free passage home, he left his business affairs in the hands of Mr Weigall in Tenterfield for another fifteen months, and remained in South Africa, at his own expense, to help Witton's brother Ernest organise the campaign to secure Witton's release.

Thomas requested a meeting with Prime Minister Edmund Barton when he stopped off in South Africa in June 1902 en route to a conference in England. Barton declined to meet him, but the Australian Prime Minister had been a curiously anonymous figure throughout this controversy. Manning Clark described him as 'a Pontius Pilot kind of liberal. He did not like to face up to big questions'. And so it seemed.

After the Wilmansrust debacle, Barton requested that Kitchener keep him informed of any more Australians being court martialled. Despite Kitchener's personal assurance, Morant and Handcock were executed without Barton's knowledge. And despite the embarrassment in parliament, the press speculation that followed, and the urgings of both Lenehan and Thomas, the executions were never debated and there was no inquiry. Was Barton concerned about Imperial unity during a time of war? Despite Wilmansrust, did he still have faith in British justice? Did he believe they got what they deserved? Sadly, 'Tosspot Toby' as he was known because of his voracious appetite, left no personal diaries and never put his personal feelings on the record. When he arrived in London he received a knighthood for services rendered, an honour that was savagely satirised by

Bulletin artist Norman Lindsay. It depicted Barton holding a bloodied knife with which he cut the throat of a kangaroo (Australian troops) whilst reaching out with the other for a glittering crown that was winging its way over from England courtesy of Joseph Chamberlain. Barton retired from politics the following year and became a judge in Australia's newly constituted High Court where the proof required to send a man to his death would surely be more conclusive than that offered in the Morant and Handcock case.

However, back in Australia, efforts to bring Witton's plight to the attention of the British authorities contrasted sharply with Barton's lack of action. Witton's brother approached Isaac Isaacs, who was a Victorian Member of Parliament. He had been opposed to the war and had been the first to quiz Prime Minister Barton when news of the executions reached Australia. Isaacs was also Australia's most eminent legal expert and went on to become Attorney-General of the Commonwealth in 1905 and the first Australian-born Governor General.

Isaacs' legal review was hampered, like all those who came after him, by the fact that he did not have a full copy of the courts-martial transcripts. The British government had not yet condescended to send copies of the proceedings. A summary of the proceedings was finally sent in June 1903, but disappeared from the parliamentary archives. The only person to ever have quoted from it was Major-General Hutton, during his campaign to have Lenehan dismissed.

Isaacs was forced to use the outlines of the trial that appeared in *The Times* and the *Telegraph*, but still managed to make a convincing case for Witton's release. The legal opinion of an eminent Australian further undermined the assurances of the British government that the trial was a fair one and Isaacs drew up a petition to King Edward VII. One hundred thousand people signed the petition – a staggering number considering it was before the age of the mass media and the population of Australia was only four million at the time. However, getting the petition to the King proved more difficult than getting the signatures for the largest petition ever to have left Australia. On reading it, Witton remarked: 'It was a clear and truthful summary of my case. I read it and re-read it, and felt that my release was assured; such a petition could not be long refused.'

It was sent to the War Office in London, who promised to present it to the King, but sat on it instead.

Thomas also unsuccessfully sought a meeting with the Secretary for State for the Colonies, Joseph Chamberlain, during his visit to Pretoria in 1903. However Chamberlain also declined to meet the Australian and New Zealand Association who were also anxious to press him for Witton's release.

The Australian and New Zealand Association was formed in April 1903 to collect signatures for a petition to supplement the Australian one. Although Chamberlain declined to meet them in Cape Town, he did agree to direct a petition to the appropriate officials. In the general spirit of reconciliation that had sprung up after the war, even Boer leaders such as Daniel Malan and Louis Botha made statements supporting Witton's release. As Botha put it, when asked if he wanted to see Witton remain in prison, 'No we do not, and we're sorry that the other men [Morant and Handcock] were shot. We all did things during the war we are sorry for in peace.'

But like the Australian petition, it made no impression on British officialdom, which appeared impervious to the mounting international criticism. Chamberlain informed the Governor of the Cape Colony that the King had received a dispatch on the matter, but had not felt moved to issue any 'special instructions'. High Commissioner Alfred Milner also declined to support another joint English–Dutch petition for Witton's release presented by a Pretoria Amnesty Committee because it concerned a crime which he regarded was, 'an outrage upon the laws of civilised warfare'. However the committee did prevail upon a sympathetic Prime Minister of the Cape Colony, Sir Gordon Sprigg, to write to London and motions calling for Witton's release were passed in both the Cape and Natal Legislatures.

The Owl, a South African magazine with a similarly uncompromising style as *The Bulletin*, also championed Witton's cause. One bitingly satirical cartoon depicted monocled, cigar-smoking War Office officials sitting on Witton whilst his cell door was held closed by the mailed fist of the German eagle – a direct reference to the suspicion of German involvement. Witton also got support from other South African newspapers such as *The Pretoria News* and *The Cape Times* likened Witton's predicament to that of Alfred Dreyfus,[†] who had also been a prisoner of conscience. Indeed, Witton's case became known as 'the second Dreyfus case' and calls were made for a proper civil retrial – an offer the British never took up. This must have been particularly galling for the British, as they had done much to secure Dreyfus's release from French prison and saw it as a mark of their liberal conscience and racial tolerance.

Though the British would not be pressured into releasing Witton, the steady barrage of criticism from both without and within did have an effect. Witton was told that his sentence would be reviewed, but only after he'd served three years. But it was almost too late. He fell seriously ill with typhoid and came perilously close to death.

[†] *Alfred Dreyfus – a Jewish officer wrongly exiled by the French in 1898 for passing military secrets to the Germans – was released and exonerated after further investigations and the stain removed from his record.*

Thomas finally left South Africa for Australia in July 1903 and on his arrival in Tenterfield immediately encountered official resistance to his efforts to help Witton. He was contacted by the Witton Defence Committee to help them in their campaign. However Thomas was still listed as a Reserve Officer and, realising that his assistance would create a conflict of interest, he wrote to New South Wales Premier, John See on September 19 and told him:

> [H]e wished to publish certain facts in connection with the case of Lieutenant Witton, but as he is upon the Reserve of Officers of the Australian Forces, and as it may be thought he ought not, as such, to publish any military matters, he wishes in the event of that view being taken, to resign altogether from the Defence Forces.

See then consulted Hutton, who replied that any information that members of the courts martial gave him was given in breach of the oath he took and, 'if it is the intention of Captain and Honorary Major Thomas to publish impugning the decision of the Court-Martial it would be well for that Officer to forward his resignation in anticipation of such statements.'

Thomas countered that he, 'did not intend to "publish matters impugning the decision of the Court-Martial", but he had been asked to publish the plain facts of the case and proposed to do so. As the General Officer Commanding and the Minister considers he ought to resign from the Defence Forces before he can do so, he accordingly encloses his resignation.'

Thomas also stated that at the time of the courts martials, he was not attached to any corps and appeared for the defence as a private practioner of law. His resignation was accepted on November 16, 1903 and Thomas never again used the title 'Major'.

But Witton and Thomas were not the only ones suffering from Imperial intransigence. Major Lenehan had been given an ultimatum the previous year – resign or be dismissed. He refused to resign and Hutton waged a two-year campaign to see him retired.

On May 13, 1902, Hutton recommended to the Governor General that Major Lenehan be retired from the Commonwealth Military Forces of New South Wales. He gave Lenehan's reprimand for culpable neglect 'in connection with such serious and particularly disgraceful events in the Regiment under his command' and the reflection it cast upon the honour of the troops he was commanding as his reasons.

But after consulting the War Office and his Cabinet, Secretary for Defence Sir John Forrest declined to retire Lenehan, as he had been given the lightest possible sentence available to the court.

Hutton continued his vendetta, saying that he had formed a very poor opinion of Lenehan during his command of the forces (1893 to 96) and the New South Wales Mounted Rifles in South Africa, and had 'never heard a good word said for him in either Peace or War'. He also believed Lenehan was unfit to hold a commission because the court of inquiry also investigated charges against him of 'attempted murder, fabricating evidence, complicity in all cases of shooting at the Spelonken, insulting behaviour to a young lady, stealing ivory, and a suggestion of cattle lifting'.

Hutton also wrote to Major-General Sir William Kelly who was Adjutant General of the Army in South Africa. He agreed that Lenehan was 'a thoroughly bad lot' and deserved to be shot alongside Morant and Handcock, but the evidence couldn't be found. Despite the speculative and unfounded nature of these allegations, Hutton forwarded them to Forrest.

After further investigations it was discovered that the

War Office had nothing more against Major Lenehan other than what he was convicted of by the courts martial. On June 30, 1903 over a year after Hutton tried to have him dismissed, the Australian Government approved his appointment to the Australian Field Artillery (New South Wales).

But it was not until late 1904 that Lenehan and Witton received the justice they sought. By mid-1904 Lenehan's request for an inquiry into the circumstances surrounding his departure from South Africa had been on the table for over two years. Australian Prime Minister John Watson said that the holding of an inquiry 'would imply that doubt exists in our minds, and we have no doubt'. Hutton was ordered to reinstate Lenehan, but he was determined that the Prime Minister would not have the last word. When it came to light that he had tried, unsuccessfully, to obtain a statement from a Lieutenant-Colonel Bridges to the effect that Lenehan had 'acted dishonourably with regard to money matters', the Defence Minister's patience finally snapped:

> I desire to express my entire disapproval of the manner in which the General Officer Commanding, by means of a confidential communication to Lieutenant-Colonel Bridges, reflects on the integrity of Major Lenehan on what appears to be unreliable information, for the acceptance of which the General Officer Commanding is responsible. Unnecessary delay occurred in carrying out my instructions of the 23rd May and so far I do not consider that the General Officer Commanding has afforded any satisfactory explanation.

Hutton sought to justify his actions by claiming he only did it for the honour and good name of the Commonwealth and regretted that he had been overruled in the matter.

This great sense of military honour did not extend to certain sections of the British Army. Captain Robertson, who had been forced by Colonel Hall to resign his command of the BVC and was told he would not be employed again by the British Army, was retained for months during the courts martials as a prosecution witness, at the princely sum of £1 per day and was given a first-class return passage to England before being re-employed as a lieutenant in Kitchener's Fighting Scouts. Likewise, Captain Taylor's career was unaffected by his connection to the BVC scandals. His conduct in the Spelonken did not deter Kitchener from again appointing him to a position of responsibility. Taylor later served as acting Provost Marshal of Kroonstad!

Lenehan was reinstated as a major in the Australian Army and put in charge of an artillery battery. He may have restored his reputation in the eyes of the Australian Government, but he found the War Office in a less generous mood when he tried to claim pay, gratuity and compensation for the personal effects he was forced to abandon. They admitted that there was £51.9.8 owing to him, but added insult to injury by refusing to pay it on the grounds that he was jointly responsible for the deficit of £585.19.1 in the regiment's accounts. He was also denied forty days' sea pay for his return journey, as he did not return home with his unit, the New South Wales Mounted Infantry.

Withholding these monies was both spiteful and unjustified, but the War Office made no apologies, saying they, 'could not ignore the grave responsibility of Major Lenehan, as Commanding Officer, for the irregularities in his command, which brought disgrace and discredit on our arms, not only in the eyes of the enemy but the whole civilised world'.

It was not until 1911 that the Australian Government stopped appealing Lenehan's case with the War Office.

WITTON WAS STILL LANGUISHING IN prison on July 14, 1904 when Winston Churchill rose for the second time in the House of Commons to ask the government what their position was on the issue of Witton's release. Witton was still there on July 19 when Churchill asked for a third time. Churchill's questions came in the wake of resolutions asking for Witton's release being passed in the Legislative Councils of both the Cape and Natal and a personal visit to AG Lyttleton, the new Secretary of State for the Colonies, by James Logan of the Cape Council.

Then, out of the blue, on August 10, Witton was freed. He was released into the care of Logan and when Churchill again returned to the question in the Commons, the Secretary of State for War, Mr Arnold-Foster, announced that 'His Majesty the King has been pleased to order that Witton be released' to resounding cheers. It was a bitter-sweet moment for Witton, who discovered that his father had died the month before. On hearing of his father's illness, he had petitioned Lyttleton for his early release on compassionate grounds, but was again told that his case would not be reviewed until February 1905. That was only six weeks before he was released. Which particular appeal produced the sudden and dramatic change of heart is impossible to say, but the British hard-line was conspicuously out of step with the rest of the civilised world. Even their former enemy, whose men he had been found guilty of murdering, felt it was time to forgive and forget. Before he left England, Witton was interviewed by the press and said that he did not hold any grudges against the British Government and the whole episode was best forgotten.

Whilst Witton was on his way home, Hutton, that

strutting little Imperial peacock, got his come-uppance when he was caught sending coded telegrams to London. He refused to give a transcript to the defence minister, saying the telegrams had been sent confidentially to the British Secretary of State for War. Even though he was an Imperial officer, he was in the employ of the Australian Government and answerable to them – a fact that seemed to have escaped him during the Lenehan affair. The story was leaked to the press and was followed by an announcement that a military board headed by a minister would replace the post of General Officer Commanding. Fearing this could be the end of his covert mission to establish an Australian expeditionary force, Hutton relented. But it was too late. Hutton's contract was not renewed and he sailed for home in late 1904. In England he was regarded as a failure and was never again consulted on matters of colonial or Imperial defence.

Witton finally arrived home in November 1904 to a warm handshake from former Prime Minister Deakin. Safely back in Australia, he promptly went back on everything he said before leaving England. He fulfilled Morant's prophecy that 'as sure as God made pippins, if you let one of us go he'll yap' by writing *Scapegoats of the Empire,* his version of the events that led to the executions and his own imprisonment.

When it was published in 1907 by DW Paterson of Melbourne, its release proved as controversial as its contents. Again, only a handful of first edition copies ever saw the light of day, as the publisher's warehouse mysteriously caught fire. It was rumoured those that survived were bought up and destroyed by the British Government to avoid the truth coming out. A relative of Miss Christina Lawson, Witton's girlfriend at the time, claimed that Kitchener had the hangman burn them publicly in the prison yard. Only a handful of copies survived. A consignment of surviving books were also said to have been intercepted and burned by British authorities at the port in Cape Town. But the truth could not be destroyed so easily and the scapegoats finally got their say when a second edition was printed and became widely available.

Scapegoats ensured a hot reception for Lord Kitchener when he arrived in Australia in late 1909 to review Australia's forces and advise on defence policy. The hope that any ill-feeling might have dissipated as this turbulent decade drew to a close was quickly dispelled. Victory in South Africa may have made him a God of the Empire, but he had aroused a fierce antipathy amongst those who served under him.

Evidence of this came at the South African Soldiers' Association meeting in Melbourne. A resolution was put to the members that those who had served under Kitchener should play a part in welcoming him to Australia. This motion was greeted with a 'volcanic outburst of indignation'. Speaker after speaker condemned him for being anti-Australian and the Wilmansrust affair and the treatment meted out to the Bushveldt Carbineers were cited as proof of this.

The Melbourne *Truth* denounced him as 'anti-Australian to his backbone and spinal marrow' and 'a military martinet and an autocratic automation driver'. They accused him of trying to break the 'spirited self-respect' of the Australian servicemen 'to tame them into disciplinary efficiency' and as a result, 'The Majority of returned Contingenteers have no more love for Kitchener than he has for them'.

The editorial ended with a warning:

The Big Wigs and the Plutes, and the half-moon proboscises are already commencing preparations for the patriotic reception of the lordly general . . . But the garden variety people and the toilers would

do well to take their cue from the men who know
him, and view him with extreme disfavour.

Some of that ill-feeling must have been evident, because
observers commented that throughout the trip the normally inscrutable, 'Sphinx-like' Kitchener had the air of
'a man concealing some secret about himself which he
dared not share with anyone'.

Bathurst town officials lobbied hard to get him to
unveil their war memorial. When the great man agreed,
there followed a flurry of activity to ensure everything
was ready for the big day. They had laid the founda-
tions of the memorial seven years before, but had yet to
build it. Kitchener performed the unveiling on January 10, 1910, little knowing that his presence would
create a myth as enduring as the one that started circulating when he left Pretoria after confirming the death
sentences on Morant and Handcock.

The memorial did not include the name of Peter
Handcock, who was a native of Bathurst. It has long
been believed that Kitchener refused to open it unless
his name was removed. When Handcock's widow
threatened to turn up with her children to disrupt
the ceremony, she was told by police to stay away. The
Handcock family said she remained bitter about
this to the end of her life, describing it as the 'final
injustice'.

However, local archives suggest the exclusion of
Handcock's name was not the work of Lord Kitchener,
but of corpulent town councillors. The original list
from 1902 not only excluded Handcock but others that
served in South Africa, and also included one man who
never went to war! Of the ninety-four men who went
to war from Bathurst, four died and one was shot by
his own side. Handcock's demise was widely reported
in the local press and his parents left Bathurst as a result

of the persistent tittle-tattle. It is unlikely that such a story would just be forgotten in a small country town. One of Handcock's relatives even claimed to have a photograph, taken in 1910, showing that a name had been chiselled off the memorial. Though it did not indicate which name had been removed, Handcock's son, Peter, also insisted, 'Make no mistake, the name was on the memorial prior to the unveiling'.

John Martin, a long-time resident of Bathurst, sent me the following account, which would seem to confirm the Handcock family's claims:

> Dad at the time of the unveiling ceremony, would have been twenty-one years old, and was a member of the Portland band. The band, along with a number of other local bands, had been invited to play at the ceremony for the unveiling of the memorial [at Bathurst] by Lord Kitchener. Dad played the euphonium, and we still have it in the family.
>
> As Dad told the story, everyone was kept waiting as Lord Kitchener was late arriving for the ceremony. Then he (Lord Kitchener) refused to unveil the memorial until Lieutenant Handcock was removed from the honour roll of veterans. More waiting. After this was done, Kitchener climbed onto the dais, mumbled a few words, unveiling the Memorial, immediately climbed back down, got into his transport, and drove off.
>
> There had been a substantial banquet prepared in Kitchener's honour, and the organisers were left in a quandary, not knowing what they should do with the food. After discussions, they said, 'Let the bands people have it', and Dad always remarked that he'd never had such a feed in his life.

Following the publication of Frederick Cutlack's *Breaker Morant – A Horseman Who Made History* in 1962, it was proposed that Handcock's name should be added to the memorial. Though this had the support of the local RSL (Returned Serviceman's League) branch, the council was split over the issue. A motion to refer the matter to the British War Office was defeated and the motion to add Handcock's name to the memorial was carried. But there was another compelling reason to restore his name to the memorial. As *The Western Advocate* reported,

> Perhaps these accidents to a splendid memorial have been co-incidental, but it does seem strange indeed that each time the damage occurs – the story about the Australians in South Africa is revived. Perhaps if the name of Lieut. Handcock were restored to the Bathurst memorial further damage to it might cease.'

Finally, on March 2, 1964, almost sixty-two years to the day since his execution, Handcock's name was added to the memorial, and the local paper noted that the mysterious cracks that had plagued the memorial had stopped appearing.

The Breaker had to wait another forty years before his name appeared on any memorial, although there were a number of unsuccessful bids to have his name added to the monument in Adelaide where he joined up. In 1999, to mark the centenary of the Boer War, the local RSL included the name of Harry Harbord Morant on the list of men who left the South Australian town of Renmark to serve in South Africa. His name has never died in this neat little riverside town. There is still a Morant at the old Banglore farmstead who marches on ANZAC Day and the Renmark Hotel's 'Breaker Bar' celebrates the time he rode his horse up their stairs for a bet.

But a century later, key questions still remain unanswered. Did Morant and Handcock get a fair trial? Was all the evidence presented? Did Kitchener give orders to take no prisoners? Some have already made up their minds. A plaque with the words 'Murdered by Kitchener' was anonymously attached to the Bathurst memorial next to Handcock's name. A bold statement, but it couldn't be true . . . could it?

12

New Evidence

Boer women, wives with children, were rounded up,
and died
In British prison compounds, an act the world decried!
What better way to show them that 'Justice'
would be done
Than to shift the blame from 'Big Brass', and lay
the guilt on one,
A self-reliant trooper of the independent school,
An offence to General Kitchener of Army red-tape rule?

'The Death of Breaker Morant' by Louis H Clark

ONE HUNDRED YEARS AFTER THE COURTS martial, Australia remains divided on the guilt of Morant and Handcock. The pendulum has swung backwards and forwards as articles, books, academic papers, a play and a film have made this one of the most enduring controversies in Australia's short history.

After the publication of Witton's book in 1907, the overall feeling in the court of public opinion was that they were, as Witton described them, 'scapegoats of the [British] Empire'. This general feeling persisted until the early 1960s when Frederick Cutlack, the little boy who 'the Breaker' gave his quart pot to when he left Renmark to join up in Adelaide, wrote *Breaker*

Morant – A Horseman Who Made History. Cutlack's book breathed new life into an old legend in the more liberal atmosphere of the 1960s, when the old order was being challenged on many fronts. It was decided to add Handcock's name to the Bathurst memorial.

Cutlack also inspired a new generation of Australians to take up the cudgel. A play by Ken Ross and a novel by Kit Denton, both entitled *Breaker Morant* and released in the early 1970s, brought the story back into the mainstream, but it was director Bruce Beresford's eponymous 1979 film that pushed Morant's story to the forefront of national (and international) consciousness. It's the common complaint of the historian that popular films give historical events or characters a mythological gloss they do not merit, and a rash of new books was published in the wake of the film. However, far from mythologising the Breaker, Shields and Carnegie's *Breaker Morant – Balladist and Bushveldt Carbineer*, Kit Denton's *Closed File* and Arthur Davey's *Breaker Morant and the Bushveldt Carbineers* began a backlash against what they saw as the beatification of a cold-blooded murderer. With the aid of new evidence, Morant and his deeds were presented in a much darker light.

Since Davey's 1987 book, historians have continued to follow a critical line on Morant without providing conclusive evidence of his guilt, or clearing up the many inconsistencies that surrounded the execution. The debate has stalled in no man's land, and at the centenary of his execution, key issues remain unresolved.

The Holy Grail for researchers has been the 'missing' courts-martial transcripts that were never released by the British. Like so many aspects of this extraordinary story, all kinds of myths and legends surround them. St John Brodrick declined to release the transcripts in the aftermath of the execution because it was not believed to be in the public interest. It has been claimed that to ensure posterity would be kind to him, Kitchener edited the war archives when he was Minister for War, and the last copy of the transcripts was signed out of the Public Records Office by one of his staff. It has also been variously claimed by British authorities that they were destroyed as a matter of procedure, because until 1913 there was no law requiring the retention of such historic documents, or that the Luftwaffe destroyed them in an air raid during World War II. However, although he chose not to publicise it at the time, one of Kit Denton's London researchers discovered that the transcripts did exist in the Public Records Office, but would not be released until 2019. Fact or fiction? Only time will tell.

The research for this book added a few more layers to the myth, including a chain of coincidences through which at least two copies were identified – one in America and one in England. The first set became available in 1998 when a solicitor's firm closed down in Lincoln. Amazingly, amongst the papers that were disposed of was a copy of the Morant courts martial transcripts. They were sold to an American private collector who declined my requests to examine them.

The second copy was offered to a friend at an antique book sale in Melton Mowbray by an 'elderly gentleman farmer from Essex'. All efforts to trace him proved unsuccessful.

Implicit in this great quest has been the unshakeable belief that some great undiscovered secret lies within those papers – incontrovertible evidence proving either the innocence or guilt of Morant and Handcock. However, this notion has been sustained more by myth than probability. It should be remembered that the purpose of the military courts martial was not to weigh innocence and guilt, but to maintain discipline in the ranks by setting an example and to underpin the military command structure. Also, Witton had access to Thomas' papers when he wrote *Scapegoats of the Empire* and published everything to the prisoners' favour.

One good reason for keeping the transcripts out of the public domain is that it keeps the ongoing speculation about the Morant courts martial at just that – speculation. The various published accounts of the trial reveal major inconsistencies between Lord Kitchener's telegram and the actual events, but without access to the full transcripts, the 'guilty' verdict retains the imprimatur of British justice. However, Wilmansrust proved that British military justice could be perverted and the Jameson Raid underlines the fact that Whitehall was not above covering up indiscretions – especially in time of war.

The Jameson Raid was little more than a thinly veiled coup d'état, despite attempts to make it look like a popular uprising. Jameson was backed by the 'gold bugs', Rhodes and Wernher-Beit, and covertly supported by Secretary of State for the Colonies, Joseph Chamberlain. He had supplied guns and ceded Rhodes' Chartered Company a vital corridor of land in British Bechuanaland to support the raid once it became an uprising. Although the uprising was aborted, Jameson went ahead anyway, but received no support from The Rand. He was captured along with his men and returned to The British to be tried and imprisoned.

There was a parliamentary inquiry into the events surrounding the raid and, unbelievably, Chamberlain, the prime suspect himself, served on that very same parliamentary committee of inquiry. Although Rhodes, Wernher-Beit and Jameson all had correspondence that would have ended his career, none of it ever came to light. The 'gold-bugs' were promised that their company charters would not be revoked and Chamberlain secretly visited Jameson in prison to ensure his silence. A 'fall-guy' was found in the shape of Sir Graham Bower,

Imperial Secretary for the Cape, but Edward Fairfield, who handled the London end of the negotiations, would not be sacrificed. Fortuitously for Chamberlain, he died of a stroke shortly after being told to fall on his sword, and with the evidence sealed, Chamberlain was able to say, hand on heart, that he knew nothing about the raid. He blamed any misunderstanding on Fairfield, saying that he had simply misunderstood the orders he had issued as he was extremely deaf!

The transcripts' only real historical value would be as a record of who said what and of the actual words Morant used to defend himself, especially as Witton claimed that Morant's retorts were so 'straight and so bitter that they resulted in the collapse of the Prosecutor after a very few questions had been asked'.

Unfortunately, Witton, with typical Victorian reserve, omitted the details of this contretemps from his book. Hopefully, the typists employed for the trial had no such scruples.

Given all this, the research for this book concentrated not on unearthing the transcripts but on new evidence – evidence not admitted in the original courts martial. However incomplete, the legal opinions and accounts of the courts martial that have been published, along with Kitchener's telegram to the Australian Government, enabled me to summarise the main points at issue in the original trial:

1. Vengeance was not a defence because:
    (i)   Hunt was not mutilated after the attack on Viljoen's Farm.
    (ii) Vengence is only allowed in very extreme cases and is not a defence.
2. The BVC officers were not entitled to hold a 'drumhead' court martial and execute Visser because:
    (i)   The prisoner had been held too long before being executed. Vengeance might have been

accepted had he been killed immediately after they captured him.

(ii) Visser had no item of Hunt's clothes in his possession when he was captured, he was not wearing khaki and, no orders were given to execute Boers wearing khaki.

3. The execution of Boers by other units was irrelevant because, as the Judge Advocate put it, 'two wrongs don't make a right'.

4. Orders to 'take no prisoners' were never issued by Lord Kitchener, or on his behalf, by his Military Secretary.

5. The defence of Pietersburg by the prisoners during the trial did not entitle them to an acquittal under a custom of war established by Wellington.

The challenge was to discover if there was any other relevant evidence that the courts martial reasonably could and should have included. The British had over three months to assemble their 'best evidence', but Thomas was only given a day and the oppressive atmosphere that surrounded the court of inquiry, plus the reluctance of the British authorities made it difficult for the accused to get the witnesses they requested. Yet, in the aftermath of the executions there were many accounts from returned soldiers disputing the evidence given at the trial and backing the accounts given by BVC officers. What did those statements reveal? What about the letters and diaries of those close to Kitchener at the time? What about the myriad dusty archives that still awaited examination in Britain, Australia and South Africa?

NEW EVIDENCE – THE MUTILATION OF HUNT

The first critical point of the trial was the prosecution's refusal to accept that Captain Hunt had been murdered and mutilated, despite testimonies from Reverend Reuter who prepared his body for burial and the BVC Surgeon, Johnston, who testified that the injuries appeared to have been inflicted before death.

However, an unpublished statement from Adjutant James Edwards, who arrived at Reuter's Farm the day after Hunt was shot, tells a very different story. He got a witness statement of particular importance which was never admitted in evidence. Furthermore, in a letter he wrote to his father in Australia shortly after the trial, he revealed what happened that fateful night:

> The Boers were waiting having seen the British climb the mountain. Capt. Hunt saw that the enemy were prepared for the attack, but decided to go the whole way. Charging across the front garden he endeavoured to climb the high verandah stoep and was shot through the lungs. Capt. Hunt . . . then crawled to cover badly wounded. The order was given to retire and the men fell back. Captain Hunt lay where he fell, his native servant [Aaron] attending to him.

Crucially, Edwards secured the only independent account of what happened to Hunt after the BVC retreated from two German farmers. Hearing the shooting, they climbed the heights overlooking the farm and as it got light witnessed what happened next through binoculars.

> The Boers approached Captain Hunt and appeared to speak to him for some time. Then a Boer, Viljoen's brother, came from the house, pointed his rifle at Hunt's head, fired then stamped upon him. The body was carried into the house and stripped of its clothing and jewellery.

The Germans' statement confirms the events witnessed by Hunt's native servant and the injuries described are consistent with those found on Hunt's corpse by Reverend Reuter.

The savage treatment of trooper Yates, who was captured by Boers after the attack on Viljoen's Farm and later found by Morant naked, beaten and tied to a wagon wheel, would also have supported the allegation that Hunt was stamped to death after the attack. Interestingly, although Yates remained in the BVC throughout the period of Morant's reprisals, he did not sign the letter to Colonel Hall which got their officers arrested and was not called to testify at the subsequent courts martial.

Had this proof of Hunt's horrible murder and mutilation been presented at the time it would have backed Thomas' claim that vengeance was Morant's motive for killing Boer prisoners. Morant made this statement in court:

> Capt. Hunt had been my most intimate friend in South Africa. We were engaged to two sisters in England. He joined the BVC to be in the same regiment as myself . . . I had implicit confidence in him and regarded his orders as authoritative and bona fide. Until Capt. Hunt's body was found stripped and mutilated I shot no prisoners. I resolved, as his successor and survivor, to carry out the orders he had impressed upon me.

But why did Yates and Edwards' evidence not come to light at the trial? Their statements would have been of vital import to the defence as it was obtained from an independent witness and totally contradicts the prosecution's claims that Hunt was not abused and that Visser had no items of Hunt's clothing in his possession. Officer Commanding of the BVC, Major Lenehan, stated that his Adjutant (Edwards) was so intimidated by the pressure applied on him during the court of inquiry that he refused to speak, except in the presence of another Australian. We can only assume he only felt it was safe to speak out after the trial was over.

As a postscript to this incident, there was also another recorded instance of a British soldier being stamped to death in revenge for incidents that took place in the field. In his book *The Boer Fight for Freedom*, Michael Davitt describes what took place following an attack on a Boer convoy that had been captured by the British at Graspan in the Orange Free State in June 1901. During the Boer attempts to liberate the convoy, British soldiers used Boer women and children as human shields. As a result, eight women and two children were killed. According to Davitt: 'When the Boers perceived this they ceased firing . . . roared like ferocious animals . . . as if they were mad dogs struck down the Tommies.' According to witness statements from British survivors, several members of the 5th and 6th Australian Imperial Bushmen were killed and wounded even though they had surrendered and had their hands raised. A Boer jumped on one who was lying wounded on the ground crushing his breastbone.

NEW EVIDENCE – A CULTURE OF MURDER

Further research in the northern Transvaal revealed that the murder of Hunt was no random act of savagery. The Reuter family has lived on the Medingen Mission, near Duwielskloof, since 1878. Mrs Krause is the granddaughter of the Reverend Reuter – the missionary who lived near Viljoen's Farm where Hunt was killed and who testified to the state of Hunt's body. He was on very good terms with the BVC and Mrs Krause still has photographs of her family visiting them at Fort Edward. Details of what really happened the night Hunt was killed have been passed down to her. Mrs Krause's memory of the details that took place that night is still quite clear.

She said that Captain Hunt had visited her grandfather on the night he attacked Viljoen's Farm, which was some six to seven miles away. He debated as to whether he should approach the farmhouse unarmed and ask them to surrender. Reverend Reuter told him that he'd be mad to do that because certain atrocities had been committed in the area by the BVC against the local Boer population. Two children under ten years of age had been shot in the back when they ran away from an approaching patrol. In another incident, a captured Boer was ordered to dig his own grave so when he was shot he just rolled into it. Who killed these Boers was not known, but it raised the question whether there was a culture of murder operating in the Spelonken.

Despite warnings from Reuter, and earlier from Taylor, Hunt still apparently didn't believe that the Boers would shoot him if he approached clearly unarmed. However he stuck to his original tactical approach and was in full view when he approached the verandah and shouted at the Boers to surrender. He was wounded and Eland was killed in the first volley that came from the house.

Other murders had taken place prior to Hunt's death, which had led to the establishment of the 'culture of murder' that Reverend Reuter had alluded to. New research has also put the shadowy figure of Taylor firmly in the frame for those killings,

STATEMENT BY MR CLARKSON I.D.
(Intelligence Dept.)

On the 18th May, 1901 (Saturday) our party consisting of Mr. Malcolm Clark (in charge), F.C. Dring, A. Earle, du Plessis and myself were coming into Pietersburg with some surrendered Burghers and their families. We were coming along the old govt. Coach Road and when we were about half way up the Buffels Hill, we were suddenly fired on by about 45 Boers from the Bush – they were about 10 (ten) yards from the Road. Du Plessis escaped untouched by the first volley. I was hit in the upper part of the leg and knocked to the ground; the other three were killed at once being riddled with bullets.

We had with us one wagon and 4 spiders – following us at some distance were about 18 surrendered burghers with their families and about 300 head of cattle; the Boers took away with them old Steyn's son and all the livestock with the exception of the trek oxen and donkeys in the yoke.

Our Kaffir scouts had just come back to us and reported 'all clear' when the Boers opened fire.

The only two Boers whose names I could discover were V.C. [Veldt-cornets] Coetzee and Jacobs. I could identify Coetzee anywhere and think I could pick up Jacobs.

The Boers left the three bodies at the side of the road and scattered some Dum-Dum bullets over them.

Our wagon was also taken with 22 rifles and a quantity of ammunition.

We were given no chance to 'hands up' by the Boers – who said afterwards that they did not know that there were so few of us.

I was taken by the Boers in a wagon to Mr Gray's Stores where I was well treated. Mr Gray is a burgher but has not been fighting.

[Sgd] M. Scott Lieut. Colonel [who took down Clarkson's statement]
Commandant, Pietersburg

A 1953 letter to Captain Ramon De Bertodano, Intelligence Officer for northern Transvaal, from JRA Kelly, a former trooper in Kitchener's Fighting Scouts, revealed how Captain Taylor settled Clark's score:

Were you on the drum-head courts martial of Corporal Jacob, a member of Beyers commando? He was the man who treacherously shot Malcolm Clark, sent out with a proclamation by Lord Kitchener. Beyers to give his due, disowned Jacobs and outlawed him. Bulala Taylor caught him through information volunteered by natives. He was tried and condemned to be hanged, Barney Williams the old Rhodesian hangman, (a particular pal of mine – he stole a horse for me at Willowmore in the Cape when I was dismounted). Barney got £1 to hang him which he did at the sawmills just outside Pietersburg.

More evidence of 'Bulala' Taylor's ruthlessness was found at a farm called Paardekraal, behind Hanglip, which is near Louis Trichardt. In either August or September 1901, a patrol of Kitchener's Fighting Scouts led by Captain Taylor killed Van Den Berg, one of Beyers' commando, in cold blood in front of his wife and children. Unfortunately, this incident did not come to light until some years after the war when the Botha Government formed a commission to investigate claims that Boer land had been taken by the British and given to their own supporters by way of compensation, rewards or bribes for services rendered.

The author of the report that follows, Melt van Niekerk, opens by saying that he returned from Europe after the Boer War and took a post in the civil service. When the Union of South Africa was formed, he then took a job in the Department of Land Affairs and became part of the inquiry team. The chairman of Botha's inquiry was a Mr Wheelwright, who was a magistrate in Pietersburg and was very familiar with the Bushveldt Carbineers' case, as he had succeeded Enraght-Moony as native commissioner. The other members of the inquiry were Granville Nicholson, a member of parliament for Zoutpansberg, and Mr Koes Grobler, previously a member of 2nd Volksraad of the South African Republic, with the author as secretary. Van Niekerk wrote this report to put the murder of Van Den Berg on the record. What follows is a translation of that original report.

Nicholson, who also worked for the Department of Land Affairs, told him how he came across the Van Den Berg story during an inspection tour. He was crossing a farm called 'Perdejlaas' when:

> [H]e saw a woman [Mrs Van Den Berg] walking in the veldt holding her apron with one hand, and picking up something which she put in it. At first he thought she was picking up wood or dung to make fire with, but when he went closer he realised she was picking up bones. He asked what she was doing and she told him that she was gathering the bones of her husband which were scattered all over and that she wished to bury them. She told him about the tragic way in which her husband had died.

Years later, when the members of the commission were interviewing Boer farmers about their lost land, Nicholson suggested paying a visit to the farm to hear the woman's stories. She recognised Nicholson immediately and retold the story.

The farm was given to them after the Magato War, a few years before the Boer War. General Joubert had set it aside for future commandos and animals because of the relatively healthy environment its high altitude offered both man and beast away from the disease-ridden valley floors.

Her husband had been a member of General Beyers' commando from the beginning of the war. He frequently suffered from fevers and the last time he returned from the commando, Beyers told him to take a long rest and not to return until he was properly fit. He slowly regained his strength and was walking around on the day the soldiers came over the hill from the direction of Louis Trichardt. He got his gun and went to a kopje overlooking the house and told his wife:

> [I]f the soldiers should ask me where my husband was, I was to tell them that he was not at home but that he went for a walk on the veldt. However, if they should try and do anything to me I was to go to the corner of the house and wave to him with my bonnet. He would then try to drive them away by shooting at them from the hill.

The soldiers, a detachment of Kitchener's Fighting Scouts, were accompanied by a Boer interpreter called Devenish from Pietersburg, who didn't believe the story she told them about her husband. In order to intimidate her:

> They used bad language against me and said he was killing somewhere and was afraid to come out. The soldiers started killing my fowls and ducks and hung them on the saddles of their horses. I got frightened and was afraid that they would assault me too, and I walked to the corner of the house and waved my bonnet.
>
> When my husband saw it he thought that something was very wrong and he started to shoot at the soldiers who were walking in the yard trying to catch the fowls. The soldiers fled to the back of the house and took position there. Devenish followed them. The second shot out of my husband's gun hit one of the soldiers and he fell alongside the horse.

After a while, the soldiers sent Devenish with a white flag to Van Den Berg with a message that they would allow him to stay on the farm and carry on farming if he handed over his gun. They would also not blame him for shooting at them because they realised that he was still part of the commando. Van Den Berg accepted the conditions offered to him saying he was too ill to fight any more. The soldiers left with Van Den Berg's gun, but left the wounded soldier (Greenfield) behind. The Van Den Bergs attended to him to the best of their ability, but he died a few days later. Mrs Van Den Berg remarked that they could not understand why they didn't return for him, but her husband made a coffin and he was buried on their farm.

A few weeks later her husband got ill again and was very weak when another patrol of Kitchener's Fighting Scouts appeared on the horizon. Her husband told her to tell them about the deal he had made with the other patrol, but, as Mrs Van Den Berg quickly discovered, they had not come to negotiate:

> When the second number of soldiers arrived they surrounded the house immediately and parked the small mule wagon which they had with them near the house . . . The attitude they took immediately made me realise that something was wrong. The Officer-in-Charge was very commanding and shouted to the soldiers. I went outside and when the officer saw me he asked me where my husband was. I indicated to him that my husband was very ill and that he was delirious most of the time because of the fever. He, however, demanded in a very brutal way that my husband had to come outside. I went inside again and told my husband what the officer had said. He told me to tell the officer that he had surrendered his weapon and that the other officer had given him a guarantee that he could stay on the farm. He said that I had to tell him that he was in any case too ill to come out.
>
> The officer was very angry and did not want to listen to any reason. He told me to tell my husband that he had to come outside or he would go in and

bring him out. It was very painful but I delivered the message to my husband and encouraged him that he should try to get up and come out. I sincerely hoped that they just wanted to see my husband. My husband had a very bad headache and the wet cloth which I wrapped around his head was still on his head. He struggled to the dining room and looked at the officer for a few seconds and it [was] as if he had a premonition because he turned to me where myself and my daughter with the youngest child in her arms stood in the room and he told me that I must greet him because they were going to shoot him. He kissed me, my daughter and the child. The officer came in and ordered my husband to go outside, he pushed him through the door. I prayed in silence to God to spare the life of my husband.

In front of the door there were a few blue gum trees and a footpath that led through the trees. There were approximately 15 soldiers and when my husband had walked for ten or fifteen yards, the Officer gave a command and fifteen bullets pierced through my husband's body. He did not fall immediately but walked a step further before he fell down. It was an awful moment for me and the children.

The British soldiers told me to gather a few things which I needed for the children and to get onto the wagon with the children. They did not allow me to have a last look at the body of my husband. They did not bury my husband but only put his body in a shallow furrow which was made with my husband's plough and scraped some soil over the body. They gave me only ten to fifteen minutes to gather the things I needed and when the children and I got onto the wagon, they had already set fire to our house.

I was told later that the British Officer was a

> Capt. Taylor and he got the nickname of 'Bulala'
> Taylor, which means to kill, because he was such a
> brutal person. They took me and the children to
> a concentration camp in Pietersburg.

Nicholson asked Mrs Van den Berg whether she had
reported the incident to the authorities. She said that she
had contacted the interpreter for the first patrol,
Devenish, who was in Pietersburg, to confirm her story
and that:

> Devenish said that he knew that her husband was
> given the assurance that he could stay on the farm
> after he had surrendered his gun. He knew it
> because he was the interpreter. When the case was
> heard, Mrs Van Den Berg also gave evidence, but
> nothing came of it. The Magistrate said that her
> husband must have done something wrong other-
> wise they would not have shot him. Nothing else
> was done in respect of the case and Mrs Van Den
> Berg said she could not do anything more.

She also told them that after the war she and the children were allowed to leave the concentration camp and
returned to the farm. On the day that Mr Nicholson first
saw her, she was busy collecting up her husband's
bones.

> Not many people lived in that area and the body
> was most probably torn to pieces by wild animals
> and his bones carried into the bushes. Mrs Van Den
> Berg found the skull of her husband approximately
> 500 yards from the place they had left his body.
> She recognised the skull when she looked at the
> teeth. She found his shoes with the bones of his
> feet still in them at the same place. After she had
> gathered as many of the bones as she could find,
> they buried them on the spot where her husband
> was shot.

Van Niekerk concludes by saying that Mr Van Den Berg's grave became the venue where the Day of the Covenant is held every year.

Confirmation of Mrs Van Den Berg's story came in a letter written to Captain De Bertodano by a soldier who served in the Transvaal at the same time as the BVC. He recounted the same incident with a few minor variations:

> A Boer shot one of Bulala Taylor's advanced scouts while he was riding away from a farm in Wylie-spoort where they had warned the woman to come into the internment camp at Pietersburg as she was being worried by natives. The scout was probably called Greenfield, and he got off to tighten the girth on his horse when the Boer shot him in the back. Taylor's lot went back and watched the house and some nights later the Boer returned. A patrol under a man called Mickey Henderson and Taylor went out to the farm. Taylor and Henderson knocked on the door and the man came out in his shirt and trousers, was recognized, and told to walk across the yard at which the whole patrol riddled him with bullets, and buried him next to his victim.

The trooper who wrote the above letter also said that this story never came out officially and no quarter was given in the Spelonken after this incident. It was clearly understood by both sides that it was a fight to the death.

Tales about the murderous exploits of 'Bulala' Taylor still reverberate through the Spelonken a century later. Dr Botha, the local general practitioner for the Duwiel-skloof area, recalled Alfred Piet Lepboa – a black patient he had with an Afrikaans *pedi*, or middle name. Normally, black South Africans have an English first name and an African *pedi* name. When Dr Botha commented on it, the patient told him the remarkable story of how his father saved the life of a burgher during the Boer War.

Piet Visser and one of his relatives, who were members of the local commando, were being pursued by a group of BVC 'like wild game' near Lemondo Kop. Piet's partner was shot dead, but he kept running until he reached a native kraal called Mamaliba. The Boer told him that a man called 'Bulala' Taylor led the patrol and would have killed him if he had caught him. On pain of death, old man Lepboa hid Piet the Boer in a hole in the ground normally used for storing grain. When Taylor and his posse arrived he threatened to shoot him if he didn't tell him where the Boer was. Lepboa bared his chest and said that he did not come through his kraal and he could shoot him if he didn't believe him. The soldiers searched the kraal, but fortunately didn't find the hiding place. Piet and Lepboa became good friends after that and some fourteen years later when the next little Lepboa was born, he was named Piet. Piet had been passed down from generation to generation ever since to preserve the story of Lepboa's unique act of kindness and bravery and his friendship with Piet Visser.

These incidents confirm that a culture of murder had been established in the Spelonken prior to Morant's arrival and was ingrained in the local psyche. Captain Taylor was the chief perpetrator, menacing both the Boer and the native population. Morant, although he resisted it at first, was drawn into this vicious cycle through the killing of Best, Eland and Hunt.

IN SOMETHING OF AN UNDERSTATEMENT, Boer War biographer Sir Arthur Conan Doyle said of the guerrilla campaign, '[The] War had lost much of the good humour which marked its onset. A fiercer feeling has been engendered on both sides.'

NEW EVIDENCE – THE WEARING OF KHAKI

The statement that Lieutenant Edwards obtained from the Germans about the death of Hunt also mentions that Hunt's body had been stripped, which means that his clothes had been taken and were in the possession of someone in Viljoen's commando. Morant claimed that the first Boer he executed, Visser, was found wearing a khaki shirt and had Hunt's trousers, which was hotly disputed by the prosecution and their witnesses. In addition, Major Bolton, the chief prosecutor, denied the existence of any order to shoot Boers wearing khaki and Morant's right to conduct a 'drum-head' or field court martial, which had no legal standing.

The wearing of khaki by Boers was as contentious an issue as the white flag and train-wrecking. Throughout the war there were many recorded instances of British troops being lured into ambushes by Boers wearing khaki. Major McKnight testified that Boers were wearing khaki when they attacked the 5th Victorians at Wilmansrust with the purpose of spreading confusion. Boers he mistook for British soldiers took him prisoner.

Deneys Reitz, in his much quoted front-line account of the guerrilla campaign, *Commando*, insists that the Boers didn't know about the British proclamation that Boers wearing khaki were to be shot until after the war.

However Reitz had been involved in several incidents involving the wearing of khaki and knew the score. There was enough anecdotal evidence that shooting Boers in khaki was British policy, even if there was no formal declaration by the British. Any soldier, in any war, who wears the uniform of his enemy, knows he will be treated as a spy and executed if caught. Reitz was part of a Boer commando that overran a British post guarded by the 17th Lancers in September 1900. He was one of many Boers who swapped the rough jackets they had fashioned out of grain bags for a British Warm and uniform. One of his commando, Piet de Ruyt, was left behind in a pub wearing his khaki and was captured and shot by the British.

In a much-publicised incident, Reitz's commando also killed a Captain Watson and a trooper after pretending to be British. They had not removed the British Army insignia after 'liberating' the uniforms.

Two of General Smuts' raiding party into Cape Colony were shot near Port Elizabeth in September 1901 for wearing khaki.

However an entry in the diary of Major Bolton's boss, Provost Marshal Poore, responsible for discipline in the field, not only contradicted Bolton's denial that there was no policy to shoot Boers in khaki, but also the court's assertion that drum-head court martials were illegal. On October 31, 1901, Poore noted, 'Most of De Wet's men were dressed in our uniform, so Lord K. has issued an order to say that all men caught in our uniform are to be tried on the spot and the sentence confirmed by the commanding officer'.

Wasn't that exactly what Morant did? He was the Officer Commanding at Fort Edward after Hunt's death. There can be no doubt that in issuing the order described by Poore, the military command knew that, given the conditions in the field, justice would be summary.

In the previous section, an example of what Taylor called 'justice' was cited and he was never brought to book. In their letter to Colonel Hall, the disgruntled BVC clearly described the two meetings Taylor had with Robertson that resulted in the deaths of the first six Boers and then Van Buuren. How did they differ from the meetings Morant had with Handcock, Witton and Picton before he ordered the deaths of the twelve Boers he was accused of murdering? The first Boer, Visser, was not shot until the next day because they captured him in an exposed position and it would not have been safe to convene a court martial in the open veldt.

Despite the fact that the Provost Marshal, and presumably other senior officers, were aware of the order and how it was to be applied, the courts martial rejected the defence motion that Visser was rightly court martialled and shot. If there was any doubt as to what Poore meant, Kitchener himself confirmed both the existence and the spirit of the policy in a cable to Lord Roberts on November 3, 1901. At that very moment, the court of inquiry was investigating the charges against the Bushveldt Carbineers and Kitchener admits that the order was retrospective:

> In certain cases of Boers captured disguised in British uniforms I have had them shot, but as the habit of so disguising themselves before an attack is becoming prevalent, I think I should give general instructions to Commanders that Boers wearing British uniform should be shot on capture.

A further statement made by St John Brodrick, British Secretary of State for War, in the House of Commons in May 1902, confirms that Kitchener's request was not only known about, but sanctioned by London:

> Boers captured in British uniforms were liable to be tried by courts martial and shot . . . Lord Kitchener had already executed some of the enemy committing this breach of the customs of civilised warfare.

NEW EVIDENCE – CUSTOMS OF WAR

Two days before Morant and Handcock were executed, Kitchener told Lord Roberts that '. . . punishment may deter. It is the only case of this sort that has occurred.' However, the BVC were by no means the only British unit to execute Boers. This became one of the main planks of Thomas' defence – that by shooting Boers, the BVC only followed the same policy as other irregular units. In the degenerate struggle that was known as guerrilla warfare, shooting prisoners had become a custom of war.

After Pretoria – The Guerrilla War was a popular series of illustrated magazines published during the Boer War. Part 38 features an illustrated story entitled *An Oath of Vengeance* about Lieutenant White of the Bushmen Corps who was shot by Boers displaying the white flag. The reporter notes: 'At the funeral his comrades replaced their hats on their heads and joined hands together and swore most solemnly never again to recognise the white flag.'

THOMAS PAKENHAM'S HISTORY OF THE Boer War states that the shooting of prisoners was the work of colonial irregular units. This claim flies in the face of clear evidence that British units also shot Boers out of hand. One of many such examples appears in the official history of the Gordon Highlanders, whose regimental pride had been severely dented in a number of train-wrecking incidents, including the Naboomspruit massacre. On August 10, 1901, a month after Naboomspruit, another train was attacked on the same line, but this time the carriage carrying the military escort was armoured and the Gordons returned rapid fire. Some nineteen Boers died and an eyewitness account recalled the end of the action:

> [F]rom behind an ant heap a Boer shouted, '. . . Put up the white flag and we will know what to do with you'. Fire was directed on the ant heap and the Boer came out with hands up and said, 'Gentlemen we are brothers spare me'. He was immediately shot.

> This man was afterwards found to be electrician to (train-wrecker) Jack Hindon and had a coil of wire round his wrist connected to a mine.

Although they discovered the coil of wire around his wrist, this was only after they had shot him. The fact he was a train-wrecker was felt to be the justification enough for shooting an unarmed man who had, by their own admission, surrendered. As the Gordons lost no-one in the attack, it must be assumed that this shooting was payback for the earlier deaths at Naboomspruit.

Other train-wreckers, such as Carl Cremer, who invented the crude but effective anti-train mine using a sawn-off rifle and dynamite, met a similar fate. Following a botched attack on a train which the British had loaded with Boer civilians, he lost his glasses and, unable to see without them, stood still with his hands up. He was shot dead where he stood, even though the Boers had abandoned the attack and retreated.

Yet, Judge Advocate General, Colonel James St Clair, in a reply to a question to Lord Kitchener about executing train-wreckers, declared:

> I can find nothing in the Laws and Customs of War on the subject of train wrecking . . . As long as we allow the Boer belligerent rights they cannot, in my opinion, be criminally prosecuted for stopping our trains.

A COLONIAL UNIT WHO DID MERIT their notorious reputation was the Canadian Scouts, who became infamous for their solemn vow never to take prisoners. An old *Bulletin* contributor who served thirteen months as a non-commissioned officer in South Africa, weighed into the debate about whether orders were given to shoot prisoners with a scathing attack on a unit widely regarded as worse than the BVC:

The Canadians [Scouts] are far the worst in this respect and they will tell you with much satisfaction of scalpings and necktie parties . . . The hanging by the Canadians in American fashion (that is with revolver accompaniment) of four Boer surrenderers because of an alleged white flag incident some time before, I have seen indignantly denied by a Canadian colonel in England. If that colonel did not know it was quite true, he ought to have known because nine Canadians out of ten can give him all the information about the story . . . the average Canadian is simply a white Red Indian and should be absolutely prohibited from taking part in civilised warfare.

Captain King of the Canadian Scouts testified at the courts martial that they also had orders not to take prisoners. Boers caught train-wrecking, wearing khaki or murdering British soldiers were dealt with summarily after they lost their founder and leader, 'Gat' (Gattling Gun) Howard, as a result of Boer treachery. His principal avenger was a colourful but little-known Australian character called Charlie Ross, whose misadventures in South Africa closely paralleled those of Breaker Morant.

Charlie Ross was born in 1837 in the outback town of Orange, New South Wales. When he was only seven years old, he stowed away to America where he was adopted by Red Indians. The tracking skills Charlie learned from the Indians secured him a position as a scout in the American army where he fought in three Indian wars. After a spell in the Canadian Mounties, where he rose to the rank of Colonel, Ross joined the many hopefuls when the gold rush began in the Yukon in 1897.

During his military service, he served with the infamous General Hutton who re-organised the Canadian volunteer forces before doing the same for New South

Wales. When the Boer War began, Hutton arranged for Ross to be sent to South Africa with the 2nd Canadian Contingent. He served as Hutton's second in command and fought at the bloody battle of Sannas Post at which five Victoria Crosses and five Distinguished Service Orders were awarded. Charlie was awarded one of the DSOs.

The turning point for Ross came when he met 'Gat' Howard, a businessman he had known in Canada. Howard had left the Canadians to set up his own irregular unit, the Canadian Scouts, and recommended Ross for a commission.

On February 17, 1901, a year before Morant and Handcock were executed, 'Gat' Howard was shot dead when taking a Boer surrender after they raised the white flag.

The death of Howard had the same effect on Ross as the deaths of Best, Hunt and Eland had on Morant. As Ross and the rest of the scouts stood round Howard's grave, he made them swear an oath never to take prisoners again. To signify this oath, they wore black feathers in their hatbands once they had taken a life. In *Born to Fight*, Neil Speed's forthcoming biography on the life of Charlie Ross, a group photograph taken shortly after the death of 'Gat' Howard shows eighty-three members of the Canadian Scouts, including their new commanding officer Major Charlie Ross. In the photo, fifteen black feathers can be counted, but due to the broad brim of the Canadian 'lemon squeezer' and the hats being worn pushed back to show as much face as possible for the photograph, many others may also have worn the black feather. The Canadians achieved certain notoriety amongst irregular units that resulted in the Boers putting a £200 bounty on Charlie's head, but it was never collected. The *modus operandi* of the Canadian Scouts was an open secret amongst other units:

> The Bushveldt Carbineers, were lambs, compared
> to some of the other corps. Take the Canadian
> Scouts for instance. They were simply notorious for
> shooting prisoners, even before their Colonel 'Gat'
> Howard, was murdered . . . And since that time it
> has been their boast that they never bring a prisoner
> to camp.

Despite the rumours surrounding his business dealing and the Canadians take no prisoners policy, Charlie Ross ended the war as a Major-General.

Although Thomas produced several witnesses from other units who testified that they too had received and carried out orders to take no prisoners, the Judge Advocate protested that the evidence was 'irrelevant' and that, 'two wrongs don't make a right'. The two Judge Advocate Generals, St Clair and Pemberton, agreed with him in their legal opinions: 'A heap of irrelevant evidence was admitted by the Court on the part of the defence despite the rule of the Judge Advocate who I consider was justified in protesting.'

However, you cannot try one man for a crime whilst overlooking evidence that others are committing the same crime with impunity and then call it justice! This selective application of military justice suggests that the customs of war only became war crimes once they threatened to become public and implicate the military and political hierarchy.

WHEN KITCHENER CONFIRMED THE death sentences on Morant and Handcock and then told Lord Roberts, 'there were no mitigating circumstances', he conveniently forgot that like Morant, he too had sought similar vengeance against the Dervishes for the 1885 murder of General Gordon whom he had hero-worshipped and hoped to emulate. Like Hunt, Gordon suffered a grisly death. After he was decapitated, his head was staked and put on show. Kitchener exacted a terrible price for Gordon's death during the 1897 expedition he led to the Sudan. It was characterised by the savagery of the British troops on a vastly inferior enemy.

Kitchener set the tone by riding through Berber on a white charger and had the Dervish commander put in chains and dragged through the streets and horse-whipped as he went. Presumably, this was his way of spreading 'light and civilisation' to the darker corners of the world. Private Teigh described the action at the battle of Atbara on April 8, 1897:

> [We] were soon inside amongst the Dervishes, slaughtering them. Everyone they saw they had a shot at or stabbed them with our bayonets, whether he was dead or alive, for we thought of the hard-ships they had put us to and also the long, dreary marches across the desert before we came to them. When we were on the march I could hear the troops saying that they would make sure that every Dervish they passed was dead before leaving them, and they kept their word. But it was a horrible sight to see the dead women, men and children. It made my blood run cold.

Trooper Cox recorded the carnage that followed:

> Dead Dervishes, donkeys, ponies, camels and in places women and children lay dead and wounded in indescribable confusion – the smell was a bit like a slaughter house. The disgusting sanitary arrange-ments were much in evidence, likewise the so-called humane conduct of the Englishman, who except in a very few occasions, where officers were on the spot to prevent it, spared nothing except the animals . . . not a man got off. Wounded or no, bay-

onets were shoved through anything human in the most brutal and cold-blooded fashion. Instance – a man (Dervish) dropped his weapons and threw up his hands for mercy in front of one of the 79th who turned round and appealed to a Sergeant who said,

'Put him out of his misery Sandy. We don't want none of these buggers 'ere'. The private turned round and bayoneted him through the neck and again through the back as he fell.

The slaughter was even worse at the decisive battle of Omdurman which took place on September 2, 1897. The Dervishes lost 12,000 men to Kitchener's forty-eight. He then ordered his men to kill the wounded. Winston Churchill, a war correspondent at the time, remarked in a letter home to his mother, 'I shall merely say that the victory at Omdurman was disgraced by the slaughter of the wounded and that Kitchener was responsible for this'.

When asked by Lord Cromer whether he ordered the killing of the wounded, Kitchener said 'No'. This denial prompted Cromer to say, 'it is sometimes difficult to extract the whole truth from him. He is inclined to keep back facts which he does not wish to be known.'

Not content with taking revenge on the wounded, Kitchener had his gunners shoot holes in the tomb of the Mahdi, the spiritual leader who sparked the revolt. He then beheaded the cadever and threw it into the Nile. He kept the skull for an inkstand, which earned him a dressing down from Queen Victoria, who remarked, 'he's gone too far this time'.

Churchill repeated the allegations in his 1899 book *The River War*, which was released just as the Boer War began. Of the slaughter at Omdurman he said:

[M]ust personally record that there was a very general impression that the fewer the prisoners the greater would be the satisfaction of the commander. The sentiment that the British soldier is incapable of brutality is one which never fails to win the meed of popular applause: but there are, in fact, a considerable proportion of cruel men in every army. The mistaken impression I have alluded to encouraged this class. The unmeasured terms in which the Dervishes had been described in the newspapers, and the idea which had been laboriously circulated of avenging Gordon, had inflamed their passions, and had led them to believe that it was quite correct to regard their enemy as vermin – unfit to live. The result was that there were many wounded dervishes killed . . . A certain number how many I can not tell, but certainly not less than a hundred – wounded Arabs were dispatched although they threw down their arms and appealed for quarter.

Then, after criticising Kitchener's lack of concern for his own wounded, he concluded:

The General, who never spared himself, cared little for others. He treated all men like machines – from the private soldiers whose salutes he disdained, to the superior officers he rigidly controlled. The comrade who served with him and under him for many years in peace and peril was flung aside incontinently as soon as he ceased to be of use. The Sirdar only looked to the soldiers who could march and fight. The wounded Egyptian, and latterly the wounded British soldier, did not excite his interest, and of all the departments of his army the one neglected was that connected with the care of the sick and injured. The lamentable episode of the Mahdi's tomb has already been noticed. The stern and unpitying spirit of the commander was communicated to his troops, and the victories which marked the progress of the River war were accompanied by acts of brutality not always justified by the harsh customs of savage warfare.

Private Cox added that the justification given for the slaughter he witnessed was their 'frightful cruel habits and Gordon's murder'.

Private Teigh noted that after the decisive battle at Omdurman, Kitchener put a notice in Army Orders that said that General Gordon's death had now been revenged, thanked the men for their pluck and regretted the losses. War, it seems, does strange things to people, especially their memories!

SHORT MEMORIES WERE ALSO IN evidence during the first courts martial and later in the Judge Advocate General's office. After Morant and Handcock helped defend Pietersburg from a Boer attack, the court had the power to dismiss the charges against the prisoners under a precedent established almost a century before by Wellington during the Peninsula War, had it felt so inclined.

The 'Iron Duke' was a strict disciplinarian. He infamously described his yeomanry as 'scum of the earth' and bitterly opposed the end of flogging in 1830. However, he felt that men should be punished for a misdemeanour not, as was the case in the Boer War, as an example to others. To this end, he established the following custom: 'The performance of a duty of honour and trust after knowledge of a military offence ought to convey a pardon.'

It has been said that Thomas showed his lack of legal experience by failing to argue this point. However, Major Bolton's daughter, in a letter to author Frederick Cutlack half a century later, confirmed that Thomas did invoke Wellington's custom of war, but the court declined to exercise its discretion. The reason commonly given is that Wellington established a custom, not a law, and the court was free to act on its own impulse. Neither was it mentioned in the court's recommendation to mercy or in the Judge Advocate General's legal opinion.

It could not be claimed that it was a custom with no modern precedents. Only the previous year, Baden-Powell, who had himself escaped a charge of murdering a captured African chief during the Matabele Uprising, invoked this custom during the siege of Mafeking.

One of his non-commissioned officers was charged with murdering a *Telegraph* journalist, but during the siege the prisoner was called to help defend the town. In recognition of the 'duty of honour' the soldier had performed, Baden-Powell acquitted him of all charges.

NEW EVIDENCE – 'TAKE NO PRISONERS'
During the courts martial, Morant was asked under which part of the Military Code he shot the Boers, to which he replied: 'We caught 'em and shot 'em under "Rule .303".' Rule .303 was a cartridge from the standard-issue Lee Metford rifle. Not only was it a memorable line, but it formed the crux of Thomas's defence, that they were acting under orders to take no prisoners.

Morant named a high-ranking officer, Kitchener's Military Secretary, Lieutenant-Colonel Hubert Hamilton, as the man who issued the order to Captain Hunt on Kitchener's behalf. Hamilton simply denied he had given any such order, and in the absence of written evidence the central part of Thomas's defence collapsed. However, the existence of these orders has remained a hot issue amongst historians, because in 1902, acting under orders issued by a superior officer was a legitimate defence, and if proved they would have been acquitted. In his report to the New South Wales Parliament,

Commanding Officer of the BVC, Major Lenehan, revealed that Morant and Handcock had both been told that if they'd said it was Lenehan and not Army HQ who issued the orders to take no prisoners then 'nothing could happen to them' (because Lenehan was the Field Officer Commanding and above them in rank). But even with the whole British military system ranged against them, Morant and Handcock preferred to die rather than betray a comrade.

However, the Morant trial was not the first time that allegations of a take no prisoners policy were made against Kitchener. That same allegation had dogged him from the first days of his command and made for a fractious relationship with London, who he saw as interfering with his efforts to end the war.

The first allegation was made on February 6, 1901, when an article appeared in *The Cape Town News* under the pseudonym of 'A British Officer'. It disclosed that Kitchener had issued instructions to exterminate the elusive De Wet's commando should they be caught. The 'officer' concluded:

> This is an act not only so cruel, but so mean and cowardly that I have difficulty in convincing myself that it could ever have been contemplated by an English officer. I received the order personally from a General of the highest rank holding one of the first positions in South Africa and the order was repeated twice so there could be no mistake.

By jailing Albert Cartwright, the editor who refused to reveal his source, for a year, Kitchener revealed an uncommon sensitivity about this issue, but could not suppress the story. On February 26, 1901, John Dillon, an Irish Nationalist MP, read out the same story in the House of Commons:

And the word has been passed round privately that
no prisoners are to be taken. That is, all the men
found fighting are to be shot. This order was given
to me personally by a General, one of the highest
rank in South Africa. So there is no mistake about
it. The instructions given to columns closing around
De Wet north of the Orange River are that all men
are to be shot so that no tales may be told.

Dillon read from another letter by a soldier that had
been published in *The Liverpool Courier*: 'Lord Kitchener has issued orders that no man has to bring in any
Boer prisoners. If he does, he has to give him half his
rations for the prisoner's keep.'

He also quoted a third letter from a soldier serving with
the Royal Welsh Regiment that was published in *The
Wolverhampton Express and Star*: 'We take no prisoners
now . . . There happened to be a few wounded Boers left.
We put them through the mill. Every one was killed.'

During the courts martial, many witnesses from other
units testified that they had received orders to take no
prisoners. Trooper Frank Hall confirmed that the same
orders were issued to the BVC, even before Hunt and
Morant arrived, and talked about the mixed reaction of
the men:

We were fed up with false proclamations from Lord
Kitchener on such a date and this even previous to
the death of Capt. Hunt . . . These proclamations
were accepted by the men in various spirit. By the
very green with absolute credulity, by the older
hands with contempt, while the others seeing the
required daring on one hand and the inhumanity on
the other, had no opinion, and were consequently
the most miserable.

How Trooper Hall knew the proclamations were
'false' is a mystery, as he had no real wealth of military

experience. He was only twenty-one when he joined in May 1901, and left in November once his six-month contract was up. Perhaps he took them as such because he didn't trust his own officers. However, it was a policy some units carried out without question. A diary entry written by Walker Henderson Thompson of the 3rd Bushmen recalls how,

> Guards over the Boers sometimes got very tired and treated the Boers very well. One example of it was the Mounted Fusiliers. After a long march they were tired and it was very wet and cold and thought it would be easier to mind corpses than live men so they bayoneted about 30 Boers and lay down and had a good sleep.

In the small country town of Burra, South Australia, where Bruce Beresford's 1979 film was shot, the townsfolk staged a retrial of the Breaker in 1988. It caught the imagination of people all over the world and archival material, which had been gathering dust in attics for decades, flooded in. One correspondent from South Africa recalled what his great-uncle, Joe Devine, a lieutenant in the British Army who had been in the siege of Ladysmith, had told him:

> He maintained that the Boer War was the 'last gentleman's war' . . . except for those wretched Australians. He told me that acting under verbal orders, which he had heard, they shot their prisoners and any Boer who was in bits of British (uniform) were to be shot too.

Although the three Burra Justices of the Peace who presided over the retrial found there was enough circumstantial evidence of a take no prisoners policy to deliver a 'not guilty' verdict, there was still nothing to prove the order came *direct* from Army HQ. But

Kitchener was an autocrat and preferred to run the whole show himself, as one of his staff explained, 'He is a complete autocrat, does exactly as he pleases and won't pay attention to red-tape regulations and to keeping records of telegrams and letters . . . there is very little correspondence except by wire and in the field almost every order is given verbally.'

Kitchener may have been careful not to issue illegal orders in writing, but there was always the chance that one of his senior officers might have noted it down in confidence. The diary of Provost Marshal Poore contained the vital admission. In his diary entry for October 7 1901, he reveals:

> At about 6 pm Bolton (Wilts Regiment) – Assistant Provost Marshal Pietersburg – arrived with some papers about rather bad things which have been taking place North of Pietersburg – The Bushveldt Carbineers accepted the surrender of 8 Boers and after taking them along for some days shot them. *If they had intended to do this they should not have accepted a surrender in the first instance.* [Emphasis added]

Poore, in effect, admits the existence of a take no prisoners policy. Had this been an unguarded comment by a lowly field officer, then it could be dismissed as speculation, but the source is unimpeachable and the inference clear. Poore, as Provost Marshal, was responsible for discipline in the army and, as we have seen, he was intimately connected with the formation of the BVC, instrumental in gathering the evidence that sent them to their deaths, responsible for their incarceration and even drilled the firing squad that shot them. He was well aware of what the BVC's brief was in the Spelonken, the rules under which they were operating and their legal status. Poore simply reaffirmed the technically correct interpretation of the take no prisoners order that was in operation. Poore had already proved that he was willing to turn a blind eye to illegal tactics when it suited him. He knew about Kitchener's policy of putting civilians on trains to prevent train-wrecking, but did nothing about it.

It has long been imagined that a carte blanche order had been issued to shoot Boer prisoners in any circumstances, but the directive was more subtle than that. 'Take no prisoners' meant literally what it said – Boers could be shot so long as they had not surrendered first. Morant was right about receiving orders, but wrong in the way he chose to interpret them. This was Morant's big mistake. All the Boers Morant shot had already been taken prisoner. In effect, Morant and Handcock were executed for failing to correctly interpret an illegal order – and it was illegal. Lieutenant Lachlan Gordon-Duff of the Gordon Highlanders illustrated how this policy should have been applied in practice when his unit was involved in a skirmish on November 27, 1900:

> 40 Boers tried to surrender to us the other day and were not allowed to and a fight ensued in which they fought well but were wasted; it is rather extraordinary how they still go on.

Witton confirmed that the BVC had misunderstood the take no prisoners order in a comment he made in relation to a similar incident that took place after the trial. On hearing a report that a British unit had shot Boers who had been trying to surrender, he admitted: 'I later understood this to be the correct interpretation of the order to "take no prisoners".'

In other words, shooting Boers was permissible, so long as it *looked like* a proper fight. When the first six Boers were shot by Sergeant Oldham and a report was sent to Colonel Hall, he replied, 'This report will not do. How could disarmed men assume the offensive? Send something more probable.'

This was a clear directive as to how the take no prisoners policy should operate. It also explains why Lieutenant Hannam was the only member of the BVC the court of inquiry found had no case to answer. He was responsible for killing two children and wounding a third when he ordered his men to open fire on Boer wagons he knew to contain civilians. Some of his men purposely fired over the top and only the screams of children from the wagon caused the BVC patrol to stop firing. On the face of it, his actions were no different to the other officers, except that he ordered his patrol to open fire *before* the Boers surrendered.

It is clear that the BVC was as guilty of ignorance of military law and custom as they were of shooting Boers. Indeed, so inexperienced were Australian officers in the field, that the British refused anyone above the rank of major. The courts-martial panel did cite lack of experience and ignorance of military law in their recommendation to mercy, but, hardly surprisingly, it made no impression on Kitchener.

Orders were communicated to the front either by cipher – punched holes in scroll paper which were deciphered and read out at parade – or passed down the chain of command verbally. This ensured there was no embarrassing paper trail leading back to HQ and any allegations could be easily denied.

In the event of trouble the *Manual of Military Law* afforded HQ another safeguard – as Morant and Handcock found out to their cost. In the courts martial the prosecution argued that military law distinctly said that a soldier must not carry out an order he *knows* to be illegal, but how does a soldier know what was official and what was not?

Taking the example of khaki, Kitchener admitted to

Roberts that he had ordered Boers wearing khaki be shot in 'certain cases', prior to his issuing of a general order some months later. Morant also told troopers who protested when he decided to shoot Visser that he had orders to shoot Boers in khaki. They all believed those orders to be bogus, yet by Kitchener's admission, this policy was in operation before it became a formal order. How was an irregular soldier with no military experience expected to distinguish between one verbal order to shoot Boers that was official and another? That was the paradox facing men like Morant and Handcock in the field during the Boer War. Many statements made at the time confirm the abovementioned scenario. The ex-*Bulletin* contributor again cited the Canadian Scouts as an example:

> There are columns, such as the Canadian Scouts, in which it is understood right through that prisoners are not to be taken, but are to be shot right off. The commanding officer does not line his men up and say, 'I____, hereby give orders' etc. But there are other ways of achieving the same result.

These orders were to be viewed as encouragement and guidance, not strict instructions, and in order for such a risky policy to operate properly it also relied on a certain unity or esprit du corps amongst the unit concerned. The Canadian Scouts demonstrated this quality when their leader Gat Howard was killed by Boer treachery, but the same could not be said of the fractious BVC. Unlike the Canadians or Gordons, they had no desire to avenge Captain Hunt and Sergeant Eland. One possible reason is that under the lax command of Captain Robertson, BVC troopers were able to appropriate Boer cattle. However, that practice was discontinued after the arrival of Hunt and Morant. Captain Taylor became the sole beneficiary – the cattle being driven north to his farm in Rhodesia.

At best, Kitchener's apologists can claim that Morant misinterpreted a general order aimed at giving men in the field some latitude in matters of discipline in what had degenerated into an ugly war. However, given the malign presence of Taylor and the culture of murder he established, it is more likely that Taylor clearly spelt out the meaning of these 'instructions' for Morant.

At worst, Kitchener and his inner circle were guilty of establishing an extermination policy, then cynically covering it up to protect their reputations. When the activities of the BVC threatened to become public, Kitchener and Poore, as two of the architects of the policy, both had a vested interest in ensuring 'justice' was seen to be done. Either way, it was denied under oath that any order to shoot prisoners was issued. This denied the accused men, who had admitted shooting Boers under orders, any prospect of mitigation in respect to their death sentences – a point Kitchener stressed in his telegrams to both Roberts and the Australian Governor General.

Also, if the same people who made and implemented the take no prisoners policy also tried and executed Morant and Handcock, it raises serious doubts about the impartiality of the courts martial themselves. It would appear that the little knot of British officers who huddled together on the veldt to watch Morant and Handcock die 'game' all shared the same guilty secret. Little wonder that Kitchener busied himself elsewhere, and that Poore was 'visibly shocked' and Henderson, the Director of Military Intelligence, felt the need to ask for God's forgiveness.

IN PRACTICE, COURTS MARTIAL WERE meant to be independent forums, but in reality, the job of the British military was to ensure discipline was maintained in the ranks and to underpin the Army command structure, not to seek truth and justice. That much can be seen in the case of the first New Zealander shot in World War I, Trooper Frank Hughes. He had previously escaped the death penalty three times for desertion, but on the fourth occasion British Commander-in-Chief, Field Marshal Sir Douglas Haig, pre-empted the verdict of the court martial with the comment, 'Oh, no, he's got to die this time as an example.'

With regard to the typical court martial the film *Breaker Morant* did us a disservice by portraying the courts martial as something like a civilian court. The fact that Major Thomas only got one day to prepare for a capital case is a further indication of the standard of proof required by a British military court martial. It should also be pointed out that one day was actually an exception as most men did not have the luxury of legal counsel – a few words from a 'Soldier's Friend', their commanding officer, was usually all they got. All but one of the six trials was held in a public courtroom in Pietersburg, but any similarity between military and civilian law ended at the front door.

Men who came before a court martial were guilty until proved innocent. Punishment was often harsh and the fraternity of the officer class underpinned this system of rough justice. Public school, India, Free-masonry and the officer's mess were all powerful levers used to ensure that the punitive system of justice was maintained. In such a system, where the onus of proof is not as rigorous as in a civil court, injustices are inevitable. During the century since the execution of Morant and Handcock there have been reforms aimed at bringing military law into line with civilian law, which can be summarised by the phrase, 'a soldier is also a citizen'.

As we have seen, doubts about the guilty verdicts returned in the BVC courts martial have existed from the outset. On May 24, 1988, eighty-six years after the original trial, the citizens of Burra, South Australia, decided to put the evidence to the test in a re-creation of the trial that included both new and original evidence. The three Justices of the Peace who presided over the re-enactment felt that there was insufficient evidence and found them 'not guilty'. In the aftermath, the then Education Minister, Greg Crafter, began a campaign to have Morant's name added to the Adelaide War Memorial – a move which was criticised by author Kit Denton who turned against the man whose legend he created with his book *The Breaker*. However, the Burra verdict was supported by the former Chief Justice of South Australia, Dr Howard Zelling, who made the following comments in a letter to *The Adelaide Advertiser* on June 7, 1988:

> I have followed with interest the comments regarding Breaker Morant. I cannot see how Mr Denton can say Morant's guilt was clear when neither Morant nor his co-accused received a proper trial which the law says every accused person and a fortiori an accused person on trial for his life shall have.
>
> The summing up was so appallingly bad that no proper trial was had on either charge on which the accused were convicted. The major faults, which are the same in both summings up, are;
> * There is no direction on onus of proof.
> * There is no direction on the standard of proof – where an onus lay on the accused – as it did on some cases in those days.
> * There is no definition of what constitutes provocation at law.
> * There is a misdirection as to intending the natural consequences of one's acts.
> * There is no direction on the defence of honest and reasonable, but mistaken belief in facts

when if true might have afforded a defence.

* The defence case on any defence is never put in either summing up. The so-called summing up was, in short, a speech for the prosecution in each case.

Neither summing up would survive for one minute before a Court of Criminal Appeal (or a court martial appeal court for that matter). The foregoing should suffice to show that no debate is needed, as suggested by the Lord Mayor, and the Minister for Education is right in his views.

Whilst an Australian re-trial could be criticised for being partisan, a public debate on April 30, 2001, hosted by the Pietersburg Historical Society in the town in which Morant and Handcock were tried ninety-nine years before, also concluded that there was 'insufficient evidence' to justify the death penalty.

In order to execute a man the evidence must be incontrovertible and, clearly, this was not the case. In the 21st century, three words safeguard our liberty from the kind of arbitrary justice that was meted out to Morant and Handcock – *beyond reasonable doubt*. That is the standard of proof required by civilised society, but even by the rudimentary standards of a British military courts martial in 1902, the verdict against Morant and Handcock can no longer be reasonably regarded as a safe conviction given the contradictory evidence that has been produced since the original verdict was handed down. It should also be noted that despite many instances quoted in this book, only Morant and Handcock were tried and executed for shooting Boer prisoners.

Almost as though he suspected that history would demand an answer, Kitchener did give his opinion on legal matters:

[I]t does no good to act without the fullest inquiry and strictly on legal lines. A hasty judgment creates a martyr, and unless Military Law is strictly followed, a sense of injustice having been done is the result.

Pity he didn't follow his own advice! For me, the Australian reporter who wrote to *The Bathurst Advertiser* in the aftermath of the executions said it best:

What had been done by them was strictly in accordance with instructions and if they deserved death for their actions – at least a thousand others should have been shot in gloomy Pretoria gaol.

13

Loose Ends

Whate'er the final verdict from the Boer War long ago,
His ballads live, still vibrant with his talent's fitful glow,
And through their stirring rhythm it's difficult to see
A man who'd kill Dutch prisoners, and a
German missionary;
A man who loved the Outback, with bright
stars overhead,
With his saddle for a pillow and his blanket
for a bed . . .

'The Death of "Breaker" Morant' by Louis H Clark

THE BREAKER MORANT STORY DOESN'T end there. There are still loose ends, and important questions remain unanswered. For the past century, rumours of a conspiracy have persisted and now there is evidence that if Morant et al. were guilty, then they were not alone. Who else was involved? How deep did it go? Was it, as Thomas suggested, an international conspiracy that reached the upper echelons of the British and German Governments, or was it more local than that?

Kitchener's deception not only ensured Morant, Handcock and Witton took the blame for all the killings, but it allowed the real culprit to go scot free. The comment in *The Times* that 'Taylor's charge sheet was the same as that of Morant – yet he was acquitted' was echoed by many critics and commentators once details of the case came to light.

Captain Taylor's reputation as 'Bulala', the killer, preceded him, but Kitchener still made him Intelligence Officer cum Commissioner for Native Affairs and controlled him directly. His own Intelligence Officer, Captain De Bertodano, warned him about Taylor, but he was ignored. The only conclusion can be that Kitchener approved of Taylor's methods. 'Bulala' and his hand-picked private army established a 'culture of murder' in the Spelonken and it was he who inducted the vulnerable and vengeful Morant into his criminal fraternity. It was Taylor who ordered the first seven killings and told Morant's patrol to 'go out and avenge your brother officer' after Hunt's death. Like Robertson, Morant was nominal commander of Fort Edward after Hunt's death, but Taylor was the real power. Ex-Captain Robertson described him as 'Kitchener's spy', and from various statements made by the men of the BVC, it was taken as read that if Taylor approved, then Army HQ approved. Morant could not have shot Boer prisoners unless Taylor approved. Going back over the accounts of the various shootings, Taylor was the common denominator in every one of the twenty deaths that they were tried for at the courts martial and, as we have revealed, many others he was never called to account for. In each case, Morant consulted Taylor before shooting Boers – as though he needed his permission or approval first.

Morant killed twelve Boers in the belief they were connected to Hunt's death. He asked the eight Boers what had happened to Captain Hunt, and when they replied that he was dead, he shot them and retorted, 'That's for Captain Hunt'. Who supplied that information? Taylor was the intelligence officer, and as Morant had commented to Major Lenehan, Taylor's was 'the most reliable intelligence I've come across'.

Once the killings threatened to become public, Kitchener pulled Taylor out. Despite the evidence Enraght-Moony uncovered, the accusations of other BVC troopers and the testimony of ex-Captain Robertson, a star prosecution witness, Taylor escaped justice. He could not be convicted, as he knew too much and had powerful friends such as Cecil Rhodes. In the case of a native he shot through the head, Taylor claimed he meant to shoot over his head, but aimed too low! His defence was accepted and he was the only one acquitted. It made a mockery of Britain's tough stance on Boers who mistreated or killed natives. Both of the executed Boer commandants, Lotter and Scheepers, were found guilty of similar charges with less evidence against them.

What also rankles is that Taylor's true position in the Spelonken and the relationship to Army HQ was never fully disclosed at the trial. From the evidence given by BVC troopers, Enraght-Moony and ex-Captain Robertson, there is little doubt he was running the show at Fort Edward. As Morant and Handcock had refused to implicate Major Lenehan, and Colonel Hall had been sent to India, Taylor, and not Morant, was the superior officer, and if it could be established that he ordered the shooting of the prisoners, Morant and Handcock would have been protected. However, Taylor cleverly retreated behind his civilian status as intelligence officer cum native commissioner when charges were laid. It was claimed he held no military rank.

Taylor also escaped justice because he was able to buy Morant's silence on this issue. During the trial, Morant did not mention Taylor's role, and when Taylor said he had no knowledge of any orders to shoot prisoners, Morant did not jump up and accuse him of lying as he had done with other witnesses, even though confirmation from Taylor would have gone a long way to establishing the main pillar of his defence.

The reason for Morant's silence became apparent once the trial for the murder of the missionary Heese got underway. The accused erroneously believed that the principal crime for which they were being tried was the killing of Heese. It was the only charge they denied and offered an alibi for.

As has been detailed, the prosecution's case was far from conclusive, but at the eleventh hour, Handcock produced two Boer women who confirmed he was 'visiting' them on the afternoon Heese was murdered. That gave him a cast-iron alibi and the case collapsed. But who were those women? Both Mrs Schiels's sons worked for Taylor and his intelligence unit was based at Mrs Bristow's farm. The only explanation for this carefully coordinated evidence is that there was an agreement not to incriminate one another, a gamble that would have paid off had their lives really hinged on the Heese verdict.

A military court acquitted Taylor, leaving what Kit Denton described as 'a sick taste on the tongue'. All kinds of feeble excuses have been offered for this travesty of justice. The most common is that there were doubts about the court's jurisdiction over a semi-official civilian. Although he was clearly acting in a military capacity, he was tried as a civilian by a general court martial or military court, which actually had a greater propensity for awarding the death sentence than the more formal field general court martial that tried Morant and Handcock. The general court martial had no trouble sending many civilians and Boer rebels, commandants Lotter and Scheepers amongst them, to their deaths, so why not Taylor?

Despite claims to the contrary, white witnesses did

come forward to back up the charges against Taylor. Captain Robertson, the prosecution's star witness, testified to Taylor's role in the killings, as did Sergeant Morrison, who took the order to kill the first group of six Boers directly from Taylor. Enraght-Moony even had documentary evidence of Taylor's murder of natives, but the political will simply wasn't there. The one fact that has been missed time and again by historians is that *the same witnesses and the same testimonies that implicated Morant and Handcock also pointed the finger at Taylor. Yet they were not used to secure a guilty verdict in Taylor's case.*

Taylor stood trial, but it was a sham. Twenty murders took place in the Spelonken, but only thirteen were paid for. The fact that Kitchener tried to blame all twenty on Morant and Handcock in his telegrams to London also points towards Taylor being protected. Kitchener avoided Roberts' question about who appointed the accused officers to their positions. He feared that any focus on Taylor would lead back to his role in the Spelonken.

If any further proof were needed that Taylor was Kitchener's man, we need look no further than the medal roll for the South Rhodesian Volunteers where Captain Alfred Taylor's honours are listed. He was entitled to the Queens South Africa medals with clasps for Rhodesia, Relief of Mafeking and Transvaal and is also on the roll for the Kings South Africa Medal with clasps 1901 and 1902. Alongside his name it says 'for special services under Lord Kitchener June 1901– April 1902'. The Commander-in-Chief went to extraordinary lengths to protect his man. Kitchener ensured that Taylor was tried as a civilian, not a serviceman. This perhaps answers the question why the court of inquiry took so long. In World War I deserters were charged, tried and shot in twenty-four hours, yet the BVC courts martial took four months to complete. Why did Kitchener wait so long when he had so much to lose and had London breathing down his neck? The explanation came in a letter from Colonel St Clair, the Judge Advocate who presided over the courts martial of the Bushveldt Carbineers, to Sir Francis Jeune:

> Taylor was not tried by a Court Martial under the Army Act as at date of trial he had ceased to be subject to military law for three months.

The courts martial began almost three months to the day from Taylor's arrest – just long enough for him to escape through the back door. Colonel St Clair clearly felt that Taylor had a case to answer and had the court martial panel found them all guilty, it would have been harder to justify the executions of Morant and Handcock alone. A military court could hand down a not guilty verdict without recourse to the military legal team, whereas a court martial involved all kinds of formalities and was open to outside scrutiny.

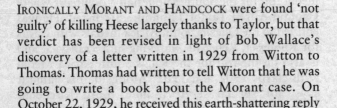

IRONICALLY MORANT AND HANDCOCK were found 'not guilty' of killing Heese largely thanks to Taylor, but that verdict has been revised in light of Bob Wallace's discovery of a letter written in 1929 from Witton to Thomas. Thomas had written to tell Witton that he was going to write a book about the Morant case. On October 22, 1929, he received this earth-shattering reply from Witton:

> But you must not forget Kitchener held Handcock's 'confession' in which he implicated me as an accessory no doubt unwittingly done while in a high shivery nervous state – but that accounts for the

reason why only Morant, Handcock and myself were punished and the War Office so adamant in my case. Had there been no Heese case the shooting of prisoners would not have worried them much. But the shooting of Heese was a premeditated and most cold-blooded affair. Handcock with his own lips described it to me. I consider that I am the one and only one that suffered unjustly (apart from yourself). Morant and Handcock being acquitted my lips were sealed.

In the preface to his 1974 book *The Australians at the Boer War*, historian Bob Wallace tells of the shock he felt at the moment he discovered the letter, and was in no doubt about the effect it would have had on Thomas:

I felt so stunned that as I looked across the room it seemed hard to realise that nothing else round me had changed in those few minutes . . . the effect on Major J.F. Thomas would have been shattering.

Thomas' single comment in a note attached to the original letter conveys his sense of resignation and defeat: 'I think it's best if we just forget the whole thing.'

Not surprisingly, Thomas's book never appeared, and Witton's letter has been taken at face value and Morant and Handcock are now adjudged to have murdered Heese. However, Witton's insistence in his 1929 letter to Thomas that he played a passive role in the cover up of the Heese murder is clearly at odds with his account of the events that led up to Handcock's 'confession' in *Scapegoats of the Empire*. After being kept in solitary confinement for weeks, with no access to legal counsel, he was pressured by the 'court of inquisition' to say that Morant gave the orders to shoot the prisoners and the missionary. When Handcock refused, he was sent back to solitary confinement to think it over before he was brought before the panel a second time. Witton said:

> Is it possible to conceive such an iniquity perpetrated in these days of supposed civilisation? – man charged with numerous murders shut up alone, without a soul from whom he could seek advice; condemned before he was tried. There could only be one ending; Handcock's mind gave way, and he was not responsible for his actions he was forced into making a statement which incriminated himself and Lieutenant Morant.

Handcock was obviously suffering from some kind of mental disorientation and no confession obtained under such duress would stand up to legal scrutiny today. There is no documentary evidence that the 'confession' actually existed – far less what was in it. Prosecutor Major Bolton, who made reference to it in correspondence, rightly suggested that it would 'clear up the whole matter', but it was clear that he had never seen it. Neither is it mentioned in the notebooks of the Judge Advocate General, Colonel St Clair, who had taken such care in assembling a watertight case. If it did exist he may have considered that the manner in which it was obtained had tainted it as evidence. Handcock may also have made admissions that were detrimental to the prosecution case and it was excluded, as according to military law, the whole confession would have to be admitted as evidence – not just selected parts. Yet, Witton, despite everything he said, believed Handcock. By his own admission he was not present when Morant allegedly told Handcock to go out and shoot Heese. So why did Witton change his mind in the intervening twenty-two years between writing his book and writing to Thomas?

Witton makes it clear both in his book and in his letter to Thomas that he felt that Handcock's 'confession' implicated him in the Heese killing, hence the reason he was found guilty of murder. However, legal opinions given after the trial suggest that was not the case. Both Judge Advocate Generals who reviewed the case agreed that Witton deserved the death sentence because he was part of the illegal court martial that sentenced Visser to death, and they did not believe that he shot one of the eight Boers in self-defence because he tried to grab his rifle.

Is there a hint of resentment in his comment, 'I consider that I am the one and only one that suffered unjustly (apart from yourself)'? Morant and Handcock had become folk heroes, whilst Witton had been forgotten and was shortly to lose his wife to cancer. Most likely he had put the whole affair behind him and wanted it left it the past. A new book by Thomas would have reignited the controversy, and this was the easiest way to dissuade him from writing it.

Other than Witton's letter, no other evidence has ever been produced to link Morant and Handcock to the death of Heese, despite the claims of the fifteen ex-BVC members who detailed the murders in a report to Colonel Hall. In fact, the chief eyewitness, Silas, described seeing a man in a corporal's uniform wearing non-military headgear and riding a poorly maintained horse. Who was he? One of Taylor's scouts? A Boer? Members of the BVC had been reprimanded for selling khaki uniforms to the Boers. In any event, the description of neither the man nor the horse sounded like Veterinary Lieutenant Peter Handcock.

Morant and Handcock were accused because on the day the missionary was shot, Morant was seen speaking to Heese, and Handcock left the fort shortly afterwards with a gun. The implication was that Morant told Handcock to shoot Heese because he saw the bodies of the eight Boers. But there is an important link missing from the chain of command. Evidence gathered later by Heese's family revealed that Heese went to see Taylor after the shooting of the eight Boers, swore at him, and then announced his intention to report the incident when he reached Pietersburg. After he left, Morant went to see Taylor, then spoke to Handcock, who rode off an hour later. Yet, despite Taylor being the common denominator in all the killings and the officer who ordered the death of the only other dissenter, Van Buuren, *it has never been suggested that Taylor might have been involved in the killing of Heese*. He would have known that none of the BVC would have been keen to shoot a Pastor and he had his own unit of trusted men who could have followed Heese without detection from Fort Edward. If Handcock was involved, would he, as the evidence suggests, have been sent out alone on such a mission? Who else was there? Taylor also had much to fear from an investigation. If news of the shootings became public, it would expose Kitchener and his hidden agenda.

I did hear about a tantalising piece of evidence that might finally settle this argument – if it ever comes to light. During a visit to South Africa in 2002 I met a local historian, Dr Louis Chavingon, who kindly gave me a guided tour around the Pietersburg/Fort Edward area. Throughout our many discussions about the Morant affair the issue of Heese came up, but was never satisfactorily resolved. One night he confided that there was something that might finally identify the guilty party.

Around five years ago Mrs Brand, a respected lady historian from the Pietersburg area, was employed by a local Pretoria church to sift through the papers of the late Dr Punt, a noted Boer War historian. He had collected material from all over the world, including Australia. Amongst this mountain of paperwork was one tiny scrap of paper with the following written on it:

'*I didn't murder the Boers, but I did shoot the mission-ary*'. At first she couldn't think what this could possibly relate to, then recalled that a Pastor Heese had been killed during the time of the BVC. Subsequent inquiries led Mrs Brand to a copy of Kit Denton's *Closed File*, which reproduced Handcock's last letter to his sister in Bathurst. The bottom of the letter appears to be ridged – as though a piece were torn off. The researcher made a trace copy of the tear and the handwriting, both of which appears to match Handcock's letter.

Unfortunately, it was some time later that Dr Chavin-gon heard about the discovery and before he could verify the find, the church had sold the archive to an Australian and it had been shipped overseas. The name of the buyer is unknown. The trace copy still exists, but without the original scrap of paper there is no proof that there was an original and therefore handwriting and true scientific tests to prove that both fragments were part of the same piece of paper cannot be conducted.

Other equally confusing snippets of new informa-tion continue to emerge, but for each push in one direction there seems to be a pull in the other direction. Author Bill Woolmore asked if it was coincidence that corporal Sharpe was reprimanded for selling his uniform to the Boers and the person Silas saw on the road was wearing a corporal's uniform? On the other hand, armoury historian, Steve Playford, noted that Silas said that the person he saw in the corporal's uniform was carrying a Mauser rifle, which would indi-cate a Boer, except that Handcock used a Mauser instead of the standard British Lee Enfield. In the group photo of the BVC officers, Handcock (pictured on the left of frame), is wearing a Mauser bandolier. During the courts martial when he and the other accused defended Pietersburg against a Boer attack, Handcock also used a Mauser. So, was the person Silas saw a Boer in corporal Sharpe's uniform, or Handcock disguised as a corporal? It appears that the identity of Heese's killer will remain a mystery a little longer.

There are still many unanswered questions and inconsistencies surrounding the Heese case, but the accepted theory that Morant and Handcock did it just because Witton said so is far from convincing.

THE LAST OF THE GREAT MYTHS surrounding the Breaker is that Morant and Handcock were executed because the Kaiser demanded retribution for the slaying of Heese. As I have established, Thomas began the rumour that external forces were involved after Major-General Kelly rejected his plea for a stay of execution on the grounds that the case had stirred up 'grave political trouble'. Thomas took Kelly's reference to mean German intervention over Heese, and the myth snowballed from there.

From the time of the courts martial until now, most informed opinion maintained that the death of Heese was the main issue, not the shooting of the Boers. However, memos between the officers compiling the case show that they had little evidence in the Heese case, and Bolton even suggested dropping it. Bolton's request to use a barrister to try the more legally complex Heese case was also denied. From the testimonies by both the BVC troopers and the officers, Kitchener knew that a guilty verdict would be easier to secure in the cases of the Boers. Judge Advocate General, Colonel James St Clair was confident that he could 'prove several charges' in the cases involving the Boers. The belief that Heese was the only case they had to defend was a fatal miscalculation on the part of the prisoners, but is yet more evidence that Kitchener was more concerned with covering his tracks with regard to his own policy.

It has never been considered that the 'grave political trouble' Kelly alluded to could refer to anything other than pressure from the German Government over Heese. No evidence of German collusion has ever been produced, and after his death it was quickly established that Heese was a British citizen, which would have negated any German demand for retribution.

The killing of Heese had caused an outcry in Germany and prompted exchanges between the British and German Governments, but prompted no action from Kitchener and other killings took place after the death of Heese.

The fact of the matter is that Kitchener cared little for the German missionaries as he regarded them as Boer spies. Three months before Heese was killed the War Office fielded complaints from the German Embassy about the harsh treatment of missionaries. Kitchener replied that his policy was to treat all missionaries who had not 'deliberately violated their neutrality' like 'all other law abiding non-belligerents'. However, he stressed that it was 'impossible to consider the attitude of some of these gentlemen as being neutral' and 'their neutrality has not been beyond grave suspicion'. These same allegations were again brought to Kitchener's notice, only a month after Heese's death. War Office documents also show that Kitchener kept updated lists of missionaries and their whereabouts.

The 'political difficulties' mentioned by Kelly emanated from a fiery speech given in Edinburgh on October 10, 1901 by Secretary of State for the Colonies, Joseph Chamberlain. In it he attacked the mounting continental criticism of the way Britain was prosecuting the war and accused the Germans of committing worse barbarities in the past:

There is one charge that undoubtedly does affect the

government. It is that we have been too lenient
towards our opponents. It is that we have not dealt
with the rebels or with guerrilla bands with sufficient severity . . . I think that the time has come –
is coming – when measures of greater severity may
be necessary, and if that time comes we can find
precedents of anything that we may do in the
actions of those nations who now criticize our 'bar-
barity' and 'cruelty', but whose example in Poland,
in the Caucasus, in Almeria, in Tongking, in Bosnia,
in the Franco–German War, whose examples we
have never even approached.

Chamberlain's speech caused a storm of protest in
Germany, where there was already heavy popular pressure for Germany to enter the war on the side of the
Boers. Rallies were held outside the Reichstag and huge
petitions presented to government ministers urging
Germany to declare war. A small regional conflict was
in danger of escalating into a world war. However, the
German Government refused to be dragged in and
maintained its 'neutral' stance.

Also, the idea that Britain would have danced like
marionettes to the German tune and ordered the execution of two of their own men is not borne out by the
attitudes of the time. After Chamberlain's speech, the
British press and Government were bullish and, if anything, it was the Germans who were trying to calm the
situation down. Had Germany wished to enter the war,
there were any number of pretexts and opportunities for
them to do so before Heese. Britain and Germany would
have their day, but not for another decade.

However, Chamberlain's ill-timed attack on Germany
made the British Government ultra-sensitive to any allegations of British war crimes. No sooner had that storm
been weathered than sketchy details came through about
the involvement of BVC officers in the shooting of Boer

prisoners and a missionary with German connections. Quick action was needed as contrary to Chamberlain's claim in his Edinburgh speech that the time had not yet arrived to introduce 'measures of greater severity' against the Boers, Kitchener was not the only one to issue orders to shoot Boers. Secretary of State for War, St John Brodrick, had proscribed the death penalty as early as May 1901. Following an incident at Vlakfontein where British soldiers were allegedly shot by Boer guerrillas after they had surrendered, Brodrick issued the following order:

> [M]embers of any commando by which such an outrage may be committed who may be captured and after trial proved to have been present on such occasion will be held guilty whether they actually committed the deed or not; that the leader . . . will be sentenced to death and other members . . . punished by death or less sentence, according to the degree of their complicity.

Once again, official diktats from the highest sources give lie to the claims of the prosecution, politicians and media that the British would never issue orders to shoot Boer prisoners.

British ministers saw that their double standard might now be exposed and quickly passed judgment on Morant and Handcock. Perhaps the missing question from Brodrick, to which Chamberlain made the enigmatic reply 'Two ought to be sufficient' was, how many executions will it take to get the international press off our backs? It worked. The execution of Morant and Handcock demonstrated their stern attitude to atrocities and silenced their continental critics.

Unluckily for Morant and Handcock, the expediency of the British Government overlapped with Kitchener's – to the same end, but for different reasons. The British Government wanted them dead because they killed prisoners, and not to act firmly would be seen as hypocritical, which allowed Kitchener to blame the BVC and cover his backside. Had Chamberlain not made that speech, the British Government might have examined the case more closely. Therefore, was it the issue of shooting prisoners generally and not Heese specifically that caused the 'grave political trouble' Kelly spoke of?

THE UNEQUAL JUSTICE METED OUT to the three Boer commandants Scheepers, Lotter and Kritzinger yields further evidence that politicians and soldiers were quite prepared to use executions for political or strategic ends. At the end of 1901, the Boers were still resisting and Kitchener was determined to make an example of the Boer commandants he had captured.

Lotter was executed for two murders and whipping a British subject – an ex-Boer who surrendered – and then trying to incite his brother to do likewise. Photographs of the wounds on the ex-Boer's back were circulated as evidence of Boer brutality. Lotter was shot on October 12, 1901.

Gideon Scheepers, at twenty-two, was the youngest and most dashing of all the Boer guerrilla leaders. After serving with Cronje and De Wet, he was sent south with Kritzinger to wreck trains, recruit Cape rebels and burn the farms of Cape traitors. This was in retaliation for the British burning Boer farms. Forty-five thousand British troops pursued 3000 Boer guerrillas, but couldn't catch Scheepers. He was only caught when he was left at a farm suffering from abdominal pains. He was tried on thirty charges of murder, seven of arson, and rough handling 'barbaric' treatment of natives. On one occasion he captured two men he believed to be traitors and made them draw lots. He shot one and sent the other back to his leader with a message.

Scheepers maintained that British law was no more superior than theirs; he had the right to shoot spies, as did the British, and in burning farms he was doing exactly what the British were doing in Transvaal, and was following orders from superiors. He denied some of the killings, saying others had done them, but freely admitted flogging 'Kaffir spies' and executing Afrikaner traitors. He claimed he was a British subject, but was born near Middleburg in eastern Transvaal.

He was executed in public at Church Square in Pretoria on January 18, 1902 by the Coldstream Guards. Like Morant, he died 'game'. He saluted his open grave and asked not to be bound or blindfolded, but his requests were ignored. In a final indignity, the officer commanding the firing party ordered him to be dropped into the grave instead of lowered. 'It made me feel sick', remarked one of the firing party. In their desire to ensure he didn't become a martyr, they threw his hat and the chair he was tied to into the grave and covered the contents with unslaked lime. Rebellion was part of the Boer tradition, and they had been shocked by the executions. It seemed fighting for liberty had been outlawed.

Many members of parliament, including Winston Churchill, thought it folly to create Boer martyrs. The trials of Boer leaders had aroused opinion in the United States, Germany, Holland and France. The US Senator for Colorado, Henry Moor-Teller, asked the US President to intervene and ask for mercy in Scheepers' case, but the plea came too late. Anxious to prove to the press and international opinion that it was a just sentence, the Secretary of State for War, St John Brodrick, released the trial transcripts.

Kritzinger almost became the third Boer leader to be executed after being wounded and captured whilst trying to help his wounded comrades escape a British patrol on December 16, 1901.

Kritzinger was charged with a similar set of offences as Scheepers – murder, robbery and train-wrecking. However, he was acquitted on April 7, 1902 when a letter was found in which he admonished those who burned the farms of ex-Boer 'traitors' living on the Cape. After the executions of Morant and Handcock, the press saw it as further proof of the impartiality of British justice, but was it impartiality or expediency? It might be argued that Kitchener was merely returning the chivalrous gesture made by Commandant De La Rey after he captured Lord Methuen. Every man in his commando, right down to the predicant, demanded that Methuen be executed immediately, but De La Rey decided to let him go despite the vehement protests. That may have some influence on his decision, but by sparing Kritzinger, Kitchener was also able to make a conciliatory gesture to the Boers and repair the good name of British justice at a stroke. Kritzinger's trial just happened to coincide with peace moves being initiated by the Boers.

On March 15, 1902, it was reported in Sydney's *Daily Telegraph* that Kritzinger's trial had been postponed because 'the evidence to hand is not complete'.

On March 24, acting President of the Transvaal, Mr Shalk W Burger, and party had arrived in Pretoria under the white flag of truce to meet Kitchener. They were then transported in a sealed train through enemy lines, as Lenin would later be, to Kroonstad to meet with other Boer leaders. Steyn and De Wet wanted independence, but Burger and Botha were happy to accept autonomy.

On March 27, Burger declared the forthcoming Friday a day to pray for peace. He believed the only road to peace was unconditional surrender.

On April 7, Kritzinger was acquitted of all charges.

On May 31, the peace declaration was signed at Vereeniging.

ALTHOUGH KITCHENER PRECEDED George Orwell's scathing critique of politics and power *1984* (written in 1948), by almost half a century, he was an early exponent of Big Brother's maxim – if you're going to tell a lie make it a *big* one. Putting all the evidence on a simple time line, there can be no doubt that Kitchener orchestrated the cover-up. He framed his case without telling the British or Australian Governments, secured a 'guilty' verdict, got the go ahead to execute Morant and Handcock on the basis of misleading information that did not represent all the facts and played on London's self-induced neurosis about prisoner atrocities. After the executions, Kitchener leaked the story to the media, which forced the British Government to back his story before the courts martial transcripts reached England. By the time they realised the case was not as cut and dry as Kitchener had claimed, the war was over, Kitchener was a hero, and suppressing the transcripts ensured that the damage was limited. It was bold, audacious, and arrogant even, but Kitchener got away with it – as he had done in the Sudan.

It has been suggested that because Kitchener commuted a death sentence on an Australian early in the war he had no bias against antipodeans. However, it should be pointed out that about ninety per cent of all death sentences were commuted and in the case of that Australian he had nothing to lose. Let's be clear, Morant and Handcock were made scapegoats for Kitchener not because they were Australian, *but because they were convenient*. It is clear from the various incidents described that the British regarded the colonials as lesser mortals and Kitchener knew executing two Australians would excite less press speculation and minimise the political fallout and the chance of further investigations.

In the end, it was nothing to do with the German

missionary, or the German Kaiser. It was not an international conspiracy, not even a national one, but a very local one designed to protect the reputation of a man who was prepared to lie, perjure and kill to protect it.

14

Rebel With a Cause?

Ten rifles spat those fateful shots that echoed
down the years,
When they executed 'Breaker' of the
Bushveldt Carbineers,
Fearlessly he faced them, erect, with lifted head,
'Shoot straight . . . don't make a mess of it,' were the
last words he said;
So was Morant a murderer, or did the soldiers fire
At a great and misjudged hero, a scapegoat of the Empire?

'The Death of "Breaker" Morant' by Louis H Clark

KIT DENTON, IN CORRESPONDENCE WITH a lady from
Adelaide in the 1980s, said of 'Breaker' Morant:

> The best description I know of him came from an
> old, old man who first told me about him over ten
> years ago. That fellow was an Adelaidian, had
> served with Morant in South Africa and called him,
> 'the bravest, bad bastard that ever lived' and I
> suspect that's close enough to the truth.

Love them or hate them, ambiguous figures like Morant
exist in every culture, but where does Morant fit into
the Australian psyche. 'Breaker' Morant may have been
wrongly executed, but he was no pillar of virtue. We

cannot ignore him, but neither can we build a monument to him. Why have Australians identified so strongly with the Breaker, whilst the British have hardly acknowledged him? There seem to be a number of reasons ranging from the maner of his death, the Australian preference for 'popular' rather than officially proscribed heroes, and the fact that he has become caught up in the search for the Australian identity.

Major Leneham revealed that Morant and Handcock had been offered a reprieve if they would only say that it was he and not Army HQ that gave the order to shoot prisoners. They refused and died with the truth on their lips.

This ultimate act of mateship is at odds with his critics' image of Morant as a profligate, selfish, ruthless, cruel, untrustworthy murderer who lied as easily about his origins as he did about the murders of thirteen men. If that were all true, why didn't he take the easy way out? He was offered a horse and a clear ride to the Portuguese border on many occasions during his incarceration. Did he put too much faith in British justice, or did he decide, somewhere along the line, that enough was enough and it was time to make a grand gesture? This book has examined all the reasons why Morant should not have been shot, without considering the proposition that he *wanted to die*. Was Morant the first modern hero – or anti-hero?

The Rebel by Albert Camus was first published in 1951, pre-dating the beatniks, James Dean and the counter-culture of the 1960s. It explores the role of the rebel in history. There are many ways to interpret an act of rebellion, but Camus suggests,

> Immediately the slave refuses to obey the humiliating orders of his master, he rejects the condition of slavery. The act of rebellion carries him beyond the

point he reached by simply refusing. He exceeds the bounds that he established for his antagonist and demands that he should now be treated as an equal. What was, originally, an obstinate resistance on the part of the rebel, becomes the rebel personified. He proceeds to put self-respect above everything else and proclaims that it is preferable to life itself. It becomes, for him, the supreme blessing. Having previously been willing to compromise, the slave suddenly adopts the attitude of All or Nothing. Knowledge is born and conscience awakened. As a last resort he is willing to accept the final defeat, which is death, rather than be deprived of the last sacrament which he would call, for example, freedom. Better to die on one's feet than to live on one's knees.

Camus perfectly articulated the subconscious process of reason Morant may have gone through during his imprisonment and trial. He believed he carried out his duty based on the orders of his superiors, orders he knew others had also received and acted on. Yet, like a slave, he had been punished for the misdeeds of his master (Kitchener). Though he was offered his freedom, if he would only betray a comrade or run away, his actions indicate he had already decided that self-respect was above self-preservation. It is this noble act of self-sacrifice that the ordinary person identifies with in Morant and has carried the name of this rebel into mythology. It is an innate, immutable feeling that everyone can identify with, and no amount of persuasion and moralising will shake it. The rebel lives in all of us. We may not all be able to perform such an act of self-sacrifice ourselves, but we can still recognise it in others.

Morant's first biographer, Frank Renar, saw that very quality in him, and though he believed that Morant did not deserve to be lionised, it was he who started the process. He could not resist the parallel between Morant and the knights of old. It is all there. Morant left Devon in 1901, a disillusioned man having failed to win back the affection of his father. He had for once taken the steady road and served faithfully, but led no charges and won no medals. He joined the BVC, a far more risky proposition than Baden-Powell's police, in order to win those plaudits. This 'debt of honour' he felt he owed his father is a recurrent theme in reminiscences by his friends and acquaintances. Harking back to what an old bush mate said of his banishment to Australia, self-sacrifice and honour were, at a deeper personal level, important to Morant: '. . . he left the land of his birth accused of a social transgression and – rather than destroy the good name of one who had a chivalrous claim upon him – he destroyed himself.'

Once in the BVC, he did his utmost to gain recognition. He distinguished himself as leader of B Squadron and then turned the lazy, corrupt wastrels of A Squadron into an efficient and feared fighting force. But for the death of Hunt and the prisoner of war imbroglio, his daring capture of Commandant Kelly might have earned him a Distinguished Service Order. Like Dante, he felt doomed to wander interminably round the seven circles of hell without any hope of redemption. Renar felt he was properly punished, but he could not get over the inherent tragedy and gallantry of a man who risked all to repair the hurt he had caused, and gave his life in the process. Camus says of the decision to die:

> If an individual actually consents to die, and, when the occasion arises, accepts death as a consequence of his rebellion, he demonstrates that he is willing to sacrifice himself for the sake of a common good which he considers more important than his own destiny. If he prefers the risk of death to a denial of rights that he defends, it is because he considers that

the latter are more important than he is. He acts, therefore, in the name of certain values which are still indeterminate but which he feels are common to himself and to all men.

That Morant was just a larrikin is a common rejoinder, but it is an oversimplification of a much more complex character. Larrikins don't die to make a political point – they just go on raging against the world until they're found dead in a ditch. Morant was well read, had a lyrical soul and was alive to his situation. He knew all was lost. Hunt, his entree back into English society, was dead, and his reputation ruined whatever the outcome of the courts martial. 'He gambled with his chances all through life, and the cards ran out against him,' as Paterson put it. He knew there was nowhere left to go. He couldn't go back to the bush and now he could never return to England. All that was left was a final noble gesture. And in death he achieved what he could not in life.

IMAGINING HARRY MORANT'S LAST moments on the veldt as he awaited his executioners' bullets, I see the face not of a man, but of a boy. 'You've got it wrong again Harry!' says the stern voice of an unforgiving father. Harry Morant was born on the wrong side of the blanket and died on the wrong side of the law. His life story reads like a Greek tragedy, and as Renar remarked, 'for as hard as he tried he could not outrun the Erinyes which pursued him'.

Morant's defiance of the officers who offered him a deal, his behaviour in court, his final iconoclasm and his epitaph were a *cri de coeur* from a man who felt unjustly done by from the cradle to the grave.

All his life his honour had been questioned, and

although he had worn his sackcloth with humility, he was not forgiven. Now he was going to have his say. His hero Byron, whose tomes he carried with him and whose deeds and verse he tried to emulate, claimed he was 'born to resistance' and died fighting for Greek independence in 1824. Morant also saw the gates of Valhalla open before him and also chose a hero's death. They were both aged thirty-six.

Many great writers have searched for the bon mots to convey the classical tragedy of Morant's life – the strong ambivalence aroused by the tale of this chivalrous n'er-do-well whose life was wasted, yet his destiny fulfilled.

For my part, I have yet to hear anything better than the words of Morant's good mate and patron JCL Fitz-patrick. From *The Good Old Days of Molong*, one of the many books of reminiscences he wrote in his later years, comes the following:

> I have met in wayside hamlets, far out back in New South Wales and Queensland occupying the hum-blest positions or indulging in the wildest orgies as they knocked down their remittance – money men whose fathers and brothers occupy positions of great eminence in that land which, with all its faults, is today the envy of the other nations of the earth. They are the harum scarum elements of the country from which they come – the Harry Morants and the Sir Harry De Houghtons of the aristocracy; and they came along to us or are sent here, so that their fires may burn out – so that they may end or die, and they generally do the latter, for a 'short life and a merry one' is the motto which, for the most part, these wild spirits, filled with love of adventure and strong drink, have emblazoned upon the banners under which they fight.

For Australians, Morant's willingness to take a bullet for a mate and the fact that he stuck to the truth when he might have escaped with a lie, encapsulated the rebel heart of Eureka and the Southern Cross which still beats beneath our more sophisticated veneer. As Henry Lawson put it in *Freedom on the Wallaby*:

> So we must fly the rebel flag
> As others did before us,
> And we must sing a rebel song
> And join in rebel chorus.

However, there is a general reluctance amongst historians to include popular heroes in Australia's relatively short and bloodless history. The 'bogey of barbarism', as Manning Clark described it, has worried historians and social commentators ever since Australia first showed any pretension to civilisation. They proscribed the championing of the convict, the Eureka pioneers and the bushranger, without first considering whether the bogeymen had a valid point. Did the Eureka 'diggers' and Ned Kelly make a point about truth, justice and the social inequities of their time? Did Morant have a point about the callousness of war? Did they not all force a change in attitudes and laws that enable us to enjoy the democracy and freedom we take for granted today?

Ironically, going to war to support the Empire was seen as the way to cleanse Australia's convict spirit and enoble her heroes. However, that argument would hold more water if we had not named our cities and streets after men who devised and administered one of the most insidious social experiments in human history. Nonetheless, Clark is adamant about the mythologising of Morant:

> Once again Australia and its savage past caused its victims to celebrate as a folk hero a liar, a thief and a drunken lout, a scoundrel, a believer in the rule of fist and a murderer of innocent people.

Every culture has its popular heroes, names that will never appear on the sanitised national pantheon. Maybe it's better that way. The Breaker will serve to remind Australians what happens when you get involved in other people's wars and that governments don't always tell the truth. As Camus observed, the rebel does have his role in history.

THE BREAKER HAS ALSO BECOME part of the ongoing search for the Australian identity. His execution came just after Federation, when Australia was still trying to define and enshrine what was distinctly Australian, whilst still maintaining the Imperial connection. There was no blueprint for a British colony going it alone – new laws, principles and national characteristics would have to evolve over time. It was both unfortunate and opportune that when Australia became a nation, it was fighting a war.

At a base level, the public did not believe that Morant and Handcock were given a 'fair go', which was recognised as more of a fundamental principle in Australia than in Britain. Implicit in British military law and the way it operated was the attitude that the lower-class ranks accepted the right of the upper-class officers to punish them. The Boer War had already demonstrated to the average 'digger' that there were intrinsic philosophical differences between the Poms and the Aussies, and the Wilmansrust, Morant, Handcock and Witton cases merely reinforced this. Maybe no-one had yet defined what was and wasn't Australian, but it wasn't about asking your citizens to volunteer for war, giving them orders and then shooting them for carrying them out. Prophetically, Renar recognised that whatever Morant's limitations as a hero, we might find something of value in his death:

> [T]he grievance has arisen, perhaps to be the muddy
> source from which will rise a river of regeneration
> for Australia, just now mad with Jingoism. Is it the
> fate of 'The Breaker' wearing his blood-besmeared
> halo to lead Australians back to the path of Right?

Morant and Handcock did indeed 'lead Australians back to the path of Right' and left an important legacy in the form of Section 98 of the 1903 *Defence Act*, which decreed that never again could an Australian serviceman be tried by a 'foreign' court martial.

In a retrospective on Morant and the Bushveldt Carbineers, Boer War historian Craig Wilcox wondered why Morant and Handcock did not think to claim Australian citizenship when charged. In 1902, being an Australian servicemen did not grant you immunity from prosecution by the British military as it did in later wars. Going back to the reply Trooper Parry's father received from the War Office after Wilmansrust and the contract Morant signed in Adelaide, Australian servicemen in the Boer War were legally and severally soldiers of the British Crown. Moreover, Morant and Handcock had left their Australian units and joined the BVC, which was raised as an Imperial irregular unit. Thomas warned the irregulars who returned to Australia with him that by joining British irregular units they were sacrificing any protection they had as Australians, but as Clark pointed out, no-one foresaw that this was the price Australia would have to pay for 'the Imperial connection'.

Australia did not have a Defence Act when Morant and Handcock were shot, and it was not until 1904 that one was promulgated. It was part of the ongoing struggle over the scope of Australia's defence policy and who would command its forces. In 1901, the first Defence Minister, Sir John Forrest, who had no experience of military affairs, was forced to modify a Draft

Bill that was drawn up by the six commandants of the six colonial forces – three of whom were Imperial officers and three of whom had served in the British Army. If passed it would have effectively allowed the British to deploy Australian troops overseas and vested control of Australian forces not in the new Commonwealth Government of Australia but it the hands of the Commander-in-Chief of British forces. Even after Forrest removed those offending sections, there were still strenuous objections to it in the House of Representatives and the Bill was abandoned.

Hutton drafted a second *Defence Act* in 1903. He tried to achieve his own Imperial ends through the Bill, again forcing Forrest to amend it. Even then, the Opposition accused Forrest of being 'strongly imperialist' and numerous changes were made before the Bill was finally passed. These prevented conscription outside times of war or a direct attack on Australia.

What sparked Section 98 was Forrest's recommendation that the Australian forces adopt the British *Army Act* as its disciplinary code because it would be an extremely complex and time-consuming task to formulate its own. Mindful of the shortcomings of the arrangement during the Boer War that saw Australia with no control over the discipline of its own troops, members only agreed on the proviso that Australia held the power of veto over disciplinary matters. The importance of Section 98 was not realised until the British tried to execute Australian servicemen in World War I. In that war alone, 121 Australians were sentenced to death by British military courts martial, but, due to Section 98, none were executed,[†] despite the entreaties of the British commanders.

† *Two Australian troopers, Sweeney and Braithwaite, were shot in World War I, but both belonged to New Zealand units which did not pass legislation preventing its servicemen being executed.*

It has been erroneously claimed that Section 98 was created as a reaction to the executions of Morant and Handcock. The legislation was, in fact, modelled on earlier colonial legislation: New South Wales (1871), Queensland (1884) and Tasmania (1885), which were all modelled on the Canadian legislation of 1868. But all those pieces of legislation had one clear aim – to ensure that local units would remain under local control – something Australia lost sight of in the Boer War. As neither of the earlier drafts of the *Defence Act* contained Section 98 it is a reasonable conclusion that by the time Forrest presented his Second Bill in 1903, the Wilmansrust, Morant, Handcock and Witton cases all provided the *political impetus* for its inclusion in the final bill. Politics is essentially no different now than it was a century ago. It is driven by media, issues and public opinion and there is nothing like popular outrage to galvanise a politician into action.

JF Thomas, who defended Morant and Handcock and had an ongoing interest in Australian military affairs, had no doubt that Section 98 was inspired by the two men he could not save. In the frontispiece of his personal copy of Witton's book *Scapegoats of the Empire*, Thomas noted:

> These officers were truly scapegoats – shot or imprisoned not so much for their own sins but for those of the system of militarism in which they were involved and which was responsible for the drastic instructions secretly issued from high places to Irregular Corps. against the indomitable Boers. In the later European wars Regular Army Officers were not given the opportunity to season themselves by victimising Colonial Officers, as was the case in the South African war.

For that alone we owe them a debt of thanks, because without that legislation, there is little doubt that World

Wars I and II would have produced many more Morants and Handcocks.

THE BELIEF THAT MORANT AND HANDCOCK did not get a fair go found a new resonance eighty years later when Australia again found itself in the aftermath of a messy war. Part of the reason for the phenomenal success of the film *Breaker Morant* was timing. It was released in 1980, just after Vietnam, a war in which 'Uncle Sam' had got Australia to do what General Hutton and the British never could – conscript Australians to serve overseas.

The 60s had, like most things, come late to Australia, and under Gough Whitlam we embarked on a journey of exploration of the Australian identity. *Breaker Morant* happened along at the right moment for both the public and the film-makers. It perfectly articulated that sense of who we are and what we're about, and the public feeling about the wisdom of sending Australians to fight someone else's war. We empathised with Morant's feeling of injustice and he became the perfect metaphor for the futility of war.

In every war there is a character like Morant – a rebellious Renaissance spirit who ends up on the wrong side of the 'great cause' and is shot, imprisoned or sent to his certain death. In doing so, he rises above the hum-drum of propaganda and jingoism and reminds us that the bad guys aren't always the ones wearing the black hats.

The Boer War and Vietnam were over sixty years apart, but they had many parallels. When Morant was shot, man had not yet flown, but by the time Lieutenant William Calley[†] was on trial, man was about to land on the moon, but he was still fighting the same stupid wars. The Boer War had Morant's iconoclastic comment, 'This is what comes of Empire building' and Vietnam had Calley's, 'You're looking to hang someone aren't you?' Although the nature and circumstances of their crimes differed, both became scapegoats for covert policies to eliminate the enemy conceived by men with similar names and policies – Kitchener and Kissinger. The latter's comment to a Senate inquiry that, 'Foreign policy isn't missionary work', says it all. The two cases spanned the 20th century and brought into sharp focus the unfailingly brutal nature of warfare and the destructive power of patriotism which blighted a century of incredible technological progress.

Through the sacrifice of Morant and Calley, the myth is exposed. The 'war machine' is the real enemy – that unseen political/military/bureaucratic conspiracy that persuades ordinary men that it is noble to sacrifice themselves for nebulous concepts like The Empire, *Lebensraum* or The Domino Theory. Breaker Morant's is a powerful story with a strong moral for Australians, but the message is a universal one. After Vietnam, it was no longer acceptable for young men to be sacrificed on the altar of war. If Morant is to be a hero, let him be an anti-war hero because his refusal to betray his senior officer exposed the hypocrisy at the heart of the British Empire and the business of war for what it is – victory regardless of the human cost. As President Kruger said, 'War is just a continuation of politics by another means.'

Once the information in this book becomes public, I hope an inquiry will be set up to investigate the executions of Morant and Handcock, as New Zealand did for their servicemen executed in the Great War with

---

† *Calley was accused of murdering civilians in a raid on My Lai in 1968. He was tried and found guilty, but not executed. He too claimed he was acting on orders, which was also denied. Operation Phoenix – of which Calley was the tip of the iceberg – was a covert operation to terrorise the civilian population into submission, rather like Kitchener's farm-burning programme.*

Canada about to follow suit.[†] If it is concluded that they were wrongly executed, then their names should be placed on the honour roll. They volunteered to fight for their country and it's the least their country can do for them.

It's also time the RSL stopped being so hypocritical. The recent ABC television series *Australians at War* put on the record what has been known for decades – that Morant and Handcock were not the only Australians to kill prisoners of war. If they can consider reconciliation with the Japanese, who were guilty of far worse crimes, then they should be able to find it within themselves to consider new evidence that might redeem two of their own. It seems hard lines that a soldier can be forgiven by his enemies, but not by their own countrymen. The ANZAC spirit was based on never leaving a mate behind, but Morant and Handcock were and have not been given a 'fair go', which is an intrinsic part of the Australian ethos. It is easier to say that they were convicted in a court of their peers and ignore the contrary evidence that has been presented. If reconsidering the case of Morant and Handcock means questioning our mythological relationship with Britain and accepting that whilst we were partners we were not always treated as equals – so be it.

Australia became a nation one hundred years ago and one of its most solemn responsibilities was to ensure that its citizens got proper justice. Edmund Barton abdicated that responsibility and it's time the present administration stepped up to the mark. Anything less would be un-Australian. As Abraham Lincoln put it, 'Fellow citizens, we cannot escape history'.

† *The New Zealand Government commissioned an ex-Judge to examine the evidence against the New Zealanders executed during the Great War. On the balance of evidence it was felt that they were unfairly executed and a Bill to pardon those men is currently making its way through Parliament. Canada is also beginning that same process.*

Epilogue

Shoot Straight, You Bastards! is a cautionary tale of a vainglorious man called Kitchener who hated having his photo taken, but was prepared to put his own self-interest above the institution he claimed to serve, the law of the land and of God. He gained the fame and adoration he craved, but fell short of his ultimate goal, to become the Viceroy of India, and, as all men must do, faced his Judgment Day on June 5, 1916. The following dispatch appeared in *The Sydney Morning Herald*:

OFFICIAL ANNOUNCEMENT

The following cable from the Secretary of State for the Colonies has been received by his Excellency the Governor General:

LONDON, JUNE 6

Deeply regret to inform you that H.M.S. *Hampshire* proceeding to Russia with Lord Kitchener and staff on board, was sunk by a mine or torpedoed west of the Orkneys last night in a heavy sea.

There is little hope of any survivors.
(signed BONAR LAW)

In the decades since the sinking of HMS *Hampshire*, it has been variously rumoured that it was the work of Irish Fenians or Fritz Joubert Duquesne, a Boer working as a German agent, and that Kitchener didn't slip off the deck, but was pushed into the cold, grey North Sea. Had his past caught up with him? Who knows?

KITCHENER'S BOOTS AND GREATCOAT POCKETS *filled with freezing water as they dragged him down into the darkness to meet the Almighty God that made him. A strange serenity had replaced the initial electric shock he felt when his warm body hit the freezing water. That had been followed by blind panic as he clawed his way back to the oily surface where the piteous screams of the dying rent the air as men were poached like eggs in the boiling sea and giant tongues of hellfire licked across the smoke blackened sky above him. The whole scene reminded him of one of those hideous medieval tableaux of Hades.*

As he continued drifting downwards, Kitchener remembered a hospital visit and an old salt, who had been plucked from the sea minus both legs, telling him that drowning was a pleasant experience, once the brain is starved of oxygen and you stop struggling and surrender.

Maybe there's something in that, he thought, and was suddenly struck by the irony that the less than exotic Scottish Orkneys would be the final resting place of Lord Kitchener of Khartoum. He was just consoling himself with the thought that at least all his secrets would be safe in Davy Jones' locker, when he saw a bright light ahead.

If hell is up there, then heaven must be down here, he reasoned dimly through rapidly fading senses.

This is it. I am about to learn the great secret. *But as he neared the light he saw the faces of those he had condemned waiting patiently for him 'on the other side', standing next to the Seat of Judgment.*

Afterword

Last year, the release of *Shoot Straight, You Bastards!* was accompanied by speculation that it had all been said before and no-one would be interested. How wrong can you be? *Shoot Straight, You Bastards!* received blanket media coverage and demonstrated that the 'Morant Affair' still has the power to arouse powerful emotions.

When news of the executions of Morant and Handcock broke, Australia was at war, patriotic passions were high, communication slow and there were no Australian correspondents on the ground. In such circumstances it is easy to understand how Morant and Handcock were demonised, but press opinion changed once conflicting evidence emerged that contradicted Kitchener's deceitful telegram to the Australian Government.

However, more than a century on, with the benefit of hindsight and with a greater appreciation of the realities of war and much published research, it is less easy to understand how the idea that they got what they deserved still prevails in some quarters. Wading through broadsheets where error-strewn opinion pieces masqueraded as fact, I often had to remind myself that this was the 21st, not the 19th century.

Predictably, The Returned Services League (RSL) and Australian War Memorial (AWM), who have long been opponents of any attempt to challenge the original verdict, were unmoved. Although the AWM refused to hold a public debate and tried to downplay the centenary of their execution, the event was marked with a ceremony in Melbourne, as well as ceremonies in a number of other regional centres and in Pretoria where a new stone was dedicated at their grave. Senator Julian McGuaran of Gippsland also acknowledged the historic landmark by asking questions in the Senate.

The first edition of *Shoot Straight, You Bastards!* forced the AWM to respond publicly. Those statements are dealt with comprehensively in the following material. But their contradictory admissions that Morant and Handcock were made an example of and other equally guilty parties were not punished, whilst still arguing they got a fair trial only confirms the popular belief that they were 'scapegoats'. They seemed more concerned with the cult of Morant, than whether he received a fair trial.

The success of the first edition of *Shoot Straight, You Bastards!* and the sterling research work done by retired Colonel Barry Caligari prompted me to begin work on the material that follows. Barry's long-standing interest in the 'Breaker' Morant saga and understanding of the workings of military law enabled us to examine the courts martial in more detail. Traditionally, historians have stuck to examining the evidence presented at the courts martial, but no-one had looked at the legal detail to see whether the trial adhered to the required legal procedures. The following material confirms that the AWM's argument that the courts martial must have been fair because it lasted six weeks is based more on blind faith in British justice than any objective assessment of the facts.

I believe this to be the most comprehensive deconstruction of the Morant courts martial ever undertaken. The case that they did not receive a fair trial is now clearly made and needs a champion to carry it forward to our political masters with the recommendation that it be re-examined, by an independent judicial review if necessary. New Zealand has already set a precedent with its re-examination of World War I court martials. Following Senator McGuaran's questions in the Senate, Veterans' Affairs Minister, Danna Vale, promised to review any new information and we look forward to her response.

By necessity, the following material is more technical and because it will be presented as a self-contained document it repeats material used in the main body of this book, but this is essential to a clear understanding of the context in which the argument is being made.

Once again I am deeply indebted to many good souls who helped me revise and expand this new edition. Barry Caligari must come top of the list for his tireless work on the following material and Steve Playford for his unstinting attention to detail. My heartfelt thanks for all their help and support goes to Iris Bleszynski, Louis Chavingon, Tim Fischer, David Hallet, Anthony Hoy, Brian Meldon, Julian McGauran, Jim McJannett, Paul Naish, Koos Roets, Ted Robel, Geoffrey Robertson, Piet Steytler, Helen Styles, Beech Thomas and Joe West.

The Morant Affair: Murder or Justice?

CONTENTS

INTRODUCTION

One hundred years after the execution of Lieutenants Morant and Handcock, the so-called 'scapegoats of the [British] Empire' is still the most controversial chapter of Australia's short military history. As noted by historian Craig Wilcox in the recently published, *Australia's Boer War: The War in South Africa 1899–1902*, the Morant Affair has cast a shadow over other heroic deeds, such as the defence of Eland's River and individuals such as Lieutenant Neville Howse, the first Australian to ever be awarded a Victoria Cross. This will continue whilst public opinion remains sceptical about the official version of events. Actions taken by the government of the day and later administrations to defend the position of Major Robert Lenehan,[1] secure the release of Lieutenant George Witton and to ensure that never again were Australian servicemen subjected to the arbitrary justice of foreign court martials, indicate serious misgivings about the executions.

Despite a century of scepticism, the custodians of our military history, The Australian War Memorial (AWM) and The Returned Services League (RSL), have both maintained the establishment line that the courts martial were fair and the sentences justified.[2] But historians are not lawyers and these institutions have based their argument on a subjective *historical* viewpoint and ignored compelling *legal* evidence to the contrary that dates back to Issac Isaacs' first review of the case in 1902. However, recent admissions by Morant's chief critic, AWM historian, Craig Wilcox, that the courts martial in question delivered only, 'partial justice',[3] and that the long-held belief that Morant and Handcock were 'scapegoats' was at least 'half true',[4] suggest that the weight of recent evidence is making their previous 'hard line' more difficult to defend. Furthermore, he concedes that, '[Captain] *Taylor's escape was shameful*'[5] and '*Kitchener wanted to make an example of Morant and Handcock*',[6] whilst Peter Stanley of the AWM concurs that: 'Morant and Handcock weren't the only British soldiers to kill Boers . . . others should have been charged with crimes as bad and no one would pretend that Lord Kitchener was not a ruthless commander in an increasingly brutal war.'[7]

Comments such as, 'our concern is that Bleszynski's book might entrench Morant as a national hero'[8] from RSL President Major-General Peter Phillips and, 'I don't think he's the hero some people make him out to be'[9] from the AWM's Geoffrey Blainey suggests that they have confused *moral* justice with *legal* justice. They appear more concerned with the cult of Morant, or what Manning Clark termed 'the bogey of barbarism', the Australian penchant for glorifying those who take the law into their own hands. However, the moral high ground can only be claimed if British conduct and justice were above reproach. That Morant shot Boers and deserved some punishment is not in dispute, but the severity of the sentence, the discharge of other equally guilty parties at what was supposed to be an impartial courts martial and Kitchener's denial that he issued orders to shoot prisoners most certainly are.

But however one feels about Morant the man and the crimes for which he was convicted, in a democracy the ends must never be allowed to justify the means where the law is concerned. Where men have been tried for their lives there is no such thing as Wilcox's 'partial justice'. If the original verdict is not 'beyond reasonable doubt' then it must be tested.

Despite the concessions made above, the AWM reacted to the publication of fresh evidence rather like the original court of inquiry. They held an in-house review behind closed doors, acted as both judge and jury and then used their own publication, *Wartime*, to dismiss it out of hand.[10] Questions in the Senate from National Party Senator Julian McGauran to the Director of the AWM, Major-General Steve Gower, and letters to Veterans' Affairs Minister, Danna Vale, met with a similarly negative response. However, the Veterans' Affairs Minister did offer to consider any fresh evidence on the matter. The authors of this paper, supported by learned legal and historical opinion, believe that there is a compelling case for a full judicial review and that it should be conducted by someone, outside of the AWM or RSL, with the appropriate legal experience.

To rectify this miscarriage of justice it would be necessary for the British authorities or the Australian Parliament to order an independent judicial review – as done recently in New Zealand with the cases of those servicemen executed during World War I. If it is found that the legal process was flawed then the convictions must be quashed, a pardon granted and the names of Morant, Handcock and Witton posthumously added to either the Roll of Honour or the Commemorative Roll (for Australians who served in Imperial units). Only when this issue has been properly investigated will it finally be laid to rest.

SUMMARY

At the end of November 1900, having captured all the main population centres, Lord Roberts, Commander-in-Chief of British forces in South Africa, declared the Boer War 'practically over', handed over command to General Kitchener and returned to England. In an effort to wear down British resolve, the Boers adopted a strategy of guerrilla warfare and Kitchener responded by introducing 'scorched earth', 'concentration camp', and 'block-house' policies to terrorise resistance and isolate the guerrillas from their supporting population. In addition, he deployed numerous 'irregular' units that showed little regard for the text-book conduct of war. The Boers reciprocated in kind and the war entered a spiral of violence, which became increasingly more spiteful, and brutal, as the war dragged on.

His failure to defeat the small and scattered Boer commandos with the largest army the British had ever assembled caused great frustration and challenged Kitchener's military pre-eminence. Criticism from within the army as well as from home and abroad increased, and Kitchener's callousness, lack of compassion, competence and fitness for command came under intense scrutiny. By

September 1901, rumours were rife that he was about to be relieved of his command and to make matters worse, news came in that a 'German' missionary, named Heese, had been murdered in northern Transvaal where an irregular unit, the Bushveldt Carbineers (BVC), was based. The situation worsened in early October when he received a copy of a letter compiled and signed by fifteen members of the BVC, which detailed other alleged atrocities. Kitchener realised that without decisive action the fragile peace process he had tentatively re-opened with the Boers was doomed and a damaging row with Britain's critics would follow. He recalled the BVC from Fort Edward and ordered the arrest of the BVC officers.

His legal department informed him that there was insufficient evidence to guarantee a conviction in the Heese case, so to ensure the successful outcome he needed, Kitchener cobbled together several cases of shooting Boer prisoners, which had previously been ignored. Ample historical evidence exists that Kitchener's brutal treatment of the civilian population desensitised moral sensibilities on both sides and that the shooting of prisoners by both sides had become prevalent during the latter stages of guerrilla warfare.

This paper will explore Kitchener's callous and clever plan to neutralise the adverse effects of the Heese case, regain the initiative and improve his tarnished credentials with the Boers, and in so doing, foster peace talks and be rid of South Africa. This plan, to a large degree, depended on the protection of three officers (Captain Alfred Taylor, Captain James Huntley Robertson and Colonel Francis Hall) from the full force of the law and preventing Hall from giving evidence, which could further discredit Kitchener. The favourable treatment extended to these officers was to the detriment of the other accused. By his actions, Kitchener ensured that the defence was ill-prepared and that evidence vital to the defence was not presented at the court of inquiry, in any summary of evidence, or during the eventual courts martial. It has also been speculated that the suppression of the courts-martial transcripts supports a cover-up by British authorities, who knew the proceedings would not stand up to independent legal scrutiny.

This theme has been pursued by a number of learned legal minds during the past century. Issac Isaacs first commented on the case[11] in the declaration that accompanied the petition of 100,000 names sent to King Edward VII on September 17, 1902, in an attempt to secure the release of Lieutenant George Witton, whose death sentence had been commuted to life imprisonment. Witton only served two and a half years and lived to write a damning account of the controversy entitled, *Scapegoats of The Empire*.

In more recent times, critical legal comment on the Morant case has been passed by the former Chief-Justice of South Australia, Dr Howard Zelling,[12] John Francis QC, Geoffrey Robertson QC, Professor Helen Styles, lecturer in international law at Macquarie University and member of the Advisory Committee on international humanitarian law to the Australian Red Cross, NSW, and Kevin Rudd,[13] Labor's shadow spokesman for international affairs.

This paper concentrates on legal and historical issues that arose before, during and after the courts martial. Incorrect process and failure to comply with the Rules of Procedure or the entering of a plea in bar of trial, jeopardised a fair hearing and the resultant findings were 'unsafe'. The fact that most official records relating to the courts martial are missing is not a reasonable argument for ignoring this injustice. The availability of other primary sources compensates for the absence of official records and gives a sufficiently clear picture to demonstrate, firstly, an unequivocal doubt where 'beyond reasonable doubt' was the legal yardstick for guilt of the accused, and, secondly, a systematic perversion of legal process.

Official records

The official documents relating to the court of inquiry and the courts martial are missing. One theory holds that a conspiracy of silence within the British Government has prevented these records from being made public, as to do so would, in some way, prove that those convicted were wrongly convicted. As early as April 9, 1902, the British Government announced that all courts-martial proceedings would be subject to the usual embargo.[14] A letter from the Public Records Office (PRO) dated July 7, 1997, confirmed the embargo had applied on individual courts martial for 75 years and, for some documents, 100 years. In addition, the PRO pamphlet on Records Information states that, 'papers for trials between 1850 and 1914 . . . were destroyed by bombing in 1940'. Kit Denton, however, in his book *Closed File*, gives good reasons to believe that the relevant records in the 'Morant Affair' were 'destroyed under statute'.[15] Philip Magnus in *Kitchener* records that Kitchener removed official documents from the War Office files[16] and destroyed private correspondence.[17] If true this would suggest that the historical perspective has been skewed strongly in favour of Kitchener's version of events.

The Manual of Military Law

The *Manual of Military Law*, 4th Edition, 1899, is rarely, if ever, quoted in bibliographies dealing with the Morant Affair, yet it was the law under which the BVC officers were arrested, incarcerated, investigated, tried, convicted, condemned and executed. It is, however, a rare book and a search of libraries throughout Australia and the AWM revealed only one copy at the State Library of Victoria. This edition incorporated the *Criminal Evidence Act* 1898 which was, apparently, the only 'law' Boers were entitled to receive in a military court.[18] Contrary to some accounts, the *Hague Conventions*, although ratified by Britain in September 1899, did not apply to the Boer War with the possible exception of Article 8 relating to Prisoners of War. Thus 'civilized nations' only had the Customs of War (Chapter 14), the *Declaration of St Petersburg* 1868 and the *Geneva Conventions* 1864 to guide them during war at the turn of the 20th century. The military law clearly sanctions the shooting of prisoners, the right to ignore the white flag and even appears to condone summary execution as an option in certain cases of treachery.

The Minute Book of Letters

This is the most significant and revealing official document still available. This manuscript record maintained by the Office of the Deputy Judge Advocate General, Army Headquarters, Pretoria, details the legal opinion provided to Kitchener and his command on courts martial, military courts and the other legal matters that arose during the Boer War. The senior legal adviser, Colonel James St Clair, Deputy Judge Advocate General (DJAG) was a qualified barrister. His assistant, Colonel AR Pemberton was also designated Deputy Judge Advocate General (DJAG). The log provides legal comment on the court of inquiry, the framing of charges and the review of sentences imposed at the courts martial of the BVC officers.

Other primary sources

Without access to official courts-martial proceedings, heavy reliance is placed on primary sources, which are mostly accounts by interested parties. Lieutenant GR Witton in his book *Scapegoats of The Empire*, a book based on eyewitness accounts, official court documents and input from the defending officer Major Thomas, has supplied the most information on the Morant affair. Witton, of course, was a convicted felon for his part in the incident. Human nature, being what it is, would suggest Witton's version of events could be tainted by self-interest and loyalty to his fallen mates, even though his sentence had been remitted at the time of writing. But his account has withstood the test of time and generally provides a condensed but sound account, especially of the Visser case and the eight Boers case. His additional eyewitness accounts are generally corroborated by other sources. Witton was severely constrained from straying too far from the truth. There were official documents and other participants in the affair who could criticise and condemn his version.

Major Lenehan, Commanding Officer, BVC, made his own account available through Frank Fox of *The Bulletin* in the book titled *Bushman and Buccaneer*, using the pseudonym Frank Renar, published in 1902. Interestingly enough though, there is no indication that either Lenehan or Witton obtained the official transcripts of the proceedings of their courts martial available from the Judge Advocate General in London within seven years of the trials for a cost not 'exceeding twopence for every folio of seventy-two words'.[19] However, correspondence between Major Thomas, Witton and 'Banjo' Patterson indicate that Thomas retained his copy of the official courts-martial proceedings.

Margaret Carnegie and Frank Shields, authors of *In Search of Breaker Morant*, and Arthur Davey, editor of *Breaker Morant and The Bushveldt Carbineers*, have provided a wealth of information from official documents, personal diaries, letters and interviews, which often differ dramatically in accuracy, content and description of the same events. Nevertheless, these accounts do add to the understanding and provide a valuable tool in a matter desperately short on detail.

However, both of the above works, and more recent historians, give too much credence to De Bertodano's memoirs, which have been used by Morant's critics to support their contention that Morant and Handcock were guilty and that the courts martial were fair and impartial. By any standards these memoirs lack credibility. His account leading up to and including the Morant affair is based on hearsay and remains, generally, uncorroborated. Captain de Bertodano's own conduct does not stand up to close scrutiny.

De Bertodano was born in Australia in 1871 and moved to Great Britain in 1895. He was present during the Matabele War and joined the Boer War as a captain in an infantry unit in 1900. Later Captain de Bertodano served as an intelligence officer in Kitchener's HQ in Pretoria.

Before joining the intelligence department, he was

Commissioner of Kroonstaat. According to the court of inquiry that was convened to look into twenty charges of fraud, theft and embezzlement laid against him, he was 'untrustworthy'.[20] Although nine charges were proved, he escaped punishment by threatening to 'spill the beans about what's really happening in the Transvaal'.[21] Whatever he knew, it was enough to secure him a transfer to intelligence where he was soon up to his old tricks again. The Judge Advocate's Office, Pretoria, around October 24, 1901, raised questions about de Bertodano's own men 'who appear to be in his [de Bertodano's] employ . . . supplying cattle and horses to the enemy'.[22]

De Bertodano's narrative contains many obvious factual errors and contradictions. Although urged to publish his 'true' story, de Bertodano never took the opportunity to subject his account to public scrutiny and criticism as had Witton. De Bertodano did not commence his memoirs until the 1950s when he was over eighty years old and 'the only one left of the H.Q.'s staff still alive since Birdwood died 2 years ago'.[23] If acquiescence by contemporaries was sought, de Bertodano's timing is convenient and self-serving. Regardless of notes, his memory of events after fifty years must be questioned. The personal diaries, which De Bertodano claims to have used to compile his memoir, are still in the possession of his son, but have not been published or opened up for scrutiny.[24] Until they are made available his memoir must be treated with great scepticism.

The centenary of the executions in 2002 saw two new books published, the first edition of this book, *Shoot Straight You Bastards!* and *The Bushveldt Carbineers and The Pietersburg Light Horse* by Bill Woolmore. Using new documentary evidence, both expanded on previous research and made the case for a re-examination of the Morant Affair. Research for the first edition uncovered the most significant new primary source in the shape of the diary of Provost Marshal Major Robert Montague Poore. Poore was intimately connected to both Kitchener and the

BVC trials and was in a position to know which orders were extant. His diary entries provided valuable new insights into the most controversial aspects of this case.

The BCV regiment was predominantly Australian. Interestingly, despite the claim of Trooper Cochrane that 'we cannot return home with the stigma of these crimes attached to our names',[25] only about ten Australians publicly expressed a view on the incidents. Were they shamed or stunned by all the fuss? In addition, there was a concerted effort to stifle any information about the trial and executions. This can be attributed to the efforts of General Kitchener and his mentors in Whitehall who also refused to waive the normal 75-year embargo on the courts-martial transcripts, though they did not hesitate when there was an international outcry over the earlier execution of Boer commandant Gideon Scheepers.[26]

GENERAL LORD KITCHENER, GCB, KCMG, COMMANDER-IN-CHIEF, SOUTH AFRICA 1901–1902

Kitchener is generally described as a 'doer', an iron man, the one who could make things happen. The British public held Kitchener in high regard after Sudan and, to a lesser degree, the Boer War. He became a national icon, the personification of what the British Empire stood for. This stern Victorian father figure projected British dominance, authority, stability and security. The adulation of Kitchener is considered to be somewhat misplaced today.

Kitchener's first notable success, Omdurman, saw his Royal Engineer skills and organisational ability come to the fore when he prepared an army to defeat Dervish barbarism in Sudan and avenge the defeat, death and subsequent mutilation and desecration of the body of General Gordon. In just a few hours, Dervish losses at the Battle of Omdurman amounted to over twelve thousand men. Losses on the British side amounted to about fifty. The Dervish tribesmen faced overwhelming modern firepower. No quarter was given and no compassion shown.

Winston Churchill remarked: 'I shall merely say that the victory at Omdurman was disgraced by the inhuman slaughter of the wounded and that Kitchener was responsible for this.'[27] Even the British public and parliament felt a little queasy.

At Fashoda, Kitchener stared down the French with uncustomary finesse. The incident only involved a small military force never in contact. But, more importantly, it was a notable moral victory.

An indisposed Lord Roberts, Commander-in-Chief, South Africa, directed his Chief of Staff, Kitchener, to pursue the Boer leader, General Piet Cronje. Cronje went to ground and formed a laager (defensive position) at Paardeberg. Unlike Omdurman, Kitchener faced a well-armed, entrenched Boer force surrounded by natural obstacles and flat, open ground. Kitchener expected the battle to be over in a few hours. His tactics were more suited for fighting tribesmen than a modern army. Troops in close order were forced to persist with frontal attacks into withering Boer fire. The attack stalled. Instead of commanding, Kitchener was reduced to berating troops in the field out of frustration over his own shortcomings. Kitchener ignored hard learnt lessons in fighting the Boers and, as a result, suffered tragic losses. 'As soon as Roberts heard the news of the outcome of the day-long battle he rushed to Paardeberg and overruled Kitchener's argument that the assault be renewed.'[28] The nickname 'K of Chaos' gathered momentum.

Kitchener is acknowledged as a callous commander devoid of all compassion. Pakenham, author of the authoritative work *The Boer War*, notes: 'No one could imagine Kitchener, like Wellington, [could be] sickened by the sufferings of his own soldiers. He preferred to be thought a monster than to be thought sentimental. He flaunted his indifference to pain, he allowed oriental punishments, like the lopping of hands and legs for trivial offences, to be continued after his conquest of the Sudan, gloated in the desecration of the Mahdi's tomb . . . he himself toyed with the skull, and said it might be fun to make it into an ink-stand or a drinking cup.'[29] Queen Victoria was not amused.

Pakenham continues that: 'Even Kitchener's intimate friends – and he did have a small circle of men (his 'band of boys') with whom he could relax – were appalled by the callous way he talked. They were also aware of other flaws in his character. In private he would occasionally give way to outbursts of self-destructive rage.'[30] (Several years later in India, Hubert Hamilton, William Birdwood, Frank Maxwell and Raymond Marker still comprised Kitchener's 'Happy band of boys'.)[31]

Characteristically, Kitchener was always more concerned with ends rather than means. He was an accomplished liar when the occasion suited him. He lied about conditions in Boer concentration camps.[32] He lied to the British Parliament over the number of armed natives assisting the British in South Africa.[33] He denied issuing an order that captured Boers would be summarily executed; yet he did.[34] He lied when seeking Crown concurrence to the sentences imposed on the accused in the Morant affair. He lied to the Australian Prime Minister, after the Wilmansrust debacle,[35] when he promised, to inform him of any Australians he intended to try in future. At the time he made that promise, Morant, Handcock, Witton, Picton, Taylor and Lenehan were all in custody awaiting trial. In the end, Edmund Barton found out about the executions from the returned Major Lenehan before Kitchener told a final lie to the Governor-General about the circumstances surrounding the execution of Morant and Handcock.[36] Anyone with the slightest doubt about Kitchener's use of intrigue, deceit and treachery only need to refer to his calculated and methodical destruction of Lord Curzon, the Viceroy of India, in 1905.

Other frequent criticisms of Kitchener concerned his obsession with verbal orders, his reluctance to delegate authority and his desire to control everything. In regard to verbal orders, Philip Magnus, in *Kitchner*, relates that in the Sudan campaign, Kitchener 'normally exercised his command by issuing verbal orders'.[37] General, Sir Ian Hamilton, who served as Kitchener's Chief of Staff, observed in his book, *The Commander*, that: 'It was one of the oddest traits in the Sirdar's [Kitchener's] extraordinary character that he abhorred having to write things down.'[38] General Kelly-Kenny, at Paardeberg, complained that: 'Kitchener was not the man to use a staff properly even when he had one. "No written orders of any sort. Kitchener only sends verbal messages – takes my Staff and my troops on no order or system".'[39]

Kitchener's reluctance to commit to the written word also extended to his use of unofficial channels when official channels failed to deliver his desired outcome. Kitchener's network of aristocratic matrons and strategically located acolytes yielded significant influence in the corridors of British power. They kept Kitchener up to date on events and ensured his message was constantly heard where it counted most.

Carnegie and Shields believe that Kitchener's 'own staff, who were subject to his sullen moods and his bullying, nevertheless succumbed to a magnetism in his personality and would go to their death or lie in their teeth for him. He worked a punishing day, unwilling to delegate responsibility in the smallest detail to anyone else. He liked to issue orders orally, however, when necessary he could formulate a series of lucidly worded telegrams.'[40]

It is easy to exaggerate a few human flaws and claim this to be proof of a personality trait. But Kitchener was a one-man band who was not comfortable confiding or delegating responsibility. This eventually led to his fall from power in Cabinet during World War I. There is no doubt that Kitchener had a brilliant mind, which was only surpassed by his courage and thoroughness in planning. He organised and executed plans, with little outside assistance, through application, determination and a punishing work ethic. But his obsession with verbal orders, intrigue, duplicity and, at times, treachery, coupled with his lack of compassion also distinguishes his character. As Lord

Curzon, Viceroy of India, remarked about his Commander-in-Chief: 'He stands aloof and alone, a molten mass of devouring energy and burning ambition, without anybody to control or guide it in the right direction.'[41]

After a year as commander, Kitchener was coming under increasing pressure on a number of fronts. First and foremost there was his own burning ambition to become the Viceroy of India. He had already been promised Commander-in-Chief, India, but even this second prize was frustrated by his inability to come to grips with the remnant bands of Boers – a constant challenge to his competency and past distinguished record. Excluding Africans, it is estimated that a total of 450,000 British and Dominion troops fought around 65,000 Boers at the peak of the Boer War. At the peace talks in May 1902, it was estimated 200,000 British troops remained to counter 15,000 Boers.

Unable to fulfil his ambition or the expectations of the British public, Kitchener slipped into the depths of despair. The government's decision to continue the war at all costs met with his disapproval. On July 21, 1901, Kitchener believed that: 'if the war is to continue until the enemy surrenders unconditionally . . . [it would be better] "to make a clean sweep of the Boer population of South Africa".'[42] Correspondence with St John Brodrick, the Secretary of State for War, and Field Marshal Lord Roberts, Commander-in-Chief, Great Britain, and newspaper reports towards the end of 1901 reveal a rather fragile and desperate Kitchener, verging on paranoia as can be gauged from the following quotes.

In mid-October, 1901, Kitchener informed the Secretary of State for War that: 'I do not want any incentive to do what is possible to finish . . . I think I hate the country, the people, the whole thing more every day.'[43] And 'If you think someone else could do better out here, I hope you will not hesitate for a moment in replacing me.'[44]

On October 19, Roberts, in a secret personal letter, informed Kitchener: 'The Government are getting anxious that your health would not be able to stand the strain you are now undergoing . . . I have told Brodrick that I am prepared to return to South Africa to take your place.'[45] Lord Roberts was now seventy years old, twenty years Kitchener's senior.

In late October, 'The last straw that broke Kitchener's self-confidence' was the defeat of Benson's column in eastern Transvaal.[46]

On November 1, Kitchener responded to Roberts with: 'I see the papers say I am not much good as a strategist . . . can you get anyone to do it better, if so please do not hesitate. A new man at the head might evolve some new ideas for finishing the war.'[47]

November 1, also saw a letter from Milner to Chamberlain pleading for Kitchener's removal from South Africa: 'If I may make a suggestion? Is it not possible to tell Kitchener that he is wanted in India.'[48]

In early November, Kitchener wrote to Roberts: 'there are strong rumours current everywhere that I am to be relieved of my command . . . Perhaps a new commander might be able to do something more than I can do to hasten the end of the war.'[49]

Also in November, *The Spectator* denounces Kitchener and calls for his removal.[50] Questions were raised in Cabinet concerning Kitchener's mental state[51] and General Sir Ian Hamilton was dispatched to South Africa as his Chief of Staff on November 15, 1901, with secret orders to report back on the Commander-in-Chief's state of mind.[52] Pakenham concludes: 'Kitchener's own sense of isolation at GHQ had reached a climax. Even with his "band of boys" he found ordinary human contact impossible.'[53]

Despair and incompetence were not in Kitchener's mind when he assumed command. His focus was more likely concerned with failure to pacify the northern Transvaal. This spectacularly rugged country lent itself to guerrilla warfare and provided the Boers with sanctuary in Portuguese Mozambique.

His efforts to eradicate these guerrilla bands were not improved by Joseph Chamberlain, Secretary for the

Colonies, who denied his repeated demands to be allowed
to take various punitive measures. He started by 'refusing
him a free hand to crush the guerrillas by banishment,
confiscation and execution'.[54] On August 7, 1901, Kitchener 'threatened confiscation of the land of burghers [Boer
citizen/ militiaman] in or supporting commando'.[55] He also
proclaimed that every burgher under arms after September 15 would be sentenced to perpetual banishment.[56]
Other wild schemes to exile Boer wives or to transplant the
Boer race onto some remote island were also given short
shrift by London.[57] However, as Commander-in-Chief
there were a number of draconian sanctions, within the
rule of law, he could impose unilaterally to end the war
and the irregular units he formed to take on the Boers in
the veldt were the perfect conduit.

THE BUSHVELDT CARBINEERS (BVC)

Boer excesses in northeast Transvaal prompted concerned
citizens of the Pietersburg area to seek Kitchener's authorisation to raise a local corps to deal with the threat,
seemingly, beyond the capability of regular British forces.
To meet this objective, Kitchener ordered Provost Marshal,
Major Robert Montague Poore, who would play a prominent part in the BVC story, to raise a tough and determined
irregular unit of hard riding marksmen, inured to personal
hardship and living off the land, to rid the Spelonken district of Boers.[58]

Major Jervis, a friend of Morant and author of *Half a
Life*, describes the scene as follows:

> 'As I have already explained, the Bushveldt Carbi-
> neers was an irregular "scallywag" corps enlisted
> from South Africans, Cape Dutch, and time-expired
> volunteers from the Yeomanry and Dominions
> troops, and was raised for the specific purpose of
> clearing a vast tract of semi-tropical, malarious
> country around Pietersburg and Barberton. By this
> time, the middle of the year 1901, hostilities had

degenerated into a loose form of guerrilla warfare, and some of the smaller commandos of Boers were led by men who had held no recognised command so long as the forces of the Free State and Transvaal were operating as organised bodies. The natural result of this type of warfare is a general deterioration in discipline with the concomitant disregard of the laws governing warfare. There was every excuse for this falling-off, because the Boers were desperate and at the last gasp, and the British troops exasperated at their dogged determination to continue when it was obvious that the end was a foregone conclusion.

There had been several cases of abuse of the white flag in the Bushveldt area, and it was recognised that the leaders of the commandos in this part of the country were conducting the campaign with less regard for the laws of warfare than was the case in other parts of South Africa. The Bushveldt Carbineers realised on enlistment that they were specially recruited to deal with particularly desperate bands of men, and for this reason the regiment had attracted a rather tougher crowd than was normally to be found in these irregular units of mounted infantry.'[59]

In July 1901, the BVC was based in Pietersburg under the overall command of India and Afghanistan veteran, Colonel Francis Hall, with an old mate of Morant's, Major Robert Lenehan, as Commanding Officer. Captain Robertson who, by all accounts, was a miserable failure and his detachment little more than a rabble, commanded A Squadron, located at Fort Hendrina 100 miles north of Pietersburg. Robertson, along with the least effective members of his squadron, was recalled to Pietersburg where he faced an inquiry into alleged illegal activities, including the shooting of six Boer prisoners and Trooper Van Buuren – a Boer member of the BVC. Another officer also implicated in these alleged illegal acts was Captain Taylor, supposedly responsible for 'natives and intelligence'[60] in the Spelonken Area and who answered to the Military Intelligence Department, AHQ, Pretoria and, on some matters, to the Area Commander, Colonel Hall at Pietersburg. It was Taylor, not Robertson, who ordered the shootings of the six Boers,[61] although Robertson confirmed the order and the next day ordered the death of Van Buuren.[62] However, it raised questions as to who was really in charge at Fort Edward.

No disciplinary action was taken against either officer and Robertson was replaced by Captain Frederick Percy Hunt in mid-July 1901 – the man who Morant would later describe as 'the best mate I had in the world.'[63] He had previously served as an officer in the 13th Hussars,[64] French's Scouts and Kitchener's Scouts[65] before being appointed to the BVC.[66] It was at this point that Lieutenant Harry Harbord Morant and a number of men from B Squadron were seconded to and, in effect, became A Squadron and Fort Hendrina was re-christened Fort Edward.

Hunt's background, experience and formal knowledge of military matters, including law, would, it was hoped, return the BVC to some semblance of normalcy. But, like Taylor and Robertson, Hunt issued orders that prisoners were to be shot. He told Morant that Kitchener's military secretary, Lieutenant Colonel Hubert Hamilton,[67] relayed a verbal message from Kitchener to this effect before he left Pretoria for Fort Edward. According to the other Hamilton on Kitchener's staff, Ian, this was quite consistent with the duties of a military secretary: 'He [Hubert Hamilton] is more than a military secretary in as much as he is, to a very great extent, the instrument used by Lord K. for issuing orders regarding the movement of troops, and conduct of operations.'[68]

It is difficult to believe that Hunt would have acted on his own recognisance, given that the issue of shooting prisoners had just seen the officer commanding and most of A Squadron recalled to Pietersburg. If the issue had so concerned Hall and the British authorities then Hunt would have delivered quite a different message from AHQ. Therefore, either Hunt was not instructed by Hall to cease the practice of shooting prisoners or he sincerely believed Kitchener's edict to shoot prisoners took precedence, or some combination of the two. The frustration of battle-weary and ill Boers surrendering, only to rejoin their commandos at a later date, inflamed the situation.[69]

Hunt's order to shoot prisoners was resisted by some members of his unit, including Morant, until Hunt himself was shot and captured by the Viljoen commando on the night of August 5, 1901, during a night attack on a farmhouse. His mutilated and desecrated body was recovered the next day.[70] Morant, as Kitchener did in the Sudan, now sought revenge for the barbaric treatment suffered by his best friend, Hunt, and vowed to shoot any Boer he believed to be associated with the Viljoen commando: 'Remember the Boers mutilated my friend Hunt. I shot those who did it. We had our orders; I only obeyed them when Hunt was murdered. I did it. Picton and Witton had nothing to do with it; I told them so at the Court-martial.'[71]

The fact that Morant carried out his superior's orders spurred on by personal vengeance is neither here nor there. The critical issues are whether Hunt gave such an order, whether the order emanated from Kitchener and whether Morant was entitled to believe the order was legal. These are critical questions as they not only have a bearing on Morant's guilt, but also goes to Kitchener's culpability in the whole matter.

Hamilton denied under oath giving the 'take no prisoners' order to Hunt on Kitchener's behalf. If it were proved he lied, Hamilton would have been guilty of perjury and it would damage his long-standing claim that the trial was fair. However, had Morant been able to prove his startling allegation that the orders came from Kitchener via Hamilton – the ultimate responsibility would have passed up the line and rested with the Commander-in-Chief.[72]

Therefore, if proof of the orders does exist – history will have to be re-written.

In the month following the death of Hunt, twelve prisoners and a 'German' missionary were shot. These incidents became subject to military charges being laid against some BVC officers. In a letter to his commanding officer, Major Lenehan, Morant reported that the capture of Veldt-Cornet Kelly on September 23, 1901, 'renders this district free from the enemy'.[73] The incidents, which led to the indictments, are summarised below.

The six Boers case – July 2, 1901

The intelligence officer, Captain Taylor, incited a BVC patrol to intercept and shoot six Boer prisoners being escorted into Fort Edward. Captain Robertson was present and acquiesced in this incitement. Squadron Sergeant Major Morrison relayed Robertson's order to shoot the prisoners to Sergeant Oldham, officer-in-charge of the firing party.

Participants: Captain Taylor, Captain Robertson.

Troopers: Eden, Brown, SSM Morrison, Heath, Sergeant Oldham, Dale, Arnold.

The Van Buuren case – July 4, 1901

The day after the first killings, a Boer member of the BVC, Van Buuren, was observed in animated conversation with the families of the six Boers who came to claim their bodies. Van Buuren was widely regarded as a spy and none of the men were keen to go out on patrol with him lest he give them away to the enemy.

Robertson and Taylor ordered Lieutenant Handcock to shoot Van Buuren during a patrol on July 4, 1901 – an act witnessed by trooper Muir Churton.[74] However, the official report stated that Boers ambushed Van Buuren.[75]

A report on the incident was falsified. Lenehan was charged with culpable neglect by omitting to make a report it was his duty to make.

The Visser case – August 10, 1901
A patrol led by Morant, but incited by Taylor, pursued the Viljoen Commando responsible for Captain Hunt's death, captured a wounded Boer named Visser wearing items of British uniform, an offence understood to warrant summary execution, which was carried out the next day.[76]

Participants: Lieutenants Morant, Handcock, Witton, Picton.

Ten troopers including, Silke, Honey, Thomson, Botha.

The eight Boers case – August 23, 1901
Taylor's intelligence reports indicated eight Boers were being escorted into Fort Edward. Morant, Handcock and Witton, among others, went out and took control of the prisoners and shot them. Witton notes: 'One of them, a big, powerful Dutchman, made a rush at me and seized the end of my rifle, with the intention of taking it and shooting me, but I simplified matters by pulling the trigger and shooting him . . . he was recognised by Ledeboer, the intelligence agent, as a most notorious scoundrel who had previously threatened to shoot him, and was the head of a band of marauders.'[77] Morant believed these Boers had been associated with the Viljoen commando.

Morant's presumption is disputed on the grounds that one of the Boers, WD Vahrmeijer, was a teacher.[78] Boer commandos were made up of civilians from all walks of life and it should be noted that the Boer who shot dead two Tasmanians as they entered Pietersburg was also a teacher.[79] In any event, one of Taylor's men, Ledeboer,[80] who was supposedly one of de Bertodano's 'angels', identified one of the eight Boers as 'the head of a band of marauders.'

Participants: Lieutenants Morant, Handcock, Witton, Sergeant-Major Hammett.

Troopers: Duckett, Thomson.

The Heese case – August 23, 1901
Whilst travelling from Elim Hospital to Pietersburg, Heese spoke to the eight Boers referred to above who expressed a fear that they were about to be shot. Later Heese saw their personal effects lying by the side of the road.[81] Realising they had been shot he went to see Captain Taylor at Fort Edward and threatened to tell the authorities in Pietersburg. As he left, Morant warned him that there were Boers on the road ahead and he should postpone his journey, but the Pastor wished to proceed and had a pass from Taylor authorising the journey. A few hours down the road Heese and his driver were shot by persons unknown. His body was not recovered until several days later.

Participants: Persons unknown.

The three Boers case – September 7, 1901
A witness, Trooper Botha stated that: 'the three Boers were being brought in by Captain Taylor's Police, and were shot by five of the Carbineers; he reported what had been done to Morant in the presence of Major Lenehan'.[82] Morant believed these Boers were associated with the Viljoen commando.[83]

Participants: Lieutenants Morant, Handcock, Corporal McMahon.

Troopers: Botha, Thomson.

THE CURIOUS DECISION TO INDICT
In general both sides endeavoured to treat prisoners properly. The loss of Pretoria in June 1901 left the Boers without an established POW facility, making the disposal of prisoners difficult. At the same time, British denial measures left the Boers in rags and barefooted. In an attempt to solve both problems, the Boers often stripped prisoners naked and released them to find their own tortuous route home exposed to the elements. On the other

hand, when pressed, the Boers left their wounded on the battlefield, confident of British succour. But prisoners were shot and these instances were sufficiently prevalent to be documented, variously justified and then ignored by both sides.[84] Thus the curious outcome in the Morant affair is not that the accused were found guilty and sentenced to death for shooting prisoners but that *they were prosecuted in the first place*. According to evidence given during the trial, numerous similar shootings occurred on both sides throughout the war. Neither the prosecution nor the bench contested this fact.[85]

To demonstrate the level of raw emotion never far below the surface, Sergeant Eland, a well-respected member of the BVC killed alongside Captain Hunt, wrote a letter to his mother shortly before he died regarding the wrecking of a train carrying Gordon Highlanders on July 4, 1901. Lieutenant Best, a friend of Morant and Hunt's, was amongst the dead. Eland commented that the Boers 'seem to have shot men down in cold blood. If we had come up with that party of Boers that night we would not have taken any prisoners.'[86] The Gordon Highlanders exacted their revenge on the wreckers during two subsequent raids – shooting a number dead after they had surrendered.[87] A letter dated September 6, 1901, to Mrs Heckford from Alfred Haserick of the native pass office summarises the prevailing attitude towards train wreckers: 'I would like nothing better than to have command of 200 men, my duty to catch this band – about 160 strong chiefly Hollanders and Irish – jail birds many of them. I do not think I would have to report many as captured did I get hold of them. "160 killed" would be the report.'[88]

In addition, Pakenham notes that at least one unit took an oath not to take prisoners, while individuals routinely shot wounded Boers because they were wearing khaki.[89] The unit Pakenham referred to was, in fact, The Canadian Scouts. Following the death of their Commanding Officer, 'Gat' Howard in January 1901, who was ambushed by Boers whilst taking a white flag, unit members joined hands and took a solemn vow over his grave never to take prisoners again. The wearing of a black feather in the hatband indicated that an individual had shot a Boer prisoner. A regimental photo shows a number of Canadian Scouts sporting the black feather.[90] Warner states: 'Wearing one's enemy's uniform was a risky procedure, for when they were apprehended – which they often were – they were promptly shot.'[91]

Churchill refers to the shooting of prisoners and summarises thus: 'The long-drawn struggle bred shocking evils . . . However, very few persons were executed [for such crimes]. Kitchener shot with impartial rigour *a* British officer and some colonial troopers *convicted long after their offence* of having killed some Boer prisoners.'[92] [Emphasis added]

This relates to the Morant affair and again highlights the rare prosecution of offenders for shooting prisoners. On the Boer side, a Barend Cilliers, while serving under General PR Botha, summarily executed a British prisoner, Lieutenant Boyle. No action was taken by the Boer command at the time and after the war he was acquitted of the offence.[93] In fact, Kitchener himself stated, 'It is the only case of this sort that has occurred',[94] which is partly true, but only insomuch as no other British or colonial servicemen had been charged with shooting Boers during his tenure as Commander-in-Chief. But as Churchill observed, a 'satisfactory' resolution of the Heese murder may have deflected further criticism of his command and improved his tarnished credentials with the Boers.

The Pietersburg Church of England Chaplain, the Reverend Joshua Brough, noted: 'In the matter of shooting the missionary [Heese], [it was] the only one of the crimes charged which really excited any moral indignation.'[95] In other words, of all the incidents, the only one that was unusual was the shooting of a civilian German missionary who, it was discovered later, was, in fact, a British subject.[96] De Bertodano also agrees that the 'Heese murder was the crucial event without which the whole matter might have been allowed to blow over'.[97] The Chaplain commented further: 'I have heard it said that the execution [Morant and Handcock] convinced the Boers of British fairness, and made them ready to come to terms.' And he concluded: 'and never, I should think, has a feebler charge been brought before a court.'[98]

The curious decision to indict the BVC officers on stale common knowledge crimes, previously ignored by commanders, assured guilty verdicts. If those already 'guilty' of shooting prisoners were also indicted for the unsolved Heese case, which was said to have caused 'grave political trouble', then justice would have been done, regardless of the outcome of that particular trial. If this stratagem brought peace and Kitchener could rid himself of South Africa then whatever sacrifice others had to make on his altar of ambition was well worth it – always ends, never means. Even Handcock, often portrayed as dumb and unquestioning, cut through the thin veneer of military justice with the comment, 'our graves were dug before we left the Spelonken'.[99]

Considering Kitchener's track record of brutality there is no doubt he was capable of executing a few colonials to achieve his ends. As he rightly calculated, the fate of a few colonials excited little indignation from the public 'back home'.

Today, there is ready acceptance of Kitchener's ruthlessness – it is almost taken for granted. But the military had its book of rules – the *Manual of Military Law* 1899 – and its processes under the watchful eye of the Judge Advocate General Sir Francis Jeune. Evasion of laid down procedures, or manipulation, would be recorded *one way or the other*, in the annals of history. Few would believe the ambitious Lord Kitchener would flagrantly pervert the processes or leave behind any incriminating evidence that might put his career at risk. But a century on the proof is clear.

As Wilcox says in *Australia's Boer War*, army command and staff knew about the shootings of prisoners shortly after the incidents occurred. Yet, no attempt was made to stop the practice or punish the perpetrators.[100] If fair and impartial justice were the objective, then an assessment of who knew what and when they knew it should have been a feature of the court of inquiry, but once again the investigators proved curiously reticent to establish *all* the facts surrounding the murders in the Spelonken.

WHO KNEW WHAT AND WHEN

To believe that Kitchener played the role of an impartial commander is to ignore his very nature and his well-established track record. Such a belief would also misunderstand the normal army chain of command and functions of a HQ. In general, HQ collect, collate and analyse information and react to the results by creating and issuing operational, administrative and logistic plans to achieve military objectives. As already noted, Kitchener was in the habit of bypassing staff and commanders and issuing verbal orders. This form of command and control for those less capable, can lead to chaos but it has the advantage of leaving no paper trail, allowing affordable denial and distorting historical reference.

It has been argued that Kitchener would not have had the time or opportunity to become personally involved in the Morant affair. But this is clearly not the case given that he found time to close AHQ on one occasion to allow the staff to search for his lost pet starling,[101] frequently supervised many of the 'model drives' in early 1902,[102] and had a habit of withdrawing to his room for several days to sulk following military disasters – a practice Hamilton described as 'churching it'. (Benson,[103] Methuen,[104] and Hamilton[105]) During these absences Kitchener's staff were able enough to function without him. This view also ignores Kitchener's obsession with reputation, ambition and determination to avoid being implicated in the BVC murders.

It is also a well-known fact that he took a personal interest in every detail of his officers' performance in the field and personally oversaw the reorganisation of the

Intelligence Department. Deficient and understaffed under Roberts – Kitchener revolutionised it. Coloured maps of each theatre of conflict covered the walls of his office and were used to plan the great sweeps and drives that became a feature of his command. He took intelligence briefings from Director of Intelligence, Colonel David Henderson, twice daily.[106] He also assumed personal responsibility for Transvaal, where the BVC killings took place, so it would be natural for Kitchener to take a close interest in the investigation.[107] Indeed, he found the time to remove Taylor and Hall from scrutiny and personally order the arrests, incarceration and court of inquiry in the Morant affair.

History reveals that Kitchener was always prepared to personally involve himself at the lowest levels of command to achieve his ends. In this case he had a detailed knowledge of what and when things happened. There was a telegraph wire between Fort Edward and Pietersburg and, as will be established later in this paper, senior officers in Pietersburg knew about the killing of Boer prisoners long before the arrest of BVC officers, yet took no action to prevent the practice. Davey produces ample documentary evidence to show Kitchener ignored early warnings about Taylor's character and mounting evidence of murder against him, but once it became apparent that Kitchener could no longer turn back the tide, he opted to protect him.[108] It should also be remembered that a powerful figure like General Kitchener with the authority of a Commander-in-Chief, only needs to express, or signal, a desired outcome, either overtly or covertly, to virtually guarantee his wishes are accommodated. Kitchener was the last old-style Commander-in-Chief who enjoyed supreme power. In later wars, commanders were under the direct control of politicians.

On April 8, 1901, General Plumer's column secured Pietersburg: 'After placing the area from Pineaars River to Pietersburg under the command of Lieut-Colonel [promoted Colonel, July 21, 1901] F. H. Hall, the British used Pietersburg as a base for further operations.'[109] Colonel Hall,

Royal Artillery, was a seasoned veteran of the Afghan War (1878–1880) and the Boer War. After action in the relief of Kimberly and the battles of Modder River and Majersfontein (mentioned in dispatches three times), he became the Officer Commanding Lines of Communication and Area Commander situated at Pietersburg. This was an important post. The garrison provided security for northern Transvaal (the only area of South Africa not subdued by the British) and also secured the approaches and lines of communication to Pretoria. Kitchener would not place such a critical command in the hands of an officer who did not warrant his complete confidence and trust. Hall allocated units to operational areas and outlined their missions. Subordinate commanders, with the apparent exception of Captain Taylor, reported to him. Taylor reported to Kitchener.

The following chronology of the incidents that led to the BVC indictments outlines the knowledge that filtered back to Pietersburg and Pretoria and the culpable lack of disciplinary action taken by the military authorities.

The six Boers case
By mid-July 1901, some BVC members in the Spelonken had been implicated in a number of crimes. Silke notes: 'We relieved Captain Robinson [sic] and party (B.V.C.) who had to go to Pietersburg to attend an enquiry on four charges, murder, cowardice, rape and robbery.'[110] In late July 1901, Sergeant Major Morrison, Sergeant Grey and several other BVC men broke arrest, stole rum and absconded to Pietersburg where they were re-arrested: 'A preliminary enquiry was made at headquarters when Morrison and a fellow N.C.O. Sergeant Grey disclosed what had been going on in the Spelonken.'[111] As a result of these investigations Colonel Hall discharged Morrison and Grey and obliged Captain Robertson to resign his commission.[112] Thus Robertson was not arrested, relieved of command or disciplined for his part in any wrongdoing. Despite being implicated in seven murders he was allowed to resign his commission, an administrative procedure, to avoid punishment – a most

improper action. Robertson's resignation would need Hall's recommendation and justification before Kitchener could approve it. Therefore Kitchener had early warning of problems in the BVC. Taylor was also implicated in similar crimes but both Hall and Kitchener initially exonerated him. Robertson was recalled in mid-July and about three months later his accomplice in crime, Taylor, was recalled, both resigning under Kitchener's authorisation for exactly the same reason.

Hall replaced Robertson with Hunt, with instructions to restore discipline to A Squadron, which was now largely made up of men from B Squadron. Yet the shootings continued.

The Van Buuren case

On July 4, 1901, BVC Trooper Van Buuren was allegedly shot by Handcock after a consultation between Robertson and Taylor.[113] *The Times* of April 17, 1902, reported extensively on the trials and noted: 'Lieutenant Edwards [Adjutant, BVC] deposed that he received a confidential letter from Captain Hunt, of which a copy was made, the original being forwarded to Pretoria. A postscript to the original had since been torn off (the copy). The postscript read "Will also write details of death of Van Buuren; Handcock shot him".'[114]

Did Pretoria learn of the circumstances surrounding the death of Van Buuren shortly after Hunt assumed command in mid-July 1901?

The Visser case

Captain Hunt was killed on the night of August 5, 1901, but it took a few days for the relief patrol to arrive and begin the pursuit of the Viljoen commando. The commando was attacked on August 9, and a wounded Boer named Visser was captured wearing khaki and had in his possession trousers belonging to Hunt and binoculars belonging to Sergeant Eland. He was executed the next day. Within the week, Lieutenant Picton, who commanded the firing party, reported the matter to his commanding officer, Major Lenehan, and to Colonel Hall.[115] Major Lenehan corroborated Lieutenant Picton's testimony and also reported the matter to Hall.[116] Witton commented: 'No action was taken, not even a notice or message was sent intimating that such practices were to be discontinued. This tended to convince me that the orders and the interpretation of the orders regarding prisoners as transmitted to me by Lieutenant Morant were authentic, and that such proceedings were not only permitted, but were approved of by the headquarters authorities.'[117]

This was a reasonable assumption on the part of Witton. It was also the second case of shooting Boer prisoner(s), yet neither Hall nor Lenehan, in full knowledge of the details, took any action to discourage a recurrence.

The eight Boers case
On August 23, 1901, eight Boer prisoners were shot. Witton noted: 'The authorities there [Pietersburg] were well aware of the facts.'[118] Morant and Handcock also made the same allegation at the courts martial.[119]

The Heese case
Hall notified the Superintendent of the Berlin Missionary Society in Pietersburg, the Reverend ORP Krause, of Heese's death in early September and implied that Boers had killed him.[120] In return, Krause provided Hall with the nearest thing to an eyewitness report from an African named Silas.[121] Although it failed to identify the perpetrators, this unsolicited statement was believable and certainly contained sufficient information to warn Pretoria and to provoke an inquiry. But other than sending Major Lenehan to make inquires there was no obvious response from Pretoria or Hall at the time.[122]

The three Boers case
On September 12, 1901, one witness, Botha, whose evidence was corroborated, claims Lenehan was present

when he discussed the shootings with Morant. On return
to Pietersburg Major Lenehan maintains he briefed Colonel
Hall about the shooting of the Boer prisoners.[123] This was
the third case of shooting prisoners and still no caution
was issued. In addition, the knowledge of these 'crimes' did
not see the perpetrators relieved of command nor did it
prevent Lenehan and Hall from sending Morant and Witton
to apprehend Veldt-Cornet Kelly and his commando.

The capture of Veldt-Coronet Kelly

Veldt-Coronet Kelly was threatening to kill 'a thousand
Englishmen' if he was approached. Several artillery pieces
were also reported to be accompanying Kelly.[124] Morant,
with thirty men, surrounded Kelly's laager and captured
the group without a shot being fired or a captured Boer
mistreated. On his return Morant received the following
message from Colonel Hall: 'Very glad to hear of your
success, and should like to have an account of what must
have been a good bit of work.'[125]

The subsequent courts martial mentioned the action
favourably in its proceedings. The message also provides a
good indication of how well the telegraph between Fort
Edward and Pietersburg kept Colonel Hall informed.

The 'Cochrane Letter'

What finally brought matters to a head was not the killing
of Heese, but a letter dated October 4, 1901, from fifteen
troopers and non-commissioned officers to Colonel Hall
outlining illegal activity in the BVC.[126] Their outline of
wrongdoing (which implicated not only Morant, Handcock and Witton, but Taylor, Robertson and Hannam
also) was substantially correct, but contained little not
already known to Hall. It was this letter and, as will be
discussed later, the imminent arrival of new native
commissioner, Francis Enraght-Moony, in the Spelonken
that prompted Pretoria to investigate the matters raised.
The Provost Marshal, Pretoria (Major Poore) 'took a
number of sworn statements from members of the BVC'

on October 7, 1901, and it is reported Kitchener witnessed some of these depositions.[127]

This, in itself, was a curious development as in dealing with the six Boers incident Hall acted to remove Robertson without, apparently, referring the matter to Kitchener. But upon receipt of the letter from the fifteen BVC troopers and non-commissioned officers, Hall immediately informed Kitchener. Instead of referring the matter back to Hall for investigation, as would be normal procedure, Kitchener became personally involved in the investigation. This would only make sense if Kitchener already knew about the killings in the Spelonken and was concerned that they might become public knowledge. By early October the plot had begun to unravel and to ensure he was not implicated Kitchener planned the posting of Hall and the resignation of Taylor.

Taylor's replacement

Breaker Morant and the Bushveldt Carbineers by Professor Arthur Davey supports the establishment line that the legal process was impartial and argues that the grounds of Morant's defence were baseless. Whilst it does reveal that his downfall was brought about by his own men, who informed Colonel Hall of the killings in the Spelonken, it also lays bare the bones of the conspiracy that was about to unfold. It shows that the real catalyst for Kitchener's arrest of the BVC officers was the investigations by Francis Enraght-Moony, the new civilian native commissioner, who had replaced Taylor. Military personnel had assumed civil responsibilities until civil structures could be established in the now annexed Transvaal. Davey states that Enraght-Moony's arrival had an 'important bearing on events' and from the brief exchange of letters he published, it is clear that it was he who exposed Taylor's murder of natives. When Enraght-Moony confronted Colonel Hall about Taylor, Hall replied that 'Taylor was sent up without reference to Col. Hall', had been appointed 'over his head',[128] and was not responsible to him. Kitchener appointed Taylor personally, and only when details of his reign of terror leaked out could he be persuaded to remove him.

If Hall distanced himself from Taylor when his killing of natives came to light,[129] would Hall also have distanced himself from Kitchener once the killing of the Boer prisoners became public knowledge? Given the damning letter Kitchener had received from the disgruntled BVC there is little doubt that Enraght-Moony would have found out everything. He was on his way to Fort Edward when Kitchener recalled the entire BVC detachment on October 16, 1901, and then ordered the arrest of its officers. Better to make the arrests and conduct the investigation yourself than have Enraght-Moony and his superior, Lord Milner (who was actively lobbying for Kitchener's removal in England), bring the whole career-ending scandal to light.

Hall silenced

In spite of Colonel Hall's position, knowledge and involvement in all these matters, he was 'suddenly recalled by the War Office, relieved of his command, and sent out of the country to India'[130] shortly before the courts martial commenced – without even having made a statement. The need to 'suddenly' relieve an operational commander holding a key appointment and send him to India in January 1902 defies belief. At this point in time, Kitchener was trying desperately to hold his whole world together. Yet he meekly accepted the removal of his experienced commander in northern Transvaal, which then came under increased Boer pressure as a result of the withdrawal and reorganisation of the BVC in Pietersburg. By November 1901, the Boer commander, Assistant Commandant General CF Beyers was back in control of the Spelonken and enjoying the hospitality of the again intimidated local populace.

The posting of Hall could only occur at Kitchener's request or with his concurrence. Hall was a material witness in all of the cases. He was certainly aware of all the circumstances in the six Boers case in view of the inquiry and administrative action taken. In the Visser case, both the officer in charge of the firing party and the BVC commanding officer briefed him. He was aware of some detail in the three Boers case, the Heese case and probably the eight Boers case. Hall would also be aware of what Kitchener's HQ knew and when they knew it. Of all the suspicious events that occurred during the subsequent arrest and prosecution of BVC officers, the posting of Hall is the most telling. The office of the Deputy Judge Advocate General, Pretoria, also considered Hall a material witness, required to take the stand at the courts martial and commented on his absence.[131]

In regard to Hall's urgent recall, it has been suggested by Davey that: 'Hall's command at Pietersburg was a mixed one, consisting of British regular Battalions, the Bushveldt Carbineers and only a small artillery component. He was out of his element as a gunnery officer.'[132] He concluded that Hall's posting might have resulted from the return of five artillery batteries to India in late 1901. Apart from there being little relationship between five batteries of artillery and the rank of colonel, the army promotion and appointment system does not function in the manner suggested. Officers promoted to colonel and above generally lose their corps identity and assume non-corps command and staff appointments. It would be normal for an arms colonel to assume responsibility as formation commander responsible for infantry units and artillery sub-units.

One would also have thought that a 'sudden posting' would entail a degree of haste and would see the senior unit commander filling a cold seat. Yet, Hall's replacement, Colonel SH Harrison, arrived before Hall had even departed. It appears the only urgency was to ensure Hall's absence from the leisurely-arranged courts martial.

The real reason for Hall's urgent posting was Kitchener's fear that he would implicate him, and others, in acts of commission or omission if he gave evidence at the court of inquiry, summary of evidence, or courts martial. Unless he agreed to fall on his sword it is difficult to see how Hall could defend his own actions without implicating those officers higher up the command chain. Hall was soon to be joined in India by his new Commander-in-Chief, Kitchener, later in 1902.[133] The fortunes of war began to smile on Colonel Hall. His service on half pay[134] ended on July 21, 1902, and a Companion of the Order of the Bath (CB) was awarded on July 29, 1902. After an unusually short tour of duty in India, Hall assumed as a substantive Colonel on Staff, Royal Artillery, Salisbury Plains, a 'plum' corps appointment, on February 6, 1903. Thus, at a time when the British Army was experiencing demobilisation and many senior officers were wondering where their futures lay, Hall was promoted to substantive rank.

While still at Pietersburg, Hall kept a close eye on the progress of the court of inquiry, which was conducted in a tent outside the commandant's office, anxious that the whole business be kept quiet. That his absence might disadvantage his own officers was of no consequence to him.

ARREST, SOLITARY CONFINEMENT, COURT OF INQUIRY AND SUMMARY OF EVIDENCE

Although Hall was responsible for good order and military discipline in the area, it was Kitchener who took a personal interest in the incidents in the Spelonken. On October 16, 1901, he ordered the close arrest[135] of the accused and convened a court of inquiry to report on the alleged incidents.[136] The actual arrests and solitary confinement took place on October 23 and 24, 1901. Witton relates his experience as follows: 'The officer commanding the fort then informed me that I was a military prisoner under his charge, and if I attempted to escape, or went outside the wire entanglements, I would be shot; that I was not to communicate with anyone outside, and all correspondence was to be sent through him.'[137]

The accused did not speak to each other or see each other, apart from the encounter at the court of inquiry in

December 1901, for three months after their arrest. They were placed in solitary confinement in different parts of the garrison until charge sheets were served on January 15, 1902. Under the circumstances the reason for subjecting the accused to solitary confinement is hard to justify, let alone for three months. With the exception of Witton, who had no active service but raised a gun detachment, all of the accused had good service records and earned their commissions on the basis of commendable active service. The official reason for solitary confinement was to prevent the accused from speaking to each other.[138] But close arrest would have the same effect: 'The Queen's Regulations direct that an officer under close arrest shall not leave his quarters or tent except to take exercise under supervision.'[139] Jarvis, grateful he did not join the BVC as proposed by Morant, assumed the accused had been placed under 'close arrest' as 'Close arrest of an officer does not mean that he is locked up in a barred cell'. Jarvis believed that Morant did not expect to be 'sentenced to anything more severe than dismissal from the Army'.[140]

The unreasonable term of solitary confinement and prolonged court of inquiry can only be explained as a deliberate ploy to unnerve the prisoners, see Hall urgently posted to avoid questioning and to facilitate Taylor's evasion of a court martial. It also kept the accused out of circulation and ignorant of their legal rights. From the letters written during their incarceration it appears that the accused never seemed to appreciate the gravity of their situation or that the death penalty was a possibility.[141] The total censorship of all communications guaranteed Kitchener's desire to prevent intervention by any third party, like the Australian Government, as occurred in the Wilmansrust affair.[142] Thus the accused, ignorant of military law and held incommunicado, were obliged to face a court of inquiry held in camera and rely on the notion of British justice for protection whilst all the while Kitchener connived against them.

The court of inquiry was established to determine if

crimes had been committed. Witton records that the court convened around November 6, 1901,[143] it 'sat daily for nearly a month and was supposed to be held in camera'.[144] Renar notes that the court 'conducted its deliberations in strict secrecy, and made none of its findings public'.[145]

The official view states 'no unreasonable delay took place . . . in assembling the court of enquiry, or subsequently in convening the Court Martial'.[146] This is not true. The *Minute Book of Letters* confirms that all staff action on the proceedings of the court of inquiry was complete and recommendations forwarded to the Adjutant General on November 21, 1901 only two weeks after the court of inquiry convened.[147] Yet, it took almost eight more wasted weeks before formal charges were laid and courts martial convened. There were two principal reasons for the long and unnecessary delay.

Firstly, there was the need to process the posting of Colonel Hall to India so he would not be called as a witness at the courts martial. The Adjutant General, Sir William Kelly, who was responsible to Kitchener for the personnel administration of the army, arranged this. Aware of the communication of October 4, 1901, between the BVC dissidents and Hall, he went through the motions of having his provost marshals in Pretoria investigate the matter in early October. Kelly and his staff then prepared the court of inquiry and the general courts martial at Kitchener's instigation and was, therefore, well aware of Hall's importance as a witness. However, at the same time, he was also preparing the sudden posting of Hall, as dictated by Kitchener through his military secretary. The posting was morally and legally indefensible but who was going to stand up to Kitchener? Colonel Pemberton noted Hall's absence as a witness at the courts martial. The *Minute Book of Letters* reveals: 'The prosecution was embarrassed by the absence of Lt Col Hall [sic] lately Commdg at Pietersburg to who all reports have been made from the Spelonken.'[148]

This matter is somewhat understated because Colonel Hall, by his absence, may have committed an indictable offence.[149] More importantly, the court should have been adjourned until he could appear as a witness as 'the absence of such a witness may cause the proceedings to be invalid'.[150] Conveniently, Hall was not posted to Britain but posted for a short term to India where the longer sea journey and separate command structure would make it administratively impossible for him to be recalled to take the stand in South Africa. But as Pemberton only assumed duty at the Judge Advocate's office at the conclusion of the trials, he was probably unaware of this. Questions Hall could have shed light on included:

- Given the events that saw Robertson removed, when Hunt was appointed to restore discipline at Fort Edward, why did his instructions not include an order that prisoners were not to be shot?
- What was Hall's knowledge and understanding of Kitchener's 'take no prisoners' policy?
- Why did Hall ignore several felonies when it was his duty to arrest, or relieve of command, those responsible and investigate each allegation as it arose? Why was it necessary for Kitchener to usurp this power? Were both aware of the established but unwritten policy of 'take no prisoners'?
- When was Kitchener or his HQ informed of each shooting incident?
- What exactly was Taylor's role? Did he ever command BVC troops and on whose authority? What was Hall's and Lenehan's command relationship to Taylor as an intelligence officer, civilian functionary and de facto commander of BVC? Did Taylor report directly to the Intelligence Department on all matters? If not, which matters was Hall responsible for? Was there a change in these relationships when Robertson was removed and replaced by Hunt?
- Why was Taylor allowed to resign and escape court martial?
- Why did the initial inquiry into the six Boers case exonerate Taylor yet, apparently, incriminate Robertson,

then allow him to escape disciplinary action by resignation? What part did Kitchener play in these outcomes?

The second reason for the long and unnecessary delay, to be expanded upon later, was to create the three months necessary for Captain Taylor to escape a court martial regulated by the *Army Act* in favour of a military court controlled by Kitchener. Like Hall and Robertson, Taylor was a beneficiary of Kitchener's largesse. At the time of the courts martial it was suddenly and conveniently discovered that Taylor had 'ceased to be under the military command for more than three months'. To quote Wilcox, 'Taylor's escape was shameful',[151] and Denton, '[Taylor's escape] leaves a sick taste on the tongue',[152] yet they and all the historians who went before them accepted this fact at face value, rather than name this deceit for what it is. The removal of Taylor from the formalities of the court martial system was just another part of Kitchener's careful stage management of the whole affair.

There are other aspects of the court of inquiry, which are just as controversial. Under the Rules of Procedure: 'Whenever any inquiry affects the character or military reputation of an officer or soldier, full opportunity must be afforded to the officer or soldier of being present throughout the inquiry.'[153] Therefore all of the accused should have attended all of the sessions but this was clearly not the case. The same Rule allows the officer or soldier to cross-examine 'any witness whose evidence, in his opinion, affects his character'.

Comments by Witton and Lenehan indicate these provisions were not observed. Witton states that he attended the court of inquiry and 'on this occasion Lieutenants Morant, Handcock and Picton were present'.[154] In his 1929 letter, Witton states he did not 'see' any of the other accused for the three months. Lenehan states: 'I have since ascertained that witnesses, men of my Regiment, had already been examined secretly.'[155] If the accused attended all sittings and were allowed to question all witnesses why does Witton protest that: 'The sentences were decided upon the evidence taken at the court of inquiry, at which no one was given an opportunity of making a defence or even of denying the slanderous and lying statements made by pre-judiced and unprincipled men.'[156] Was this a deliberate tactic to conceal, from the accused, the fact that Colonel Hall would not give evidence at the inquiry to substantiate their individual accounts? And what of Colonel Hamilton, surely his evidence was critical to the findings of a court of inquiry?

Coercion was also a feature of the inquiry and there are question marks over other evidence gathered by what Witton described as a 'star chamber'. A junior British officer stationed at Pietersburg during the court of inquiry observed: 'It would be hard to convey the secrecy that sur-rounded not so much the court martial as the preparation of the case and all the details – the guarding of witnesses and the threats of punishment if any talking was done.'[157] Witton also complained: 'When the men of the Carbineers were being examined they were questioned in a most high-handed manner, and in some cases questions and answers would be taken down in writing without their knowledge; a day or so later they would be sent for again, and a long statement read over to them which they were ordered to sign . . . Others who were called and said truly that they knew nothing were treated as hostile, and were bullied and badgered, and even threatened with arrest.'[158]

There is evidence to support Witton's allegations. On April 17, 1902, in relation to the eight Boers case, *The Times* reported that Trooper Thomas gave testimony, 'that the evidence which he had given at the court of inquiry was given under pressure and was untrue'.[159]

Some of the accused were offered exoneration if they implicated Lenehan in the shooting of prisoners. Lenehan claims: 'Lieutenant Edwards, the Adjutant of the Regiment, was so pressed to give evidence against me; and such endeavours were made to intimidate him, that he refused to speak until an Australian representative was present.'

Lenehan continues: 'Both Lieutenants Morant and Handcock informed me that the court [of inquiry] stated to them that if they received orders from me to shoot prisoners nothing could happen to them as I alone was responsible.'[160]

But to Lenehan's obvious relief: 'They were too honest too perjure themselves, and save their lives at my expense, and persisted in stating as they did to the hour of their death, where the orders did come from, viz, – Headquarters.'[161]

In addition, Witton and Lenehan reported that the British authorities tried to turn Morant and Handcock against each other using similar tactics. Witton says: '[Handcock] was so completely ignorant of military law and court proceedings that he asked the president what would be the best course for him to pursue; he was advised to make a clean breast of everything, as the responsibility would rest solely on Lieutenant Morant.'

The president's underhand tactics took effect: 'There could only be one ending; Handcock's mind gave way, and when he was not responsible for his actions he was forced into making a statement which incriminated himself and Lieutenant Morant.'[162] But incriminated in what and to what degree is conveniently never revealed. There is surprisingly little evidence to support the well-established view that Handcock 'confessed' at all. The only available evidence is attributed to Witton and Bolton.

In his book Witton claimed that Handcock 'incriminated himself and Lieutenant Morant' at the court of inquiry,[163] but did not believe this admission included the Heese murder because he was 'astounded' and 'had not the slightest reason to connect him [Handcock] with it [Heese's murder]'.[164]

However, in his 1929 letter to Thomas, almost three decades after writing his book, Witton attempts to rewrite history. After three months solitary confinement, the accused were reunited on January 15, 1902. It was at about this time 'Morant told me that Handcock had broken down and confessed to everything including shooting

Heese'.[165] But apart from this contradiction, what justification is there to accept Witton's convenient and private 1929 letter in favour of the testimony given at the court martial? In *Scapegoats of The Empire* he puts the confession down to the terrible pressure Handcock was put under, yet in 1929 he discounts his previous explanation.

Major Bolton, who was part of the court of inquiry and chief prosecutor at all but the Visser trial claimed in 1907: 'There should be in existence a confession made by Handcock previous to the trial and constantly referred to at it. This I believe was made at the Court of Enquiry and could of course not be produced [Bolton tried but failed to obtain a copy of the courts martial proceedings] but if still in existence would I believe clear up the whole matter.'[166] If, as according to Davey,[167] Bolton was a member of the court of inquiry then he would have *known* if Handcock made a confession. It should be noted that there is also no mention of a confession in the Deputy Judge Advocate General's examination of the proceedings of the court of inquiry. The implications and consequences of a confession would be critical to both the legal system and the legal advice tendered to the Adjutant General and Kitchener. As a barrister, St Clair could be expected to commit such critical advice to writing in the *Minute Book of Letters* along with the rest of his comments on the court of inquiry.

Even if Handcock had admitted killing Heese during the court of inquiry the confession would have been of dubious value if obtained under duress. It would also have been inadmissible as evidence at the court martial and if it was 'constantly referred to' during the courts martial then that was a serious breach of court procedure. *No* evidence from a military court of inquiry is admissible in a court martial and a legal argument could be made that constant reference to a 'confession' unduly influenced the final verdict.

The alleged 'confession' and Witton's contradiction has become a 'bone of contention' between those who believe that Morant and Handcock were murderers and those who see them as 'scapegoats'. Although they were found 'not guilty' of the murder of Heese, Kitchener's telegram to the Australian Governor General[168] implied they were guilty by association and Witton's contradictory statement has been seen by many as the *fait accompli*. Although Handcock's 'confession' has never come to light – it has given rise to the myth that he was guilty of Heese's murder. For example, Wilcox states that 'It was soon clear that . . . Handcock had shot Heese',[169] but provides no evidence to back it up. A century on, there are plenty of theories, but still no substantive proof as to who was responsible.

It should be understood that a court of inquiry is separate, distinct and not a pre-requisite to a court martial. Again, *no* material from a military court of inquiry can be admitted as evidence to a court martial. However, there is a requirement for a 'summary (or abstract)[170] of evidence' to accompany the documents convening a court martial.[171] This summary of evidence is essential to acquaint the accused with the charges to be met, allow the court to compare testimony being given with previous witness statements and the court with the case itself.[172] A summary of evidence reduces all of the evidence given by all of the witnesses to a summary of admissible facts. The accused is present throughout, may question witnesses, and is not obliged to make a statement but he must be cautioned on any statement he does make.[173] There is a requirement for a 'true copy' of the summary of evidence to accompany the formal charge sheets handed to the accused when they were warned for trial. On January 15, 1901, 'just twelve weeks from the date of my arrest, I [Witton] was served with the charge sheets'.[174] There is no mention of a summary of evidence. This was, in fact, just one day before the first court martial was due to begin. A bullish letter he wrote to his brother in January 1902 supports the belief that he was unaware of the seriousness of the charges against him. He ended with the words: 'I shall come out of this all right, they can't surely crucify me. I reckon it will be rough if I'm cashiered.'[175]

Four days before the courts martial commenced, Colonel J St Clair wrote to the Adjutant General advising that: 'The summary has been carefully taken and should, I think, be sufficient to prove the several charges . . . as copies of the summary will have to be given to the accused when they are warned for trial I would suggest that they be made at once by the typists who have been engaged for the trial. They should be sworn to secrecy.'[176]

If this was a routine courts martial why was there a need for secrecy? Why would the Deputy Judge Advocate General say that 'the summary has been carefully taken' when there is every indication a formal summary of evidence was never taken but that an expedient alternative was used under the terms of Rules of Procedure 104 (Exception from Rules) outlined below? Was he referring to an *inferior document* conforming to the Exception from Rules as the summary?

St Clair's routine confidential memo signed on January 10, belied the urgency of the matter. This memo was setting in train a process which would require the approval of the Adjutant General; a summary typed in Pretoria requiring the signature of up to forty-one witnesses, mostly in Pietersburg over one day's travel away; correction of any amendments made by witnesses; proof-reading; reproduction of enough certified 'true copies' for the president of the court and each accused 'when they are warned for trial' on January 15, 1902. The chances of this summary being in the hands of recipients, under the circumstances outlined, were negligible. Even assuming this stringent timetable could be met, there is other information that a formal summary of evidence, under the terms of Rules of Procedure 8(A), never eventuated.

Neither Witton, Lenehan nor Thomas mentions any formal summary of evidence,[177] yet they would be expected to do so. In his diary, Silke, a witness for the prosecution, states he was called to give evidence at the court of inquiry, but there is no record he was recalled and obliged to make a further separate statement at the taking of a summary of evidence.[178] There is no evidence of any extracts from a summary of evidence in Witton's book, yet he had access to court documents dealing with his particular trials. The *Minute Book of Letters* makes detailed comment on aspects of the court of inquiry and the courts martial but there is no comment on any summary of evidence, apart from St Clair's erroneous claim.

If the proceedings of the court of inquiry cannot be used at a court martial and no subsequent summary of evidence was taken, how was the requirement to provide a summary of evidence satisfied? The only explanation is that Kitchener used extraordinary powers under Rules of Procedure 104[179] to dispense with the requirement. The Rules clearly state: 'The powers conferred in this rule should rarely be exercised except on active service and then only in absolute necessity.' The examples given for this rule to apply are during embarkation or on the line of march, neither of which is relevant to the unhurried trials in question. The surviving references are sufficient to believe that the absolute minimum requirement was provided in accordance with the notes to Rules of Procedure 104, namely, in the absence of a summary of evidence 'some means must be taken to inform the prisoner of the charge, and the names of the witnesses, and of the nature of their evidence'.[180] Witton recounts this procedure as follows: 'Towards the end of December I was again requested to attend a sitting of the court of inquiry [Witton also records the inquiry concluded early December] . . . we were informed by the president that we would be tried by court-martial at an early date, and the statements of the witnesses for the prosecution were read over to us.'[181]

Witton reinforces the view that privileged information may have been placed before the courts martial with his claim that: 'The sentences were decided upon the evidence taken at the court of inquiry, at which no one was given an opportunity of making a defence or even of denying the slanderous and lying statements made by prejudiced and unprincipled men.'[182] If a 'summary' was taken why doesn't Witton refer to further witness statements and questioning of witnesses?

In essence it can only be assumed that there was no summary of evidence taken. Kitchener used extraordinary powers, in an inappropriate context, to 'suspend' the summary of evidence 'on the grounds of military exigencies' which did not exist. He replaced the need for a summary of evidence with the minimum permissible legal requirement referred to erroneously by St Clair as a 'summary'. This 'St Clair Summary' was tainted through the possible use of witness statements taken directly from the court of inquiry and therefore not admissible as evidence at the courts martial. By revoking the requirement for a summary of evidence, Kitchener ensured Hall was excluded from making any incriminating statement.

Apart from the summary of evidence, Rules of Procedure 104 also denied the accused the legal right of 'proper opportunity of preparing his defence, and he shall be allowed free communication with his witnesses, and with any friend or legal adviser with whom he may wish to consult'.[183] Witton complained that whilst the British authorities were willing to pay up to £1 a day to secure witnesses for the prosecution, they did not expend the same energy on defence witnesses: 'when certain men, most important witnesses for the defence, were asked for, the authorities at first refused to make any inquiries as to their whereabouts . . . and later on the authorities declared that they were unable to trace the men asked for'. He also noted: 'Yet at this very time a witness most important to me was travelling by permission of the Pretoria authorities on the Pietersburg line, and had just visited Nylstroom.'[184]

The assurance Kitchener gave the Governor General of Australia in his now infamous telegram that, 'the prisoners . . . were defended by counsel', was as economical with the truth as was the rest of the communiqué.[185] They were only defended because Major JF Thomas answered a desperate plea from a fellow Australian lawyer, Major Lenehan, to defend him at the courts martial, and only discovered, when he arrived at Pietersburg that the other accused were about to be tried for murder without legal representation.[186] He also discovered that his new charges did not appear to understand the gravity of their situation. Earlier, Witton had been told that the charges against him did not warrant legal representation.[187] Later, after the death sentences had been handed down, Kitchener suppressed telegrams requesting assistance, sent by both Witton and Lenehan.[188]

Ten of the eleven capital charges were for murder. Yet it took an internal complaint from the BVC, then depositions taken by provosts and finally a court of inquiry, a total of six weeks, to establish the foundation for the charges. It then took a fully operational AHQ with all of this information another eight weeks to decide that the unauthorised shooting of Boer prisoners provided a *prima facie* case of murder. On the other hand, Izak Koen, a Boer caught wearing khaki, was taken prisoner, tried by military court and executed in a few hours.

'MARCH THE GUILTY BASTARDS IN'
The court

The general perception is that the courts martial, convened in Pietersburg on January 15, 1902, were little more than kangaroo courts acting out a pre-determined verdict and sentence. However, contrary to some views Kitchener would never overtly attempt to rig the outcome of a court martial, especially one involving the death sentence, because he knew the proceedings would be closely scrutinised by Colonel Francis Jeune, the Judge Advocate General in London, and if wrongly applied could expose the president and members of the court and himself to a charge of murder. But he could influence the outcome in other ways. The perceived injustice and lack of fair play surrounding the proceedings ultimately became the focal point of historical research. This has deflected attention from the accuracy of the verdicts and appropriateness of the sentences, arrived at on the manipulated evidence and in the absence of a plea in bar of trial on the grounds of condonation. Other justifications given for the seemingly adverse outcome of the trials include Hamilton's denial that he relayed Kitchener's orders to shoot prisoners and a strong belief the German Government demanded retribution for the murder of 'German' missionary, Daniel Heese.

The solitary defence counsel, acting on behalf of all the accused, was Major JF Thomas who previously practised law in a small country town. He joined the local reservist troop in 1894 and commanded a squadron in the first NSW contingent deployed to the Boer War in 1899 and again saw Boer War service in 1901. Despite his background he had little experience in criminal law and next to no experience in military law.

He arrived the day before the trial began and requested a delay the start until he had time to interview his clients. This was denied, but Thomas did get a day's grace, but only because the court was obliged to seek clearance from Pretoria before Thomas could represent the BVC officers. Half an hour before the courts martial commenced, he was only able to pay a 'hurried visit' to Witton.[189] Yet the *Manual of Military Law* 1899 stipulates 'a failure to give the prisoner full opportunity of preparing his defence, and free communication with others for the purpose, may invalidate the proceedings'[190] unless waived under Rules of Procedure 104. Thomas later admitted he, 'argued the case not as an army man but as a private practitioner of law'.[191] This admission was unlikely to serve the best interests of his clients in view of the differences between the two codes of law. There can be no doubt, however, that Thomas gave a spirited defence, which belied his experience. Military prosecutors, who had the benefit of witnesses being retained in Pietersburg, conducted the prosecution.[192]

Even before the opening statement could be made there was a breach of court procedures. According to Isaac Isaacs, the courts-martial panel should have included one officer from an irregular unit like the BVC.[193] This would have ensured that at least one member of the panel would have been conversant with the harsh realities of guerrilla warfare – a disparity that Morant was aware of when he commented: 'We were out fighting the Boers, not sitting comfortably behind barb-wire entanglements'.[194] As it was the courts-martial panel was composed entirely of regular British officers. Failure to observe this procedure disadvantaged the accused as Thomas based much of his defence around the issue of the Customs of War in remote areas, which differed markedly from conventional warfare.

Whilst the Customs of War should apply equally to all warfare, the Judge Advocate,[195] Major CS Copland, took a great deal of exception to evidence admitted which concerned 'orders that no prisoners were to be taken' and evidence 'to prove what had been done to their knowledge in other corps' regarding the shooting of prisoners.[196] He was obviously not aware of the legal provisions that allow the accused greater latitude in presenting their defence in serious cases.[197]

Ignorance of the law was manifest in the court of inquiry and to a lesser extent in the courts martial. The court commented on the ignorance of the accused in relation to military law and practices, which is understandable from volunteers, but not court officials and legal representatives.

The charges and the fickle law

For a conviction, the prosecution had only to prove that prisoners were shot by the BVC without authorisation. The defence argued obedience to orders, reprisals and the legal technicality that the BVC officers were only accessories whereas the principals in the shootings were not indicted. Morant accepted full responsibility for the actions of his subordinates. Simply stated, shooting prisoners is murder. The *Manual of Military Law* makes this abundantly clear and also stipulates 'ignorance of the law is no defence to a criminal charge'.[198]

14. . . . The right of killing an armed man exists
    only so long as he resists; as soon as he submits
    he is entitled to be treated as a prisoner of
    war.[199]

15. Quarter should never be refused to men who
    surrender . . . it is *seldom* justifiable for a
    combatant to take the law into his own hands
    against an unresisting enemy.[200] [Emphasis
    added]

For Morant's critics this is where the argument begins
and ends – with a literal reading of these sections of the
Manual of Military Law. Morant went against what has
grandly been described as 'British values'[201] and nothing
can mitigate his crimes. *There are, however, significant
exceptions to this law.* This area of military law is fraught
with ambiguities and loopholes, which Kitchener was able
to exploit to his advantage. Contrary to the impression
given above, the Customs of War *did* allow for the
summary execution of prisoners in certain circumstances.
They related to the following scenarios:

1. **Wearing of khaki.** Those captured 'disguised in' or
   'wearing British uniform'.
2. **Retaliation.** Those guilty of 'murder by treachery of
   individuals' exposed themselves to being 'treated otherwise than as prisoners of war'.
3. **The white flag.** Those displaying the white flag. Military law states: 'it must be understood that firing during
   an engagement does not necessarily cease on the appearance of a flag of truce and that the parties connected
   with such a flag cannot complain if its bearers are killed
   by such firing.'

The charges against the BVC officers touched on all
three areas. In each case the court ruled that the case
against them had been proven, but the verdict might have
been different had the court been in possession of all the
facts.

Boers in khaki

The shooting of Boers dressed in khaki was one of the most controversial issues of the war and perfectly illustrated the ambiguities inherent in the Customs of War and the difficulties that existed for the volunteer with no knowledge of military law. This is relevant because Morant claimed that the first Boer prisoner he shot, Visser, was wearing a khaki shirt, but the man who would soon be appointed chief prosecutor, Major Bolton, denied that any order to shoot Boers wearing khaki existed. However, there is clear documentary evidence to the contrary.

Kitchener denied ever issuing an order to shoot prisoners, let alone one sanctioning reprisals.[202] The multitude of incidents, widespread over time and space, recorded by many historians clearly proves that summary executions were carried out in the belief they were in compliance with Kitchener's orders. Kitchener's own reference to such an order is as follows,

No. 708
From Lord Kitchener to the Secretary of State for War (Telegram)
No. S664   Pretoria, 3rd November 1901,
                                    11.20 A.M.

In certain cases of Boers captured disguised in British uniform I have had them shot, but as the habit of so disguising themselves before an attack is becoming prevalent, I think I should give general instructions to Commanders that Boers wearing British uniform should be shot on capture.[203]

On March 19, 1902, shortly after the executions of Morant and Handcock, the Secretary of State for War admitted to the House of Commons: 'Boers captured in British uniforms were liable to be tried by Court Martial and shot. Lord Kitchener had already executed some of the enemy found committing this breach of the customs of civilized warfare.'[204] The statement is cleverly crafted and does not assert that the Boers shot by Kitchener were actually tried by a military court. It is contrived to make Kitchener's admission more politically palatable without misleading the House. Kitchener's telegram doesn't mention 'to be tried by court martial [military court] and shot'. Kitchener states emphatically, 'I have had them shot'. After all, a military court could also sentence 'death by hanging' which Kitchener could only confirm or commute.[205]

Historian, Craig Wilcox, writing in *The Australian* in 1999, disputed the generally accepted view that Kitchener's telegram referred to summary executions: 'I can't see it as anything more than an unanswered request to London for authority to instruct senior officers to execute Boer soldiers captured in khaki – after a proper trial . . . Even if the "order" does turn out to be the real thing, it's difficult to see how Morant could be said to have been following it. He had been in prison for a fortnight pending trial when Kitchener put pen to paper.'[206]

Three years later, in his most recent work, he continues to defend Kitchener: 'Kitchener wanted to allow column commanders to shoot such Boers [wearing khaki] without trial, as military law condoned, but London was hardly going to sanction that.'[207]

London did not have to sanction anything. The *Manual of Militray Law* gave Kitchener, the Commander-in-Chief, the power and discretion to issue such an order. The past tense used in the telegram clearly indicates he was speaking retrospectively – 'In certain cases . . . I have had them shot' – and entries in the *House of Commons Blue Books*[208] contradict the view that the order was not the 'real thing'. These House of Commons publications reveal that only four Boers were legally executed for wearing British uniform during the war – a most unlikely figure considering the controversy it generated and the anecdotal and documented evidence to the contrary. The shooting of Boers, disguised in British uniform, wearing British uniform or wearing khaki was a major issue right until the end of the war and the subject of sharp exchanges between both Smuts and Kitchener. Thus, in November 1901, when Kitchener signalled London that Boers being disguised in or wearing British uniform was a prevalent offence, the same Blue Books record that not one Boer had been legally executed for the offence during Kitchener's term as Commander-in-Chief. The four Boers who were legally executed after being tried by a military court were:

TRANSVAAL
16 Aug 1900, Pretoria, *Cordua*, Hans,
1. Violating his parole.
   First, in taking part in a movement against the British Government
   Second, was found and arrested disguised in British uniform.
2. Treacherously conspiring against British authority.

Shot in Pretoria goal, 24 Aug 1900

15 Apr 1902, Jackalsfontein, *Koen*, I.,
   Being dressed in khaki, disguised as a British soldier.
Shot on 15 Apr 1902.

ORANGE RIVER COLONY
24 Dec 1901, Vlakfontein, *Struis* (Burgher of late Orange Free State),
   Wearing British uniform.
Shot same day.

21 Jan 1902, Blanbosch Spruit, *Steyne,*C.,
   Being disguised in the uniform of the British Army when bearing arms against H.M.'s Government.

There are no cases in Natal or Cape Colony.
   Therefore, as no Boers were shot for wearing khaki

during Kitchener's tenure as Commander-in-Chief, until Christmas Eve 1901, the Boers Kitchener shot, on his own admission, could not have been condemned by military courts. They were summarily executed.[209]

The transcript of Koen's military court is one of the few that has survived and destroys the notion that if Lord Kitchener ever obtained permission from London to execute Boers in khaki it would only have been after 'a proper trial'. Koen was captured early on April 15, 1902, tried and executed by 12.45pm.

> The Court is duly sworn
> EVIDENCE
> Sergt. Meder
> Damont's Horse SWORN
>
> I found prisoner in farm to-day. He was fully dressed in khaki, disguised as a British soldier, and was wearing the badge of a Canadian. He had a bandolier, no rifle, 2 bullets were filed so as to make them explosive.
>
> Prisoner says badge and clothing were served out to him.
> Cpl. Slateler, I corroborate the above statement.
> Trooper Steyn, I corroborate the above statement.
> Damont's Horse.
>
> ---
>
> Prisoner states he was unaware of Proclamation saying all Boers caught in khaki were to be shot.
>
> | Finding | Guilty |
> | *Sentence* | To be shot. |
> | 15/4/02 | Sd. N. J. Cameron, Major |
> | | 1st Cameron Highlanders |
>
> ---
>
> | Confirmed. | Sd. Walter Kitchener |
> | | M. General Commanding[210] |

The Koen case contains a number of glaring errors. The Customs of War state:

> 11. . . . It is the duty of the enemy to be prepared against a military surprise, but not to guard himself against the treacherous attacks of individuals introduced in disguise into his camp.[211]

Perfidy not allowable.

> 43. It must, however, be observed that no deceit is allowable where an expressed or implied engagement exists that the truth should be acted or spoken. To violate such an engagement is perfidy, and contrary alike to the customs of war and the dictates of honour. For example, it is a gross breach of faith and an outrage against the customs of war, to hoist a hospital flag on a building not appropriated to the wounded, or to use a place protected by a hospital flag for any other purpose than a hospital (b).' Vattel, ii. 207; Halleck, ii. 25, et seq.[212]

Legal opinion in an earlier case similar to Koen's states:

> unless it can be proved . . . that [he] was captured in action – the fact of his wearing the badges of a British Officer will not in my opinion be sufficient to justify a charge of Perfidy against him – at present there is nothing in the papers connected with his case to show the *circumstances under which* [emphasis added] he was taken prisoner. Cannot some further evidence on this point be obtained.

> [Signed] Colonel Pemberton DJAG
> 28.3.02

> Provost Marshal, I agree with the above remarks.
> [Signed] Colonel St Clair DJAG
> 28.3.02[213]

Koen was shot under the proclamation that Kitchener never made and that Bolton knew nothing about. He was executed not for being 'disguised in' or 'wearing British uniform', but wearing khaki. Visser, Morant's first victim was wearing a khaki shirt, yet, according to the courts martial, he had no right to execute him.

In addition, there was no evidence that Koen was 'captured in action'. The testimony states: 'I found the prisoner in farm today . . . no rifle.' According to the legal opinion of Pemberton and St Clair, he should not have been convicted of treachery involving the wearing of khaki.

To make matters worse the Blue Book states it was *Lord Kitchener and not Walter Kitchener* who confirmed the sentence of Izak Koen.[214] Did General Walter Kitchener have the authority to confirm the verdict and death sentence of this military court? There seems to be a requirement for sentences over two years imprisonment to be reviewed and confirmed by the Commander-in-Chief.[215] If Morant was guilty of murder for shooting Visser under 'Rule 303', then it would appear Kitchener's brother was guilty of a similar crime.

Further evidence that Boers were being executed without formal trial comes in a letter to Lord Roberts dated November 26, 1901, from Kitchener's Chief of Staff, Colonel Ian Hamilton. It bluntly stated British policy towards Boers in khaki: 'It only makes it easier for us to get rid of them. I have bullets put into them, when I catch them in our [khaki] uniform. Only two days ago I had a man shot we caught so dressed.'[216]

Wilcox contradicts his previous claims that Boers in khaki were only shot after a proper trial with his description of any incident on page 255: 'When Garratt's column scooped up a Boer in khaki [February 1902 near Harrismith] he was court martialled and sentenced to death according to Lord Kitchener's Orders.' The Boer was made to dig his grave and was said to have died bravely.

Once again, the Blue Book has no formal record of any Boer being executed wearing khaki before December 24,

1901 or between Januayr 21, and April 15, 1902 – so it must be assumed that they were executed using Morant's 'Rule 303'.

According to the Boers, the order they believed to be in operation indicated: 'All Boer prisoners wearing khaki were to be shot.' Deneys Reitz, in his book *Commando*, says: 'We could not believe that the British were resorting to the shooting of prisoners, and it was only after many had been executed that we learnt of Kitchener's proclamation [sic] ordering the death of all Boers caught in khaki. As far as I know no steps were ever taken by the Military to acquaint us of its contents.'[217]

Critically, Reitz specifies 'caught in khaki' and not 'disguised in British uniform', which is an important distinction. Khaki was an occasional item of Boer dress and, in general, could not, by itself, be considered 'British uniform'. The Johannesburg and Pretoria commandos wore khaki uniform at the outbreak of the war. The Boers were so desperate for clothing towards the end of the war they stripped prisoners, even dead British and Boers, of clothing. In addition, at the peace talks, 'General Smuts taxed him [Kitchener] with having unfairly executed our men in the Cape, and this, too he justified, on the plea that we had used khaki uniforms to decoy his soldiers'.[218] Again, there is a distinction – not British uniform, just 'khaki'. Reitz gives a number of examples of Boers from his commando being summarily executed for wearing khaki.[219]

Dress could also be an issue on the British side. Commenting on his capture, Winston Churchill, the principal war correspondent of the *Morning Post*, relates: 'I had enough military law to know that a civilian in a half uniform who has taken an active and prominent part in a fight, even if he has not fired a shot himself, is liable to be shot at once by drumhead court martial [executed summarily].'[220]

A British born Lieutenant, Joe Devine, was working as a clerk for the Orange Free State Government when war broke out. He fled to Natal where he joined his country's cause and was part of the British force that defended Lady-smith. Many years later he told his great-nephew how the Boer war was fought: 'He maintained that the Boer War was the "last gentleman's war" . . . except for those wretched Australians. He told me that acting under verbal orders, which he had heard, they shot their prisoners and any Boer who was in bits of British (uniform) were to be shot too.'[221]

The order acknowledged by Kitchener, that all 'Boers captured disguised in British uniform' (or 'wearing British uniform') were to be summarily shot, is also illegal unless it is linked to an officially sanctioned reprisal in the terms of the Customs of War. If these incidents were reprisals then the fact was not promulgated to the enemy. Despite this omission it would still constitute a legitimate reprisal. Lord Roberts had previously authorised a number of reprisals in the Boer War when he was Commander-in-Chief, South Africa.[222]

Provost Marshal, Major Robert Poore, was in charge of discipline in the army and was the one who investigated and oversaw the execution of the BVC officers. An entry in his diary dated October 31, 1901, confirms that the trial and execution of Boers caught wearing khaki, not captured in action, disguised in British uniform, was to be summary execution: 'Most of De Wet's men were dressed in our uniform, so Lord K. has issued an order to say that all men caught in our uniform are to be tried on the spot and the sentence confirmed by the commanding officer.'[223]

This quote raises some interesting questions about the fluid nature of the rules of warfare, which, as we have seen, allowed the Commander-in-Chief quite a bit of latitude. Kitchener was supposed to review all cases where the sentence was greater than two years imprisonment, yet Poore admits that the new orders now allow for what amounted to summary execution. As demonstrated by the executions of Koen and Visser, a drum-head court martial was never to be as rigorous or impartial as a formal military court.

The date in Poore's diary again exposes Kitchener's duplicitous nature. On November 3, 1901, he cables London: 'I think I should give general instructions to Commanders that Boers wearing British uniform should be shot on capture.' However, according to Poore, Kitchener had long gone past the thinking stage and had already issued the order by October 31, 1901. It also makes nonsense of the claim by Major Bolton, chief prosecutor at the Morant trial, that he: 'had "no knowledge" of a proclamation that Boers taken in khaki were to be shot'.[224]

Witton suggests that the order to shoot Boers in khaki existed even earlier than October. He maintains Morant mentioned it as early as August 11, 1901: 'only the other day Lord Kitchener sent out a proclamation to the effect that all Boers captured wearing khaki were to be summarily shot'.[225]

In his recently published work on the Australians in the Boer War, Wilcox contradicts his earlier statement in *The Australian* by stating that orders to shoot Boers in khaki were in existence as early as September 1901.[226] Therefore, his assertion that Morant was already under arrest when the order was issued is incorrect. If Kitchener's telegram was no more than, 'an unanswered request to London for authority to instruct senior officers to execute Boer soldiers captured in khaki – after a proper trial', then Kitchener acted unilaterally.

During the Visser trial 'the president'[227] quizzed Morant about the nature of the drum-head court martial that passed sentence on the unfortunate Visser. 'Was it like this?' he asked Morant. 'No, it wasn't quite so handsome' came the retort.[228] This was a curious question given Poore's comment that they were to be tried 'on the spot'. In light of the short shrift given to Boers like Izak Koen, one wonders why Denny, 'the president', pursued this line of questioning at all. Even more curious was the legal opinion of Deputy Judge Advocate General (DJAG), Colonel Pemberton: '1.) The so-called Court was not a Court at all; it may be more justly called a consultation between 4 officers which ended in a party of subordinates being ordered to commit murder.'[229]

Colonel St Clair, the Deputy Judge Advocate General and senior legal adviser, shared this opinion. Pemberton and St Clair, like Major Bolton, appeared to be unaware of which orders had been issued and how they were to be applied in the field. Poore and Ian Hamilton, Kitchener's Chief of Staff, on the other hand, seemed very sure what Kitchener's order meant. This major discrepancy raises serious questions about the veracity of the evidence presented and the competency of the legal team administering it.

Kitchener's telegram to Brodrick was nothing less than that which it purports to be – a timely justification for past and future summary executions. However, it should be noted that although it may appear to be a draconian measure the order does comply with the provisions of the Customs of War authorising retaliation[230] and even more so in some cases involving treachery.[231] As has been discussed, Boers were summarily executed as a consequence of verbal orders or insinuations relayed by Kitchener's personal staff to field commanders. The timing of the telegram is also important, falling as it does between the arrest of the BVC officers and the court of inquiry – and at a time Kitchener was under considerable pressure from home and abroad. The so-called Morant affair was the only British prosecution for the shooting of Boer prisoners, and, under the circumstances, Kitchener could not afford to get it wrong and destroy his one chance to diffuse the 'grave political trouble' the Heese case is said to have aroused.[232]

In the final analysis, if Boers were not tried and sentenced to death by military courts for being 'disguised in' or 'wearing British uniform' and Kitchener admits to having Boers shot for what he regarded as a 'prevalent' offence, then who carried out such killings and on what authority? In the absence of any written orders the only other authority would be Kitchener's convenient and deniable verbal orders.

Other forms of retaliation

Kitchener's duplicity over the khaki issue also raises questions about the controversial 'take no prisoners' orders Morant claimed Hunt gave him. Certainly, Kitchener's determination to eliminate 'the enemy' by any means is all too evident. According to Philip Magnus, Kitchener 'demanded authority to shoot all Cape and Natal rebels out of hand'. Brodrick explained (21 June 1901) that it would be, ' "awkward" to shoot rebels out of hand'. Magnus continues: 'Kitchener was contemptuous of legal scruples by which he considered that the Cabinet was consistently swayed.'[233] Whilst rebels (citizens of the Cape or Natal fighting on the Boer side) were British subjects and shooting them might provide certain difficulties, Boer prisoners were an entirely different matter. As Commander-in-Chief, Kitchener (according to the *Manual of Military Law*) did not need London's approval to shoot them, nor was he inclined to dispose of the habits of a lifetime by adopting 'legal scruples'.

British authorities did sanction the shooting of prisoners (no distinction is made between 'handsuppers' or 'bitterenders') as measures of officially sanctioned reprisal or retaliation.[234] In fact, in certain actions involving 'murder by treachery of individuals' the perpetrators exposed themselves to being 'treated otherwise than as prisoners of war' and, therefore, outside the protection of the Customs of War.[235]

Wilcox says that St John Brodrick, Secretary of State for War, 'may' have sanctioned reprisals,[236] but there is no 'may' about it. There is a well-documented case following an infamous skirmish at Graspan in the Orange Free State in June 1901. The Boers alleged that during an attack on a wagon convoy the British used women and children as human shields. It resulted in the deaths of eight women and two children. Enraged, the Boers kept shooting after the British surrendered killing at least four and wounding others. Although London would not accede to Kitchener's requests to issue a general 'take no prisoners' order,

Brodrick reacted to Kitchener's report of the incident by establishing the following custom: 'members of any commando by which such an outrage may be committed who may be captured and after trial proved to have been present on such occasion will be held guilty whether they actually committed the deed or not; that the leader . . . will be sentenced to death, and other members . . . punished by death or less sentence, according to the degree of their complicity.'[237]

This custom does not appear to have been applied in the Visser case for which Morant, Handcock, Witton and Picton were all found guilty of murder, despite the mutilation and murder of Hunt being cited as a mitigating factor by the court martial panel in their Recommendations to Mercy.[238] Indeed, the Judge Advocate and Pemberton, the Deputy Judge Advocate General, were dismissive of any legitimate attempt to establish what the Customs of War were.[239] However, to confuse the situation further the *Manual of Military Law* states that Chapter 14, the Customs of War, 'has no official authority'[240] and explains the Customs of War as follows:

> In this manual the expression 'customs of war' has been substituted advisedly for 'laws of war'. A law to the mind of an Englishman, conveys the idea of a defined and rigid rule, which must be obeyed in all circumstances and at all risks, and the infraction of which involves a crime punishable by a legally constituted tribunal. The customs of war do not, with very few exceptions, admit of being precisely defined. They consist of principles the enforcement of which must vary considerably, according to circumstances . . . and to use 'customs' as applicable to the more elastic rules which constitute the practice, so to speak, of civilized nations in war.[241]

The Morant affair strayed into this legal and moral minefield with allegations that orders were given to shoot prisoners. The issue is complicated by what constitutes a lawful command, whether a commander must personally issue the command and when a subordinate is obliged to obey. The *Manual of Military Law* states:

> '11.) If the command were obviously illegal, the inferior would be justified in questioning, or even in refusing to execute it, as, for instance, if he were ordered to fire on a peaceable and unoffending bystander. But so long as the orders of the superior are not obviously and decidedly in opposition to the law of the land, or to *the well-known and established customs of the army*, so long must they meet prompt, immediate, and unhesitating obedience.'[242] [Emphasis added]

In Section 9 sub-section 2 of the *Army Act* states: 'it is not requisite to prove that the command was given personally by a superior. It is sufficient to show that it was given by the deputy or agent of a superior.'[243]

According to Hunt, he received an order from Kitchener's senior staff officer, Lieutenant Colonel HIW Hamilton[244] that 'All Boer prisoners were to be shot'. If this was the actual verbal order then it is clearly illegal and must not be complied with. Hunt should have been aware of the implications in complying with such an order. Testimonies given at the courts martial, even by prosecution witnesses, leave no doubt that Hunt did order his detachment to shoot prisoners.[245] What compelled Hunt to revisit the sins of his predecessor? It is often overlooked, but even before Hunt and Morant arrived at Fort Edward, Taylor and Robertson had ordered the death of six Boers and one BVC trooper. However, if Kitchener's order was, 'all Boer prisoners are to be shot as a reprisal for similar acts committed by Boers', then the order would appear to be legal.[246]

The Boers killed Lieutenant Best and eighteen other Gordon Highlanders 'in cold blood' at a train wrecking near Pietersburg on July 4, 1901. Would a ground commander find it that hard to believe that Kitchener authorised reprisals under these circumstances? And would he not look upon such an order as 'sweet justice'? In any event, the Gordon Highlanders took full revenge for the slaughter of their comrades on two occasions and went unpunished.[247] No-one was charged with the murder of Van Buuren – the most telling example of the court's selective application of the 'superior orders' principle. These circumstances were no different to Handcock murdering Boers on Morant's orders, yet the court clearly avoided exposing this hypocrisy by not charging Handcock. Morant, on the other hand, took revenge for the murder and mutilation of Hunt, who had previously reprimanded him for not shooting prisoners, and paid with his life.

It should be noted that Thomas attempted to establish the shooting of prisoners as one of 'the well-known and established customs of the army', but apparently failed to establish legal validity according to the *Manual of Military Law*. Had he done so, it might have been more difficult for the Judge Advocate to dismiss what appears, in the light of the above passage, to be a valid claim. The Judge Advocate, Major Copland, piously commented, 'two wrongs don't make a right.'[248] Maybe so, but it also does not make for justice, especially when others have committed the same crime with impunity. How many wrongs does it take to make it one of the 'established customs of the army'?

The white flag
Lastly, there is the issue of the white flag. The diary of Poore is again instructive in clearing up the issue of which orders were in circulation at the time the BVC controversy arose. As Provost Marshal he was the one man who could be relied on to know. According to his diary, he regularly met with Kitchener and his 'inner circle' to discuss field discipline. He first heard of the allegations against the BVC officers on October 7, 1901: 'At about 6 pm Bolton (Wilts Reg.) – (APM [Assistant Provost Marshal] Pietersburg)

arrived with some papers about rather bad things which have been taking place North of Pietersburg – The Bushveldt Carbineers accepted the surrender of 8 Boers and after taking them along for some days shot them. *If they had intended to do this they should not have accepted a surrender in the first place*.[249] [Emphasis added]

In this quote Poore reveals that a clear protocol for shooting Boers did exist, but the BVC breached it by taking prisoners and then waiting some days before shooting them. However, if they had shot them before they surrendered this would have been acceptable. If this interpretation is correct, then to which order was Poore referring?

Much energy has been expended over the past century in the search for written evidence to support Morant's claim that Captain Hunt issued a 'take no prisoners' order. The failure to produce any written proof has led to claims by Morant's critics that no orders existed in the first place. Wilcox asserts that: 'No written order could be produced, even in a war in which every rule and regulation was written, in triplicate, in hundreds of army record books.'[250] But although it has now been proved beyond doubt that an order to shoot Boers in khaki did exist, *no written order from Kitchener to that effect has ever been found*.

However, the order Poore was alluding to when he wrote, '. . . If they had intended to do this they should not have accepted a surrender in the first place' is documented in the *Manual of Military Law*. It pertains to the section on the Flag of Truce, which sanctioned the shooting of surrendering Boers and empowered Kitchener, as Commander-in-Chief, to issue a 'take no prisoners' order without reference to London or having to write it down.

The Customs of War, *Manual of Military Law*, 1899, explains Armistice; Flag of Truce as follows:

> 61. A flag of truce can only be used legitimately for the purpose of entering into some arrangement with the enemy. If adopted with a view to

obtain surreptitiously information of the enemy's forces or positions, it loses its character of a flag of truce, and exposes its bearer to the punishment of a spy. Great caution, however, and the most conclusive evidence is necessary before the bearer of a flag of truce can be convicted as a spy.

62. The bearer of a flag of truce cannot insist on being admitted, and should not be allowed without permission to approach sufficiently near to acquire any useful information. When an army is in position, the bearer of a flag of truce should not, without leave, be permitted to pass the outer line of sentinels or even to approach within the range of their guns. When a flag of truce is sent from a detachment during an engagement, the troops from which it is sent should halt and cease firing. The troop to which it is sent should, *if they are willing to receive it,* signal to that effect, and also cease firing, *but it must be understood that firing during an engagement does not necessarily cease on the appearance of a flag of truce and that the parties connected with such a flag cannot complain if its bearers are killed by such firing.* When it is intended to refuse admission to a flag of truce the bearer should, as soon as possible, be signalled to retire, and if he do [sic] not obey the signal he may be fired upon (a) [Emphasis added]

(a) Halleck, ii. 361; Instructions for United States Armies, Sec. vi.

There were many documented abuses of the white flag. Poore recorded: 'A brutal thing has happened to the East of Pretoria. The telegram came as follows: "*Three Boers approached one of Capt Mier's posts waving a white flag.*

Capt. Tandy walked out to them and they asked to see an officer. Capt. Tandy returned to the post and Capt. Miers rode out alone and was seen to dismount and talk for some time with the Boers who were in a group. One of the Boers then shot Miers through the back and stomach and two more shots were fired at his horse as it galloped in. The Boers then rode away. This is pretty cold blooded murder and these people are to be treated as belligerents." '[251]

The same fate befell 'Gat' Howard – Commanding Officer of the Canadian Scouts. At his graveside the colourful Australian, Charlie Ross, who succeeded Howard as commander made his men join hands and vow never to take another prisoner. Regimental photographs show many, including Ross, wearing black feathers in their hats as proof they had honoured their pledge[252] (see picture section). A Lieutenant King of the Canadian Scouts even testified to the fact that they had shot prisoners at Morant's court martial.[253]

Issuing a 'take no prisoners' order meant working at the margins of the law. Due to its controversial nature it was always a discreet policy, never a formal order and not everyone was willing to carry it out. It has been argued that orders are irrelevant – that our 'moral compass' should enable us to distinguish between right and wrong. In normal circumstances this might be true, but it is a different story in wartime. As Witton put it, 'war is designed to make men's nature both vengeful and callous'. There is clear documentary evidence that the British and colonial irregulars were operating this policy. Lieutenant Lachlan Gordon-Duff of the Gordon Highlanders demonstrated how the order should be carried out: '40 Boers tried to surrender to us the other day and were not allowed to and a fight ensued in which they fought well but were wasted; it is rather extraordinary how they still go on.'[254]

Even within the BVC there was an awareness that a protocol existed for shooting surrendering Boers – as was demonstrated when the first six Boers were shot on the orders of Robertson and Taylor on July 2, 1901: 'Sergeant

Oldham stated that the previous witness [Sergeant-Major Morrison] warned him of six Boers, and told him he was to *make them fight*, and on no account bring them in alive. The Boers were ambushed.'[255] [Emphasis added]

Again, on September 5, 1901, a similar pattern emerged during the ambush of a Boer wagon: 'When the first shot was fired by the BVC disclosing their presence the Boers shouted "We surrender", but although Lt. Hannam knew that the Boers wished to surrender and from first to last they never fired a single shot in token of their desire to surrender, he ordered his men to continue firing with the result that two little boys were killed and one little girl wounded.'[256]

All of the incidents described above adhered to Poore's dictum that if they wanted to shoot Boers they should not accept their surrender. Despite the presence of witnesses, no-one was found guilty in either of the BVC cases. Captain Taylor was charged with murder, but acquitted and Lieutenant Hannam was released from custody after the court of inquiry. So, why was Morant found guilty?

Initially, Morant showed no interest in shooting Boers and was reprimanded for bringing in prisoners by Captain Hunt. However, that all changed after Hunt was murdered and mutilated. Morant's big mistake was to shoot Boers *who had already been taken prisoner*. In the final analysis the only difference between the actions of Taylor, Hannam and Morant was that the former two shot their Boers *whilst they were trying to surrender*. Given that both parties went out with the premeditated intention of killing Boers, only a fine legal distinction separates them, but Morant's critics have no claim to the moral high ground. Commenting on the first Boers executed by the BVC on July 2, 1901, an incident that took place before either he or Morant were posted to Fort Edward, Witton confirms that it was a distinction that he did not make until after the trials: 'According to the evidence taken at the court martial, Captain Taylor on 2nd July, 1901, received intelligence that a party of six armed Boers were going into camp to surrender. The officers in charge decided to intercept these men, and not allow them to come in; they would send out a patrol and have them ambushed and shot. After a good deal of argument, a sergeant-major paraded a patrol headed by a sergeant. The men were told to go out and meet the wagon in which there were six Boers; they were to make the Boers fight, and on no account were these to be brought in alive; if the white flag was put up the men were to take no notice of it, just fire away until all the Boers were shot. *This, I afterwards learned, was the correct interpretation of the orders not to take prisoners.'*[257] [Emphasis added]

Wilcox admits that Kitchener made other proclamations such as, 'leave no living thing behind you', 'stamp out as rapidly as possible all armed resistance'[258] and 'All officers must use discretion in dealing with the white flag'. And as Witton concluded: 'These orders were interpreted in one way by the officers, and that was "No quarter, no prisoners".'[259]

How would a subordinate recognise an illegal order from an officially sanctioned reprisal to shoot Boer prisoners if the reprisals were not promulgated? Especially if a verbal order to shoot Boer prisoners came from a secretive and duplicitous Kitchener. For a volunteer with no military training to understand the different law involved, analyse the difference in relation to a particular situation and be able to conclude whether shooting prisoners is legal or illegal is a questionable ask. When asked about the rules of war during the trial Morant retorted: 'As to rules and sections, we had no Red Book, and knew nothing of them. We were out fighting the Boers, not sitting comfortably behind barb-wire entanglements; we got them and shot them under Rule 303.'[260] Witton supports this by stating that their only acquaintance with military law came during the voyage to South Africa when an officer read out bridge extracts from Queen's Regulations and Military Law with an emphasis on 'obedience to orders'.[261] While 'ignorance of the law is no excuse', 'ignorance of fact will very often be an excuse', and it was ignorance, of military law, that lay at the heart of the Morant affair.

Morant's critics have erroneously argued that even if it were proved that Kitchener had issued orders to shoot prisoners, it does not mitigate Morant's crimes and claiming that they were following orders would not have saved them at Nuremberg.

However, the evidence presented in this paper and in Chapter 12 'New Evidence' quashes the long-standing claim that orders to 'take no prisoners' were never issued and that the courts martial were fair and above board and that Morant and Handcock were the only ones shooting. It also vindicates Thomas' defence that the BVC were acting on superior orders, which were also being enforced by other units. Had Morant been able to prove his startling allegation that the orders to shoot prisoners came from Kitchener via Hamilton – the ultimate responsibility would have passed up the line and rested with the Commander-in-Chief.[262] According to Helen Styles, Lecturer in International Communication at Macquarie University and member of the Advisory Committee on International Humanitarian Law to the Australian Red Cross, NSW, both the *Manual of Military Law* and the London Charter of the Nuremberg Tribunal of 1945 held that following orders of a superior officer was a defence to responsibility for an alleged war crime. In fact, under the Nuremberg Charter it would have been Kitchener who would have been tried as a war criminal:

> . . . Even if the British military manual, which in 1901 held that following orders of a superior officer was a defence to responsibility for a war crime, was wrong in accordance with the customs of war, the London Charter of the Nuremburg Tribunal of 1945 stated that: 'The fact that the defendant acted pursuant to orders of his government or of a superior shall not free him from responsibility, *but may be considered in mitigation of punishment if the Tribunal determines that justice so requires.*'

In conclusion

In conclusion, the preceding sections confirm that the order to 'take no prisoners' did exist in the *Manual of Military Law* and covered three separate contingencies: retaliation, the wearing of khaki and the white flag. Documentary evidence has been produced to show that Boers could be and were shot under all three protocols and not always according to the letter of the law, which suggests that a more general 'take no prisoners' order was in operation. No written orders to shoot prisoners have come to light because of Kitchener's well-documented reluctance to write them down and because there was no need for him to petition London, so long as he acted within the constraints of the *Manual of Military Law*. However, as demonstrated by the issue of Boers in khaki – just because Kitchener didn't write down it doesn't mean that it didn't exist. In fact, the absence of written orders, where they clearly existed, only confirms the long-held suspicion that Kitchener gave those controversial orders verbally.

Normally commanders, especially Commanders-in-Chief, disseminate written orders through their staff systems and then to subordinate headquarters. Verbal orders are seldom given at senior levels but in such cases they are confirmed in writing to ensure uniformity, compliance and awareness of what was happening at all levels of command and within each level of command. Kitchener's use of personal staff to convey verbal order(s) to field commanders could escape the attention of staff and senior commanders and enjoy the status of being 'non-attributable'. To complete the conspiracy of silence Kitchener would rely on the fact that his personal staff would never reveal such action because of their loyalty and a sense of duty to Kitchener,[263] not to mention the severe repercussions that might ensue as a consequence of a breach of trust. There can be no doubt that Kitchener was not only capable of such deceit but was an accomplished past master at it. Carnegie believes that Kitchener 'was also cunning and he only gave verbal instructions not to take prisoners'.[264]

Denton expresses the view that: 'As a professional and very tough soldier he [Kitchener] may well have condoned secretly the sorts of actions being carried out in areas like the Spelonken; he may even have suggested the "no prisoners" approach and allowed the word to filter down unobtrusively through Colonel Hamilton and others, but he was hardly the type of man to issue a direct order of the kind which could so easily have drawn down fire on his own head.'[265]

Davey questions Carnegie's view: 'i. that Kitchener only gave verbal instructions that prisoners should not be taken (p.53); ii. that Kitchener's staff were willing to "go to their death or lie in their teeth for him" (p. 110).'[266]

But Carnegie's view is valid. The absence of written orders to subordinate commanders regarding the shooting of Boers in khaki when documentary evidence confirms their existence indicates they must have been issued verbally. In which case his staff lied. Tellingly, during the courts martial, neither the court nor the prosecution attempted to rebut the allegations from defence witnesses that they had seen or been given orders to shoot prisoners. Those who maintain the establishment line are blinded by their own political conviction and continue to ignore the undeniable evidence that there were verbal orders to shoot prisoners. The courts martial were denied this vital evidence, so although the verdicts are understandable, they are no longer 'beyond reasonable doubt'.

This paper contends that a secretive and duplicitous Kitchener used every legal and quasi-legal non-attributable device within his powers to rid the Spelonken of Boers. Kitchener also had the power to make all these actions legal for all ranks if he committed such orders and proclamations to writing as, for example, authorised reprisals. But written orders could attract criticism from the foreign powers and incur the wrath of Whitehall, which was reluctant to support some of Kitchener's more draconian solutions to the Boer problem.

Firstly, Kitchener's order to shoot surrendering Boers

by making them defend themselves then ignoring any display of the white flag was legal according to the *Manual of Military Law*, albeit immoral. This order complied with the Customs of War even though Kitchener removed the discretionary powers normally exercised by field commanders, as recorded by Poore.

Secondly, Kitchener's order to shoot surrendered Boers wearing khaki on the spot as directed by 'Proclamation' as a measure of retaliation and as recorded by Poore was also confirmed by his secret signal to Brodrick. In addition, official records show 'legal' military courts only executed four Boer prisoners during the war for this 'prevalent offence'. These four Boers, by some oversight, escaped summary execution in favour of a questionable 'legal' execution.

Thirdly, Kitchener's order to shoot all Boer prisoners was a 'catch all' if all other measures failed. It would also solve the problem of sick and war weary Boers surrendering only to rejoin their commandos at a later date. It is inconceivable Hamilton expected an experienced officer like Hunt to obey such an order. What other convincing justification or guarantee of protection accompanied Kitchener's order which compelled Hunt, to repeat the mistakes of his predecessor, Robertson? If the shooting of Boer prisoners was so unusual and inhumane why wasn't Hunt warned about continuing the practice? Why was Hunt so confident of his orders to carry out such 'dastardly' deeds that he openly acknowledged Kitchener as the culprit even though such an accusation could land Hunt in considerable trouble? Hunt's death certainly solved many problems and facilitated Kitchener's later evasive actions.

So why bother with the theatre of a court of inquiry and courts martial? Why not simply charge Morant and Handcock with failing to properly carry out army orders? The truth is that Kitchener and the British authorities did not want to admit that there were any exigencies that would allow imperial or colonial forces to shoot prisoners in what appeared to be an arbitrary manner. Would the

British public and Britain's critics make the fine distinction between what Morant did and others were doing? Boer prisoners were dead, Heese was dead and someone had to be seen to pay. According to the eminent English military historian, The Marquis of Anglesey, it was a simple case of crime and punishment: '[Morant and Handcock], in spite of recommendation to mercy, were shot on Kitchener's orders after what was, to put it leniently, an unsound court martial. It is clear that the Commander-in-Chief was determined to make an example, for there was mounting evidence of indiscipline in the numerous irregular units.'[267]

The Boer War has often been described as 'the first media war' and Britain's image had already taken a hammering in the home and international press. Chamberlain had caused an uproar in Germany with a speech he made on October 10, 1901, in Edinburgh, accusing them of carrying out atrocities during the Franco–Prussian war.[268] As already discussed, khaki was not exclusively a British form of dress and, although it was not recognised by any formal international treaty in 1901, it was generally accepted in the so-called 'civilised world' that combatants would be given quarter once the white flag had been raised. If it were then revealed that their Customs of War sanctioned Morant's actions, Britain would have suffered a humiliating loss of face. As it was, the execution of Morant and Handcock was well received in the media, both at home and internationally as proof of Britain's 'impartiality'.[269]

Despite the iniquities of the court of inquiry, which tried to intimidate, exhaust and entrap the accused and the high-handed attitude of the senior members of the courts martial, they did get a 'fair go' from the panel members. Many were stationed in Pietersburg and would have been friendly with the accused in better times. The members appeared sympathetic with, and, at times, even supportive of the accused. The leeway given to the defence frustrated the prosecution and the Judge Advocate of the court on a number of occasions.[270]

Although they found Morant, Handcock and Witton

guilty of killing Boer prisoners they issued strong Recommendations to Mercy. Thomas won the argument that the
killings were not cold blooded murder, as is often claimed,
but acts of vengeance following the murder and mutilation
of Captain Hunt, which the members accepted was proved.
They also recognised the prisoner's previous good services,
their ignorance of military law and custom and the fact
that Morant had been placed in a difficult position with
no military experience or superior to consult.[271] However,
Kitchener again showed a sleight of hand by informing
both Lord Roberts and the Governor General of Australia
that there were 'no mitigating circumstances'.[272]

The 'Not Guilty' verdict in the Heese case, which they
saw as the main charge, prompted two members of the
courts martial to send champagne to the accused in
the belief that they would be at least spared the death
penalty.[273] In their cells they had what proved to be a premature celebration.

The verdict

Major CS Copland, failed to comply with the letter of the
law during the courts martial and was again found wanting
during the sentencing procedure. The Rules of Procedure
stipulate that only one sentence can be awarded 'in respect
of all the offences of which the offender is found guilty and
that sentence shall be deemed to be awarded in respect of
each charge'.[274] Copland, however, allowed the court to
award a sentence to each guilty finding for each offender.

This failure by the courts martial to follow procedure
attracted adverse criticism from the Judge Advocate
General's Office, which cast some doubt on the safety of
some verdicts and sentences. Staff criticism forwarded to
the Adjutant General on February 20, 1902, included the
following:

Legal Opinion
Pietersburg Cases,
[To] A.G. [Adjutant General] (Major General Kelly)

The procedure followed on these trials was by trying the prisoners jointly on each charge of murder and conducting each trial to its conclusion, including the sentence.

It resulted from this mode of procedure that Lieut. Morant has been convicted three times to death.

Lieuts. Picton, Handcock and Witton have been convicted once of manslaughter and sentenced to cashiering; Lieut. Handcock has been also twice convicted of murder and sentenced to death twice.

Lieut. Witton has been convicted of murder and sentenced to death. From the above it appears that the responsibility for these illegal acts were (sic) in the following order:

1. Morant. 2. Handcock. 3. Whitton. 4. Picton.

According to rules of procedure 48 and 62 the trial on the separate charge sheets should have proceeded up to and including the findings – but that one sentence should have been awarded each prisoner for all the offences of which he was convicted.

This irregularity has not in my opinion inflicted any injustice on Lieut. Morant, but I am not prepared to say that it has not done so in the other 3 cases.

[Col. St Clair]
20-2-02[275]

Davey makes the following comments: 'with some minor reservation about procedure [Pemberton and St Clair] were in agreement with the verdicts.'[276] However, the above quote by St Clair, the senior legal adviser, must be considered substantial because multiple sentences can allow legal objection to the sentences.[277] Unfortunately, Major Thomas and the accused could not protest because they would be unaware of this breach of the Rules of Procedure until well after the verdicts were promulgated. The denial of petition on the verdicts meant the condemned were executed regardless.

Kitchener's assertion that, 'There were, in my opinion, "no extenuating circumstances"' in the Morant affair, compounds his litany of lies.[278] As already detailed there were strong Recommendations to Mercy in the Visser case, the eight Boers case and the three Boers case. The Manual of Military Law states that: 'a recommendation to mercy will be exceptional . . . owing to the prisoner's character or other exceptional circumstances, he should not suffer the full penalty which the offence would ordinarily demand.'[279]

Whereas some verdicts and sentences were questionable, the promulgation and execution of the sentences highlights Kitchener's determination to brook no opposition or interference from any quarter. Kitchener obtained Crown concurrence in the preferred punishments in a telegram on February 24, 1902.[280] He confirmed the sentences on February 25, then disappeared before the sentences were confirmed late on the morning of February 26, for execution at dawn the next day. The protests raised by the accused were greeted with the news that Kitchener could not be contacted and that the punishments had War Office concurrence and, therefore, nothing could be done.[281]

The prisoners should have had the privilege of being able to petition the confirming authority (Kitchener) and/or the reviewing authorities using normal channels (Kitchener).[282] 'An officer should not be disposed to push to extremes his right to bring his complaint before the Sovereign.'[283] [Emphasis added] This right was frustrated. To further ensure the sentences could not be stayed, all communications between the prisoners and the outside world were withheld which was consistent with the general level of secrecy surrounding the whole affair.

All of the above legal process, from arrest to punishment, was conducted in total secrecy instigated at the highest level. Neither Lord Roberts, nor the British Government knew anything of killings and court martials until early January 1902 when a returning British surgeon wrote to Roberts.[284] In a private letter from St John Brodrick to Kitchener, dated February 22, 1902, the Secretary of State for War states: 'Your report of the Court Martial on Bush Veldt Carabineers [sic] came to hand last night. It is a most deplorable performance and, if it gets out, as I fear it will, even the strong measures we are taking will not undo the disgrace it inflicts on our Colonial Forces.'

The impartial Minister went on to say he would have shot Witton also![285] In a telegram to Kitchener on February 24, 1902, St John Brodrick remarked: 'As the incident will probably become public, I should like to be furnished with the fullest particulars and the evidence by mail.'[286] He complained that although he had kept the Morant affair quiet, he was embarrassed when the findings and sentences were listed in Army Orders without his knowledge.[287]

Unluckier still was the Australian Government. The first 'official' advice it received was from Major Lenehan on return from South Africa. He personally reported the matter to Major General E Hutton, General Officer Commanding, Commonwealth Forces. Hutton relayed Lenehan's startling allegations to the Secretary for Defence on March 27, 1902, regarding 'certain occurrences in connection with Australian Officers serving under him [Lenehan] and to himself, and I have the honour to request that a cable communication may be sent to the Commander-in-Chief, South Africa, on the subject'.[288] These communications give substance to the view that 'strong measures' were taken to keep the whole legal process secret. It would also explain the news blackout after the sentences were carried out. The lengths the authorities went to is hard to justify on any grounds other than the ambition of Kitchener himself. The Secretary intimated that the secrecy was a response to conceal 'the disgrace it inflicts on our Colonial Forces', but as secrecy is an anathema to British justice, other motives must be attributed.

The evidence presented to the courts martial was

seriously deficient. Kitchener denied giving an order to shoot prisoners, yet he did. Hunt asserts Hamilton gave him such an order, which Hamilton denied but whose evidence could not be tested. It also begs belief to expect Hamilton would admit in court that he relayed a verbal order to Hunt, which Kitchener would deny issuing. As mentioned, Hamilton's integrity was seriously questioned to the extent that another of Kitchener's acolytes, Lieutenant-Colonel Henry Rawlinson, considered him the 'enemy'.[289] The one person, apart from Kitchener, who could provide critical evidence on these matters, was Hall. However, Kitchener conveniently removed Hall before he could give evidence to the investigation or the courts martial. More importantly, the secret telegram Kitchener did send to the Secretary of State for War concerning shooting captured Boers, provided evidence of summary executions withheld from the courts martial.

Having no previous experience in shooting British officers, Kitchener provided a brief and misleading summary of the courts martial proceedings to obtain the hasty 'concurrence' of a partial and gullible Secretary of State for War. But such was Kitchener's haste to be rid of the whole messy business that he contravened the terms of his empowering Court-Martial Warrant, which was facilitated by an incompetent British minister.

COURT-MARTIAL WARRANTS

Only the Court-Martial Warrant issued to the Commanders-in-Chief by the Crown authorises them to convene a general courts martial and confirm verdicts and sentences awarded – except in the cases of British officers. Colonel St Clair, DJAG, was of the opinion that 'the warrant held by the C in C which I presume is according to Form IV on p.765. Man. Mil. Law.'[290]

One would think that the DJAG would not 'presume' but be in no doubt about the exact nature of the particular warrant. This warrant states in part:

'Provided always, that if by the sentence of any General Court-Martial a *Commissioned Officer*, other than a native Commissioned Officer, *has been sentenced to suffer Death*, or Penal Servitude, or to be cashiered or dismissed from Our Service, you shall in such cases, as also in the case of any other General Court-Martial in which you shall think fit so to do, *transmit the proceedings* to Our Judge-Advocate-General, in order that he may lay the same before Us and afterwards send them to Our Commander-in-Chief, or, in his absence, to the Adjutant-General of Our Forces, *for Our decision* thereupon.' [Emphasis added]

Apart from St Clair being careless in his opinion, Kitchener was obliged to, 'transmit the proceedings of any General Court-Martial to Our Judge-Advocate-General, in order that he may lay the same before us'. But Kitchener submitted his preferred sentences without the actual proceedings to St John Brodrick, the Secretary of State for War. In the *Manual of Military Law* 1899 proceedings are specifically described as follows:

'At a court-martial the judge-advocate, or, if there is none, the president, shall record or cause to be recorded all transactions of that court, and shall be responsible for the accuracy of the record (in these rules referred to as the proceedings);'[291]

The *Concise Oxford Dictionary* defines proceedings as 'published report of discussion or conference'.

Kitchener's cursory telegram to Brodrick, dated February 21, 1902, stated:

'Your No. 636. Lieutenant Morant, Lieutenant Hancock [sic], Lieutenant Whitton [sic], Lieutenant Picton and Major Lenehan, the Officer Commanding the Bushveldt Carabineers [sic], have been tried by General Court Martial. Trial received today, resulted in convicting of Morant of 3 separate murders, Handcock, 2 murders and 1 manslaughter; Whitton, 1 murder and 1 manslaughter, Picton, 1 manslaughter; Lenehan neglecting to report knowledge acquired after fact. The murders were of Boer prisoners, in a spirit of revenge, for alleged ill-treatment of 1 of their officers, Lieutenant Hunt, who was shot in action. No such ill-treatment was proved. Sentence, the first 3, death; Picton, cashiered; Lenehan will be removed. As corps had been disbanded some time ago for irregularities, dismissal of Lenehan not necessary, and he will be ordered to Australia. I propose to confirm sentences on Morant, who originated crimes, on Handcock, who carried out several cold-blooded murders, and, in the case of Whitton [sic], who was present, but under influence, commutation to penal servitude for life. Do you concur? There are other cases against Morant and Handcock, including a charge of murder of German. Plea in evidence was not sufficient to convict.'

The Secretary replied three days later:

'The circumstances of these deplorable occurrences, and the evidence which has led to the conviction of these 5 officers, are not before us in sufficient detail to enable a judgment to be formed here of the relative guilt of those convicted. We are prepared to support the conclusion you have arrived at. If you have any doubt as to reprieving Whitton [sic], I could only express our opinion if all the facts and circumstances were communicated, which would cause delay, and I fully rely on your judgment.'

This exchange of barest details between Kitchener and Brodrick can hardly be recognised as 'proceedings' in the terms of the Warrant or the *Manual of Military Law* description. Even Kitchener's scant summary encapsulating the proceedings of five trials taken over one month is untrue and misleading in at least two significant aspects. In addition, legal opinion on the proceedings by the St Clair and Pemberton were not entered in the *Minute Book of Letters* until February 28, 1902 – the day after the executions and seven days after Kitchener's telegram. Did Kitchener characteristically notify Brodrick without the benefit of legal opinion? For his part Brodrick acknowledges in his reply that Kitchener provided insufficient detail to enable a judgment to be made, even though the warrant demands his decision to be based on the proceedings of the courts martial.

The mandatory Crown review of the sentences was frustrated by Kitchener's submission of a deceitful summary in place of the required courts martial proceedings. If the purpose of seeking Crown concurrence was to allow the sentences to be reviewed independently and impartially by someone who was in possession of all the facts then this purpose was clearly frustrated. Any fair assessment of the process outlined would have to conclude that the sentences did not receive Crown concurrence based on the facts and are, therefore, questionable.

Adding weight to the argument that a Crown review may well have arrived at quite a different conclusion are the comments of Sir Francis Jeune, Judge Advocate General in London. Kitchener's Warrant stipulated that Jeune and not Brodrick should have received the proceedings for Crown review. In April 1902, just after the executions hit the headlines in both Australia and England, Lord Roberts informed Kitchener: 'We have had some difficulty with Sir Francis Jeune in regard to General Courts Martial. I proposed that you should have the power of confirming the sentences as is the practice in India. He argued that this would be unfair to the officers who like to think that their cases are submitted to the King before being finally decided. Unfortunately the first General Court Martial sent home under the new rules somewhat supported Jeune's contention that officers officiating as Judge Advocate General are not sufficiently versed in law to warrant the conduct of Courts Martial being left altogether with them.'[292]

In another part of the same letter Roberts reveals: 'It would be as well to warn St Clair and his assistants that their work is being very carefully scrutinised by the JA General here.' Hardly a ringing endorsement of the administration of justice that Morant's critics have always maintained was fair and above board.

The failure to punish Taylor must also be questioned. In early February 1902, following the conclusion of the three Boers case against Morant and Handcock, the same court then convened to hear the charges against 'Captain' Alfred Taylor. The court, however, underwent a dramatic change in jurisdiction. He was to be tried by a military court instead of a court martial.[293]

THE MILITARY COURT OF EX-CAPTAIN ALFRED TAYLOR

Captain Alfred Taylor, an Irishman of great experience in South Africa, became attracted to the field of intelligence culminating in his appointment to Kitchener's intelligence branch. His official appointment appears to have been acting native commissioner and intelligence officer. His record of service in the British Army is as elusive as the man himself. Even the Judge Advocate's Office had difficulty in determining the exact nature of Taylor's commission.[294] His appointment was in line with Kitchener's general approach to the war being waged in northern Transvaal – endorsing brutality. Carnegie notes: 'Kitchener's plan to defeat the enemy by turning Boer territory into a vast desert needed ruthless men. Taylor was ruthless. An Intelligence officer who knew the Spelonken area and its people – he was Kitchener's man for the job.'[295]

Witton notes that 'as far as the natives were concerned, he [Taylor] had a free hand and the power of life and death; he was known and feared by them from the Zambezi to the Spelonken, and was called by them 'Bulala' which means to kill, to slay'.[296]

Kitchener's personal interest in Taylor is substantial and well documented, as shown by the following passages:

- May 11, 1901. Taylor burnt down the village of Lois Trichardt on the orders of Kitchener. (Colonel Grenfell's column)[297]
- 'I [Taylor] went with the column [Grenfell's] to Pietersburg and was sent for by the Commander-in-Chief and was congratulated on the work I had accomplished.'[298]
- In May 1901, de Bertodano alleges he tried to have Taylor relieved. The matter was discussed with Kitchener but no action taken.[299] Obviously Kitchener preferred Taylor's effective brutality to de Bertodano's unproductive and questionable morality.
- August 30, 1901. The new civilian Minister for Native Affairs (GY Lagden) wrote to the Director of Military Intelligence (DMI) (Colonel Henderson) concerning a 'conversation with you and with Lord Kitchener about Taylor . . . Lord Kitchener suggested that we should take Taylor over'.[300]
- September 2, 1901. Even after AHQ was made aware of Taylor's involvement in the shooting of the six Boers, Van Buuren, the eight Boers and the three Boers, the Director of Military Intelligence congratulated Taylor commenting, 'Your success . . . is much appreciated, and Lord Kitchener hopes to hear of your further successes'.[301]
- September 11, 1901. A letter from Enraght-Moony to the Minister for Native Affairs stated: 'This is of course confidential and not to be used in discussing the matter with C-in-C [Kitchener], Taylor was sent up without reference to Col. Hall.'[302]
- September 27, 1901. Kitchener finally relented and the Director of Military Intelligence issued orders for Taylor to return to Pretoria for administrative reasons.[303]

Earlier in July 1901, Taylor briefed a patrol of BVC to intercept and shoot six Boers. An inquiry into this and other matters implicated Captain Robertson. Consequently, the formation commander, Colonel Hall, obliged

Robertson to resign. Despite eyewitness statements that Taylor had issued the order, no blame was attached to Taylor for his decisive part in the incident.

When Kitchener set up his dragnet to ensnare only BVC officers implicated in the shooting of prisoners he could hardly ignore Taylor's part in the six Boers case, which was common knowledge. Taylor, however, like Colonel Hall, knew more than the secretive Kitchener would want revealed in regard to the shadier side of operations designed to rid the Spelonken of Boers, such as, looting, dispossession, killing Africans, arming Africans and rough justice in regard to Boers. Therefore the dilemma facing Kitchener was that justice had to be seen to be done, by arresting Taylor, along with the BVC accused of similar crimes, yet not to the extent of sacrificing the future use of Taylor's considerable talents.

Thus, the second inquiry in November 1901 included the six Boers case and this time Taylor was implicated. As far as is known, he suffered the same treatment as his fellow officers with one exception. Taylor was allowed to resign his commission at about the same time as he was arrested (a privilege already received by Taylor's co-accused ex-Captain Robertson who turned King's evidence). Consequently, as the trial did not begin until three months after his unpublicised resignation and arrest, Taylor was not tried by a court martial as an officer but by a military court as a civilian. On February 28, 1902, the Deputy Judge Advocate General, Pretoria, sent the trial documents to the Judge Adjutant General, Great Britain, with the notation: 'The record of a Military Court held under Martial law for the trial of Alfred Taylor an intelligence agent. The latter was not tried by a Court-Martial under the Army Act. As at date of trial he had ceased to be subject to military law for more than three months. A full report on these cases has been sent to the Secretary of State for War by this mail.'[304]

The authority for this distinction can be found in The Customs of War – Military Occupation:

'47. The special tribunals created by an invader for carrying into effect the rule of military occupation in the case of individual offenders are usually military courts framed on the model and carried on their proceedings after the manner of a courts-martial. Technically, however, courts so established by an English general would not be courts-martial within the meaning of the Army Act, *but courts established and regulated only by the will of the general*.'[305] [Emphasis added]

Obviously the phrase emphasised did not escape the attention of Kitchener, because it virtually meant, regardless of the finding of a military court, he could impose any penalty which took his fancy at the time, unlike a courts martial where his options were severely limited by the *Army Act*. Good news for ex-Captain Taylor, but not so good for his fellow officers facing a court martial on similar charges.

The resignation of Taylor was not published in British Army Orders because, as a Rhodesian, his resignation may have been processed through Rhodesia in accordance with the *Army Act*, Section 175, which states that this can be done: 'Provided that nothing in this Act shall affect the application to such persons of any Act passed by the legislature of a colony.' If Taylor's resignation was processed and promulgated in Rhodesia and not in AHQ Army Orders then Kitchener's protection of Taylor would not appear obvious and Taylor's co-accused would remain ignorant of the fact until his military court occurred. Why does the three months required to escape a court martial dovetail so neatly with the wasted three months the accused spent incommunicado in solitary confinement? Why, under the circumstances, did Kitchener allow Taylor to resign his commission and not let him face the full force of the law as convention demanded? After all, Enraght-Moony had secured the evidence and according to

Pakenham, Kitchener was 'wild' about the indiscretions committed by his troops.

The obvious answer to the last question is that Taylor was an extremely experienced, efficient and ruthless intelligence operative who, like de Bertodano, knew too much and therefore warranted Kitchener's protection. Section 9 sub-section 2 of the *Army Act* may also have had something to do with it. Again it reads: 'it is not requisite to prove that the command was given personally by a superior. It is sufficient to show that it was given by the deputy or agent of a superior.'[306] If it came to light that Taylor was an 'agent' of Kitchener's and was found guilty of ordering the deaths of Boer prisoners – then Thomas' defence of superior orders would implicate Kitchener directly.

The composition of the courts martial in the three Boers case remained the same for the military trial of ex-Captain Taylor. Witton notes that 'Captain Taylor was afterwards tried by court-martial for having ordered the shooting of the six Boers'[307] and also that 'The court then sat to hear the charges against Captain Alfred Taylor'.[308] However, Witton was not aware the nature and jurisdiction of the court had changed.[309] In addition, Witton refers to Robertson (giving King's evidence)[310] as 'ex-captain' because he had resigned but continues to refer to Taylor as 'captain', oblivious to Taylor's changed status.[311] However, *The Times* reported on April 17, 1902, that: 'On February 7 the military court sat to hear the charges against Alfred Taylor.'

Taylor was charged with incitement to murder, yet eleven separate charges were recommended by the court of inquiry.[312] Taylor was, in one way or another, involved in all of the charges against all of the accused. In the absence of Colonel Hall, the only witnesses arraigned against him were the disgraced ex-Captain Robertson and two senior non-commissioned officers (Oldham and Morrison) over whom Taylor, in theory at least, exercised no direct command function. In addition, all the damning written evidence found by Enraght-Moony and sent to the intelligence department[313] was not admitted into evidence and an incriminating file concerning the case was 'stolen' from Captain Taylor's office.[314] Again, the tactic was not to tamper with the court only to withhold any incriminating witnesses and evidence.

What had not been 'lost' was easily explained away. One of the charges against Taylor was that he shot in the head a native who refused to give him details of Boer movements. Taylor's plea that he had intended to shoot over his head but aimed too low was accepted.[315]

Not surprisingly, Taylor was acquitted by Kitchener's arranged military court and despite his reputation continued in military service as a civilian for the rest of the war.[316] The South Rhodesian medal roll confirms he received The King's South Africa Medal with clasps for 1901 and 1902 'for special services under Lord Kitchener June 1901–April 1902',[317] proof, if any more was needed, that he was Kitchener's 'man'. Although evidence at the courts martial implicated Taylor in other incidents, further indictments did not ensue. It can also be concluded that both Captain Hunt and Captain Taylor were both pursuing Kitchener's dream of ridding the Spelonken of Boers. The reason for this single-minded objective is most likely found in the verbal orders relayed to commanders in the field by Kitchener's personal staff officers. Taylor did not admit to knowing of orders to not take prisoners, but admitted to knowing that Hunt had issued such orders. That, as a superior officer, he allowed such orders to be implemented without taking any action whatever was an offence and an act of condonation that no-one seemed to notice.

By the admission of their own legal experts and many others since, British justice provided a below average performance during the Morant affair. There are grave questions of justice surrounding the findings and sentencing at the courts martial, the use of inadmissible material; the withholding of evidence; the lack of defence experience and preparation; the failure of at least one material witness to take the stand; the furtive executions denying petition, Crown concurrence secured through deceit and the high degree of secrecy accompanying the legal process, aided and abetted at the highest levels of public office. The greatest tragedy, however, was the failure of the prosecution to acknowledge a clear case of condonation, despite displaying a clear familiarity with the term.[318]

CONDONATION

Condonation, the excusing of an offence by virtue of mitigating circumstances, takes two forms – in the first, a superior annuls the offence by acceptance of the conduct or by failure to discipline an offender; in the second, the offence is excused by an act of bravery by the offender 'after the knowledge of a military offence committed'. Both forms are relevant to the BVC courts martial – the first was pleaded somewhat weakly by Major Thomas, however it is the second that deserved more of the court's attention.

The first mention of condonation appears in the Australian petition to His Majesty the King in December 1902 requesting a pardon for Witton.[319] The petition was based on the opinion of Isaac Isaacs (1855–1943), a noted legislator, jurist and counsel (later Chief Justice and Governor General of Australia). The petition reviews the known evidence as supplied by participants and newspaper reports in the absence of official records. In paragraph 12, the petition raises the issue of condonation in the following terms:

> Clode, at page 103, states the general principles thus – 'The discharge of duty involves condonation', and quotes the Duke of Wellington as writing 'The performance of a duty of honour and trust after knowledge of a military offence ought to convey a pardon'.[320]

The reason why such an eminent jurist did not mention the *Manual of Military Law* in relation to condonation is because the manual hardly mentions the subject.

The British Government's attitude to the issue of condonation raised by Isaacs in paragraph 12 of the petition cannot be determined because the official 'file on which this petition was considered 110/Cape/833 has apparently been destroyed. The file referred to marked up to 110/Colonies/19(1907) and apparently all these papers have been destroyed' as at October 24, 1919.[321]

With regard to the second and most common type of condonation, Morant, Handcock and Witton were involved in three incidents, which, to a greater or lesser degree, qualify as acts of condonation under the above definition. Hall and Lenehan, aware that military offences had been committed, took no disciplinary action, but signalled condonation of past actions by sending him in command, on an arduous and dangerous mission over one hundred miles away from base. Apart from that, Morant was commended on the mission by Colonel Hall. This action could be classed as a type one condonation by invoking the principles of:

(a) The discharge of duty involves condonation, and
(b) The performance of a duty of honour and trust after knowledge of a military offence ought to convey a pardon.

On January 23, 1902, during the court martial into the Visser case, there was an attack on the fort at Pietersburg by Beyers'[322] commando. Although Wilcox says that, 'their [Morant and Handcock's] role in the defence was trivial'[323] others, who were there, saw it differently: 'Morant joined Handcock as soon as the firing commenced, and they climbed together on to the flat roof of the fort, in the most exposed position. Disregarding any cover, they fought as only such brave and fearless men can fight. Handcock in particular, in his cool and silent manner, did splendid work.'[324]

Renar noted that they were 'brought out of their cells to help fight for the lives and freedom of their gaolers . . . Morant was in command at his own prison, and right gallantly he held himself, fighting like the brave man that he was, and having probably in his heart more hope than fear of death, since an evil fate threatened him just then so sorely. The others too, Lenehan, Picton, Handcock and Witton, showed out as men of courage.'[325]

Even Lord Kitchener himself acknowledged the spirited defence of Pietersburg and was, therefore, aware of the details that the prisoners were called to arms and that a plea of condonation would result: '. . . the attack upon the town [Pietersburg] was not equally successful. This commenced at 4.20 am on the 24th January, and, after 20 minutes' sharp firing, resulted in the complete repulse of General Beyers, who retired, leaving three of his followers killed, and three dangerously wounded within 300 yards of our defences. Great steadiness was show by the Volunteer Town Guard, who turned out with promptitude to support the troops in garrison.'[326]

It should also be noted that Handcock was credited with bagging Marthinus Pretorius, Beyers' fighting leader.

Again, on January 31, 1902, en route from Pretoria to Pietersburg, the train halted near Warm Baths Station as Boers were sighted on the rail line. 'A member of the court came to our little sheep-truck and for the second time during our trial we were ordered to stand to arms.' No contact was made with Boers.[327]

A plea of condonation should also have been entered once it was revealed that senior officers were made aware of the offences soon after they were committed but failed to reprimand, caution or remove the offenders from duty or positions of command. This relates to the first type of condonation mentioned in the preamble and meant that the offences were 'condoned by competent military authority' in accordance with Rules of Procedure 36(A)(2) or condoned 'by the deliberate act of some superior authority', Rules of Procedure 34, Note A.

Some time after the war, Bolton's daughter, Mrs Bagshaw, recalled that Thomas did enter a plea of condonation (second type): 'It is quite true that Morant was released on parole to help defend the town, and the other officer defending him did all he could to get him off or his sentence reduced on that account.'[328]

However, there is no evidence that a plea of condonation was entered because 'If he offers a plea in bar the court shall record it as well as his general plea', Rules of Procedure 36(B). There is no mention of the Beyers' attack by any member of the courts martial or in any available court document and nor was it mentioned in mitigation.[329] In addition, a plea in bar of trial on the grounds of condonation would, if proven, require the trial to be adjourned for the plea to be confirmed. Even if a plea of condonation is not proven it must be recorded on court documents. No such endorsement exists on available court documents or official summaries of the court findings and sentences.

The absence of a plea of condonation by the defence may be attributed to the following: firstly, the long period of solitary confinement denied them visits from a Chaplin, never mind the chance to seek legal advice or prepare any kind of defence. When Major Thomas arrived he had no time to prepare a defence before the trial commenced and admitted that he approached the trial 'as a private practitioner of law of a British Colony'.[330] His lack of military experience would have tragic and fatal consequences for the accused because condonation is a rare plea in civil law.

Secondly, the defendants could not brief Major Thomas on condonation because even the members of the court martial remarked on their ignorance of military law. The *Manual of Military Law* 1899, (4th Edition) scarcely mentions condonation; the 1907 and 1914 editions (5th and 6th Editions) do not even mention condonation in the index whereas the 1929 edition (7th Edition) provides a page in explanation. Yet the principle had not changed since the time of the Duke of Wellington and codification by Clode.

Thirdly, even if the members of the court martial were aware a plea of condonation was warranted they are not obliged to express an opinion on the conduct of the prosecution or defence as long as both progress in accordance with the Rules of Procedure.

Pakenham gives an example of condonation at the Siege

of Mafeking. An artillery officer named Murchison was tried and sentenced to death by Colonel RS Baden-Powell for the murder of *The Daily Chronicle* correspondent, named Parslow, 'but later released because of gallant services in the siege'.[331]

The 1899 *Manual of Military Law* Rules of Procedure 36(A)(2) outlines the procedure for a plea in bar of trial on the grounds the offence had been condoned.[332] Although the principle had not changed, the 1929 edition added to Rules of Procedure 36(A)(2) that: 'The fact that after trial, but before confirmation, the accused has been employed on active operations does not affect the legal validity of the sentence, but affords grounds for a pardon.'[333] The Murchison case takes this process one stage further. This precedent dictates that after sentence has been confirmed any act by the condemned man involving the 'performance of a duty of honour and trust' also conveys a pardon. Sir Isaac Isaac's opinion was that the plea of condonation remained valid, even after a sentence had commenced. British comment on this opinion cannot be determined as this file is missing.

A pardon is the remission (forgiveness) of legal consequences of a crime or conviction. In the Murchison case the trial and sentencing was complete when a 'duty of honour and trust' arose, yet condonation was still granted. But the two qualifying acts of condonation displayed by the BVC officers were not even mentioned at the courts martial. As there appears to be no impediment to a plea of condonation after sentences have been carried out and there is adequate evidence to support the plea of condonation at the courts martial of Morant, Handcock and Witton, they should be pardoned of the legal consequences of their convictions.

This point is supported not only by Issac Isaacs, but by contemporary opinion. The *Australian Dictionary of Biography* notes: 'The acquittal [of Morant] whilst certainly open on the evidence, is with hindsight best supported by the defence of condonation based on the call to service during the attack on Pietersburg.'[334]

The last word on the condonation issue should go to Melbourne QC Charles Francis. In a recent newspaper article on the Morant affair he commented:

'While expressing no views on the facts that gave rise to the court martial of Breaker Morant and Peter Handcock ('Morant Deserves A Break' February 6th, 2002) their conviction was clearly wrong in law.

Early in the 19th century the Duke of Wellington propounded the military legal principle of condonation.

No soldier facing court martial could be required to perform military duties until his trial ended. If he were placed on military duties, that was a condonation of any offence previously committed and thereafter could not be tried for it.

During the process of Morant and Handcock's trial, the Boer attacked the unit where they were imprisoned.

They were temporarily released to fight valiantly in a successful defence action. Consequently, when the trial resumed, the court had an express duty immediately to discharge them, as their offence, if any, had been condoned.

Kitchener would well have known their conviction was wrongful.

Because of these executions, the Australian Government in the first days of World War I made Australian participation conditional upon no British court martial having the right to execute an Australian.'[335]

It should be borne in mind that this defence of Pietersburg took place during the first court martial and Francis Jeune would have known about this oversight when Roberts commented to Kitchener: 'Unfortunately the first General Court Martial sent home under the new rules somewhat supported Jeune's contention that officers officiating as Judge Advocate General are not sufficiently versed in law to warrant the conduct of Courts Martial being left altogether with them.'[336]

CONCLUSION

The BVC officers were the only British or colonial servicemen prosecuted for the shooting of Boer prisoners during Kitchener's time as Commander-in-Chief. Even by the draconian standards of British military law, their treatment appears to have been unduly harsh and contravened a number of rules and regulations enshrined in an Army Act designed to ensure servicemen got a fair trial. In the past, any such suggestion has been waved away by Morant's critics on the grounds that he was found guilty and deserved his fate, whilst others claim that no objective assessment can ever be made until the elusive court martial transcripts surface. However, there is sufficient evidence from both official and private sources to compensate for the loss of most official records in the Morant affair and to raise serious questions about the veracity of the whole legal process, from the court of inquiry right through to the executions.

Kitchener raised the BVC as an irregular unit to rid the Spelonken of Boers. This unit was manned with hardened veterans with the skills and temperament to accomplish the task. There were, however, episodes of illegality and lawlessness, including the shooting of several Boer prisoners, which marred the reputation of the BVC. With the exception of officially sanctioned reprisals, the shooting of prisoners is manifestly illegal and the penalty is death. But, to be just, the law must be applied universally, without fear or favour. Few of those responsible for shooting prisoners on either side in the Boer War were taken to task. In the Morant affair not all of those involved in the shooting of prisoners were indicted, not all of those indicted were treated impartially and senior officers failed to discourage the crimes or remove the perpetrators when the offences were committed. The singling out of a particular group for special attention is not justice but persecution.

In August 1901, a 'German' missionary was murdered which had the potential to intensify Kitchener's despair and perceived incompetence and further inflame the strident criticism of Britain by the international community. A vigorous resolution of the Heese case was essential despite strong suspicions there was insufficient evidence to guarantee a conviction.

Under the circumstances Kitchener had to act decisively and avoid an embarrassing failure in court. He fashioned the charges from a number of previously ignored and tolerated incidents of shooting of Boer prisoners and included the Heese case as an adjunct. The accused would be convicted of at least one offence at the courts martial, in which case the outcome of the last trial to be conducted, the Heese case, would be almost irrelevant because the 'guilty' would pay the penalty, even in the face of strong recommendations to mercy. Such an outcome would stifle Kitchener's many critics in South Africa, at home and abroad. It would also promote him as a credible, fair, decisive and authoritative figure that could gain the trust of Boers and cultivate a return to peace talks – a scenario that was already under discussion. In the three months after the executions, peace talks were proposed and accepted, culminating in the Vereeniging Peace Treaty of May 31, 1902.

Kitchener's plan, to a large extent, depended on the protection of three officers; Colonel FH Hall, Captain Alfred Taylor and Captain James Robertson. Both Hall and Taylor were variously aware of what information was forwarded to Kitchener's HQ, when it was delivered and what reaction it received. Much of this information would not be to Kitchener's credit. To avoid discrediting Kitchener whilst defending themselves, both were protected from the full force of the law and extended considerable privilege in relation to the legal process.

Hall cleared Taylor of involvement in the six Boers case but there were too many loose ends. When Kitchener indicted BVC officers on similar offences Taylor was swept along with a tide of seemingly righteous indignation. The court of inquiry recommended eleven charges against Taylor but he faced one charge of incitement to murder in relation to the six Boers case and one charge of murdering a native. Taylor, and not Morant, is the common denominator in all of the killings. In addition to this favoured treatment, Taylor was allowed to resign his commission despite strong documentary evidence that he was a murderer. It would appear that even some of those attending the court were not aware of the changed jurisdiction of the court and of Taylor's new status, that is, that Taylor was being tried as a civilian by a military court, instead of being court martialled as an officer.

Hall was more deeply involved than Taylor because of his rank and responsibility; resignation was not an option. So Hall had to be prevented from being called as a witness at the court of inquiry, a summary of evidence or the courts martial. Evidence that supports this belief includes the fact that Hall did not order the arrest or detention of the accused and he did not convene the court of inquiry, yet as formation commander he could be expected to do so. This ensured he did not become entangled in the legal process. In addition, the court of inquiry contravened the rules of procedure and also ensured the accused never knew who all the witnesses were, nor were they given the opportunity to question them.

Thus the arrest and solitary confinement of the accused, for three months, bereft of any consideration, was not designed to prevent the accused from talking to each other as claimed officially. It was meant to provide the time necessary to prepare Colonel Hall's posting to India so he could not be recalled to take the stand at the courts martial as anticipated. His absence was not only an indictable offence but the courts should have been adjourned to accommodate this 'essential witness' because without his attendance the proceedings of the courts martial could be rendered invalid. This waste of time also catered for the qualifying period, which allowed Captain Taylor to resign his commission and revert to civilian status without alerting the accused or counsel to what was happening around them.

In addition, the extraordinary but unjustified measures taken to waive the requirement for a summary of evidence, were, once again, designed to prevent Hall and Taylor from making statements or being questioned. However, the end result was that 'privileged' information from the court of inquiry was probably used to satisfy even the minimum legal requirement of documentation required for convening the courts martial.

The absence of Hall at any of the legal proceedings and the protection of Taylor altered the eventual outcome of all the courts martial. Their privileged treatment also exposes, and amply demonstrates, the manipulative and deceitful nature of Kitchener in achieving his ends, even when it meant perverting the course of justice.

The courts martial themselves were in striking contrast to the court of inquiry. The main blemish concerned the failure of Major CS Copland to carry out his responsibilities in regard to the Rules of Procedure. His reluctance to allow the traditional leeway normally given to the defence in serious matters was amply demonstrated. But his failure to comply with the Rules regarding verdicts and sentencing caused the Judge Advocate's office to cast doubt on the safety of the verdicts and sentences against those other than Morant. The most damning failure of the trials, however, was to allow evidence to be withheld. Kitchener's denial he ever ordered Boer prisoners shot, robbed the system of any semblance of justice.

The central argument at the courts martial amounted to whether the accused had Kitchener's authorisation to shoot Boer prisoners. The Judge Advocate ruled any evidence confirming the widespread practice of shooting prisoners as irrelevant. But Kitchener had devised a number of ways to rid the Spelonken of Boers.

Firstly, Kitchener issued a 'proclamation' that Boers

wearing khaki were to be summarily executed (according to Poore's Diary, 'on the spot'), as retaliation for treachery. The Secretary of State for War was advised of this fact. A few of the Boers tried before military courts and 'legally' executed for this 'prevalent' offence were condemned because they violated Kitchener's 'proclamation'.

Secondly, Boers were not allowed to surrender. According to Poore's Diary, Kitchener removed the ground commander's discretion in relation to the white flag. Boers were to be made to fight and any display of the white flag was to be ignored and those attempting to 'surrender' were to be shot.

Thirdly, there was strong evidence of a 'catch all' order that was relayed by Kitchener's personal staff authorising the shooting of Boer prisoners, the details of which remain obscure. In the case of the BVC, there is no doubt Hunt ordered prisoners be shot in the full knowledge of Robertson's downfall and disciplined those who ignored it. Why wasn't Hunt ordered to refrain from such practises? What convincing justification did Hamilton offer Hunt, an experienced veteran, to take this path? Why would Hunt leave himself open to serious charges by attributing an 'illegal order' to Kitchener himself? Hunt's untimely demise was indeed fortuitous for Kitchener, as Hamilton could not be challenged in his questionable testimony. And no wonder, Kitchener denied issuing an order to shoot prisoners, yet he did as proven by his 'proclamation', Poore's diary entries and Kitchener's admission to the Secretary of State for War that he had 'had them shot'.

The care taken by Kitchener to avoid any hitches once the BVC sentences were promulgated also deserves comment. Kitchener obtained Crown concurrence to the sentences by submitting an inadequate and deceitful document in contravention of his Warrant. He then ensured that no cables or outside communication could be made to frustrate his will. He then absented himself to avoid receiving any petition. It was their *right* to appeal to the King and Kitchener was, at the very least, morally obliged to hear the petition before the execution. But Kitchener's plan was brilliantly implemented down to the last detail.

The whole legal process was then shrouded in secrecy. Amply supported by the leading political and military figures in the country and at home, Kitchener was so successful in his pursuit of secrecy that no word about the Morant affair filtered back to Australia during the four months of investigation and trials. In addition, news of the executions of Morant and Handcock did not reach Australia for a month after the event. This measure alone stifled any chance of Australian intervention that could again embarrass Kitchener.

Finally, the convictions of Morant, Handcock and Witton satisfied Kitchener's plan in spite of the acquittal in the Heese case. The defence counsel had been a country lawyer before volunteering as an infantry officer in the Boer War. Regardless of his background, he could never realistically expect to get his clients acquitted of all the major charges in light of the rigged evidence. In fact, the absence of defence preparation could render the courts martial invalid. Kitchener's only probable concern was that a plea of condonation might be entered on behalf of Morant, Handcock and Witton in regard to the three separate incidents that justified such a plea. But the inexperience of Thomas sealed the fate of his clients. Condonation is a rare feature of civil law and receives the barest mention in the 1899 *Manual of Military Law*. It contains no explanation of the principles involved in condonation or any example of its application. This would explain why a most learned jurist like Isaac Isaacs did not refer to the *Manual of Military Law* in the petition to secure a pardon for Witton in 1902. What hope did Thomas have? For whatever reason, the plea of condonation was not entered and this failure was by far the single most important travesty of justice.

Whatever the shortcomings of Major Thomas' defence, many eminent legal minds have raised questions about the veracity of the courts martial. Geoffrey Robertson QC has been involved in many high-profile war-crimes trials during his illustrious career. His reading of the 'Morant Affair' also indicates the existence of serious legal flaws:

> Examples abound in military courts of wrongful convictions – from Dreyfus to General Yamashita – and of wrongful acquittals (eg: of Col. Medina over the Mai Lai massacre). 'Breaker' Morant's trial was a particularly unattractive use of legal proceedings against lower ranks as a means of covering up the guilt of more senior officers, who gave or approved the unlawful 'shoot to kill' order, and possibly the 'command responsibility' of Kitchener himself. Morant may have been all too happy to obey the unlawful order, of course, in which case he deserved punishment. But it was morally wrong to use him as a scapegoat for an unlawful policy. I have considered a good deal of material about the trial itself, and consider that it was unfair in a number of respects: the convictions of Morant and Handcock must in consequence be regarded, prima facie, as unsafe.

Robertson's opinion is supported by Lecturer in International Communication at Macquarie University and member of the Advisory Committee on International Humanitarian Law to the Australian Red Cross, NSW, Helen Styles:

> I agree strongly with the argument that Morant and Handcock and Witton deserve to have the conviction quashed as unsound on 'technical grounds'. They deserve to be pardoned on the basis of military practice and opinion juris, in accordance with Wellington's belief that 'The performance of a duty of honour and trust after knowledge of a military offence ought to convey a pardon'. It is particularly significant that this argument was raised by the prominent Australian jurist Sir Isaac Isaacs in the petition for Witton's release in 1902, but was

not entered as a plea in bar of trial in the court martial that led to an unsafe conviction and the execution of Morant and Handcock.

In conclusion, there is reasonable doubt in relation to the manipulated legal process, which masqueraded as British justice during the Morant affair in Pietersburg, early in 1902. As in the Wilmansrust affair the convictions should be quashed on 'technical grounds' without prejudice to the British Government. In any case, Morant, Handcock and Witton deserve to be pardoned on the basis of Wellington's belief that: 'The performance of a duty of honour and trust after knowledge of a military offence ought to convey a pardon.'

Almost as though he knew history would demand an answer, Kitchener did give his opinion on legal matters,

'[I]t does no good to act without the fullest inquiry and strictly on legal lines. A hasty judgement creates a martyr, and unless Military Law is strictly followed, a sense of injustice having been done is the result.'

A proper independent judicial review should now be announced without delay to ensure that Lord Kitchener is taken at his word.

ENDNOTES

1   For an account of the treatment of Lenehan *see* Bleszynski, Nick. *Shoot Straight You Bastards! The Truth Behind the Killing of 'Breaker' Morant* (Updated edition). Sydney: Random House, 2003, pp. 23–25, 431–433; Bridges, Barry. 1978, 'Lord Kitchener and the Morant-Handcock executions', *Journal of the Royal Australian Historical Society*, Vol. 73, No. 1.

2   *The Bulletin*, 'Justice denied', 29 February 2002, p. 26; *Wartime*, Issue 18, pp. 14–16.

3   *Wartime*, Issue 18, p. 15.

4   Wilcox, Craig. *Australia's Boer War: The War in South Africa 1899–1902.* Oxford University Press, 2002, p. 296.

5   *Wartime*, Issue 18, p. 15.

6   Ibid.

7   *Wartime*, Issue 18, p. 66.

8   *The Bulletin*, op cit., p. 26.

9   *The Daily Telegraph*, 'Breaking the Morant "hero myth"', 20 November 2002, p. 7.

10   *Wartime*, Issue 18, p. 66.

11   Witton, George. *Scapegoats of the Empire: The story of the Bushveldt Carbineers*. London: Angus & Robertson, 1982, pp. 197–206.

12   Bleszynski, op cit., pp. 482–483.

13   *The Daily Telegraph*, 'Court in the middle', 18 June 2002, p. 15.

14   Carnegie, Margaret and Shields, Frank. *In Search of Breaker Morant*. Armadale, Vic: H.H. Stephenson, 1979, p. 117.

15   Denton, Kit. *Closed File*. Adelaide: Rigby, 1983, p. 93.

16   Magnus, Sir Philip. *Kitchener*. New York: E.P. Dutton & Co., 1959, p. xi.

17   Ibid., p. 194.

18   Minute Book of Letters, p. 1563.

19   War Office Great Britain, *Manual of Military Law* (MML), 4th Edition. HMSO, London, 1899, p. 653.

20   Commission of Enquiry into the Late Administration of the Kroonstad District, 1901, Free State Archives, Bloemfontein.

21   Fuller, J.F.C. *The Last of The Gentlemans Wars*. London: Faber & Faber, 1937, pp. 159–160.

22   Public Records Office (PRO), War Office (WO), 93/41, Minute Book of Letters from Judge Advocate, Pretoria, p. 916.

23   For further details on de Bertodano *see* Bleszynski, op cit., pp. 179–182; *see also* Woolmore, William. *The Bushveldt Carbineers and the Pietersburg Light Horse*. Melbourne: Slouch Hat Publications, 2002, pp. 296–301.

24   Ibid., p. 224.

25   Ibid., p. 81.

26   Bleszynski, op cit. pp. 500–501.

27   Ibid., p. 469.

28   Smurthwaite, David, *The Boer War 1899–1902*, Hamlyn History, Great Britain, 1999, p. 106.

29   Pakenham, Thomas. *The Boer War*. London: Abacus, 1996, p. 315.

30   Ibid., p. 315.

31   Magnus, op cit.

32   Pakenham, op cit., p. 494.

33   Pakenham, op cit., p. 547.

34   Carnegie, op cit., p. 120.

35   A precursor to the BVC courts martial. In July 1901 three members of the 5th Victorians were sentenced to death for treason. They were overheard saying that they should refuse to serve under a British officer (Brigadier-General Beatson) who had accused them of being 'white-livered curs' after they were over-run by Boers during a night attack. Kitchener commuted their sentences to various terms in prison. When news of their imprisonment reached

Australia the government asked questions and Australians in London petitioned the King. The Victorians were released after 'legal flaws' were suddenly discovered in the court proceedings.

36   Witton, op cit., p. 155.
37   Magnus, op cit., p. 114.
38   Hamilton I. *The Commander*, pp. 99–112, as quoted in Pakenham, op cit., p. 335.
39   Kelly-Kenny, General, Diary, February 18–19, 1900, after the battle of Paardeberg, as quoted in Pakenham, op cit., p. 335.
40   Carnegie, op cit., p. 110.
41   Magnus, op cit., p. 203.
42   Carnegie, op cit., p. 148.
43   Pakenham, op cit., p. 461.
44   Pakenham, op cit., p. 535.
45   Carver, Lord., *The National Army Museum Book of the Boer War Field Marshall Lord Carver*. London: Sedgwick & Jackson, 1999, p. 240.
46   Pakenham, op cit., p. 536; Carver, ibid., pp. 238–239.
47   Carver, op cit., p. 241.
48   King, Peter. *The Viceroy's Fall*. London: Sidgwick & Jackson, 1986, p. 56.
49   Pakenham, op cit., p. 535.
50   Ibid.
51   Pakenham, op cit., p. 536.
52   Roberts to Colonel Ian Hamilton November 26, 1901, File no. 2/3/1–33, Hamilton 2/3/3–4, Hamilton papers, King's College, London, Liddel-Hart Military Archives.
53   Pakenham, op cit., p. 539.
54   Pakenham, op cit., p. 535.
55   Carver, op cit., p. 250.
56   Reitz, Denys. *Commando*. Great Britain: Faber & Faber, 1932, p. 218; Pakenham, op cit., p. 522.
57   Bleszynski, op cit., p. 207.
58   Bleszynski., op cit., pp. 189–192.
59   Jarvis, C.S. *Half a Life*. London: J Murray, 1943, p. 127.
60   Witton, op cit. p. 139.
61   Davey, Arthur. *Breaker Morant and The Bushveldt Carbineers*. South Africa: Van Riebuck Society, 1987, pp. 82–83, 131.
62   Davey, op cit., p. 131.
63   Denton, op cit., p. 126.
64   Davey believes Hunt previously served with the 13th Hussars, op cit., p.xlii.
65   Carnegie, op cit., p. 62.
66   Witton, op cit., p. 113.
67   The total loyalty and dedication of Colonel H.I.W. Hamilton to Kitchener can be amply demonstrated by his conduct in the downfall of Curzon, the Viceroy of India. King, loc cit.

68 Hamilton., op cit., File no. 2/3/7, December 12, 1901.

69 Witton, op cit., p. 59.

70 Witton, op cit., p. 55 (*see* Appendices 1 to Annexes A and B attached for endorsement of court martial).

71 Witton, op cit., p. 154.

72 The MML states that 'condoned by competent military authority' in accordance with Rules of Procedure 36(A)(2) or condoned '*by the deliberate act of some superior authority*' Rules of Procedure 34, Note A are both valid defences.

73 Renar, Frank. *Bushman and Buccaneer*. Sydney: H.T. Dunn, 1902, p. 28.

74 Carnegie, op cit., p. 56 (interview with Shields); *see also* Denton, op cit., pp. 107–108 and Davey, op cit., pp. 95–98 (Trooper E. Powell deposition).

75 Davey, op cit., p. ??.

76 Carnegie, op cit., p. 84.

77 Witton, op cit., p. 63.

78 Davey, op cit., p. 195.

79 Carnegie, op cit., pp. 47–48.

80 Davey, op cit., p. 59.

81 The Shulenberg Papers, 'Daniel Heese: A Biographical sketch' by Pastor Paul Burr, Chapter 10 – Heese's Death.

82 Ibid., p. 135.

83 Witton, op cit., p. 136.

84 Bleszynski, op cit. pp. 462–479.

85 Witton, op cit., p. 116

86 Davey, op cit., p. 22.

87 Bleszynski, op cit., pp. 463–464.

88 Unpublished letter, Alfred E. Haserick, Native Pass Office, Pretoria, September 6, 1901 to Mrs Heckford (protégé of Frank Eland's mother).

89 Pakenham, op cit., pp. 538, 541, 560, 561.

90 Bleszynski, op cit, pp. 464–467.

91 Warner, Philip. *Field Marshal Earl Haig*. London: Cassells Military Paperbacks, 1991, p. 79.

92 Churchill, Winston S. *My Early Life*. Glasgow: Fontana Books, 1979, pp. 361–362.

93 Davey, op cit., p. 166; Woolmore, op cit., p. 39.

94 Carnegie, op cit., p. 136.

95 Witton, op cit., p. 225.

96 Carnegie, op cit., p. 87; Davey, op cit., p. 36.

97 Davey, op cit., liv.

98 Witton, op cit., p. 225.

99 Renar, op cit., p. 42.

100 Wilcox, op cit., p. 276.

101 Pakenham, op cit., p. 539.

[102]   Hamilton to Roberts, January 17, 1902, Hamilton papers 2/3/12; Hamilton to Roberts, February 21, 1902, Hamilton papers 2/3/16.

[103]   Pakenham, op cit., p. 536.

[104]   Carver, op cit., pp. 246–247; Pakenham, op cit., p. 549.

[105]   Hamilton , op cit., File no. 2/2/7–9, March 16, 1902.

[106]   Hamilton, op cit., File no. 2/3/8, December 16, 1901.

[107]   Ibid.

[108]   Davey, op cit p. 67–70, xlviii

[109]   Wallace, R.L. *The Australians at the Boer War*. Canberra: AGPS, 1976, p. 319.

[110]   Carnegie, op cit., p. 63; *see also* Witton, op cit., p. 49. *See* Davey, op cit., p. 23 and Chapter V.

[111]   Carnegie, op cit., p. 66; see also Witton, op cit., pp. 50–51.

[112]   'An Army Order published on 5 October reported briefly that Lieutenant J.H. Robertson had been permitted to resign his appointment on 10 September 1901', Army Order 422, October 5, 1901 (Military Governor Pretoria 262); Davey, op cit., p. xlvi, note 126.

[113]   Davey, op cit., p. 131.

[114]   Davey, op cit., p. 130.

[115]   Witton, op cit., p. 84.

[116]   Witton, op cit., p. 85.

[117]   Witton, op cit., pp. 60–61.

[118]   Witton, op cit., p. 76.

[119]   Carnegie, op cit., p. 125.

[120]   Denton, op cit., p. 112.

[121]   Davey, op cit., pp. 39–41.

[122]   Davey, op cit., p. 41.

[123]   Wallace, op cit., p. 376.

[124]   Witton, op cit., p. 69.

[125]   Witton, op cit., p. 72.

[126]   Davey, op cit., p. 78.

[127]   Davey, op cit., pp. 74, 75.

[128]   Davey, op cit., pp. 68–69.

[129]   Davey, op cit., pp. 67–68.

[130]   Witton, op cit., p. 51.

[131]   PRO, WO, 93/41, op. cit., p. 1400.

[132]   Davey, op cit., preface l.

[133]   Magnus, op cit., p. 194.

[134]   MML, 4th Edition, 1899, op cit., p. 518.

[135]   Kitchener to Broderick, Confidential Telegram No.S886, dated February 25, 1902, as quoted by Carnegie, op cit., p. 136.

[136]   Ward, E.D.W., The Under Secretary of State, dated March 29, 1905, as quoted by Carnegie, op cit., p. 179.

[137]   Witton, op cit., p. 73.

[138]   Ward, as quoted by Carnegie, op cit., p. 181.

[139] MML, 4th Edition. 1899, op cit., p. 32.

[140] Jarvis, op cit., p. 131.

[141] Bleszynski, op cit., pp. 295–298.

[142] Six months earlier Australians were court martialed for inciting mutiny, found guilty and sentenced to death. These sentences were commuted to imprisonment by Kitchener. However, *'When the three men had been six weeks in English prisons, the War Office issued an instruction for their immediate release'* after intervention by the Australian Government: Wallace, op cit., p. 333.

[143] Witton, op cit., pp. 73, 74.

[144] Witton, op cit., p. 78.

[145] Renar, op cit., p. 32.

[146] Ward, as quoted by Carnegie, op cit., p. 182.

[147] PRO, WO, 93/41, op cit., pp. 1018, 1019.

[148] PRO, WO, 93/41, op cit., p. 1400.

[149] MML, 4th Edition, 1899, op cit., p. 350.

[150] MML, 4th Edition, 1899, op cit., p. 584.

[151] Wartime, Issue 18, p. 15.

[152] Denton, op cit. p. 115.

[153] MML, 4th Edition, 1899, op cit., p. 666.

[154] Witton, op cit., p. 79.

[155] Carnegie, op cit., p. 124.

[156] Witton, op cit., p. 154.

[157] Cutlack, F.M. *Breaker Morant – A Horseman Who Made History*. Sydney: Ure Smith, 1962, pp. 97–98.

[158] Witton, op cit., pp. 77–78.

[159] Davey, op cit., p. 132.

[160] Carnegie, op cit., p. 124–125.

[161] Carnegie, op cit., p. 125.

[162] Witton., op cit., p. 78.

[163] Ibid.

[164] Witton, op cit., p. 75.

[165] Witton, op cit., p. 245.

[166] Davey, op cit., p. 199.

[167] Davey, op cit., p. 75.

[168] *The Times*, 'The trial of Officers for the murder of Boer prisoners', April 17, 1902, quoted in Davey, op cit., p. 137.

[169] Wilcox, op cit., p. 290.

[170] RPSA Where an officer is charged with an offence under the Army Act the investigation shall, if he requires it be held, and the evidence taken in his presence in writing , 'in the same manner' as that for a soldier. In other cases, a 'abstract of evidence' makes out a case against an officer, in absentia, and does not contain much detail. For this reason it does not include witness statements. It is delivered to the accused not less than 24 hours before

his trial and is laid before the court on assembly. Thus 'abstracts of evidence' do not appear to apply in any of the courts-martial under consideration. MML, 4th Edition, 1899, op cit., p. 579.

171   MML, 4th Edition, 1899, op cit., p. 50.

172   MML, 4th Edition, 1899, op cit., p. 40.

173   MML, 4th Edition, 1899, op cit., p. 39.

174   Witton, op cit., p. 81.

175   Bleszynski., op cit., p. 298.

176   PRO, WO, 93/41, p. 1189.

177   MML, 4th Edition, 1899, op cit., Rules of Procedure 4 and 8, pp. 574, 579.

178   Carnegie, op cit., p. 106.

179   MML, 4th Edition, 1899, op cit., p. 656.

180   MML, 4th Edition, 1899, op cit., p. 657.

181   Witton, op cit., p. 79. Colonel Carter, the president of the court of inquiry, which concluded six weeks previously, had submitted the proceedings to the Deputy Judge Advocate General Pretoria, but he was now involved in the indictment process, which is highly questionable. In what capacity was he acting – President of the Court of Inquiry or Commanding Officer, Wiltshire Regiment? The responsibility should have rested with Colonel Hall.

182   Witton, op cit., p. 154.

183   MML, 4th Edition, 1899, op cit., p. 583.

184   Witton, op cit., p. 80.

185   *The Times*, 'The trial of Officers for the murder of Boer prisoners', April 17, 1902, quoted in Davey, op cit., p. 137.

186   Thomas, Major James Francis quoted from *Tenterfield Star*, October 6, 1903.

187   Witton, op cit., p. 80.

188   Witton, op cit., p. 151.

189   Witton, op cit., p. 82.

190   MML, 4th Edition, 1899, op cit., p. 583.

191   Hoy, Anthony. 'Tenterfield Battler', *The Bulletin*, Sydney, 4 April 2000, p. 36.

192   Carnegie, op cit., p. 105; Witton, op cit., p. 80; *see also* MML, 4th Edition, 1899, op cit., p. 593.

193   Witton, op cit., p. 205.

194   Witton, op cit., p. 84.

195   The Judge Advocate of a court martial has no special qualifications and only acts as such for the duration of a court martial. He has no relationship with the Judge Advocate's Office, where most staff usually have military legal qualifications.

196   Witton, op cit., p. 116.

197   MML, 4th Edition, 1899, op cit., p. 58.

198   MML, 4th Edition, 1899, op cit., p. 112.

199   MML, 4th Edition, 1899, op cit., p. 288.

200   Ibid.

201   *Wartime*, Issue 18, p. 66.

202   Renar, op cit., p. 35.

203   Carnegie, op cit., p. 120.

204   Carnegie, op cit., p. 48.

205   PRO, WO, 93/41, op cit., p. 1163 (military court – Commandant G.J. Scheifers).

206   Wilcox, Craig. 'Morant a victim? Give me a break', *The Australian*, 13 May 1999.

207   Wilcox, op cit., p. 230.

208   House of Commons, The Blue Book Cd 981, Accounts and Papers 1902, Vol. LVII, Army (Martial Law in South Africa), HMSO, London 1902; House of Commons, The Blue Book Cd 1423, Accounts and Papers 1903, Vol. XXXVIII, Army (Martial Law in South Africa), HMSO, London, 1903.

209   PRO, WO, 93/41, op cit., pp. 862–1636 (11 October 1901 to 21 April 1902).

210   National Archives of South Africa, National Archive Repository, PMO 54, PM 3727.

211   MML, 4th Edition, 1899, p. 287.

212   MML, 4th Edition, 1899, p. 296.

213   Minute Book Of Letters, p. 1556 dated 29 March 1902. [??]

214   Ibid.

215   The House of Commons, Blue Book Cd 1423, Accounts and Papers 1903, Vol. XXXVIII, Army (Martial Law in South Africa), HMSO, London, 1903, p. 80.

216   Hamilton to Roberts, November 26, 1901, Hamilton papers 2/3/2.

217   Reitz, op cit., p. 233.

218   Reitz, op cit., p. 316; *see also* Witton, op cit., p. 116.

219   Reitz, op cit., pp. 242, 255.

220   Churchill, op cit., p. 264.

221   Bleszynski, op cit., pp. 475–476. Original letter from Doryn Pote to David Jennings, 29 June 1988, in author's possession.

222   MML, 7th Edition, 1929, op cit., p. 344, note 2 and p. 345, note 1.

223   Personal diary of Provost Marshal Robert Montague Poore, October 31, 1901. Diary held at Liddel-Hart Military Archive, King's College, London.

224   Witton, op cit., p. 117.

225   Witton, op cit., p. 58.

226   Wilcox, op cit., p. 236.

227   Witton, op cit., p. 84.

228   Witton, op cit., pp. 83–84.

229   Davey, op cit., p. 140.

230   MML, 4th Edition, 1899, Ch. XIV, paras 11 and 31, pp. 287, 292.

231 MML, 4th Edition, p. 287, para.11

232 Churchill, op cit., pp. 361–362.

233 Magnus, op cit., pp. 184–185.

234 MML, 4th Edition, 1899, op cit., pp. 287, 292.

235 MML 4th Edition, 1899, op cit., p. 287

236 Wilcox, op cit., p. 235

237 Davitt, Michael. *The Boer Fight For Freedom*. pp. 505, 515–516.

238 Witton, op cit., pp. 158–161.

239 Davey, op cit., p. 140.

240 MML, 4th Edition, 1899, op cit., p. 285 Note (a).

241 MML, 4th Edition, 1899, op cit., p. 3.

242 MML, 4th Edition, 1899, op cit., p. 22.

243 MML, 4th Edition, 1899, op cit., p. 330.

244 Davey provides a glowing report on Hamilton (Preface, pp. xxxiv, xxxv) but 'Hammy' lacked integrity and loyalty according to another of Kitchener's 'Band of Boys' Colonel Rawlinson: Carver, op cit., p. 249.

245 *The Times*, 'The trial of Officers for the murder of Boer prisoners', April 17, 1902, quoted in Davey, op cit., p. 137; Davey, op cit., pp. 127–129.

246 MML, 4th Edition, 1899, op cit., p. 292, para 31: '*an unjust execution of prisoners by the enemy may be followed by the execution of an equal number of number of prisoners by their opponents.*'

247 Bleszynski, op cit., pp. 104–202, 463–464; Greenhill, Gardyne Captain. *The Life of a Regiment: The History of The Gordon Highlanders*, Vol. 3, pp. 51–55.

248 Witton, op cit., p. 131

249 Poore, op cit.

250 Wilcox, Craig. 'Ned Kelly in Khaki', *The Weekend Australian*, 23/24 February 2002, p. 22.

251 Poore., op cit., September 27, 1901.

252 Bleszynski, op cit., pp. 464–467.

253 *The Times,* 'The trial of Officers for the murder of Boer prisoners', April 17, 1902, quoted in Davey, op cit., p. 137; Davey, op cit., pp. 133–134.

254 Bleszynski, op cit., p. 477.

255 Bleszynski, op cit., p. 201.

256 Witton, op cit., p. 61; Davey, op cit., p. 80.

257 Witton, op cit., pp. 47–48.

258 Wilcox, op cit., p. 235.

259 Witton, op cit., p. 76.

260 Witton, op cit., p. 84.

261 Witton, op cit., p. 8.

262 The Manual of Military Law states that 'condoned by competent military authority' in accordance with Rules of Procedure

36(A)(2) or condoned '*by the deliberate act of some superior authority*' Rules of Procedure 34, Note A are both valid defences.

263 *See* note 44 above.

264 Carnegie, op cit., p. 53.

265 Denton, op cit., p. 110.

266 Davey, op cit., p. xxvii.

267 *The Bulletin*, 19 February 2002, p. 10.

268 *See* note 256.

269 Witton, op cit., p. 157.

270 PRO, WO, 93/41, p. 1400; *see also* Witton, op cit., p. 116.

271 Witton op cit., pp. 158–161.

272 Bleszynski, op cit., p. 359.

273 Renar, op cit., p. 36.

274 MML, 4th Edition, 1899, op cit., pp. 616–617.

275 PRO, WO, 93/41, op cit., p. 1400.

276 Davey, op cit., p. 114.

277 MML, 4th Edition, 1899, op cit., p. 617.

278 Witton, op cit., p. 155.

279 MML, 4th Edition, 1899, op cit., p. 65.

280 Carnegie, op cit., p. 135; PRO, WO, 30/S7/22, 1900–1902, Kitchener Papers, Letters Y127.

281 Witton, op cit., pp. 150–151; Carnegie, op cit., p. 144.

282 MML, 4th Edition, 1899, op cit., p. 67 and p. 362.

283 MML, 4th Edition, 1899, op cit., p. 363.

284 *See* Bleszynski, op cit., pp. 310–314 for a full account of the secrecy Kitchener shrouded the trial in.

285 Public Records Office (PRO), War Office (WO), 30/S7/22, 1900–1902, Kitchener Papers, Letters Y128.

286 Carnegie, op cit., p. 135.

287 Carnegie, op cit., p. 115.

288 Australian War Memorial, file 02/673.

289 Carver, op cit., p. 249.

290 PRO WO 93/41, op cit., p. 938 dated October 31, 1901.

291 MML, 4th Edition, 1899, p. 650.

292 National Army Museum, cipher Roberts to Kitchener, April 26, 1902.

293 Davey, op cit., p. 143.

294 PRO, WO 93/41, op cit., p. 1152.

295 Carnegie, op cit., p. 55.

296 Witton, op cit., p. 46. See also *The Sydney Morning Herald*, April 4, 1902; Davey, op cit., p 55.

297 Davey, op cit., p. 45.

298 Davey, op cit., p. 219.

299 Davey, op cit., p. 55.

300 Davey, op cit., p. 67.

301 Davey, op cit., p. 66.

302   Davey, op cit., pp. 68–69.

303   Davey, op cit., p. 69.

304   PRO, WO, 93/41, p. 1400.

305   MML, 4th Edition, 1899, op cit., p. 297.

306   *See* note 209.

307   Witton, op cit., p. 49.

308   Witton, op cit., p. 137.

309   Ibid.

310   MML, 4th Edition, 1899, op cit., p. 96.

311   Witton, op cit., p. 137.

312   Davey, op cit., p. xlvii.

313   PRO, WO, 93/41, p. 1024.

314   Davey, op cit., p. 72.

315   Witton, op cit., p. 140.

316   *The Times*, 'The trial of Officers for the murder of Boer prisoners', April 17, 1902 quoted in Davey, op cit., p. 137.

317   Bleszynski, op cit., pp. 489–490.

318   Witton, op cit., p. 130, the Judge Advocate, Copland, uses the phrase '*condoned or ignored*'.

319   The original Petition on file 110/Cape/833 was destroyed in 1907. A copy of the Petition can be found on file PRO WO32/9116.

320   Clode, C. M. *Military Forces of the Crown*, 1869, Vol. 1, p. 103.

321   Public Records Office (PRO), Home Office (HO), 144/580 (George Ramsdale Witton).

322   Assistant Commandant General C. F. Beyers was appointed Boer commander in the Zoutspansberg and Waterberg; Davey, op cit., p. lix.

323   Witton, op cit., p 294.

324   Witton, op cit., p. 89.

325   Renar, op cit., p. 34.

326   Dispatched by General Lord Kitchener, dated 8 Feb 1902House of Commons, Blue Book Cd 965, South African Dispatches.

327   Witton, op cit., p. 111.

328   Cutlack, op cit., p. 94.

329   Davey, op cit., p. 116.

330   Australian War Memorial, File 02/673.

331   Pakenham, op cit., p. 403.

332   MML, 4th Edition, 1899, op cit., p. 603.

333   MML, 7th Edition, 1929, op cit., p. 640.

334   Todd, Robert. 'Morant, Harry Harbord (1864?–1902)', *Australian Dictionary of Biography*, Vol.10, 1891–1939, Carlton, Vic: Melbourne University Press, 1986, p. 582.

335   *Melbourne Sun Herald*, 'My Say', 13 February 2002.

336   See note 279.

Historical Sources

There are six standard published texts on 'Breaker' Morant which give the basic outline of his life and the circumstances surrounding his death and were extremely useful throughout my research:

Carnegie, Margaret and Shields, Frank. *In Search of Breaker Morant: Balladist and Bushveldt Carbineer*. Armadale, Vic: H.H. Stephenson, 1979.

Cutlack, Frederick. *Breaker Morant: A horseman who made history*. Sydney: Ure Smith, 1962.

Davey, Arthur. *Breaker Morant and The Bushveldt Carbineers*. South Africa: Van Riebeck Society, 1987.

Denton, Kit. *Closed File*. Adelaide: Rigby, 1983.

Renar, Frank. *Bushman and Buccaneer: Harry Morant – his 'ventures and verses*. Sydney: H.T. Dunn, 1902.

Witton, George. *Scapegoats of The Empire: The story of the Bushveldt Carbineers*. London: Angus & Robertson, 1982.

To that list I would add two soon to be published books. The first is a definitive and long overdue chronology of all of Morant's writings by Ted Robl entitled *The Backblock Bard* from which I obtained information on Morant's poetry (contact the author at roblt@bigpond.com). The second is a comprehensive unit history of the BVC by Bill Woolmore entitled *The Bushveldt Carbineers and The Pietersburg Light Horse* (Melbourne: Slouch Hat Publications, 2002).

Below is a select bibliography of my principal sources

Abbott, J.H.M. *Tommy Cornstalk*. London: Longmans, Green & Co., 1902.

Arthur, Sir George. *The Life of Lord Kitchener: Vols I, II and III*. London: McMillan, 1920.

Australian War Memorial. *Australians at War, 1885–1972: Photographs from the collection of the Australian War Memorial selected by Peter Stanley and Michael McKernan*. Sydney: Collins, 1984.

Bates, Daisy. *The Passing of the Aboriginies: A lifetime spent amongst the natives of Australia*. London: John Murray, 1944.

Blackburn, Julia. *Daisy Bates in the Desert*. London: Secker & Warburg, 1994.

Bufton, John. *The Tasmanians in the Transvaal War*. Newton, Tas: S.G. Loone, 1905.

Camus, Albert. *The Rebel*. London: Hamish Hamilton, 1953.

Cannon, Michael. *The Roaring Days*. Mornington, Vic: Today's Australian Publishing Company, 1998.

Carver, Lord. *The National Army Museum Book of the Boer War Field Marshal Lord Carver*. London: Sidgwick & Jackson, 1999.

Churchill, Winston S. *My Early Life: A roving commission*. Glasgow: Fontana Books, 1979.

Clark, Manning. *A History of Australia (Vols 4 and 5)*. Carlton, Vic: Melbourne University Press, 1981.

Clark, Manning. *Henry Lawson: The man and the legend*. South Melbourne: Sun Books, 1985.

Coetzer, Owen. *The Anglo–Boer War: The road to infamy*. William Waterman, 1996.

Cole, Tom. *Hell West and Crooked*. Sydney: Collins, 1988.

Corvisier, André (Ed). *A Dictionary of Military History and the Art of War* (translated from the French by Chris Turner). Oxford; Cambridge, Mass.: Blackwell, 1994.

Couch-Keen, Glenda. *Equestrienne Australis: The story of Australia's horsewomen*. Springton, SA: G. Couch-Keen for The Side-Saddle Association of SA, 1990.

Crowther, Margaret Anne. *The Workhouse System (1834–1929): The history of an English social institution*. Methuen, 1983.

De Wet, C.R. *Three Years War: October 1899–1902* (translated from the Dutch), Westminster: Constable, 1902.

Doyle, Sir Arthur Conan. *The Great Boer War* (17th ed.). London: George Bell & Sons, 1903.

Drooglever, R.W.F. (Ed) *From The Front: The observations of Mr A.B. (Banjo) Patterson, special war correspondent in South Africa, November 1899 to July 1900.* Sydney: Pan Macmillan, 2000.

Evans, Roger. *The Forgotten Heroes of Bridgwater.* 1990 (self-published: available from evansroger@lineone.net).

Farwell, Byron. *The Great Boer War.* Wordsworth Editions Ltd, 1999.

Field, L.M. *The Forgotten War: Australian involvement in the South African conflict of 1899–1902.* Carlton, Vic: Melbourne University Press, 1979.

Fitzpatrick, J.C.L. *The Good Old Days of Molong.* Parramatta, NSW: Cumberland Argus Ltd, 1913.

Fuller, J.F.C. *The Last of the Gentlemen's Wars: A subaltern's journal of the war in South Africa, 1899–1902.* London: Faber & Faber, 1937.

Gordon, J.M. *Chronicles of a Gay Gordon.* London: Cassell, 1921.

Gordon-Duff, Lachlan. *With the Gordon Highlanders to the Boer War and Beyond.* Travis Books, 1998.

Greenhill Gardyne, A.D. *The Life of a Regiment: The history of the Gordon Highlanders.* Gordon Highlanders Regiment, 1939.

Hickman, A.S. *Rhodesia Served The Queen (Vols 1 and 2).* Salisbury, 1970.

Hill, Ernestine. *Kabbarli: A Personal Memoir of Daisy Bates.* Sydney: Angus & Robertson, 1973.

Idriess, Ion. L. *Cattle King.* Sydney: Angus & Robertson, 1936.

Jackson, Tabitha. *The Boer War.* London: Channel 4 Books, 1999.

Jarvis, C.S. *Half a Life.* London: J Murray, 1943.

Jenkin, Graham. *Songs of the Great Australian Balladists.* Adelaide: Rigby, 1978.

King, Peter. *The Viceroy's Fall: How Kitchener destroyed Curzon.* London: Sidgwick & Jackson, 1986.

Kruger, Rayne: *Goodbye Dolly Grey: The story of the Boer War*. London: Pimlico, 1996.

Le May, G.H.L. *British Supremacy in South Africa 1899–1907*. Oxford: Clarendon Press, 1965.

Lindsay, Norman. *Bohemians of The Bulletin*. Angus & Robertson, 1965.

Magnus, Sir Philip. *Kitchener: Portrait of an Imperialist*. New York: E.P. Dutton & Co., 1959.

Magoffin, Richard. *Fair Dinkum Matilda*. Charters Towers, Qld: Mimosa Press, 1973.

Magoffin, Richard. *The Political Paterson*. Kynuna, Qld: Matilda Expo, 1998.

Marsh, Peter T. *Joseph Chamberlain: Entrepreneur in Politics*. New Haven: Yale University Press, 1994.

Martin, Allan. *Henry Parkes: A Biography*. Carlton, Vic: Melbourne University Press, 1980.

Martin, Ralph G. *Lady Randolph Churchill (Vol II)*. Cassel, 1972.

Maurice, Sir Frederick. *History of the war in South Africa, 1899–1902 (Vol 4)*. London: Hurst & Blackett, 1906–1910.

May, Henry John. *Music of the Guns: Based on two journals of the Boer War*. London: Jarrolds, 1970.

Meredith, John (Ed). *Omdurman Dairies 1898*. Leo Cooper, 1998.

Meredith, John. *The Breaker's Mate: Will Ogilvie in Australia*. Kenthurst, NSW: Kangaroo Press, 1996.

Mitchell, Sally. *Daily Life in Victorian England*. Westport, Conn.: Greenwood Press, 1996.

Mordike, John. *An Army for a Nation: A history of Australian military developments, 1880–1914*. North Sydney: Allen & Unwin in association with the Department of Defence, 1992.

Neillands, Robin (Ed). *The Dervish Wars: Gordon and Kitchener in the Sudan, 1880–1898*. John Murray, 1996.

Packenham, Thomas. *The Boer War*. London: Abacus, 1996.

Packenham, Thomas. *The Scramble For Africa*. London: Weidenfeld & Nicolson, 1991.

Palmer, Rick (Ed). *The Shearer's Strike 1891–1991: A Celebration*. Rockhampton, Qld: University of Central Queensland, 1992.

Palmer, Vance. *The Legend of the Nineties*. Melbourne Municipal Press, 1960.

Parker, Geoffrey (Ed). *The Cambridge Illustrated History of Warfare: The triumph of the West*. Cambridge University Press, 1995.

Pollock, John. *Kitchener: The Road to Omdurman*. London: Constable, 1998.

Pugsley, Christopher. *On the Fringe of Hell: New Zealanders and military discipline in the First World War*. Auckland: Hodder & Stoughton, 1991.

Putkowski, Julian and Sykes, Julian. *Shot at Dawn: Executions in World War One by authority of the British Army Act*. Wharncliffe Publishing, 1989.

Quiller-Couch, Sir Arthur (Ed). *The Oxford Book of English Verse, 1250–1918*. Oxford: The Clarendon Press, 1939.

Reitz, Deneys. *Commando: A Boer journal of the Boer War*. Great Britain: Faber & Faber, 1932.

Robins, Joseph. *The Lost Children: A study of charity children in Ireland, 1700–1900*. Dublin: Institute of Public Administration, 1980.

Robinson, Judy. *Bushman of the Red Heart: Central Australian cameleer and explorer Ben Nicker, 1908–1942*. Rockhampton, Qld: Central Queensland University Press, 1999.

Roderick, Colin. *Banjo Paterson: A poet by accident*. North Sydney: Allen & Unwin, 1993.

Salter, Elizabeth. *Daisy Bates: 'The Great White Queen of the Never Never'*. Sydney: Angus & Robertson, 1971.

Smurthwaite, David. *The Boer War 1899–1902*. Great Britain: Hamlyn History, 1999.

Sommerville, Edith and Ross, Martin. *Some Experiences of an Irish R.M.* Longman Green, 1899.

Souter, Gavin. *Lion and Kangaroo: The initiation of Australia*. Sydney: Collins, 1976.

Speed, Neil. *Born To Fight*. 2002 (contact the author at SpeedNG@bigpond.com).

Spies, S.B. *Methods of Barbarism? Roberts and Kitchener and civilians in the Boer Republics, January 1900–May 1902*. Cape Town: Human & Rousseau, 1977.

Stack, John. *Lieutenant Calley: His Own Story (as told to John Stack)*. New York: Viking Press, 1971.

Stirling, J. *The Colonials in South Africa, 1899–1902* (2nd edition). London: 1990.

Svensen, Steven. *The Shearer's War: The Story of the 1891 Shearer's Strike*. St Lucia, Qld: University of Queensland Press, 1889.

Todd, Robert. 'Morant, Harry Harbord (1864?–1902)', *Australian Dictionary of Biography*, Vol. 10, 1891–1939. Carlton, Vic: Melbourne University Press, 1986.

Valentine, Douglas. *The Phoneix Program*. New York: Morrow, 1990.

Viljoen, Benjamin. *My Reminiscences of the Boer War*. 1902 (available at the State Library of Victoria).

Wallace, Robert L. *The Australians at the Boer War*. Canberra: Australian War Memorial/ Australian Government Publishing Service, 1976.

Wallace, Robert L. *The Circumstances Surrounding the Seige of Elands River Post: A Boer War study*. Loftus, NSW: Australian Military History Publications, 2000.

Warner, Philip. *Field Marshall Earl Haig*. London: Cassells Military Paperbacks, 1991.

Warner, Philip. *Kitchener: The Man Behind the Legend*. New York: Atheneum, 1986.

Wilde, William. *Australian Poets and Their Works: A reader's guide*. Melbourne: Oxford University Press, 1996.

Wongtschowski, B.E.H. *Between Woodrush and Wolkberg*. South Africa, 1987.

Articles, Papers and Unpublished Material

'Events Prior to Eland's River in August 1900 in which J.F. Thomas took part', Mitchell Library, Sydney (Ref: At69).

'Report of Commission of Enquiry into the Late Admini-
stration of the Kroonstad District since the Annexation'
(De Bertodano), Archives of the Orange Free State,
Bloemfontein (Ref: ORC 44).

'The Boer War: Army, Nation and Empire', collected
Australian War Memorial papers from the 1999 Boer War
conference.

'The Breaker Morant File', North Devon Athenaeum, Barn-
stable.

'The Memoirs of the Marquis De Moral (De Bertodano)', BE 3
National Archives of Zimbabwe.

Australia, House of Commons, *Parliamentary Debates*,
Vol. 105, 8 April 1902; Vol. 138, 14 July 1904.

Australia, House of Representatives, *Debates*, 2 April
1902.

Australia, NSW Parliamentary Debates, Vol. 7, 28 May 1902,
26 June 1902, 8 July 1902, 9 September 1902.

Australian War Memorial. Bench Depositions, Police Court
Muttaburra, Queensland showing records of litigation
involving Morant, April 1888 to January 1889 (Accession
No: PR84/019).

Baker, G.F. The Care and Education of Children in Union
Workhouses of Somerset, 1834–1870, MA thesis, University of London. [2 bdls]

Bennett, Dr John. 2001, 'Doubting Thomas', *Law Society
Journal*, Vol 39(9), p 70.

Bridges, Barry. 1978, 'Lord Kitchener and the Morant–
Handcock Executions', *Journal of the Royal Australian
Historical Society*, Vol. 73, No.1.

Burr, Pastor Paul. 'Daniel Heese: A biographical sketch'.

Cape Colony, Legislative Council, *Debates*, 8 April 1904.

Carnegie, Margaret. 'Recollections of Breaker Morant', Oxley
Library, Brisbane (Ref: OM79.002/17).

Chamberlain, Max. 1982, 'The Characteristics of Australia's Boer War Volunteers', *Historical Studies*, Vol. 20,
No. 78.

Chamberlain, Max. 1985, 'The Williamsrust Affair: A defence

of the 5th Victorian Mounted Rifles', *Journal of The Australian War Memorial*, Vol. 6, p 47.

Colony of Natal, Legislative Assembly, *Debates*, June 1904.

Glenister, Richard. 1984, Desertion without execution: Decisions that saved Australian Imperial Force deserters from the firing squad in WWI, BA (Hons) thesis, La Trobe University.

Hamilton, The Papers of Colonel Ian, Liddel-Hart Military Archive, King's College, London, File no 2/3/1–33, 2/3/3–4.

Kitchener, Lord, The Masonic Records of, Masonic Hall, London.

Lewis, Peter N and Morrison, Angela. 'George Whyte-Melville: A Grand Man and a Golfer', The Royal and Ancient Golf Club of St Andrews Trust, 1999.

Northgate Union Workhouse of Bridgewater, The Records of (1860–1882), held at The Somerset County Archives Office, Exeter.

Playford, Steve. 'The Rifles That Blazed .303', *Australian Shooter Magazine*, 1999.

Poore, The Papers of Brigader General Robert Montague (1886–1938), Liddel-Hart Military Archive, King's College, London.

Poore, Provost Marshal Major Robert Montague, Personal diary of (1900–1902), Liddel-Hart Military Archives King's College, London.

Rubin, Professor Gerry. 1988, 'Military Law in World War One', *RUSI Journal* (Royal United Services Institute).

Schulenberg, Dr. C.A.R. 1981, 'Die Bushveldt Carbineers', *Historia*, No.1.

Shaw, John (Ed). 'The Death Penalty' and 'The Defence Act', in *The Australian Encyclopedia* (Collins, 1984).

van Nieker, Melt. 'The Van Den Berg Murder', in *War Crimes? 1899–1902*, compiled by R.F. Odendaal.

Wallace, Robert L. 'Major J.F. Thomas – A Bushman in the Boer War'.

War Office Documents – WO 93/41, Army Order No. 497

12 February 1902; No. 506 28 February 1902.

Wilcox, Craig. 2000, 'Lost in the Translation', *Memento Magazine*, National Archives of Australia (Refs: NAA: A661/665; NAA: CP1/33, E).

Willmansrust Affair: An account by Major McKnight of the 5th Victorian Bushmen (held in the Museum of Tasmania).

Official Publications

War Office Great Britain, Manual of Military Law, HMSO, London, 1899, 4th Ed.; 1907, 5th Ed.; 1914, 6th Ed.; 1929, 7th Ed.

The Monthly Army List 1901–03.

House of Commons, The Blue Book Cd 981, Accounts and Papers 1902, Vol. LVII, Army (Martial Law in South Africa), HMSO, London, 1902.

House of Commons, The Blue Book Cd 1423, Accounts and Papers 1903, Vol. XXXVIII, Army (Martial Law in South Africa), HMSO, London, 1903.

Official Records

Australian War Memorial, AWM 02/673 and 03/673, Major Lenehan.

Mitchell Library, AM, 78, Witton to Thomas, 21 October 1929.

National Archives of Australia, Series A11085/1, item B3A/1B, Major Lenehan.

National Archives of Australia, Series A6661/1, item 665, Kitchener's reply to Governor General on Morant Affair.

National Archives of Australia, Series B168/0, item 1902/2085, Major Lenehan and Lieutenant Witton.

National Archives of South Africa (NASA), National Archive Repository, PMO 54, PM3727 (Izak Koen).

Public Records Office, Kew. Home Office HO144/580/ A63460 (George Ramsdale Witton, Prisoner).

War Office, WO 32/9116, Petition, G. R. Witton (original file 110/Cape/833 destroyed).

War Office, WO 30/S7/22, 1900–1902, Kitchener Papers, Letter Y127–Y128.

War Office, WO 93/41, Minute Book of Letters from Judge Advocate, Pretoria.

Transvaal Archives, Pretoria

Colonial Secretary (Pretoria) 1902: Letterbook I, pp. 5–8/ 11–13/ 14–17/ 18–20/ 24/ 27–31/ 33–34/ 67–70/ 77–78/; Letterbook II, pp. 33–34/ 37–46/ 47–62/ 71–76/ 79/ 80–82/ 87–89/ 94.

Military Governor of Pretoria: 263, p. 24.

PMO (Provost Marshal, Pretoria): 50 (3415/02), 76 (File p. 60), 3198/02, 81 MC40

Secretary for Native Affairs: 2, 11, 24, 27, 29, 31 September 1901, 26 October 1901, 12 December 1901, 24 December 1902.

S.T.A: 15/02 (CS58)

Public Records Office, London

WO 93/41 (Letterbook of Provost Marshal General St Clair).

WO 32/8007 (Proceedings of Court of Enquiry concerning Boer attack on detachment of Major General Beatsons force at Wilmansrust, Transvaal, 1901).

Film/Television Productions

Australians at War, 2001, ABC TV.

Breaker Morant, 1972, ABC TV.

Breaker Morant (motion picture), 1979, South Australian Film Corporation.

Kitchener – The Empire's Flawed Hero, 'Reputations' series, June 1998, BBC TV.

The Boer War, September 1999, BBC TV.

The Boer War, October/ November 1999, Channel 4 TV.

Bulletin References

The Bulletin was an excellent source for material about Morant's days in Australia, the Boer War and the aftermath of his execution.

2/12/1899	5/4/1902	6/1/1903
6/1/1900	12/4/1902	21/2/1903
13/1/1900	3/5/1902	6/1/1904
27/1/1900	10/5/1902	6/1/1910
10/2/1900	17/5/1902	13/1/1910
10/3/1900	24/5/1902	25/2/1947
5/10/1901	31/5/1902	13/3/1947
15/2/1902	7/6/1902	4/9/1955
17/2/1902	14/6/1902	7/3/1960
21/2/1903	28/6/1902	10/4/1979
6/3/1902	11/9/1902	2/12/1980
28/3/1902	27/12/1902	6/11/1986

Other Newspaper Sources

Bathurst Free Press: 26 April 1901.

Brisbane Courier: 22, 23 September 1891.

Electronic Mail and Guardian: 7 July 1998.

Financial Times: 28 May 1997.

Sunday Telegraph: 21, 28 June1998.

Sunday Times: 23 November 1997, 30 August 1999.

Sydney *Daily Telegraph*: 3, 15, 25, 27, 28, 29 March 1902; 3, 4, 5, 6, 7, 8, 10 April 1902; 5, 13 August 1904; 13 November 1904.

The Adelaide Advertiser: 12, 13 January 1900; 27 January 1900; October 1901; 12 April 1902; April 1988; 24, 25, 26, 29 May 1988; 7 June 1988.

The Adelaide Observer: 12 April 1902.

The Age: 28 September 1901.

The Argus: 9 January 1901; 1 February 1902; 12 August 1909.

The Australian Law Journal: 15 May 1929.

The Australian: 20 July 1999.

The Barnet Press: 1868–1883.

The Bideford Gazette: November 1900–March 1901.

The Daily Telegraph: 18, 27 April 1998; 6, 8, 13 June 1998; 7 November 1998.

The Guardian: 27 May 1998.

The Leader: 7, 12 April 1902.

The Northern Miner: 3 November 1883; 13, 27 March 1884; 16, 21, 23, 25 April 1884; April/May 1902, 20 May 1902.

The Otago Daily Times: 10 April 1902.

The Sun: 28 May 1961.

The Sydney Mail: 12 April 1902.

The Sydney Morning Herald: 31 March 1902; 4, 9 April 1902; 16 June 1923; 3, 4 May 1988.

The Tenterfield Star: 10, 26 January 1900; 20 and 21 February 1900; 15 May 1900; 29 June 1900; 4, 17 July 1900; 7 August 1900; 7, 11 September 1900; 23, 24, 26 October 1900; 29 November 1900; 6 October 1903; 12 August 1942.

The Times: 5, 17 April 1902; 16 February 1998; 2 September 1998; 28 February 1992; 23 November 1997.

Town and Country Journal: 1, 15 February 1902; 29 March 1902; 5, 12 April 1902; 3, 13 May 1902.

Weekly Truth: 21 August 1909.